FINANCIAL MANAGEMENT IN THE SPORT INDUSTRY

Now in a fully revised and updated third edition, this essential textbook introduces the fundamentals of sport finance and sound financial management in the sport industry. It is still the only textbook to explain every aspect of finance from the perspective of the sport management practitioner, explaining key concepts and showing how to apply them in practice in the context of sport.

The text begins by covering finance basics and the tools and techniques of financial quantification, using industry examples to apply the principles of financial management to sport. It then goes further, to show how financial management works specifically in the sport industry. Discussions include interpreting financial statements, debt and equity financing, capital budgeting, facility financing, economic impact, risk and return, time value of money, and more. The final part of the book examines financial management in four sectors of the industry: public sector sport, collegiate athletics, professional sport, and international sport. It provides an in-depth analysis of the mechanics of financial management within each of these sport sectors. Useful features, such as sidebars, concept checks, practice problems, case analysis, and case questions will help students engage more deeply with financial techniques and encourage problem-solving skills. This new edition includes a completely new chapter on international sport, reflecting the globalized nature of the modern sport industry, as well as expanded coverage of current issues such as digital media finance, recent legal cases affecting collegiate sport, and the central importance of collective bargaining.

Financial Management in the Sport Industry is an essential textbook for any undergraduate or postgraduate course in sport finance, and an invaluable supplement to any course in sport business or sport management. It is also an important reference for all sport management practitioners looking to improve their understanding of finance.

The book is accompanied by updated and expanded online ancillary materials, including an instructor's manual, PowerPoint slides, and an image bank.

Matthew T. Brown is Interim Dean of the College of Hospitality, Retail and Sport Management at the University of South Carolina, USA, where he teaches and researches in the areas of sport business and finance. Brown has served as the Chief Financial Officer of the Southern Ohio Copperheads and Treasurer of the Board of Directors of the Southern Ohio Collegiate Baseball Club. He served as Treasurer of the North American Society for Sport Management from 2006 to 2012. In 2003, Brown was named the Jefferson College Alumnus of the Year and in 2018 he received the Garth Paton Distinguished Service Award, North American Society for Sport Management.

Daniel A. Rascher teaches and publishes research on sports business topics and consults to the sports industry. At SportsEconomics and OSKR, he has worked on over 150 sports business engagements. He is Co-Director of the Sport Management Program at the University of San Francisco, USA. He has been named Research Fellow of the North American Society for Sport Management and received the Lifetime Achievement Award from the Applied Sport Management Association. Dr. Rascher has testified as an expert witness in federal and state courts, in arbitration proceedings, and provided public testimony numerous times to state and local governments.

Mark S. Nagel is Professor in the Department of Sport and Entertainment Management at the University of South Carolina, USA. Prior to joining the department, Nagel was director of the Graduate Sport Management Program at Georgia State University. He currently serves as an adjunct faculty member at the University of San Francisco, and Saint Mary's College of California. Nagel served as Treasurer for the North American Society for Sport Management and the Sport and Recreation Law Association. He is also the Associate Director of the College Sport Research Institute, USA. He has been named Research Fellow of the North American Society for Sport Management and has been active in a variety of sport consulting projects.

Chad D. McEvoy is Vice Provost for Faculty Affairs at Northern Illinois University, USA. He previously served as President of the Sport Marketing Association and as editor of two academic journals in the sport management discipline. His professional affiliations include the North American Society for Sport Management and the Sport Marketing Association. He served as a panelist before the prestigious Knight Commission on Intercollegiate Athletics in a discussion on the effectiveness of NCAA penalties for rules violations. Dr. McEvoy's professional industry experience is in intercollegiate athletics marketing.

THIRD EDITION

FINANCIAL MANAGEMENT IN THE SPORT INDUSTRY

Matthew T. Brown,

Daniel A. Rascher,

Mark S. Nagel,

and

Chad D. McEvoy

Routledge
Taylor & Francis Group

LONDON AND NEW YORK

Third edition published 2021
by Routledge
2 Park Square, Milton Park, Abingdon, Oxon OX14 4RN

and by Routledge
52 Vanderbilt Avenue, New York, NY 10017

Routledge is an imprint of the Taylor & Francis Group, an informa business

First edition published 2010
Second edition published by Routledge 2017

British Library Cataloguing-in-Publication Data
A catalogue record for this book is available from the British Library

Library of Congress Cataloging-in-Publication Data
Names: Brown, Matthew T., editor. | Rascher, Daniel A., editor. |
Nagel, Mark S., editor. | McEvoy, Chad D., 1971– editor.
Title: Financial management in the sport industry / [edited by] Matthew T. Brown,
Daniel A. Rascher, Mark S. Nagel and Chad D. McEvoy.
Description: Third edition. | Abingdon, Oxon; New York, NY: Routledge, 2021. |
Includes bibliographical references and index.
Identifiers: LCCN 2020041808 | Subjects: LCSH: Sports--Finance. |
Sports administration. | Sports–Economic aspects.
Classification: LCC GV716 .F555 2021 | DDC 338.4/7796–dc23
LC record available at https://lccn.loc.gov/2020041808

ISBN: 978-0-367-26092-7 (hbk)
ISBN: 978-0-367-32121-5 (pbk)
ISBN: 978-0-429-31674-6 (ebk)

Typeset in Palatino
by Newgen Publishing UK

Visit the eResources: www.routledge.com/9780367321215

CONTENTS

CONTRIBUTOR BIOGRAPHIES

Tom. H. Regan is an Associate Professor and Interim Chair of the Department of Sport and Entertainment Management at the University of South Carolina, USA. His research focuses on the business of sport and entertainment and economic impact of sport teams and venues.

Nicholas M. Watanabe is Associate Professor in the Department of Sport and Entertainment Management at the University of South Carolina, USA. His research interests lie in sports economics, big data and analytics, sport finance, social media, communication, international sport, and collegiate athletics.

GLOSSARY

80/20 rule   The expectation that 80% of needed funds to reach a capital campaign goal will come from 20% of the donors, based on past giving patterns.

90/10 rule   The expectation that 90% of needed funds to reach a capital campaign goal will come from 10% of the donors, based on past giving patterns.

accounting profit   Profit earned when revenues exceed costs and expenses over a particular period of time. Accounting profit does not necessarily accurately reflect the results of an individual's or organization's financial decisions.

accounts receivable   Money owed by a company's customers.

accrual basis accounting   An accounting method that recognizes income when it is earned and expenses when they are incurred, rather than when the money is exchanged.

acid-test ratio   *See* quick ratio.

administration   Another term for bankruptcy.

allocated revenues   Revenues transferred by a school to its athletic department.

annual coupon interest payment   A periodic return paid to the owner of a bond.

annuity   A series of equal payments or receipts made at regular intervals.

antitrust exemption   An exemption from the antitrust laws, which prohibit unfair restraint of trade and the creation of monopolies. Through Congressional or judicial action, some entities have been granted exemption from some or all antitrust laws. Major League Baseball enjoys a much stronger antitrust exemption than any of the other US professional sport leagues.

arm's length   Describes a buyer and seller who are not related to each other in any way, whether they are individuals, businesses, or estates; they have no familial relationship, neither company is a subsidiary of the other, neither company has an ownership interest in the other, and there is no financial relationship between the parties.

arms race   The continuous building of bigger and better athletic facilities for the sole purpose of landing key recruits.

assessed value   The product of the fair market value of a property and its assessment ratio (see formula, p. 443).

assessment ratio   The percentage of a property's value that is subject to taxation.

asset-backed securities (ABS)   Bonds guaranteed by a franchise's COI or expected revenue streams.

asset-based approach   An approach to valuing an asset, a business, or an interest or equity in a business by determining what it would cost to re-create the business or asset. Also termed cost approach.

assets   What a company owns, including items such as cash, inventory, and accounts receivable.

athletic support group (ASG)   An organization responsible for an athletic department's annual giving programs, also known as a booster club.

auction-rate bond   A form of long-term debt that acts like short-term debt, in which interest rates are reset through auctions typically held no more than 35 days apart.

balance sheet A snapshot of the financial condition of an organization at a specific point in time.

bankruptcy The process of liquidation or reorganization of an insolvent firm.

base budget The expenditure level necessary to maintain last year's service level at next year's prices.

basis point A unit, representing one-hundredth of a percent, used in measuring changes in financial rates.

benefit principle The idea that those who benefit from a particular project ought to be the ones taxed to pay for it.

beta coefficient (B) A measurement of the volatility of a stock compared to market return, reflecting the degree to which the stock increases or decreases with an increase or decrease in the overall market.

board of directors An elected group whose job is to select the executives and top-level management of the company.

bond A promise to pay back borrowed money plus interest to the investor who has purchased the bond; a financial mechanism for raising capital by using debt as opposed to equity.

bond rating An estimation of the likelihood of a bond issuer's making payments in full.

Bosman ruling Court ruling allowing European soccer players to move to a new team without that team paying a transfer fee.

budget A set of financial statements based on projections resulting from a particular scenario, generally the most likely or hoped-for scenario.

budget time horizon The shortest time period that can be predicted with a reasonable degree of certainty on the basis of past business decisions and commitments.

business planning horizon The period for which forecasts can be made with a reasonable degree of confidence, generally three to five years.

call premium A fee charged to a borrower for repaying the principal on a bond prior to the maturity date (see formula, p. 230).

call provision Provision allowing a borrower to repay a debt before the maturity date.

campaign case statement In fundraising, a pitch to donors that answers all critical questions regarding the campaign, suggests why an individual should support the campaign, and informs the reader how he or she can give to the campaign.

capital The long-term, fixed assets that are used in production.

capital asset pricing model (CAPM) A method of analysis of the relationship between risk and rate of return, built on the notion that a stock's required rate of return is equal to the risk-free rate of return plus a risk premium, with the risk reflecting the portfolio's diversification.

capital budgeting The process of evaluating, comparing, and selecting capital projects to achieve the best return on investment over time. Also known as capital investment appraisal.

capital campaign An intensive effort to raise funds in a given time frame through gifts and pledges for a specific purpose.

capital expenditure The funds used to acquire capital assets that will help the organization earn future revenues or reduce future costs.

capital expenditure budget A forecast of the expenses and income related to a capital investment.

capital gain   The increase in a stock's price since purchase.

capital gains yield   For a bond, the annualized percentage change in the price relative to the current price.

capital markets   Markets for intermediate or long-term debt, as well as corporate stocks.

capital structure   The amount of debt and equity that a firm has.

capitalism   An economic system in which the majority of capital is privately owned.

capture rate   The portion of an organization's spending that is spent locally.

cash basis accounting   An accounting method that recognizes transactions when money is either received or paid out.

cash budget   A forecast of how much cash an organization will have on hand in a specific time period and how much it will need to meet expenses during that time.

casual visitor   A visitor attending a sporting event who was already in town for a different reason.

central revenues   Earnings that are paid directly to a league and then distributed to member organizations.

certificate of deposit (CD)   An FDIC-insured debt instrument issued by banks and savings and loans with a fixed term and a specific interest rate. Certificates of deposit are intended to be held until maturity, and penalties are incurred if the depositor removes the money prior to the term's completion.

certificate of participation (COP)   Financial instrument that a government agency or a non-profit corporation sets up to build a facility, often sold to one or more financial institutions to obtain the initial capital for construction. The agency or non-profit leases the facility either directly to the tenant(s) or to a facility operator and uses the lease payments to pay off the COP.

closed league   League requiring a majority of owner approval for a new team to enter the league.

coefficient of variation (CV)   A measure of the stand-alone risk of an investment (see formula, p. 85).

collateral   Asset(s) pledged to a lender to be used as repayment of a loan in the event of default.

collective bargaining   The process that occurs when workers in a company or league agree to negotiate as one unit with management to determine salaries and other working conditions.

collusion   Secret agreement or cooperation for an illegal purpose.

common stock   Ownership shares of an organization.

comparables analysis   In a feasibility study for a sport facility, a comparison of similar cities to the one where the new facility is proposed, with the idea that if facilities are successful in those cities, a similar facility may be successful in the subject city.

competitive analysis   In a feasibility study for a new sport facility, the investigation of existing facilities that might compete with the proposed facility.

competitive balance   The condition under which every franchise, if it executes sound management strategy, has a reasonable opportunity to compete for a playoff spot at least every couple of seasons.

competitive issue A bond issue in which a municipality publishes a notice of sale, seeking bids from underwriters. The underwriter submitting the lowest bid, or lowest interest rate, will be selected to underwrite the bonds.

compound interest Interest that is calculated on both the principal investment and the interest generated by that investment.

conglomerate A large corporation composed of many smaller firms.

construction impact The amount of money that comes into a community during the construction phase of a building that would not otherwise have entered the community.

Consumer Price Index (CPI) The result of a calculation based on the prices of roughly 80,000 goods and services in more than 200 categories reflecting the current lifestyle of the typical American consumer, intended to reflect the overall change in real prices during a period.

contingent liabilities Debts that may or may not occur.

contractually obligated income (COI) A revenue stream that a team receives under a multi-year contract. These revenue sources may serve as collateral for a loan.

controlling interest An ownership interest that effectively controls the business.

convertible bond A bond that offers some of the features of both equity and debt. The investor has the option to convert the bond into a fixed number of shares of stock in the company, at a stock price agreed upon at the issuance of the bond.

cord cutting Customers who get rid of their traditional cable packages in favor of alternative internet-based or wireless services.

corporate depth The extent of a market's corporate base, including the number of headquarters of Fortune 500 companies in the local area.

corporate veil Legal separation between a business owner and the organization, intended to eliminate personal liability.

correlation coefficient A measure of how closely the returns of an asset move relative to the returns of another asset held in a portfolio.

cost approach *See* asset-based approach.

cost-benefit analysis An analysis or study of the cost of a project in relation to its potential benefits.

cost of goods sold (COGS) Those costs that are directly attributable to the production of goods or products, including raw materials and labor costs.

coupon rate The rate that a bond issuer pays for the use of money; equivalent to an interest rate.

covariance The degree to which two variables change together; in finance, it helps us find assets that move differently from those already held in a portfolio.

credit An increase to a liability or equity account, entered on the right-hand side of a ledger.

current expenditure A short-term expense that is completely written off during the same year as the expense is incurred.

current liabilities Liabilities due within one year.

current ratio A formula that measures a company's ability to meet its current liabilities with its current assets (see formula, p. 60).

current yield   For a bond, the amount earned annually from an interest payment compared with the price, expressed as a percentage return (see formula, p. 231).

debit   An increase to an asset or expense account, entered on the left-hand side of a ledger.

debt financing   A method of raising capital in which an organization borrows money that must be repaid over a period of time, usually with interest.

debt ratio   A measure of an organization's leverage, sometimes referred to as the debt-to-assets ratio (see formula, p. 64).

decision package   A discrete addition to a reduced-level budget to maintain an existing program, serve an increased workload, or add a new program.

decision unit   An individual or unit where budget decisions are made, responsible for creating decision packages in zero-based budgeting.

default   The failure of an organization to fulfill its obligations toward a loan, often because it ceases operations or enters bankruptcy.

default risk   The risk that a borrower will not pay back the principal of a debt plus interest.

default risk premium (DRP)   Premium added to the nominal interest rate to account for the risk that the borrower might default.

deferred compensation   Salary whose payment is delayed under contractual terms; also known as deferred salary.

demand   The quantity of a product or service desired by consumers.

department-generated revenues   Funds generated independently by an athletic department and its programs.

depreciation   The allocation of an item's loss of value over a period of time.

depreciation recapture   Additional taxes that must be paid on an item that is found to have a higher salvage value than was initially estimated.

direct impact   Expenditures on a project or event that contribute to economic impact.

discount factor (DF)   *See* discount rate (1).

discount rate   (1) A measure of risk or uncertainty used in present value calculations; also called capitalization rate. (2) The rate charged by the Federal Reserve on loans made to member banks. (3) The rate of return required to justify an investment.

discounted cash flow (DCF) analysis   A valuation method based on the idea that the fair market value of an asset is equal to the present value of its expected future cash flows.

discounted payback period   The number of years required to recover an initial capital investment, discounting the investment's cash flows at the investment's cost of capital.

displaced spending   Money spent by a local resident on an event that would have been spent elsewhere in the local economy if the event had not occurred.

distributed club ownership model   A league structure under which individual owners, rather than the league office, own and control teams. *See also* franchise ownership model.

diversifiable risk   The portion of a stock's risk that can be removed through a well-diversified portfolio.

dividends   Periodic payments made to shareholders of a company, as a way of distributing profits to the shareholders.

dollar return The return on an investment measured by subtracting the amount invested from the amount received (see formula, p. 73).

double-declining balance depreciation A variation of straight-line depreciation in which a much higher amount of depreciation is allocated to the early years of the depreciation schedule.

double-entry bookkeeping A method of recording financial transactions where each transaction is entered or recorded twice, once on the debit side of the accounting records and once on the credit side.

draft lottery A lottery used in the NBA to determine the draft order of the non-playoff teams, in which a poorer record provides a greater chance to "win" the highest picks in the draft.

dynamic ticket pricing A pricing strategy in which ticket prices are altered instantly (like a stock price on a stock exchange) as demand increases or decreases.

earnings before interest and taxes (EBIT) A useful measure of income or profit (see formula, p. 64).

economic cycle A cycle consisting of four stages—growth, peak, recession, and recovery—and typically lasting for just under six years.

economic depression An extreme recession, lasting two or more years.

economic growth The part of the economic cycle when the economy is increasing in real terms (faster than the rate of inflation).

economic impact The net economic change in a host community resulting from spending attributed to an event or facility.

economic profit Profit that remains when opportunity costs are subtracted.

economics "The study of how people choose to allocate their scarce resources" (Wessel, 2000 [Ch. 5 References]).

efficiency principle The notion that a tax should be easy to understand, simple for government to collect, low in compliance costs, and difficult to evade.

eminent domain The government taking of private property for public use.

endowed gift Funds donated to a department in perpetuity that are invested, with only a portion of the annual investment return used for the gift's specific purposes.

entrepreneur A person who establishes a business venture and assumes the financial risk for it.

equity financing Financing in which an organization exchanges a share or portion of ownership for money.

esports Competitive video games that are organized with teams, players, tournaments, etc. in a similar manner to traditional sports.

excise tax Tax on goods and services that may be imposed within a city, county, or state.

expansion fee A fee charged to the owners of the newly established franchise when a professional sport league expands, to compensate current league owners for the short-term decrease in shared revenue from media contracts and licensed merchandise.

expected rate of return The sum of each possible outcome (return) on an investment multiplied by the outcome's probability.

expected return on a portfolio The weighted average of the expected returns of a set of assets (see formula, p. 86).

expense budget A list of a business unit's primary activities, with a dollar amount allocated to each.

expenses   Funds flowing out of an organization as costs of doing business.

express partnership   A general partnership created by a contract between the parties.

fair market value   The net price for an asset that would result in a transaction between a willing buyer and a willing seller, neither of whom is under compulsion to buy or sell, both having reasonable knowledge of the relevant facts, and the two parties being at arm's length.

fair tax   A national sales tax proposal that would repeal all current federal taxes and replace them with a tax on retail products and services.

fair value   The transaction price of two specific parties taking into account the advantages or disadvantages each one will gain from the transaction.

feasibility study   A study conducted to determine whether a project is likely to be successful, considering such items as engineering, land use, financing, demand, and economic impact.

federal funds rate   The interest rate on overnight loans between banks.

Federal Reserve   The central bank of the United States. It is the primary organizing body that attempts to maintain the overall economic health of the United States.

fiduciary duty   The responsibility of a company's management to act in the best interests of all shareholders.

finance   The science of fund management, applying concepts from accounting, economics, and statistics.

financial management   A sector within firms that is concerned with the acquisition and use of funds to meet the goal of wealth maximization.

financing analysis   An assessment of how much money will be needed for a project, such as facility construction.

fiscal policy   The use of government revenue collection and spending to influence the economy.

fiscal year   A 12-month period over which a company budgets its money.

fixed costs   Expenses that do not vary with volume of sales.

flat tax   A federal levy that would require every American to pay the same income tax rate, rather than rates based on each taxpayer's yearly income.

forecast   A prediction and quantification of future events for the purpose of budgeting.

franchise free agency   The ability of a team to relocate to another city when it is not obligated to a facility through a lease or a municipality through an agreement.

franchise ownership model   A league structure under which individual owners, rather than the league office, own and control teams. *See also* distributed club ownership model.

free ride   To benefit at another's expense without expending a usual cost or effort.

Freedom of Information request   Request filed by a citizen under the Freedom of Information Act to discover, for example, where and how a government agency is spending its money.

future value (FV)   The worth of an asset at a certain date in the future, determined by calculating the change in value of money when an interest rate is applied over the intervening period of time.

general obligation bonds (GOBs)   Bonds issued by a local government, lasting about 20 years and secured by tax revenues and the issuing entity's ability to impose new taxes, with interest paid each year directly out of the entity's general funds.

general partnership   The joining of two or more individuals with the intent to own and operate a business.

generally accepted accounting principles (GAAP)   A standard set of guidelines and procedures for financial reporting.

gift financing   Charitable donations, either cash or in-kind, made to an organization.

globalization   The integration of economies into one "world economy."

going concern   An organization that we assume, for budgeting purposes, will operate indefinitely.

government financing   Funding provided by federal, state, or municipal sources, including land use, tax abatements, direct financing, state and municipal appropriations, and infrastructure improvements.

grant   Monetary aid that does not have to be repaid.

Great Society   A set of initiatives, including Medicare and Medicaid, intended to combat poverty, passed in the 1960s during President Lyndon B. Johnson's administration.

gross domestic product (GDP)   The market value of all final goods and services produced within the borders of a county, state, country, or other region in a year.

gross domestic sport product (GDSP)   The market value of a nation's output of sport-related goods and services in a given year. This includes the value added to the economy by the sport industry, as well as the gross product originating from the sport industry.

horizontal equity   The idea that individuals with similar incomes should pay similar amounts of a tax.

implied partnership   A general partnership that is not established by a contract but created by the parties' merely acting as partners.

income approach   An approach to valuing an asset, a business, or an interest or equity in a business, under which income or cash flow serves as the basis for the value of the business or asset.

income statement   A statement of a company's income over a specified period of time, typically issued on an annual or quarterly basis. Also called a statement of earnings or profit and loss statement.

incremental budget   A budget arrived at by either decreasing or increasing last year's budget, based on projected changes in operations and conditions.

incremental cash flow   Cash flow created through the implementation of a new project.

incremental spending   Spending above and beyond what a person would have spent had an event not taken place.

incremental visitor   A visitor who came to town because of an event and would not have come to town otherwise.

indirect economic impact   Economic impact that represents the circulation of initial expenditures (direct impacts) in an economy.

induced economic impact   The effect of direct and indirect economic impacts on earnings and employment.

inflation   The devaluation of money over time.

inflation premium (IP)   The portion of an investment's return that compensates the investor for loss of purchasing power over time, calculated by determining the expected average inflation rate over the life of the security.

inheritance (death) tax   A levy on an estate applied when the owner dies.

initial cost   The actual cost of starting a project, adjusted for any installation, delivery, or packing costs; discounts to the initial price; the sale of existing equipment or machinery; and taxes.

initial public offering (IPO)   The offering of shares of a company to the public in order to generate cash for the business, when no shares had previously been available.

interest   The cost of borrowing money.

interest coverage ratio   A measure of a firm's ability to pay the interest on its debt. Sometimes called the times interest earned ratio (see formula, p. 64).

interest rate risk   The risk of a decrease in the value of a security due to an increase in interest rates.

internal rate of return (IRR)   The discount rate at which the present value of estimated cash flows is equal to the initial cost of the investment.

inventory turnover ratio   A measure of how often a company sells and replaces its inventory over a specified period of time, typically a year.

investment risk   A measure of the likelihood of low or negative future returns.

investments   Security choices made by individual and institutional investors as they build portfolios.

jock taxes   Special taxes that apply to professional athletes' income earned in a particular city, county, or state.

joint use agreement   A formal agreement for the sharing of a facility between two or more parties.

junk bond   A bond with a significant chance of default and a high coupon rate, receiving a bond rating below BBB.

laissez-faire   Describes an economic policy in which the government has little involvement in the business environment beyond setting and enforcing rudimentary laws.

large-cap company   A publicly traded company that has a market capitalization of at least $5 billion.

Larry Bird exception   A provision that allows NBA teams to re-sign their "own" potential free agents for salaries that would otherwise cause the team to exceed the designated yearly salary cap; so named because the Boston Celtics were concerned that the loss of Larry Bird to free agency would devastate the team.

league think   The philosophy, initially advocated by NFL commissioner Pete Rozelle, that team owners should think of the overall financial health of the league as their first priority and individual franchise profits as a secondary concern.

leakage   The movement of money out of a geographic region.

lease revenue bond   A version of revenue bond in which the revenue stream backing the payment of the bond is a lease.

level of risk   A comparative evaluation of risk, determined by comparing the risk of one asset or firm to that of another. Some firms or assets have a lower degree of risk and some have a higher degree of risk.

leverage   How a company chooses to finance its operation with debt versus equity. A company that relies extensively on borrowing money is considered to be heavily leveraged. Such a company faces greater risk of financial problems than one not so reliant on debt.

liabilities   The financial obligations or debts owed by an organization to others.

limited liability corporation/limited liability partnership (LLC/LLP)   A business structure under which shareholders' distributions are taxed as ordinary income and shareholders are shielded from personal liability.

limited partner   A partner who is liable only for his or her direct financial contribution and is not permitted to participate formally in the company's operation.

line-item budgeting   Approach in which line items, also known as objects of expenditure, are the main focus of analysis, authorization, and control.

liquidation   The sale of an organization's assets piece by piece, effectively removing the firm from existence.

liquidation value   The value of assets when they are not used together (i.e., the value obtained when a company's assets are sold separately, piece by piece).

liquidity   The ease and speed with which an asset can be converted to cash.

liquidity premium (LP)   A premium added to the interest rate of a security that cannot be converted to cash in a short amount of time at a reasonable price. Also called the marketability premium.

liquidity spread   The difference between a long-term interest rate and a short-term interest rate.

loan   A sum of money borrowed from a financial intermediary, such as a bank or insurance company, that must be paid back over a specific period of time and with interest, the fee for borrowing the money.

loan pool   A league-financed fund from which franchises can borrow at relatively low cost.

local market   The area in which a franchise operates, with distinct differences in population, economic activity, and passion for sport.

local option sales tax   A special-purpose tax levied at the municipal level.

local revenues   Team earnings from home ticket sales, local television and radio, advertising, and sponsorship, shared within the league.

lockout   A decision by management to suspend production while it negotiates with labor.

London Interbank Offered Rate (LIBOR)   A benchmark interest rate based on the average interest rate that banks in the London interbank market pay to borrow unsecured funds from one another.

long-term liabilities   Liabilities due after one year.

loss-of-value insurance   Insurance coverage that pays if an athlete experiences a significant injury that negatively alters their career.

luxury tax   A fee imposed on franchises that exceed a salary threshold.

M1   A measure of liquid assets in the form of cash and checking accounts in the total money supply.

M2   A measure of liquid assets in the form of cash and checking accounts (see M1) plus all money in savings accounts and certificates of deposit in the total money supply.

M3   A measure of liquid assets in the form of cash and checking accounts (see M1) plus all money in savings accounts and certificates of deposit (see M2) plus the assets and liabilities, including long-term deposits, of financial institutions.

macroeconomics   The study of forces that affect numerous or even all sectors of the overall economy.

major gift   A donation worth $25,000 or more.

market approach   A method of valuing an asset, a business, or an interest or equity in a business that relies on prices that similar assets sell for in the marketplace.

market capitalization   The market price of a company, equal to the number of outstanding shares multiplied by the price per share.

market demand   The demand within a marketplace for a facility.

market multiples approach   A type of market approach based on the premise that the value of a business enterprise depends on what investors in a competitive market actually pay to own equity or shares of stock in similar companies.

market risk   The portion of a stock's risk that cannot be eliminated through a diversified portfolio; it is measured by the degree to which the stock moves with the market.

market transactions approach   A type of market approach in which the value of a company is determined by reference to the value of comparable firms that have been sold within a reasonably recent period of time, with appropriate adjustments for the time value of money.

market value   An estimate of the value of a company according to the stock market (see formula, p. 66).

marketability   A measure of the readiness with which an asset may be sold or liquidated.

maturity risk premium (MRP)   A premium added to the interest rate of a security that accounts for interest rate risk.

media equivalency   Analysis that measures the exposure for a sponsor (the number of people seeing the sponsor's ad or signage) and determines what it would cost to achieve the same exposure through some other form of media.

membership   Club ownership type where individuals wishing to invest in a club are required to purchase a membership. A fan-owned team.

microeconomics   The study of issues, such as supply, demand, and pricing, that occur at the firm level.

mid-year convention   The practice of using June 30 as the accounting date for a cash flow when an analyst does not have the exact details of the cash flow over the year.

mill   A measure of tax rates equal to 1/1,000 of a dollar, or 1/10 of a penny.

millage/millage rate   The tax rate approved by a public body such as a state or local government, city council, school board, special purpose district, or county council to meet the budgetary needs of each entity; the total of the levies by the city, county, school district, and any special districts in which a particular resident lives.

minority discount   Discount applied to the purchase price of stock when the purchaser receives no controlling interest.

minority partner   An owner who holds less than a 50% stake in a jointly owned business.

mixed cost   An expense that includes both fixed and variable elements.

modified internal rate of return (MIRR)   The discount rate at which the present value of a project's cost is equal to the present value of the project's terminal value.

modified zero-based budgeting (MZBB) A budgeting concept that starts at a base higher than zero and matches spending levels with services to be performed.

monetary policy Policy the government sets to control the supply, availability, and cost of money.

money markets Markets for highly liquid, short-term securities.

monopoly The status of an individual or organization that has no viable competition and, hence, complete control of the distribution of a product or service.

multiple owners/private investment syndicate model An ownership model in which individuals pool their resources to purchase a franchise and incorporate as a partnership, LLC, or the like. The most common model of team ownership.

multiple owners/publicly traded corporation model An ownership model in which a franchise is governed by a board of directors who are elected by shareholder vote. The board of directors appoints the team's senior management. With the exception of the Green Bay Packers, this model is not currently used in the United States.

multiplier A variable that measures the change in output for each and every industry as a result of the injection of one dollar of direct impact into any of those industries, to help researchers quantify indirect and induced economic impacts.

multiplier effect The ripple effects of initial spending (direct impacts), consisting of indirect and induced impacts.

municipal bond A bond for which the borrower is a city.

naming rights The right to place a firm's name on a facility; a form of sponsorship.

National Association of Intercollegiate Athletics (NAIA) One of three main governing bodies overseeing college sport in the United States.

National Collegiate Athletic Association (NCAA) The largest of the three main governing bodies overseeing college sport in the United States, and the primary governing body; formerly the Intercollegiate Athletic Association of the United States.

National Junior College Athletic Association (NJCAA) One of the three main governing bodies overseeing college sport in the United States, with membership made up of junior and community colleges.

NCAA Division I One of three classifications of NCAA university membership. Division I includes subclassifications based on football sponsorship: (a) Football Bowl Subdivision (FBS), schools that participate in bowl games; (b) Football Championship Subdivision (FCS), schools that participate in the NCAA-run football championship; and (c) other, schools that do not sponsor football at all.

NCAA Division II One of three classifications of NCAA university membership, requiring the institution to sponsor a minimum of ten sports.

NCAA Division III One of three classifications of NCAA university membership, requiring the institution to sponsor a minimum of ten sports. Athletes cannot receive financial aid related to their athletic ability in this division.

negotiated issue A bond issue for which a municipality selects one underwriter and the municipality and underwriter negotiate the terms of the sale.

net assessed value   Taxable worth of property, the difference between total assessed value and tax-exempt property.

net present value (NPV)   The present value of a project's future cash flows less the project's initial cost; also, a capital budgeting method based on this calculation.

net profit margin ratio   A measure of the effectiveness and efficiency of a company's operations (see formula, p. 65).

net working capital (NWC)   The cash needed to run a business on a daily basis (measured in annual dollars needed), which is not available to be given to the owners of the business because it is needed for operations. It is calculated by subtracting current liabilities from current assets.

NIL cap   The maximum amount that student-athletes can be paid for use of their names, images, and likenesses.

nominal exchange rate   The market values that are displayed on a given day for foreign currency exchange.

nominal interest rate   The interest rate actually charged for a given marketable security, consisting of the real risk-free rate of interest plus multiple risk premiums. These include risk premiums based on the risk of time and the level of risk, which reflect the riskiness of the security itself, and premiums reflecting inflation and liquidity. Also called the quoted interest rate (see formula, p. 80).

nominal risk-free rate   The real risk-free rate of interest plus an inflation premium (see formula, p. 80).

nominal value   The face value of money.

non-excludable   Describes a good that a producer cannot prevent someone from consuming or from enjoying.

non-profit organization   An organization not conducted for the profit of owners. Typically, a non-profit organization's activities are devoted to charitable activities, such as education. Revenues generated by non-profit organizations are treated differently for tax purposes from those of for-profit entities.

non-rival   Describes a good that can be consumed by one person without preventing another person from consuming it.

North American Industrial Classification System (NAICS)   A classification system used by the US Census Bureau to measure and track economic activity in the United States. The sport industry is not classified as a distinct industry and is scattered across at least 12 different NAICS-defined industries.

offset language   Language in a contract that states that if a released player is owed compensation, that compensation will be lowered by the amount the future team may pay for the player's services.

open league   A league that allows teams the ability to freely enter the league.

operations impact   The economic impact of a facility generated through its daily operation.

opportunity cost   The cost of a financial decision in terms of forgone alternatives. For example, often part of the public's financing for a stadium involves giving away the land or leasing it for a below-market rate. The public's total cost is not just what it directly spends to support building the facility, but also what it "loses" by not utilizing the land in another manner.

over-the-top (OTT)   The delivery of content via the internet rather than through a traditional cable provider.

owners' equity   An estimate of the ownership value of a company. Also called shareholders' equity or stockholders' equity.

parachute payments   Payments made to relegated teams to reduce the financial impact of relegation.

pay-as-you-go approach   A financing method where projects are paid for with current assets rather than borrowed funds.

payback period   The number of years required to recover an initial capital investment.

payments in lieu of taxes (PILOT)   Payments made to a local government instead of franchise, property, or sales taxes.

periodic expense   An expense that does not occur regularly throughout the year but must be budgeted for during the year, such as new vehicles, retirement bonuses, and other one-time events.

permanent seat license (PSL)   The right to purchase tickets for a specific seat location, for the life of the facility, with fewer restrictions on exchange or sale than those for personal seat licenses.

perpetual growth rate   An expected annual growth rate in a dividend payment, in perpetuity.

perpetuity   An annuity that has no scheduled ending. Also, "in perpetuity": without an ending date.

personal seat license (PSL)   The right to purchase tickets for a specific seat location, sometimes limited to a period of time that may not match the expected lifespan of the facility.

planning   The establishment of objectives and the formulation, evaluation, and selection of the policies, strategies, tactics, and actions required to achieve those objectives.

player draft   The process by which a league assigns incoming players throughout the league.

point system   System in which donors to athletic programs earn points based on their giving characteristics, which qualify them to purchase tickets for high-demand events or tickets in a desired location.

pooled debt   A debt instrument that has the backing of an entire league rather than an individual team, usually providing a more favorable interest rate than the individual franchise could obtain.

portfolio   A combination of financial assets held by an investor.

positive externalities   Benefits produced by an event that are not captured by the event owners or sport facility being used; also termed overflow benefits.

present value   The current value of a payment that will be received or paid in the future, computed by applying a discount rate that measures risk and uncertainty.

price   What one party (the buyer) must give to obtain what is offered by another party (the seller).

price elasticity of demand   The percentage decrease in the number of units sold compared to the percentage increase in the unit price.

price-to-earnings (P/E) ratio   An estimate of how much money investors will pay for each dollar of a company's earnings, used widely to measure corporate performance and value (see formula, p. 67).

price-to-revenue (P/R) ratio Transaction price divided by total annual revenues, a common starting point for franchise valuation.

primary research The generation of information specifically for the purpose of a study.

prime rate The rate banks charge their "best" customers, usually those that are the largest and most stable or have been with the bank the longest.

private financing Financing that does not use public dollars.

probability distribution A list of all possible outcomes of an investment in terms of expected rates of return, with a probability assigned to each outcome.

production opportunities The reason a company needs capital and the possibility that the money can be turned into more money or benefits.

profit maximization The pursuit of the highest profits possible as an organization's primary goal.

program budget A budget in which expenditures are based primarily on units of work and secondarily on the character and object of the work.

program planning budgeting system (PPBS) An approach to developing a program budget that focuses on outputs rather than inputs, with an emphasis on organizational effectiveness, not spending.

promotion Teams moving to higher leagues by finishing at the top of the standings at the end of the season.

property tax A government levy based on the value of property, including real property (land and structures built on the land or improvements made to the land) and personal property (everything else that has value, such as automobiles, trucks, furniture, and equipment).

prospect Any individual, foundation, corporation, or organization that has the potential and likelihood to give to an organization.

psychic impact The emotional impact on a community of having a local sport team or hosting national or international events.

public facility authority (PFA) bond A type of municipal bond used for the construction, renovation, or improvement of public facilities.

public financing The use of public funds to finance a project. For the construction of an arena or facility, tax revenues are typically used to retire debt service.

public good A good that is non-rival and non-excludable.

public/private partnership A collaboration between the public and private sectors.

public sector sport Sport programs offered to serve societal need rather than profit potential.

quantitative easing The purchase from banks of poorly performing loans or loans likely to soon be poorly performing by the central bank of a country. This increases the individual banks' latitude under their reserve requirement to issue new loans and their confidence in pursuing additional loan applicants because their "worst" loans have been removed from their financial books.

quick ratio A measure of a company's ability to meet its current liabilities with its current assets, not including inventory (see formula, p. 61).

rate of return The gain or loss of an investment over a period of time (see formula, p. 73).

real exchange rate Foreign currency exchange rate that takes into account the differing levels of inflation between two countries.

real risk-free rate The rate of interest on a riskless security if inflation were not expected; the rate of interest on a short-term US Treasury bill in an inflation-free environment.

real value The value of money after inflation is taken into account; often referred to as purchasing power.

recession Two consecutive quarters or more of negative growth in a nation's gross domestic product.

reduced-level budget In zero-based budgeting, a budget that results from cutting the base budget by a predetermined percentage.

reinvestment rate risk Risk related to declining interest rates, primarily affecting short-term bills; the risk measures loss of income that would occur if the interest rate on a bond has fallen at the time the funds are reinvested.

related-party transaction A transaction between two businesses that have some form of pre-existing relationship.

relegation System under which, after each season, a certain number of the "worst performing" clubs will be "sent down" or relegated to a lower division.

relevant risk The contribution of a single stock to the riskiness of a diversified portfolio.

required rate of return The profit that an investor would require from a particular investment, whether in stocks or bonds, in order to consider it worth purchasing, given the riskiness of the investment.

reserve clause An agreement among owners that ties a player to a team in perpetuity.

residual value What a business or asset will be worth at the end of the period for which cash flows are projected.

retained earnings A portion of earnings that a firm saves in order to finance operations or acquire assets.

return on assets (ROA) A similar measure to the return on equity ratio with a similar formula except that total assets is used as the denominator in the calculation instead of shareholders'/owners' equity. Also referred to as return on investment (ROI).

return on equity capital The combination of dividend payments and capital gains on an investment.

return on equity ratio A measure of the rate of return a company's owners or shareholders are receiving on their investment (see formula, p. 66).

return on investment (ROI) *See* return on assets.

revenue bonds A form of public finance that is paid off solely from specific, well-defined sources, such as hotel taxes, ticket taxes, or other sources of public funding. Also, bonds that are secured by the revenues to be generated by the project being funded. If the source of funding does not meet expectations, the bonds will not be paid off in full.

revenue budget A forecast of revenues based on projections of the organization's sales.

revenue sharing The sharing of revenues among teams in a league to support weaker franchises and maintain the competitive balance in the league.

revenues   Income generated from business activities, such as the sale of goods or services.

reverse time-switcher   A local resident who leaves town during an event period because of the event.

risk   A measure of the chance that some unfavorable event will occur.

risk averse   A quality that investors tend to display: when presented with two alternatives for investment with the same expected rate of return, most investors will select the investment with the lower risk.

risk-free rate   The interest paid on risk-free investments that pay a guaranteed return, such as US Treasury bills.

risk of time   The fact that risk increases as the length of time funds are invested increases.

risk premium   The difference between the rate of return for a risky investment and the risk-free rate.

rule of thirds   The expectation that the top ten gifts to a campaign will account for 33% of the campaign's total goal, based on past giving patterns.

salary arbitration   A process whereby an independent judge determines whether the salary that a team submits for a player or the salary that the player requests will be paid.

salary cap   A limit on the compensation an employer may provide to employees; in sport, a salary cap restricts salaries for teams across an entire league.

salary slotting   League-established rules or recommendations regarding initial compensation provided to a player based on draft positioning.

sales tax   A tax on the sale of certain goods and services.

scalping   Pejorative term for the resale of tickets.

scarcity   Lack of sufficient supply of an item or a resource to meet current demand.

secondary research   The analysis of data that have already been generated for other purposes but might provide information for a study.

secondary ticket market   The market for the reselling of tickets.

secured claim   A debt for which the borrower provided collateral.

securitization   The use of contractually obligated future revenue as collateral for issued debt.

security market line (SML)   A formula for evaluating the risk and return merits of an investment (see formula, p. 90).

self-sustaining   Describes an athletic department whose revenues cover its operating expenses.

sensitivity analysis   The process of developing several forecasts under different scenarios and assigning probabilities to each scenario to arrive at an acceptable forecast.

serial bond   A bond requiring regular payments on principal and interest over the life of the bond.

Sherman Antitrust Act   An 1890 law that forbids contracts or other actions among businesses that would restrict competition.

simple interest   Interest that is calculated only on principal.

sin taxes   Taxes on alcohol and tobacco.

single-entity structure   A league structure in which owners purchase shares in the league rather than in an individual franchise.

single owner/private investor model   An ownership model in which one individual owns the firm.

small-cap stock   The stock of a publicly traded company with a market capitalization between $250 million and $1 billion.

socialistic   Describes an economic system where the government takes an active role in owning and administering the means of production.

sole proprietorship   A business that is legally owned and operated by a single individual.

solidarity payments   Payments from league rights and commercial agreements guaranteed to clubs in an open league.

sponsorship   A form of advertising in which a firm pays for exposure that supports the firm's marketing objectives.

Sports Broadcasting Act (SBA)   A 1961 law providing an antitrust exemption that permitted professional sport leagues to sell their television rights as a league package.

stadium-related revenue source   A non-shared source of revenue from sales related to the venue where a team plays, such as the sale of luxury suites.

stand-alone risk   The risk that an asset would present if only that single asset were held.

standard deviation (SD)   A measure of variability in a distribution of numbers, denoted σ.

statement of cash flows   A report that tracks cash in and cash out of an organization and provides data as to whether a company has sufficient cash on hand to meet its debts and obligations.

step cost   An expense that is constant within ranges of use but differs between ranges.

stock   A share of ownership in a company.

stock exchange/stock market   An organization that provides a place and means for brokers to trade stocks and other securities.

stock market index   A measure of a section or sections of a stock market.

stock option   A contract that allows a party to purchase a specified number of shares of stock for a certain price.

straight-line depreciation   A depreciation method in which the total cost of the item, less its estimated salvage value, is divided by its useful life to determine its yearly depreciation allowance.

strategic planning   The process of defining a vision for an organization and creating goals and objectives to help achieve this vision.

strategic planning horizon   The far future, planning for which is concerned with the long-term aspirations of the organization and management.

strategic value   The value that a buyer would be willing to pay in order to obtain certain assets because it has the ability to use the assets in a way to get more value out of them than a typical buyer would.

subchapter C corporation   A business structure under which the company may seek investors and conduct business activities around the world. The corporation must hold annual meetings, elect a board of directors, and provide specific annual paperwork to the government and to shareholders. Often called a C corp.

subchapter S corporation   A business structure under which shareholders' distributions are taxed as ordinary income and shareholders are shielded from personal liability. Often called an S corp.

sum-of-years'-digits depreciation   A method of depreciation that takes the non-linear loss of value into account.

surplus   The amount of an asset or resource that exceeds the portion that is utilized.

sustainability   Meeting today's needs without compromising future generations' ability to meet their own needs.

synergistic premium   An additional amount that a buyer would be willing to pay for an asset or business because ownership would provide benefits beyond those of owning the asset or business as a stand-alone investment.

synthetic fixed-rate bond   A bond that has elements of both a fixed-rate bond and a variable-rate bond.

T-accounts   The method accountants have historically used to track revenues and expenses and to create accounts to be entered on balance sheets and income statements.

tax abatement   A government's forgoing of collection of taxes.

tax increment financing (TIF)   The use of only additional or new taxes generated from a certain source, such as property taxes, to help finance a sport facility. Once the facility is built, any increases in tax revenues resulting from the improvement of the area are used to pay off the tax increment bond.

tax rate   The total rate of tax that an individual or business pays; the total of levies by the city, county, school district, and any special districts in which the tax-payer resides.

tax receipts   Tax revenues from all sources received by a municipality.

tax subsidy   The use of tax receipts to fund a program or business.

term bond   A bond paid in a single payment made at the end of the loan period.

terminal value   The future value of a project's cash inflows compounded at the project's cost of capital.

territorial rights   The exclusive control of a predetermined area (typically an entire metropolitan area), which enables a professional sport team to market exclusively in that area without fear of the presence of another franchise.

time-switcher   A visitor who would have come to town at another time, but opted to come to town during an event period in order to attend the event.

time value of money   The yearly, monthly, or daily changes in the purchasing power of money.

total asset turnover ratio   A measure of how efficiently a company is utilizing its assets to make money (see formula, p. 62).

total expected return   The rate of return expected on an asset or a portfolio of assets when all terms of gain are combined.

tourism tax   Tax on hotel stays or rental cars; may also include food and beverage taxes in certain districts.

tournament theory   An economic theory where prize money should be structured to elicit more effort from competitors.

trade credit   An agreement between a manufacturer and a retailer that after the manufacturer ships its product to the retailer for sale, the retailer may delay payment for a period of time, according to the terms.

traditional gifts table   A table of targeted amounts and numbers of gifts for a capital campaign, developed according to a specific formula.

transfer   The movement of a player in the soccer labor market. Transfers often involve a fee paid by one club to another.

transfer pricing   The pricing of assets transferred within an organization.

units of production depreciation   Depreciation calculated by dividing the total number of items produced during a given year by the total number of items the asset will produce during its useful life.

unsecured claim   A debt for which the investor has no right to seize any assets from the company or person who borrowed the money.

use tax   A levy imposed on certain goods and services that are purchased outside the state and brought into the state.

valuation date   The specific date selected for the valuation of a business or asset.

value added tax (VAT)   A consumption tax levied on any value that is added to a product.

value over replacement player (VORP)   The production that a player can provide over that which is readily available for "free" (league minimum). Teams should allocate financial resources to players based upon their ability to provide production.

variable cost   An expense that changes with volume of sales.

variable ticket pricing (VTP)   A method of placing various values on entry to games, with higher initial prices for highly demanded games and lower prices for lower-demanded games.

vertical equity   The idea that a tax should not cause poorer persons to bear a disproportionate share.

volatility   The amount of fluctuation that occurs in a series of similar investment returns and the degree to which the returns deviate from the average. More volatility translates into greater risk.

wealth maximization   Maximizing the overall value of the firm. This is the goal or outcome of financial management for most organizations.

weighted average cost of capital (WACC)   In a capital expenditure, the weighted average of the cost of each of the funding sources.

win maximization   The pursuit of winning as a primary goal.

wins above replacement (WAR)   A method of analyzing a player's performance to determine how much the player contributes to on-field success beyond what an easily obtainable player, such as a minor league player at the same position or an unsigned free agent, can contribute.

yield curve   The graphic depiction of interest rates against time to maturity for bonds with equal credit quality, including government bonds.

yield to maturity (YTM)   The percentage rate of return that a bond would provide if held until its maturity date, often used to denote the total annualized return from owning a specific bond. It is the same as the total expected return.

zero-based budgeting (ZBB)   A budgeting approach and financial management strategy that requires building a budget from a zero base rather than from the previous year's budget.

Finance Basics

CHAPTER 1

Introduction to Sport Finance

Matthew T. Brown

KEY CONCEPTS

capital markets
debt financing
distributed club ownership model
economic cycle
economic depression
economic growth
equity financing
finance
financial management
gift financing
government financing
gross domestic product (GDP)
gross domestic sport product (GDSP)
investments

money markets
multiple owners/private investment
   syndicate model
multiple owners/publicly traded
   corporation model
North American Industry
   Classification System (NAICS)
retained earnings
Sherman Antitrust Act
single-entity structure
single owner/private investor model
sustainability
wealth maximization

INTRODUCTION

Why is an understanding of financial management important? Consider the example of the construction of a new stadium or arena. This area of sport finance is often in the news because a new stadium or arena directly impacts local residents, businesses, and government. Here are a few examples:

- Allegiant Stadium, home of the Las Vegas Raiders, opened in 2020 at a cost of $1.9 billion. The domed venue seats 65,000 and offers 70 premium suites and 6,000 club seats. The stadium's capacity can be expanded to 72,500 for special events like the Super Bowl.
- The City of Columbia, South Carolina, paid approximately $29 million to build Segra Park to bring minor league baseball back to the state's capital. The $35 million ballpark opened in 2016 and seats 8,000 for baseball games and 14,000 for concerts. The city used revenues from its hospitality

tax to pay off bonds used to finance the new stadium's construction. The Savannah Sand Gnats announced in 2015 that they would relocate to Columbia for the 2016 season. Hardball Capital, the team's owner and manager of the stadium, contributed approximately $6 million toward construction costs.

- In 2020, the Texas Rangers replaced Globe Life Park, built for $191 million in 2004, with Globe Life Field. The $1.1 billion stadium features a retractable roof, with seating for 40,300 fans. It has 12 suites located behind home plate and an additional 71 long-term suites and 16 party suites.
- Tottenham Hotspur Stadium, which opened in London in 2019, seats 62,303. Home to Tottenham Hotspur Football Club of the English Premier League (EPL), its retractable pitch made it the first purpose-built stadium for the National Football League (NFL) in Europe. The £1 billion ($1.31 billion) venue was privately financed by the club, primarily via a £637 million senior loan from a group of banks that included Bank of America Merrill Lynch, Goldman Sachs, and HSBC. The loan had a maturity date of April 2022. In 2019, the club converted £525 million of the loan into bonds in the US with maturities ranging from 15 to 30 years.
- For the Minnesota Twins, a new stadium meant access to previously unavailable revenue. The Twins shared the Hubert H. Humphrey Metrodome with the Minnesota Vikings. The facility was poorly designed, not only for watching a baseball game but also for generating baseball revenue. The Twins received almost nothing from luxury suite rentals; rather, the money from luxury suite sales went to the Vikings. The City of Minneapolis kept a portion of revenue generated from parking, concessions, and in-stadium advertising. In their new ballpark, Target Field, the Twins have kept almost all revenue, including revenue from naming rights, premium seats, and luxury suites. The average ticket price for a premium seat when the stadium opened was approximately $52 per game. A membership fee of $1,000 to $2,000 was also charged to premium seat ticket holders for access to the exclusive club areas within the stadium (Roberts & Murr, 2008).
- Texas A&M University expanded and renovated Kyle Field, its football stadium, in a $450 million project. More than 20,000 seats were added, bringing the stadium's capacity to more than 102,000 and making Kyle Field the largest stadium in the Southeastern Conference (SEC).
- SoFi Stadium, home of the Los Angeles Rams and Los Angeles Chargers of the NFL, opened in 2020. The new stadium became the permanent home for the two recently relocated teams. The $5 billion stadium is part of Hollywood Park, a 298-acre sports and entertainment complex built in Inglewood, California. In addition to being the home of two NFL teams, the venue will host the Super Bowl in 2022, the College Football Championship Game in 2023, and the opening and closing ceremonies of the Olympic Games in 2028.

These examples represent the revenue side of constructing new venues—the large price tags of which put them in the news. But what about other financial management issues related to a facility's construction, for example, how the revenue is shared and how ongoing operating expenses will be met? To consider these issues and how they can impact a community, let's look at the

Indianapolis Colts. Lucas Oil Stadium, the replacement to the RCA Dome, immediately generated new revenue for the Colts after the team moved into its new home; however, none of the new stadium-generated revenue went to the Capital Improvement Board (CIB). The CIB is the governmental entity that operates the stadium and manages its debt service—the cash required over a specific time period for repayment of the principal and interest on the debt ("Indy wrestles," 2009).

The $675 million stadium was paid for through a municipal bond issue backed primarily by a 1% tax increase on prepared food in nine counties surrounding Indianapolis. However, the revenue generated through the increased tax covers only the facility's debt service. No funds were made available for the operation of the facility. With the tax revenue allotted for debt service and stadium revenue going to the Colts, the CIB has been operating the stadium at a $20 million annual deficit ("Indy wrestles," 2009). As a result of poor financial management—specifically plans and forecasts relating to the operating costs of the new stadium—state officials had to act. The citizens of the metropolitan area likely will be required to pay for the stadium's operating costs through some form of tax increase.

As the above examples show, the revenue generated in these new venues attracts a large amount of media attention. However, financial management issues related to the construction and operation of the venues are often ignored, overlooked, or perhaps not understood. When this happens, as in the case of Indianapolis, the importance of understanding financial management becomes clear.

In this chapter, we will introduce you to key concepts in finance, many of which will be discussed in greater depth in later chapters. You may encounter terms with which you are unfamiliar. To gain a working knowledge of these terms, refer to the Glossary at the start of the book.

WHAT IS FINANCE?

Finance, the science of fund management, includes application of concepts from accounting, economics, and statistics. Within the world of finance, there are three interrelated sectors: (1) money and capital markets, (2) investments, and (3) financial management (Brigham & Houston, 2019). **Money markets** are markets for highly liquid, short-term securities; **capital markets** are markets for intermediate or long-term debt, as well as corporate stock. Hence, the money and capital markets sector includes securities markets such as the New York Stock Exchange and the Chicago Mercantile Exchange. Investment banking falls within this sector as well, as do insurance and mutual fund management.

As opposed to this first sector, the focus of the **investments** sector is on security choices made by individual and institutional investors as they build portfolios. Merrill Lynch and Edward Jones are companies operating within this sector.

The **financial management** sector involves decisions within firms regarding the acquisition or use of funds, usually with the goal or outcome of **wealth maximization**, or maximizing the overall value of the firm. To achieve wealth maximization, the finance department forecasts future revenues and plans future expenses. In sport, this may include calculating cash flow increases resulting from a move to a new facility (as shown in the chapter introduction) and determining how much the organization can increase player payroll as a result of the forecast. The finance department also performs a portion of the control function of management. Through coordination with other departments in the organization, the finance department pursues efficiency of operation and resource utilization. The finance department makes investment and financing decisions, working with financial markets and investment firms when necessary. The type of debt financing to be used when constructing a new stadium is one example of these decisions.

A firm in the sport industry may be structured as a for-profit, not-for-profit, or governmental entity. For-profit sport enterprises have many commonalities with other types of for-profit business. Hence, the financial management of a sport organization is often quite similar to the financial management of organizations in other industries. These commonalities include value creation, or increasing the value of a firm over time, and revenue growth. However, there are areas of difference. One major difference is the diverse objectives of firm owners within sport (Foster, Greyser, & Walsh, 2005). Although sport organizations usually compete for wealth maximization, an owner in professional sport might not be interested in this goal. Rather, the owner may be more interested in winning championships or in seeking celebrity status by being one of a select few professional sport franchise owners. Another goal of the owner may be to protect a community asset. The differing objectives of owners can harm the competitive balance in a league, particularly in terms of winning championships. For example, an extremely wealthy owner with a willingness to incur losses over several seasons can create an imbalance in competition. As a result, at the beginning of a season, only a few teams may have a realistic chance of winning a championship. Leagues have reacted by implementing salary constraints, revenue sharing, and other similar mechanisms that create both competition between franchises on the field and cooperation regarding financial management off the field.

FIVE WAYS TO FINANCE THE OPERATION OF A SPORT ORGANIZATION

Whether an owner's objective is wealth maximization or winning and whether the sport organization is for-profit, not-for-profit, or governmental, a manager in the sport industry will encounter five methods used to finance the organization (see Exhibit 1.1). These include three methods typically used by for-profit companies to finance their operations: debt, equity, and reinvestment of retained earnings. In sport, two additional financing methods are often available: government funding and gifts. Examples of each will be seen throughout this text. A brief introduction to each is presented here.

Debt

When an organization borrows money that must be repaid over a period of time, usually with interest, **debt financing** is being used. Typically in sport, teams issue bonds or borrow from lending institutions (or in some instances their league) to finance operations through debt. Tottenham Hotspur financed

EXHIBIT 1.1	Methods used to finance sport organizations.	
METHOD	**DEFINITION**	**EXAMPLE**
Debt	Borrowing money that must be repaid over time, usually with interest	Construction of Yankee Stadium
Equity	Exchanging a share or portion of ownership of the organization for money	Green Bay Packers' renovation of Lambeau Field
Retained earnings	Reinvestment of prior earnings	Packers Franchise Preservation Fund
Government	Funding provided by federal, state, or municipal sources, including land use, tax abatements, direct stadium financing, state and municipal appropriations, and infrastructure improvements	Tax-backed bonds issued by the City of Arlington, TX to support AT&T Stadium
Gift	Charitable donations, either cash or in-kind	Donations totaling $85.4 million to Texas A&M with most money going toward Kyle Field

their new stadium in this way. As noted previously, the team borrowed £637 million from Bank of America Merrill Lynch, Goldman Sachs, and HSBC. It then converted £525 million of these loans into bonds. ("Tottenham hails," 2019). Debt financing may be either short-term or long-term; short-term debt obligations are those repaid in less than one year, and long-term obligations are those repaid in more than one year. A key point of financing operations with debt is that the lender does not gain an ownership interest in the organization. The sport organization's obligation is limited to the repayment of the debt.

Equity

In contrast to debt financing, in **equity financing** the owners exchange a share or portion of their ownership for money. The organization, therefore, obtains funds for operations without incurring debt and without having to repay a specific amount of money at a given time. A drawback is that ownership interest will be diluted and the original owners may lose control as additional investors are added. Stephen M. Ross used equity financing to raise capital after he purchased the Miami Dolphins in 2009. He sold minority interests in the team to several partners, including singers Marc Anthony and Gloria Estefan (Talalay, 2009). Few sport organizations issue stock, a common form of equity financing outside the sport industry. One of the few, the Green Bay Packers, used $143 million of stock proceeds to help finance the renovation of Lambeau Field ("History of Green Bay Packers," 2015).

Two reasons account for the fact that professional team sport organizations do not typically issue stock to raise equity capital. One reason is that little can remain hidden when a company is publicly traded. To comply with Securities and Exchange Commission (SEC) regulations in the United States, publicly traded organizations must file annual reports detailing the accounting activities of the organization. A team that claims financial hardship in seeking public funding for a new stadium may have difficulty convincing the municipality of the need if financial reports reveal significant positive cash flow. A second reason is that teams that issue stock must answer to their shareholders. Stockholder demands for profitability might run counter to the goal of winning on the field (for example, the team might be unable to acquire a player at the trading deadline because of the near-term financial loss that would result from the acquisition). Concern over public ownership is so great that the NFL does not allow its teams to be publicly owned. The league instituted a ban on public ownership in 1960 (Florio, 2011).

As noted above, the Green Bay Packers are an exception to the norm and the NFL rule. To keep the franchise from leaving Green Bay, Wisconsin, the team went public in 1923, and today the Packers continue to be exempt from the NFL's prohibition on issuing shares. However, unlike those of a typical publicly traded company, the Packers' shares do not appreciate in value and are not traded on a stock exchange.

Despite sport organizations' reluctance to use equity financing, teams in leagues other than the NFL have raised significant amounts of capital by doing so. The Cleveland Indians raised $60 million through the team's initial public offering (IPO) in 1998. The Florida Panthers, Boston Celtics, Vancouver Canucks, and Colorado Avalanche all have used equity financing. Today, however, these teams are privately held.

Retained Earnings

In addition to financing through debt and equity, organizations can finance operations or the acquisition of assets through the reinvestment of prior earnings. The portion of earnings that a firm saves in order to fund operations or acquire assets is termed **retained earnings.** The reinvestment of retained earnings is generally considered a type of equity financing, as this financing method is often used by publicly traded companies when they choose to reinvest earnings rather than pay them to shareholders as dividends. However, in sport, financing through the reinvestment of retained earnings should be considered separately from equity financing, because organizations in the industry—with the exception of sporting goods manufacturers and retail stores—are typically privately held. Although earnings may be distributed to team owners, in sport they are often used to finance the acquisition of players, improve operations, or make other investments.

The Green Bay Packers reinvest retained earnings to maintain a competitive and successful football operation and to preserve the franchise and its traditions. However, because the franchise is owned by its shareholders and not a single, wealthy individual, the organization is at a disadvantage when reacting to business challenges. A wealthy owner is able to use personal funds to infuse cash into a sport organization. One method that the Packers use to overcome this disadvantage is the Packers Franchise Preservation Fund. By providing liquidity, the fund is intended to improve the sustainability of the corporation and franchise. The fund is held as a part of the team's corporate reserve fund. At the end of the 2020 fiscal year, the corporate reserve fund totaled $385 million (Williams, 2020).

Government Funding

In the sport industry, it is common for private organizations, such as professional sports teams, to receive funding from governmental sources. In addition, public high schools and universities typically receive a portion of their financing through direct or indirect government funding, and this funding may support sport programs at these schools. For all sport organizations, **government financing** may be provided by federal, state, or municipal sources and may include land use, tax abatements, direct stadium financing, state and municipal appropriations, and infrastructure improvements. Between 2010 and 2017, $2.7 billion in tax-free municipal debt was issued for the renovation or construction of professional sport stadiums (Sangha, 2017). Exhibit 1.2 provides examples of direct stadium financing from government sources.

Gifts

Gift financing includes charitable donations, either cash or in-kind, made to an organization. Gift financing is a primary source of operating and investing income for major collegiate sports programs. It is also a supplemental source for minor college programs and non-profit sport organizations. According to the National Collegiate Athletic Association (2019), colleges received $2.89 billion in athletic department donations during 2020, which was 15.9% of overall revenues. Of this total, Division I Autonomy athletic departments received $1.93 billion (Chapter 14 includes an in-depth analysis). See Exhibit 1.3 for donations to NCAA Division I athletic departments.

College athletic programs use revenue from gifts to offset the rising costs of collegiate sport, build or renovate facilities, and increase endowments (see Exhibit 1.4). Duke University, for example, raised $340 million in its Building Champions fundraising campaign ("Athletics raises," 2017). The campaign supported all 27 varsity sports and helped finance the Scott Family Athletics Performance Center. Further, $50 million was added to its endowment to support scholarships and programs. In total, 107 new endowed scholarships and program endowments were created. Other institutions use gift financing to offset losses in institutional (government) financing resulting from cuts in state government funds to colleges and universities. Most institutions, like Duke, are seeking to increase their athletic department endowments to provide financial flexibility across programmatic needs.

OVERVIEW OF THE INDUSTRY

The sport industry is large and diverse. This makes classifying the industry and measuring its size and scope difficult. Further, how sport is defined affects estimates of industry size. For example, Business Wire estimated that the global

EXHIBIT 1.2   Select tax-backed stadium/arena bond issues.

STADIUM/ARENA	ISSUER	SECURITY
AT&T Stadium	City of Arlington, Texas	Sales tax, hotel tax, rental car tax
Camden Yards	Maryland Sports Authority	State appropriation
Guaranteed Rate Field	Illinois Sports Authority	Hotel tax, state appropriation
Great American Ballpark	Hamilton County, Ohio	Sales tax
Cleveland Browns Stadium	City of Cleveland, Ohio	City appropriation
Comerica Park	Detroit/Wayne County Stadium Authority	Hotel tax, car rental tax
State Farm Stadium	Arizona Sports and Tourism Authority	Hotel tax, car rental tax, jock tax, sales tax
Toyota Center	Houston-Harris County Sports Authority	Hotel tax, car rental tax
Marlins Park	Miami Dade County	Hotel tax, tourism tax, county appropriations
Target Field	Hennepin County	Sales tax
Amway Center	City of Orlando, Florida	Hotel tax, city appropriations

Sources: UBS Wealth Management Research (2012); Sangha (2017).

EXHIBIT 1.3   2018 NCAA Division I median athletic department donations by subdivision (in millions).

NCAA DIVISION I SUBDIVISION	2014	2015	2016	2017	2018
FBS Autonomy	$19.1	$21.0	$21.5	$23.1	$23.9
FBS Non-Autonomy	$3.1	$3.3	$3.3	$3.7	$3.8
FCS	$1.0	$0.9	$1.1	$1.0	$1.1
Non-Football	$0.6	$0.7	$0.7	$0.9	$0.8

Source: NCAA Financial Database (2019).

EXHIBIT 1.4 Top donor contributions to athletic departments in the SEC (2018).	
INSTITUTION*	**AMOUNT**
TEXAS A&M UNIVERSITY	$94,175,383
UNIVERSITY OF GEORGIA	$67,772,093
UNIVERSITY OF FLORIDA	$46,015,298
UNIVERSITY OF SOUTH CAROLINA	$38,059,706
THE UNIVERSITY OF TENNESSEE	$35,704,713
AUBURN UNIVERSITY	$35,683,958
LOUISIANA STATE UNIVERSITY	$35,070,680
UNIVERSITY OF MISSISSIPPI	$34,144,898
THE UNIVERSITY OF ALABAMA	$30,213,518
UNIVERSITY OF MISSOURI-COLUMBIA	$26,511,039
UNIVERSITY OF ARKANSAS	$24,247,462
MISSISSIPPI STATE UNIVERSITY	$23,888,969
UNIVERSITY OF KENTUCKY	$21,543,756

* As a private institution, Vanderbilt University did not report its data.

Source: College Athletics Financial Information Database (2019).

sports industry was a $488.5 billion industry in 2018, whereas Plunkett Research (2018) estimated the value to be $1.3 trillion, or three times as large. Why is there such a difference in estimates? Business Wire and Plunkett Research are likely using two different definitions of the sport industry.

In the United States, federal agencies use the **North American Industry Classification System (NAICS)**, developed by the US Census Bureau, to measure and track the business economy. Each business is classified as part of a larger industry. However, the sport industry is not classified as an industry in the NAICS. Instead, the sport industry as it is commonly conceived is scattered across at least 12 different industries in the NAICS (see Exhibit 1.5). The largest grouping of sport businesses is within the Arts, Entertainment, and Recreation segment (NAICS 71).

The Arts, Entertainment, and Recreation segment is described as follows by the US Department of Labor's Bureau of Labor Statistics (BLS). This segment employs a large number of seasonal and part-time workers. Those employed in the industry tend to be younger than employees in other industries, and wages are relatively low. As of 2018, the BLS forecast for the industry as a whole was promising. Barring long-term COVID-19-related recessionary trends, rising incomes and increasing leisure time over the next ten years should lead to an

EXHIBIT 1.5   NAICS codes for sport businesses.

CODE	INDUSTRY	SUBINDUSTRY	SPORT BUSINESS TYPES
237	Construction	Heavy and Civil Engineering Construction	Field Construction
315	Manufacturing	Apparel Knitting Mills	Sport Apparel
335	Manufacturing	Electrical Equipment, Appliance, and Component Manufacturing	Stadium Lighting
339	Manufacturing	Miscellaneous Manufacturing	Sporting Goods Manufacturing
423	Wholesale Trade	Merchant Wholesalers, Durable Goods	Sporting Goods Wholesale
424	Wholesale Trade	Merchant Wholesalers, Nondurable Goods	Sportswear
451	Retail Trade	Sporting Goods, Hobby, Book, and Music Stores	Sporting Goods
453	Retail Trade	Miscellaneous Store Retailers	Used Sporting Goods
515	Information	Broadcasting (except Internet)	Sports Television
516	Information	Internet	Sport Internet Sites
532	Real Estate and Rental Leasing	Rental and Leasing Services	Sports Equipment Rental
561	Administrative and Support and Waste Management and Remediation Services	Administrative and Support Services	Ticketing
611	Educational Services	Educational Services	Sport and Recreation Instruction
621	Health Care and Social Assistance	Ambulatory Health Care Services	Sports Physical Therapists
711	Arts, Entertainment, and Recreation	Performing Arts, Spectator Sports, and Related Industries	Spectator Sports

EXHIBIT 1.5   Cont.

CODE	INDUSTRY	SUBINDUSTRY	SPORT BUSINESS TYPES
712	Arts, Entertainment, and Recreation	Museums, Historical Sites, and Similar Institutions	Halls of Fame
713	Arts, Entertainment, and Recreation	Amusement, Gambling, and Recreation Industries	Recreation and Club Sports
722	Accommodation and Food Services	Food Services and Drinking Places	Concessions
811	Other Services (except Public Administration)	Repair and Maintenance	Sport Equipment Repair
813	Other Services (except Public Administration)	Religious, Grantmaking, Civic, Professional, and Similar Organizations	Leagues and Governing Bodies

Source: www.census.gov/cgi-bin/sssd/naics/naicsrch?chart=2017.

increase in demand in this sector, with employment growing 5.0% by 2028 ("Employment by," 2018). Almost all leisure-time activities, other than watching movies, are included in this industry sector.

The BLS classifies this sector into three large subsectors: live performances or events; historical, cultural, or educational exhibits; and recreation or leisure activities. The live performances or events subsector includes professional sports, commercial sport clubs, sport promotion companies and agencies, and dog and horse racing facilities. Privately owned museums, such as the National Baseball Hall of Fame and Museum, are found in the subsection for historical, cultural, or educational exhibits. The recreation and leisure activities subsector includes golf courses, fitness facilities, bowling centers, and health clubs. The BLS further divides the subsectors of the Arts, Entertainment, and Recreation segment, assigning NAICS codes to smaller divisions. Exhibit 1.6 lists the codes for spectator and recreational sport divisions. These subsectors range from sport teams and clubs to bowling centers and marinas.

FINANCIAL SIZE OF THE SPORT INDUSTRY

Academicians and sport industry professionals frequently discuss, quote, and cite the size of the sport industry in specific countries. For example, in 2020 it was estimated that the sport industry in the United Kingdom (UK) was a £39 billion ($51.1 billion) industry, with grassroots sport being its largest sector (Sport England, 2020). In the United States, the size of the sport industry grew from $47 billion in 1986 to $152 billion in 1995, a real annual growth rate of 8.8% (Rascher, 2001). King (2002) stated that the industry in the United States grew

EXHIBIT 1.6   Sport-related business divisions within NAICS Code 71: Arts, Entertainment, and Recreation.

NAICS CODE	DEFINITION
711211	Sports Teams and Clubs
711212	Racetracks
711219	Other Spectator Sports
711310	Promoters of Performing Arts, Sports, and Similar Events with Facilities
711320	Promoters of Performing Arts, Sports, and Similar Events without Facilities
711410	Agents and Managers for Artists, Athletes, Entertainers, and Other Public Figures
712110	Museums
713910	Golf Courses and Country Clubs
713920	Skiing Facilities
713930	Marinas
713940	Fitness and Recreational Sports Centers
713950	Bowling Centers
713990	All Other Amusement and Recreation Industries

Source: www.census.gov/cgi-bin/sssd/naics/naicsrch?chart_code=71&search=2017%20 NAICS%20Search.

to $195 billion in 2001 (an annual growth rate of 4.24% since 1995). Milano and Chelladurai (2011) estimated that the industry's size in 2005 fell somewhere in a range from a conservative number of $168.5 billion, which would indicate a slight decline in the industry's size, to a liberal estimate of $207.5 billion, which would indicate modest growth.[1] Plunkett Research estimated the industry's size to be $485 billion in 2015, and more recently (2018) they stated it had grown to $539.7 billion. Did the US sport industry really grow by $332 billion or more from 2005 to 2018? Were different industry definitions once again used in measurements of the size and scope of the industry? Or were different methods used in calculations of the size of the industry?

We can determine the size of any industry by calculating its gross product. We measure the overall size of an economy by its **gross domestic product**

---

1   The authors used data from the US Census Bureau's Economic Census to develop their estimate of industry size.

(GDP). GDP is the market value of the goods and services produced within the borders of a county, state, country, or other region in a given year. To determine the size of the sport industry, we calculate the **gross domestic sport product (GDSP)**. GDSP is defined as the market value of a nation's output of sport-related goods and services in a given year. This includes the value added to the economy by the sport industry, as well as the gross product originating from the sport industry.

Efforts to measure GDSP must avoid a double count (one of the guidelines for calculating GDP), that is, the duplication of dollars that could be accounted for in two or more ways. Double counting often results in errors in estimates of the sport industry when secondary spending is included in the calculation. For example, players' salaries should not be counted, because this amount is included in ticket prices. When organizations set ticket prices, they account for the salaries of professional athletes, as these are essentially a production cost or cost of goods sold (see Chapter 2). As an intermediary cost of production, salaries should not be counted separately from ticket revenue in calculations of industry size. To count them separately is to count them twice.

In the first major study on the size of the United States' sport industry, *Sports Inc.* magazine calculated the industry's size at $47 billion (Sandomir, 1988). However, the study did not follow US Department of Commerce rules for computing GDP and made no effort to determine the economic impact of the industry on the United States (Meek, 1997). Meek performed a study that did avoid double counting and resulted in the figure of $152.2 billion for the size of the sport industry. Street and Smith's *Sports Business Journal* determined that $194.64 billion was spent in sports during 2001 (King, 2002). In a subsequent description of this report's methodology, Broughton (2002) noted that the amount reported was not a measure of the size of the industry but only a measure of sport-related spending. The author stated that when traditional economic standards were applied (i.e., avoidance of double counting), the size of the industry was measured to be $31.76 billion. Milano and Chelladurai (2011) followed the methodology of Meek and the US Department of Commerce's rules for calculating GDSP when they developed their ranged estimate of industry size (between $168.5 billion and $207.5 billion). In their ranged approach, all debatable GDSP expenditures were removed from the industry size estimate to arrive at the lower number, and all debatable expenditures were included in the higher number. Milano and Chelladurai's moderate estimate of industry size is $189.4 billion. Here, the estimate includes fractions of the debatable expenses.

Exhibit 1.7 shows a 22-year comparison between Milano and Chelladurai's study, which used 2005 data, and Meek's study, which used 1995 data, and data from the most recent Economic Census (2017). Data are compared in six areas: (1) entertainment and recreation, (2) products and services, (3) non-sports-related advertising, (4) sport investment, (5) sport net exports, and (6) sport-related government expenditures. The largest sector of the industry is sport products (e.g., Louisville Sluggers) and services (e.g., tennis lessons), accounting for over half of GDSP.

STRUCTURE OF SPORT BUSINESSES

The structure of a firm affects the tax and legal obligations of that firm. Different structures offer different benefits. For example, a firm's options for raising

EXHIBIT 1.7   1995, 2005, and 2017 GDSP comparisons (in 2017 dollars).

INDUSTRY SECTOR	1995 ESTIMATE (BILLIONS $)	MODERATE 2005 ESTIMATE (BILLIONS $)	2017 ESTIMATE (BILLIONS $)
Entertainment and recreation	44.27	48.79	69.68
Products and services	93.36	105.68	143.60
Non-sport-related advertising	7.54	14.78	19.83
Sport investment	11.84	22.97	35.34
Sport net exports	–4.71	–3.53	–4.52
Sport-related government expenditures		0.66	1.68
Total	152.2	189.34	265.6

Source: Meek (1997); Milano and Chelladurai (2011); US Census Bureau (2020).

funds are based on its business structure, as is the personal legal liability of its managers and employees. As we will discuss in Chapter 5, several different structures are available to business entities. These structures include governmental, non-profit, sole proprietorship, partnership, limited liability corporation (LLC), subchapter S corporation, and C corporation. Each structure has unique advantages and disadvantages that affect the financial management of the organization.

Collegiate athletic departments are classified as governmental or nonprofit businesses, depending on whether the department is a part of a state college or university, such as University of North Carolina–Chapel Hill, or is a part of a private university, such as Duke University.

In professional sports, most franchises are operated as for-profit businesses. They are structured under various ownership models. After describing these ownership models, we will discuss the structures of sport leagues, conferences, and associations.

Franchise Ownership Models

Most franchises are formed under one of three ownership models (Foster, Greyser, & Walsh, 2005): single owner/private investor model, multiple owners/private investment syndicate model, or multiple owners/publicly traded corporation model.

SINGLE OWNER/PRIVATE INVESTOR MODEL

In the **single owner/private investor model**, one individual, often an independently wealthy person, owns the firm. The owner may play an active role in the operation of the franchise, or, after selecting key managers, the owner may be hands off. For example, the Los Angeles Clippers are owned by former Microsoft CEO Steve Ballmer. Ballmer purchased the franchise in 2014 for $2 billion.

MULTIPLE OWNERS/PRIVATE INVESTMENT SYNDICATE MODEL

The most common model for team ownership is the **multiple owners/private investment syndicate model**. It is the most common for two reasons. First, the value of franchises has risen so high that it is rare for one individual to be able to afford to purchase a franchise on his or her own. Second, as discussed previously, the publicly traded corporation model has many disadvantages versus the private investment model—and one league, the NFL, even forbids it.

When individuals pool their resources to purchase a franchise and incorporate as a partnership, LLC, or the like, they are forming an ownership group under the multiple owners/private investment syndicate model. For example, in 1995 a group of long-time friends and fans including Fred Hanser, William DeWitt, Jr., and Andrew Baur purchased the St. Louis Cardinals. Each ownership group is governed by an investment syndicate document, which outlines the decision rights of the owners, including who will represent them in league meetings. Sometimes the ownership group has a dominant individual who appears to be a single owner, as was the case for many years after an ownership group purchased the New York Yankees, and George Steinbrenner was viewed as the sole owner of the team. Any disputes that arise among the owners may be resolved through arbitration or legal action (see Sidebar 1.A).

SIDEBAR 1.A   Atlanta Spirit LLC

In 2003, Time Warner was in the process of selling the Atlanta Hawks (National Basketball Association [NBA]), Atlanta Thrashers (National Hockey League [NHL]), and Philips Arena to a single buyer, David McDavid. However, questions were raised about McDavid's ability to finance the purchase. At about the same time, Michael Gearon, Jr., and Rutherford Seydel spoke with Time Warner about the possibility of purchasing the assets. The response from Time Warner was that they could make the purchase if outside financing was not used and if the agreement could be completed within a week. Gearon and Seydel approached sports investment banker John Moag to help find additional partners. Bruce Levenson, Ed Peskowitz, and Steve Belkin were soon added to the investment group. With four additional minority partners, the Atlanta Spirit LLC was born. In total, nine men were members of the partnership, with five—Belkin, Levenson, Peskowitz, Gearon, and Seydel—holding majority interest. From the time Gearon and Seydel first met with Time Warner to discuss the purchase of the assets, only eight days elapsed until the partnership was formed (King & Lombardo, 2005).

The partnership agreement called for management by consensus, with the majority partners sharing three controlling votes: one for Belkin, one for Levenson and Peskowitz, and one for Gearon and Seydel.

Belkin was to represent the group with the NBA, and Levenson was to represent the group with the NHL. The two would, according to the partnership agreement, be bound to act according to consensus (King & Lombardo, 2005).

An early sign of disagreement among the partners caused Belkin to have a "put" option placed into the ownership agreement, whereby he could sell his shares of the partnership for 85% above their fair market value beginning in June 2006. Disagreements over minor issues then arose, relating to the initial financing of the LLC, ticket allotment for the NBA All-Star Game, titles of partners in media guides and other publications, and player payroll budgets. Finally, the authority to trade players caused a split among the three voting groups of majority owners. The lack of a defined managing partner became a major issue (King & Lombardo, 2005).

When NBA commissioner David Stern became aware of the issues between the partners, he asked the NBA's executive vice president of legal and business affairs, Joel Litvin, to intervene. Stern was concerned that the disagreements among the majority owners could harm the Hawks' basketball operations and, therefore, harm the NBA. When Litvin could not resolve the conflict, Stern met with the owners face to face and ordered the group to resolve their issues. After this meeting, Belkin, the Spirit's representative to the NBA, vetoed a trade that the other partners favored. The trade was to bring Joe Johnson to the Hawks for two future first-round draft picks. Belkin cited his role as the NBA team governor as his reason for acting counter to the remaining partners' preferences. He wrote,

> Both the NBA and NHL require that a single individual be designated by each team "to manage the business and affairs of the team and to act for and bind the team." I served in that role as NBA Governor of the Hawks. I was fine with a "3-vote system" on all matters that did not conflict with league requirements and I abided by that system.
>
> King & Lombardo, 2005, para. 48

The board of managers voted 2–0 to trade Joe Johnson and informed Belkin that they would remove him as NBA governor if he interfered with the trade. After his veto, the managing board removed Belkin as NBA governor, and on August 8, 2005, Belkin countered with a temporary restraining order. By August 19, Levenson, Peskowitz, Gearon, and Seydel agreed to buy out Belkin's share and pay him more than the 85% premium to have him leave.

Three and a half years later, the buyout amount still had not been determined, because the contract outlining the buyout process was vague and the group could not agree on a process or a price. When Belkin agreed to the buyout in 2005, the price was to be determined by up to three appraisals (see Chapter 10). The first appraiser was to be hired by Belkin and the second by either party objecting to the findings of the first appraisal. However, both sides objected to the first appraisal, and the contract did not state what process should be followed if both objected. Both wanted to select the second appraiser. The parties had agreed to litigate contract disputes in Maryland, so a state circuit court judge heard the facts. The judge ruled that Belkin had the right to select the second appraiser. The judge also ruled that since Levenson, Peskowitz, Gearon, and Seydel had missed the deadline to pay the price set by the second appraiser, Belkin could buy them out at cost. This decision was overturned at the appellate level. A new trial then began in February 2009 (Swartz, 2009).

After six years of legal dispute, the owners finally settled out of court. Belkin's 30% share of the teams was purchased by the remaining owners. Gearon and Levenson were named as managing partners of the Hawks, the Thrashers, and Philips Arena (Swartz, 2010). Shortly thereafter, the remaining owners disclosed that the Atlanta Thrashers had incurred operating losses greater than $130 million from 2005 through 2010, while the franchise value dropped by more than $50 million. In June 2011, the Thrashers were sold for $170 million to True North Sports and Entertainment and relocated to Winnipeg. No Atlanta-area investors were interested in purchasing the team due to the past ownership issues. The $170 million sale price included a $60 million relocation fee, which was split by the remaining NHL teams. Therefore, Atlanta Spirit netted only $110 million from the sale of the hockey team (Burnside, 2011).

Soon, the group began to seek to sell the Hawks, too. A failed attempt to sell the team occurred in late 2011. In September 2014 Levenson announced—after several offensive and racially insensitive emails were exposed in the press—that he was going to sell his controlling interest in the team (Lee, 2014). In January 2015 all owners announced that 100% of the Hawks and operating rights to Philips Arena were for sale. When the sale was announced, Levenson and his partners Peskowitz and Foreman owned 50.1% of the team; Gearon, Seydel, and Turner owned 32.3%; and Steven Price and his New York-based ownership group, which had bought a portion of the team during the summer of 2014, owned 17.6% (Vivlamore, 2015). By April, the Hawks and Philips Arena operating rights were sold to a group led by Anthony Ressler for $850 million ("Hawks announce sale," 2015).

MULTIPLE OWNERS/PUBLICLY TRADED CORPORATION MODEL

The third model of ownership is the **multiple owners/publicly traded corporation model**. With the exception of the Green Bay Packers, this model is not used in the United States. Typically, it is employed by European professional soccer franchises, such as Manchester United, whose shares are traded on the New York Stock Exchange with the symbol MANU. Other examples include AS Roma (ASR) and Juventus (JUVE), whose shares are traded on the Italian Stock Exchange (Borsa Italiana); Borussia Dortmund shares are traded in Germany on the Xetra exchange. On the London Stock Exchange, shares in the Scottish Celtic Football Club (CCP) can be bought and sold. Under this model, a franchise is governed by a board of directors, elected by shareholder vote. The board appoints the team's senior management. In the case of the Packers, the NFL restricts the franchise's shareholders, as shares cannot be traded on the open market and anti-takeover provisions prevent any one individual from amassing a majority of the team's shares and thereby becoming the team's majority owner.

Although only one US sport franchise is publicly owned by stockholders, some franchises are owned by publicly traded corporations, such as Comcast and Cablevision. For example, Comcast owns the Philadelphia Flyers via its subsidiary Comcast Spectacor. Corporations such as Time Warner, Disney, News Corp, Cablevision, and Anheuser-Busch have owned US sport franchises in the past.

League Structures

The structure of a team's league affects the financial management of a sport organization, as well. Leagues operate to ensure the viability of the league. Decisions made at the league level include admissions criteria, the structure of competition, revenue sharing, and player relations. These decisions affect the financial management of member teams (see Chapters 14, 15, and 16), and the structure of the league also affects member teams' financial management.

A league may be structured either as a single entity or with distributed club ownership (Foster, Greyser, & Walsh, 2005).

SINGLE-ENTITY OWNERSHIP MODEL

With a **single-entity structure**, a single group or an individual owns the league and all of the teams that compete within that league. This structure is frequently used with new or start-up leagues. For example, the American Basketball League (ABL) was owned by a group of investors, the Women's National Basketball Association (WNBA) by the NBA, Major League Soccer (MLS) by a group of investors, and the XFL (2020) by Alpha Entertainment.

An advantage of the single-entity structure is that antitrust law does not apply, as it does to leagues that use the distributed club ownership model. Collusion, agreements that eliminate competition, and other violations of anti-trust law are not possible when one entity owns a league and all of its teams. Therefore, single-entity leagues can place franchises in preferred cities and assign players to specific teams in specific cities. For example, the WNBA, in an effort to build a loyal following, assigned Lisa Leslie to the Los Angeles Sparks franchise. Leslie was a well-known collegiate player in southern California, as she had competed at USC. The league also assigned Sheryl Swoops, a standout basketball star at Texas Tech, to the Houston Comets. The assignment of players to teams also allows a league to promote competitive balance within the league so that no one team dominates competition.

A financial advantage for single-entity leagues is that player salary costs are constrained. Players sign contracts with the league, so there is no bidding for players on an open market. In 2019, the average MLS salary was $345,867. Zlatan Ibrahimovic was the league's top earner at $7.2 million guaranteed (Prince-Wright, 2019), and the minimum salary for league senior players was $70,250 and for the team's reserve players, $56,250 ("MLS salaries," 2019). The league's salary philosophy is to pay for impact players while constraining costs on defenders and goalkeepers (Keh, 2014). As another example, in 2008 the Arena Football League (AFL) was considering reorganizing as a single-entity league in the hope of reducing costs, including salary costs. The AFL had a

$25 million operating loss prior to suspending its operations indefinitely in 2008 (Lombardo, 2008). The AFL resumed play in 2010 but did not change its structure. Unfortunately for the league, debts assumed during reorganization and failure to contain costs led to its subsequent filing for Chapter 7 bankruptcy in 2019, thereby fully ceasing operations (Chang, 2019).

A drawback to single-entity status is that it provides little economic incentive at the club level (Foster, Greyser, & Walsh, 2005). For the franchises, there is no benefit to operating well, as the benefits are completely shared with the other franchises in the league, although the losses are also equally shared. This is one of the reasons why the WNBA and NBA Development League are moving away from the single-entity structure and toward the distributed club ownership model (Lombardo, 2008).

In addition, single-entity leagues have been challenged in court under the **Sherman Antitrust Act** (1890). The Act forbids contracts and other actions among businesses in restraint of trade. In *Fraser v. MLS* (1998), players were seeking to end the practice of league-negotiated contracts. They felt that negotiating with the league eliminated competition for player services among teams and thereby reduced their earnings potential. In *Fraser*, the court reaffirmed that, for leagues structured as a single entity, the Sherman Act does not apply. The court affirmed that the league and its investors (team operators) functioned as a single entity and, therefore, were a single economic unit.

DISTRIBUTED CLUB OWNERSHIP MODEL

The **distributed club ownership model** is used by Major League Baseball (MLB), the NBA, the NHL, NFL, EPL, and most global leagues. Under this league structure, each individual franchise has its own ownership group. League-wide revenues, such as those from national television contracts, are collected at the league level and distributed to each team to cover net costs. Leagues sometimes are structured as non-profit organizations governed by representatives from each team. The NFL was the first league in the US to receive non-profit status in 1942 (Fornwalt, 2018). Today, leagues operating as non-profits include the NHL and the PGA and Ladies Professional Golf Association (LPGA) Tours. These entities qualify as 501(c)(6) corporations, as they work to promote their industries rather than operating as for-profit enterprises. Revenues earned are taxed, however. For example, money that goes to the NHL for television contracts and merchandise flows to its teams, which operate as for-profit entities and, therefore, pay taxes on this revenue. As noted, the NFL used to be structured as a non-profit. So did Major League Baseball. However, MLB opted to forgo its non-profit status in 2007; the NFL did the same in 2015[2] (Harwell & Hobson, 2015). NASCAR and the NBA operate as for-profit companies.

Whether a league is structured as non-profit or for-profit, team representatives select a commissioner to run its daily operations. Leagues may own affiliated entities, as well. For example, the NFL owns and operates NFL Enterprises, which includes NFL.com and Sunday Ticket, and NFL Properties, the licensing arm of the league.

---

2 Congress has estimated that the NFL's move to for-profit status will generate an additional $10 million annually in tax revenue.

With this structure, conflicts related to the financial management of the league can arise. Large-market franchises and small-market franchises tend to have differing philosophies on revenue sharing, for example. League and club conflicts often arise over territorial rights. A player and a league may come into conflict, as well. Disputes often end up in court, and the resulting court decisions affect the structure of the distributed club ownership model.

Many of these disputes fall under antitrust law. In contrast to court decisions involving single-ownership leagues, courts have consistently ruled that leagues structured under the distributed club ownership model are subject to antitrust law. The only exception is MLB, which was granted an exemption from antitrust law in *Federal Baseball Club v. National League* (1922), a decision reaffirmed in *Flood v. Kuhn* (1972). Courts have stated that a degree of cooperation at the league level is warranted in order for the league to create its product, but they also have noted that teams conduct activities separate from the league, such as entering into local radio and television contracts. Hence, the teams and leagues are separate legal entities and subject to the Sherman Act. In *NFL v. NASL* (1982), the court ruled that the NFL was subject to US antitrust law. The court reaffirmed this in *McNeil v. NFL* (1992) and *Sullivan v. NFL* (1994). In *McNeil*, the court found that the league's "Plan B" free agency was more restrictive than reasonably necessary to maintain competitive balance within the league. Further, "Plan B" free agency caused economic harm to the players. This decision led to unrestricted free agency in the NFL. An earlier case, *Mackey v. NFL* (1976), led to the end of the league's reserve system, which essentially bound a player to one team over his career.

As for the NBA, the courts ruled in 1971 that the league was subject to antitrust law. Prior to *Haywood v. NBA* (1971), the NBA required graduating high school players to wait four years before becoming eligible to play in the league. The court's decision in *Haywood* allowed high school graduates and college attendees (prior to graduation) to declare themselves eligible for the NBA draft.

FINANCIAL AND ECONOMIC FACTORS AFFECTING SPORT

Many factors affect the economics of sport, but five must be watched closely: (1) the impact of the current economic cycle on sport, (2) the effects of television revenues, (3) the relationship between sport teams and real estate holdings, (4) a continued push for sustainability in sport, and (5) the impact of politics on the governance of sport.

Economic Cycle

The **economic cycle** is made up of four stages—growth, peak, recession, and recovery—and typically lasts just under six years. As the economy cycles through periods of growth and contraction, the sport industry is affected.

Economic growth occurs when the economy is increasing in real terms (faster than the rate of inflation). Evidence of economic growth includes increases in employment, industrial production, sales, personal income, and GDP. During periods of economic growth, the sport industry has benefited greatly, as during the 1990s and 2010s. Most leagues, both major and minor, added teams; new leagues, such as the WNBA, ABL, the National Women's Soccer League (NWSL), were formed; and teams and athletic departments across the globe spent billions constructing new stadiums and arenas.

When the economy contracts, either declining or growing at a rate that is not higher than inflation, it can enter a recession or depression. A recession occurs when GDP is negative for two consecutive quarters (six months) and usually lasts for six to 18 months. An **economic depression** is an extreme recession, lasting two or more years.

When the economy contracts, the sport industry is affected, as during the economic downturns of 2001, 2007–2009, and 2020. The sport industry relies on the discretionary income of spectators and participants, and as a result is sensitive to changes in the economy. From December 2007 to June 2009 (dates established by the Bureau of Labor Statistics), the United States experienced the Great Recession. The impact of this recession can be seen in the statistics for 2005 to 2015 for employment in the arts, entertainment, and recreation industry, of which sport is a major part (see Exhibit 1.8a). As the economy entered the recession and spending slowed in December 2007, many jobs within the industry were shed. From December 2007 to December 2010, approximately 115,000 jobs were lost.

As a result of the COVID-19 pandemic, the US economy entered into a recession in March 2020. While the economic slowdown is ongoing as of August 2020, the impact of the sudden closure of sport can be seen in Exhibit 1.8b. Between March 2020 and April 2020, a staggering 1.3 million jobs were shed in this sector. As governmental restrictions were lifted and businesses began to reopen, 420,000 jobs were added back by June 2020. Still, 857,000 were lost through June.

During the Great Recession, not only did the slowdown in spending by spectators and participants affect jobs within the industry, but leagues also ceased operation (e.g., the AFL), teams declared bankruptcy (e.g., the Phoenix Coyotes) or ceased operation (e.g., the Columbia Inferno), construction slowed

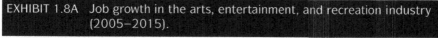

EXHIBIT 1.8A   Job growth in the arts, entertainment, and recreation industry (2005–2015).

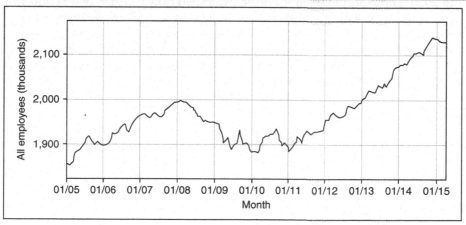

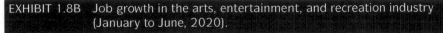

EXHIBIT 1.8B   Job growth in the arts, entertainment, and recreation industry (January to June, 2020).

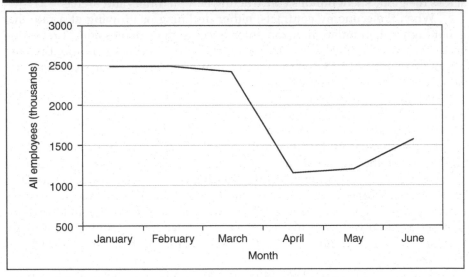

or stopped altogether, and sponsorship revenue declined. *Sports Business Daily* noted the following impacts of the Great Recession:

- The Dallas Cowboys failed to have a naming rights deal signed by the completion of their new stadium in 2009. Although companies were interested, they were not willing to pay the price the team was seeking. Four years passed before the naming rights were finally sold.
- MLB teams cut ticket prices in 2009, hoping to keep fans coming to ballparks despite an unemployment rate approaching 10% nationwide during the summer.
- Automotive advertising spending was down $100 million at the end of 2008 ("Economy could affect," 2008).

The total impact of the 2020 recession on sport is still unknown. However, we can examine the short-term impact based on what has been seen through July 2020. The World Economic Forum examined how COVID-19 was affecting sport leagues in April 2020 (Hall, 2020). The industry was examined across three sectors: (a) broadcasting (sales and media rights), (b) commercial (sponsorship and advertising), and (c) game day revenues (ticketing and hospitality). Without games played and postponed seasons resumed, the ability of leagues to distribute broadcasting revenue back to clubs would be limited. As noted in the study, no games means no television deals and no game day income. No income means no teams.

Patrick Rishe, an economist at Washington University in St. Louis, estimated that the shutdown of professional and college sport in the US would cost $12 billion in revenue, with that number doubling if college and professional football were not played in the fall of 2020 ("Sudden vanishing," 2020). As an illustration on a micro level, Barry Alvarez, athletic director at the University of Wisconsin, estimated that their program would lose $60 million due to the COVID-19 pandemic. He added that the amount would grow to over $100 million if the university is not able to play football during the 2020–2021 academic year (Milewski, 2020).

As a consequence of both the Great Recession and the COVID-19 pandemic, some sport organizations were more affected than others, and some industry segments were affected more than others. In the following sections, we will discuss several sport industry segments that have been especially sensitive to changes in economic conditions.

UNITED STATES OLYMPIC COMMITTEE

With the postponement of the 2020 Olympic Games in Tokyo to 2021, the United States Olympic Committee (USOC) faces a unique financial challenge. In a normal economic slowdown, the renewal of sport sponsorships is affected (Last, 2009)—and sport has become more reliant than ever on revenue from corporate sponsorships. Add to that additional costs related to the delay of the Olympic Games; the challenge is compounded. The USOC receives no direct government funding, unlike other National Olympic Committees (NOCs) around the globe. Therefore, the USOC relies heavily on corporate support, and sponsorship revenue accounted for 45.8% of its $316.6 million budget in 2018. In 2008, as the last recession was deepening, most USOC sponsorship agreements expired following the Summer Olympic Games. Several corporations ended their sponsorships. Home Depot and Bank of America did not renew their 16-year sponsorships, and General Motors, a sponsor since 1984, did not renew. Kodak, which had been associated with the Olympic Games since 1896, ended its sponsorship, too. John Hancock also decided not to renew its sponsorship, although the company had been an Olympic sponsor since 1994. Each sponsorship agreement was worth between $4 million and $5 million on average per year. Considering the sponsorship losses from these companies alone, the USOC had to replace more than $16 million and as much as $20 million in annual revenue. Additional losses in revenue occurred, too. For example, Anheuser-Busch agreed to return as a sponsor, but it lowered the level of its commitment (Macur, 2009; Pells, 2009).

As the economy began to recover, the USOC added BP, Procter & Gamble, and Deloitte as sponsors prior to the 2010 Vancouver Olympics, thereby offsetting some of the earlier losses (Mickle, 2010). By the 2012 Summer Olympic Games, as the effects of the Great Recession waned, the USOC added new sponsors Kellogg's and DeVry through 2016 and renewed BP and Nike. Combined, these sponsorship agreements were worth $38.8 million (Mickle, 2012). Chobani, Budweiser, and AT&T also renewed their agreements.

During the latest recession, the USOC, like so many other organizations impacted by business closures due to COVID-19, requested governmental assistance. The organization lobbied congress for $200 million to be included in the coronavirus relief CARES Act (Hobson, 2020). Part of the request, $50 million, was for the United States' Olympic athletes to replace lost income due to the postponement of the games. The remaining $150 million was for the 55 national governing bodies (NGBs) overseeing each Olympic sport in the US. While many sport organizations received temporary government funding, the USOC's request was denied. Forty-one of the 55 NGBs reported that cancelled events from March to June led to lost revenue of approximately $122 million.

Without this support, the USOC announced 10–20% budget cuts through the 2024 Olympic year (Bachman, 2020). The cuts were needed to maintain 2020 levels of funding to NGBs and athletes for the rescheduled 2021 games.

COLLEGIATE ATHLETICS

Today, college athletics is having its business model challenged in court (see Chapter 14), plus it is facing the financial impact of cancelled, postponed, and modified seasons in 2020. Further, college athletics is significantly affected by changing economic conditions. For example, as the economy expanded during the late 1980s and through the 1990s, Stanford University built its athletic department endowment to over $500 million. In 2008, when the financial markets collapsed, Stanford saw the size of the endowment shrink 20–30%. As a result, the university eliminated 21 athletic department staff positions and reduced the department's budget by $7 million. When the coronavirus pandemic hit in 2020, severe moves were made to offset the financial impact on the program. Stanford cut 11 of 36 sports at the end of the 2020–2021 academic year. Impacted were 240 student-athletes and 22 coaches. The cut teams had won a combined 20 national championships and the athletes in those programs had won 27 Olympic medals. These programs were cut as a result of a projected $12 million deficit, growing to a best-case $25 million deficit due to the impact of the pandemic. Over three years, Stanford estimated that the department would accumulate $70 million in losses (Scarborough, 2020).

Through June 2020, 18 schools at the highest level of college athletics in the US joined Stanford in making cuts to programs (Cash, 2020). In Division I of the NCAA, game day and television revenues from football and men's basketball generate enough revenues to offset the operating costs of much of the remaining programs (see Chapter 14 for a detailed analysis). A cancelled spring 2020 NCAA basketball tournament and altered fall 2020 football games have led to revenue shortfalls across the entire department leading to the reduction of non-revenue programs. Across the universities announcing cuts, 57 teams have been eliminated. Hard hit were baseball, softball, wrestling, men's and women's lacrosse, men's and women's tennis, and men's and women's golf.

One aspect of college sports that typically does not seem to be impacted by an economic slowdown is coaching salaries. This was true during the Great Recession. From 2007 to 2014, men's head basketball coaching salaries increased 102%, increasing 93% for head football coaches. Even coaches of smaller teams saw increases in pay. Tennis coaches, for example, saw their pay increase 20% over the same period (McGregor, 2014). However, it has been different during the 2020 pandemic. Furloughs and pay cuts have hit coaches at major programs. Coaches and athletic administrators at schools like Boise State, South Carolina, Colorado, Minnesota, Kansas, Arizona, Florida State, and Michigan have seen reductions in their 2020–2021 salaries ("The coronavirus," 2020).

Some observers feared that economic slowdowns would further increase the disparity between the larger NCAA Division I–FBS schools and the smaller ones. While the full impact of the 2020 economic downturn is unknown, this seemed to be the case in 2009, when not all athletic departments were affected by the downturn. Although most schools experienced a decrease in ticket revenue for 2009, larger programs were able to offset those losses. The University of Georgia expected ticket revenue for football to be down $2.5 million to

$3.0 million in 2009. The university, however, had just signed an eight-year, $92.8 million marketing and media rights contract. Further, as a member of the SEC, the school received $11 million from the conference in 2009 and expected to receive an additional $6.2 million in 2010 as a result of the conference's new television contract with CBS and ESPN. Other examples of larger schools not experiencing significant impact from economic downturns include the University of Michigan's athletic department, which enjoyed a $9 million surplus at the end of fiscal year 2008. Also in 2008, the University of Florida was able to increase its athletic budget by $5.9 million, and the University of Texas's football program generated $73 million in revenue during the 2008 football season (Schlabach, 2009).

For most big-time college athletic programs, the Great Recession only temporarily slowed growth in budgets. Some colleges used new funds to add sand volleyball teams after the Great Recession ended. As a result, NCAA Divisions I–III have approved the sport for NCAA championship status. Twelve new college football teams began play in 2013, and 11 more athletic departments added teams over the following three years. Further, when the new College Football Playoff began in 2014, bowl game payouts grew post-recession to just over $505 million, an increase of approximately $200 million per year. This growth was due mostly to increases in the media rights fees associated with the six bowls and national championship game belonging to the College Football Playoff ("College bowl payouts," 2015).

WOMEN'S PROFESSIONAL SPORTS

Women's professional sports are extremely sensitive to changes in the economy (Kreidler, 2009). For example, amidst the Great Recession and after the 2008 season ended, the Houston Comets of the WNBA folded. The Comets were one of the league's most successful franchises and one of six teams not owned by NBA-affiliated parties (see "Case Analysis: The Growth of a League" at the end of the chapter). The team's demise created fear within the league and among its followers that NBA owners—who owned eight of the 13 teams remaining in the league at the time—would shut down teams that were not making money (or even possibly the league itself) in efforts to cut costs, as several NBA franchises were having financial difficulties. However, the only additional WNBA team to fold during the Great Recession was the Sacramento Monarchs. The Atlanta Dream was added to replace the Houston Comets, and the Detroit Shock moved to Tulsa in 2010. Overall, the WNBA lost only one franchise.

The Ladies Professional Golf Association (LPGA) also struggled during the Great Recession. The LPGA had difficulties renewing sponsorships as the recession began. This led to a decrease in the number of tour stops, from 37 events in 2008 to 29 in 2009. The financial situation became so bad that tour players removed LPGA commissioner Carolyn Bivens from her position, replacing her with Michael Whan in January 2010. At the height of the recession, in 2010, the LPGA tour held only 24 events. As the economy improved, events were added back to the LPGA schedule, and by 2014 they were back to 33 tour events.

After global COVID-19 pandemic closures, women's professional sport leagues began to reopen during the 2020 summer. There was a fear that gains in popularity made in 2019 and early 2020 would be lost (Ingle, 2020). While it is too soon to determine the long-ranging impact of the COVID-19 recession on women's sports, the short-term impact can be examined. In England, the FA Women's Super League season was cancelled, while the men's season returned. However, in Germany the Frauen Bundesliga resumed play in June 2020. There are other bright spots for women's sports too. While much of traditional sports programming was halted due to league shutdowns, several women's sporting events saw record television ratings. The April 17, 2020 WNBA draft had its highest ratings in 16 years and second highest rating ever (Fine, 2020). Sabrina Ionescu was selected as the first draft pick, and her New York Liberty jersey sold out online within an hour of the pick. Further, she signed an endorsement deal with Nike which some estimate to be the biggest endorsement deal in the history of women's professional basketball. The NWSL's Challenge Cup, the league's solution to a potential cancelled 2020 season, drew a record 653,000 on television for its final game. Prior to this, its record viewership was 190,000 from a game in 2014, with its 2019 championship only recording 166,000 viewers (Williams, 2020). Likewise, the WNBA's 2020 opening weekend of play saw viewership up 69% over the opening weekend in 2019. The ratings success led ESPN to add 13 games to its original 24-game broadcast schedule (Negley, 2020).

NASCAR

NASCAR was the first major North American sport to return during the COVID-19 pandemic. Prior to its return, the league used the global shutdown of business and stay-at-home mandates to build an audience through virtual racing. In a partnership between NASCAR, iRacing, and Fox Sports, NASCAR set televised esport rating records. Its first event of the eNASCAR Pro Invitational iRacing Series drew 903,000 viewers (Long, 2020). The previous record for an esport televised event was 770,000 viewers for a Mortal Kombat event. Viewership of the eNASCAR events was similar to that of its second level, Xfinity racing series. Through its seven televised events, the virtual race series averaged one million viewers, reaching a high of 1.3 million during its run.

With its virtual racing success, some of the financial impact of the 2020 recession was lessened. However, NASCAR has proven vulnerable to changing economic conditions. Just prior to the Great Recession's beginning, a top NASCAR team had to generate between $20 million and $25 million in revenues per year, of which $15 million to $20 million would come from the team's primary sponsors. When the economy slowed, sponsors became hard to find (Newton, 2008).

As the economy slowed and sponsor opportunities vanished toward the end of the 2007 season, Petty Enterprises, one of the best-known and most historic NASCAR teams, explored the idea of merging its team with another team or selling to another team (Caraviello, 2007). The team had won 268 races between 1949 and 1999 but could no longer afford to compete. In another example, Chip Ganassi Racing shut down operation of its number 40 car during the 2008 season. The team could not find a sponsor for the car and decided to focus its efforts on its two remaining cars.

At the same time, higher gasoline costs affected NASCAR more than other leagues (Klayman, 2008). Many NASCAR fans travel long distances to see races, often traveling in recreational vehicles. High gasoline costs affected the ability of some fans to drive to the races. In 2008, the average percentage drop in ticket sales at NASCAR Sprint Cup races was in the mid-single-digit range as gas prices reached $4 per gallon.

Since the recession ended, sponsorship has grown slowly, while the cost of fielding a competitive team has dropped from its peak of $30 million (Sigalos, 2018). However, attendance and television ratings have yet to rebound to pre-recession levels (Mickle & Bauerlein, 2017).

Television Revenue

Another important factor in sport finance is television revenue. It is a guaranteed form of revenue, with long-term contracts in place between leagues, conferences, teams, and networks. Fortunately for sport teams and leagues, television revenues somewhat insulate the industry from short-term slowdowns in the economy, such as the recession of 2007–2009. Even with postponed events in 2020 and empty or partially filled stadiums, television revenues provide some financial stability for leagues and teams. For example, the NFL's television contract will bring in close to $10 billion in revenue in 2020 ("TV money," 2020). ESPN and Turner pay the NBA about $2.6 billion annually. With games lost in the NHL, NBA, and MLB in 2020, networks and leagues will have to work together to offset lost advertising revenue with monies owed to leagues thereby impacting future league revenues (Soshnick, 2020).

Post-pandemic, long-term contracts will likely provide financial protection. The English Premier League (EPL) sold its 2020–2022 British and global rights for $12 billion (£9.2 billion) ("English Premier," 2019). The NFL's current contracts extend through the 2022 season, while MLB's run through 2021, and the NBA's extend from 2016 through 2025.

At the collegiate level, the SEC ended its long-time partnership with CBS for its Saturday afternoon football games. CBS is paying $55 million per year through 2023. ESPN will begin paying the league approximately $300 million for the same package of games in 2024. Further it created the SEC Network with ESPN in 2014. The league's television package will last for 20 years and is worth $400 million annually (Glass, 2014).

Television revenues have also provided NASCAR with some insulation. Even with attendance down at tracks and ratings in decline, the league holds a ten-year agreement with NBC and Fox for $8.2 billion. The contract runs through 2025 (Pockrass, 2013).

Real Estate

The development of real estate surrounding sport venues has become a popular means to generate additional revenue. As teams in some communities have found it more difficult to fund stadiums and arenas with public tax dollars, teams have turned to real estate development to help meet the debt service for privately financed facilities. The most successful example is L.A. Live. This development, which encompasses 27 acres surrounding the Staples Center in Los Angeles, features complementary entertainment venues, including broadcast studios, restaurants, movie theaters, music clubs, and the Grammy Museum. AEG owns both the development and the Staples Center, as well as the Los Angeles Kings of the NHL and a portion of the Los Angeles Lakers. Both the Kings and the Lakers play home games in the Staples Center. L.A. Live has long-term leases with ESPN, Ritz Carlton, Regal Theaters, and the Grammy Museum, to name a few. Other successful examples of real estate developments around sport venues include Xfinity Live! in Philadelphia, Fourth Street Live! in Louisville, and Baltimore's Power Plant Live!

Two new entertainment districts opened in 2019 and are becoming the norm (Cripe, 2019). Texas Live! opened in Arlington, Texas. It is a $250 million development located next to AT&T Stadium. The district includes a Live! By Loews hotel and the Texas Rangers new ballpark, Globe Life Field. The entertainment district was designed by the Rangers, the City of Arlington, and the Cordish Companies, a real estate partner with several professional sport teams. Over 200,000 square feet of dining and entertainment space can be found in the district. San Francisco saw the opening of Chase Center and Thrive City in the city's Mission Bay neighborhood. Thrive City was created by the Golden State Warriors and Kaiser Permanente to promote health and wellness in the area. The 11-acre mixed-use district was privately financed.

Sustainability

When sustainability or sustainable development is discussed today, it is typically in relation to the "green" movement. However, sustainability and venue construction and usage have been topics of discussion in the sport industry for many years. The 1987 Brundtland Report defined **sustainability** as meeting today's needs without compromising future generations' ability to meet their own needs. In sport, the glut of sport arenas built for mega-sporting events such as the Olympics or World Cup and even the overbuilding of publicly financed arenas in metropolitan areas have been questioned.

Previously, the New York City metropolitan area had five sporting arenas, with three of the five losing money: Izod Center, Prudential Center, and Nassau Coliseum. In New Jersey, the Devils left the Izod Center for the new, publicly subsidized Prudential Center and then asked the state to demolish the Izod Center in order to eliminate competition for events from the older arena. Further, it offered $2 million for the building to be closed. Officials from New Jersey announced the closing of the facility in March 2015, after a planned performance by the Ringling Bros. and Barnum & Bailey Circus (Sherman, 2015). The Izod Center, run by the New Jersey Sports and Exposition Authority, was also the home of the Nets. The Devils attempted to convince the Nets to move with them to the Prudential Center, in hopes that the newer arena would host more events and become profitable. However, the Nets moved to the new Barclays Center in Brooklyn. Meanwhile, Madison Square Garden underwent a $1 billion renovation, and the New York Islanders decided to leave the Nassau Coliseum for Brooklyn. When all five arenas were in operation, there were 100,000 seats to fill on a nightly basis within a 30-mile radius—not including the remaining stadiums and the performing arts complexes and theaters operating in the area (Bagli, 2009). Of the arenas still operating, Madison Square Garden has three anchor tenants, Barclays Center one, Prudential Center one, and Nassau Coliseum one. The Nassau Coliseum was refurbished and reopened in 2017. It is now the anchor of NYCB LIVE. The $180 million renovation is also the temporary home of the New York Islanders, who left their brief stay at the Barclays Center and are on their way to the new UBS Arena in Queens (opening in 2021). With an estimated 200 event dates needed per year to produce a profit, these five arenas are competing for event dates with each other. The Izod Center, the first casualty of the competition, lost both of its anchor tenants and saw the number of concerts held at the venue fall to eight to ten per year, down from 18 to 24 before Barclays and Prudential opened (Sherman, 2015).

Many other cities have experienced similar problems with sustainable development, though on a much smaller scale than New York's. Glendale, Arizona's Gila River Arena has struggled financially and must compete for events with Phoenix's Talking Stick Resort Arena and Arizona State's on-campus Desert Financial Arena. In Minnesota, the Target Center, owned by the City of Minneapolis, competes directly with the Xcel Energy Center in St. Paul, a publicly subsidized facility. Both facilities have lost money in the past. Finally, in Columbus, Ohio, the NHL's Blue Jackets sold money-losing Nationwide Arena to the Franklin County Convention Facilities Authority in 2012 for $42.5 million (Caruso, 2012). Nationwide Arena competes for events with Ohio State's Schottenstein Center (Bagli, 2009).

Questions regarding the sustainable development of venues have also been raised in connection with Olympic sport and FIFA's World Cup. The Brazilian government spent about $3.6 billion on new and refurbished stadiums for the 2014 World Cup. Today, four of the 12 stadiums host few events outside of weddings and other receptions ("FIFA returns," 2015). In addition, the country spent over $13 billion to host the Olympics two years later. Many of the venues constructed for the games proved to be too big and too expensive for the ongoing hosting of events. A planned auction to sell Olympic venues to private owners failed to generate interest beyond one potential bidder. Within a year of the games ending, venues began to deteriorate. The Olympic pool turned orange and Maracana Stadium had its power cut due to $930,000 in unpaid bills (Davis, 2017).

Ozanian (2020) notes that the cost of the Tokyo Olympics was $12.6 billion and is expected to rise by $2.7 billion due to the games' postponement to 2021. The initial projection for the cost of the games was $7.3 billion when the bid to host was submitted. In China, according to Matheson (2008), the Olympics became an economic disaster as sport-related infrastructure projects led to little long-term economic growth. Improvements to airports, highways, and transit systems that were needed during the games will provide long-term benefits, but the sports infrastructure cannot easily be converted to other uses.

Beijing and Rio are not alone in experiencing losses from unused facilities constructed for hosting specific international events and their attendees. Of the ten new stadiums built in South Korea to host the 2002 World Cup, most are unused today. Montreal finished paying for its Olympic Stadium 30 years after hosting the 1976 games. The facility was largely unused when debt obligations were finally met. Full-service hotels in Lillehammer, Norway, built to handle the influx of visitors for the games, struggled after the 1994 Winter Olympics. Forty percent had gone bankrupt a few years after the games ended.

Politics

Since *Federal Baseball* (1922), the case in which the US Supreme Court held that MLB is not subject to the Sherman Antitrust Act, sport and government have been intertwined. Changes in the nation's political climate can have a significant impact on the industry. NASCAR, for example, benefited from its relationship with several members of Congress after Congress passed the financial services bailout bill in 2008. The bill included language that classified motorsports facilities as "amusement parks and other entertainment complexes." Hence, track owners could depreciate the cost of new fixed assets over a seven-year period rather than a 15-year period, and taxes paid by track owners would be reduced in the years immediately following the capital expenditures ("Bailout bill includes," 2008).

Changes to the depreciation schedule positively affected NASCAR. However, some potential laws debated in Congress could have a significant impact on the sport industry. Important examples are legislative proposals relating to college athletics and changes to US tax law.

PROPOSED LEGISLATION AFFECTING COLLEGE ATHLETICS

The NCAA is facing forced changes to its business model resulting from several losses in US federal courts. The Ninth US Circuit Court of Appeals ruled that attempts by the NCAA to limit education-related benefits do not abide by rules set forth in the Sherman Act. The court found fault in the NCAA's limitation on the kinds of compensation athletes could receive related to their education (Kendall, Radnofsky, & Higgins, 2020). While the courts have only recently begun to reject the NCAA's antitrust defenses, the courts also have failed to give student-athletes unrestricted rights to income. From Ed O'Bannon's win related to the use of his name, image, and likeness in an NCAA video game, the NCAA has faced continued losses related to its long-standing business model.

In response to recent court rules and the passing of numerous and slightly different state laws relating to athletes' rights to compensation, the NCAA is working to have Congress pass the Intercollegiate Amateur Sports Act of 2020 (Dellenger, 2020b). If passed, the bill would give the NCAA antitrust protection and provide protection from lawsuits and state laws related to athletes' names, image, and likeness (NIL) compensation. In addition, the act would give full control to the NCAA to create rules for NIL and other forms of compensation.

The NCAA argues that without protection from antitrust law and state laws regulating NIL compensation, gender equity in athletic programs would be threatened. Further, the NCAA claims the legislation is needed as current NIL laws passed by states would create tax liabilities for athletes, would create an employer–employee relationship between athletes and their schools, and cause corruption related to unregulated NIL rights deals for athletes. The NCAA also claims the law is needed as differing state laws related to NIL would impact competitive balance within the NCAA and within its conferences (Dellenger, 2020b).

Some in Congress are skeptical of this proposed legislation. Senators Cory Booker and Richard Blumenthal are in the process of creating an athlete's "bill of rights" which might become a part of any federal NIL bill. Many in Congress are skeptical of the NCAA's ability to self-regulate and have begun to demand full-scale reform of the organization (Dellenger, 2020a). Whatever the outcome of these proposed pieces of legislation, the NCAA and its member schools are continuing to adapt to changes to the college business model resulting from court decisions and state legislation impacting revenues and expenses within collegiate athletics.

CHANGES TO TAX LAW

The Tax Cuts and Jobs Act was signed into law by President Trump on December 22, 2017. The $1.5 trillion tax reform law impacted the sport industry in the United States. First, employers can no longer deduct expenses related to their entertainment activities. The tax act repealed the ability for corporations to deduct 50% of the cost of entertainment, amusement, or recreation that is directly related to, or associated with, the businesses. Therefore, the cost of tickets used to entertain clients or prospective clients at sporting events is no longer deductible. Further, the act eliminated the ability of a donor to deduct 80% of the cost paid for seating rights in college sport. No longer can gifts to a booster club be deducted when tied to the ability to purchase seats or improve the quality of the seats purchased (Nussbaum et al., 2018).

Since 2001, the so-called jock tax has been applied in more and more jurisdictions (see Chapter 15). When Michael Jordan won his first NBA Championship in Los Angeles, the California Franchise Tax Board notified Jordan that he would owe state income taxes for the days he spent in California playing in the finals. The State of Illinois then created its own tax, known as "Michael Jordan's Revenge," taxing athletes who live in other states but play games in Illinois. The practice of taxing athletes who live out of state but play within the state grew. It has been estimated that in 2012, professional athletes playing in California contributed $216.8 million in tax revenues for the state (Cicalese, 2015).

Changes in tax law are often instituted to facilitate changes in the way industries conduct business. Current tax law in the United Kingdom, for example, may limit the further globalization of sport, as it may limit the continued expansion of the NFL, NHL, and NBA into London if it is not changed. The NFL, for example, has played games in London consistently since 2007 and may be considering relocating a team to that city. Under the UK's tax code, non-resident athletes can be taxed not only on the salary they earn while playing in London but also on their worldwide endorsement income. Typically, endorsement income is taxed only in the athlete's home country, but both the United Kingdom and the United States tax the total endorsement income of any athlete who plays on their soil.

In the United Kingdom, non-resident athletes are taxed on endorsement income based on the ratio of the number of days spent training and competing in the country versus the number of days spent training and competing outside the country. The tax rate on this income could reach as high as 45% (the United Kingdom's maximum tax rate in 2020). Currently, NFL players who compete in only one game in London are not greatly affected, and they can take a foreign tax credit on their US income tax return for any taxes withheld by the United Kingdom.

If the NFL were to move a team to London, the amount of tax owed by players on that team would become a significant issue. With 8 to 12 games being played by the team in London, about half of a player's salary could be taxed at the United Kingdom's maximum rate of 45%. In the United States, the maximum tax rate in 2020 was 37%. Since the foreign tax credit benefit is limited to the income tax filer's US tax rate, a player whose team is based in London would pay more in taxes than a player whose team is based in the United States. Nitti (2012) provides an example of how a player would be affected, using maximum tax rates of 50% in the United Kingdom and 30% in the United States. Suppose Player X earns $8 million in salary with his London-based team, and $5 million of his salary is earned in the United Kingdom. In the United Kingdom, as a non-resident player he will be taxed at 50% and owe $2.5 million. In the United States, as a US citizen he will owe federal tax at 30% on the full $8 million he earned. His US tax bill would be $2.4 million. His foreign tax credit is limited to the $5 million he earned in the United Kingdom multiplied by his US tax rate of 30%, or $1.5 million. Therefore, Player X would pay $900,000 to the United States ($2.4 million minus $1.5 million) and $2.5 million to the United Kingdom, for a total of $3.4 million and an effective tax rate of 42.5%. Therefore, according to laws in place in 2012, he would pay $1 million more in taxes than a player who earned $8 million playing for a United States-based team. Add to this the fact that any endorsement income the player earned would be allocated to his UK earnings, according to the method previously discussed. For a London-based team in a league with a hard salary cap, it might be difficult to attract talented free agents, as the tax difference would reduce their net incomes significantly.

CONCLUSION

The sport industry is large and diverse, with many factors that affect financial management within the industry. Financial managers strive to maximize wealth by forecasting revenues, planning for expenses, arranging financing, and making investment decisions. However, a team owner's objective might not be to maximize wealth. Goals other than wealth maximization have resulted in salary constraints, revenue sharing, and other control mechanisms under which financial managers in the industry must function.

In addition to debt and equity financing, sport organizations rely on retained earnings, government financing, and gift financing. These forms of financing will be used to varying degrees depending on the subsector of the industry in which the organization functions. The ownership structure of a team and the structure of the league will also affect financing decisions.

Growth in the sport industry is linked to the performance of the economy as a whole. Newer leagues are more likely to be affected by sudden changes in the economy, as are organizations without long-term guaranteed forms of revenue. Teams often attempt to bolster revenues through initiatives such as real estate development. Such initiatives, however, may further increase teams' exposure to changes in the economy. Financial managers in sport must be aware of factors that might affect the operation of their organization and must be pro-active to protect valuable sources of revenue.

Concept Check

1. What are the five forms of financing, and how is each used within sport?
2. What is financial management? How does financial management differ in the sport industry as compared to other industries?
3. Why does the definition of the sport industry affect the calculation of its size? How should the industry be defined?

4. Which has the greater impact on financial management: the structure of a league or the structure of a team?
5. Many factors affect the economics of sport. What are some not discussed in the chapter? How do they affect financial management within the industry?
6. Why is sustainability in the sport industry linked to the green movement?
7. What legislative actions currently being considered in Congress might affect the financial management of sport?

Case Analysis

The Growth of a League

For many years, women's professional basketball struggled for consistency in the United States. Since 1978, when the Women's Professional Basketball League (WBL) was formed, leagues have had difficulty surviving beyond a few seasons. The WBL lasted for only three seasons, and it was ten years before a second professional league, the Liberty Basketball Association (LBA), was launched. The LBA folded after only one exhibition game. A year later, another league was created: the Women's World Basketball Association. Although this league was more successful than the LBA, it too folded shortly into its first season. Finally, 1996 saw the launch of the American Basketball League, and the Women's National Basketball Association launched a year later. The ABL lasted for two and a half seasons (Jenkins, 2009). The WNBA entered its 24th season in 2015.

The WNBA began as a single-entity league in 1996, with its first season starting in June 1997. It was formed by the NBA Board of Governors and owned by the league. Since its founding, the number of franchises and the franchise locations have fluctuated. The league's first 16 players were dispersed to the inaugural eight teams, and the rest of the players were selected by the teams via a draft ("History of the WNBA," 2015). The Women's National Basketball Players Association (WNBPA) was formed soon thereafter and negotiated its first collective bargaining agreement (CBA) with the WNBA in 1999. This was the first CBA in women's professional sports. Under this CBA, rookie minimum salary increased by 75%, and veteran minimum salary doubled. Year-round health coverage and a retirement plan were provided. Contracts became guaranteed, and players earned a collective share of league licensing income ("About the WNBPA," 2015).

The WNBA introduced a draft lottery in 2001, and in 2003 the league and the WNBPA signed a new CBA. This CBA created the first free agency system in women's sports ("About the WNBPA," 2015). The most significant change during this time frame, however, was the NBA Board of Governors' vote to allow individual team ownership, moving the league from a single-entity model to a distributed club ownership model. Further, teams could be owned by non-NBA owners and could be located in non-NBA markets. On January 28, 2003, the Mohegan Tribe, located in Connecticut, became the first non-NBA owner in league history when it was awarded the Orlando Miracle franchise ("WNBA's greatest moments," 2015).

In 2005, the Chicago Sky became the second WNBA franchise to be owned and run by a non-NBA entity (the team's first season was 2006), and the Washington Mystics were transferred from Wizards owner Abe Pollin to Lincoln Holdings, LLC ("WNBA's greatest moments," 2015). Sheila Johnson then became the first female owner in the league. The Los Angeles Sparks became independently owned in 2006, as did the Houston Comets in 2007, although the Comets folded prior to the 2009 season. The sixth independently owned team was the expansion team Atlanta Dream, which began play in 2008 ("WNBA expands," 2007). The Tulsa Shock became independently owned, as well, when they relocated from Detroit.

The league also began to move toward profitability. Its first television agreement under which it would receive a rights fee was an eight-year agreement (2009–2016) signed with ABC, ESPN, and ESPN2. Teams including the Phoenix Mercury and Los Angeles Sparks sold sponsorship rights to their uniforms, with LifeLock appearing on Phoenix's uniform and Farmers Insurance on the Sparks' uniform.

In 2008, as the league continued to move away from its single-entity status and closer to profitability, the third CBA was signed. This six-year agreement set the WNBA salary cap at $803,000 per team in 2009 and increased it to $900,000 by 2013. For players with three-plus years of WNBA experience, the minimum salary was $51,000. The maximum salary for a player with six or more years was $99,500. Rookies received a minimum of $35,190 (*Women's National*, 2008). After the 2009 season, the Sacramento Monarchs folded, and the league has played with 12 teams since then. Seven of the 12 are owned by entities outside the NBA (Atlanta Dream, Chicago Sky, Connecticut Sun, Dallas Wings, Las Vegas Aces, Los Angeles Sparks, and Seattle Storm).

The fourth CBA was signed in 2014 and continues through 2021. This CBA added a 12th roster spot to each team. Maximum salary was set at $107,000 in 2014 and increases during the term of the CBA. The minimum salary was set at $37,950, with veterans with over three years' experience receiving a minimum of $50,000. A soft salary cap of $750,000 per team was set. Teams can exceed the cap by 4% ("WNBA salaries 2015," 2015).

The league's viability is still a subject of concern. The Sparks lost money each year after the team was purchased from the league in 2006. The team was scheduled to lose more than $1 million in 2014, when it was put up for sale. Magic Johnson purchased the team after it had been on the market for two months (D'Hippolito, 2014). Though ESPN and ABC extended the television agreement with the league in 2016 through 2022 and Twitter also streamed 20 games per year from 2017 to 2020 the league still has tight budgets ("We got," 2018). For example, teams fly coach and player salaries average $70,000. With a new CBA due after the 2021 season, there have been calls for greater financial transparency as star players push to see increased salaries, improved travel conditions, and a season that is less condensed.

Case Questions

1. Why was the WNBA structured as a single-entity league when it was founded? What advantages and disadvantages did the structure provide to the league?

2. What impact did the first CBA have on the WNBA, and how did each of the CBAs affect the league's profitability?
3. What factors have caused the WNBA to move away from the single-entity structure?
4. For new leagues, why is the single-entity structure appealing? At some point, do start-up leagues have to move away from this structure? Why or why not?

References

About the WNBPA. (2015). Retrieved from http://wnbpa.com/about/.

Athletics raises $340 million in Duke Forward campaign. (2017, August 15). *GoDuke.com*. Retrieved from https://goduke.com/news/2017/8/15/211661442.aspx.

Bachman, R. (2020, April 21). Coronavirus prompts budget cut for U.S. Olympic & Paralympic committee. *The Wall Street Journal*. Retrieved from www.wsj.com/articles/coronavirus-fallout-prompts-u-s-olympic-paralympic-committee-to-cut-budget-10-20-11587492104.

Bagli, C.V. (2009, June 29). As arenas sprout, a scramble to keep them filled. *The New York Times*. Retrieved from www.nytimes.com/2009/06/29/nyregion/29arenas.html.

Bailout bill includes tax breaks for NASCAR tracks, facilities. (2008, October 6). *Sports Business Daily*. Retrieved from www.sportsbusinessdaily.com/article/124459.

Brigham, E.F., & Houston, J.F. (2019). *Fundamentals of financial management* (15th ed.). Mason, OH: Cengage Learning.

Broughton, D. (2002, March 11–17). Methodology. *Sports Business Journal*, 4(47), 25–26.

Brundtland, G.H. (1987, March). *Our common future: Report of the world commission on environment and development*. New York: Oxford University Press.

Burnside, S. (2011, May 30). Owners to blame for Thrashers' failure. *ESPN.com*. Retrieved from http://sports.espn.go.com/nhl/columns/story?columnist=burnside_scott&id=6611534.

Business Wire. (2019). Sports—$614 billion global market opportunities & strategies to 2022. Retrieved from www.businesswire.com/news/home/20190514005472/en/Sports---614-Billion-Global-Market-Opportunities.

Caraviello, D. (2007, September 17). Economic reality forces Pettys to explore change. *NASCAR.com*. Retrieved from http://about.nascar.com/2007/news/headlines/cup/09/17/kpetty.blabonte.petty.partnership.

Caruso, D. (2012, March 30). Taxpayers now own Nationwide Arena. *The Columbus Dispatch*. Retrieved from http://bluejacketsxtra.dispatch.com/content/stories/2012/03/30/taxpayers-now-own-nationwide-arena.html.

Cash, M. (2020, July 8). Cincinnati, Stanford, and 17 other Division I schools are permanently eliminating dozens of sports programs in an unexpected loss from the pandemic. *Insider*. Retrieved from www.insider.com/college-sports-programs-cut-due-to-coronavirus-pandemic-2020-7.

Chang, D. (2019, November 27). Arena Football League shuts down, files for bankruptcy after 3 decades. *NBC Boston*. Retrieved from www.nbcboston.com/news/sports/arena-football-league-bankruptcy/2032975/#:~:text=is%20no%20more.-,The%20AFL%20announced%20Wednesday%20it%20filed%20for%20Chapter%207%20bankruptcy,AFL%20Commissioner%20Randall%20Boe%20said.

Cicalese, C.R. (2015, February 3). The tax man collects from everyone, even the jocks. *Above the Law Redline*. Retrieved from www.atlredline.com/the-tax-man-collects-from-everyone-even-the-jocks-1682470238.

College Athletics Financial Information Database. (2019). *Knight Commission on Intercollegiate Athletics*. Retrieved from http://cafidatabase.knightcommission.org/about.

College bowl payouts surpass $500 million. (2015, April 11). *ESPN.com*. Retrieved from http://espn.go.com/college-football/story/_/id/12688517/college-bowl-game-payouts-surpass-500-million-first-year-college-football-playoff.

The coronavirus and college sports: NCAA reopening plans, latest news, program cuts, more. (2020, July 31). *ESPN.com*. Retrieved from www.espn.com/college-football/story/_/id/29036650/the-coronavirus-college-sports-ncaa-reopening-plans-latest-news-program-cuts-more.

Cripe, K. (2019, October 28). 3 major sports and entertainment districts competing for your event. *Meetings Today*. Retrieved from www.meetingstoday.com/magazines/article-details/articleid/33995/title/new-sports-entertainment-districts-event?viewall=true.

D'Hippolito, J. (2014, February 5). Magic Johnson steps in to rescue Los Angeles Sparks. *The New York Times*. Retrieved from www.nytimes.com/2014/02/06/sports/basketball/magic-johnson-steps-in-to-rescue-los-angeles-sparks.html?_r=0.

Davis, S. (2017, June 15). The Rio Olympics were a financial disaster and it keeps getting worse. *Business Insider*. Retrieved from www.businessinsider.com/rio-olympics-financial-disaster-2017-6.

Dellenger, R. (2020a, July 22). 'It's time for substantive reform': Senators demand more from Mark Emmert, NCAA in hearing. *Sports Illustrated*. Retrieved from www.si.com/college/2020/07/22/senate-demands-more-reform-from-ncaa-mark-emmert.

Dellenger, R. (2020b, July 31). NCAA presents Congress with bold proposal for NIL legislation. *Sports Illustrated*. Retrieved from www.si.com/college/2020/07/31/ncaa-sends-congress-nil-legislation-proposal.

Economy could affect Cowboys' stadium naming-rights search. (2008, October 20). *Sports Business Daily*. Retrieved from www.sportsbusinessdaily.com/article/124822.

Employment by detailed occupation. (2018). *Bureau of Labor Statistics*. Retrieved from www.bls.gov/emp/tables/emp-by-detailed-occupation.htm.

English Premier League broadcast rights rise to $12 billion. (2019, May 21). *USA Today*. Retrieved from www.usatoday.com/story/sports/soccer/2019/05/21/english-premier-league-broadcast-rights-rise-to-12-billion/39500789/.

Federal Baseball Club v. National League, 259 U.S. 200 (1922).

FIFA returns $100M to Brazil; World Cup costs $15 billion. (2015, January 20). *USA Today*. Retrieved from www.usatoday.com/story/sports/soccer/2015/01/20/fifa-returns-100m-to-brazil-world-cup-cost-15-billion/22050583/.

Fine, M. (2020, April 29). Covid-19 and women's sports: Another casualty of gender inequality? *Forbes.com*. Retrieved from www.forbes.com/sites/melaniefine/2020/04/29/covid-19-and-womens-sports-another-casualty-of-gender-inequity/#190510e361b0.

Flood v. Kuhn, 407 U.S. 258 (1972).

Florio, M. (2011, November 7). Partial public ownership of Vikings doesn't mesh with league rules. *NBC Sports*. Retrieved from http://profootballtalk.nbcsports.com/2011/11/07/partial-public-ownership-of-vikings-doesnt-mesh-with-league-rules/.

Fornwalt, A. (2018, July 20). Should Congress reconsider the tax exemption of pro sports organizations? *Tax Foundation*. Retrieved from https://taxfoundation.org/congress-reconsider-tax-exemption-pro-sports-organizations/.

Foster, G., Greyser, S.A., & Walsh, B. (2005). *The business of sports*. New York: South-Western College Publishers.

Fraser v. Major League Soccer, LLC, 180 F.R.D. 178 (D. Mass. 1998).

Glass, A. (2014, August 14). SEC network: What you should know. *Forbes.com*. Retrieved from www.forbes.com/sites/alanaglass/2014/08/14/sec-network-what-you-should-know/.

Hall, S. (2020, April 9). This is how COVID-19 is affecting the world of sports. *World Economic Forum*. Retrieved from www.weforum.org/agenda/2020/04/sports-covid19-coronavirus-excersise-specators-media-coverage/.

Harwell, D., & Hobson, W. (2015, April 28). The NFL is dropping its tax-exempt status. Why that ends up helping them out. *The Washington Post.* Retrieved from www.washingtonpost.com/news/business/wp/2015/04/28/the-nfl-is-dropping-its-tax-exempt-status-why-that-ends-up-helping-them-out/.

Hawks announce sale for $850M to Anthony Ressler-led group. (2015, April 23). *ESPN.com.* Retrieved from http://espn.go.com/nba/story/_/id/12744168/atlanta-hawks-antony-ressler-led-group-agree-sale-850-million.

Haywood v. National Basketball Association, 401 U.S. 1204 (1971).

History of Green Bay Packers (2015). Retrieved from http://shareholder.broadridge.com/packers.

History of the WNBA (2015). Retrieved from www.wnba.com/history/.

Hobson, W. (2020, March 26). USOPC asked for $200 million in the coronavirus stimulus bill to 'sustain American athletes'. *The Washington Post.* Retrieved from www.washingtonpost.com/sports/2020/03/26/usopc-asked-200-million-federal-stimulus-money/.

Indy wrestles with venue deficits. (2009, March 18). *VTPulse,* 8(9), 20–25.

Ingle, S. (2020, May 24). Covid-19 has rocked women's sport but its future remains bright. *The Guardian.* Retrieved from www.theguardian.com/sport/2020/may/24/covid-19-has-rocked-womens-sport-but-its-future-remains-bright.

Jenkins, S. (2009). History of women's basketball. Retrieved from www.wnba.com/about_us/jenkins_feature.html.

Keh, A. (2014, October 26). Many in MLS playing largely for love of the game. *The New York Times.* Retrieved from www.nytimes.com/2014/10/27/sports/soccer/many-in-mls-playing-largely-for-love-of-the-game-.html?_r=0.

Kendall, B., Radnofsky, L., & Higgins, L. (2020, May 18). NCAA takes another court hit on athlete compensation. *The Wall Street Journal.* Retrieved from www.wsj.com/articles/ncaa-takes-another-court-hit-on-athlete-compensation-11589826409.

King, B. (2002, March 11–17). Passion that can't be counted puts billions of dollars in play. *Sports Business Journal,* 4(47), 25–26.

King, B., & Lombardo, J. (2005, September 19). Atlanta partnership, formed in 8 days, dissolved in sea of squabbles. *Sports Business Journal.* Retrieved from www.sportsbusinessjournal.com/article/46968.

Klayman, B. (2008, June 30). High gasoline prices pinch NASCAR fans. *USA Today.* Retrieved from www.usatoday.com/money/industries/energy/2008-06-30-nascar-gas_N.htm.

Kreidler, M. (2009, July 24). State of uncertainty for women's sports. *ESPN.com.* Retrieved from http://sports.espn.go.com/espn/pring?id=4352885&type=story.

Last, J.V. (2009, January 30). Are pro sports too big to fail? *The Wall Street Journal,* p. W11.

Lee, M. (2014, September 11). A blunder-filled era for Atlanta Hawks ownership nears its end. *The Washington Post.* Retrieved from www.washingtonpost.com/news/sports/wp/2014/09/11/a-blunder-filled-era-for-atlanta-hawks-ownership-nears-its-end/.

Lombardo, J. (2008, February 25). A new play for the AFL? *Sports Business Journal.* Retrieved from www.sportsbusinessjournal.com/article/58179.

Long, D. (2020, March 14). eNASCAR race draws record TV audience for eSports event. *NBC Sports.* Retrieved from https://nascar.nbcsports.com/2020/03/24/dale-jr-denny-hamlin-nascar-iracing-tv-viewership-esports/.

Mackey v. National Football League, 543 F2d 606 (1976).

Macur, J. (2009, January 12). For U.S.O.C., sponsorships become a challenge. *New York Times.* Retrieved from www.nytimes.com/2009/01/12/sports/olympics/12olympics.html.

Matheson, V. (2008, August 22). Caught under a mountain of Olympic debt. *The Boston Globe.* Retrieved from www.boston.com/bostonglobe/editorial_opinion/oped/articles/2008/08/22/caught_under_a_mountain_of_olympic_debt/.

McGregor, J. (2014, April 7). Here's what the average fulltime professor made last year. *The Washington Post.* Retrieved from www.washingtonpost.com/blogs/on-leadership/wp/2014/04/07/heres-what-the-average-full-time-professor-made-last-year/.

McNeil v. National Football League, 790 F. Supp. (D. Minn. 1992).

Meek, A. (1997). An estimate of the size and supported economic activity of the sports industry in the United States. *Sport Marketing Quarterly,* 6(4), 15–22.

Mickle, T. (2010, February 15). USOC adding BP as sponsor. *Sports Business Journal.* Retrieved from www.sportsbusinessjournal.com/article/64822.

Mickle, T. (2012, January 2). USOC enters Olympic year on strong footing with new sponsors, renewals. *Sports Business Journal.* Retrieved from www.sportsbusinessdaily.com/Journal/Issues/2012/01/02/Olympics/USOC-sponsors.aspx.

Mickle, T., & Baujerlein, V. (2017, February 21). Nascar, once a cultural icon, hits the skids. *The Wall Street Journal.* Retrieved from www.wsj.com/articles/long-in-victory-lane-nascar-hits-the-skids-1487686349?utm_source=newsletter&utm_medium=email&utm_campaign=newsletter_axiosam.

Milano, M., & Chelladurai, P. (2011). Gross domestic sport product: The size of the sport industry in the United States. *Journal of Sport Management,* 25, 24–35.

Milewski, T.D. (2020, July 22). Wisconsin Athletics' revenue hit from COVID-19 could pass $100 million without a football season. *Wisconsin State Journal.* Retrieved from https://madison.com/wsj/sports/college/football/wisconsin-athletics-revenue-hit-from-covid-19-could-pass-100-million-without-a-football-season/article_8bdf70cc-1927-53b1-a70d-ae5f77482064.html.

MLS salaries: Ibra earning record $7.2m in '19. (2019, June 12). *ESPN.com.* Retrieved from www.espn.com/soccer/major-league-soccer/story/3874490/mls-salaries-ibra-earning-record-$72m-in-19.

National Collegiate Athletic Association. (2019). *NCAA Financial Database.* Retrieved from www.ncaa.org/about/resources/research/finances-intercollegiate-athletics-database.

National Football League v. North American Soccer League, 459 U.S. 1074 (1982).

Negley, C. (2020, July 26). ESPN puts WNBA on main channels, garners historic numbers. *Yahoo! Sports.* Retrieved from https://sports.yahoo.com/espn-4-game-average-wnba-viewership-up-63-percent-over-2019-season-201902094.html.

Newton, D. (2008, July 1). With Ganassi pulling the plug on a team, question remains: Will it get worse? *ESPN.com.* Retrieved from http://sports.espn.go.com/espn/pring?id=3470082&type=story.

Nitti, T. (2012, October 29). One reason the NFL will never permanently relocate a team to London: The U.K.'s tax treatment of nonresident athletes. *Forbes.* Retrieved from www.forbes.com/sites/anthonynitti/2012/10/29/one-reason-the-nfl-will-never-permanently-relocate-a-team-to-london-the-u-k-s-tax-treatment-of-nonresident-athletes/.

Nussbaum, A.H., Oram, J., Parnes, A., & Zeicer, A. (2018, January 3). Tax reform's effect on the sports industry. *Proskauer Tax Talks.* Retrieved from www.proskauertaxtalks.com/2018/01/tax-reforms-effect-on-the-sports-industry/.

Ozanian, M. (2020, March 25). Postponement of Tokyo Olympics expected to increase games' cost by $2.7 billion. *Forbes.* Retrieved from www.forbes.com/sites/mikeozanian/2020/03/25/postponement-of-tokyo-olympics-expected-to-increase-its-cost-by-27-billion/#2af6eaf81b7c.

Pells, E. (2009, June 3). Bank of America wants more out of USOC sponsorship. *The Seattle Times.* Retrieved from http://seattletimes.nwsource.com/html/sports/2009264103_apolyusocsponsor.html.

Plunkett Research (2018). Sports & recreation industry statistics and market size overview. Retrieved from www.plunkettresearch.com/statistics/Industry-Statistics-Sports-Industry-Statistic-and-Market-Size-Overview/.

Pockrass, B. (2013, August 15). How NASCAR landed a staggering TV deal despite ratings decline. *The Sporting News*. Retrieved from www.sportingnews.com/nascar/story/2013-08-15/nascar-tv-coverage-network-contract-fox-sports-1-nbc-deal-ratings.

Prince-Wright, J. (2019, June 12). 2019 MLS player salary list released. *NBC Sports*. Retrieved from https://soccer.nbcsports.com/2019/06/12/2019-mls-player-salary-list-released/.

Rascher, D. (2001, August 1). What is the size of the sports industry? *Sports Economics Perspectives*, 1(1). Retrieved from www.sportseconomics.com.

Roberts, J.L., & Murr, A. (2008, October 20). If you build it, will they pay? *Newsweek*, E6–E8.

Sandomir, R. (1988, November 14). The $50-billion sports industry. *Sports Inc.*, 14–23.

Sangha, J. (2017, July 27). Prospects of sports stadium financing in the U.S. *MunicipalBonds.com*. Retrieved from www.municipalbonds.com/investing-strategies/sports-stadium-financing/.

Scarborough, A. (2020, July 8). Stanford to cut 11 varsity sports, cites pandemic as breaking point. *ESPN.com*. Retrieved from www.espn.com/college-sports/story/_/id/29429478/stanford-cut-11-varsity-sports-cites-pandemic-breaking-point.

Schlabach, M. (2009, July 14). Programs struggle to balance budget. *ESPN.com*. Retrieved from http://sports.espn.go.com/print?id=4314195&type=story.

Sherman, T. (2015, January 18). Izod Center shutdown may take longer than expected. *NJ.com*. Retrieved from www.nj.com/news/index.ssf/2015/01/turning_out_the_lights_the_last_acts_at_the_izod_c.html.

Sigalos, M. (2018, May 27). Why Americans have fallen out of love with NASCAR. *CNBC*. Retrieved from www.cnbc.com/2018/05/27/nascar-racing-fans-sponsors-viewers.html.

Soshnick, S. (2020, March 25). Leagues and networks forced to reevaluate TV deals due to sports blackout. *Fortune*. Retrieved from https://fortune.com/2020/03/25/nba-mlb-nhl-sports-blackout-leagues-tv-deals/.

Sport England. (2020). *Economic development*. Retrieved from www.sportengland.org/why-were-here/economic-development.

Sudden vanishing of sports due to coronavirus will cost at least $12 billion, analysis says. (2020, May 1). *ESPN.com*. Retrieved from www.espn.com/espn/otl/story/_/id/29110487/sudden-vanishing-sports-due-coronavirus-cost-least-12-billion-analysis-says.

Sullivan v. National Football League, 34 F3d 1091 (1994).

Swartz, K.E. (2009, January 24). Atlanta Spirit circus resumes. *The Atlanta Journal-Constitution*. Retrieved from www.ajc.com/services/content/printedition/2009/01/24/spirit0124.html.

Swartz, K.E. (2010, December 22). Hawks, Thrashers ownership group settle lawsuit. *The Atlanta Journal-Constitution*. Retrieved from www.ajc.com/news/sports/hawks-thrashers-ownership-group-settle-lawsuit/nQn89/.

Talalay, S. (2009, July 21). Marc Anthony buys stake in Miami Dolphins. *South Florida Sun-Sentinel*. Retrieved from www.sun-sentinel.com/sports/miami-dolphins/sfl-marc-anthony-dolphins-s072009,0,3720783.story.

Tottenham hails stadium financing deal. (2019, September 23). *SportBusiness*. Retrieved from www.sportbusiness.com/news/tottenham-hails-stadium-financing-deal/.

TV money gives NFL leg up if fans can't fill teams' coffers. (2020, June 13). *USA Today*. Retrieved from www.usatoday.com/story/sports/nfl/2020/06/13/tv-money-gives-nfl-leg-up-if-fans-cant-fill-teams-coffers/111957448/.

UBS Wealth Management Research. (2012). Retrieved from www.scribd.com/doc/92368114/Stadium-Bonds.

US Census Bureau. (2020). *2017 Economic Census*. Retrieved from www.census.gov/programs-surveys/economic-census.html.

Vivlamore, C. (2015, June 2). 100 percent of Hawks up for sale. *The Atlanta Journal-Constitution*. Retrieved from www.ajc.com/news/sports/basketball/breaking-news-100-percent-of-hawks-up-for-sale/njfLd/.

We got next! The history of the WNBA. (2018, October 1). National Women's History Museum. Retrieved from www.womenshistory.org/articles/we-got-next.

Williams, B. (2020, July 29). NWSL draws record 653,000 TV audience for Challenge Cup. *SportBusiness*. Retrieved from www.sportbusiness.com/news/nwsl-draws-record-653000-tv-audience-for-nwsl-challenge-cup-final/.

Williams, N. (2020, July 6). Green Bay Packers say possibility of no fans at Lambeau this year. *Milwaukee Business Journal*. Retrieved from www.bizjournals.com/milwaukee/news/2020/07/06/green-bay-packers-say-possibility-of-no-fans-in-st.html.

WNBA expands to Atlanta. (2007, October 17). Retrieved from www.wnba.com/dream/expansionrelease_071012.html.

WNBA salaries 2015. (2015). Retrieved from www.altiusdirectory.com/Sports/wnba-salaries.php.

WNBA's greatest moments. (2015). Retrieved from www.wnba.com/about_us/greatest_moments_020508.html.

Women's National Basketball Association collective bargaining agreement. (2008, January 24). Retrieved from www.wnbpa.com/documents/2008WNBACBA_003.pdf.

CHAPTER 2

Analyzing Financial Statements and Ratios

Chad D. McEvoy

KEY CONCEPTS

accounts receivable
accrual basis accounting
acid-test ratio
assets
balance sheet
cash basis accounting
contingent liabilities
cost of goods sold (COGS)
credits
current liabilities
current ratio
debits
debt ratio
double-entry bookkeeping
earnings before interest and
    taxes (EBIT)
expenses
fiscal year

generally accepted accounting
    principles (GAAP)
income statement
interest coverage ratio
inventory turnover ratio
leverage
liabilities
liquidity
long-term liabilities
market value
net profit margin ratio
owners' equity
price-to-earnings ratio (P/E ratio)
quick ratio
return on equity ratio
revenues
statement of cash flows
T-accounts
total asset turnover ratio

INTRODUCTION

The 2003 publication of *Moneyball: The art of winning an unfair game* popularized the use of objective, evidence-based decision making in the sport industry. Michael Lewis's book details the inner workings of the front office of the Oakland Athletics baseball club and how Athletics General Manager Billy Beane and his staff used objective data and statistical analysis to gain a competitive advantage over other Major League Baseball teams, most of which could afford to out-spend the Athletics dramatically for talent.

Over the past two decades, the use of data analytics and objective deci-sion making in financial analysis has blossomed, both in sports and throughout nearly all industries. Just as baseball general managers use analytical tools—such as on-base plus slugging percentage (OPS), value over replacement player (VORP), and wins above replacement player (WAR or WARP)—to scrutinize players' production and value objectively, financial analysts use accounting data, summarized in documents such as balance sheets and income statements, to compute metrics that allow them to examine the financial strength and performance of an organization. The results of this type of financial analysis provide insights to a variety of the organization's stakeholders, including its management, customers, current and potential investors, lenders, and suppliers. Each of these stakeholders may be concerned with the past, present, and likely future financial performance and status of the organization. Just as a baseball executive is disadvantaged by not fully understanding objective statistical analysis (as described in *Moneyball*), so too is a manager in the sport industry who does not grasp the tools of financial analysis.

This chapter will provide a foundation for understanding financial analysis. It focuses first on a brief primer regarding standard accounting principles and double-entry bookkeeping. Second, this chapter introduces financial statements, such as the balance sheet, that use accounting data to provide a summary of financial performance. The final portion of the chapter focuses on the computation of financial ratios that provide objective interpretations of the data provided by key financial statements.

ACCOUNTING BASICS

Most business organizations, including those in the sport industry, utilize a system of accounting known as **double-entry bookkeeping**. As its name suggests, this system requires that every entry on an account have a corresponding entry to a different account. Double-entry bookkeeping is required under **generally accepted accounting principles (GAAP)**, which are a standard set of guidelines and procedures for financial reporting. This section will briefly explain the use of T-accounts and double-entry bookkeeping, in order to provide the background necessary to understand financial statements and ratios.

During start-up, an organization creates a chart of accounts, which specifies the individual accounts to which its financial transactions will be recorded. The major types of accounts are liability accounts, for legal debts or obligations; equity accounts, to track funds contributed by the owner plus retained earnings or losses; asset accounts, for funds or items (such as real estate) that the organization possesses; and expense accounts, to track money that is spent in the course of operating the organization.

To record financial transactions and track the organization's revenues and expenses, accountants historically have used **T-accounts**. Today, large organizations often rely on industry-specific accounting information systems, and small companies use computer software (such as QuickBooks) to create entries to accounts that are then used in the automatic generation of financial statements. Though software is available and has simplified the accounting process, an understanding of T-accounts will aid a manager's comprehension of double-entry bookkeeping and balance sheets, income statements, and statements of cash flows, which are discussed later in this chapter.

A T-account is created on a ledger. **Credits** reflect increases to liability or equity accounts, and they are entered on the right-hand side of the ledger.

EXHIBIT 2.1	The effects of debits and credits on the various account types.	
ACCOUNT TYPE	**DEBIT THE ACCOUNT FOR**	**CREDIT THE ACCOUNT FOR**
Asset	Increases +	Decreases –
Expense	Increases +	Decreases –
Revenue	Decreases –	Increases +
Liability	Decreases –	Increases +
Equity	Decreases –	Increases +

Debits show increases to asset or expense accounts, and these are entered on the left-hand side of the ledger (see Exhibit 2.1). The "T" suggests the division of the ledger page into right- and left-hand columns. In the past, the ledger page was an actual sheet of paper on which figures were written by hand; now, financial data are stored in a database, but some software packages still display the numbers in a form that resembles a ledger page.

In double-entry bookkeeping, any entry on one account—for example, a debit in an organization's cash account—must be accompanied by a corresponding simultaneous entry in another account, so that the net result across the accounts is zero. In other words, the accounts must balance. See Sidebar 2.A.

FINANCIAL STATEMENTS

Just as a general manager or coach/manager reviews statistical records in order to evaluate the performance of a sports team, the manager of a business organization examines data to evaluate the organization's financial health and performance. The primary source of this type of data is the company's financial statements. Financial statements are the equivalent of box scores or statistics sheets, allowing managers to assess the organization's financial status.

The three basic financial statements are the balance sheet, the income statement, and the statement of cash flows. Each of these is examined in this chapter. These financial statements are constructed from the organization's accounting records. Their preparation typically follows generally accepted accounting principles, or GAAP, as mentioned earlier.

Publicly traded companies—those whose stock is traded on one of the many stock exchanges that exist in the United States (such as the New York Stock Exchange [NYSE] and National Association of Securities Dealers Automated Quotations [NASDAQ]) and internationally (such as the Toronto, London, and Tokyo stock exchanges)—are required to release their financial statements to the public regularly. Public companies in the United States release annual reports to the Securities and Exchange Commission (SEC) through a Form 10-K. These reports, which can also include information about a company's history, products, market segment, research and development, and subsidiary activities, are widely available online through companies' websites, as well as through various online resources. As with publicly traded companies, non-profit philanthropic organizations are also required to provide their financial statements on a regular basis and make them available to the public. This rule applies to collegiate athletic departments in the United States, as we will discuss in Chapter 14. Private firms, including the vast majority of North American professional sport organizations, are generally not required to disclose financial statements or other related information to the public.

SIDEBAR 2.A   Understanding Double-entry Bookkeeping through a Tennis Club's T-accounts

To understand how double-entry bookkeeping and T-accounts work, let's examine transactions for a tennis club by looking at the T-account form shown in (A).

(A)

	T-account
Debits	*Credits*

Every month, the club mails a monthly membership bill to one of the club's members, Customer A. The monthly membership fee is $200. This bill constitutes a transaction, which is recorded as a debit, or increase, in the tennis club's accounts receivable account. The accounts receivable account reflects money owed to the club by its customers for services or products provided on credit (meaning a promise to pay within a defined period of time). Accounts receivable appears as a short-term asset on the tennis club's balance sheet, as will be explained later in the chapter when we discuss financial statements.

The second entry to be made for this transaction is a credit, representing an increase, in the membership revenue account. This account will appear on the club's income statement, also to be discussed later in this chapter. This first transaction (marked 1) is shown in T-account form (B).

(B)

	Cash
Debits	*Credits*
(1) $200	

	Membership Revenue
Debits	*Credits*
	(1) $200

The club also has a cash account (or bank account), which is an asset account. Form (C) presents the T-account for cash.

(C)

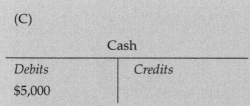

Cash

Debits	Credits
$5,000	

    The cash account shown in (C) is the current balance of the account, indicating that the tennis club currently has $5,000 cash in the bank—probably in a checking account. If Customer A writes a check to the tennis club to pay her $200 monthly membership fee, this transaction (marked 2) is recorded in the T-accounts as shown in (D).

(D)

Accounts Receivable

Debits	Credits
(1) $200	(2) $200

Cash

Debits	Credits
$5,000	

    The club's accounts receivable account is credited with $200, as Customer A has now paid her bill and no longer owes that amount to the club. The accounts receivable account now has a zero balance, reflecting the fact that nothing is currently owed to the club. The club's cash account is debited $200 (an increase), as the amount that Customer A paid is deposited in the checking account. At the end of the financial reporting period (monthly for many organizations), the T-account entries are finalized and financial reports are prepared. These reports provide each account's end-of-period total, as shown in (E).

(E)

Membership Revenue

Debits	Credits
	(1) $200

Accounts Receivable

Debits	Credits
$0	

Cash

Debits	Credits
$5,200	

    The T-accounts show that the tennis club has generated $200 in membership revenue, which will be reflected on the club's income statement.

Accounts receivable has a zero balance, as discussed previously. Finally, the cash account grows to $5,200, and this will be reflected on the club's balance sheet.

This example, and the information it conveys, provides an extremely basic illustration of accounting principles and double-entry bookkeeping. Further accounting background, including courses and readings, is essential for individuals who intend to work in the financial operations of sport organizations, but this material is beyond the scope of this text.

To illustrate concepts relating to financial statements, as well as other concepts discussed in this chapter, we will examine financial statements for Nike, an Oregon-based sports footwear and apparel company which has grown to become a global leader in the industry over the past half-century. Nike is a publicly held corporation whose stock is traded on the New York Stock Exchange. As such, Nike is required to release its financial data to the public on both a quarterly and an annual basis. We will present the company's financial statements from its 2019 annual report. The statements are provided and will be discussed throughout the chapter.

SIDEBAR 2.B   Publicly Traded Companies in the Sport Industry

Shares of stock in dozens of sport industry organizations are available for trade on various stock exchanges, including both well-known exchanges, such as the NYSE and NASDAQ, and smaller ones, such as the American Stock Exchange (AMEX). Examples of publicly traded sport organizations include sports apparel and sporting goods companies such as Nike, Reebok, and Callaway Golf; media companies, including Walt Disney (which owns ESPN), The Madison Square Garden Company (MSG), and Comcast; and motorsports companies such as International Speedway Corp. and Speedway Motorsports, each of which owns and operates NASCAR racetracks. Not represented among publicly traded companies are professional sport franchises. Currently, no major North American professional team is a publicly traded corporation, although some teams are subsidiaries, or parts, of publicly traded corporations. In the 1980s and 1990s, certain franchises—such as the Boston Celtics, Florida Panthers, and Cleveland Indians— sold stock through major exchanges; however, each of those teams has since privatized its ownership.

The Balance Sheet

The balance sheet is a picture or snapshot of the financial condition of an organization at a specific point in time. The balance sheet is unique among the financial statements in that it represents the organization's financial condition *on the date on which it is prepared* (thus the reference to a snapshot or picture), whereas the other two financial statements reflect the organization's financial performance over a period of time.

The balance sheet is organized in three primary sections: assets, liabilities, and owners' equity. A company's **assets** are what it owns, including items such as cash, inventory, and accounts receivable, or the money a company is owed by customers. **Liabilities**, conversely, are the organization's financial obligations or debts owed to others. **Owners' equity**, which is also referred to as shareholders' equity or stockholders' equity, is an estimated measure of the ownership value of the company; it includes paid-in capital and retained earnings (see Exhibit 2.2, **K** and **L**).

On the balance sheet, owners' equity is equal to the company's assets minus its liabilities. Stated differently, the balance sheet is always truly "in balance," as the assets—the first half of the statement—must equal the total of the liabilities and owners' equity—the second half of the balance sheet. This balance is assured through the use under GAAP of double-entry bookkeeping, where each transaction is entered or recorded twice, once on the debit side of the accounting records and once on the credit side, as discussed earlier in this chapter. Hence, the balance sheet can be viewed through the lens of T-accounts, as shown below, where assets are listed on the debit (left) side of the T, while liabilities and owners' equity are listed on the credit (right) side.

Balance Sheet

Assets	Liabilities Owners' Equity

The result of this accounting system is a "balanced sheet," where the sum of the organization's assets is equal to the combined sum of its liabilities and owners' equity. Exhibit 2.2 shows Nike's balance sheet as of May 31, 2019. Note on Exhibit 2.2 that Nike's assets of $23 billion in 2019 were equal to the total of its liabilities and shareholders' equity:

$$assests = liabilities + shareholders' equity$$
$$\$23,717,000,000 = \$14,677,000,000 + \$9,040,000,000$$

Asset accounts on a balance sheet are listed in order of **liquidity**, or how quickly the asset can be converted into cash, with the most liquid assets listed first. Hence, cash will almost always be the first asset listed, at the top of the balance sheet. Further, assets are typically divided into the categories of *current assets* and *long-term assets*. Current assets (Exhibit 2.2, **A**), are those that are likely to be converted to cash within one year's time and long-term assets are those that will take longer than a year to convert (Exhibit 2.2, **C**). Liabilities are similarly listed according to their maturity, or when the liability or debt is due to be paid by the organization. Liabilities with the earliest maturity dates are listed first. Liabilities due within one year are labeled **current liabilities** (Exhibit 2.2, **E**), and those due after one year are labeled **long-term liabilities** (Exhibit 2.2, **G**). Common examples of current liabilities include employee salaries and accounts payable, or purchases from suppliers on credit, whereas long-term liabilities include mortgage loans for facility construction or renovation and employee pension obligations. Note that Nike's balance sheet does not explicitly list total liabilities; however, this figure can be quickly calculated by adding the three

EXHIBIT 2.2 Nike balance sheet.

Nike, Inc.
Consolidated Balance Sheets
(Dollars in millions)

		May 31, 2019	May 31, 2018
	ASSETS		
	Current assets:		
A	Cash and equivalents	$4,466	$4,249
	Short-term investments	$197	$996
	Accounts receivable, net	$4,272	$3,498
	Inventories	$5,622	$5,261
	Prepaid expenses and other current assets	$1,968	$1,130
B	Total current assets	$16,525	$15,134
C	Property, plant and equipment, net	$4,744	$4,454
	Identifiable intangible assets, net	$283	$285
	Goodwill	$154	$154
	Deferred income taxes and other assets	$2,011	$2,509
D	**TOTAL ASSETS**	**$23,717**	**$22,536**

EXHIBIT 2.2   Cont.

	LIABILITIES AND SHAREHOLDERS' EQUITY		
E	Current liabilities:		
	Current portion of long-term debt	$6	$6
	Notes payable	$9	$336
	Accounts payable	$2,612	$2,279
	Accrued liabilities	$5,010	$3,269
	Income taxes payable	$229	$150
F	Total current liabilities	$7,866	$6,040
G	Long-term debt	$3,464	$3,468
H	Deferred income taxes and other liabilities	$3,347	$3,216
I	Commitments and contingencies (Note 18)		
	Redeemable preferred stock	$0	$0
	Shareholders' equity:		
J	Common stock at stated value:		
	Class A convertible—315 and 329 shares outstanding	$0	$0
	Class B—1,253 and 1,272 shares outstanding	$3	$3
K	Capital in excess of stated value	$7,163	$6,384
	Accumulated other comprehensive income (loss)	$231	($92)
L	Retained earnings	$1,643	$3,517
M	Total shareholders' equity	$9,040	$9,812
	TOTAL LIABILITIES AND SHAREHOLDERS' EQUITY	$23,717	$22,536

Source: Nike (2019). Access the full report, cited in References, for Notes and other background information.

primary liabilities listed (Exhibit 2.2, F+G+H), or by subtracting total owners' equity (Exhibit 2.2, M) from total assets (Exhibit 2.2, D).

As stated previously, owners' equity, or assets minus liabilities, represents an estimate of the value or ownership stake of the company (Exhibit 2.2, **M**). It should be noted that this figure is often a very rough and inaccurate estimate, for several reasons. First, asset and liability figures represent the items' value at the time of purchase, not necessarily their present value. For example, land bought decades ago would be listed as an asset on the balance sheet at the price that was paid for the land when it was purchased, even if that land has increased in value many times since then. Second, the assets listed on the balance sheet often do not include intangible assets, such as branding, management expertise, or product positioning. Nike's balance sheet, for example, does not account for the value of its brand and the "swoosh" mark developed through countless marketing campaigns over the past 50 years. Third, the balance sheet does not include **contingent liabilities**, debts that may or may not occur, such as the result of ongoing litigation against the company. Contingent liabilities are frequently disclosed in a notes or footnotes section associated with the balance sheet and other financial statements. These can be found with Nike's financial statements in a quick online search for their corporate annual report.

If you compare Nike's balance sheet in Exhibit 2.2 to that of its sports apparel rivals Under Armour or Adidas, you may notice considerable differences in terminology. GAAP establishes standard procedures for accounting and the reporting of information on financial statements, but it allows considerable flexibility for companies to report their financial data in a manner that is appropriate for their particular business enterprise. If you find terminology in a balance sheet or another financial statement unfamiliar or confusing, note that many of these terms and concepts will be explained throughout this chapter.

The Income Statement

The **income statement**, also referred to as the statement of earnings, operating statement, or profit-and-loss statement, shows the organization's income over a specified period of time and is typically issued on an annual or quarterly basis. For the specified time period, the income statement lists the organization's **revenues**, or income generated from business activities, such as the sale of goods or services, and the organization's **expenses**, or funds flowing out of the organization as costs of doing business. Exhibit 2.3 shows Nike's income statement from its 2019 annual report. When expenses are subtracted from revenues, the resulting figure is the organization's net income (or net loss, if expenses were greater than revenues over the period of time). Net income is frequently referred to as profits or earnings (Exhibit 2.3, **G**).

An organization's books may be kept on a cash basis or an accrual basis, and it is important to note the differences between these two methods and the resulting impact on the income statement. **Cash basis accounting** recognizes transactions when money is either received or paid out. **Accrual basis accounting**, on the other hand, accounts for income when it is earned and expenses when they are incurred, rather than when the money is exchanged. For example, if Nike makes a major sale in fiscal year (FY) 1 but does not actually receive payment until FY 2, under accrual basis accounting, the sale is

EXHIBIT 2.3   Nike income statement.

		2019	2018	2017
	Nike, Inc. **Consolidated Statements of Income** **(In millions, except per share data)**			
		YEAR ENDED MAY 31,		
A	Revenues	$39,117	$36,397	$34,350
B	Cost of sales	$21,643	$20,441	$19,038
	Gross profit	$17,474	$15,956	$15,312
	Demand creation expense	$3,753	$3,577	$3,341
	Operating overhead expense	$8,949	$7,934	$7,222
C	Total selling and administrative expense	$12,702	$11,511	$10,563
D	Interest expense (income), net	$49	$54	$59
E	Other (income) expense, net	–$78	$66	–$196
F	Income before income taxes	$4,801	$4,325	$4,886
	Income tax expense	$772	$2,392	$646
G	**NET INCOME**	**$4,029**	**$1,933**	**$4,240**
	Earnings per common share:			
	Basic	$2.55	$1.19	$2.56
	Diluted	$2.49	$1.17	$2.51
	Weighted average common shares outstanding:			
	Basic	$1,579.70	$1,623.80	$1,657.80
	Diluted	$1,618.40	$1,659.10	$1,692.00

Source: Nike (2019).

included as revenue on Nike's FY 1 income statement. Note that a **fiscal year** is a 12-month period over which a company budgets its money; it may or may not begin in January, and so the term *fiscal year* distinguishes it from the calendar year. As shown on its financial statements, Nike's fiscal year ends on May 31 of each year, and thus, its new fiscal year begins the next day on June 1. Under cash basis accounting, the money would be included as revenue only when it is received in FY 2. Some sole proprietorships and other businesses utilize cash basis accounting, but most corporations and partnerships are required by GAAP to follow accrual basis accounting. The limitation of cash basis accounting, as it pertains to the income statement, is that sales made during a particular time period cannot be recognized on the income statement if payment has not yet been received, even if payment is forthcoming. Under accrual basis accounting, the lag time between when a transaction is made and when payment is exchanged is acknowledged through another financial statement, the statement of cash flows, to be discussed later in this chapter.

SIDEBAR 2.C   The Birth and Growth of Nike

As detailed in Nike founder Phil Knight's 2018 memoir, the story of the Nike corporation is a fascinating one. Knight and University of Oregon track coach Bill Bowerman founded Nike in 1964 under the name Blue Ribbon Sports, with the company's original focus on developing better running shoes. The company opened their first retail store in 1966 and sold the first Nike branded shoes in 1972, which became famous for their soles made originally with the Bowerman family's waffle iron. In the following years, Nike quickly became recognizable for its swoosh brand, its entry into the basketball market with the endorsement of Michael Jordan, and its "Just Do It" marketing campaign. Throughout its history, Nike has diversified its business into a variety of related categories, often through corporate acquisitions, including Cole Haan (upscale footwear), Bauer (hockey), and Umbro (soccer). More recently in the 2000s, Nike has refocused its business on core lines by divesting, or selling, some divisions, including the three business acquisitions listed previously. While companies like Under Armour and Adidas have periodically gained ground in terms of sales and revenue, Nike remains in its long-held dominant top position in the athletic footwear and apparel market.

Experts disagree about whether income statements truly reflect actual earnings or profit (Higgins, Koski, & Mitton, 2018; Shapiro & Balbirer, 2000). One reason why they might not is that when firms account for depreciation (the reduction in value of an asset due to age or use, discussed in Chapter 5), a number of options are available, and the approach chosen can greatly influence expenses, and thus net income or loss, on the income statement. A related issue is taxation. Accounting decisions—particularly in regard to depreciation and inventory—are frequently influenced by the goal of minimizing taxes. This can result in financial statements, especially income statements, that lack objectivity. Another issue is how the company accounts for expenditures in the areas of research and development (R&D) and advertising. These two areas represent investments in the future revenues of the company, yet they are typically accounted as expenditures when they are spent rather than in the future, when their benefits are reaped. If a company makes cuts in these areas in difficult times, the result may be an increased net income (or decreased net loss) in the short term. Such action could, however, be harmful to the long-term future of the company.

The Statement of Cash Flows

For any company to be successful in the long term, it must generate more cash than it spends, a condition known as *positive cash flow.* Negative cash flows may be sustainable in the short term, but few companies can survive long periods of spending more than they generate. The income statement and balance sheet, however, do not provide insight into this simple fact.

Whereas the income statement provides information about the revenues and expenses flowing into and out from an organization, the **statement of cash flows** tracks cash in and cash out. The ability to track cash coming into and going out of the business is of particular importance to an organization that uses accrual basis accounting. The cash flows statement provides information as to whether the company has sufficient cash on hand to meet its debts and obligations, which is not provided by the balance sheet or the income statement of firms that use accrual basis accounting. In addition to revealing differences between accrual basis accounting and cash transactions, the statement of cash flows is free from the influence of non-cash expenses, such as depreciation—unlike the income statement. On the income statement, the depreciation of an asset such as a stadium or an office building is listed as an expense, yet depreciation does not reflect any true monetary expenditure. The statement of cash flows provides a simpler examination of cash generated and spent. Exhibit 2.4 is Nike's statement of cash flows from its 2019 annual report. As is evident in Exhibit 2.4, **D**, Nike had more cash available at the end of its 2019 fiscal year than at the end of FY 2018 or FY 2017.

Whereas the balance sheet states the status of the company's assets, liabilities, and equity at a single point in time, without showing trends over time, the statement of cash flows examines cash transactions over a period of time and so can provide additional context for the information in a balance sheet.

Cash flow statements are typically organized in three sections: operations, investing, and financing; these appear in Exhibit 2.4, **A**, **B**, and **C**, respectively. *Operations* refers to the organization's cash flows from normal business operations, such as cash flowing in from the sale of products or services, or cash flowing out to pay employees' salaries. *Investing* activities include the buying and selling of fixed assets, such as the purchase of property. *Financing* refers to the company's debt and equity financing, such as the sale of stock or repayment of a loan.

FINANCIAL RATIOS

Just as the general manager of a baseball team can take a database of statistics and compute various figures, such as batting average, slugging percentage, and earned run average, in order to evaluate teams and players, a business manager

EXHIBIT 2.4 Nike statement of cash flows.

Nike, Inc. Consolidated Statements of Cash Flow (Dollars in millions)			
	YEAR ENDED MAY 31,		
	2019	**2018**	**2017**
A Cash provided by operations:			
Net income	$4,029	$1,933	$4,240
Adjustments to reconcile net income to net cash provided by operations:			
Depreciation	$705	$747	$706
Deferred income taxes	$34	$647	($273)
Stock-based compensation	$325	$218	$215
Amortization and other	$15	$27	$10
Net foreign currency adjustments	$233	($99)	($117)
Changes in certain working capital components and other assets and liabilities:			
(Increase) decrease in accounts receivable	($270)	$187	($426)
(Increase) decrease in inventories	($490)	($255)	($231)
(Increase) decrease in prepaid expenses and other current and non-current assets	($203)	$35	($120)
Increase (decrease) in accounts payable, accrued liabilities and other current and non-current liabilities	$1,525	$1,515	($158)
Cash provided by operations	$5,903	$4,955	$3,846
B Cash provided (used) by investing activities:			
Purchases of short-term investments	($2,037)	($4,783)	($5,928)
Maturities of short-term investments	$1,715	$3,613	$3,623
Sales of short-term investments	$2,072	$2,496	$2,423
Additions to property, plant and equipment	($1,119)	($1,028)	($1,105)
Disposals of property, plant and equipment	$5	$3	$13
Other investing activities	$0	($25)	($34)
Cash provided (used) by investing activities	($264)	$276	($1,008)

EXHIBIT 2.4   Cont.

C	**Cash used by financing activities:**			
	Net proceeds from long-term debt issuance	$0	$0	$1,482
	Long-term debt payments, including current portion	($6)	($6)	($44)
	Increase (decrease) in notes payable	($325)	$13	$327
	Payments on capital lease and other financing obligations	($27)	($23)	($17)
	Proceeds from exercise of stock options and other stock issuances	$700	$733	$489
	Repurchase of common stock	($4,286)	($4,254)	($3,223)
	Dividends—common and preferred	($1,332)	($1,243)	($1,133)
	Tax payments for net share settlement of equity awards	($17)	($55)	($29)
	Cash used by financing activities	($5,293)	($4,835)	($2,148)
	Effect of exchange rate changes on cash and equivalents	($129)	$45	($20)
	Net increase (decrease) in cash and equivalents	$217	$441	$670
	Cash and equivalents, beginning of year	$4,249	$3,808	$3,138
D	**CASH AND EQUIVALENTS, END OF YEAR**	$4,466	$4,249	$3,808
	Supplemental disclosure of cash flow information:			
	Cash paid during the year for:			
	Interest, net of capitalized interest	$153	$125	$98
	Income taxes	$757	$529	$703
	Non-cash additions to property, plant and equipment	$160	$294	$266
	Dividends declared and not paid	$347	$320	$300

Source: Nike (2019).

EXHIBIT 2.5   Summary of key financial ratios.

RATIO	DESCRIPTION	FORMULA
Liquidity Ratios		
current ratio	The organization's ability to meet its current liabilities (those due within a year) with its current assets	$\dfrac{\text{current assents}}{\text{current liabilities}}$
quick ratio	The organization's ability to meet its current liabilities with current assets other than inventory	$\dfrac{\text{current assets} - \text{inventory}}{\text{current liabilities}}$
Asset Management Ratios		
total asset turnover ratio	How efficiently the organization is utilizing its assets to make money	$\dfrac{\text{net sales}}{\text{average total assets}}$
inventory turnover ratio	How often the organization sells and replaces its inventory over a specified period of time	$\dfrac{\text{cost of goods sold}}{\text{average inventory}}$

EXHIBIT 2.5   Cont.

RATIO	DESCRIPTION	FORMULA
Leverage Ratios		
debt ratio	How the organization finances its operation with debt and equity	$\dfrac{\text{total liabilities}}{\text{total assets}}$
interest coverage ratio	The organization's ability to pay the interest on its debt owed	$\dfrac{\text{earnings before interest and taxes (EBIT)}}{\text{interest expense}}$
Profitability Ratios		
net profit margin	The percentage of the organization's total sales or revenues that was net profit or income	$\dfrac{\text{net income}}{\text{sales or revenues}}$
Market Value Ratios		
market value	An estimate of the organization's worth according to the stock market	price per share of common stock × number of outstanding shares
price-to-earnings ratio	An estimate of how much money investors will pay for each dollar of the organization's earnings	$\dfrac{\text{price per share of common stock}}{\text{earning per share}}$

can utilize accounting data provided in the financial statements discussed above in order to make similar types of analyses. For example, instead of dividing at bats by hits to find batting average, the business manager might divide net income by shareholders'/owners' equity to calculate a metric called return on equity. The remainder of this chapter focuses on the computation and analysis of similar measures, known as financial ratios. Reasons why financial managers engage in ratio analysis include:

1. To evaluate how well a company is operating in the current time period.
2. To compare its current performance to its past performance.
3. To compare its current and historical performance to industry standards.
4. To study the efficiency of its operations.

Financial ratios provide key information about the condition and performance of a company and are, therefore, vital for managers to understand. This chapter will focus on many of the most important and commonly used ratios. These ratios are organized into five sections based on their type: liquidity, asset management, financial leverage, profitability, and market value. Exhibit 2.5 summarizes these ratios.

Liquidity Ratios

Recall that liquidity refers to the ability to convert an asset into cash quickly. Liquidity ratios measure an organization's ability to pay its short-term liabilities or debts with its short-term assets. A company that lacks sufficient short-term assets, such as cash, inventory, and accounts receivable, to pay off debts that are coming due in the near future may be forced to refinance its debts or borrow additional money in order to meet its financial obligations.

CURRENT RATIO

The most commonly used liquidity measure is the current ratio. The **current ratio** measures the organization's ability to meet its current liabilities (those due within a year) with its current assets. The following formula is used to calculate the current ratio:

$$\text{current ratio} = \frac{\text{current assets}}{\text{current liabilities}}$$

Both current assets and current liabilities are found on the balance sheet. By using data from Exhibit 2.2, **B** and **F**, we can calculate Nike's current ratio for May 31, 2019, as follows:

$$\text{current ratio} = \frac{\$16,525,000,000}{\$7,866,000,000} = 2.10$$

(We add six zeros to each of the values from the balance sheet because the figures in Exhibit 2.2, except for stock share information, represent millions, as is stated near the top of the balance sheet.) The current ratio suggests that Nike has the ability to cover its short-term liabilities more than two times over with current assets.

In general, a higher current ratio figure is preferable, as it represents a healthy ability to cover debts with assets such as cash and accounts receivable.

The higher a company's current ratio, the less likely it is that the company will need to convert longer-term assets into cash or borrow money to cover liabilities. It is possible, however, for a current ratio to be too high. This may represent inefficient company management that is not maximizing the use of its cash balance or that is carrying excessive inventory (Helfert, 2002). A current ratio near 2:1 is commonly viewed as a good target for many companies (Helfert, 2002). With this standard, Nike's current ratio of 2.10 is at an appropriate level.

It should be noted, however, that current ratio values—as well as most other financial ratios—must be evaluated in context, especially when we are using them as comparative tools. The first context in which financial ratios should be viewed is against other firms within the same industry. Before we make a judgment as to whether Nike's current ratio is appropriate, we should compare it to that of rival companies, such as Adidas or Under Armour. Another important context for comparison is the company's own history. We examine financial ratios relative to their values in previous time periods to evaluate trends in the company's financial position.

QUICK/ACID-TEST RATIO

Another frequently used measure of liquidity is the **quick ratio**, also known as the **acid-test ratio**. Like the current ratio, the quick ratio provides information about the organization's ability to meet its current liabilities with current assets. The quick ratio, however, does not include inventory among current assets. If a company faces a financial emergency and needs to convert assets into cash in order to meet pending obligations, inventory is likely to be difficult to convert into cash as quickly as other assets. It may take months for a company to sell its inventory at full value, or the company may have to discount the inventory deeply to sell it rapidly. According to Higgins, Koski, & Mitton (2018), sellers may receive 40% or less of an inventory's book value through a liquidation sale. Because inventory is viewed as the least liquid of a company's current assets, the quick ratio is often useful as a more conservative alternative to the current ratio.

The quick ratio is simply a modified version of the current ratio. It is calculated as follows:

$$\text{quick ratio} = \frac{\text{current assets} - \text{inventory}}{\text{current liabilities}}$$

The inventory value is found on the balance sheet within the current assets section (Exhibit 2.2, **A**). Nike's quick ratio for May 31, 2019, is calculated as follows:

$$\text{quick ratio} = \frac{\left(\$16,525,000,000 - \$5,622,000,000\right)}{\$7,866,000,000} = 1.39$$

Nike can cover its short-term liabilities 1.39 times over with its current assets other than inventory. For an apparel company with significant inventory, this signifies that Nike is not overly encumbered with short-term debt and has sufficient assets to cover that debt if necessary. As an aside, note that Nike possessed more than $5 billion in inventory at this point in time in 2019, which provides a glimpse into the enormous size and scale of this business organization.

Asset Management Ratios

How effectively a company utilizes its assets and resources to generate sales revenue is important information for business managers. All companies have a limited amount of resources. Those that are most efficient and effective in using those limited resources to produce sales are likely to be successful. Several ratios measure companies' asset management. These ratios are also sometimes referred to as turnover ratios or activity ratios. Two of the most common are the total asset turnover ratio and the inventory turnover ratio.

TOTAL ASSET TURNOVER RATIO

One measure of how efficiently an organization is utilizing its assets to make money is the **total asset turnover ratio**. This ratio requires information from both the company's balance sheet and its income statement, in the following formula:

$$\text{total asset turnover ratio} = \frac{\text{net sales}}{\text{average total assets}}$$

The net sales value, sometimes labeled as net revenues or just revenues in the case of Nike, is found on the income statement (see Exhibit 2.3, **A**); for Nike in 2019, this figure was $39,117,000,000. Total assets, which include both current assets and long-term assets, are listed on the balance sheet. To find average total assets, we average the company's total assets at the beginning and at the end of the period of interest, often the fiscal year. For Nike, these asset values are given in Exhibit 2.2, **D**. Total assets at the end of the 2019 fiscal year were $23,717,000,000. The beginning-of-period total assets are assumed to be identical to total assets at the end of the previous period—in this case, May 31, 2018—which were $22,536,000,000. We average these two figures to find the average total assets value. The entire calculation proceeds as follows:

$$\text{total asset turnover ratio} = \frac{\$39,117,000,000}{\$(23,717,000,000 + 22,536,000,000)/2}$$

$$= \frac{\$39,117,000,000}{\$23,126,500,000}$$

$$= 1.69$$

In 2019 Nike's revenues exceeded assets by a considerable amount, suggesting that the company is using its assets efficiently. As with other ratios, these values should be compared to the organization's own historical values, as well as to those of industry competitors.

INVENTORY TURNOVER RATIO

Another ratio that is useful in evaluating asset management is the **inventory turnover ratio**, which measures how often a company sells and replaces its inventory over a specified period of time, typically a year. For some firms, particularly those in manufacturing and retail, this is an especially important ratio, as inventory is often a large asset for these companies. A manufacturer—like Nike—that must sell a high volume of relatively low-priced products in order to be profitable must turn over its existing inventory frequently. If the inventory is sitting in warehouses and on shelves rather than being sold in a timely manner, it will be difficult for the company to be financially successful. Inventory turnover ratio is calculated with the following formula:

$$\text{inventory turnover ratio} = \frac{\text{cost of goods sold}}{\text{average inventory}}$$

Cost of goods sold (COGS) includes those costs that are directly attributable to the production of goods or products to be sold, including raw materials and labor costs (Exhibit 2.3, **B**). Cost of goods sold, sometimes labeled *cost of sales*, is typically listed immediately after net sales (or net revenues), near the top of the income statement. Recall that inventory is found on the balance sheet and that we calculate average inventory by finding the average of the inventory values at the beginning and the end of the time period of interest (Exhibit 2.2, **A**).

By using data from Exhibits 2.2 and 2.3, we calculate Nike's inventory turnover ratio for the 2019 fiscal year as follows:

$$\text{inventory turnover ratio} = \frac{\$21,643,000,000}{\left[(\$5,622,000,000 + \$5,261,000,000)/2\right]}$$

$$= \frac{\$21,643,000,000}{\$5,441,500,000}$$

$$= 3.98$$

To interpret this figure, we may say that Nike turned over, or sold and replenished, its inventory nearly four times during 2019. Of course, in general, a higher value is preferred. Once again, note that this value is difficult to interpret without comparisons to industry competitors and the company's own history. This particular ratio is especially industry-specific. Industries in which very low-cost items are sold, such as groceries, are likely to see their inventory turn over much more rapidly than industries in which high-priced luxury items are sold, such as jewelry or yachts. Inventory turnover ratio values should reflect these differences. In the apparel industry, a common benchmark for the inventory turnover ratio is a value of four, as apparel companies often sell seasonal merchandise for the four seasons—winter, spring, summer, and fall. The value of 3.97 for Nike in 2019 is right in line with this standard.

Leverage Ratios

Leverage refers to how a company chooses to finance its operation with debt versus equity. A company that relies extensively on borrowing money to operate is considered to be heavily leveraged. Such a company faces greater risk of financial problems than one not so reliant on debt.

DEBT RATIO

A useful financial leverage ratio is the **debt ratio**, sometimes referred to as the debt-to-assets ratio. The debt ratio is a quite simple yet telling measure of an organization's leverage. It is calculated with the formula:

$$\text{debt ratio} = \frac{\text{total liabilities}}{\text{total assets}}$$

Both total liabilities and total assets are found on the balance sheet. Total assets (Exhibit 2.2, **D**) is equal to current plus long-term assets, and total liabilities (Exhibit 2.2, **F+G+H**) is equal to current plus long-term liabilities. While many balance statements specifically list total liabilities, Nike's does not, and thus the current and long-term liabilities must be summed together. A low debt ratio is generally preferable, as a higher value signifies heavier borrowing and increased financial risk. This ratio is unique among those presented in this chapter; with all other ratios, a higher value is preferred to a lower one. From the data in Exhibit 2.2, we calculate Nike's debt ratio for May 31, 2019 as follows:

$$\text{debt ratio} = \frac{\$14,677,000,000}{\$23,717,000,000} = 0.619 \text{ or } 61.9\%$$

Nike's debt was a little more than three-fifths of the value of its assets. Note that the debt ratio is often reported in percentage form, in this case 61.9%. Money borrowed from creditors makes up 61.9% of the value of Nike's assets. This ratio may be somewhat high, as a preferable debt ratio is typically closer to 30 or 40% (or less), but this again is a data point that should be compared to industry standards and the company's own historical data.

INTEREST COVERAGE RATIO

Another tool for understanding a company's financial leverage is the **interest coverage ratio**, sometimes called the times interest earned ratio. As the name of this ratio implies, the interest coverage ratio measures a firm's ability to pay the interest on its debt. Consider this on an individual level: persons who carry a debt balance on a credit card—as millions do—know that, while they might not be able to pay the full balance by the next payment due date, they must at least pay a minimum amount, which is often approximately equivalent to the interest on the balance. This concept applies at the organizational level, as well. Many companies may not be able to pay the full amount of debt owed in the short term, but a company that cannot at least pay the interest on its debt is at risk for significant financial problems. The interest coverage ratio measures a company's ability to pay interest on debt out of income or earnings. It is calculated with the following formula:

$$\text{interest coverage ratio} = \frac{\text{earnigs before interest and taxes (EBIT)}}{\text{interest expense}}$$

The interest coverage ratio formula involves a term that is common in financial analysis and accounting: **earnings before interest and taxes (EBIT)**. EBIT, found on the income statement (Exhibit 2.3, **D**), is defined as follows:

$$\text{EBIT} = \text{operating revenue} - \text{operating expenses} + \text{non-operating income}$$

EBIT can be challenging to find as companies use different terminology and items on their income statements. In examining Nike's income statement, EBIT can be found a couple of different ways. First, by taking revenues (Exhibit 2.3, **A**) and subtracting all related operating expenses (Exhibit 2.3, **B, C, & E**), EBIT is found. Note that "Other (income) expense, net" (Exhibit 2.3, **E**) is in parentheses, meaning that it is an income number, not an expense, and thus should be added rather than subtracted in the calculation above. An alternative method for identifying EBIT on Nike's income statement is to take "Income before income taxes" (Exhibit 2.3, **F**) and to add "interest expense" (Exhibit 2.3, **D**) to find EBIT, noting that EBIT is defined as earnings before accounting for interest and tax expenses. After finding EBIT, interest expense (Exhibit 2.3, **D**) is the denominator for this ratio. Using data from Nike's income statement (Exhibit 2.3), we calculate the company's interest coverage ratio for FY 2019 as follows:

$$\text{interest coverage ratio} = \frac{\$4,850,000,000}{\$49,000,000} = 98.98$$

The interest coverage ratio value of 98.98 suggests that Nike can cover its interest expense nearly 100 times over with its earnings or operating income.

Profitability Ratios

A primary purpose of a for-profit business is, of course, to generate a profit. A number of financial ratios measure the profitability of a company. We will discuss two of the most useful profitability ratios: net profit margin and return on equity. These ratios evaluate the performance of the company and its management in controlling expenses and generating profit.

NET PROFIT MARGIN RATIO

A widely used profitability ratio is net profit margin. The **net profit margin ratio**, the percentage of total sales or revenues that was net profit or income, measures the effectiveness and efficiency of the organization's operations. A higher value indicates that the company is efficient in its production and operations. A low net profit margin may reflect inefficient operations and poor management, as well as a company that would be at risk financially if sales were to decline. Net profit margin is calculated as follows:

$$\text{net profit margin} = \frac{\text{net income}}{\text{sales or revenues}}$$

Both net income (Exhibit 2.3, **G**) and sales or revenues (Exhibit 2.3, **A**) may be found on the income statement. Recall that net income is essentially the "bottom line" of the income statement itself and is traditionally listed near or at the end of the income statement. The sales or revenues value is commonly listed at the beginning of the income statement. From data in Exhibit 2.3, we calculate Nike's net profit margin for FY 2019 as follows:

$$\text{net profit margin} = \frac{\$4,029,000,000}{\$39,117,000,000} = 10.30\%$$

Net profit margin is reported in percentage form, as it represents the percentage of sales that returned to the company's owners in the form of profits on their capital. Nike's net profit margin for FY 2019 was slightly greater than 10%. In other words, Nike spent 90% of the money generated by sales in FY 2019 on everything from manufacturing to employee pay to advertising, while slightly more than 10% was returned to the owners as profit. Again, we must compare this value to the company's own history and to industry competitors in order to draw valid conclusions, although a 10% net profit margin is generally considered solid.

RETURN ON EQUITY RATIO

Another important measure of profitability is the **return on equity ratio**, which measures the rate of return a company's owners or shareholders are receiving on their investment. Like net profit margin, return on equity bases a measure of efficiency on net income. The return on equity ratio, however, compares net income to shareholders' or owners' equity instead of to revenues. The formula is:

$$\text{return on equity} = \frac{\text{net income}}{\text{shareholders' or owners' equity}}$$

As stated earlier, net income is typically found near the end of the income statement (Exhibit 2.3, **G**). Shareholders' or owners' equity is found on the balance sheet (Exhibit 2.2, **M**). Nike's return on equity for FY 2019 is calculated as follows, from data in Exhibits 2.2 and 2.3:

$$\text{return on equity} = \frac{\$4,029,000,000}{\$9,040,000,000} = 44.57\%$$

Like net profit margin, return on equity is reported in percentage form, as it represents the percentage of ownership stake or equity that the company's owners realized as profit during a period of time. Nike's return on equity for the 2019 fiscal year was nearly 45%. To examine profitability further, some investors examine a similar measure known as *return on assets*, which is also sometimes referred to as *return on investment*. The formula for return on assets is similar to return on equity, except that total assets is used as the denominator in the calculation instead of shareholders'/owners' equity.

Market Value Ratios

The final set of financial ratios that we will consider is helpful in estimating the book value of a company. The two ratios discussed in this section, market value and price-to-earnings ratio, are quick methods to estimate a company's value. Valuation is discussed further in Chapter 10.

MARKET VALUE RATIO

Perhaps the quickest method of estimating the value of a company is to find its **market value** according to the stock market. A company's market value may be computed with the following formula:

$$\text{market value} = \text{price per share of common stock} \times \text{number of outstanding shares}$$

Although this method for estimating a company's worth is convenient and easy, it is not necessarily the most precise method. One notable problem is that stock prices often reflect investors' speculation about the future potential of a company rather than its present performance (see the discussion of valuation in Chapter 10).

To estimate the value of Nike, we can refer to stock information found on the company's balance sheet in the stockholders' equity section (Exhibit 2.2, J). Nike possesses two forms of common stock – Class A and Class B. Class B is its most widely used with 1.253 billion shares outstanding, or in circulation. As discussed in the notes of their annual report, another 315 million stock shares exist that can be converted into Class B shares. By adding these together, Nike had 1.568 billion stock shares outstanding at the end of the 2019 fiscal year.

Stock price is not typically provided on financial statements. Fortunately, numerous sites on the internet provide historical stock price data. Nike's stock closed at $77.14 at the end of trading on May 31, 2019, on the New York Stock Exchange. Therefore, the market value of Nike on that date was:

$$\text{market value} = 1,568,000,000 \text{ shares} \times \$77.14 = \$120,955,520,000$$

According to the stock market, Nike was worth more than $120 billion as of May 2019. It is highly unlikely that Nike's primary investors could sell the company for that high amount, however; its high market value reflects the speculative nature of the stock market.

PRICE-TO-EARNINGS RATIO

The **price-to-earnings ratio**, or **P/E ratio**, is a widely used measure of corporate performance and value, particularly among stock market investors. The P/E ratio estimates how much investors will pay for each dollar of a company's earnings. One of the strengths of the P/E ratio is that its scaled nature allows comparisons of the market values of companies of all sizes. The P/E ratio is calculated with the following formula:

$$\text{price-to-earnings ratio} = \frac{\text{price per share of common stock}}{\text{earnings per share}}$$

To calculate the P/E ratio, we must first determine earnings per share. We can do this by using the following formula:

$$\text{earning per share} = \frac{\text{net income}}{\text{number of outstanding shares of common stock}}$$

Recall that net income is found on the income statement (Exhibit 2.3, **G**), and outstanding stock share information is found on the balance sheet (Exhibit 2.2, **J**). Once we have found earnings per share, we divide the stock price by earnings per share to find the P/E ratio. By using data from Exhibits 2.2 and 2.3, along with the May 31, 2019 stock price, we determine Nike's P/E ratio as follows:

$$\text{price-to-earnings ratio} = \frac{\$77.14}{(\$4,029,000,000 / 1,568,000,000)}$$

$$= \frac{\$77.14}{\$2.57}$$

$$= 30.02$$

Simply put, Nike's stock price in May 2019 was more than 30 times the company's earnings.

When calculating the P/E ratio, be careful in your use of the data. In this example, we multiplied the net income figure by 1,000,000, because the income statement gives net income in thousands. The stock share data, however, should not be multiplied by 1,000,000. Doing so would result in a wildly inaccurate P/E ratio value. It is important to be precise here.

In general, a higher P/E ratio is preferred, but not always. A high P/E ratio can signify subpar earnings or net income, which, of course, is not desirable. Because stock price is a component of the P/E ratio formula, P/E ratio values are heavily influenced by investors' speculation about a company's potential for growth and success in the future, reflected in the stock price. Companies with high P/E ratio values are often perceived to have high growth potential. In this regard, a P/E ratio says as much about investors' beliefs about the future of a company as it does about present performance (Higgins, Koski, & Mitton, 2018). Nike's somewhat high P/E ratio may represent positive beliefs on the part of investors, but it could also signify merely that the stock is trading at an overly high value given the company's actual financial performance.

CONCLUSION

The ability to examine, understand, and calculate financial statements and financial ratios is vital for a financial manager in the sport industry—or any industry, for that matter. Financial statements are comparable to box scores or statistical data that the manager/coach or general manager must be able to read and comprehend in order to understand the performance of players and the team. Financial ratios are analytical tools that help managers evaluate statistical data, just as a calculation tool such as earned run average or slugging percentage helps a baseball executive, or a quarterback's passer rating helps a football executive. This chapter discussed several categories of financial ratios and provided two important examples for each category. Remember that the ratios discussed in this chapter represent just a few important and commonly used financial ratios, and many more are available to help you analyze companies' performance. Bear in mind that financial ratios should not be examined in isolation, but rather must be compared to the company's own historical data and to competitors' ratios. These provide the context necessary for understanding a company's performance and condition.

Concept Check

1. What is a T-account and how is it utilized in double-entry bookkeeping?
2. What are the three major sections of the balance sheet? For each of these sections, provide at least one example of the items that would be found there.
3. What is the primary difference between an income statement and a statement of cash flows?
4. What is the purpose of computing financial ratios?
5. If an organization's current ratio value is below 1.00, what might that suggest about the organization?
6. What information do leverage ratios provide?
7. Why is the price-to-earnings ratio so widely used among investors?
8. This chapter repeatedly states that financial ratios are most valuable when viewed in comparison to the organization's historical ratio values and competitors' values. Why is this context valuable when examining financial ratio values?

Practice Problem

Choose a competitor of Nike's in the athletic footwear and apparel industry and conduct an internet search for that company's most recent annual report and financial statements. Some competitors are headquartered beyond the United States, such as Adidas and Asics, which may provide challenges with currency conversions, so you may wish to choose an American company such as Under Armour or Sketchers. Once you have found the company's financial statements online, use those statements to compute the ten financial ratios discussed in this chapter.

Case Analysis

Financial Analysis Comparison of Nike and a Competitor

While it has been challenged over time by competitors such as Reebok, Adidas, and Under Armour, Nike remains the dominant player globally in the athletic footwear and apparel industry. Use the financial ratios for the company that you computed in the Practice Problem and the financial ratios for Nike provided throughout this chapter to compare the financial health of Nike and its competitor. Answer the following questions.

Case Questions

1. In what ratio areas is Nike stronger than its competitor?
2. In what ratio areas is the competitor stronger than Nike?
3. If you were an investor considering purchasing stock in either Nike or another competitor, which company would you choose? Explain and support your answer.
4. If you were a bank manager or other investor considering a request to loan money to either Nike or a competitor, to which company would you choose to provide a loan? Explain and support your answer.

References

Helfert, E.A. (2002). *Techniques of financial analysis: A guide to value creation* (11th ed.). New York: McGraw-Hill/Irwin.

Higgins, R.C., Koski, J.L., & Mitton, T. (2018). *Analysis for financial management* (12th ed.). New York: McGraw-Hill/Irwin.

Knight, P. (2018). *Shoe Dog: A memoir by the creator of Nike*. New York: Simon and Schuster.

Nike. (2019). 2019 annual report. Retrieved from http://investors.nike.com/files/doc_financials/2014/docs/nike-2014-form-10K.pdf.   https://investors.nike.com/investors/news-events-and-reports/default.aspx.

Shapiro, A.C., & Balbirer, S.D. (2000). *Modern corporate finance: A multidisciplinary approach to value creation*. Upper Saddle River, NJ: Prentice Hall.

CHAPTER 3

Risk

Matthew T. Brown

KEY CONCEPTS

auction-rate bond
beta coefficient
capital asset pricing model (CAPM)
central revenues
coefficient of variation (CV)
correlation coefficient
covariance
default risk premium (DRP)
deferred compensation
diversifiable risk
dollar return
expected rate of return
expected return on a portfolio
inflation
inflation premium (IP)
interest
interest rate risk
investment risk
level of risk
liquidity premium (LP)
loan pool
local revenues
London Interbank Offered Rate
  (LIBOR)

market risk
maturity risk premium (MRP)
nominal interest rate
nominal risk-free rate
portfolio
probability distribution
rate of return
real risk-free rate
reinvestment rate risk
relevant risk
required rate of return
revenue sharing
risk
risk averse
risk-free rate
risk of time
risk premium
security market line (SML)
stand-alone risk
standard deviation (SD)
synthetic fixed-rate bond
volatility

INTRODUCTION

Risk is often overlooked in sport management. It affects many areas of finance, including interest rates, bond rates, estimates of cash flows, the cost of capital, and capital structure. A good understanding of risk will greatly assist with financial analysis, as well. **Risk** measures the chance that some unfavorable event will occur. In finance, we often examine the risks of assets. The choice to invest in an asset suggests that the return on the investment is expected to be proportional to the risk involved with the investment (Groppelli & Nikbakht, 2018). The measurement of risk is, therefore, paramount for prudent financial management.

Unfortunately, little has been written about financial risk in sport. Perhaps this is due to the general feeling that the business of sport, especially professional sport, is recession proof. In a *Wall Street Journal* article, Last (2009) asked, "Are pro sports too big to fail?" (p. W11). As the US economy slowed in 2008, some in sport declared that the industry was indeed recession proof. In general, the belief was that during periods of economic uncertainty people turn to sport to escape the economic realities of life. Last probed this idea in his *Wall Street Journal* article.

Beginning with the idea that in a struggling economy the weak go out of business first, Last noted that minor professional sports have shown signs that an economic slowdown can have a significant impact. The Arena Football League (AFL), in existence since 1987, cancelled its 2009 season. Shortly thereafter, the league declared bankruptcy. Subsequent to Last's article, the league's assets were purchased by a new entity, Arena Football One, on December 8, 2009, and the league relaunched on April 2, 2010 ("Key dates," 2013). The AFL lasted until operations ceased in November 2019 when accumulated debt from its previous incarnation forced the league to shut down (Barrabi, 2020). The LPGA tour also experienced troubles in 2009 as it eliminated three tour events and cut $5 million in prize money, and that year the WNBA saw the Houston Comets, its premier franchise, cease operations, as discussed in Chapter 1.

During the late 2000s, however, the major professional sport leagues showed some signs of strength. Television ratings for NFL regular season games were strong in 2008. During the 2009 off-season, the top three free agents in professional baseball signed for a combined $423 million. This was a 7.1% increase from 2008. Professional baseball attendance in 2008 was only slightly below its all-time high of 79.5 million in 2007. Although teams and leagues laid off employees in 2008 and 2009, and some NFL teams struggled to sell out playoff games in January 2009, teams continue to build new stadiums and fans continue to pay more for parking, concessions, and tickets.

Just over ten years later, a greater risk seems to be facing the business of sport. With the spread of COVID-19 and the resulting pandemic, the industry is facing financial uncertainty unlike any time in recent history. The United Nations' Department of Economic and Social Affairs (2020) examined the impact of COVID-19 on sport. Notably, the department analyzed how the cancellation or postponement of sporting events is impacting the global value of sports. Further the report examined the millions of jobs at risk for those working for teams and leagues, as well as related sectors like sporting goods and sporting services (travel, tourism, media, etc.).

The global impact on the sport business is unprecedented. It was estimated that British sport would see a loss of over £700 million between Football League, Rugby Football Union, and the England and Wales Cricket Board (Ingle, 2020). At the club level, Tottenham Hotspur borrowed £175 million from the Bank of England to cover the short-term financial impact COVID-19 caused on the team's operations (Nelson, 2020). The government in New Zealand gave its sports sector NZ$265 million as funding and revenue for sports organizations within the country was non-existent ("NZ gives," 2020). In the United States, the financial impact on sport is estimated to be $12 billion, with the amount doubling if the college and professional football seasons are cancelled ("Sudden vanishing," 2020).

With the transmission of COVID-19 lessening in Japan, Nippon Professional Baseball (NPB) began play three months after the season was originally scheduled to begin. The J-League began soon thereafter. While sport has restarted, and games are being played, there is still a large financial impact of the paused and delayed seasons. The two leagues are expected to lose half of the year's revenues. The total number of games played, and their related revenues, have been reduced in both leagues. In NPB, the All-Star game was cancelled and the post-season Climax Series will either be cancelled or reduced. Regular season games, once fans were allowed in the stadiums, were restricted to 5,000. With approximately half of team revenues coming from game day sources, the impact is significant (King, 2020).

So, what is risk? Is sport affected by recession as any other industry would be affected? Is sport more affected by the COVID pandemic than other industries? How does risk affect the financial management of sport teams, leagues, and properties? This chapter discusses risk and how concepts related to risk apply in sport.

RELATIONSHIP BETWEEN RATE OF RETURN AND RISK

When a sport organization makes an investment, it expects that the money invested today will earn more in the future. The gain or loss of an investment over a period of time is the **rate of return**. Measuring return allows the organization to know the financial performance of its investment. We can measure the return on any type of investment—from an investment in a new player to the investment in a stadium renovation. The easiest way to measure the return of an investment is in dollar terms. **Dollar return** is simply the result of subtracting the amount invested from the amount received:

$$\text{dollar return} = \text{amount received} - \text{amount invested}$$

However, this method of measuring return is problematic. First, the size or scale of the investment is important. Without knowing the size of the investment, we cannot meaningfully evaluate the sufficiency of the return. Second, the timing of the return is important (see the discussion of time value of money in Chapter 4). Hence, the preferred method is to calculate a measure called the *rate of return*, or *percentage return*, rather than dollar return. Rate of return corrects for differences in the scale of investments, and, when calculated on an annual basis, it also solves the timing problem. Rate of return is calculated as follows:

$$\text{rate of return} = \frac{\text{amount received} - \text{amount invested}}{\text{amount invested}}$$

This formula standardizes the investment's return by measuring the return per investment unit.

EXHIBIT 3.1   Relationship between risk and return.

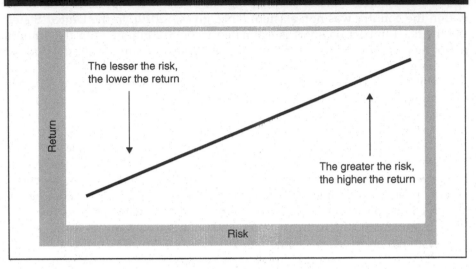

In a more technical definition, risk measures the volatility of rates of return (Groppelli & Nikbakht, 2018). When investing in a new facility, for example, the organization should forecast the expected cash flows, or return, of the new project and how those cash flows will impact the organization's overall finances. Obviously, those forecasts could turn out to be wrong, because investments do not always return what we expect. The less certain we are that an investment will return what we expect, the higher the rate of return we demand will be, in order to compensate for the risk. As risk increases for the stadium project, the rate of return required to invest in that project also increases. Exhibit 3.1 illustrates this relationship.

Volatility is the amount of fluctuation that occurs in a series of similar investment returns and the degree to which those returns deviate from the average. More volatility translates into greater risk.

Time is a factor in risk. Cash today is worth more to an investor than the same cash in the future, because the future is uncertain (see Sidebar 3.A). When money is invested, there is always uncertainty as to whether the investment will be repaid. Similarly, when a bank lends money, it takes the risk that the loan may not be repaid. The investor or lender must be compensated for risking today's cash, or it will lack incentive to make the investment or loan. For example, if a friend asks you to lend him money to help finance the purchase of a minor league baseball franchise, you might decide to lend him $1 million in cash. You are giving up the safety of having that $1 million in cash today in exchange for an uncertain future return. The franchise might lose money and your friend might not be able to repay your investment. As a result, you might ask that the $1 million be paid back one year from now, along with an additional $70,000 return for your $1 million investment. The rate of return would be 7%, which is the $70,000 additional return divided by the initial investment amount of $1 million. To convince you to give up the safety of your $1 million cash, your friend will have to pay an additional $70,000, to compensate for the risk associated with the future return on your money. The financial principle underlying the request for an additional $70,000 is that there is more risk in the future than the present. There is also more risk in larger investments, all else being equal. If you were asked to invest $2 million, your risk would increase and you likely would ask for a return greater than 7%. The rate of return required increases as risk increases.

SIDEBAR 3.A July 1 is Bobby Bonilla Day

Today's dollar is worth more than tomorrow's. In professional sport, risk affects players as they negotiate salary, especially when deferred compensation is part of the negotiation. **Deferred compensation,** or deferred salary, is salary whose payment is delayed under contractual terms. In the National Football League, teams structure contracts with deferred compensation due to strict salary cap rules that limit the amount a team can spend on player payroll in a given season. In other leagues, teams sometimes take a "buy now, pay later" approach and use deferred salaries to do so. One of these teams, the Arizona Diamondbacks, nearly went bankrupt as a result. According to Birger (2009), the Diamondbacks almost became the first team to win a major sports championship one year and declare bankruptcy the next. Financial problems arose because the team overspent on free agents. Over its first seven years of operation, the Diamondbacks lost $353 million. Due to resulting cash flow shortages, the team's management convinced free agents to accept contracts with large, backloaded deferred salary payments. In 2009, the team still owed just over $58 million to players who were no longer with the organization.

The Diamondbacks paid off $16 million in deferred salary in 2009. Further, they paid $15 million, $14 million, and $13 million in 2010, 2011, and 2012, respectively. In 2013 the team paid less than $1.5 million in deferred salary (Rovell, 2009; "#20 Arizona Diamondbacks," 2011).

Agent David Falk has referred to deferred salary as "funny money" (Conrad, 2006), as the deferred portion of a player's contract is not always guaranteed (especially in the NFL). Even if deferred salary is guaranteed, if a team declares bankruptcy a player may never be paid in full. Mario Lemieux, a player for the NHL's Pittsburgh Penguins, knows this well. On October 13, 1998, the Pittsburgh Penguins filed Chapter 11 bankruptcy. As a result, 200 individuals and businesses became unsecured creditors (Anderson, 2005).

At the time the Penguins declared bankruptcy, they owed $114.3 million. Of that amount, $55.2 million was secured debt (e.g., money owed to banks) and $1.4 million was priority debt (e.g., money owed to the IRS). The unsecured debt was $57.7 million, and the three largest unsecured creditors were Lemieux, Fox Sports Net, and SMG (Anderson, 2005). Under US bankruptcy law, unsecured creditors are paid last, and they often receive less than 50% of what is owed. As a major creditor (Lemieux held over half of the team's unsecured debt), Lemieux had a large incentive to find a way to salvage the $32.5 million in deferred compensation owed to him (Sandomir, 1999). Four plans were presented to the bankruptcy judge. The unsecured creditors committee backed

Lemieux's plan, under which Lemieux offered to forgive $7.5 million of debt owed to him and transfer another $20 million of debt into equity, so that only $5 million of his claim remained. The court approved Lemieux's plan on June 24, 1999 (Anderson, 2005). Although Lemieux received only $5 million of the deferred salary owed to him (15.4% of the original amount owed), he also received controlling interest in the Penguins. Lemieux became one of only a few former players to own a major league team (Sandomir, 1999). Ten other players were unsecured creditors at the time of the bankruptcy filing, as well. Combined, they were owed $7.4 million (Anderson, 2005).

During the period in which Lemieux, together with Ron Burkle, has co-owned the Penguins, the team has won the Stanley Cup three times, sold out 12 straight seasons (entering the 2019/2020 hockey season), and moved into the PPG Paints Arena ("Front office," 2020). At the beginning of the 2019 season, Forbes ranked the Penguins the eleventh most valuable NHL franchise, at $665 million ("The List," 2019).

The most famous (or perhaps infamous) deferred payment involves Bobby Bonilla, the New York Mets, and Bernie Madoff, the financier who was sentenced to 150 years in prison for running the biggest Ponzi scheme* in US history and defrauding his investors out of $65 billion. In 2011, the Mets began to pay Bonilla, a 47-year-old former player, $1.19 million each year for 25 years on July 1, now commonly referred to as "Bobby Bonilla Day." This series of payments resulted from an agreement between the Mets and Bonilla on January 3, 2000, when the Mets bought out the final year of Bonilla's contract with the team, worth $5.9 million. Bonilla was to be paid the amount owed, plus a compounded 8% rate, beginning in 2011 (Sielski, 2010).

In the short term, the Mets freed up cash to sign several free agents in 2000, who earned a combined $15.1 million that year. The team reached the World Series for the first time since 1986. But since 2000, the team has had little success and reached the post-season only one time. Now that Bonilla's payments have come due, Sielski argues that the Mets' short-term gain was not worth its long-term risk, as the team will pay Bonilla $29,831,205 in principal and interest over the 25-year period.

The Mets did plan to mitigate the long-term financial risk posed by Bonilla's salary deferral. Team owner Fred Wilpon, close friends with Bernie Madoff, made many investments with Madoff beginning in 1985. As Wilpon built teams through the 1980s and into the 1990s, he used money from Madoff investments—returning about 18% annually—to fund player acquisition. The Mets then began placing liquid assets into Madoff accounts and paid expenses with proceeds from the money Madoff "earned" the team. When Wilpon agreed to the structure of Bonilla's buyout, he thought he would make more from the deferral than Bonilla. The Mets' investments in the Madoff account would have had to earn an 8% return on the $5.9 million investment to pay Bonilla. With the Madoff account supposedly returning double-digit amounts, the Mets calculated that they would generate a profit of between $60 million and $70 million from the deferral (Winegardner, 2012).

The Mets and owner Wilpon were not fortunate, however. Three years before the payments to Bonilla were to begin, the Madoff Ponzi scheme was exposed. Wilpon's investments and much of his income evaporated. Lured to the deferment of $5.9 million by the prospect of increasing it ten times, the Mets had no money set aside to pay the amount they had guaranteed Bonilla. Without an emergency loan from MLB, the Mets might have had to enter bankruptcy (Winegardner, 2012).

* Ponzi schemes lure investors by promising them unusually higher than normal returns on investments. The person running the Ponzi scheme uses money from new investors to pay off returns promised to older investors. To the old investors, this makes their investments seem profitable, though no profit is actually being made. They are simply being given what the new investors bring in. The investment strategies that are supposedly used to produce the amazing profits are often held as secrets, which the person running the scheme claims to do in order to protect the business. Later in the scheme, the con artist merely tells the investors how much they are "making," without providing any actual returns. Ponzi schemes collapse when new investors become hard to find and the flow of cash to older investors dries up, too many current investors request their returns at one time, or the operator takes the investment money and runs.

MEASURING RISK

One way to measure risk is to determine the chance of making a profit or loss by investing in a project or asset. The simplest way to do this is to break the risk into two components: level of risk and risk of time (Groppelli & Nikbakht, 2018).

Level of Risk

Level of risk is a comparative evaluation of risk, determined by comparing the risk of one asset or firm to that of another. For example, the risk associated with an NFL franchise is much less than that of a franchise in another major professional sport league. This is true because a high percentage of the league's income is guaranteed via long-term television contracts and because the league has strict rules that control its largest expense, player salary. As this example suggests, level of risk may be viewed as variability of income. Similarly, within a league, for example MLB, the risk of owning a franchise such as the Boston Red Sox is much less than that of a franchise in a small market, such as Kansas City. Some franchises have a low level of risk, while others have a high level.

Risk-free investments are short-term investments deemed to have no chance of loss. For example, US Treasury securities with a 90-day maturity are backed by the federal government's guarantee to pay. The interest paid on risk-free investments that provide a guaranteed return is termed the **risk-free rate**. (**Interest** is the cost of borrowing money.) As the level of risk for an investment increases above zero, the risk-free rate increases by a **risk premium**, the

EXHIBIT 3.2   Risk premiums and level of risk.

TYPE	RISK-FREE RATE	TIME RISK PREMIUM	LEVEL OF RISK PREMIUM	INTEREST RATE (TOTAL RISK)
30-Year US Treasury Bonds	0.11%	1.22%	0.00%	1.33%
30-Year Municipal Bonds (AAA Insured)	0.11%	1.22%	0.17%	1.50%
30-Year Municipal Bonds (AA)	0.11%	1.22%	0.37%	1.70%
30-Year Corporate Bonds (AAA)	0.11%	1.22%	0.81%	2.14%

Note: Rates as of July 2020.

difference between rate of return for the risky investment and the risk-free rate. Therefore, total risk includes the risk-free rate plus a risk premium, or

$$\text{total risk} = \text{risk-free rate} + \text{risk premium}$$

Exhibit 3.2 lists differences in rates of return for bonds based on their level of risk. (For a discussion of bonds, see Chapter 7.) As all the bonds listed in the exhibit are 30-year bonds, the difference in interest rates is attributable to the bonds' level of risk. The 30-year US Treasury bond yields less than the 30-year AAA-rated corporate bond because less risk is associated with investing in US Treasury bonds. Investors will seek a risk premium, here 0.81%, for AAA-rated corporate bonds because they carry a greater risk than do US Treasury bonds.

The risk associated with owning a sport franchise affects the franchise's cost of borrowing money. Franchises with lower risk have a lower discount rate or required rate of return; that is, they pay lower rates to borrow money. Therefore, the return for a low-risk franchise will receive a better valuation in the marketplace than the same return generated by a high-risk franchise. In essence, the market rate reflects the chance that the investors will receive their money back. An investment in a large-market Major League Baseball team is more likely to be paid back than an investment in a small-market team, so the large-market team offers a lower return. Similarly, investments in NFL franchises are less risky than investments in franchises in other major sporting leagues, and NFL franchises find it easier and less expensive to borrow money.

The impact of a franchise's level of risk on its ability to borrow was clear during the Great Recession, which the Bureau of Labor Statistics indicates began in December 2007 and ended in June 2009. From September 2008 through May 2009, only teams in large markets or with strong brands were able to execute debt deals. Franchises that were able to acquire or extend debt included the Pittsburgh Steelers, New York Yankees, and Dallas Cowboys. In May 2009, the Orlando Magic became the first mid-tier team to receive a loan in a nine-month period, a $100 million loan from Goldman Sachs. The team, however, paid a high rate for the loan—450 interest points over LIBOR. (**LIBOR, the London Interbank Offered Rate,** is a benchmark interest rate based on the rate that banks in the London interbank market pay to borrow unsecured funds from one another.) Prior to the credit market freeze in 2008, the Magic likely would have had to pay only 200 interest points over LIBOR (Kaplan & Lombardo, 2009).

During the 2020 pandemic, governmental programs provided low interest loans to sport franchises to protect from borrowing at higher rates as happened during the Great Recession. As franchise revenue streams were negatively impacted, the rate for loans would have risen due to the increased level of risk from the decreasing revenues without these programs. As noted by King (2020), Tottenham's £175 million loan came from the Bank of England through its COVID Corporate Financing Facility. The interest rate was set at 0.5% and is fully repayable by the end of April 2021, with a club option to redraw for another year. This loan mechanism was to cover staffing costs and working capital, not player acquisition costs. Similar governmental programs related to short-term COVID financing were seen across the globe. In the United States, the $660 billion Paycheck Protection Program (PPP) provided small businesses, including many sport franchises, loans to cover support for ongoing operations if the business lacked a means to generate revenue during the pandemic. When used for the loan's stated purpose, the amount borrowed would be forgiven by the government. Over 100 Minor League Baseball (MiLB) teams received up to $76.25 million in total from this loan program. It was estimated that MiLB teams would lose on average 90% of annual revenues due to the impact of COVID-19 on 2020 operations (Holdman & Adcox, 2020).

Risk of Time

The second component of risk is the **risk of time**, the fact that risk increases as the length of time funds are invested increases (Groppelli & Nikbakht, 2018). Exhibit 3.3 illustrates the impact of time on risk. In this table, the risk-free rate

EXHIBIT 3.3   The impact of time on risk.

TYPE	RISK-FREE RATE	RISK PREMIUM	INTEREST RATE (TOTAL RISK)
90-Day Treasury Bills	0.11%	0.00%	0.11%
52-Week Treasury Bills	0.11%	0.03%	0.14%
2-Year Government Notes	0.11%	0.03%	0.14%
5-Year Government Notes	0.11%	0.18%	0.29%
10-Year Government Notes	0.11%	0.53%	0.64%
30-Year Government Bonds	0.11%	1.22%	1.33%

Note: Rates as of July 2020.

is 0.11%, which was the auction rate of 90-day Treasury bills on July 17, 2020. As all of the securities in the table are issued by the federal government, the differences in interest rate, which reflects total risk, are attributable to the risk of time. As the length of time between issue date and maturity date increases, the risk premium increases. This increase reflects the risk of time.

DETERMINANTS OF INTEREST RATES

The interest rate on a given debt security, called the **nominal interest rate**, consists of the real risk-free rate of interest plus multiple risk premiums. These include risk premiums based on the risk of time and the level of risk, which reflect the riskiness of the security itself, and premiums reflecting **inflation** (the devaluation of money over time) and liquidity (the marketability of the security—how quickly it can be turned into cash). (These premiums are defined and discussed below.) The nominal interest rate, or quoted interest rate, on a marketable security is expressed as:

$$\text{nominal interest rate} = k = k^* + \text{IP} + \text{DRP} + \text{LP} + \text{MRP}$$

where k^* = real risk-free rate of interest
    IP = inflation premium
    DRP = default risk premium
    LP = liquidity premium
    MRP = maturity risk premium

The **real risk-free rate** of interest, k^*, is the rate of interest on a riskless security if inflation were not expected. It can also be viewed as the rate of interest on a short-term US Treasury bill in an inflation-free environment. In Exhibit 3.3, the real risk-free rate is 0.11%. The **nominal**, or quoted, **risk-free rate** of interest, k_{RF}, on a security such as a US Treasury bill is the real risk-free rate (k^*) plus an inflation premium (IP). Therefore,

$$\text{nominal risk-free rate} = k_{RF} = k^* + \text{IP}$$

The **inflation premium (IP)** is the portion of an investment's return that compensates the investor for loss of purchasing power over time. We calculate it by determining the expected average inflation rate over the life of the security. (See Chapter 4.)

To account for the risk that a borrower might default, a **default risk premium (DRP)** is added to the nominal interest rate. If the borrower defaults, the investor will receive less than the promised return. The default risk of US Treasury securities is zero, so these securities have no default risk premium. As the riskiness of the borrower increases, the default risk increases. The greater the default risk, the higher the default risk premium and the higher the interest rate. (This concept is similar to the level of risk discussed earlier and illustrated in Exhibit 3.2.)

The terms of a bond contract and the financial strength of the entity issuing the bond are factors in default risk. Moody's Investor Service, Fitch Ratings, and Standard and Poor's Corporation (S&P) all assign quality ratings to bond issues. These ratings measure the likelihood that the bond will go into default. The highest ratings are Aaa (Moody's) and AAA (Fitch and S&P). These bonds

EXHIBIT 3.4   Guide to bond ratings.

AGENCY			
FITCH	**S&P**	**MOODY'S**	**RISK**
AAA	AAA	Aaa	Highest credit quality, with smallest degree of risk
AA	AA	Aa	Very high credit quality and very low credit risk
A	A	A	High credit quality and low credit risk; economic situation can impact risk
BBB	BBB	Baa	Good credit quality, with moderate credit risk
BB	BB	Ba	Speculative, with questionable credit quality
B	B	B	Highly speculative, with high credit risk
CCC	CCC	Caa	Substantial credit risk, with poor credit quality
CC	CC	Ca	Very high level of credit risk, usually in default on deposit obligations
C	C	C	Exceptionally high level of credit risk, typically in default, with low potential recovery values

are very safe, with little default risk. Exhibit 3.4 provides an overview of the bond ratings used by the three agencies.

Another premium included in the nominal interest rate is the **liquidity premium (LP)**, also referred to as the marketability premium. It is added for securities that are not liquid. A security is considered liquid if it can be sold in a short amount of time at a reasonable price.

Because an increase or decrease in interest rates affects the value of outstanding securities, the **maturity risk premium (MRP)** accounts for the risk of a change in the value of a security resulting from changes in interest rates. **Interest rate risk** is the risk that interest rates will increase, causing a decline in the value of the security. Increases in interest rates affect long-term securities more than short-term securities, so interest rate risk is higher for long-term securities. Hence, the maturity risk premium increases as the security's yield to maturity (the rate of return anticipated on the security) increases.

Declining interest rates also pose a risk, called **reinvestment rate risk**. This primarily affects short-term bills, and it increases as the maturity of the bill decreases. This risk reflects the fact that the investor may lose income if at the time the funds are reinvested the interest rate on the bonds has gone down.

For any investment, if we know the real risk-free rate of interest and the risk premiums, we can calculate the nominal interest rate. As previously discussed, the nominal interest rate on a marketable security is:

$$\text{nominal interest rate} = k = k^* + \text{IP} + \text{DRP} + \text{LP} + \text{MRP}$$

To calculate the nominal interest rate (k) for a five-year US Treasury bond, we add the real risk-free rate of interest (k^*), inflation premium (IP), default risk premium (DRP), liquidity premium (LP), and maturity risk premium (MRP). Treasury securities have essentially no default or liquidity risk, so DRP = 0 and LP = 0. Hence, for a Treasury bond with $k^* = 0.5\%$, IP = 3.4%, and MRP = 0.2%,

$$k = k^* + IP + DRP + LP + MRP$$

$$= 0.5\% + 3.4\% + 0\% + 0\% + 0.2\%$$

$$= 4.1\%$$

The nominal interest rate for this five-year US Treasury bond is 4.1%.

RISK AND INVESTMENT RETURNS

Investment risk measures the likelihood of low or negative future returns. As the chance for a low or negative investment return increases, the riskiness of the investment increases. Typically, investment risk focuses on the future performance of a company's stock, so this concept applies directly to publicly traded companies. In North America, the Green Bay Packers are the only publicly traded major league team, though Madison Square Garden (MSG) includes an entertainment and venue portfolio including the New York Knicks and Rangers, and Liberty Braves Group (BATRK) is a holding company that includes the Atlanta Braves and its ballpark. US collegiate sport teams are subsets of larger governmental or non-profit educational entities and, therefore, are not publicly traded. For European teams, shares of Manchester United (MANU), Juventus (JUVE. Italy), and Borussia Dortmund (BVB.Germany) are publicly traded. In addition, the major sporting goods manufacturers are publicly traded. However, the concept of investment risk can be applied beyond publicly traded companies, especially in consideration of stand-alone risk.

Stand-Alone Return and Risk

One approach to analyzing investment return and risk is to consider the investor's risk as if only one asset were held. This is **stand-alone risk**. When analyzing the investment, we examine the stand-alone expected rate of return and stand-alone risk in isolation from other investments.

CALCULATING STAND-ALONE EXPECTED RATE OF RETURN

A potential investor who is considering buying a professional sport franchise, for example, should not invest unless the expected rate of return is high enough to compensate for the perceived risk of the investment. According to data from *Forbes*, the average value of an NFL franchise increased 38% in 2015, 19% in 2016, and 6.8% in 2017. The three-year average increase was 21.1%. Just before the 2018 season began, Carolina Panthers owner Jerry Richardson sold the team to David Tepper (Newton, 2018). The three-year average increase in the Panthers' value from 2015 to 2017 was 22.9%. Since the expected rate of return was 1.8% more than the league's average increase, Mr. Tepper might have been eager to purchase the franchise; therefore, he would consider paying a premium on the team's price. Because investment risk, or the uncertainty of future cash flows, is a component of value, a higher team value reflects lesser risk. Mr. Tepper purchased the Panthers for $2.275 billion, an NFL record price (Newton, 2018).

This example provides a simple analysis of expected rate of return. A more thorough analysis involves evaluating probabilities. A **probability distribution** is a list of all possible outcomes (projected returns) of an investment, with a probability assigned to each outcome. The sum of all probabilities must equal 1.0. Exhibit 3.5 lists the probabilities of investment returns in two NFL franchises. The **expected rate of return** for an investment is the sum of each possible outcome multiplied by its probability. For Franchise X, the expected rate of return of $142.8 million is the sum of the three probable returns. Each *probable return* is the product of the projected return and the probability of that outcome occurring. The expected rate of return for Franchise Y, $139.5 million, was calculated in the same way. Mathematically, the expected rate of return ($\hat{k}$) is expressed as follows:

$$\text{expected rate of return} = \hat{k} = \sum_{i=1}^{n} P_i k_i$$

where i = a specific occurrence[*]
  n = the number of occurrences[*]
  P_i = the probability of occurrence
  k_i = the possible outcome

[*] i and n, as part of summation, will not be defined in subsequent formulas.

For NFL Franchise X, the investor estimates a 35% chance of a low return of $134.5 million, a 50% chance of an average return of $142.4 million, and a 15%

EXHIBIT 3.5	Projected returns and probabilities for two franchise investments (millions).		
PROBABLE OUTCOME	PROJECTED RETURN (k)	WEIGHT OR PROBABILITY (P)	PROBABLE RETURN (P × k)
NFL Franchise X			
Low	$134.5	0.35	$47.08
Average	$142.4	0.50	$71.20
High	$163.5	0.15	$24.53
Expected rate of return			$142.80
NFL Franchise Y			
Low	$119.0	0.20	$23.80
Average	$134.5	0.40	$53.80
High	$154.7	0.40	$61.87
Expected rate of return			$139.47

chance of a high return of $163.5 million (see Exhibit 3.5). The expected rate of return for Franchise X is calculated as follows:

$$\hat{k}_{\text{Franchise x}} = \sum_{i=1}^{n} P_i k_i$$

$$= .35(\$134.5) + .5(\$142.4) + .15(\$163.5)$$

$$= \$142.8 \, \text{million}$$

Note that the return that is actually earned during a given period of time is the *realized rate of return* ($\bar{k}$). The realized rate of return usually differs from the expected rate of return.

When the number of possible outcomes is practically unlimited, we use a continuous probability distribution to calculate the expected rate of return. The **standard deviation (SD**, denoted by σ) is a measure of variability in a distribution of numbers and, in the case of an investment, indicates the riskiness of the investment. A lower-risk investment will take the form of a tighter, or more peaked, distribution curve. Investments with probability distributions that have wider dispersion from the expected value are riskier. In Exhibit 3.6, the distribution with the tallest peak is the one with the lowest standard deviation (σ = 0.3) and the lowest risk.

The standard deviation of a probability distribution is calculated as follows:

$$\text{standard deviation} = \sigma = \sqrt{\sum_{i=1}^{n} \left(k_i - \hat{k}\right)^2 P_i}$$

where k_i, = the outcome of a specific occurrence
$\hat{k}$ = the expected return
P_i = the probability of the return

We calculate the standard deviation of the investment in Franchise X as follows:

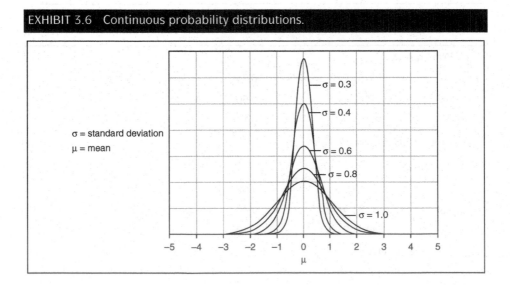

EXHIBIT 3.6   Continuous probability distributions.

σ = standard deviation
μ = mean

σ = 0.3
σ = 0.4
σ = 0.6
σ = 0.8
σ = 1.0

1. Find the expected rate of return (entity) from the previous calculation:

$$\hat{k}_{\text{Franchise X}} = \$142.8 \text{ million}$$

2. Subtract the expected rate of return $\left(\hat{k}_{\text{Franchise X}}\right)$ from each possible outcome (k_i) to obtain a list of deviations (see Exhibit 3.5 for each possible outcome for Franchise X):

$$\text{Deviation}_i = k_i - \hat{k}_{\text{Franchise X}}$$

$$\text{Deviation}_1 = (134.5 - 142.8) = -8.3$$

$$\text{Deviation}_2 = (142.4 - 142.8) = -0.4$$

$$\text{Deviation}_3 = (163.5 - 142.8) = 20.7$$

3. Calculate the variance (σ^2) of the probability distribution. To do this, take the square of each deviation, multiply this value by the probability of its corresponding outcome, and sum these values:

$$\sigma^2 = .35(-8.3)^2 + .5(-0.4)^2 + .15(20.7)^2$$

$$= 24.11 + 0.08 + 64.27$$

$$= 88.46$$

4. Take the square root of the variance:

$$\sigma = \sqrt{88.46} = 9.41$$

CALCULATING STAND-ALONE RISK

The coefficient of variation (CV) measures the stand-alone risk of an invest ment. It is useful when we are comparing the expected returns on two alternative projects whose returns are not the same. A lower CV suggests less risk, since the CV indicates risk per unit of return. To calculate the CV, we divide the standard deviation (σ) by the expected return ($\hat{k}$):

$$\text{coefficient of variation } (CV) = \frac{\sigma}{\hat{k}}$$

Return to Exhibit 3.5 to view the expected rates of return for two possible investments. For Franchise X, $\hat{k}$ = \$142.8 million and σ = 9.41. For Franchise Y, $\hat{k}$ = \$139.47 million and σ = 13.66. With this information, we can calculate the CV for each investment:

$$CV_X = \frac{\sigma_X}{\hat{k}_X} = \frac{9.41}{142.8} = .066$$

and

$$CV_Y = \frac{\sigma_Y}{\hat{k}_Y} = \frac{13.66}{139.47} = .098$$

The CVs of the two alternatives confirm that the lower-risk investment for the potential team owner is Franchise X, as it has less risk per unit of return.

Investors tend to be **risk averse**: when presented with two investment alternatives with the same expected rate of return, most investors will select the alternative with the lower risk. Hence, most investors will seek a higher rate of return for riskier investments and require a risk premium.

Portfolio Return and Risk

By holding more than one asset, an investor can eliminate some of the risk inherent in the individual assets. Hence, most financial assets are held in **portfolios**—combinations of assets held by individual investors—and investors are concerned with portfolio return and portfolio risk.

An investor chooses assets with the goal of maximizing the return of the overall portfolio while minimizing overall risk. To do so, the investor examines both the expected rate of return and risk of each individual asset and the degree to which each asset affects the rate of return and risk for the entire portfolio.

CALCULATING PORTFOLIO EXPECTED RATE OF RETURN

To calculate the **expected return on a portfolio** $\left(\hat{k}_p\right)$, we sum the weighted average of the expected returns of each asset:

$$\text{expected return on a portfolio} = \hat{k}_p = \sum_{i=1}^{n} w_i \hat{k}_i$$

where w_i = the weight (percentage) of the total portfolio invested in an individual asset

$\hat{k}_i$ = the expected rate of return of the asset

For example, suppose Portfolio 1 is valued at $1 million, with $200,000 invested in each of five companies, and the following returns can be expected for the stocks held in the portfolio:

STOCK	$\hat{k}$
Company A	10.0%
Company B	9.5%
Company C	11.5%
Company D	3.5%
Company E	6.0%

To calculate the expected return on Portfolio 1, we proceed as follows:

$$\text{expected return on a portfolio} = \hat{k}_p = \sum_{i=1}^{n} w_i \hat{k}_i$$

$$= w_1\hat{k}_1 + w_2\hat{k}_2 + \ldots + w_n\hat{k}_n$$

$$= 0.2(10.0\%) + 0.2(9.5\%) + 0.2(11.5\%) + 0.2(3.5\%) + 0.2(6.0\%)$$

$$= 8.1\%$$

If the owner of Portfolio 1 decided to invest in the NFL's Buffalo Bills, with an average annual return of 2.9%, the expected return of the portfolio would decrease. Suppose the portfolio's owner purchased $1,000,000 of the Bills. The portfolio now would be as follows:

PORTFOLIO A: STOCK	$\hat{k}$
Company A	10.0%
Company B	9.5%
Company C	11.5%
Company D	3.5%
Company E	6.0%
Bills	2.9%

The total value of the portfolio would now be $2 million, with $200,000 invested in each of companies A through E and $1 million invested in the Bills. Each of assets A through E makes up 10% of Portfolio 1 and has a weight of 0.1. The investment in the Bills has a weight of 0.5. Now,

$$\hat{k}_p = w_1\hat{k}_1 + w_2\hat{k}_2 + \cdots w_n\hat{k}_n$$

$$= 0.1(10.0\%) + 0.1(9.5\%) + 0.1(11.5\%) + 0.1(3.5\%) + 0.1(6.0\%) + 0.5(7.0\%)$$

$$= 7.55\%$$

CALCULATING PORTFOLIO RISK

Calculating a portfolio's risk (σ_p) is not as simple as computing the weighted average of the individual assets' standard deviations. The portfolio risk is actually smaller than the weighted average of the individual assets' standard deviations—this is why portfolios are so attractive to investors. A portfolio's risk depends not just on the standard deviations of the individual assets' risks but also on the correlation (degree of relationship) between those risks. If securities are added to a portfolio that have low standard deviations but that have the same patterns of movement and dispersion around the expected rate of return as the assets already held in the portfolio, the risk of the portfolio will remain unchanged.

The **correlation coefficient** (r) measures the degree of the relationship between two variables. In portfolio analysis, the correlation coefficient measures how closely the returns of an asset move relative to the returns of the other assets held in the portfolio. The measure ranges from +1.0, where the two variables move in the exact same way, to −1.0, where the two variables move exactly opposite to each other. When there is no correlation between the variables, $r = 0.0$. Typically, the correlation between assets in a portfolio is positive but less than +1.0.

Correlations reflect the degree to which *two* assets change together. A correlation cannot be calculated for an entire portfolio. We can, however, calculate multiple correlations between various combinations held within a portfolio. More usually, when we analyze a portfolio we select one individual asset to be represented by one variable, with the rest of the portfolio represented by the second variable.

A general rule on diversification states that as an investor adds assets to a portfolio the riskiness of the portfolio decreases, as long as the assets are not perfectly positively correlated. If the assets already in the portfolio are highly correlated, diversifying the portfolio does little to reduce its risk if the new asset is perfectly positively correlated with the existing portfolio. By adding assets that are not perfectly correlated to the existing portfolio mix, the investor can eliminate some but not all risk. A truly riskless portfolio does not exist.

The correlation coefficient of two assets is calculated as follows:

$$\text{correlation coefficient of two assets} = r_{x,y} = \frac{\sum_{i=1}^{n} \frac{\left(\overline{k}_{x,i} - \hat{k}_{x,i}\right)\left(\overline{k}_{y,i} - \hat{k}_{y,i}\right)}{n}}{\sigma_x \sigma_y}$$

where $\overline{k}$ = the actual rate of return
$\hat{k}$ = the expected rate of return
σ = the standard deviation

The volatility (entity) of the two assets (x, y) relative to each other is measured in the numerator. In the denominator, the product of the two assets' standard deviations standardizes the **covariance**—the degree to which two variables change together—between the assets (Groppelli & Nikbakht, 2018). Because the covariance is standardized, the correlation coefficient helps the investor find the assets that move differently from those already held in a portfolio. Groppelli and Nikbakht add that the equation can also be expressed as

$$\text{correlation coefficient of two assets} = r_{x,y} = \frac{\text{covariance}(x, y)}{\sigma_x \sigma_y}$$

Exhibit 3.7 illustrates the concept of covariance. The chart depicts the rates of return for stocks X and Y over a five-year period. The two stocks represent a perfectly negative correlation ($r = -1.0$). When the rate of return rises for Stock X, Stock Y's return falls. When Stock Y's return rises, Stock X's return falls.

The key to building a portfolio that reduces overall risk is that it must not contain assets that are all highly positively correlated. Holding a well-diversified portfolio is less risky than holding a stock as a solitary asset, and holding two highly *negatively* correlated assets is less risky than holding a stock as a solitary asset. Brigham and Houston (2018) add that almost half of the riskiness of an individual stock can be eliminated if that stock is held in a well-diversified portfolio (one containing 40 or more stocks). Note, however, that a completely diversified portfolio will lose money if the whole market is in decline, as a diversified portfolio will move as the market moves.

EXHIBIT 3.7 The rates of return for stocks X and Y over a five-year period.

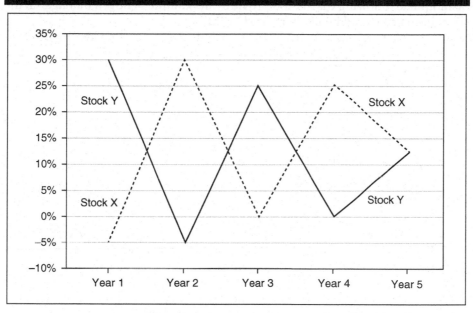

ANALYZING THE RELATION BETWEEN PORTFOLIO RATE OF RETURN AND PORTFOLIO RISK

Capital asset pricing model. The **capital asset pricing model (CAPM)** provides a means to analyze the relationship between risk and rate of return. A stock or bond's **required rate of return** is the profit that an investor would require in order to consider the investment worth purchasing, given its riskiness. The CAPM is built on the notion that this required rate of return is equal to the risk-free rate of return plus a risk premium, with the risk reflecting the portfolio's diversification. Under this model, the **relevant risk** of a stock is its contribution to the riskiness of a diversified portfolio.

CAPM divides risk into two components: diversifiable risk and market risk. **Diversifiable risk** is the portion of a stock's risk that can be removed through a well-diversified portfolio. This type of risk is caused by events that are unique to the company issuing the stock. **Market risk** is the portion of a stock's risk that cannot be eliminated. It is caused by factors that affect most organizations similarly (the economy, inflation, interest rates, and so forth). Market risk is measured by the degree to which the stock moves with the market. Market risk, therefore, is the relevant risk under CAPM. It determines the impact of an individual stock on the overall portfolio's risk.

CAPM incorporates the concept of the **beta coefficient** (β), or the volatility of a stock compared to market return, in its model (see the next section for more information about the beta coefficient). In addition to a stock's beta, the model factors in the average investor's risk aversion to determine the return that an investor would require from a particular stock. Groppelli and Nikbakht (2018) add that, although CAPM is primarily applicable to the analysis of securities, investors and managers can also use the model to evaluate the risk and return merits of an organization's investments and assets. For a majority of the businesses in the sport industry, CAPM would most likely be used in this fashion. The following discussion provides an example of how a manager in the sport industry would be likely to use CAPM.

The **security market line (SML)** formula for evaluating the merit of an investment expresses the risk/return relationship as follows:

$$\text{required return on investment} = k_i = k_{RF} + (k_M - k_{RF})\beta$$

where k_i = the rate of return required for the investment
k_{RF} = the nominal risk-free rate of interest
k_M = the expected average stock market return
β = the beta of the firm's investments

For example, to evaluate an investment in a new arena, the organization would first estimate the nominal risk-free rate (k_{RF}) based on US Treasury secur-ities. For an arena with a 30-year useful life, the nominal risk-free rate (k_{RF}), based on the interest rate of a 30-year US Treasury bond, is currently 1.33% (see Exhibit 3.2). Next, it is necessary to calculate the beta (β) of the organization's portfolio of assets. We will assume that this value is 1.3. Finally, the organiza-tion will estimate the market's expected rate of return (k_M). We will assume a value of 8.0%. This is the forecaster's best guess at how the market will per-form, on average, over the next year, based on past performance. For example, the average annual growth rate of the S&P 500 was slightly under 10% through 2019. By using the SML equation, we calculate the required return on the invest-ment in the facility as follows:

$$\text{required return on investment} = k_i = k_{RF} + (k_M - k_{RF})\beta$$

$$= 1.33\% + (8.0\% - 1.33\%)1.3$$

$$= 1.33\% + 8.67\%$$

$$= 10.00\%$$

If the franchise can earn 10.0% on the equity capital—the money the firm is reinvesting in itself by investing in the arena—the owners of the team should be willing to invest in the new facility, based on its risk and return merits as evaluated under CAPM. Earnings would likely come from increased revenues generated by the new arena, especially from luxury suites, club seats, naming rights, and personal seating licenses.

Beta coefficient. As discussed above, CAPM incorporates the concept of beta (β). Beta reflects the degree to which a stock increases or decreases with the increase or decrease of the overall market. An average-risk stock is a stock that tends to move with the market. Such a stock has a beta of 1.0. A stock that is twice as volatile as the market will have a beta of 2.0, and a stock that is half as volatile will have a beta of 0.5. As volatility increases, risk increases. Therefore, stocks with betas greater than 1.0 are riskier than the market, and those with betas less than 1.0 are less risky than the market. Beta is the most relevant measure of any stock's risk.

Betas for securities are available from sources such as Bloomberg. Exhibit 3.8 lists the beta coefficients for the stocks of 13 companies in the sport industry. The table reveals that the stocks of sporting goods retail organizations have risk

EXHIBIT 3.8   Beta coefficients for sport-related companies (July 2020).

	SYMBOL	BETA
Motorsports		
Dover Motorsports Inc.	DVD	0.51
Sporting Goods Retail		
Dick's Sporting Goods	DKS	1.61
Hibbett Sports, Inc.	HIBB	1.60
Foot Locker, Inc.	FL	1.33
Zumiez, Inc.	ZUMZ	1.82
Sporting Goods Manufacturers		
Nike, Inc.	NKE	0.81
Under Armour, Inc.	UA	1.19
Callaway Golf Co.	ELY	1.97
Crocs Incorporated	CROX	1.88
Columbia Sportswear Co.	COLM	0.68
Sport and Entertainment Organizations		
World Wrestling Entertainment, Inc.	WWE	1.49
Live Nation Entertainment, Inc.	LYV	1.10
Electronic Arts Inc.	EA	0.93

Source: Yahoo! Finance (2020).

greater than the market ($\beta > 1.0$), whereas the sole stock in motorsports has risk less than the market, with a beta below 1.0.

The beta of a portfolio is the weighted average of the betas of the individual securities:

$$\text{beta of portfolio} = \beta_p = \sum_{i=1}^{n} w_i \beta_i$$

where w_i = the weight of the ith security

β_i = the beta of the ith security

For example, suppose an investor has a portfolio of three sport-related stocks:

COMPANY	BETA	WEIGHT
Dover Motorsports	0.51	40%
Foot Locker	1.33	30%
Under Armour	1.19	30%

For this portfolio,

$$\beta_p = \sum_{i=1}^{n} w_i \beta_i$$

$$= w_1\beta_1 + w_2\beta_2 + w_3\beta_3$$

$$= .4(0.51) + .3(1.33) + .3(1.19)$$

$$= 0.96$$

The beta for this portfolio indicates that it has slightly below-average risk.

SOURCES OF RISK

Groppelli and Nikbakht (2018) discuss sources of risk that may affect an organization's returns. They divide risk into three categories: external business activity, industry and company risk, and global risk. Risk related to external business activity arises from economic conditions, political developments, and inflation. Examples of industry and company risk include risks common to a particular industry, technological changes, and environmental and social concerns. Finally, global sources of risk include changes to regulations regarding import and export activities, expropriation, and changes in exchange rates.

This section discusses how some of these risks, including economic conditions, political developments, and global issues, affect sport.

Economic Conditions

One source of risk related to external business activity is the economic conditions of the time. From 2009 through 2020, most of the world saw a record long period of economic growth. For example, in the United States the economic expansion lasted 128 months, ending in February 2020 as the global economy slowed due to the COVID-19 pandemic (Tilley, 2020). While the long-term impacts on the sport industry as a result of the pandemic are unknown, the Great Recession, which began in late 2007 and lasted through June 2009, shows how a slowing economy can have a major impact on financial management in sport.

CAPITAL FINANCE

As lending standards tighten in a credit crisis, the economy's impact on the bond market affects teams' and cities' capital financing endeavors. In 2008, for example, debt became more expensive as a result of the recession and accompanying banking crisis. During this time, the Arlington, Texas, city council sought to refinance a portion of the municipal bonds that it had used to finance part of the Dallas Cowboys' new stadium. The municipal bonds were initially issued in 2005 as **synthetic fixed-rate bonds**, bonds that have elements of both a fixed-rate bond and a variable-rate bond. Their interest rate ranged from 3% to 4%. The tightening credit market caused an increase in the interest rate during the spring of 2008, to 7%. Three months later, the rate climbed to 8%, and it peaked at 9% during the summer of 2008, resulting in a $500,000 increase in Arlington's monthly interest payment (Schrock, 2008). The city sought to refinance the bonds at a fixed rate of approximately 6% ("Cowboys, city council," 2008). In total, the city was seeking to refinance $164 million of the synthetic fixed-rate bonds.

After encountering difficulty refinancing, the city decided to attempt to refinance only a portion of the bonds. Arlington converted $104 million of the $164 million to a fixed rate of approximately 6%. The city also financed $10 million in closing costs, which included bond insurance and fees required to terminate the previous financing agreement. The remaining $60 million was left on the fluctuating rate. Due to the changes in the bond market, the debt service costs to the city increased by $44 million over the life of the issue (Ahles & Schrock, 2008).

At about the same time, Jerry Jones, the Dallas Cowboys' owner, announced that the team had refinanced $435 million worth of debt for AT&T Stadium. The variable rates from the initial offering had fluctuated dramatically during the year, increasing the required bond payments and the cost of the overall project. This led the Cowboys to refinance at a fixed rate of 5% ("Cowboys refinance $435m," 2008).

Both the city of Arlington and the team were affected by the risk associated with variable-rate bonds. The tightening credit market led to an increase in rates, raising the total cost to finance the project and affecting the operating budgets of the team and the city.

Auction-rate bonds, a common method of financing facility construction, can also be negatively impacted by changes in the bond market. An **auction-rate bond** is a form of long-term debt that acts like short-term debt, in which interest rates are reset through auctions held no more than 35 days apart (Schnitzler, 2008). They are supposed to reduce the borrowing costs for long-term financing, as these costs are linked to short-term interest rates rather than 20- or 30-year interest rates (see Exhibit 3.3 for examples of how rates vary for various bond terms). In 2007, the New York Giants sold seven series of bonds totaling $650 million. The March 24, 2008 auction, however, failed to attract enough bidders. When there are not enough bidders for this type of bond, a penalty interest rate is calculated based on the terms of the offer. The team was obliged to pay 22% interest on $53 million in bonds. Additionally, the team began paying 11.5% on the $70.85 million in bonds that were successfully auctioned that day. As a result, the Giants chose to redeem $100 million of the bonds ("NFL Giants redeeming," 2008).

The State of Indiana financed the entire $700 million Lucas Oil Stadium with auction-rate bonds. As a result, like the Giants, the state was exposed to the risk of drastic changes in interest rates. Unlike the Giants, however, the maximum interest rate the state had to pay was 15% (Schnitzler, 2008).

OPERATING BUDGETS

In addition to affecting capital finance, a recession can also have an effect on operating budgets. In 2009, for example, MLB attendance was down 6.6% from 2008 (Brown, 2010). During this period, to keep fans coming to games, sport organizations resorted to discounting tickets and providing ticket promotions. These included two-for-one tickets, family nights, gas card deals, e-savers, dollar nights, college nights, and "economic stimulus plans" for fans (Fisher, 2008). With the combination of fewer fans coming to games and the fact that those who were attending were taking advantage of discounts and promotions, revenues from ticket sales were down for most clubs in 2009. Short-term advertising and sponsorship revenues also decreased. However, for professional teams and major college programs, long-term contracts with sponsors and media rights partners softened the full impact of the slowing economy.

For sport organizations, risk is reduced when revenues are guaranteed. Teams with greater percentages of guaranteed income have less risk than those with lower percentages of guaranteed income. For many sport organizations, their most significant revenue comes from sources protected by long-term contracts ("Struggling economy likely," 2008). For example, during the Great Recession the Southeastern Conference signed a long-term media rights deal with CBS and ESPN that significantly increased member school revenues, despite the slowdown in the economy and the struggle to sell season tickets that some schools faced. Similarly, in 2009 the NBA had just completed the first year of an eight-year, $7.5 billion deal with ESPN, ABC, and Turner (Kaplan & Lombardo, 2009).

However, the timing of the expiration of long-term contracts does affect leagues. For example, in 2009 the PGA Tour lost five automotive title sponsors and was threatened with losing more. Thirteen of its events were sponsored by banks, investment firms, and credit card companies. As long as financial markets remained in turmoil, the PGA Tour and other sport organizations were at risk of losing sponsors. In the case of the PGA Tour, each sponsorship agreement was worth approximately $32 million over four years ("Struggling economy likely," 2008).

With the 2020 pandemic-induced recession, the impact on operating budgets is already being seen. As games are played to empty or capacity-restricted stadiums, revenues derived from ticketing, concessions, merchandise sales, and parking are non-existent or severely restricted. For MiLB teams, there will be an 18-month period without significant revenues due to the cancellation of their 2020 season (Couch & Calloway, 2020). However, the full and long-term impact will not be known for some time due to the current economic stimulus programs enacted by governments across the globe. These programs provide short-term protection. An analysis in the *Sports Business Journal* estimates that the Paycheck Protection Program loan in the United States was used by more than 600 sports organizations in 2020. In total the US sport industry received an estimated $665.9 million which helped preserve roughly 36,000 jobs (McCormick & Broughton, 2020). With the future of live sporting events unknown at this time, the full impact of the COVID-19 pandemic on operating budgets likely will be severe once governmental subsidies run out.

LEAGUE LOAN POOLS

League loan pools are also affected by economic conditions. Because the risk of an individual franchise is greater than the risk of an entire league (this is similar to the risk of an individual asset being greater than the risk of a portfolio), leagues borrow to create **loan pools** that provide capital to affiliated franchises at reduced cost. The NBA, for example, created its loan pool in 2003 and renewed the $1.96 billion debt in May 2009. Seventeen NBA teams borrowed from the fund. Due to the condition of the credit markets in 2009, the cost to borrow from the pool rose from 75 points over LIBOR to approximately

175 points over LIBOR (i.e., by 1%) (Lombardo & Kaplan, 2011). By 2017, the economy was strong. Combined with the league's labor peace, lucrative media rights deals, and valuable young demographics, the league was able to refinance $300 million of its debt for 3.6% rather than the 5.5% when the previous bonds were sold (Kaplan & Lombardo, 2017). In total, the NBA's credit facility had grown to $3.5 billion by 2017 with approximately 67% of teams borrowing for a variety of team expenses.

Major League Baseball, the NFL, and NHL also took advantage of the strong economy and refinanced debt while also expanding the size of their loan pools. MLB increased its debt pool to almost $2 billion after it signed a new collective bargaining agreement with its players. Teams were allowed to increase borrowing from $75 million each to $100 million (Kaplan, 2013). Likewise, the NFL increased the amount its teams could borrow while also increasing its overall credit facility to $2.7 billion (Kaplan, 2017). In expanding its loan pool to $1.7 billion, the NHL allowed Canadian teams to borrow for the first time (Kaplan & Thomas, 2016). Teams from Canada originally could not borrow because of issues with the Canadian government.

Political Developments

Changes in the political environment can also affect financial risk in sport. Policy decisions at the local, state, and national levels directly impact the business of sport. For example, at the local and state levels, policy is set regarding the public funding of venues, state income tax rates for athletes, and amusement tax rates on ticket revenues. Federal policy on sport often includes antitrust regulations and labor relations laws. Over time, policy may shift as the attitudes and beliefs of the electorate change and as the values of society shift. Financial managers must be aware how changes in the political environment may affect the sport industry.

The Great Recession impacted sport as public policy shifted as a result of the economic crisis. In 2008, with the federal government bailouts of the financial sector and the automobile industry in the US, members of Congress asked whether sponsorship spending by firms receiving taxpayer support is a prudent use of public money ("Struggling economy likely," 2008). In 2009, companies in the financial sector had $2.47 billion in obligated payments for naming rights to US and Canadian sports venues (Lefton & Mickle, 2009). Banking was the fourth largest category in sport sponsorship spending, at $900 million. Additionally, banks spent $122.3 million on advertising in sport (Lefton & Mickle, 2009).

As mentioned earlier in this chapter, the recession caused by the COVID-19 pandemic led to government programs designed to support industries harmed by the virus's spread. In the US, early reports show the impact of the program on the sporting industry. The $665.9 million provided to the industry was highly scrutinized and led to some of the awarded monies being returned. The most visible example was the Los Angeles Lakers. The Lakers received a loan from the PPP designed for small businesses, despite having a franchise value over $4 billion dollars. US Treasury Secretary Steve Mnuchin stated, "I never expected in a million years that the Los Angeles Lakers, which, I'm a big fan of the team, but I'm not a big fan of the fact that they took a $4.6 million loan" (Cillizza, 2020, para. 5). While the rules set for companies to receive PPP loans applied to the Lakers, public outcry over the Lakers receiving money, while other small businesses did not, led the Lakers to quickly return the money. Similar outcry was seen in England where fans criticized Tottenham and Newcastle United for seeking large governmental loans (Keh & Das, 2020).

While public scrutiny and outcry led the Lakers to return money, many sport organizations benefited from the PPP loans. The National Women's Soccer League (NWSL) received funding, which was used to save the league's eighth season (Keh & Das, 2020). The primary use of the funds was to provide player salaries for two months of the season. Exhibit 3.9 lists sporting teams and organizations receiving PPP loans. Reporting was done by the Small Business Administration using a range of funding which is shown in the exhibit.

EXHIBIT 3.9   A sampling of teams and leagues receiving PPP loans.

	RANGE
Major League Soccer	
DC United	$1–2 million
Inter Miami	$1–2 million
Orlando City	$2–5 million
Seattle Sounders	$2–5 million
Professional Sport Leagues	
Big 3 Basketball	$0.9 million
Major League Rugby	$1–2 million
National Women's Soccer League	$1–2 million
Premier Lacrosse League	$1–2 million
College Athletic Conferences	
Big Sky Conference	$0.15–0.35 million
Conference USA	$0.35–1 million
Northeast Conference	$0.15–0.35 million
Minor League Baseball	
Asheville Tourists	$0.15–0.35 million
Charleston RiverDogs	$0.35–1 million
Columbia Fireflies	$0.35–1 million
National Governing Bodies	
USA Hockey	$2–5 million
US Ski & Snowboarding	$2–5 million
USA Swimming	$1–2 million

Sources: Evans, 2020; Holdman & Adcox, 2020; McCormick & Broughton, 2020.

Global Issues

As business becomes more global, financial managers face new issues. In North America, the league most affected by global issues on a consistent basis is the National Hockey League. This league has the highest percentage of Canadian franchises. Most of the Canadian franchise revenue is earned in Canadian dollars, whereas the NHL's collective bargaining agreement requires that all player contracts be paid in US dollars. As a result, most of the expenses of these franchises are in US dollars. As the Canadian dollar strengthens relative to the US dollar, a Canadian team's revenue increases while its expenses decrease. As a result, Canadian teams become more profitable. But when the US dollar strengthens again, the Canadian teams' primary expense, player salaries, increases and reduces the profits of these franchises. Fluctuations in the exchange rate between the Canadian dollar and US dollar, therefore, affect the profitability not only of the Canadian teams but also of the US teams and the league as a whole.

This impact can be seen when examining the league over ten seasons (2008/2009 to 2018/2019). For the 2008/2009 NHL season, the salary cap rose to $56.7 million ("NHL salary cap," 2008), increasing for the fourth straight year. As the salary cap is tied directly to overall league revenues, the increase in the cap was attributable to record attendance (ticket revenues are the source of a majority of team and league revenues) and the strength of the Canadian dollar. While the Canadian dollar remained strong compared to the US dollar in 2008/2009 the cap continued to rise (Burnside, 2008). The collective bargaining agreement with the players includes not only a salary cap but also a salary floor, the minimum amount a team can spend on player payroll. The salary floor grew to $40.7 million for the 2008/2009 season. Some teams in smaller, non-traditional US markets complained that they could no longer turn a profit, even with revenue sharing. These teams included the Phoenix Coyotes (who were in bankruptcy at the time), the Atlanta Thrashers (who were sold and relocated to Winnipeg in 2011), the Nashville Predators, the Florida Panthers, and the Columbus Blue Jackets ("NHL owners growing," 2008).

By 2016, the Canadian dollar hit a 13-year low as compared to the US dollar ("NHL expects," 2016). The league stated that the slide of the Canadian dollar would cost it $200 million as approximately one-third of its revenue comes from Canada. As the owners and players split revenues 50-50, the players lost a majority of their salary held in escrow by the league (approximately 18%). During 2017, the Canadian dollar strengthened and therefore created more salary cap room for teams and offsetting losses in 2016 (Campbell, 2017). Importantly for the players, the time that their salary cap rose the most was during times of a strong Canadian dollar (2008, 2011, and 2014).

In Europe, differing income tax rates between countries impact team profitability and quality. When in England the top income tax rate rose to 50% in 2010, the high tax rate and fluctuations in currency value (e.g., the British pound versus the euro) impacted Premier League players. They could have seen their salary decrease by a third in 2010 as compared to 2009 (Gibson, 2009). However, players in Europe often structure their contract values based on net (after tax) earnings; therefore, the EPL teams had to make up the difference in salary resulting from the tax increase, so that the players' net salaries remained the same. Also, continental European players typically ask EPL clubs to pay them in euros. Hence, like the NHL, EPL clubs have to account for fluctuations in exchange rates.

REVENUE SHARING AND RISK

Each individual franchise or athletic department operates within its own financial environment, facing risk that sometimes is unique to that franchise or department. However, franchises and athletic departments also cooperate in several ways even while their teams are competing on the field, and one of the ways is in financial management. In both college athletics and professional sport, leagues use **revenue sharing** to support weaker franchises and maintain the competitive balance within the league. A byproduct of revenue sharing is that each individual organization's risk is lessened. Revenues are shared through pools under several models, discussed below. See Sidebar 3.B for a discussion of revenue sharing in the NHL.

Revenue Pools

Each league has two basic pools of revenue that may or may not be shared by teams within the league: central and local. **Central revenues** are revenues paid directly to the league. These revenues are then distributed to member organizations. Typically, net costs of operating the league, association, or conference are deducted prior to distribution. In professional sport, the degree to which teams share central revenues is governed by the league's collective bargaining agreement. In collegiate sport, central revenue sharing is a product of NCAA membership agreements and conference affiliation (Foster, Greyser, & Walsh, 2005). For example, the revenue from the CBS television contract to broadcast the NCAA Men's Basketball Tournament goes first to the NCAA. Then, based on a predetermined formula, the NCAA sends the revenue to member institutions. For NCAA Division I–FBS schools, a majority of the revenue from football broadcasts flows through conference offices. Similarly, revenue from the SEC's television contract with CBS and the SEC Network is sent to the conference, which deducts expenses and forwards the revenue to member institutions.

SIDEBAR 3.B   Reducing Risk at the Franchise Level

Over the past 15 years, leagues have moved to reduce risk at the franchise level. MLB increased the sharing of local revenues, and the NFL began modestly sharing local revenues. The league that changed its revenue sharing model most drastically, however, was the National Hockey League. Prior to locking out the players in 2004, the owners of franchises and league management decided that the financial structure of the league needed modification. During the 2002/2003 NHL season, with total revenues of $1.996 billion and total expenses of $2.269 billion, the league had an operating loss of $273 million. As the league lacked a salary cap, player costs had risen to 75% of total league revenues. This was the highest percentage for player salary of all leagues in North America. Further, 19 NHL franchises lost an average of $18 million. For the 11 teams making a profit that year, the average profit was $6.4 million. Only two teams earned over $10 million.

When the NHL lockout ended, the league had implemented a hard salary cap and had increased revenue sharing. Player salary was capped at 54% of league revenues, if league revenues were below $2.2 billion. The cap amount increased slightly if league revenues increased above the $2.2 billion mark. The sharing of local revenues was increased to assist small-market teams that were struggling financially under the old system.

As of 2015, the NHL salary cap is determined by calculating the midpoint of total hockey-related revenues (as defined in the league's collective bargaining agreement). The players receive 50% of hockey-related revenues. The salary cap is set at 15% above the midpoint of these revenues, with a salary floor at 15% below the midpoint. All teams in the league must spend to at least the salary floor. The NHL's salary cap was expected to be approximately $81.5 million during the 2019/2020 season, with the salary floor at $60.2 million ("NHL salary cap," 2019).

Local revenues, such as those from teams' home ticket sales, local television and radio, advertising, and sponsorship, are also shared. The specific revenues that are shared and the degree to which they are shared vary by league. For example, MLB teams pay 48% of local revenues into a pool of money which is then divided equally among all teams. The difference between what a team pays in and what it receives is either a net payment into the revenue sharing pool or a net receipt. In the current CBA, however, the top 13 clubs by market size are disqualified from revenue sharing receipts. Their funds instead go to support player benefits and clubs who were payees into the revenue sharing plan.

Revenue Sharing Models

Each league uses one of three models for sharing revenue (Foster, Greyser, & Walsh, 2005). Under the first, the league provides increased revenue allocations to teams with low local revenues. MLB uses this model, as does the NBA.

Under the second model, the league provides equal allocations to all teams in the league. For the most part, this is how the NFL currently shares revenue. Under the current CBA, players receive approximately 47% to 48.8% of all revenues; the percentage shared with players varies by revenue source. The league's central revenues are shared equally among all clubs. The players receive a lower share of local revenues, and very little of local revenue is now shared among clubs. In a previous CBA, players received 59.9% of *all* league revenues, both central and local. Because of the great disparity in revenues generated locally within the NFL, under that CBA the owners had to provide higher revenues to clubs with smaller local revenue pools.

By examining revenues for two NFL franchises, Team X and Team Y, we can see why a group of owners sought to change the revenue sharing model.

EXHIBIT 3.10 Comparison of revenues of two NFL teams.		
REVENUE TYPE	**TEAM X**	**TEAM Y**
Local	$89,000,000	$49,000,000
Central	$111,000,000	$111,000,000
Total	$200,000,000	$160,000,000

Team X is located in a medium/large market with a newly renovated stadium, and Team Y is located in a small market with an older facility. Revenues for each team are shown in Exhibit 3.10.

The salary cap under the prior CBA, which was set at a percentage of total revenues, affected Team Y more than Team X, because Team Y earned less in local revenue. With a $105 million cap, Team X's ratio of player salary to total revenue is 0.53 ($105,000,000/$200,000,000). For Team Y, the ratio is 0.66 ($105,000,000/$160,000,000).

At the college level, the SEC uses an equal allocation formula for distributing conference media revenues to member institutions. Most college conferences distribute revenues in a similar fashion.

The third revenue sharing model favors teams that generate higher revenue. The Premier League, the elite football (soccer) league in England, uses this model. Franchises are rewarded for the effective financial management of their clubs.

CONCLUSION

Risk affects the financial management of all sport organizations. Interest rates, bond rates, estimates of cash flow, and the cost of capital are all affected by changes in risk, as are rates of return. Because cash today is worth more to an investor than the same cash in the future, risk premiums compensate investors for risking today's cash. These premiums include an inflation premium, default risk premium, liquidity premium, and maturity risk premium.

An investment may be evaluated as a stand-alone investment or as a part of a larger portfolio of investments. For a stand-alone investment, the expected rate of return must be higher than the perceived risk. When considering whether to add an investment to a portfolio, the investor will examine how the new asset would affect the risk and return of the portfolio. The goal is to maximize the return of the portfolio while minimizing risk. Diversification is an important approach to reducing the risk of a portfolio. Financial managers use the capital asset pricing model to analyze the relationship between risk and rate of return for securities. CAPM allows the manager to analyze diversifiable and market risk by incorporating the beta coefficient of a security or a portfolio of securities, by using the security market line formula. Typically, CAPM is used to analyze securities; however, an investor or manager can use it to evaluate the risk and return merits of an organization's investments and assets.

Managers in sport organizations must be aware of risks that may affect the organization's finances. Leagues have been proactive in reducing the risks that member clubs face—but there is no risk-free investment. Managers must strive to analyze risk carefully to protect the organization's financial assets.

Concept Check

1. How does risk affect the financial management of sport organizations?
2. Describe the process of determining a nominal interest rate.
3. Of MLB, the NBA, and the NHL, which league has the most risk, and which has the least? Why?
4. What must players and agents understand about risk? How should an agent structure a player's contract if it contains deferred compensation?
5. What risk factors should a team consider when deciding whether to build and fund a new venue? How are the risk factors different if a municipality is funding the construction?
6. If you were advising an investor interested in purchasing a sport franchise, what advice would you give?
7. Among NCAA men's basketball teams, which team would you expect to have the highest value? Why? How do you think conference affiliation affects value among these teams?

Practice Problems

1. You have the opportunity to purchase NFL Franchise A. The probability distribution of expected returns for the franchise is as follows:

PROBABILITY	RATE OF RETURN
0.1	–20%
0.2	0%
0.4	7%
0.2	15%
0.1	25%

What is the expected rate of return for an investment in Franchise A? What is the standard deviation?

2. An owner of several sport assets holds the following portfolio:

ASSET	INVESTMENT	BETA
Team A	$100,000,000	0.5
Team B	$100,000,000	1.0
Facility A	$100,000,000	1.5
Total	$300,000,000	

What is the beta of this portfolio?

3. Boggs Sports Holdings has a total investment of $500 million in five companies:

	INVESTMENT (IN MILLIONS)	BETA
Company A	$130	0.3
Company B	$160	1.5
Company C	$70	3.2
Company D	$90	2.0
Company E	$50	1.0
Total	$500	

What is the beta of this portfolio?

4. For the portfolio described in Problem 3, if the risk-free rate is 10% and the market risk premium is 5%, what is Boggs's required rate of return?

5. You have been hired as the manager of a portfolio of ten sport assets that are held in equal dollar amounts. The current beta of the portfolio is 1.9, and the beta of Asset A is 2.1. If Asset A is sold and the proceeds are used to purchase a replacement asset, what beta would the replacement asset have to have in order to lower the portfolio beta to 1.6?

6. The Sports Investment Fund has a total investment of $5 million in the following portfolio:

	INVESTMENT	BETA
Asset A	$900,000	1.2
Asset B	$1,100,000	−0.4
Asset C	$1,000,000	1.5
Asset D	$2,000,000	0.9
Total	$5,000,000	

The market's expected rate of return is 10%, and the risk-free rate is 4%. What is the required rate of return?

7. Following is a distribution of returns:

PROBABILITY	RETURN
0.4	$35
0.5	$24
0.1	−$15

What is the coefficient of variation of the expected dollar return?

Case Analysis

Risk and Team Values

Risk directly affects the values of professional teams. Groppelli and Nikbakht (2018) state that to maximize the value of a firm, managers must focus on increasing the growth rate of cash flows and reducing the risk or uncertainty of those cash flows. One measure of an organization's risk is its credit rating. According to Fitch Ratings (2002), factors affecting the risk of cash flows and, therefore, the credit rating of leagues and teams, include player salary restraints, national television contracts, revenue sharing among member clubs, league influence on team financial matters, debt limits, and the relationship with the players' union.

Exhibit 3.11 compares the average franchise value for the NFL and MLB from 2015 through 2019. The fact that the average value of an NFL franchise is more than 61% greater than that of the average MLB franchise in 2019 is due in part to differing levels of risk.

Fitch Ratings discussed the factors that led to its conclusion that the NFL has the highest credit rating of all leagues. Primarily, the NFL is best able to withstand economic slowdowns that affect sponsorships, naming rights agreements, and the disposable income of fans. Its risk is reduced by lucrative long-term contracts with its media partners, strong relations with the NFL Players Association (NFLPA), and the willingness of team owners to be proactive in working together for the betterment of the league. The teams cooperate on merchandising and licensing revenues and have agreed to the creation of a league-funded loan pool to help individual franchises build new stadiums that will increase local revenues. Further, the league is the most competitively balanced from top to bottom, thanks to its hard salary cap and salary floor. The hard cap controls the largest team expense, reducing the risk of team financial losses and improving the league's creditworthiness. The NFL also limits the debt that a franchise can incur, reducing risk for both the league and its teams.

Fitch Ratings rates the creditworthiness of MLB lower than that of the NFL because MLB is exposed to greater risk. Although revenue sharing has increased under the latest MLB CBA, the league does not have a hard salary cap, and although labor relations have improved through 2019, MLB and the players association have a history of poor relations.

Fitch Ratings notes that as MLB moves its economic model closer to that of the NFL, its risk will decrease and its rating will improve. This can be seen

EXHIBIT 3.11	Average value (in billions) of NFL and MLB franchises from 2015 to 2019.				
	2015	**2016**	**2017**	**2018**	**2019**
NFL	$1.97	$2.34	$2.50	$2.57	$2.86
MLB	$1.20	$1.30	$1.54	$1.65	$1.78
Source: Data compiled from Forbes.com.					

in the narrowing gap between franchise values of the NFL and MLB from 2016 to 2019. During that time frame, MLB values increased at a greater rate than NFL values, as MLB signed a new CBA increasing revenue sharing and had secured more money from its television rights deals and increased the value of Major League Baseball Advanced Media (MLBAM) and the revenues derived from MLBAM. MLB's television rights deals are now worth more than twice what the league was receiving under its previous rights deals. However, after the NFL's new broadcasting deals began, revenues received by each team from media rights increased significantly. This new revenue resulted in NFL team values growing 19% in 2016, while MLB values grew 8%.

The importance of acquiring and securing revenue sources and the impact of doing so on risk and value is evident in an examination of collegiate football teams (see Exhibit 3.12). *Forbes* and *Yahoo* calculated the value of NCAA Division I–FBS teams in its reporting on the revenues of athletic programs. Exhibit 3.12 lists the 20 most valuable football teams in 2019. The average

EXHIBIT 3.12   Valuations of college football teams in 2019 (millions).

UNIVERSITY	CONFERENCE	VALUE
Texas A&M	SEC	$147
Texas	Big XII	$147
Michigan	Big 10	$139
Alabama	SEC	$134
Ohio State	Big 10	$132
Oklahoma	Big XII	$129
Georgia	SEC	$125
Notre Dame	Independent	$120
Florida	SEC	$117
Auburn	SEC	$117
LSU	SEC	$114
Tennessee	SEC	$113
Penn State	Big 10	$104
Oregon	Pac 12	$96
Florida State	ACC	$96
South Carolina	SEC	$95
Arkansas	SEC	$95
USC	Pac 12	$93
Washington	Pac 12	$92
Nebraska	Big 10	$91

Sources: Data compiled from Forbes.com and Yahoo.com (2019).

value of these teams was $114.8 million. The list clearly indicates that teams in conferences with higher cash flows and lower risk or uncertainty of those cash flows are more highly valued than teams in conferences without lucrative long-term media contracts. (In Notre Dame's case, the team itself has secured these contracts.) For example, the SEC has nine of the 20 most valuable teams, according to *Forbes* and *Yahoo*. The league has a lucrative contract to broadcast football games nationally, and revenue from that contract flows back to its member schools. Further, the league launched the SEC Network in partnership with ESPN in August 2014. Notre Dame's contract with NBC provides similar revenues. The Big 10, with four teams listed, created its own television network to generate revenues for member institutions.

A recent history of winning has little impact on a team's value. Texas has struggled for several years but is tied as the most valuable program. Clemson has been one of the most dominant teams in the past four years but is not ranked due to the Atlantic Coast Conference's (ACC) relatively poor national television contract as compared to the SEC and Big 10.

Case Questions

1. What current economic conditions might affect the credit rating of a team or league?
2. Which teams' credit ratings might be most negatively affected during a recession?
3. What must the NFL do to maintain its high credit rating?
4. What can MLB do to improve its credit rating?

References

#20 Arizona Diamondbacks. (2011). *Forbes.com*. Retrieved from www.forbes.com/lists/2011/33/baseball-valuations-11_Arizona-Diamondbacks_337798.html.

Ahles, A., & Schrock, S. (2008, December 3). Arlington refinances much of its debt for Cowboys stadium. *Star-Telegram*. Retrieved from www.star-telegram.com/330/v-print/story/1071095.html.

Anderson, S. (2005, August 20). Penguins pay off nearly all creditors. *Pittsburgh Post-Gazette*. Retrieved from www.post-gazette.com/pg/05232/557229.stm.

Barrabi, T. (2020, June 2). Bankrupt Arena Football League holds auction, will sell off assets. *Fox Business*. Retrieved from www.foxbusiness.com/sports/arena-football-league-online-auction-bankruptcy.

Birger, J. (2009, February 19). Baseball battles the slump. *CNN Money.com*. Retrieved from http://money.cnn.com/2009/02/18/magazines/fortune/birger_baseball.fortune/index.htm.

Brigham, E.F., & Houston, J.F. (2018). *Fundamentals of financial management* (15th ed.). Mason, OH: Cengage Learning.

Brown, M. (2010, March 15). Total yearly MLB attendance 1901 to present. *The Biz of Baseball*. Retrieved from http://bizofbaseball.com/index.php?option=com_content&view=article&id=4190&Itemid=185.

Burnside, S. (2008, July 6). Memo to owners: The cap is what you wanted; make it work. *ESPN.com*. Retrieved from http://sports.espn.go.com/nhl/columns/story?columnist=burnside_scott&id=3475686.

Campbell, K. (2017, July 10). Improving Canadian dollar is very good news for the NHL. *The Hockey News*. Retrieved from https://thehockeynews.com/news/article/improving-canadian-dollar-is-very-good-news-for-the-nhl.

Cillizza, C. (2020, April 28). How, exactly, did the LA Lakers get a 'small business' loan? *CNN Politics*. Retrieved from www.cnn.com/2020/04/28/politics/lakers-ppp-small-business/index.html.

Conrad, M. (2006). *The business of sports: A primer for journalists*. Mahwah, NJ: Lawrence Erlbaum Associates.

Couch, G., & Calloway, B. (2020, June 30). A summer without Lugnuts baseball: How COVID-19 is impacting the club, city, fans and players. *Lansing State Journal*. Retrieved from www.lansingstatejournal.com/story/sports/columnists/graham-couch/2020/06/30/no-minor-league-baseball-summer-covid-19-lugnuts-city-of-lansing/3255760001/.

Cowboys, city council having issues with stadium-financed bonds. (2008, September 3). *Sports Business Daily*. Retrieved from www.sportsbusinessdaily.com/article/123692.

Cowboys refinance $435m worth of debt for new $1.1b stadium. (2008, December 5). *Sports Business Daily*. Retrieved from www.sportsbusinessdaily.com/article/126048.

Department of Economic and Social Affairs. (2020, May 15). *The impact of COVID-19 on sport, physical activity and well-being and its effects on social development*. New York: United Nations.

Evans, P. (2020, July 8). Sports get PPP assist. *Front Office Sports*. Retrieved from https://frontofficesports.com/paycheck-protection-program-in-sports/.

Fisher, E. (2008, July 7). Cheap seats. *Sports Business Journal*. Retrieved from www.sportsbusinessjournal.com/article/59474.

Fitch Ratings. (2002, September 16). *Economics of professional sports: Rating sports transactions*. New York: Author.

Forbes.com. (2019). College football's most valuable teams. Data compiled from www.forbes.com/sites/chrissmith/2019/09/12/college-football-most-valuable-clemson-texas-am/#775a83bda2e7.

Foster, G., Greyser, S.A., & Walsh, B. (2005). *The business of sports*. New York: South-Western College Publishers.

Front office: Executive staff. (2020). *NHL.com*. Retrieved from http://penguins.nhl.com/club/page.htm?id=56529.

Gibson, O. (2009, July 17). Tax burden will end Premier League's domination. *The Guardian*. Retrieved from www.theguardian.com/football/2009/jul/17/deloitte-premier-league-la-liga-taxes.

Groppelli, A.A., & Nikbakht, E. (2018). *Finance* (7th ed.). Hauppauge, NY: Barron's Educational Series.

Holdman, J., & Adcox, S. (2020, July 11). SC law firms, churches, builders, sports teams received major federal COVID-19 lifelines. *Post and Courier*. Retrieved from www.postandcourier.com/business/sc-law-firms-churches-builders-sports-teams-received-major-federal-covid-19-lifelines/article_fecdff82-co5e-11ea-86d6-b76e5e8ddco8.html.

Ingle, S. (2020, May 5). British sport faces devastating £700m black hole from Covid-19 pandemic. *The Guardian*. Retrieved from www.theguardian.com/sport/2020/may/05/british-sport-devastating-700m-black-hole-covid-19-pandemic.

Kaplan, D. (2013, April 8). MLB will expand loan pool. *Sports Business Journal*. Retrieved from www.sportsbusinessdaily.com/Journal/Issues/2013/04/08/Finance/MLB-loan-pool.aspx.

Kaplan, D. (2017, September 4). NFL ups loan-pool financing to $2.7B. *Sports Business Journal*. Retrieved from www.sportsbusinessdaily.com/Journal/Issues/2017/09/04/Leagues-and-Governing-Bodies/NFL-finance.aspx.

Kaplan, D., & Lombardo, J. (2009, May 11–17). $100M loan for arena is pure magic. *Sports Business Journal*, 22(4), 1, 27.

Kaplan, D., & Lombardo, J. (2017, January 30). Strong outlook cuts borrowing cost for NBA. *Sports Business Journal*. Retrieved from www.sportsbusinessdaily.com/Journal/Issues/2017/01/30/Leagues-and-Governing-Bodies/NBA-borrowing.aspx.

Kaplan, D., & Thomas, I. (2016, January 25). NHL welcomes Canadian teams to loan pool. *Sports Business Daily.* Retrieved from www.sportsbusinessdaily.com/Journal/ Issues/2016/01/25/Leagues-and-Governing-Bodies/NHL-loan-pool.aspx.

Keh, A., & Das, A. (2020, July 2). Federal loan saved a soccer season nearly lost to the pandemic. *The New York Times.* Retrieved from www.nytimes.com/2020/07/02/ sports/soccer/nwsl-ppp-loan.html.

Key dates. (2013, September 9). *Arenafootball.com.* Retrieved from www.arenafootball. com/history/key-dates.html.

King, T. (2020, June 26). Japanese sport sets out on the long road back. *SportBusiness.* Retrieved from www.sportbusiness.com/2020/06/japanese-sport-sets-out-on-the-long-road-back/.

Last, J.V. (2009, January 30). Are pro sports too big to fail? *The Wall Street Journal,* p. W11.

Lefton, T., & Mickle, T. (2009, March 2). Beaten-up banks. *Sports Business Journal.* Retrieved from www.sportsbusinessjournal.com/article/61682.

The List. (2019). *Forbes.com.* Retrieved from www.forbes.com/nhl-valuations/list/#tab: overall.

Lombardo, J., & Kaplan, D. (2011, January 11). NBA increases league loan pool to $2.3B. *Sports Business Journal.* Retrieved from www.sportsbusinessdaily.com/Journal/ Issues/2011/01/20110117/Leagues-and-Governing-Bodies/NBA-loan-pool.aspx.

McCormick, B., & Broughton, D. (2020, July 13). $665M in PPP loans saves 36K jobs. *Sports Business Journal.* Retrieved from www.sportsbusinessdaily.com/Journal/ Issues/2020/07/13/Leagues-and-Governing-Bodies/PPP.aspx.

Nelson, A. (2020, June 5). Tottenham secures £175m Bank of England loan to combat Covid-19 impact. *Sport Business.* Retrieved from www.sportbusiness.com/news/ tottenham-secures-175m-bank-of-england-loan-to-combat-covid-19-impact/.

Newton, D. (2018, July 8). Sale of Panthers franchise to David Tepper finalized. *ESPN. com.* Retrieved from www.espn.com/nfl/story/_/id/24049997/sale-panthers-david-tepper-finalized.

NFL Giants redeeming $100m in auction-rate bonds for stadium. (2008, April 16). *Sports Business Daily.* Retrieved from www.sportsbusinessdaily.com/article/120079.

NHL owners growing wary of league's revenue-sharing system. (2008, October 13). *Sports Business Daily.* Retrieved from www.sportsbusinessdaily.com/article/124637.

NHL salary cap ceiling rises to $56.7m for 08–09 season. (2008, June 27). *Sports Business Daily.* Retrieved from www.sportsbusinessdaily.com/article/121958.

NHL salary cap officially set at $81.5 million for 2019–20. (2019, June 22). *Sportsnet.ca.* Retrieved from www.sportsnet.ca/hockey/nhl/nhl-salary-cap-officially-set-81-5-million-2019-20/.

NZ gives sports sector $157 million boost to get through COVID-19. (2020, May 16). *Reuters.* Retrieved from www.reuters.com/article/us-health-coronavirus-sport-newzealand/nz-gives-sports-sector-157-.

Rovell, D. (2009, August 7). Diamondbacks to pay Gilkey until 2017. *CNBC.* Retrieved from www.cnbc.com/id/32333349.

Sandomir, R. (1999, September 2). Hockey: Lemieux is finally the emperor of the Penguins. *The New York Times.* Retrieved from www.nytimes.com/1999/09/02/sports/hockey-lemieux-is-finally-the-emperor-of-the-penguins.html.

Schnitzler, P. (2008, February 25). State debt tactics backfire. *Indianapolis Business Journal.* Retrieved from www.ibj.com/html/detail_page.asp?content=11607.

Schrock, S. (2008, November 11). New game plan for refinancing. *Star-Telegram.* Retrieved from www.star-telegram.com/stadium/story/1041607.html.

Sielski, M. (2010, July 1). There's no accounting for this. *The Wall Street Journal.* Retrieved from http://online.wsj.com/news/articles/SB10001424052748703426004575339013108198050.

Struggling economy likely to pose problems for sports. (2008, October 6). *Sports Business Daily.* Retrieved from www.sportsbusinessdaily.com/article/124438.

Sudden vanishing of sports due to coronavirus will cost at least $12 billion, analysis says. (2020, May 1). *ESPN.com*. Retrieved from www.espn.com/espn/otl/story/_/id/29110487/sudden-vanishing-sports-due-coronavirus-cost-least-12-billion-analysis-says.

Tilley, M. (2020, June 8). U.S. enters recession, ending longest economic expansion in U.S. history. *Talkbusiness.net*. Retrieved from https://talkbusiness.net/2020/06/nber-u-s-enters-recession-ending-longest-economic-expansion-in-u-s-history/.

Winegardner, M. (2012, May 3). Paying it forward. *ESPN the Magazine*. Retrieved from http://espn.go.com/mlb/story/_/id/7879021/mlb-new-york-mets-pay-bobby-bonilla-millions-years-come-espn-magaz.

Yahoo.com. (2019). College football's 25 most valuable teams. Data compiled from www.yahoo.com/news/college-football-25-most-valuable-182024139.html.

Yahoo! Finance. (2020). Retrieved from http://finance.yahoo.com.

■ ■ ■ ■

CHAPTER 4

Time Value of Money

Mark S. Nagel

KEY CONCEPTS

annuity	nominal value
compound interest	perpetuity
consumer price index (CPI)	present value (PV)
default	real value
discount rate	simple interest
future value (FV)	time value of money

INTRODUCTION

Imagine a sports agent asking clients if they would rather have a payment of $100,000, $102,000, $110,000, or $120,000. The obvious choice is to take the $120,000. But if the agent were to ask a client if he wanted $100,000 immediately, $102,000 to be paid one year from now, $110,000 in 18 months, or $120,000 in three years, which should the athlete choose? The choice can be made properly only with an understanding of the yearly, monthly, or even daily changes in the purchasing power of money—known as the **time value of money**. A variety of financial and economic concepts—including inflation, risk, future value of money and annuities, liquidity, present value of money and annuities, and interim compounding—must be understood before the time value of money can be applied to real-world sport management problems. Each of these concepts affects the answer to questions such as the one posed at the beginning of this paragraph.

INFLATION

If someone were to travel back in time to 1955, she would experience instant sticker shock. Prices for nearly all items would be lower—just ask someone 30 years older than you about what it used to cost to buy things. A dollar could purchase more goods or services in the 1960s than in the 2020s. This loss of purchasing power, or **real value**, is the result of inflation. Prices tend to increase over time, and the value of money tends to decrease, even though the **nominal value**, or face value, of money remains the same.

Inflation Rate

The inflation rate affects all financial decisions, particularly those related to long-term investments. Hence, financial managers are wise to understand and monitor the inflation rate. Organizations that invest their money for future purchases must ensure that they are receiving interest that at least matches the rate of inflation, or the real value of their investment will decrease. Although the nominal value of a dollar has remained the same over the past 25 years, the real value of that dollar has dramatically decreased; in other words, the products or services that that dollar can purchase have diminished.

To understand the effect of inflation, consider a recreation center that places $10,000 into a checking account and receives no interest. The rate of inflation will gradually erode the value of the money. For instance, if the annual rate of inflation is 2%, the real value of the $10,000 will decrease by 2% over the year, even though the account experiences no loss in nominal value (the account balance remains the same). Conversely, if the recreation center saves $10,000 in a bank account for one year and receives 3% interest, and the rate of inflation is 2%, the realized change in purchasing power can be calculated as follows:

$$\$10,000 \times .03 = \$300 (\text{interest received})$$

$$\$10,000 \times .02 = \$200 (\text{purchasing power lost})$$

$$\text{real change in value} = \text{interest received} - \text{purchasing power lost}$$

$$= \$300 - 200$$

$$= \$100$$

Although the organization now has $10,300 in its account, the ability to purchase products has increased by $100. The recreation center may wish to explore investments that receive higher returns relative to inflation.

Consumer Price Index

Economists compute the inflation rate by studying changes in the **consumer price index (CPI)**. The CPI is the result of a calculation based on the prices of goods and services in more than 200 categories reflecting the current lifestyle of the typical American consumer, to determine the overall change in real prices during a period (Bureau of Labor Statistics, n.d.). The Bureau of Labor Statistics (BLS), which is the government agency responsible for calculating the CPI, allocates the 200-plus smaller categories into eight larger categories: (1) food and beverages, (2) housing, (3) clothing, (4) transportation, (5) medical care, (6) recreation, (7) education and communication, and (8) other; and estimates the percentage of spending for each category for a typical US household. The CPI helps consumers understand the difference between the real value and nominal value of money and how the purchasing power of their money is changing. The nominal amount of money needed to purchase products or services typically increases over time, but economists and financial managers are interested in the real value of dollars—the purchasing power those dollars retain.

The Bureau of Labor Statistics tracks the CPI and provides monthly charts for various products and services, as well as information for various cities and regions throughout the country (visit www.bls.gov/cpi/home.htm#tables). The BLS website also provides a "CPI Inflation Calculator" (http://data.bls. gov/cgi-bin/cpicalc.pl) that indicates the change in the value of money over a specified period. For instance, by using the calculator, one can quickly determine that $100 in 1989 had the same buying power as $190.81 had in 2015. In March 2009, in the midst of a significant economic slowdown, the CPI *decreased* over a 12-month period, for the first time since 1955 (Zigler, 2009). Furthermore, from 2009 to 2015 the CPI increased no more than 3% per year, indicating a continuing low rate of inflation for the goods and services that comprise the CPI. Interestingly, the cost of energy has decreased from 2017 to 2019 as the United States has rapidly increased the production of a variety of energy sources.

In addition to tracking the CPI, financial managers need to understand that individual items or services may experience inflation-related changes that deviate from the overall rate. Financial managers must understand the forces working within their industries, because even if the overall inflation rate remains relatively stable, an increase in prices for certain items—for example, travel or sporting equipment—could have a major negative impact on their organization.

Despite tremendous growth in the popularity of Major League Baseball from 1950 to 1990, ticket prices actually decreased in real terms. Andrew Zimbalist (1992) noted that if 1950 MLB ticket prices were adjusted for inflation, they would average $8.74, whereas the average cost of an MLB ticket in 1990 was $7.95. However, from 1991 to 2001, the average ticket price increased by 120%, while the CPI increased only 30% (Corwin, 2001). MLB tickets have continued to increase in price since 2001, which has caused some observers to question whether teams may be pricing out many of their core customers, as well as future generations of fans (Herbert, 2009).

SIDEBAR 4.A   Present and Past Prices

Are prices always higher in the present than in the past? In other words, does purchasing power always decrease over time? When prices are adjusted for inflation, one of the fastest-growing products or services over the last 30 years is college tuition. From 1986 to 2012 the overall inflation rate increased 115.06%, but college tuition and fees increased *498.31%* (Wadsworth, 2012)! That means over that time it became nearly five times as expensive to attend college. College tuition continues to increase at a much higher rate than the general rate of inflation. Projections indicate that college tuition is likely to continue to increase dramatically, with one projection estimating that from 2015 to 2033 the average tuition cost for a private university will increase from $134,600 to $323,900 ("Tutorial— the real cost of higher education," n.d.). Exhibit 4.1 indicates the various

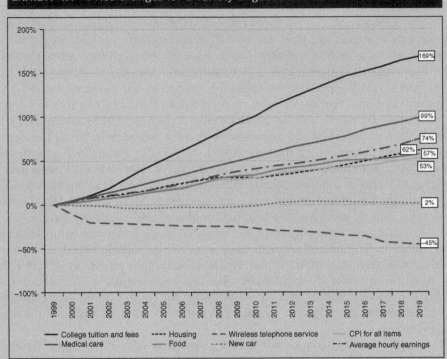

EXHIBIT 4.1   Price changes for a variety of goods and services 1999–2019.

change in "real" prices that have occurred across a number of different products and services. While the "real" cost of wireless telephone service has decreased dramatically, the cost of attending college has risen at a much faster rate than medical care, housing, food, and the overall CPI for all tracked items. As noted by economist Mark Perry, the "greater the degree of government involvement in the provision of a good or service the greater the price increases over time" (2019, para. 11). The huge increases in college tuition and the cost of textbooks have resulted in students' relying heavily on loans to attend college, with roughly 70% of American students using loans to finance their college education. In 2019, roughly 45 million Americans owed $1.6 trillion in student loans (Fields, 2019).

Now let's consider what has happened to the price of gasoline. If you ask anyone who was alive during the 1970s when there was a serious gas crisis and actual shortages occurred, they can tell you that high gasoline prices can have a massive negative impact upon the overall economy and the morale of its citizens. Certainly, gasoline is more expensive in nominal terms now than it was in the past. However, we must consider the rate of inflation to determine whether the purchasing power for gas has increased, decreased, or remained relatively unchanged for consumers.

Changes in gasoline prices typically result in extensive media attention and complaints from consumers. Exhibit 4.2 shows how the

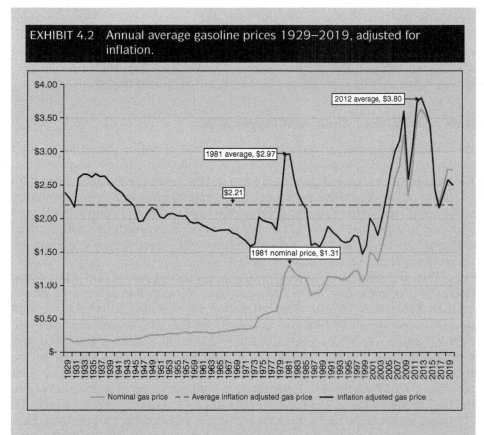

EXHIBIT 4.2   Annual average gasoline prices 1929–2019, adjusted for inflation.

cost of gasoline, adjusted for inflation, changed from 1929 to 2019. During World War II gasoline was expensive due to shortages, as most of the country's gasoline supply was used for military purposes. From 1945 to 1970, the "real" price of gasoline steadily decreased. However, during the late 1970s, unrest in the Middle East and economic conditions in the United States resulted in a large increase in prices. In the first part of the 21st century gasoline prices encountered dramatic increases and decreases: gasoline reached near record highs in 2008, dropped dramatically by 2010, increased to near-record levels again in 2012, and began to fall precipitously again in 2013. Interestingly, from 2013 to 2017, gasoline prices dropped considerably as the United States discovered new sources of oil and had periods where it became a net exporter of oil and other refined fuels (Olson, 2018). Partially in reaction to this additional worldwide supply, a few other countries altered their oil production to affect the price. While the typical consumer only sees the "sticker price" for oil and other products, only by adjusting nominal price to inflation can one see exactly how much a product really costs the consumer.

RISK

Like inflation, risk—uncertainty about the future and future returns—may also affect the value of money. Risk often leads to financial losses. It is much harder to predict what will happen in the sport industry in five years than in five days. For this reason, most sport managers are reluctant to invest cash for a long period of time unless the expected payoff from the investment is significant. Typically, financial managers contemplate the risk versus the reward of an investment before making any financial decision, but they are especially particular when making investments that will extend far into the future.

Deferred Salaries: Team and Player Risk

With deferred salaries, players and teams try to optimize the value of their money over time. A team might contemplate deferring players' salaries when it needs additional cash in the short term to sign new players, attract or retain coaching or administrative personnel, make capital improvements, or enhance some other facet of the operation. When the team defers a portion of a player's contract, it hopes that retaining the money for other expenditures will result in enhanced revenues, and that those revenues will exceed future expenditures when the deferred salaries must be paid.

The Arizona Diamondbacks made a successful run at the 2001 World Series by assuming long-term financial risks through the deferral of player salaries. Prominent players—Randy Johnson, Steve Finley, Curt Schilling, and others—were signed to lucrative contracts for the 2001 season that deferred over $16 million to future years (on top of $37 million that the team had previously deferred for the 1998 through 2000 seasons) (Rovell, 2001). In the short term, deferring salaries helped the Diamondbacks field a team that won the 2001 World Series. Unfortunately, anticipated revenue increases from the highly successful season did not materialize. During the years following the 2001 season, the Diamondbacks were not able to retain many players from their championship team because the commitments to deferred salaries drained the team's cash reserves. The team was forced to borrow money to pay the deferred salaries coming due, and veteran players who left the team via free agency or for retirement were often replaced with rookies and other less experienced and, often, less skilled players. Though the new players did not cost the team nearly as much money to employ, the team's fortunes on the field dramatically decreased. By 2004, the team had fallen to a Major League worst 51–111. It was not until 2007 that the Diamondbacks recovered sufficiently to achieve a winning record. As stated in Chapter 3, at the start of the 2009 season the team still owed $58 million in deferred salaries, most of it resulting from player contracts signed in the early 2000s (Birger, 2009).

For players, deferred salary is also a risk. The future payments owed to players are valuable only if the team remains financially viable and able to pay. Deferred money becomes worthless if the organization defaults on (fails to fulfill) its obligations. A default could result from the organization's ceasing operations or entering certain types of bankruptcy. In 1998 when the Pittsburgh Penguins could not pay $35 million in deferred salary owed to Mario Lemieux, he became the primary owner and assumed control of the team (Hoffman, 1998). Although this situation was certainly unusual, Lemieux's case caused alarm for numerous players who were owed deferred salaries. For many players, deferred salaries are their safety net—money to be used for retirement. The potential of losing that money is a risk that the player and his or her agent must consider when negotiating deferred compensation. When the NHL's Phoenix Coyotes (now the Arizona Coyotes) declared bankruptcy in 2009, concern arose that deferred salaries might not be paid once the bankruptcy case was concluded ("Q&A part 2," 2009). Fortunately, the league was able to arrange a sale, and the franchise continued normal financial operations. In professional leagues, if the financial survival of the league is in serious doubt, players should exercise great caution in accepting deferred salary payments.

Even long-time and iconic professional sport franchises can experience financial difficulty. Under owner Frank McCourt, the Los Angeles Dodgers were financially mismanaged to the point that the team was unable to make payroll for deferred salaries and current employees in May 2011 ("Los Angeles Dodgers lack cash," 2011). After watching one of Major League Baseball's most storied franchises become financially insolvent, commissioner Bud Selig took control of the team and mandated that all financial transactions by the club be approved by Tom Schieffer, MLB's appointed advisor. In 2012, MLB brokered the sale of the Dodgers from McCourt to an investment group headed by Mark Walter of Guggenheim Partners for $2 billion (Markazi, 2012).

SIDEBAR 4.B   Bernie Madoff Scandal nearly Derails the New York Mets

In 2009, disgraced financier Bernie Madoff was convicted of 11 federal felonies in connection with his ongoing operation of a Ponzi scheme (see Sidebar 3.A in Chapter 3 for additional information). One of Madoff's long-time investors and a close friend was New York Mets owner Fred Wilpon, who consistently enjoyed an 18% return on his investments with Madoff in the 1980s and 1990s. Once the Madoff scandal began to unravel, it became apparent that much of Wilpon's fortune, and some of the Mets' money utilized for operating expenses, had been invested with Madoff (Winegardner, 2012). The Mets, typically one of the highest-spending teams in MLB, slashed their payroll to approximately $93 million in 2012, after it had been over $133 million in 2011 (Rubin, 2012). The team had to borrow money from MLB to meet their financial obligations in 2011 (Winegardner, 2012).

Policies on Deferred Salaries

The deferral of salaries is certainly not a new phenomenon in sport finance. During the early 1970s, teams in the American Basketball Association (ABA) and the NBA battled to acquire the services of players. To attract and retain players, the ABA instituted the "Dolgoff Plan" (Pluto, 1990): teams in the ABA would offer multimillion-dollar contracts to potential players but would defer a large portion of each contract. To help the potential player and the player's agent feel secure that the future payments would be made, the team often invested money for the player's deferred salary in an annuity (a fixed future payment plan) with a prominent corporation. Although the NBA criticized the ABA's plan, teams in the ABA were able to attract enough quality players that *all* professional basketball players' salaries dramatically increased, and eventually, in

1976, the leagues merged (Pluto, 1990). Although some of the deferred money was never paid out, in some cases former ABA players received money long after the ABA had merged with the NBA. Examples include current basketball commentator Len Elmore, whose deferred compensation included $80,000 each year for 1981 to 1984 plus $105,000 for 1985. Former ABA player and NBA coach Dan Issel received semimonthly deferred payments beginning in 1974 and continuing until 1983; he received an additional $12,000 per year from 1989 to 1999 (Pluto, 1990).

Until recently, the NFL, NBA, and NHL had few contracts with deferred compensation, though MLB has for years had many players who defer some of their money. In 2013, there was only one NHL player with deferred money and a small number in the NFL and NBA (Dave, 2013). It appears that the number of players receiving deferred compensation in the NBA, NFL, and NHL has grown slightly over the past seven years and has become a more important component of negotiated collective bargaining agreements. Conversely, in 2018, Mets fan Michael Mayer tweeted a list of over 25 MLB players who had a deferred compensation plan (Crawford, 2018). Some of the major North American professional sport leagues have attempted to address the risks of deferred salaries.

- MLB: Teams must show that deferred money is fully funded within two years of the associated playing season.
- NFL: The team must place deferred payments in a league fund for administration and future disbursement. In most cases, deferred money cannot exceed 50% of the first $2 million of the yearly contract and 75% of the yearly salary exceeding $2 million.
- NBA: Only 25% of a total contract value may be deferred.
- The NHL does not restrict teams regarding deferred payments. ("CBA Breakdown," n.d.; "NFL CBA Series: Rovell, 2001; Deferred Compensation," 2013; Tyler, 2017.)

The Challenge of Multi-Year Contracts

Multi-year contracts present an interesting challenge for teams in Major League Baseball, the National Basketball Association, and the National Hockey League, as those contracts are typically guaranteed to the players regardless of their future ability. In teams' fight to obtain or retain prominent players, longer-term contracts are an important recruiting and retention tool. The team, of course, must attempt to sign longer-term contracts only with players who are likely to remain motivated and productive in the future. Players who sign long-term guaranteed contracts and then become injured or perform poorly will limit their teams' future financial options.

The purchasing power of future compensation is difficult to calculate when contracts extend for long periods of time. The team must predict not only the player's future performance ability but also the appropriate compensation. For players and their agents, future compensation must account not only for performance but also for inflation. For example, MLB All-Star outfielder Johnny Damon's compensation for each of the 2006 through 2009 seasons was $13 million, meaning that even with minimal inflation during that time, Damon saw a yearly decrease in the purchasing power of his salary ("*USA Today* salaries databases," 2009). Similarly, in the NBA, Atlanta Hawks forward Al Horford's contract mandated that he be paid exactly $12 million in each of the 2013/2014, 2014/2015, and 2015/2016 seasons ("Salaries," n.d.). With his contract paying the same amount each year, Horford's purchasing power decreased each year as a result of inflation. Interestingly, when Horford signed a contract in 2019 with the Philadelphia 76ers, his compensation *decreased* each year by $500,000 from $28,000,000 million in the 2019–2020 season to $26,500,000 in the 2022–2023 season ("Al Horford," n.d.). In MLB, All-Star Manny Machado signed one of the richest contracts in sports history with the San Diego Padres in 2019, but his salary for the 2020–2028 seasons would be exactly $30,000,000 ("Manny Machado," n.d.). Even with the eroding of his purchasing power during his employment, he will likely still have plenty of money to maintain a high standard of living.

When the Cleveland Browns drafted wide receiver Braylon Edwards in 2005, he signed a contract that included a $6.5 million signing bonus. Lamont Smith, Edwards's agent, remarked, "It was a priority for us ... because we believe in the time value of money. When you wait for your money, you are providing the team with an interest-free loan" (Mullen, 2005, para. 24). For star NFL players, the signing bonus not only ensures that much of their contract money is guaranteed but also assures them that inflation will not erode the purchasing power of their compensation. The majority of NFL players must play each week with the risk that injury or poor performance may lead to termination of their (non-guaranteed) contracts.

The use of long-term contracts to circumvent salary cap rules (see Chapter 15) was a significant component of the National Hockey League's 2013 CBA. In an effort to circumvent the cap, numerous teams had signed players to contracts exceeding ten years and $80 million. In some cases, players were signed to contracts that extended payments into their late thirties and early forties, long after their ability as effective players would have waned. Under the new CBA, some of these contracts would be penalized at a much tougher rate than under the old CBA.

FUTURE VALUE

To determine the costs and benefits of financial decisions such as deferring salaries, financial managers must understand and be able to compute the **future value (FV)** of a payment—the value of that payment at a certain date in the future, which we determine by calculating the change in value of money when an interest rate is applied over the intervening period of time. Initial computations of future value provide a nominal value of money; financial managers must then assess the expected rate of inflation and, potentially, provide an estimate of risk to determine the real value of money after time. The question posed at the opening of this chapter dealt with a $100,000, $102,000, $110,000, or $120,000 payment. In a situation like this, a financial manager or agent can appropriately advise a client which payment to take only by understanding the present and future value of a dollar.

Suppose a sport organization invests $100 in a savings bond that pays 5% interest annually for five years. To determine what the value of the investment will be after one year, we perform a simple calculation:

$$\text{original investment} + \text{interest} = \text{future value}$$

$$\$100 + (5\%)(\$100) = \$105$$

To determine the value beyond one year, we must distinguish between simple and compound interest. **Simple interest** is calculated only on principal. After year 1, under simple interest the investment of $100 would continue to grow at a rate of $5 per year, for a total value of $125 after five years. **Compound interest**, on the other hand, is calculated on principal and on the interest generated by that principal. Thus, determining the value of an investment under compound interest requires the following formula:

$$FV = PV(1+i)^n$$

where FV = future value
  PV = the present value of the initial investment (principal)
   i = rate of interest per period
   n = number of periods

As an example, again consider the sport organization that invests in a savings bond. With compound interest, the calculation is as follows:

$$FV = 100 \times (1.05)^5$$

$$= 100 \times (1.05 \times 1.05 \times 1.05 \times 1.05 \times 1.05)$$

$$= 100 \times 1.2763$$

$$= 127.63$$

Fortunately, it is not necessary to memorize this formula; with a table we can look up values rather than calculate them (see Table A.1 in the Appendix). The future value table gives a future value interest factor (FVIF). To find the FVIF, determine the number of periods (in this example the periods are expressed in years) of the investment. Find this row in the table, and then move across to the column for the interest rate. The number in this cell is the FVIF. Now, simply multiply the FVIF by the initial investment.

For an investment at 5% interest for five years, the FVIF is 1.2763. Multiplying this factor by $100 (the initial investment) yields $127.63. Notice that this value is higher than the $125 that would be received under simple interest. To see a dramatic difference in simple versus compound interest, change the time period from five to 20 years and the amount invested to $100,000. With simple interest, the future value is $100,000 + (20 [years] ×5,000 [simple interest]) = $200,000. With compound interest, the future value is $100,000 × 2.6533 = $265,330. This example illustrates why financial managers prefer to receive compound interest on their investments and why Albert Einstein is believed to have remarked that the most powerful force in the universe is compound interest.

Annuities and Perpetuities

Often, the value of an investment is paid out or received not in one lump sum but over time in multiple payments or receipts. Any series of equal payments or receipts made at regular intervals is termed an **annuity**. Annuity payments may occur annually, quarterly, monthly, or at any other regular interval. Examples of annuities include regularly scheduled mortgage payments, individual retirement account (IRA) contributions, loan payments, and pension payments. An annuity has a scheduled end point. If the payments or receipts were to continue forever, this would be considered a **perpetuity**. Perpetuities are rarely established, for obvious reasons. Forever is certainly a long time.

Future Value of an Annuity

The amazing financial power of a regularly funded annuity was noted by Benjamin Franklin when he once explained, "money makes money. And that money makes more money." A sport manager might wish to determine the future value of an investment that is funded on a regularly scheduled basis (an annuity). For instance, a sport team might need to determine how much money it would have after investing $1,000 per year for five years at 5% interest. The financial manager would use the following formula:

$$\text{FVA} = \text{PMT}\left(\frac{(1+i)^n - 1}{i}\right)$$

where FVA = future value of an annuity
PMT = payment
i = rate of interest per period
n = number of periods

For the example given above, the calculation would proceed as follows:

$$\text{FV} = 1,000\left(\frac{(1.05)^5 - 1}{0.05}\right)$$

$$= 1,000\left(\frac{(1.05 \times 1.05 \times 1.05 \times 1.05 \times 1.05) - 1}{0.05}\right)$$

$$= 1,000\left(\frac{1.2763 - 1}{0.05}\right)$$

$$= 1,000\left(\frac{0.2763}{0.05}\right)$$

$$= 1,000(5.5256)$$

$$= \$5,525.60$$

Fortunately, we can use a table (see Table A.2 in the Appendix) to simplify the above equation to $FV_a = PMT \times FVIFA$, where FVIFA is the future value interest factor of an annuity, from the table.

SIDEBAR 4.C   The Greatest Deal in Sports?

The idea of guaranteeing anyone money forever would cause most sport organizations to cringe. But the NBA has paid three people who have no connection to the league hundreds of millions of dollars in compensation—simply because of a deal consummated many years ago. When the NBA and ABA were discussing a merger in 1976, the NBA agreed to absorb four teams: the New York (now Brooklyn) Nets, Denver Nuggets, San Antonio Spurs, and Indiana Pacers. In addition, the owner of the Kentucky Colonels was paid $3 million to fold the team, leaving the Spirits of St. Louis as the remaining ABA team. Although the owners of the Spirits, Ozzie and Danny Silna, and their lawyer, Don Schupak, initially desired to enter the NBA, when it became apparent the NBA did not want to merge their team, they negotiated one of the greatest (for them) sport finance deals in history (Pluto, 1990; Rovell, 2002). The Spirits' owners received $2.2 million in cash plus 1/7 of a share of national television money from each of the four merged ABA teams—in perpetuity. Essentially, the Spirits' owners were guaranteed to receive 4/7 of the annual television share for an NBA team, *forever*. At the time, the value of the television contracts was minimal, but during the 1980s the Spirits' owners received roughly $8 million in television revenue. From 1990 through 1998 they received just under $41 million, and from 1998 through 2002 they received $50 million (Rovell, 2002). Despite protests, lawsuits, and buyout attempts, the Spirits' owners (who currently run an embroidery business) have retained their share of the television money. By 2012, the Spirits' owners had collected over $255 million, and at no time did they have to pay for rising salaries of players or other expenses incurred through ownership (Sandomir, 2012).

Despite the contract language guaranteeing the former owners of the Spirits of St. Louis television money in perpetuity, in 2014 the NBA announced a $500 million buyout of the majority share of the Spirits' television rights (Mandell, 2014). As part of the buyout the Silnas agreed to end their litigation with the NBA regarding new television revenue streams that have emerged in the digital environment. In addition, the deal called for an option for the NBA to purchase the remaining shares of the Spirits' television rights in the future. Many observers wondered why the Silnas would agree to end a perpetual contract that had withstood previous NBA attempts to eliminate it or buy it out. Though $500 million is certainly a significant sum, the future potential for the Silnas and their heirs would likely have exceeded billions of dollars within the next ten years. However, reports emerged that the Silnas had lost a considerable sum of money by investing with Bernie Madoff, which might have influenced their desire for a short-term infusion of cash from the settlement.

To find the FVIFA, determine the number of periods of the investment. Find this row in the table and then move across to the column for the interest rate. This is the FVIFA. Simply multiply the FVIFA by the investment amount per period. For $1,000 invested per year at 5% interest for five years, the FVIFA is 5.5256, yielding a future value of $1,000 × 5.5256 = $5,525.60.

The following examples demonstrating the use of the FVIFA show the importance of time and persistence in the creation of wealth. First, suppose two sport managers open retirement accounts and commit to invest $3,000 each year, earning 7% interest, until they retire. The first sport manager starts investing at age 25 and continues until age 65. The second investor starts at age 35 and invests until age 65. When the investors reach age 65, the first will have accumulated over 40 years of time. Her investment will have an FVIFA of 199.64. Multiplied by $3,000, this yields a future value of $598,920. The second investor will have accumulated over 30 years of time, for an FVIFA of 94.461. His future value will be $283,383. The total difference from the additional ten years of investment, with only $30,000 in cash paid in, is $315,537. Any IRA holder can use the Future Value of an Annuity table to determine how much money he or she will have upon retirement (in nominal terms), given an expected rate of return and yearly investment.

In addition to the impact of time, interest rate changes (even small ones) can have a dramatic effect on the yield of an investment. In the preceding example, the first person invested for 40 years at 7% interest, yielding $598,920. If the interest rate increased from 7% to 8%, the new FVIFA would be 259.06, and the yield would be $3,000 × 259.06 = $777,180—an increase of $178,260. If the interest rate increased to 9% per year, the overall yield would be $3,000 × 337.88 = $1,013,640. The change in an interest rate may appear small, but it can result in tremendous changes in the yield. Readers should note the importance of investigating the effect that a minor change in interest rate can have on the yield of an investment. If the interest rate increases from 7% to 8%, this is a 14% increase [(8 − 7)/7 = 14%]. An interest rate change from 7% to 10% is a percentage increase of 43% [(10 − 7)/7 = 43%]. When the Federal Reserve changes interest rates, dramatic changes in loans, investments, and other financial activities may result (see Chapter 5). Sport managers are wise to anticipate interest rate changes and plan financial activities with future rates in mind.

In some cases, the future value of an annuity may have payments that increase. This is known as a growing annuity. For instance, let's assume that an agent arranges for one of her players to contribute money to an annuity over a four-year period so that he is prepared for retirement. The agent determines that the player should contribute $2,000 in the first year and then have the contribution increase by 2% each year. The agent expects that the investment vehicle chosen will yield an interest rate of 8% per year. To determine how much money the player will have at the end of the four years, the following formula is utilized.

FUTURE VALUE OF A GROWING ANNUITY

$$FVA = PMT\left(\frac{(1+i)^n - (1+g)^n}{i-g}\right)$$

where FVA = future value of an annuity
PMT = payment
i = rate of interest per period
n = number of periods
g = growth rate

$$FV = 2,000 \left(\frac{(1+.08)^4 - (1+.02)^4}{0.08 - 0.02} \right)$$

$$= 2,000 \left(\frac{(1.36) - (1.08)}{0.06} \right)$$

$$= 2,000 \left(\frac{.28}{.06} \right)$$

$$= 2,000(4.67)$$

$$= \$9,340.00$$

Note: In the aforementioned equation and all subsequent equations for the rest of the chapter, the answers were derived by rounding to two decimal places in order to show the mechanics of computation. Results can vary depending on decimal places utilized. When computed in the sport business world, computers (which may round to four or even five decimal places) will be utilized and results can vary.

At the end of the investment period, the growing annuity will have a value of $9,340.00. Several considerations should be made when evaluating growing annuities. Of importance is underestimating the rate of potential interest. If there are changes or surprises in the investments' performance, the investor should want the expected returns to be under the reality. In addition, the investor needs to make sure that the rate of increase is sustained on a yearly basis. In many cases, employment contracts mandate that the employee contribute a certain percentage of their salary into a retirement account. If the employee has a set yearly increase in salary (e.g. 3%), the corresponding investment contributions will automatically increase as the base salary increases.

Once the future value of a single payment or of an annuity is determined, the financial manager can compare this value with the expected rate of inflation to determine the real change in value. In addition to inflation, risk levels associated with different potential interest rates may affect the decision to invest in a particular project, as discussed in Chapter 3. In some financial decisions, a lower potential return may be acceptable for an investment with lower risk. In all cases, the organization or individual is working to maximize the real value of money.

Liquidity

An understanding of inflation, a tolerance for risk, and the computation of future value are all critical to short- and long-range financial decisions. In addition, the sport manager must understand the significance of liquidity before investing capital in any project. As discussed in Chapter 2, an asset's liquidity is the readiness with which it can be converted to cash. Often, organizations own assets (such as real estate) that cannot easily be sold to raise cash to pay short-term obligations. Before committing resources to long-term investments, individuals and organizations must understand the importance of maintaining liquidity. Those who cannot effectively meet their cash obligations (payroll, facility overhead, and so forth) might be forced to alter short- and long-term financial commitments, sell assets (often at a discount) for immediate cash, or file for bankruptcy. For this reason, sport managers typically expect greater returns from investments that require a longer period until maturity or that cannot be redeemed for cash without substantial penalty. In addition, after an initial investment is made, subsequent investments of similar risk will often be considered only if higher returns can be realized.

For example, suppose a recreation center that has $20,000 in cash commits $9,000 of that amount to a capital improvement project, such as an additional basketball court, that will generate increased participation fees. However, revenue from the new court will not be realized for one year. During that time, the facility is less likely to use an additional $9,000 for another project with a similar expected return, as that would leave only $2,000 in reserve for short-term obligations or emergencies. Most likely, the financial manager would require any second project not only to offer a higher return on investment but also to return cash within one or two months.

PRESENT VALUE

Determining the future value of investments is only part of understanding the time value of money. Sport managers must also understand the concept of **present value (PV)**. Present value is today's value of a future cash flow—the current value of a payment that will be received or paid in the future. Net present value, or the comparison of the present value of future cash flows to initial cost, will be discussed in Chapter 8.

We calculate present value by applying a discount rate to the future cash flow. The discount rate, or capitalization rate, is a measure of risk or uncertainty. It is determined by the person performing the calculation, e.g., a financial manager, based on his or her estimate of future inflation rates, interest rates, and business activity.

If we revisit the problem from the opening of the chapter, one option for the player's agent is to accept $120,000 for her client, payable in three years. To determine how valuable (in today's dollars) that future $120,000 is, the agent would apply a discount rate—say, 6% for the purpose of this example. The present value could be compared with the $100,000 that the athlete could receive immediately. If the present value of $120,000 is greater than $100,000 (and assuming the athlete does not need the cash immediately), the better choice is to defer the salary. If the present value of $120,000 in three years is less than $100,000, then the athlete should take the $100,000 now.

To compute the present value, we use the following formula:

$$PV = FV\left(\frac{1}{(1+i)^n}\right)$$

where PV = present value
       FV = future value
        i = discount rate per period
       n = number of periods

For $120,000 payable in three years with a 6% discount rate,

$$PV = \$120,000\left(\frac{1}{(1+0.06)^3}\right)$$

$$= \$120,000\left(\frac{1}{(1.06\times1.06\times1.06)}\right)$$

$$= \$120,000\left(\frac{1}{1.19106}\right)$$

$$= \$120,000(0.8396)$$

$$= \$100,752$$

Notice that the present value formula is the inverse of the future value formula.

Just as we can easily compute the future value of a dollar by using a table, we can use the Present Value of $1 table (Table A.3 in the Appendix) to compute the present value of a dollar with the present value interest factor (PVIF). To find the PVIF, determine the number of periods until the income is realized and move across that column to the appropriate discount rate. For example, suppose a minor league baseball team anticipates sponsorship revenue of $15,000 to be realized in four years. What is the present value of that future payment if the discount rate is 9%? We can find the PVIF by examining Table A.3. For four periods and a 9% discount rate, the PVIF is 0.7084. Hence, the present value is 0.7084 × $15,000 = $10,626.

Often, the financial manager cannot accurately predict the future. For this reason, when financial managers estimate present values of future cash flows, they use multiple discount rates to calculate a variety of potential results. At all times, sport managers must remember that projections can change, especially over long periods of time. During the late 1970s, the inflation rate often exceeded 15%. Creditors collecting fixed long-term payments saw the purchasing power of their receipts diminish dramatically. Although inflation rates are not likely to return to such high rates in the United States, they do fluctuate from year to year. When forecasting for the future, it is advisable to employ at least three different discount rates and to consider the *worst-case* scenario the most likely outcome. This will result in any financial surprises being positive rather than negative.

To understand the present value of future money better, we can look at Table A.3 to see how changing the discount rate to adjust for risk affects the present value of a future expected payment. As the discount rate increases, the present value of the future income decreases (see Exhibit 4.3).

The present value also allows us to compare different investment opportunities to determine which is the best alternative. Suppose a minor league baseball team received two sponsorship offers, one for $15,000 and one for

EXHIBIT 4.3 Inverse relationship between present value and risk.

FUTURE INCOME	DISCOUNT RATE	PVIF, 5 YEARS	PV OF FUTURE INCOME
$10,000	12% (higher risk)	0.5674	$5,674
$10,000	6% (average risk)	0.7473	$7,473
$10,000	3% (lower risk)	0.8626	$8,626

$17,000, both to be paid in four years. Although the second payment would be higher, suppose the risk of default with this company is higher, so you choose to apply a discount rate of 12% as opposed to 9%. Which is the better investment opportunity?

Option 1: PV = 0.7084 × $15,000 = $10,626
Option 2: PV = 0.6355 × $17,000 = $10,803

Option 2 yields a higher present value and should be selected given the information provided.

It is important for sport financial managers to remember that many financial decisions are made in spite of the numbers. This is not always advisable, but in some cases decision makers may give up the higher present value of a certain project in favor of a less risky investment. In other cases, owners may be tempted to choose certain investment options for political or public-relations reasons, against financial advice. In cases like these, the financial manager must ensure that decision makers have a complete understanding of the options and the financial ramifications of each choice. Unfortunately, too often decisions are made without a thorough investigation or understanding of available financial information.

Present Value of an Annuity

A sport manager might wish to determine the present value of a series of future cash flows (an annuity). Suppose an agent negotiated a long-term sponsorship deal that called for yearly payments to an athlete of $10,000 for five years, and the agent felt that a discount rate of 10% was appropriate. We could determine the present value for each individual year and then total those amounts to determine the present value of the future cash flows. Instead, it is far easier to use a formula to calculate the present value of an annuity. Note that these calculations assume that the cash flows in each period are equal.

We can compute the present value of an annuity with the following formula:

$$PVA = PMT \left(\frac{1 - \frac{1}{(1+i)^n}}{i} \right)$$

where PVA = present value of an annuity
    PMT = payment per period
        i = discount rate
        n = number of periods

The calculation for our example would proceed as follows:

$$PVA = \$10,000 \left(\dfrac{1 - \dfrac{1}{(1+0.10)^5}}{0.10} \right)$$

$$= \$10,000 \left(\dfrac{1 - \dfrac{1}{1.10 \times 1.10 \times 1.10 \times 1.10 \times 1.10}}{0.10} \right)$$

$$= \$10,000 \left(\dfrac{1 - \dfrac{1}{1.61051}}{0.10} \right)$$

$$= \$10,000 \left(\dfrac{1 - .62092}{0.10} \right)$$

$$= \$10,000 \left(\dfrac{.37908}{0.10} \right)$$

$$= \$10,000 \, (3.7908)$$

$$= \$37,908$$

By using the present value interest factor of an annuity (PVIFA) from Table A.4 in the Appendix, we can reduce the above equation to PVA = payment × PVIFA. To determine the PVIFA, simply find the period of the annuity in the Present Value of an Annuity table and read across to the discount rate. For the calculation above, PVA = $10,000 (3.7908) = $37,908.

Consider a sport agent who has two potential sponsors for his client. Sponsor A is willing to pay the athlete $10,000 each year for five years, with a discount rate of 5%. Sponsor B is ready to pay the athlete $12,000 each year for five years, with a discount rate of 10%. Which is the better option?

Sponsor A: PV = $10,000 × 4.3295 = $43,295.00
Sponsor B: PV = $12,000 × 3.7908 = $45,489.60

Sponsor B is the better financial choice, given the information provided.

Often, the better choice between two payment options is the one that is lower in nominal terms, because, as the result of a lower discount rate, it has greater real value after discounting. Suppose Sponsor A is willing to pay $10,000 a year for five years, discounted at 4%, while Sponsor B is ready to pay the athlete $12,000 a year for five years, discounted at 12%. In this case, the better option is Sponsor A:

Sponsor A: PV = $10,000 × 4.4518 = $44,518.00
Sponsor B: PV = $12,000 × 3.6048 = $43,257.60

Many state lotteries offer winners a choice in how they receive their winnings: the winner can either receive the prize in equal payments over a predetermined number of years (often 20 or 30) or elect to receive a *portion* of the prize amount in a lump sum payment. To make a wise choice, the winner must understand the time value of money. Each winner will have different short-term financial obligations, long-term goals, tolerance for risk, and preferences for liquidity. Unfortunately, unscrupulous firms often attempt to purchase the right to future payments from winners who are unaware of the financial ramifications of their disbursement choices. Decisions regarding state lottery winnings have such importance that states have developed websites to educate winners about the financial implications of their decisions.

In some cases, determining the present value of an annuity may involve payments that are increasing or growing each period. In these situations, a different formula is utilized to determine the present value of the series of payments. Suppose that a college basketball coach is to receive a bonus for each season of her three-year employment contract. The first bonus will be $20,000 and that will increase by 10% each year. A discount rate of 4% will be applied. If the coach wanted to know what the present value of those bonuses would be, she must utilize the present value of a growing annuity formula to determine the answer. Before beginning, it is important to note if the bonus will be paid at the beginning of each year or at the end of each year. If the coach is to be paid the bonus at the start of each year, then the following formula is utilized.

PRESENT VALUE OF A GROWING ANNUITY (PAYMENTS START AT THE BEGINNING OF EACH PERIOD)

$$PVA = \frac{PMT}{i-g}\left(1-\left(\frac{1+g}{1+i}\right)^{n}\right)1+i$$

where PVA = present value of a growing annuity, payment paid at beginning of period
PMT = payment per period
i = discount rate
n = number of periods
g = growth rate

$$PVA = \frac{20,000}{.04-.10}\left(1-\left(\frac{1.10}{1.04}\right)^{3}\right)1+.04$$

$$PVA = \frac{20,000}{-.06}(1-1.06^{3})1.04$$

$$PVA = -333,333.33\ (1-1.19)\ (1.04)$$

$$PVA = -333,333.33\ (-.19)(1.04)$$

$$PVA = 63,333.33(1.04)$$

$$PVA = \$65,866.66$$

The value of $65,866.66 is generated. In this situation, the bonus appears to be more of a "signing" or "starting" bonus which means if the coach decided to quit before the season was over, the team would likely have no recourse to retrieve the bonus money. In most cases, salary bonuses are paid at the end of each period so that they encourage the employee to honor their contract. If the same series of payments were to be paid at the end of each year, the following formula would be utilized.

PRESENT VALUE OF A GROWING ANNUITY (PAYMENTS START AT THE END OF EACH PERIOD)

$$PVA = \frac{PMT}{i-g}\left(1-\left(\frac{(1+g)}{1+i}\right)^n\right)$$

where PVA = present value of a growing annuity, payments start at the end of
    each period
  PMT = payment per period
    i = discount rate
    n = number of periods
    g = growth rate

$$PVA = \frac{20,000}{.04-.10}\left(1-\left(\frac{1+.10}{1+.04}\right)^3\right)$$

$$PVA = \frac{20,000}{-.06}(1-(1.06)^3)$$

$$PVA = -333,333.33(1-(1.06)^3)$$

$$PVA = -333,333.33(1-1.19)$$

$$PVA = -333,333.33(-.19)$$

$$PVA = \$63,333.33$$

Notice that by moving the bonus payments "back" to the end of each year, the present value of the payments decreases to $63,333.33, a difference of $2,533.33! It is important to know not only the amount of a payment but also the timing for when that payment will be received.

In some cases, the athletic department might desire to structure the contract so that the bonus payments are delayed before they are disbursed. In such a situation, to determine the present value, one would need to utilize the present value of a delayed growing annuity.

If the same parameters as the previous delayed annuities were provided ($20,000 base bonus payment, 10% yearly growth, 4% discount rate applied) but the athletic department delayed the first payment for four years, the following calculations would be made.

PRESENT VALUE OF A DELAYED GROWING ANNUITY (FOUR-YEAR DELAY)

$$PVA = \frac{\dfrac{PMT}{i-g}\left(1-\left(\dfrac{1+g}{1+i}\right)^{n}\right)}{(1+r)^{y-1}}$$

where PVA = present value of a delayed growing annuity
    PMT = payment per period
        i = discount rate
        n = number of periods
        g = growth rate
        y = year (or period) of delay before initial payment

$$PVA = \frac{\dfrac{20,000}{.04-.10}\left(1-\left(\dfrac{1+.10}{1+.04}\right)^{3}\right)}{(1+.04)^{4-1}}$$

$$PVA = \frac{\dfrac{20,000}{-.06}\left(1-\left(\dfrac{1.10}{1.04}\right)^{3}\right)}{(1.04)^{3}}$$

$$PVA = \frac{\dfrac{20,000}{-.06}\left(1-(1.06)^{3}\right)}{(1.04)^{3}}$$

$$PVA = \frac{-333,333.33\left(1-1.19\right)}{1.13}$$

$$PVA = \frac{-333,333.33\left(-.19\right)}{1.13}$$

$$PVA = \frac{63,333.33}{1.13}$$

$$PVA = \$56,047.19$$

Notice that the present value has decreased to $56,047.19. If the delay was five years instead of four, the denominator portion of the equation would change from $4-1=3$ to $5-1=4$, meaning the total value will decrease due to a higher denominator.

PRESENT VALUE OF A DELAYED GROWING ANNUITY (FIVE-YEAR DELAY)

$$PVA = \frac{\dfrac{PMT}{i-g}\left(1-\left(\dfrac{(1+g)}{1+i}\right)^{n}\right)}{(1+r)^{y-1}}$$

where PVA = present value of a delayed growing annuity

PMT = payment per period

i = discount rate

n = number of periods

g = growth rate

y = year (or period) of delay before initial payment

$$PVA = \frac{\frac{20,000}{.04-.10}\left(1-\left(\frac{1+.10}{1+.04}\right)^3\right)}{\left(1+.04\right)^{5-1}}$$

$$PVA = \frac{\frac{20,000}{-.06}\left(1-\left(\frac{1.10}{1.04}\right)^3\right)}{\left(1.04\right)^4}$$

$$PVA = \frac{\frac{20,000}{-.06}\left(1-\left(1.06\right)^3\right)}{\left(1.04\right)^4}$$

$$PVA = \frac{-333,333.33\left(1-1.19\right)}{1.17}$$

$$PVA = \frac{-333,333.33\left(-.19\right)}{1.17}$$

$$PVA = \frac{63,333.33}{1.17}$$

$$PVA = \$54,131.05$$

The extra year of delay would lower the present value of the annuity to $54,131.05 for a difference of $1,916.14. The impact of delaying just one year can create a substantial difference in the present value of the series of payments. For a detailed examination of various time value of money calculations often utilized in sport, see B. David Tyler's 2017 article in *Case Studies in Sport Management*.

INTERIM YEAR COMPOUNDING

For all previous examples involving interest, we have assumed that the interest is compounded (calculated and added to principal) once per year. However, in many financial arrangements, interest is compounded each quarter, month, week, or, in some cases, day. To adjust for compounding on a basis other than annual is simple. Depending on whether you are computing the present or future value of a dollar, or of an annuity, you will simply determine the number of periods and use the appropriate table to find the factor you need for the calculation.

Suppose, for example, that a sport organization wishes to determine the future value of $1,000 invested for two years receiving 12% interest, compounded quarterly. To determine the future value, we would first find the interest rate for the compounding period. Since there are four quarters in a year, we divide the annual interest rate of 12% by four and find that the interest per quarter is 3%. Since the investment period is two years, the number of compounding periods is eight. From the future value table we find that the FVIF for eight periods at 3% interest is 1.2668, yielding a future value of $1,000 × 1.2668 = $1,266.80. Note that if the 12% interest were compounded yearly, the future value would be $1,000 × 1.2544 = $1,254.40, a difference of $12.40.

SIDEBAR 4.D William Andrews Wants His Money Now

During the early 1980s William Andrews was one of the top halfbacks in the NFL. While playing for the Atlanta Falcons from 1979 through 1983, Andrews rushed for more than 5,000 yards and accumulated more than 2,500 yards receiving. In one of his contract negotiations, Andrews agreed to a deferred compensation plan that would pay him $200,000 per year for 25 years ($5 million) after his playing career was complete. In 2001, Andrews negotiated a deal where he would give up his deferred compensation in exchange for an immediate $2 million from Hanleigh Co. (Kaplan, 2001). Although the money he received was only 40% of the total due him from the Falcons, Andrews determined that he could invest the money and receive a greater return than what the Falcons had agreed to pay him.

For Hanleigh Co., the risk of the Atlanta Falcons' defaulting on their financial obligation must have seemed minimal, as NFL teams have been stable for many years and the prospect is strong that they will remain financially solvent. Hanleigh Co. does assume risks, however, from time, inflation, and lack of liquidity. Over the length of the contract, numerous factors could diminish the value of the annual $200,000 payments. For one, inflationary pressure could diminish purchasing power. In addition, immediate payment of $2 million to Andrews meant an immediate loss of capital to Hanleigh, which could be critical if Hanleigh Co. were to need money to meet short-term financial obligations. The financial analysts at Hanleigh Co. likely investigated the investment options available to them, their level of liquidity, and their tolerance for risk, and determined that it was better to receive $200,000 per year for the remaining years of the contract than to invest the $2 million in other financial opportunities.

For William Andrews, the desire to receive immediate money must have been more important than the longer-term security of regular payments. He might have needed immediate liquidity to pay off some obligation. More likely, Andrews computed the return available from potential investments and determined it would be more profitable for him to take the immediate cash. Andrews, of course, assumes the risks associated with his investment decisions. If with the $2 million he generates more than $200,000 per year, his investment decision will have been sound. However, if his returns do not exceed his contracted payments, the decision to take immediate cash will have been in error.

Financial institutions often advertise that they compute interest payments to customers on a quarterly, monthly, weekly, or even daily basis. Before placing funds in any institution, the consumer should calculate the interest that she will receive on deposits. In some cases, interest compounded daily may not exceed the interest compounded monthly or even yearly. By understanding the concept of compounding and using the time value of money tables, investors can make informed decisions.

USING A SPREADSHEET TO CALCULATE TIME VALUE OF MONEY

Though many computations can be completed by hand or with a financial calculator, the use of spreadsheets provides a simple and efficient mechanism to determine the answers to financial calculations. Specifically, Microsoft Excel is a powerful spreadsheet program that has dramatically altered the finance and accounting landscape.

The Microsoft Excel help menu provides instructions for completing computations, including present value, future value, and payments. Excel provides a definition and explanation of the components of each calculation, as well as functions for time value of money calculations. An important consideration in building spreadsheets is ensuring that positive and negative amounts are entered appropriately.

Present Value Function

To compute present value, select the Formulas tab, choose Financial, and scroll through the list to find PV. Click on this function, and the dialog box appears as shown in Exhibit 4.4.

Note that the box prompts you to input the values Excel uses to calculate present value. In a spreadsheet cell, Excel's PV function appears as follows:

EXHIBIT 4.4 Dialog box for PV function.

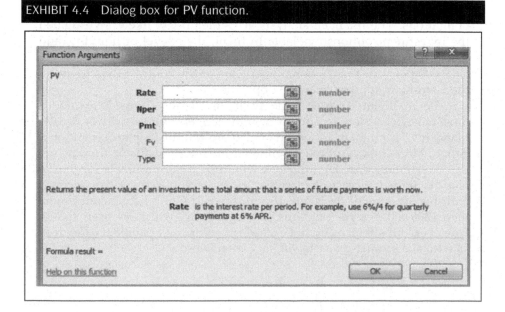

$$PV(rate,nper,pmt,fv,type)$$

where

- **rate** is the interest rate per period. For example, if you obtain an automobile loan at a 10% annual interest rate and make monthly payments, your interest rate per month is 10%/12, or 0.83%. You would enter 10%/12, or 0.83%, or 0.0083 into the formula as the rate.
- **nper** is the total number of payment periods in an annuity. For example, if you secure a four-year car loan and make monthly payments, your loan has 4 × 12 = 48 periods. You would enter 48 into the formula for nper.
- **pmt** is the payment made each period, which cannot change over the life of the annuity. Typically, pmt includes principal and interest but no other fees or taxes. For example, the monthly payments on a $10,000, four-year car loan at 12% are $263.33. You would enter −263.33 into the formula as the pmt. You have the option of omitting the pmt amount and entering a number for fv instead.
- **fv** is the future value, or a cash balance you want to attain after the last payment is made. If fv is omitted, it is assumed to be 0 (the future value of a loan, for example, is 0). For example, if you want to save $50,000 to pay for a special project in ten years, then $50,000 is the future value. You could then make a conservative guess at an interest rate and use the present value formula to determine how much you must save each month. If fv is omitted, you must include the pmt argument.
- **type** is the number 0 or 1, indicating when payments are due. Use 0 (or omit specifying type, as it will default to 0) for payments that are due at the end of each period; enter 1 for those due at the beginning of each period.

Exhibit 4.5 provides examples of the use of the present value function in Excel. Example A calculates the present value of a $50,000 payment to occur in ten years, applying various discount rates. Example B determines the present value of a $10,000-per-year annuity discounted 5% over a variety of years.

Future Value Function

To compute future value in Excel, select the Formulas tab, choose Financial, and scroll through the list to find FV. Click on this function, and the dialog box appears as shown in Exhibit 4.6. Note that the box prompts you to input the values Excel uses to calculate future value. In a spreadsheet cell, Excel's FV function appears as follows:

$$FV(rate,nper,pmt,pv,type)$$

For a description of the arguments in FV and for more information on annuity functions, see the discussion of Excel's PV function.

Exhibit 4.7 provides examples of the use of the FV function. In Example A, the future value of $10,000 is computed over ten years (compounded annually) at various interest rates. In Example B, the future value of a $5,000 annuity is computed at various interest rates.

EXHIBIT 4.5   Calculating present value with Excel's PV function.

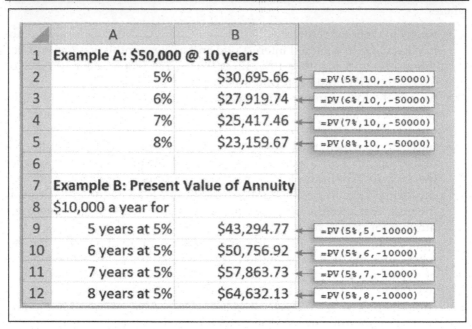

	A	B	
1	**Example A: $50,000 @ 10 years**		
2	5%	$30,695.66	=PV(5%,10,,-50000)
3	6%	$27,919.74	=PV(6%,10,,-50000)
4	7%	$25,417.46	=PV(7%,10,,-50000)
5	8%	$23,159.67	=PV(8%,10,,-50000)
6			
7	**Example B: Present Value of Annuity**		
8	$10,000 a year for		
9	5 years at 5%	$43,294.77	=PV(5%,5,-10000)
10	6 years at 5%	$50,756.92	=PV(5%,6,-10000)
11	7 years at 5%	$57,863.73	=PV(5%,7,-10000)
12	8 years at 5%	$64,632.13	=PV(5%,8,-10000)

EXHIBIT 4.6   Dialog box for the FV function.

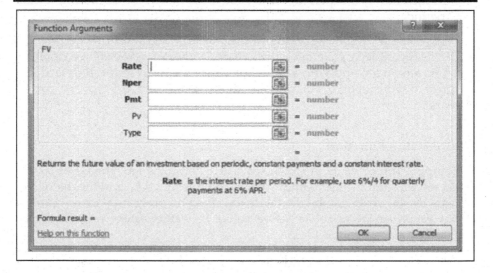

Payments Function

We can use an Excel spreadsheet to determine a loan repayment schedule. This is especially helpful when computing monthly payments for purchases such as automobiles and real estate.

EXHIBIT 4.7   Calculating future value with Excel's FV function.

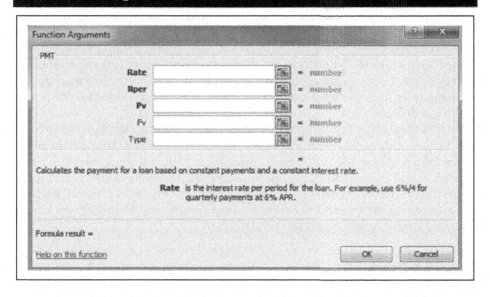

	A	B	C
1	**Example A: 10 years (compounded annually)**		
2	$ 10,000.00		
3	5%	$16,288.95	◄— =FV(5%,10,,-10000)
4	6%	$17,908.48	◄— =FV(6%,10,,-10000)
5	8%	$21,589.25	◄— =FV(8%,10,,-10000)
6	10%	$25,937.42	◄— =FV(10%,10,,-10000)
7			
8	**Example B: Future Value Annuity**		
9	$ 5,000.00		
10	10 years @ 5%	$62,889.46	◄— =FV(5%,10,-5000)
11	20 years @ 5%	$165,329.77	◄— =FV(5%,20,-5000)
12	30 years @ 5%	$332,194.24	◄— =FV(5%,30,-5000)
13	40 years @ 5%	$603,998.87	◄— =FV(5%,40,-5000)
14	50 years @ 5%	$1,046,739.98	◄— =FV(5%,50,-5000)

EXHIBIT 4.8   Dialog box for the PMT function.

Function Arguments   ? ✕

PMT

Rate [   ] 🔢 = number

Nper [   ] 🔢 = number

Pv   [   ] 🔢 = number

Fv   [   ] 🔢 = number

Type [   ] 🔢 = number

                                                    =

Calculates the payment for a loan based on constant payments and a constant interest rate.

Rate is the interest rate per period for the loan. For example, use 6%/4 for quarterly payments at 6% APR.

Formula result =

Help on this function   OK   Cancel

To compute loan payments, select the Formulas tab, choose Financial, and scroll through the list to find PMT. Click on this function, and the dialog box appears as shown in Exhibit 4.8. Note that the box prompts you to input the values Excel uses to calculate payments. In a spreadsheet cell, Excel's PMT function appears as follows:

PMT(rate,nper,pv,fv,type)

EXHIBIT 4.9   Calculating loan payments with Excel's PMT function.

	A	B	C	
1	Payments on a $100,000 loan with a 20-year term			
2		PMT	Total Amount Paid	
3	5%	($659.96) ←— =PMT(5%/12,240,100000)	($158,389.38) ←— =240*B3
4	6%	($716.43) ←— =PMT(6%/12,240,100000)	($171,943.45) ←— =240*B4
5	8%	($836.44) ←— =PMT(8%/12,240,100000)	($200,745.62) ←— =240*B5
6	10%	($965.02) ←— =PMT(10%/12,240,100000)	($231,605.19) ←— =240*B6

Exhibit 4.9 presents a series of calculations of the monthly payment for a $100,000 loan to be repaid over 20 years when different interest rates are applied. In addition, it computes the total nominal amount of all payments made over the 20-year loan period.

CONCLUSION

Let's return to the question that introduced this chapter. Which option should the athlete choose among his four potential payments? As discussed in this chapter, in order to make an informed decision, the athlete must understand or estimate his current and future need for liquidity, the potential investments available to him and the risks associated with each investment, and the current and future rates of inflation. An athlete who needs immediate cash would be compelled to take the $100,000 now, without even investigating other options. An athlete without liquidity concerns or with immediate access to a loan should investigate each potential investment's yield and the associated risks before making a decision.

It is critical not only that sport managers be able to calculate the present and future value of money, but also that they understand the immediate needs of the firm and how the time value of money, inflation, the organization's risk tolerance, and its need for liquidity influence the selection of short- and long-term strategies. Proper financial analysis can lead to long-term financial success, but a failure to understand the time value of money and to implement sound financial strategies may yield financial disaster.

Concept Check

1. Explain the concept of inflation. How does inflation affect saving and investing?
2. How does a preference for liquidity influence an individual or organization's financial decisions?
3. Explain the difference between simple and compound interest.
4. What aspects of the time value of money must professional sport organizations and athletes consider when negotiating contracts?
5. What mistake did the NBA make in its dealings with the owners of the Spirits of St. Louis?

6. What are some advantages and disadvantages of deferring salaries (both from the player's and the team's perspectives)?
7. What concerns should a sport organization contemplate when negotiating future payments from sponsorships or other long-term agreements?

Practice Problems

1. What is the real increase in value if $1,500 is invested for one year at 5% interest and the rate of inflation during that time is 1.79%?
2. A sport organization has a commitment from a sponsor for a $17,000 payment in three years. What is the present value of that money if it is discounted at (a) 3%, (b) 5%, and (c) 9%?
3. Suppose you are the financial manager for a recreation center that has signed an option to purchase new elliptical machines for $22,000 in two years. If you have an investment opportunity that guarantees 7% interest, how much must you invest to have the necessary funds to purchase the elliptical machines?
4. An athlete signs a five-year endorsement deal with a prominent sponsor. Under this deal the athlete will receive $5,000 each year for the first three years and $6,500 each year for the final two years. What is the present value of the total deal if the payments are discounted at 6%?
5. What is the future value of $12,000 invested at 8% interest, compounded yearly for ten years?
6. If an investor commits $4,500 to an IRA each year for 30 years and receives 6% interest, what will her total investment be worth at the end of the 30 years?
7. A bank offers customers the option of receiving interest compounded quarterly, semi-annually, or annually. If the rate of interest is the same, which is the best option for the customer?
8. What is the difference between $10,000 invested for ten years at 3% interest, compounded yearly, and at 8% interest, compounded semi-annually?

Case Analysis

Time Value of a Sponsorship

The director of marketing of your organization asks for your advice regarding sponsorship deals she is contemplating. She has to choose from the following: a 15-year sponsorship paying $100,000 per year, a 15-year sponsorship initially paying $75,000 per year and increasing 5% each year, and a 15-year sponsorship initially paying $45,000 per year but increasing 12% each year.

Case Questions

1. Determine the present value of each year's payment for each proposal, as well as the total present value of each proposal. For each proposal, compute two different outcomes, one with a discount rate of 5% and one with a discount rate of 10%.
2. Which proposal should the marketing director choose?

3. What questions about her firm and about the potential sponsors should she contemplate?

4. How would the decision be affected by the answers to the questions posed in #3? Fully explain your response.

References

Al Horford. (n.d.). *Spotrac*. Retrieved from www.spotrac.com/nba/philadelphia-76ers/al-horford-2199/.

Birger, J. (2009, February 19). Baseball battles the slump. *Fortune*. Retrieved from http://money.cnn.com/2009/02/18/magazines/fortune/birger_baseball.fortune/index.htm.

Bureau of Labor Statistics. (n.d.). Frequently asked questions. Retrieved from www.bls.gov/cpi/cpifaq.htm.

CBA breakdown. (n.d.). Retrieved from https://cbabreakdown.com/compensation.

Corwin, M. (2001, April 4). MLB's ticket prices risk alienating fans. Retrieved from www.yaledailynews.com/article.asp?AID=15265.

Crawford, D. (2018, July 1). Someone listed all of the future MLB deferred payments in honor of Bobby Bonilla Day. *Busted Coverage*. Retrieved from https://bustedcoverage.com/2018/07/01/someone-listed-all-of-the-future-mlb-deferred-payments-in-honor-bobby-bonilla-day/.

Dave, P. (2013, November 17). By deferring some earnings, athletes can help themselves and their teams. *The Los Angeles Times*. Retrieved from www.latimes.com/sports/la-sp-worst-sports-contracts-20131117-story.html.

Fields, S. (2019, September 30). 70% of college students graduate with debt. How did we get here? Retrieved from www.marketplace.org/2019/09/30/70-of-college-students-graduate-with-debt-how-did-we-get-here/.

Herbert, B. (2009, October 16). Pricing the kids out. *The New York Times*. Retrieved from www.nytimes.com/2009/10/17/opinion/17herbert.html?_r=1&em.

Hoffman, D. (1998, November). Penguins file for bankruptcy protection. *Stadium and Arena Financing News*, 2(21), 1.

Kaplan, D. (2001, March 12–18). Securitization era opens for athletes. *Sports Business Journal*, 3(1), 43.

Los Angeles Dodgers lack cash for end of May payroll. (2011, May 4). *The Huffington Post*. Retrieved from www.huffingtonpost.com/2011/05/04/los-angeles-dodgers-lack-_n_857610.html.

Mandell, N. (2014, January 7). Ending the greatest sports deal of all time will reportedly cost the NBA at least $500 million. *USA Today*. Retrieved from http://ftw.usatoday.com/2014/01/ending-the-greatest-sports-deal-of-all-time-will-reported-ly-cost-the-nba-at-least-500-million.

Manny Machado. (n.d.). *Spotrac*. Retrieved from www.spotrac.com/mlb/san-diego-padres/manny-machado-11638/.

Markazi, A. (2012, March 28). Price for Dodgers questioned. Retrieved from http://espn.go.com/los-angeles/mlb/story/_Zid/7747848/economist-2b-los-angeles-dodgers-makes-no-sense.

Mullen, L. (2005, August 22). The NFL's vanishing bonus. *Sports Business Journal*. Retrieved from www.sportsbusinessjournal.com/index.cfm?fuseaction=search.show_article&articleId=46518&keyword=NFL's,%20vanishing,%20bonus.

NFL CBA Series: Deferred Compensation. (2013, May 29). Retrieved from https://in2theleague.wordpress.com/2013/05/29/nfl-cba-series-deferred-compensation/.

Olson, B. (2018, December 6). U.S. becomes net exporter of oil, fuels for first time in decades. *The Wall Street Journal*. Retrieved from www.wsj.com/articles/u-s-becomes-net-exporter-of-oil-fuels-for-first-time-in-decades-1544128404.

Perry, M.J. (2019, January 11). Chart of the day … or century. Retrieved from www.aei. org/carpe-diem/chart-of-the-day-or-century/.

Pluto, T. (1990). *Loose balls.* New York: Simon & Schuster.

Q&A part 2: Revisiting the Phoenix Coyotes bankruptcy. (2009, June 1). *SportsJudge Blog.* Retrieved from http://sportsjudge.blogspot.com/2009/06/q-part-2-revisiting-phoenix-coyotes.html.

Rovell, D. (2001, May 9). Creative financing 101: Deferred salaries. Retrieved from http://espn.go.com/mlb/s/2001/0509/1193881.html.

Rovell, D. (2002, January 22). Spirit of ABA deal lives on for Silna brothers. Retrieved from http://sports.espn.go.com/espn/print?id=1295194&type=story.

Rubin, A. (2012, January 26). Mets could trim more than $50M. Retrieved from http:// espn.go.com/new-york/mlb/story/_/id/7495383/new-york-mets-largest-payroll-dropoff-ever.

Salaries. (n.d.). *ShamSports.com.* Retrieved from http://data.shamsports.com/content/pages/data/salaries/hawks.jsp.

Sandomir, R. (2012, September 6). No team, no ticket sales, but plenty of cash. *The New York Times.* Retrieved from www.nytimes.com/2012/09/07/sports/basketball/former-aba-owners-ozzie-and-daniel-silna-earn-millions-from-nba.html?pagewanted=all&_r=0.

Tutorial—The real cost of higher education. (n.d.). Retrieved from www.savingforcollege.com/tutorial101/the-real-cost-of-higher-education.

Tyler, B.D. (2017, January). Using the time value of money decision tree to calculate an athlete's contract offers. *Case Studies in Sport Management,* 6, 48–57.

USA Today salaries databases. (2009). *USA Today.* Retrieved from http://content.usatoday.com/sports/baseball/salaries/default.aspx.

Wadsworth, G.H. (2012, June 14). Skyrocketing college costs. Retrieved from http://inflationdata.com/Inflation/Inflation_Articles/Education_Inflation.asp.

Winegardner, M. (2012, May 3). Paying it forward. Retrieved from http://espn.go.com/mlb/story/_/id/7879021/mlb-new-york-mets-pay-bobby-bonilla-millions-years-come-espn-magazine.

Zigler, B. (2009, April 15). Yearly CPI falls; first time in over five decades. Retrieved from www.hardassetsinvestor.com/component/content/article/3/1519-yearly-cpi-falls-first-time-in-over-five-decades.html?year=2009&month=04&Itemid=39.

Zimbalist, A. (1992). *Baseball and billions.* New York: Basic Books.

Financial Management

CHAPTER 5

Introduction to Financial Management

Mark S. Nagel

KEY CONCEPTS

accounting profit
antitrust exemption
basis point
capitalism
certificate of deposit
collateral
corporate veil
demand
depreciation
depreciation recapture
discount rate
double-declining balance
   depreciation
economic profit
economics
eminent domain
entrepreneur
express partnership
fair tax
federal funds rate
Federal Reserve
fiscal policy
flat tax
Freedom of Information request
general partnership
globalization
Great Society
implied partnership
jock tax

laissez-faire
large-cap company
limited liability corporation (LLC)
limited liability partnership (LLP)
limited partner
loss-of-value insurance
M1, M2, M3
macroeconomics
market capitalization
microeconomics
minority partner
monetary policy
non-profit organization
opportunity cost
price
prime rate
quantitative easing
recession
scarcity
small-cap stock
socialistic
sole proprietorship
stock
stock exchange
stock market
stock market index
straight-line depreciation
subchapter C corporation (C corp)
subchapter S corporation (S corp)

sum-of-years'-digits depreciation
surplus
units-of-production depreciation

unsecured claim
value-added tax (VAT)

INTRODUCTION

In 2013, reporter Bryan Curtis asked Major League Baseball All-Star Jason Giambi why he lived in Las Vegas. Giambi casually noted, "No state [income] tax." Curtis then responded: "Very good answer" (Curtis, 2013, para. 45). Although it was not likely his intention to be so profound, Giambi's response encapsulates a number of different important elements of finance, both for individuals and organizations.

Financial management is a component of operating any business and, more important, is a necessary and critical aspect of anyone's personal life. Balancing a checkbook, determining a monthly budget, and investing for retirement are financial management activities likely familiar to many. The work of chief financial officers (CFOs), comptrollers, and other staff members in finance departments is certainly more complex and detailed than what most individuals undertake for their personal finances, but the idea of finance—the application of a series of principles to maximize wealth—applies to both individuals and businesses.

In any sizable organization the finance department will handle most of the long-term financial management issues, but it is vital that *every* member of the organization have some comprehension of finance. Understanding the basics of finance enables a manager to interact more effectively with the financial analysts whose job it is to decipher the numbers. Financial acumen is critical for career advancement in most organizations. The leaders of any department, at the least, will be involved in budgeting and forecasting decisions. The financial "Golden Rule" always applies: "He who has the gold makes the rules."

ECONOMIC PRINCIPLES

Although this book focuses on advanced financial principles, we will briefly review some fundamental economic principles that form the basis of finance. **Economics** has been defined by Walter Wessel as "the study of how people choose to allocate their scarce resources" (2000, p. 2). Key economic principles outlined in this section include: (1) demand, scarcity, surplus, and price; (2) microeconomics versus macroeconomics; and (3) wealth maximization/ profits.

Demand, Scarcity, Surplus, and Price

The choices individuals and organizations make will be influenced by the interdependent factors of demand, scarcity, surplus, and price. **Demand** is the quantity of a product or service desired by consumers; **scarcity** describes the situation when the availability of a resource does not meet current demand; **surplus** is the amount of an asset or resource that exceeds the portion that is utilized; and **price** is defined as what one party (the buyer) must give to obtain what is offered by another party (the seller). For instance, economic principles are at work when the Professional Bowlers Association (PBA) Tour announces a new event on its schedule. For the chosen bowling alley, a variety of factors influence its ability to set prices. The number of available tournament passes to be sold (scarcity and lack of it), the potential surplus of other viable sport and entertainment events in the local area, known as substitutes, and the anticipated customer demand determine the price that the alley can charge. However, even if there is high demand, if the PBA decides to schedule an additional tournament close to a current one, more tickets to PBA events become readily available for customers in this marketplace (i.e., the scarcity of tickets changes), and this may reduce the potential ticket price.

North American professional sport franchises and leagues employ the economic concept of scarcity in a variety of ways. The most prominent way is that leagues create scarcity by *not* expanding into every metropolitan area that could potentially support a franchise. With viable alternative cities available, teams often can demand financial concessions from their current metropolitan areas in exchange for their remaining in the current location. Although Charlotte and Portland are larger than some cities that currently have MLB franchises, the league has not rushed to expand into those areas and others similar to them. Current teams seeking new facilities have utilized these non-MLB cities as bargaining chips ("Will Charlotte," 2006; Rogers, 2007). Despite being the second largest metropolitan area in the United States, Los Angeles did not have an NFL team after the Los Angeles Raiders and Los Angeles Rams left the area for Oakland and St. Louis, respectively, in 1995. For a number of years, representatives of a variety of NFL teams, including the Arizona Cardinals, Jacksonville Jaguars, and Indianapolis Colts, mentioned, and in some cases actually used, the threat of moving to Los Angeles as a bargaining chip during negotiations with their home markets for a new or significantly remodeled facility (Joyner, 2006; "Lucas Oil," 2006). Despite the threats of other teams moving to Los Angeles, no NFL team entered the market until the Rams returned in 2016. The San Diego Chargers also moved to Los Angeles in 2017. Both teams were lured to the area by the promise of a new, state-of-the-art stadium in Inglewood that opened in 2020.

Leagues have established internal rules to restrict franchise movement in an effort to maintain scarcity. Most North American professional sport leagues have territorial rules restricting franchise movement within the proximity of a current team. This provides the established franchise with greater bargaining power when negotiating contracts with sponsors and media partners. For instance, even though more than 3 million people live in San Bernardino County (an area just east of Los Angeles), MLB prohibits any MLB team from moving into that area, since it is considered part of the "home market" of the Los Angeles Dodgers and the Los Angeles Angels of Anaheim (Nagel, Brown, McEvoy, & Rascher, 2007). When the Montreal Expos moved to Washington DC to become the Washington Nationals in 2005, Baltimore Orioles owner Peter Angelos was given initial control of 90% of the Nationals' regional cable television rights (in a newly created cable network called Mid-Atlantic Sports Network [MASN]) and a guaranteed sale price of $365 million if he were to sell the Orioles, as compensation for the infringement on his territory (Nagel et al., 2007). Though, according to the agreement, the Nationals' share in MASN increases by 1%

each year until it reaches 33%, with the explosion in cable television contracts for MLB teams, the Nationals are likely "losing" $60 million each year in their current arrangement with MASN (Kilgore, 2012). By protecting team territories, leagues help ensure that individual franchises will have every opportunity to exploit their scarcity power to maximize their financial position.

SIDEBAR 5.A   Kansas City's Sprint Center Still Waiting for Permanent Tenant

Completed in 2007 at a cost of $276 million, the Sprint Center in Kansas City, Missouri, operated by Anschutz Entertainment Group (AEG), is one of the largest multi-use arenas in the United States that does not have a permanent NBA or NHL tenant. However, the Sprint Center has been mentioned often as a *potential* site for a relocated NBA or NHL team, beginning even before it initially opened its doors. The NHL's Nashville Predators, New York Islanders, and Pittsburgh Penguins and the NBA's New Orleans Hornets and Sacramento Kings expressed varying degrees of interest in relocating their franchises to Kansas City, but each was able to negotiate favorable lease terms in their current metropolitan area. This has resulted in consternation among many Kansas City residents, who thought part of the city's plan for financing the arena was to acquire an anchor tenant (Unell, 2012). Former AEG CEO Tim Leiweke noted that other NHL teams had openly utilized the Sprint Center to negotiate better venue deals. Leiweke noted, "Pittsburgh used Kansas City … they were ready to move if they didn't get that deal done (in Pittsburgh) … they were moving here" (Unell, 2012, para. 14). In addition, NHL deputy commissioner Bill Daly stated, "Kansas City has never been entirely 'off our radar screen …' We have talked to potentially interested stakeholders in the past, and it's certainly a market that in the right circumstances (including a desire by our board to entertain further expansion), our league would fairly evaluate and consider" (Caldwell, 2017, para. 16). The venue has been successful under AEG's management in attracting top-quality entertainment and sporting events, such as the Big 12 Conference Men's Basketball Tournament and NCAA Championship events and NBA and NHL pre-season games, but it appears the short-term future of the venue will not involve hosting an NBA or NHL franchise, despite an anonymous NBA executive telling the SEC Network that, "Kansas City will get an NBA team at some point" (Allen, 2019, para. 1). See Chapter 11 for additional information about Kansas City's viability as a home for a major league team.

Microeconomics versus Macroeconomics

The field of economics is typically divided into microeconomics and macroeconomics. An understanding of each is critical to financial decision making. **Microeconomics** refers to the study of issues that occur at the firm level, such as supply, demand, and pricing. Many of the decisions that financial managers make are determined by microeconomic factors. Such decisions might include setting prices for athletic club memberships or tickets for an upcoming event, or deciding whether to offer a new product line or to pay for training for current employees to learn new job processes. To make these decisions, the financial manager must evaluate the microeconomic forces at work in the business.

In addition to microeconomic forces at the firm level, macroeconomic forces affect every individual and business throughout the world. **Macroeconomics** refers to the study of forces that affect numerous or even all sectors of the overall economy, such as income, unemployment, and inflation at the community, national, regional, or global level. It is critical that financial managers track economic conditions and make their best attempt to predict how macroeconomic forces will affect their operations. Of course, no one can be certain what will occur in the future, but research and planning can assist the decision-making process. If the national or state economic outlook is poor, for example, it may not be an ideal time to expand production, because customers may not be able to purchase the additional inventory. However, if economic conditions are poor but research indicates that the economy will improve soon, a business may want to expand before its competitors do, to capture the increased demand that will develop once the economic environment has changed. Since interest rates are often lower during an economic downturn, it is typically more favorable to take out loans when the overall economy is sluggish rather than when the economy is performing well. This issue will be discussed in greater detail later in this chapter.

At various levels—cities, counties, states, regions, and countries—economic conditions and outlooks differ from place to place. However, although differences certainly continue to exist in every area, regions around the world are now much more interwoven than in the past. As Thomas Friedman has discussed extensively (2000, 2005), we now have a "worldwide economy." Incidents that disrupt markets in one country can have a tremendous impact in countries on other continents. For example, in 1997, the Asian currency crisis caused economic problems in North America and Europe (Friedman, 2000). And as discussed, problems in the US housing market during the Great Recession and afterward have affected investors in other countries, because many brokerage houses around the world purchase mortgage notes sold by US lending institutions. An unexpectedly high number of these mortgages have entered foreclosure, and investors around the world have been left with little or no return on their investments. Given the **globalization** of finance—the integration of economies into one "world economy"—no longer can financial managers view macroeconomic conditions solely at the national level. The economic world will continue to shrink as technology continues to enable jobs, capital, and information to move swiftly around the world, often with merely the click of a mouse.

Financial managers usually do not compartmentalize microeconomic and macroeconomic factors in their decision-making processes. Every economic factor must be contemplated, whether it is specific to the firm or applicable to the overall economy. With proper decisions arrived at after evaluation of the appropriate economic environments, firms and individuals can achieve consistent profits and long-term wealth maximization.

Wealth Maximization/Profits

Financial managers must conduct accurate appraisals of potential and realized profits. A distinction must be made between accounting profit and economic profit. An **accounting profit** is earned when revenues exceed costs and expenses over a particular period of time (see Chapter 2). **Economic profit** is the profit remaining after the opportunity costs (costs in terms of forgone alternatives) associated with a financial decision are included. Accounting profit does not necessarily accurately reflect the results of the individual's or organization's financial decisions. For example, if an individual starts a sport promotion business and has $20,000 net income over the first year, an accounting profit of $20,000 has been realized. However, a calculation of economic profits must include the opportunity costs of not working for someone else. If the individual quit a job that paid $40,000 a year, the economic profit would not be $20,000; instead, it would be $20,000 (gained through the business activities) less $40,000 (lost by not working), for a net of *negative* $20,000.

This example is typical of new businesses. Starting a business is a risky venture, and even when the business is turning an accounting profit, the economic profit may be negative when opportunity costs are factored into the analysis. What may be more important is what will happen in the second, third, and subsequent years of the life of the business. Typically, **entrepreneurs**—people who establish a business venture and assume the financial risk for it—understand that a short-term economic loss will be overcome if and when the business becomes successful. Working for someone else may be advantageous in the short term, but most wealthy individuals at some point took risks and endured temporary losses to establish a business.

In addition to understanding the importance of generating profits and creating long-term wealth, managers should be aware that the way a business is structured can have a tremendous impact on its financial performance and on the individual risk of the owners.

BUSINESS TYPES

Most businesses start when an individual or a small group has an idea to create a new product or service or to improve a product or service that already exists. When the initial idea is born, the entrepreneurs do not necessarily think about the importance of forming the new business in a manner that will maximize their short- and long-term financial position. Usually, the primary focus is on developing the idea and determining whether it is viable in the marketplace. However, every business owner, even someone who is earning part-time income from a "hobby," should understand the ramifications of the organizational structures in his or her industry. In the sport industry, these structures include government-operated organizations, community-owned entities, non-profits, sole proprietorships, partnerships, subchapter S corporations, limited liability corporations or limited liability partnerships, and subchapter C corporations.

SIDEBAR 5.B   Entrepreneurs Changing the Sport Business Landscape

Though most people think first of professional sport and big-time college athletics when they think of sport management, entrepreneurs have created a variety of new entities that are growing in popularity. One of the most interesting is the endurance event industry. Participants compete in races that offer a variety of physical tasks, such as traditional running and swimming events, while also exposing the participants to extreme heat and cold. Among the most successful organizations in this industry is Tough Mudder (www.toughmudder.com). Co-founded in 2010 by Will Dean and Guy Livingstone, Tough Mudder courses require participants to engage in military-like endurance tasks that test both physical ability and mental perseverance. Tough Mudder initially created events that were based primarily upon teamwork and personal growth rather than competition, but it has greatly expanded the number and type of events it offers. Among its newer events, the World's Toughest Mudder presents competitors with a 24-hour challenge to determine the best athlete. Since the company's founding, it has had more than 3 million registrants for its events. In a short period of time, Tough Mudder and other companies operating within the same space have grown from small, niche organizations into international conglomerates that attract significant media and sponsor attention.

Government-Operated Organizations

It is important to remember that governments can operate businesses. In the sport industry, high school and collegiate athletic departments at public schools are ultimately operated by the government. Since the athletic department is a component of the public school, and the public school is operated by the city or county school district or the state, the government entity has ultimate authority over and responsibility for the athletic department's actions and financial performance. Chapter 14 details some of the important and unique financial considerations of intercollegiate athletic departments, and Chapter 13 discusses recreational programs, which are often subsidiaries of a government agency.

Most private businesses want minimal government involvement in their affairs. When former San Diego Padres owner Joan Kroc offered to donate all or a portion of the Padres to the City of San Diego, MLB immediately voiced its displeasure (Swank, 2004). Major League Baseball owners also rejected the suggestion of Carl Pohlad, former owner of the Minnesota Twins, that a portion of his team be sold to the State of Minnesota. If a sizable portion of the Padres or the Twins were to be owned by the government, citizens would have greater access to information about the financial operation of an MLB team, because information about how government agencies spend their money is available to citizens through **Freedom of Information requests** (requests made under the Freedom of Information Act or other laws and regulations requiring openness in government, sometimes referred to as "sunshine laws"). Fortunately for MLB, it retains an **antitrust exemption** that permits it to restrict the sale of franchises and ultimately determine who is eligible to become an owner.

SIDEBAR 5.C   Baltimore Colts Nearly Become the Property of the State of Maryland?

On March 29, 1984, Baltimore Colts fans, as well as various Baltimore and Maryland politicians, awoke to discover that their beloved team had moved during the night to Indianapolis, Indiana. The Colts, a team which was one of the best in the league in the 1950s to mid-1970s, had performed poorly on the field for roughly a decade. In addition, the team's owner, Bob Irsay, had annoyed local and state government officials with his demands for a new stadium ... that should be paid for by the public. Irsay's irascible personality and the Colts' poor play did not mesh well with government officials, who desired to see the Colts stay in town, but did not want to simply write a blank check to support new stadium construction. With Indianapolis promising favorable lease terms in their new, state-of-the-art Hoosier Dome, Irsay pushed for Baltimore and Maryland officials to increase their subsidies or the Colts would move. When it appeared the Colts might seriously consider Indianapolis's offer, Baltimore and Maryland officials proposed utilizing **eminent domain**—the government taking of private property for public use—to secure the Colts (Euchner, 1994). Though eminent domain had been and continues to be utilized to seize—for "just compensation" to its previous owner—private property to construct things such as dams, airports, freeways, schools, and other public facilities, it had not been fully vetted in a court of law as appropriate for a sport franchise. Government officials desired to seize the Colts and operate the franchise as a public entity. Fearing a potential seizure of his team, or, at the least, extensive time spent in litigation if government officials executed their plan, Irsay ordered the franchise to move in the middle of the night via 15 Mayflower trucks (Sibilla, 2014). Though Baltimore and Maryland officials would continue their eminent domain proceedings and continue to pursue legal action against the team, ultimately the Colts' quick move prevented any serious challenge from being executed since the franchise technically was no longer within the city or state jurisdictions. Despite the heartache from the Colts' rapid departure during that fateful snowy 1984 night, Baltimore would later convince Cleveland Browns owner Art Modell to move his franchise to Baltimore in 1996, largely based upon the construction of a new, publicly financed stadium.

Community-Owned Entities

Although the NFL requires its teams to be controlled by a primary individual owner, it has allowed the Green Bay Packers to maintain their ownership structure despite violating NFL rules. The Packers have a unique history and ownership structure. The Green Bay franchise, formed in 1919, was initially owned by the Indian Packing Company—hence the nickname "Packers" ("Birth of a team," n.d.). During its first few years the team was not financially successful, and in 1923 it was on the verge of folding. However, A.B. Turnbull, publisher of the *Green Bay Press-Gazette*, and four other men worked to save the team for the community ("Shareholder and financial history," n.d.). In August 1923, the Packers were re-formed as a non-profit organization called the Green Bay Packers Corporation, and stock certificates for 1,000 shares of stock were sold at $5 apiece ("Shareholder and financial history," n.d.). Because the team was established as a non-profit organization, owners of the team would not be financially rewarded. However, the initial stock sale ensured that the team would remain financially viable and that it would stay in Green Bay.

When the team encountered additional financial difficulty in 1935, the franchise was reorganized as Green Bay Packers Inc., and more shares were sold. The franchise also sold stock in 1950 at $25 per share. Unlike the earlier purchasers, who primarily lived in Green Bay, for the 1950 sale of stock, citizens across Wisconsin and former Green Bay residents living in other states came forward to purchase shares. The team no longer "belonged" to Green Bay but had become "Wisconsin's team," as over $50,000 was raised in an 11-day period ("Shareholder and financial history," n.d.). The team experienced tremendous on-field success in the 1960s under legendary coach Vince Lombardi, and as its NFL television exposure increased, the Packers began to attract fans from around the country. Many admired the rich history of the Packers and venerable Lambeau Field.

Despite the Packers' on-field success, by the 1990s the economics of the NFL had dramatically changed. The team was financially successful, but Lambeau Field was in need of considerable upgrades. Other NFL teams played in newer facilities that offered luxury suites and club seating. The Packers could continue to draw sellout crowds, but in order to maximize stadium revenues Lambeau Field needed significant remodeling. Since the team was owned by the community, raising funds would require an additional sale of stock. The NFL supported the Packers' plan to amend the articles of the corporation to offer additional shares to the general public. In November 1997 the Packers offered 400,000 shares to the general public ("Shareholder and financial history," n.d.). The response was overwhelming, and the team was able to raise millions of dollars to pay for the Lambeau Field renovations. Citizens in every state and in some foreign countries purchased shares. Many of the shares were exchanged as Christmas gifts (Wolfley, 1997).

In late 2011, the Packers opened their fifth stock sale in franchise history. Though Lambeau Field had been renovated in 1997 with proceeds from the team's fourth stock sale, the franchise hoped to renovate and expand Lambeau Field once again, with significant improvements to its scoreboards and entrance gates. More than 268,000 shares were sold at $250 apiece, yielding in excess of $67 million (Spofford, 2012). The sale helped defray total renovation costs of $143 million. Similar to the 1997 sale, the 2011/2012 offering attracted "investors" from around the world, and 250,000 new shareholders were added to the ownership roll. By 2019, the Packers had 5,009,562 outstanding shares "owned" by 361,169 different people ("Shareholders," 2019).

Owners of stock in the Packers are motivated by sentiment rather than the expectation of financial gain. Shareholders may attend an annual meeting and vote on franchise issues, but they will never receive a dividend. In addition, shares cannot be sold except back to the team, at a significant discount from the initial price ("Shareholder and financial history," n.d.). However, shares can be given or bequeathed to others. The team's unique financial structure has enabled it to remain in the small community of Green Bay (population 105,116) while the rest of the teams in the NFL play in much larger metropolitan markets.

While the Packers' ownership situation is unique in the United States, in the Canadian Football League (CFL) three teams are essentially owned by members of their community. The Edmonton Eskimos, Saskatchewan Roughriders, and Winnipeg Blue Bombers have ownership structures that resemble certain aspects of the Packers' ownership plan. Though the public-ownership model was once more common in the CFL, over the past 40 years, the league has attracted private ownership for many of its franchises. Among the three publicly operated teams, the Blue Bombers have a slightly different financial structure as there are no shareholders. Of the three franchises, the Eskimos have been the most successful on the field, having won the second most championships in the CFL. In 2019, amid concerns that the Montreal Alouettes' owners wanted to divest, the CFL purchased the franchise, creating a situation where only five of the nine CFL teams were operated by a "traditional" owner ("Alouettes sold …," 2019). In 2020, the CFL was able to sell the Montreal franchise to Sid Spiegel and Gary Stern.

Non-profits

Non-profit organizations—those that are not conducted for the profit of owners—operate under a variety of specific rules that make them distinct from for-profit enterprises. One of the main rules governing non-profits is that shareholders never receive dividends; most non-profit organizations that generate more revenues than expenses and costs will spend that money to further the organization's business interests, whereas a for-profit business's net income would likely be distributed to the shareholders as dividends. A variety of sporting events are operated by non-profit organizations. For instance, the PGA Tour is a non-profit company, and it requires that nearly all PGA Tour events be operated on a non-profit basis.

SIDEBAR 5.D   NFL Changes its Tax-exempt Status

In 2015, the National Football League elected to alter its long-standing tax-exempt status. Though the individual franchises (except for the Green Bay Packers) have always operated as for-profit entities owned by individuals or partnerships, since the 1940s the league office had resisted calls for it to change its own status. Operating as a tax-exempt organization permitted the NFL to avoid paying some potential taxes but also required it to submit select financial information to the government, including the salaries of key employees. NFL commissioner Roger Goodell's salary—$44.2 million in 2012, $35 million in 2013, $34.1 million in 2014, and $31.7 million in 2015 (Garcia, 2016)—was perceived by many members of Congress, the media, and sports fans as obscene, particularly for the head of a non-profit organization. In addition, for many years, Goodell made more money than any player, even while concerns regarding player health, particularly with greater understanding of concussion, were increasing. Though the league office often reported financial losses, former Oklahoma Senator Tom Coburn led a chorus of complaints that the exemption cost the United States millions of dollars in tax revenue each year (Belson, 2015). By reclassifying its tax status, the NFL has been able to avoid some public scrutiny of its financial operations, but it also has paid additional taxes under its new structure.

Sole Proprietorships

The vast majority of for-profit businesses in the United States operate as sole proprietorships. A **sole proprietorship** is a business that is legally owned and operated by a single individual. No formal paperwork is required to establish the business, and the paperwork necessary to sustain the business is minimal (compared to other business types). Extensive meetings to determine strategy and company direction are not necessary, as the owner can simply make decisions unilaterally. Sole proprietorships are typically easier to sell than other business types. The business exists as long as the owner is operating it, and all profits belong to the owner.

However, the simplicity of the sole proprietorship presents some drawbacks. It can be more difficult for a sole proprietorship to raise capital than for other business types. More importantly, the owner is personally liable for the business's activities. A successful lawsuit against the business can result in the owner being required to sell personal assets to pay the judgment. Most owners of sole proprietorships purchase liability insurance to guard against the financial ramifications of potential lawsuits. Because sport and recreation activities tend to have a higher likelihood of physical injury than activities provided in many other industries, owners of sole proprietorships in sport and recreation often require additional insurance or choose to convert to an alternative business structure. Some of the business structures discussed below can provide a **corporate veil** separating the business from the owner. This protection from personal liability is an important reason why business owners often choose one of these alternative structures.

SIDEBAR 5.E   Insurance a Forgotten Component of Sport Business Operations?

Insurance carriers (or the government) create an arrangement with their clients to assume significant financial obligations for outcomes that are not likely to occur. In exchange for assuming large risks, the insurance company will charge a premium, based upon the likelihood that the "risky outcome" will occur and, in that case, what amount of financial obligation will be created. People who drive a car understand the basic concept of insurance as they pay a small amount of money each month to protect against the outcome of an accident that could do significant harm to person or property. Like any insurance product, car insurance rates increase or decrease based upon various factors (age, gender, income, previous driving activities, etc.) that might predict a potential accident. In addition, the rates will fluctuate by the potential damages that could be incurred (more expensive automobiles are costlier to replace, and therefore insure, than less expensive automobiles).

The sport business industry utilizes a variety of insurance products to cover all aspects of various activities. The sport insurance market has been rapidly changing due to risk factor modifications. The entire football industry has undergone a recent transformation with the increased awareness of concussion dangers and other injuries and the resulting litigation that has occurred. Since 2011, the number of insurance carriers willing to insure various player-related risks in the NFL has decreased from over ten to just one (Fainaru & Fainaru-Wada, 2019). At the youth football level, many organizations no longer have many choices for coverage and what does exist often has rapidly increasing deductibles, causing many recreational and government-operated football programs to shut down their activities. Pop Warner Executive Director Jon Butler noted, "People say football will never go away, but if we can't get insurance, it will" (Fainaru & Fainaru-Wada, 2019, para. 4). Other contact sports have seen similar increases in costs while many insurers simply exit the industry. Alex Fairly, CEO of the Fairly Group, a risk management firm that still retains many professional sport clients, noted, "If you're football, hockey or soccer, the insurance business doesn't want you" (Fainaru & Fainaru-Wada, 2019, para. 30).

Sport-related insurance changes have also occurred in limited or non-contact sports. Most insurance carriers have always assessed risk factors (age, position played, etc.) in evaluating baseball player contracts, but over the past ten years a number of carriers that still insure contracts have altered their approach as player salaries have increased dramatically. In most cases, MLB player contracts now insured for catastrophic injury no longer cover the entire contract length. Carriers now typically cover only a portion of the contract, so if a player signs a six-year deal, an insurance carrier might offer the team a contract that would cover the first two to three years of the contract and then renew (at potentially different terms) the agreement to cover the player's final three years (Branda, 2013). The insurance company also will typically require a player to be injured for a considerable period of time (multiple months) and be verified by the insurance carrier's doctor as unable to play before any compensation is provided. In 2013, New York Yankee Alex Rodriguez needed hip surgery while he was playing under a ten-year, $275 million contract ("Claim game," 2013). The massive contract, combined with Rodriguez's age and earlier admission of steroid use (which would potentially impact the risk assumed by the insurance company), caused many to speculate as to how much money the Yankees would owe Rodriguez and how much would be covered by insurance if the injury prevented him from ever playing again (Branda, 2013). A potential outcome existed where the Yankees might have been better off financially by letting Rodriguez retire rather than rehabilitate and return to play. Rodriguez was able to return eventually and played until 2016, but his situation caused other insurance carriers to reassess their involvement in MLB.

The situation with Rodriguez did not have any impact upon *his* potential compensation. With a guaranteed contract, Rodriguez would be paid regardless of his playing status; it was just a matter of how much the Yankees would cover of the overall obligation. Though player insurance in professional team sports is typically retained by the team, in college sports some players have begun to retain **loss of value insurance** to protect themselves against injury before they play professionally. The NCAA has allowed players to retain this insurance for many years by paying for it directly or by securing the required premiums through loans (Dodd, 2017). However, recently the NCAA has permitted many players to access the Student Assistance Fund to cover their premiums ("Loss-of-value insurance FAQ," n.d.), essentially allowing the athlete's school to provide added compensation to cover against future losses due to injury. Unfortunately, even with this insurance in place, many injured athletes have realized that the coverage does not equate to a potential professional contract and they have made their own risk assessments ... and decided to skip potential games. After Notre Dame star linebacker Jaylon Smith suffered a severe and potentially career-ending injury in the 2016 Fiesta Bowl, his likely first round selection and resulting $20+ million contract vanished as he was chosen in the second round. Though insured for roughly $700,000, the potentially massive difference in compensation caused many other star players such as Stanford's Christian McCaffrey and LSU's Leonard Fournette to sit out their team's bowl games (Dodd, 2017). Fortunately, Smith later developed into an NFL star, but other players have not been so fortunate. South Carolina running back Marcus Lattimore never recovered from multiple injuries he sustained in college and though he collected approximately $1.7 million from insurance, his likely career NFL earnings if he had been healthy would have been many millions more (Dodd, 2017).

Interestingly, though most players will be paid much more to play than to be injured, some insurance policies may "encourage" some players to retire. In tennis, golf, and other individual sports, the athlete is responsible for obtaining and maintaining injury insurance. Those policies are typically maintained to protect the athlete from injury, but in the case of former star golfer Anthony Kim, his $10-million policy may have encouraged him to give up the sport. After a fast start to his career, Kim earned millions of dollars and established himself as one of the top stars of the future in American golf. Then a series of injuries resulted in Kim needing to rest and heal. While his injuries were certainly serious, there were concerns that his $10 million (or more) insurance policy would weigh against Kim ever returning to play professionally. Since there was concern that Kim might not be the same upon returning as he was before the injury, the financial equation might have been in Kim's favor to retire ... and collect the insurance. As one of Kim's friends noted, "He's trying to weigh the risks of coming back. The way he's phrased it to me is, 'If I take one swing on [the PGA] Tour, the policy is voided'" (Shipnuck, 2014, para. 9). Kim never did return to the PGA Tour.

Partnerships

A **general partnership** is simply the joining of two or more individuals with the intent to own and operate a business. The partnership agreement may divide ownership equally or unequally. Most attorneys will advise against operating a business as a 50/50 partnership, even if the owners are family members, because a 50/50 partnership can result in a stalemate. Neither partner in such a partnership can institute policy without the permission of the other, since business decisions must be approved by a majority (50.1%) of the owners. However, disproportionate ownership positions may place the **minority partner** or partners at a disadvantage. If a two-person partnership is owned with a 60/40 split, the minority partner is entitled to only 40% of the profits and only 40% of the influence in company decisions. That partner can be outvoted on any organizational issue. Typically, investors in partnerships who take minority positions are not likely to invest as much money as they would if they were receiving control.

SIDEBAR 5.F   Al Davis as Raiders General Partner

Perhaps the most intriguing partnership agreement in professional sport involves the NFL's Oakland Raiders. Al Davis had been the head coach and general manager of the Oakland Raiders in the American Football League from 1963 through 1966. After achieving on- and off-field success, he became commissioner of the AFL in 1966. At the time, the AFL and the NFL were competing to sign players and attract fans. Davis, never one to compromise easily, sought to gain an advantage over the NFL by signing the majority of the latter's star quarterbacks and instituting an aggressive marketing plan (Harris, 1986).

   Almost immediately after Davis became commissioner, however, three AFL owners secretly negotiated with the NFL to merge the leagues. When the leagues merged without Davis's input, Davis was upset, as he felt the AFL could have succeeded against the NFL. Davis felt his work made him the likely choice to become NFL commissioner after the merger. However, the NFL retained commissioner Pete Rozelle.

   After the AFL-NFL merger, Al Davis signed a ten-year contract to return to Oakland as general manager and part owner of the Raiders. He was offered a 10% stake in the team—a stake valued at approximately $1 million—for only $18,500 (Harris, 1986). More importantly, Davis was named managing general partner. Ed McGah and Wayne Valley were the other general partners.

   After continued success on the field and in the front office, Davis utilized language in the partnership agreement to his advantage. When other teams contacted him about becoming their general manager, Davis convinced McGah that McGah needed to sign over complete ownership control of the Raiders to him. McGah, in one of the most amazing incidents in sports business history, signed a contract he did not even bother to read. The contract essentially named Al Davis the Raiders' "controlling" owner (Harris, 1986). The partnership agreement that governed the franchise stipulated that if any two of the general partners agreed to a contract, the other had no recourse. Even though Valley owned the largest percentage of the team, Davis controlled the franchise and would represent the organization in all matters. Valley eventually sold his shares in the partnership after his litigation to regain control of the franchise failed. It was not until 2005 that Davis would acquire a majority of the Raiders, when he purchased shares still owned by McGah's heirs. Davis subsequently sold roughly 20% of the team for $150 million to investors in 2007 to improve the franchise's cash flow (Young, 2007).

When Al Davis died in 2011, control of the Raiders passed to his widow, Carol, and his son, Mark. Though Davis owned only 47% of the Raiders at the time of his death, his partnership agreement assured that control of the franchise would remain in his family (Tafur, 2011). Mark Davis has presided over the Raiders since his father's death, though with not nearly so much flair and controversy. However, despite the perception that he was not qualified to effectively operate the Raiders, Mark Davis was able to secure a significant amount of public money to help construct the $1.8 billion Allegiant Stadium in Las Vegas, where the Raiders moved in 2020.

A general partnership may be established either formally or informally. An **express partnership** can be created by a contract between the parties. An **implied partnership** may exist if individuals merely act as partners, such as by sharing a company checking account or by jointly signing for a business loan. Owners must understand the consequences of their actions in the course of operating a business, as a court will examine the activities of the owners when determining liabilities.

A partnership presents the same disadvantages as a sole proprietorship. The partners have personal liability for company losses or judgments. In some cases, a minority partner may be personally liable for a greater share of the company's liabilities than his or her percentage of ownership. If a partner who owns 60% of a business goes bankrupt, a judgment against the business may result in the minority partner's being required to cover financial obligations of the insolvent general partner, even though the minority partner owns only 40% of the company. For this reason, some partnerships involve **limited partners**— partners who are liable only for their direct financial contribution and do not perform any formal managerial role in the operation of the business. Limited partners must remember that the general partner or partners do have personal liability and that a judgment or other financial loss could bankrupt the general partners and, hence, the overall company. It is important to note that limited partners can hold more than 50% of the ownership in a company. A limited partner who owns 60% of an organization, for example, does not have any formal role in the company's operation but is entitled to 60% of the profits.

A partnership ends when a partner dies or goes bankrupt or when the partnership engages in any illegal activity. A partnership may also be discontinued by the courts if one of the partners is adjudicated insane. A difficulty sometimes arises in the termination of a partnership if the business is not making money. Ultimately, if the business cannot make money, the partnership will be dissolved. In some cases, however, the partners have differing opinions about the future financial viability of the company. If the partners cannot agree on whether to continue the business, a resolution may require court intervention. The court may dissolve the partnership or may determine how, and at what compensation, one or more partners may exit.

SIDEBAR 5.G   What Type of Owner do Fans Want?

In North American professional sports, the owners of most teams are individuals or groups of individuals. Typically, sports teams are not held as C corporations. In fact, the NFL bars publicly traded companies and non-profit organizations from owning franchises. The current public ownership status of the Green Bay Packers is permitted because the team was organized as a non-profit organization before the current NFL ownership rules were established (Eichelberger, 1998; "Shareholder and financial history," n.d.). The NFL once required that one individual own at least 30% of the franchise and that this owner did not control a majority interest in a team from Major League Baseball, the National Basketball Association, or the National Hockey League (Eichelberger, 1998; Chass, 2003). However, the rapidly increasing value of NFL franchises, combined with the aging of many owners, resulted in changes in the ownership rules. In 2004, the NFL altered the 30% rule to allow a primary owner to own just 20% of the team if his or her family owned another 10%. The required figures were "flipped" in 2009 to mandate that the primary owner control 10% if his or her family owned at least another 20% (Kaplan, 2009). In addition, the NFL wants each franchise to have one decision maker in attendance at league meetings. These rules ensure that individual teams are not likely to change their "organizational philosophy," since controlling ownership is retained by one individual (or family) rather than a group of shareholders (Tucker, 2003).

There have been cases of large Fortune 500 companies holding a professional sport franchise in their portfolio. George Steinbrenner purchased the New York Yankees from the Columbia Broadcasting System (CBS) in 1973. The Atlanta Braves of MLB were owned by media mogul Ted Turner for many years. The flamboyant Turner was often seen at games and on television discussing his hope for the team's on-field success (Conlin, 2008). Although Turner certainly wanted to generate a profit, he was primarily concerned with attempting to win the National League Pennant and the World Series. When Turner sold the team to AOL-Time Warner, many fans noticed a change: AOL-Time Warner operated the team much as they operated their numerous other corporate holdings (Conlin, 2008). The team was required to set a strict yearly budget. Whereas Turner was often willing to trade for talented but expensive players in the middle of the season, fans perceived AOL-Time Warner as being solely interested in achieving a specific return on investment rather than fielding the best possible team to compete for championships (Tucker, 2003).

The Disney Corporation owned the Los Angeles Angels of Anaheim from 1996 to 2003. Although Disney management initially thought it could conduct extensive cross-promotions of the team with its theme parks, movies, and other entertainment offerings, it discovered that the benefits of MLB ownership mainly pertain to the "ego gratification" of the team's owner. (An owner of a professional sport franchise will be known throughout the team's metropolitan area and potentially throughout the United States and parts of the rest of the world.) Despite the Angels' 2002 World Series win, Disney soon realized that the team could not generate the same return on investment as its other holdings and sold the team to Artie Moreno for $184 million in 2003 (King, 2003). Moreno has since inspired and annoyed many Angels fans, who appreciate that the team has spent money lavishly, but have been largely disappointed in the results ("Moreno keeps promise," 2008). For example, in December 2011 the Angels signed Albert Pujols to a $254 million, ten-year contract even though Pujols was 31 years old ("Albert Pujols, Angels," 2011). The following year, the Angels signed Josh Hamilton to a five-year, $125 million contract despite concerns that Hamilton was likely to miss many games given his age, his injury history, and personal problems experienced in his past. Unfortunately for Angels' fans, despite Moreno's largesse, which has resulted in the Angels ranking in the top ten in MLB payroll nearly every year since he acquired the team, the Angels' on-field performance has been subpar as they only made the playoffs one time from 2010 to 2019. During this time period, the Angels have not only spent considerable sums of money, but they have also had the best player in the game, Mike Trout, making it all the more baffling for fans why the team has not had more on-field success.

Subchapter S Corporations

The main financial advantage of a **subchapter S corporation** (often called an **S corp**) is that profits flow through the business to the shareholders and are taxed only once, as ordinary income to the shareholders. A second advantage is that the shareholders are shielded from personal liability (beyond their investment) by the corporate veil. A subchapter S corporation can own subsidiaries that operate independently (from a legal standpoint), which enables the S corp to be shielded from liability, as well.

Subchapter S corporations do have some significant drawbacks, particularly if the owners seek to grow the business and involve a wide variety of investors. Subchapter S corporations must be based in the United States, and all of the investors—who may number no more than 100—must be from the United States. An S corp can issue only one form of **stock** (a security that represents an ownership percentage of a company), meaning every share must have the same voting rights and dividend allotments. Many businesses that do not anticipate having a large, diversified ownership structure and do not intend to operate outside the United States choose to be incorporated as subchapter S corporations. Numerous sport businesses in the United States are S corps.

Limited Liability Corporations and Limited Liability Partnerships

Forming and operating a subchapter S corporation requires extensive paperwork and attention to detail. For this reason, many business owners choose to operate as a **limited liability corporation (LLC)** or a **limited liability partnership (LLP)**. An LLC or LLP operates in many ways like a subchapter S corporation. Profits flow through to the investors and are taxed as ordinary income. The LLC and LLP structures also provide a corporate veil against personal liability. However, LLCs and LLPs are typically easier to establish than S corps, through simple paperwork filed in the state where the LLC or LLP will initially operate. Tax forms are also much easier to fill out and file than those for a subchapter S corporation. However, because LLCs and LLPs are fairly new business entities, national standards regarding their operation are still being established and formalized. Individual states govern LLCs and LLPs in a variety of ways. In some states, rules for LLCs and LLPs have been determined through legislative or judicial action, but in other states ground rules have not been firmly established. States also differ in their laws regarding taxation of LLC and LLP owners. Investors should seek financial and legal advice regarding the formation and operation of LLCs and LLPs.

Subchapter C Corporations

When most people think of corporations, they think of Fortune 500 companies such as Disney or General Motors. Disney and General Motors are indeed corporations, but specifically they are classified as **subchapter C corporations** (often called **C corps**). Many, but not all, of the 500 largest companies in the world operate as C corporations, for the primary reason that C corporations may seek investors and conduct business activities around the world. To become a C corporation, a company must file extensive paperwork in its home state. Because of its favorable state laws, Delaware is home to many of the largest C corps, despite the fact that these companies typically do not do much, if any, business in Delaware. Once established, the corporation must hold annual meetings, elect a board of directors, and provide specific annual paperwork to the government and to shareholders.

The C corporation provides the corporate veil that protects investors from personal liability. However, unlike a subchapter S corporation, a C corporation is taxed as a separate legal entity before any profits that remain may be provided to shareholders. Since the shareholders must then pay taxes on their dividends, C corporations are said to be subject to "double taxation." For example, if a subchapter S corporation earned a $200,000 profit, that money would flow through to the owners' personal taxes. If the individual tax rate was 35%, then the owners would pay a total tax of $70,000. However, a company operated as a C corporation would first pay corporate taxes on the $200,000 profit. With a corporate tax rate of 35%, the corporation would pay $70,000 in tax, leaving $130,000. If the company were then to issue a dividend to the owners for the entire $130,000, the owners would pay 35% tax on the $130,000.

Companies organized as C corporations are not limited in their number of shareholders. In addition, a C corp can issue different classifications of stock and can sell stock to foreign nationals and institutional investors. A profitable company operated as a partnership, LLC, or subchapter S corporation may

EXHIBIT 5.1 Advantages and disadvantages of various for-profit business structures.

TYPE	ADVANTAGES	DISADVANTAGES
Sole proprietorship	Easily created and managed Flow-through taxation	Personal liability Raising capital
Partnership	Easily created Flow-through taxation	Potential management disputes Personal liability (except limited partners)
S corp	Flow-through taxation Limited liability	Limited number of potential investors Costs of formation and operation Single classification of stock can be issued
LLC/LLP	Flow-through taxation Limited liability	Undefined and inconsistent state operating standards
C corp	Limited liability Unlimited number of investors Different classifications of stock can be issued	Costs of formation and operation Double taxation

elect to change its structure to a C corporation, a process called "going public." By going public the owner or owners potentially can generate a tremendous amount of money, and other investors also can take a significant stake in the operation of the company. Decisions regarding the direction of the company are made by the majority of shareholders. If one person or group of people holds 50.1% of the stock, then that person or group has the power to set policies. In most cases, when a company goes public, no one owner retains more than 50.1% of the stock. Factions of stockholders must vote together to establish or alter company policies. In some cases, prominent founders of companies have been "forced out" of their management positions by other shareholders working in concert.

Exhibit 5.1 summarizes the advantages and disadvantages of various for-profit business structures.

STOCK MARKETS

Every company has individuals who own a percentage of the organization. Though many companies issue stock to owners, not every company is publicly traded. The vast majority of companies are privately held, meaning new investors, whether individuals or institutions, must be invited to purchase stock. The stock of companies that do go public will be listed for sale on a **stock market** or **stock exchange**. Stock exchanges exist around the world; the most prominent in the United States are the New York Stock Exchange (NYSE) and the National

Association of Securities Dealers Automated Quotations (NASDAQ). Each exchange lists the stocks of companies that are available for purchase or sale. To be listed on the exchange, a company must meet a variety of requirements, most of them relating to company capitalization, revenues, and number of outstanding shares. The stock exchange acts as the clearinghouse for brokers to buy and sell listed companies.

The New York Stock Exchange, sometimes known as the "Big Board," is the largest exchange in the world when measured by market capitalization. However, the Bombay Stock Exchange in Mumbai, India has the most public companies listed. In addition, NASDAQ—the world's first electronic stock market, which typically attracts emerging and technology companies—and a couple of other exchanges have more listings than the NYSE. Most of the industrialized nations of the world have at least one stock exchange; Canada, for example, has the Toronto Stock Exchange (TSX). Online trading has enabled investors to buy and sell stocks directly in each of these markets.

Professional Sport Franchises

Many non-North American professional sport franchises are listed on stock markets around the world. One of the more notable stock offerings was for Manchester United in 1991 (Kaplan, 2001). For many years Manchester United has been one of the most powerful brand names in sport, and when it went public its stock was quickly purchased by fans around the world. In 2003, Malcolm Glazer (owner of the NFL's Tampa Bay Buccaneers) launched a takeover bid for Manchester United. After Glazer successfully gained control of the franchise, it was delisted in 2005. Ironically, stock in the franchise was offered on the New York Stock Exchange in 2012 as part of a refinancing effort by the Glazer family.

North American professional sport franchises are currently not traded on a stock market, but some teams were listed in the past. The New England Patriots of the NFL, the Cleveland Cavaliers and Milwaukee Bucks of the NBA, and the Baltimore Orioles of MLB were all taken public in the 1960s or 1970s. Each of them has since returned to private ownership. Shares of the Boston Celtics were offered to the public in 1986, and shares of the Cleveland Indians were offered in 1998. These stocks attracted some interest, but they were initially priced too high for most investors to achieve acceptable financial returns (Much & Phillips, 1999). The Indians were taken private in 2000, and the Celtics were taken private in 2002.

Athletes Selling Their "Own" Stock

It is not uncommon for family members and other supporters to provide money to help athletes pursue their dreams. In many cases, the athlete compensates these supporters by promising a portion of the athlete's long-term earnings through a verbal or contractual agreement. In some extreme situations, athletes have had to endure legal disputes with family members or past agents regarding how much compensation was required. However, in most cases, parties invested money in hopes of a future payout from an athlete's success without a formal mechanism. However, in 2013, Fantex Brokerage Services created an environment where athletes could offer investors an opportunity to receive a portion of their future earnings from salaries, endorsements, and other sources (such as film and broadcasting roles), in exchange for buying "stock" in the athlete now. San Francisco 49ers tight end Vernon Davis and Houston Texans running back Arian Foster were among the first athletes to sell stock through the new company. Fantex paid Foster $10 million for a 20% stake in his future earnings, and that stake was resold to new investors (Rovell, 2013). Davis sold a 10% stake for $4 million. In Davis's case, Fantex announced that his 2015 investment in three Jamba Juice locations would be included in the investor's portfolio ("Fantex invites," 2015). Fantex has signed a number of other athlete deals since its foray into the sport marketplace.

SIDEBAR 5.H   What is the Dow Jones?

The performance of the overall stock market is a matter of interest to many people, not only investors. One way to examine the market's overall performance is to track a specific stock market to see how all of its stocks are performing. Since each market lists hundreds or even thousands of stocks, you might have to dissect the overall stock market into **stock market indexes** in order to examine the overall market's performance or the performance of market subsectors. The Dow Jones Industrial Average (the "Dow") is the most famous stock market index. In 1884—long before computers were available to crunch massive quantities of numbers—Charles Henry Dow created the index to attempt to track the overall market by following the price fluctuations of a few selected stocks. Dow's original index included 11 stocks. It increased to 12 stocks in 1896, 20 stocks in 1916, and then 30 in 1928. As the overall economy has changed, the companies included in the Dow have also been changed. The Dow lists only well-known and widely held **large-cap companies**, those with a **market capitalization**—the market price of a company, equal to the number of outstanding shares multiplied by the price per share—greater than $5 billion. General Electric is the only company that remains from Henry Dow's original list. The computation of the Dow uses a scaled average that accounts for stock splits.

Since the Dow contains only large-cap stocks, some investors turn to other indexes for a broader picture of the stock market's performance. The Standard and Poor's 500 (S&P 500) is a popular stock market index. Note that the S&P 500 does not list the 500 largest companies, but rather 500 companies that, together, are believed to provide an accurate indication of the overall performance of the stock market. Other popular indexes include the Russell 2000, which tracks the performance of **small-cap stocks** (stocks of companies with a market capitalization between $250 million and $1 billion), and the Wilshire 5000, which tracks the performance of all publicly traded companies in the United States. These indexes tend to move in similar directions over an extended period of time, but short-term market conditions may affect the indexes differently.

GOVERNMENT INFLUENCE ON THE BUSINESS ENVIRONMENT

The US government has a vested interest in the financial success of individuals and corporations. A prolonged poor economy hurts citizens, and since citizens may vote for many government positions, the government must at least tacitly acknowledge the state of the economy and at least appear to be addressing economic concerns. Although the United States operates under a **capitalist** economic system, in which the majority of capital is privately owned, over the past 100-plus years it has moved away from 19th-century **laissez-faire** economics—where the government meddled little in the business environment beyond setting and enforcing rudimentary laws—toward a more **socialistic** system, where the government is more actively involved in owning and administering means of production.

Two important events in the 20th century spurred the US government into taking a more active role in the business community. During the Great Depression, President Franklin D. Roosevelt enacted extensive and expensive government programs to provide food for the poor and work for the unemployed. After the economic downturn ended, many of these programs were not repealed. Then, during President Lyndon B. Johnson's administration in the 1960s, Congress passed expensive **Great Society** initiatives to combat poverty. Much of the legislation passed during Johnson's tenure, such as Medicare and Medicaid, is still active.

The long-term economic results of Roosevelt's and Johnson's policies have been mixed. Massive amounts of spending did help to spur some economic activity, but many economists believe the government's large financial commitments could have been better utilized in the private sector. The programs have clearly created an expectation among the majority of the country's citizens that the government will be actively involved in their individual and business affairs. Currently, the government's overall role in the economy encompasses a variety of areas of influence. Our discussion in this chapter will center on two important governmental functions: monetary policy and fiscal policy.

Monetary Policy and the Federal Reserve

Monetary policy is policy the government sets to control the supply, availability, and cost of money. In most cases, when monetary policy decisions are made, the vast majority of American citizens pay little attention. The **Federal Reserve**, or "Fed," is the primary organizing body that attempts to maintain the overall economic health of the United States. Established in 1913, the Federal Reserve acts as "the nation's bank," controlling the nation's currency and lending money to the government, among other functions. The Federal Reserve's main goal is to manage the economy so it grows steadily. Its secondary goal is to control inflation—the devaluation of the currency. Inflation is not unusual (see Chapter 4), but a high rate of inflation, like that encountered in the late 1970s, causes significant damage to the economy.

The Federal Reserve system includes 12 district Federal Reserve Banks and numerous member banks across the United States. Seven governors serve 14-year terms on the Federal Reserve Board, with staggered terms to ensure continuity. Each of the governors is appointed by the President of the United

States and approved by Congress. The length of time each governor serves is longer than the terms served by the President and members of Congress, to diminish political interference and enable the Federal Reserve to serve the short- and long-term financial interests of the country rather than the whims of elected politicians. Typically, the governors meet approximately every six weeks, with additional meetings scheduled if needed.

The Federal Reserve acts to

- regulate the nation's currency supply
- serve as banker for many government agencies
- lend to banks
- audit banks
- control the currency
- guard more than 10,000 tons of gold held in the New York Federal Reserve Bank
- administrate the transfer of funds via checks.

Usually, the Federal Reserve does not need to act often or dramatically to maintain the economy. Typically, the overall economy shifts gradually, and the Fed can take subtle action to attempt to nudge it in a positive direction. However, during times of concern, the Federal Reserve may need to act often. If the economy is rapidly slowing or expanding, the Fed may meet more than once every six weeks to set interest rates. Natural disasters, such as Hurricane Katrina, or terrorist acts, such as those that occurred on September 11, 2001, can cause dramatic shifts in the overall economic climate. If necessary, the Federal Reserve will meet and act multiple times in a single month.

SIDEBAR 5.I   What is the Impact of an Interest Rate Change?

The Federal Reserve typically changes the discount and federal funds rates by only a quarter of a percent at a time. If the Fed feels the economy needs a more dramatic change, it might increase or decrease the rates by a half percent or more. A hundredth of a percent is called a **basis point**. If the Federal Reserve cuts rates by one-quarter of one percent, then it has cut rates by 25 basis points. Note that a 25-basis point increase or decrease is not the same *percentage change* for different established rates. If a 10% rate is cut by 25 basis points (to 9.75%), the rate is changed by 2.5%, but if a 5% rate is cut by 25 basis points (to 4.75%), the rate has changed by 5%. Most people pay no attention to the Fed's changes in interest rates, until they start shopping for a loan. Even a small increase of 25 basis points can dramatically alter the monthly or yearly interest payment on a loan, particularly when the loan has a large principal or a long term.

For instance, a person who wishes to purchase a $250,000 house and can make a down payment of $50,000 would need a mortgage loan for the remaining $200,000. Most home mortgages have a term of 10, 15, 20, or 30 years, although some mortgages have a term of 40 or even 50 years. Exhibit 5.2 shows the effect of a small increase or decrease in rates on a monthly mortgage payment.

EXHIBIT 5.2 Monthly payment (principal and interest) for a $200,000 loan.

RATE	TERM				
	10 YEARS	15 YEARS	20 YEARS	30 YEARS	40 YEARS
3.50%	$1,977.72	$1,429.77	$1,159.92	$898.09	$774.78
3.75%	$2,001.22	$1,454.44	$1,185.78	$926.23	$805.05
4.00%	$2,024.90	$1,479.38	$1,211.96	$954.83	$835.88
4.25%	$2,048.75	$1,504.56	$1,238.47	$983.88	$867.24
4.50%	$2,072.77	$1,529.99	$1,265.30	$1,013.37	$899.13
4.75%	$2,096.95	$1,555.66	$1,292.45	$1,043.29	$931.52
5.00%	$2,121.31	$1,581.59	$1,319.91	$1,073.64	$964.39
5.25%	$2,145.83	$1,607.76	$1,347.69	$1,104.41	$997.74
5.50%	$2,170.53	$1,634.17	$1,375.77	$1,135.58	$1,031.54
5.75%	$2,195.38	$1,660.82	$1,404.17	$1,167.15	$1,065.78
6.00%	$2,220.41	$1,687.71	$1,432.86	$1,199.10	$1,100.43
6.25%	$2,245.60	$1,714.85	$1,461.86	$1,231.43	$1,135.48
6.50%	$2,270.96	$1,742.21	$1,491.15	$1,264.14	$1,170.91
6.75%	$2,296.48	$1,769.82	$1,520.73	$1,297.20	$1,206.71
7.00%	$2,322.17	$1,797.66	$1,550.60	$1,330.60	$1,242.86
8.00%	$2,426.55	$1,911.30	$1,672.88	$1,467.53	$1,390.62

Although the Federal Reserve performs many functions, it focuses primarily on two main areas: setting interest rates and monitoring the money supply. The Fed studies a variety of evaluation measures before making changes in interest rates or the money supply. These measures include unemployment claims, durable goods orders, housing starts, new factory orders, and overall consumer confidence.

SETTING INTEREST RATES

The first primary responsibility of the Federal Reserve is to set interest rates. The Fed does not mandate the rates individual lending institutions charge customers for loans for cars, homes, and so forth, but it does establish lending policies, and it sets two important interest rates. The **discount rate** is the rate at which banks may borrow money from the Federal Reserve. This rate is used primarily as a baseline for setting other rates—the vast majority of banks do not ever borrow money from the Federal Reserve, as this would be seen as a sign of financial trouble for the bank and is typically a last resort. However, banks do borrow money from other banks on a daily basis. The rate a bank charges another bank when it loans excess money through the Federal Reserve is the **federal funds rate**.

The reason banks borrow money from each other is that the Federal Reserve requires every bank to have a reserve available in case customers wish to withdraw their deposits. This reserve is essentially 10% of total deposits, although the stipulations are complex (Morris & Morris, 1999). One factor that led to the Great Depression of the 1930s was that a large number of customers visited their local branches to withdraw funds (particularly after President-elect Franklin D. Roosevelt failed to renounce formally a radical change to US dollar valuation that he had been privately discussing), and some of the banks did not have sufficient money available to give to them. A financial panic ensued as more and more customers became concerned that money was not available. This caused banks to fail. The US government has established the Federal Deposit Insurance Corporation (FDIC; not a part of the Federal Reserve) to assure citizens that their money is safe in banks. Typically, savings accounts and some (though not all) other accounts are insured by the federal government up to $250,000 in the event a bank fails.

Each day, banks determine how much money they have on deposit and how much money they have loaned to customers. Since banks earn profits by loaning money and charging interest, they benefit from loaning as much money as possible. To adhere to the Fed's reserve requirement, a bank that does not have enough money on hand on a given day must borrow from another bank (or the Federal Reserve, in dire situations) to increase its reserve. Banks that are in good financial standing can typically find other banks willing to loan them money. Each day, hundreds of banks borrow from and lend to one another to maintain their reserve requirement and maximize financial returns. It is not uncommon for a bank to borrow money from another bank one day and then loan money back to that other bank a few days later, as each bank's overall deposits fluctuate through customers' making deposits, taking out loans, and so forth. Computers enable the timely and orderly computation and transfer of money.

The Federal Reserve monitors the overall economic health of the United States (and to a lesser extent the rest of the world) and attempts to set the discount and federal funds rates at a level that will maintain the overall economic health of the nation. If the Federal Reserve believes the economy is slowing down, it may lower the interest rates in an effort to cause more money to "flow" through the economy. Lower interest rates encourage citizens and businesses to borrow money, and when a business borrows money, it will often expand its production, hire new workers, and so forth. The Federal Reserve seeks to avoid a national **recession**—two consecutive quarters of negative growth in the nation's gross domestic product—as a recession can result in a dramatic increase in unemployment.

When the Fed reduces the interest rate at which banks borrow money from one another, other interest rates typically fall as a result. For instance, some banks set their **prime rate**—the rate they charge their "best" customers— a few percentage points higher than the federal funds rate. If the federal funds rate goes down, the prime rate likely will decrease. Banks are likely to change some but not all of their rates as soon as the Federal Reserve sets its rates. Credit card rates are not changed as often as the federal funds rate, because credit card debts are **unsecured claims**, debts issued without any collateral. (**Collateral** is an asset or assets pledged to a lender to be used as repayment of a loan in the event of default.)

During times when the economy is performing well, the Federal Reserve may elect not to change the rates, but if the Fed feels the economy is performing *too* well, it may raise interest rates. An overheated economy can lead to inflation, as businesses will be expanding rapidly. When businesses increase output, they tend to require new workers, and if there are not sufficient workers available, the businesses will begin to offer much higher wages to entice workers away from other businesses. This is obviously a good environment in which to work, but only to a point. If wages increase too rapidly, inflation can become rampant. By raising interest rates, the Federal Reserve slows the rate of increase in the overall economy. It becomes more expensive for individuals and businesses to borrow money, resulting in fewer purchases and lower overall production.

For an example of how interest rate increases can dampen economic activity, consider the purchase of a house. Referring back to Exhibit 5.2 (p. 166), the difference in payment between a 30-year mortgage for $200,000 at 4.0% interest and a 30-year mortgage at 4.25% interest, for example, is $29.05 per month. When multiplied by 360 (the number of payments to be made over the 30-year period), the monthly difference results in a total additional outlay of $10,458. The difference between 4.0% and 5.0% is even more dramatic: the monthly difference of $118.81 results in a total difference of $42,772. Any individual or company that is anticipating taking out a loan would be wise to observe the Federal Reserve's actions on interest rates.

MONITORING THE MONEY SUPPLY

In addition to setting interest rates, the Federal Reserve attempts to control the overall amount of money in the economy. The public money supply is measured in three ways:

- **M1** measures liquid assets in the form of cash and checking accounts.
- **M2** includes all of the money in M1 plus all money in savings accounts and **certificates of deposit (CDs)**—FDIC-insured debt instruments issued by banks and savings and loans with a fixed term and a specific interest rate. This money is not likely to be spent as readily as M1 money.
- **M3** includes all of the money in M1 and M2 plus the assets and liabilities, including long-term deposits, of financial institutions. In 2006, the Federal Reserve announced that it would no longer publish M3 statistics, but other entities continue to estimate and publish this information.

These measures and other information help the Federal Reserve determine the likelihood that money will be spent in the near future. The M1 and M2 tables are available at www.federalreserve.gov/releases/h6/Current/.

Increasing the money supply. If the Federal Reserve believes the economy needs more money to maintain or improve its overall health, it will increase the overall money supply by creating new money with which it buys securities from banks and other financial institutions. The financial institutions in turn spend, loan, or invest the new money. The Fed must be careful that it does not create too much money. Simply "printing" more money to pay off current financial obligations is a recipe for hyperinflation. After World War I, the German government printed too many marks (the German currency at the time), and their value decreased to such an extent that people were burning their paper money, since that was more efficient than gathering wheelbarrows full of money to use to buy firewood.

SIDEBAR 5.J   What is Quantitative Easing?

When the Federal Reserve wants to stimulate the economy, it typically will reduce interest rates to spur economic activity. With lower rates, in theory, more businesses and individuals will be interested in applying for additional loans, since the cost of money will be more affordable. Consumers and businesses will use those additional loans to start businesses, buy houses, and make other purchases that will spur economic growth. But if interest rates are already at or near zero, and many of the banks are unable to loan considerably more money because their balance sheets are already carrying too many poorly performing loans, what can the Federal Reserve do in this situation to influence the behavior of banks and citizens?

Quantitative easing occurs when the central bank of a country purchases from banks poorly performing loans or loans likely soon to become poorly performing. The banks then have more "room" under their reserve requirement to issue new loans, and they will have more confidence in pursuing additional loan applicants because their "worst" loans are now removed from their financial books. Quantitative easing was initially implemented by Japan to fight deflation in 2001. The United States implemented Quantitative Easing 1 (QE1) after the 2007 financial crisis. In November 2008, the US Federal Reserve purchased $600 billion in mortgage-backed securities, which increased its holdings of debt to $2.1 trillion by the middle of 2010. Though the plan was to phase out the debt purchases, by November 2010 the Federal Reserve implemented QE2 to address an economy that had not returned to typical (by US standards) performance metrics. The plan called for an additional $600 billion of debt purchases. With the economy continuing to stagnate under the Obama administration, the Federal Reserve announced QE3 in September 2012, with promises by Federal Reserve Chairman Ben Bernanke that the massive debt purchases would continue while the economy was performing at a suboptimal level. In June 2013, Bernanke announced that the slightly improving economy would allow the Federal Reserve to decrease bond purchases from $85 billion to $65 billion a month, with additional cuts to be announced as economic conditions warranted.

The short- and long-term impact of quantitative easing programs in the United States and other countries (such as Japan, the UK, and other European nations) is difficult to quantify. Certainly, in the United States, the removal of poorly performing debt from balance sheets strengthened banks' financial solvency and ability to issue new loans. However, many of those banks did not choose to issue new debt at the level some experts anticipated. Some banks simply kept all or a significant portion of their additional financial reserves or invested it in "safer" debt instruments, rather than risk it through loans to entrepreneurs and small businesses.

The financial benefits that QE1, QE2, and QE3 have provided might not have been worth the cost. Injecting hundreds of billions of dollars into the economy did provide some benefits, even if some of the money was not directed effectively. The sheer volume of additional dollars sparked some economic growth, but there is a concern that the US economy was difficult to "evaluate" during and after the quantitative easing phases were introduced. The excess money may have caused the economy to become "overly reliant on QE's support of asset markets" ("Ten years on," 2018, para. 6) rather than on normal underlying economic factors associated with investing. In addition, though the use of quantitative easing may have assisted the economy in the short term to a certain extent, no one is exactly sure about its long-term effects and how much inflation will impact the economy in the years ahead. Also, the fact that the Federal Reserve purchased poorly performing debt instruments from banks did not mean the debts magically disappeared. Debt, whether "good" or "bad," is still debt, and when defaults occurred, the Federal Reserve wrote it off its books, essentially saying to the American taxpayers that they will have to cover those losses. Quantitative easing is essentially a "bet" that the short-term benefits of the Federal Reserve's actions will generate enough positive outcomes to overcome the unknown potential long-term dangers from massive inflation and defaults.

Decreasing the money supply. The Federal Reserve can also remove money from the economy by issuing government securities. Financial institutions usually will be interested in purchasing the newly issued securities, because they are backed by the United States government and typically provide a solid rate of return. As financial institutions purchase the securities, money is removed from the economy—until the securities are due to be repaid, with interest.

The overall supply of money in the economy is ever changing. It is not uncommon for the Federal Reserve to issue securities one day and then buy them the next.

Fiscal Policy

Another function of the government in relation to the economy is setting **fiscal policy**—governmental decisions to collect and spend money in order to influence the economy. With more than 320 million people in the United States, there are more than 320 million opinions regarding exactly how much money the government needs and where the government should spend its money. Politicians have different views regarding spending priorities, but it seems none of them ever complains about having too much money to spend. The legislative and the executive branches of the government have direct influence on the United States's fiscal policy. Congress passes a federal budget, and then the President signs it into law. Each individual state, county, and city also has a fiscal policy, which is managed by governors, mayors, city council members, and so forth. Debates regarding the collection and spending of money, at every level of government, can become contentious. Often, compromises must be made to avoid a government shutdown when the debate runs past a fiscal deadline. The fiscal policies of governments, such as decisions about taxes and depreciation, influence sport entities, as well as other businesses. In some cases, laws are enacted that specifically affect the sport industry, such as "jock tax" legislation (discussed later in this chapter).

TAXES

Governments need revenues to defray the cost of providing services. These revenues are typically raised through a variety of different taxes. Citizens who owe the government money must pay their taxes on time or incur penalties and late fees. In addition, delinquent taxes can result in criminal charges against the offending party. Notorious mobster Al Capone, a mob boss during the Prohibition era, used intimidation, physical violence, extortion, and in some cases murder to sustain his criminal enterprises. Despite these well-known violations of the law, his failure to pay federal income taxes led to Capone's eventual imprisonment in 1931.

SIDEBAR 5.K   Phil Mickelson's Golfing Success and Tax Liability

In 2013, Phil Mickelson noted that he might follow Tiger Woods's example and purchase a new residence outside the State of California. In late 2012, California passed a significant tax increase for those residents earning over $250,000, with a new 13.3% tax on incomes over $1,000,000. In January 2013 Mickelson noted his displeasure with the State of California: "If you add up all the federal (taxes) and you look at the disability and the unemployment and the Social Security and the state, my tax rate is 62, 63 percent ... I've got to make some decisions on what I am going to do" (Miceli, 2013, para. 6). Though long-time California resident Mickelson experienced a public relations backlash from some fans and members of the media, former California resident Tiger Woods noted, "I moved out of here [California] back in '96 for that reason" (Ackerman, 2013, para. 8). Mickelson later apologized for discussing his personal financial situation. Despite the attention the tax discussion generated, Mickelson had one of his best years in 2013, as he won the Scottish Open and also won the prestigious British Open for the first time. Mickelson owed to the United Kingdom 45% of his total earnings from those two events, for a British tax bill of $954,000, plus 45% of a portion of his endorsement monies earned within the UK (Murphy, 2013). Fortunately, the United States and the United Kingdom have a tax treaty that limits some of Mickelson's exposure to double taxation on income earned in foreign countries.

Every business must spend considerable time and money ensuring that it adheres to the various applicable tax codes. It is beyond the scope of this book to detail how various federal, state, and local taxes affect sport business operations. However, a sport business or an individual who understands the overall tax code and its unique aspects can save hundreds of thousands or even millions of dollars. For instance, under the Federal Insurance Contributions Act (FICA), every employee pays 2.9% of wages (technically half is paid by the employer and half is paid by the employee) for Medicare (King, 2005). Signing bonuses, however, were exempt from the 2.9% tax until December 2004, when the Internal Revenue Service (IRS) changed its interpretation of the tax regulations for signing bonuses for MLB players. Major League Baseball had long argued that signing bonuses should not be taxed as wages. Signing bonuses and wages are treated the same for federal income tax purposes, but until the 2004 ruling they were taxed differently for Medicare. When the IRS altered its rules, some players and teams realized they had been paying taxes on signing bonuses that they did not owe. Baseball agent Scott Boras understood both the previous rules and the ramifications of the new interpretation. After negotiating Carlos Beltran's $119 million contract with the New York Mets, he insisted that Beltran sign the contract prior to January 12, 2005—the date the new IRS ruling would take effect. Signing the contract prior to the deadline saved Beltran $319,000 in Medicare taxes on his $11 million signing bonus (King, 2005).

DEPRECIATION

Depreciation, the allocation of an item's loss of value over a period of time, is an important factor in the determination of a business's tax obligation. Items such as machinery, buildings (but not land), computers, and desks purchased for a business's operations have a useful life, and once their useful life is completed, they typically must be replaced. The tax code permits businesses to deduct the loss of value of business assets from their taxable income. For instance, if a fitness club purchases a computer, each year the computer will lose some of its initial value. At the end of its useful life, the business will need to replace the computer with a new one.

The IRS recognizes a variety of methods to determine the yearly loss of value of a particular item. For simplicity, this discussion will describe four of the most common methods.

Straight-line. Estimating straight-line depreciation is straightforward. We subtract the item's estimated salvage value from its total cost and divide this figure by its useful life to determine its yearly depreciation allowance. For a computer with a cost of $1,000, a useful life of five years, and no salvage value, the depreciation would be ($1000 − $0)/5 = $200 per year. The $200 is recorded as a deduction against yearly revenue. If the business had operating income of $100,000, its tax obligation would be calculated on $99,800. The $200 deduction from operating income will be applied each of the next four years.

Sum-of-years'-digits. Straight-line depreciation is simple and easy to calculate, but it is not necessarily accurate in assessing the loss of value an item experiences during its useful life. In some cases an item depreciates quickly, and in others the item retains a greater portion of its value until the completion of its useful life. The **sum-of-years'-digits** method attempts to take the non-linear loss of value into account. As in the straight-line method, we must estimate the useful life of the item. We then add up the numbers of the years of the item's life: for a life of two years, the sum is $1 + 2 = 3$; for a life of three years, it is $1 + 2 + 3 = 6$; and so on. For the computer that will be depreciated over five years, the sum is $1 + 2 + 3 + 4 + 5 = 15$. Now, for each year the item is depreciated, this figure serves as the denominator. The year number, counted in reverse, serves as the numerator. We count in reverse because most items depreciate quickly after purchase (sometimes known as decelerating depreciation), so the largest amount of depreciation is taken first. See the depreciation schedule in Exhibit 5.3.

SIDEBAR 5.L   Sport Gambling in the United States: A New Source of Tax Revenue?

Each of the states in the union has different methods of collecting taxes. Whereas many states, such as Georgia, California, and New York, charge individuals income tax, other states, such as Florida, Texas, and Washington, have no state income tax, generating revenue from other forms of taxation, such as taxes on property, sales, and tourism. The State of Nevada has long utilized taxes on tourism and gambling activities (among others) rather than income taxes to generate revenue. Other states have realized that gambling activities in various forms can be a lucrative source of state revenue (McCredie, 2008). Forty-two states have established some form of a state lottery that produces revenue (McCredie, 2008). However, for many years, sport gambling, though legal and popular in many other places around the world, was legal in only four states (Nevada, Oregon, Montana, and Delaware), with Nevada being the only state that offered "full service" sport gambling opportunities. In 2013, led by Governor Chris Christie, the State of New Jersey sued the United States for limiting sport gambling to these four states (McClam, 2013). In 2018, the US Supreme Court ruled that the federal government could not restrict sport gambling and it would be the responsibility of the states to determine their specific laws (Edelman, 2018). Within this new legal environment, some states passed laws that made sport betting legal, while others took a more cautious approach. Within the states where sport betting was legal, a variety of differences in format were in place. Some states required a person to physically be in a sport book while others permitted sport gamblers to bet online as long as they were within the state jurisdiction. Still other states created different laws, but each had one motivation: to dramatically increase their state tax revenues. Within the new legal environment, most states reported increased revenue due to sport gambling, but the amount of money was not the complete panacea for budget woes that many predicted. However, with sport gambling in most states becoming more and more popular and the future likely to attract more gambling activity, it is expected that a number of states will legalize some form of sport betting within five years of the 2018 Supreme Court ruling.

SIDEBAR 5.M   Flat and Fair Taxes: New Ways to Assess Taxes?

As long as there are organized societies there will be debates about taxes. Certainly, taxes are necessary to fund government activities, but every citizen probably has different ideas about who should pay taxes, how much each person should pay, and the proper method of collecting government revenue. The United States federal government collects a variety of taxes from individuals and businesses. These include income taxes, capital gains taxes, social security taxes, Medicare taxes, and estate taxes, among many others. In 2013, the United States tax code was 73,954 pages long, whereas the Bible is 1,291 pages and *War and Peace* is 1,444 pages ("How many pages is," 2013). There have been some disputes about the tax code length as some claim that the main or most pertinent components of the tax code are "only" about 4,000 pages long and that the other thousands of pages are merely providing additional information that the majority of people would not need to compute and file their yearly tax returns (Grossman, 2014). Even when the tax code was largely changed and "simplified" under the Tax Cuts and Jobs Act signed into law by President Donald Trump in December 2017, the size of the tax code did not become considerably smaller (Giacopelli, 2018). Within the thousands of pages of the current and past tax codes thousands of tax credits and deductions existed. The complicated and opaque system led to former Internal Revenue Service Commissioner Mark Everson retaining an accountant to compute his taxes, because he was not sure if he could understand the code. Everson noted, "I don't want to get a letter from the IRS saying I made a mistake" ("67,204-page code," para. 5). In the sport industry, as in others, businesses often argue with the IRS about what the tax code requires. For instance, the Tampa Bay Rays successfully argued in court that money they received for advance ticket sales prior to their franchise having played any games should be taxed in the year the games were played (Moskal, 2002). At the time, the tax code did not clearly state exactly how to handle that situation.

Adhering to the cumbersome federal tax laws costs a tremendous amount of time and money. It was estimated that American citizens and businesses spent over 6 billion hours and $225 billion each year in the effort to adhere to the code (Boortz & Linder, 2008). Those figures have likely increased dramatically since 2008. This time and money could certainly be spent more effectively in other pursuits—such as working to streamline businesses' operations, designing better products, and providing improved services. For individuals, a simpler tax code would afford them more time and money for investing, retirement planning, and spending leisure time with family and friends. The overall inefficiency and costs of adhering to the current tax code have concerned a variety of groups and caused many to plead for a simpler tax code (Edwards, 2006).

One of the more popular tax reform proposals is the **flat tax**. The United States currently assesses income taxes on citizens based on their yearly income, with different Americans paying different income tax rates. Under a flat tax, every American would pay the same tax rate, and the myriad deductions and tax loopholes would be eliminated. Steve Forbes advocated a 17% flat tax rate when he sought the Republican Presidential nomination in 1996 and 2000. Forbes did not win the nomination, but his flat tax idea attracted media attention and some support. Forbes continues to promote in articles, books, and speeches the merits of the flat tax as a necessary reform.

Another tax reform idea is the "**fair tax.**" During his tenure, former Georgia Congressman John Linder repeatedly introduced legislation in the US House of Representatives that would have repealed the entire current tax code and replaced it with a consumption tax. Many European countries use a similar tax called a **value-added tax (VAT)**. European countries employing the VAT also assess a variety of other taxes, but Linder's plan would eliminate all other forms of taxation at the US federal level except for a 23% national sales tax. If the fair tax were implemented, Americans would no longer need to keep receipts, hire accountants, and worry about specific deductions. They would be taxed only when they purchased retail products and services (Boortz & Linder, 2008). The more a person consumed, the higher the taxes that person would pay. The poor would pay no taxes, since the fair tax plan mandates a monthly "pre-bate" for every American to cover the tax obligation for the basic necessities of life (Boortz & Linder, 2008). The fair tax is designed to be revenue neutral, meaning the federal government would receive the same amount of revenues that it does under the current system.

The main obstacle for the flat and fair tax plans is that members of Congress support the current system. Under a complex tax code, government officials can solicit financial support from lobbyists for specific deductions and loopholes. Members of Congress, regardless of party affiliation, have little reason to seek radical reform to a system that provides them considerable financial support and political power.

If the item will depreciate slowly in the beginning (known as accelerating depreciation), the schedule will be reversed, with the largest amount depreciated in the last year. In most cases, regardless of an item's "actual" useful life, taxpayers will seek to take the largest depreciation possible as soon as possible, due to the time value of money (see Chapter 4). Deferring taxes is typically an excellent way to boost short-term profits and long-term wealth. In the event an item that initially was estimated to have no salvage value proves to have value at the end of its life, the government requires that **depreciation recapture** taxes be paid.

Double-declining balance. This depreciation method is the most aggressive in allocating loss of useful life to the early years of an asset's use. In this method, we estimate the total years of useful life and calculate the straight-line depreciation percentage. However, for **double-declining balance depreciation**, we double the estimated depreciation percentages. Then, we multiply the percentage by the remaining amount of money to be depreciated. After the depreciation calculations have been performed for the item's useful life, a certain amount of money will remain to be depreciated. This amount is the

EXHIBIT 5.3   Five-year sum-of-years'-digits depreciation schedule for a $1,000 computer with no salvage value.

YEAR	PROPORTION DEPRECIATED	AMOUNT DEPRECIATED	REMAINING AMOUNT TO BE DEPRECIATED
1	5/15	$333.33	$666.67
2	4/15	$266.67	$400.00
3	3/15	$200.00	$200.00
4	2/15	$133.33	$66.67
5	1/15	$66.67	$0

EXHIBIT 5.4   Five-year double-declining balance depreciation schedule for a $1,000 computer with a useful life of five years.

YEAR	STRAIGHT-LINE PERCENTAGE	DOUBLE-DECLINING BALANCE PERCENTAGE	AMOUNT DEPRECIATED	REMAINING AMOUNT TO BE DEPRECIATED
1	20%	40%	$400.00	$600.00
2	20%	40%	$240.00	$360.00
3	20%	40%	$144.00	$216.00
4	20%	40%	$86.40	$129.60
5	20%	40%	$51.84	$77.76

theoretical salvage value. If the actual salvage value is higher, then depreciation recapture must be paid; if the actual salvage value is lower, then additional depreciation can be taken during the last year of the item's useful life. Exhibit 5.4 shows how double-declining balance depreciation works.

Units of production. Perhaps the most accurate method for depreciation is the **units-of-production** method. For this method, we must estimate the total number of items that will be produced by the asset during its useful life. We then calculate the depreciation schedule simply by dividing the total number of items produced during a given year by the total number of items the asset will produce during its useful life. The resulting percentage is multiplied by the original purchase price to determine the yearly depreciation. Exhibit 5.5 shows the use of units-of-production depreciation for a copier costing $2,000 that is expected to produce 10,000 copies and to have zero salvage value at the end of its useful life.

EXHIBIT 5.5	Units-of-production depreciation schedule for a copier costing $2,000 that is expected to produce 10,000 copies and to have zero salvage value.			
YEAR	**# OF COPIES PRODUCED**	**DEPRECIATION PERCENTAGE**	**COPIES REMAINING**	**AMOUNT DEPRECIATED**
1	3,000	30%	7,000	$600
2	2,000	20%	5,000	$400
3	1,500	15%	3,500	$300
4	1,500	15%	2,000	$300
5	1,200	12%	800	$240
6	800	8%	0	$160

The units-of-production depreciation schedule is ideal for items that are clearly related to some sort of tangible production. For items that lose value simply due to time, the units-of-production schedule may not be optimal. As with the other depreciation schedules, if the item retains value beyond its anticipated useful life, then adjustments to taxable income may be required.

Choice of depreciation method. The choice of depreciation method is determined by a variety of factors. In some cases the federal government mandates that certain types of items be depreciated in a specific manner. In other cases the government permits individuals and businesses to use the depreciation schedule they feel is appropriate—with IRS permission, of course. For specific information about which depreciation method to use, see www.irs. gov/publications/p946/ch01.html#en_US_ publink1000107337.

JOCK TAXES

Professional athletes are subject to a variety of special taxes. Since professional sport attracts much media and fan attention, it is easy to know where and when professional athletes "work" in a particular location. California has had laws since the early 1980s requiring out-of-state residents to pay taxes on income earned while in the state. California was certainly able to collect taxes from full-time, part-time, and seasonal employees who received a W-2 from a business located in the state, but it was not until 1991 that the state realized it could track professional athletes working in California. After the Chicago Bulls defeated the Los Angeles Lakers in the NBA Championship, the State of California sent the Bulls' players and coaches a tax bill for the portion of their salaries that they earned in the state (Smith, 2007; Williams, 2003). In response, Illinois assessed its own state taxes against professional athletes. Eventually, individual cities and counties realized they could also enact and enforce **jock taxes** on highly paid, visible professional athletes.

SIDEBAR 5.N   Bill Veeck Tax Interpretation Changes Sport Finance

Bill Veeck owned numerous Major League Baseball franchises from 1941 to 1980 and was known primarily for his marketing activities. Veeck dramatically changed the way the game of baseball was promoted and presented. Though they are commonplace now, his ideas, such as providing non-baseball entertainment such as fireworks, exploding scoreboards, and on-field parades, were revolutionary when he first introduced them. His marketing acumen led to Veeck's election to the Baseball Hall of Fame in 1991.

Although Bill Veeck was known primarily for his marketing activities, perhaps his greatest contribution to the business of sports was his understanding of the US tax code and the application of depreciation. In 1959 Veeck successfully argued that the government should accept his interpretation of the depreciation laws. His financial plan was soon copied by most of the other owners in the league (Zimbalist, 1992).

The essential elements of Veeck's plan involved the depreciation of contracts for players currently on a team's roster at the time of the owner's purchase of the franchise. Traditionally, when a player/contract was purchased from another team (which happened far more often in Veeck's time than now, because most of the minor league teams were then not affiliated with a Major League club), that expense was charged off taxable income, like any other operating expense. However, when an owner bought an entire team, all assets were simply transferred to the new owner.

Veeck wished to write off the existing player contracts from his taxes. To do this, he needed to control 80% of a franchise when he (and his investors) initially purchased the team. Prior to the purchase, Veeck would establish a new organization, and the team would then sell the players and their contracts to the new organization for at least 90% (and usually higher) of the agreed upon purchase price *prior* to selling the rest of the team (name, logos, merchandise, media contracts, and so forth). Since the players/contracts had been purchased rather than transferred with the other team assets, they could be depreciated on the new organization's taxes. Veeck, and most owners who mimicked his plan, depreciated the cost of the players/contracts over three to ten years (Veeck, 1996), which considerably lowered the owners' taxable income.

Once it was accepted by the IRS, the effect of this plan was dramatic. Purchasing professional sport franchises became a valuable tax shelter, which attracted new owners who had made fortunes in other industries and dramatically increased franchise values (Zimbalist, 1992). Veeck's initial tax plan has since been altered by the Omnibus Tax Act of 2004, which permits a new owner to deduct 100% of the team's purchase price over a 15-year period (Fort, Gerrard, Lockett, et al., 2008).

Jock taxes are based on the athletes' time spent working within a particular jurisdiction. The state or local government would prefer to calculate athletes' taxes based on their time spent in the state and the number of games played in the season, but instead jock tax calculations typically are based on the athletes' "duty days." The athletes' total duty days are counted from the first day of training camp to the last day of the team's season. For example, if a professional baseball player has 225 duty days from the start of spring training in March until the conclusion of the season in early October, and he spends 25 days playing games in California, he will receive an income tax bill based on the 11% (25 days/225 days) of his yearly salary he earned in the state. Most states issue a tax credit for income taxes paid in other states, but California does not, resulting in potential double taxation (Smith, 2007).

Although jock taxes have been assessed since 1991, litigation continues regarding how much individual athletes actually owe. Scott Radinsky of the Chicago White Sox sued the State of Illinois for the manner in which it administered its jock tax against him (Rovell, 2003). Other athletes have complained that jock taxes are often assessed even when the athlete does not visit a city as part of the team's travel party. Many players on injured reserve do not travel with their team while they rehabilitate, and in those cases the player may be able to argue that he or she did not earn any salary in the state, even though the team played there.

Jock taxes are not limited to the United States. Alberta, Canada, home to the Edmonton Oilers and the Calgary Flames of the National Hockey League, began to assess jock taxes in 2003 (Schecter, 2002). When the Montreal Expos played games in Puerto Rico, players were assessed a jock tax. The special tax was passed just days before the first games. Although the players were required to pay, Major League Baseball, the participating teams, and the promoter of the games were granted a waiver absolving them of tax liability on their profits (Rovell, 2003).

The complex nature of jock taxes has resulted in many teams' hiring additional staff for their payroll departments to monitor the tax bill players and coaches may owe in various jurisdictions (Smith, 2007). Players have also had to retain accountants to ensure they adhere to the various laws. Ray Suplee, an accountant who works for a variety of professional athletes, noted, "My clients' returns are typically 12 to 15 inches thick" (Williams, 2003, p. 25). In 2015, fans became blatantly aware of the complexity of player tax obligations when Pittsburgh Pirates' outfielder Andrew McCutchen left the first page of his May 1–15 pay stub in the Wrigley Field clubhouse. Once discovered by a fan and posted online, readers could see that just in one two-week pay period, McCutchen had money withheld not only for his home city of Pittsburgh and state of Pennsylvania, but also Illinois and Missouri, states where he had played during the pay period (Bell, 2015). In addition, his pay stub indicated Arizona, Ohio, and the city of Cincinnati as potential tax recipients though there was no deduction for those jurisdictions. The first page ended with a reference to a continued list of cities and states on the next page, though McCutchen had not left that page in the clubhouse for fans to view.

Some players consider the potential state and local taxes in their decision to sign with a particular team. The old adage "It is not what you make, but what you keep" certainly applies to a well-paid professional athlete. Paying 10.3% in state income tax in California versus no state income tax in Florida could mean a difference of hundreds of thousands or even millions of dollars in taxes over the life of a multimillion-dollar contract. For some professional athletes, such as tennis players, it is easier (for tax adherence purposes) and much less expensive to live in a country, such as Monaco, where there is no income tax rather than deal with the unwieldy United States tax laws (Sweet, 2002). For an exhaustive examination of the impact of state and federal taxes on athlete compensation, please see Stanley Veliotis's (2013) article in the *Journal of Sport Management*.

SIDEBAR 5.0   The Tennessee Jock Tax

Though Tennessee has no state income tax, it did have a unique 2009 jock tax (conveniently titled a "Privilege Tax") that applied for five years to NBA and NHL players. Any player who was on a team roster that played in Tennessee paid a flat $2,500 tax per game, up to a maximum of three games and $7,500. Whether those players were members of the NBA's Memphis Grizzlies or NHL's Nashville Predators or members of a visiting team, the tax applied. However, NFL players were exempt (Butler, 2013). In addition to the unique tax, the law also mandated that the collected money be distributed to the Grizzlies' home arena and the Predators' home arena, which are owned by the Grizzlies and the Predators, respectively (Butler, 2013; Lowe, 2013). This created a situation where players were taxed by the state to subsidize the operations of a private entity, which also happened to be the employer of some of the taxed athletes. It is estimated that Tennessee collected $3.5 million from this particular tax in 2012 (Butler, 2013).

Though the Tennessee tax did not receive extensive media scrutiny, the NBA Players Association and the NHL Players Association began lobbying Tennessee to repeal the tax almost as soon as it was passed. The NHL created a $2 million pool to compensate the taxed athletes, but the NBA did not provide any financial relief, which caused former interim NBA Players Association President Ron Klempner to note, "In certain instances it can actually cost a player money to play in Memphis" (Lowe, 2013, para. 8). For example, NBA teams often sign bench players to ten-day contracts that pay a prorated portion of the league's minimum salary (ranging from $473,000 to $1.3 million in 2012/2013, depending on a player's accrued service time). If a player with no NBA service time signed a ten-day contract to play for the Memphis Grizzlies, he could have paid $7,500 in Tennessee taxes, which would exceed his total ten-day compensation. The tax was repealed in 2014 due to concerns that only taxing some professional athletes would be unconstitutional (Raunrau, 2014). However, it stayed in force until the completion of the 2015–2016 NBA season.

CONCLUSION

Management's understanding of microeconomic and macroeconomic concepts and trends is critical to the success of any sport entity. In addition, the government's monetary and fiscal policies will impact financial decision making. Successful financial managers will work within the established tax codes to minimize tax obligations legally. As governments continue to seek revenue sources, it is likely that new tax laws—some of which may be specifically targeted to sport businesses—will be passed. Successful financial managers will be able to adapt their operations quickly to remain profitable when tax changes occur.

Concept Check

1. Define microeconomics and macroeconomics. What are the main differences between the two?
2. How do professional sport leagues use the concept of scarcity when locating franchises?
3. Define and discuss monetary policy. What specific actions can the Federal Reserve take to achieve its goals?
4. List actions that a government can take to establish its fiscal policy. What are some fiscal policies specifically targeted to the sport industry?
5. What is a basis point? How does a change in a few basis points affect a loan?
6. Define inflation and explain how it might affect sport business operations.
7. What is a stock market index? What is an index designed to accomplish?
8. What considerations must teams and athletes evaluate in regard to insurance?
9. Explain the important differences between general and limited partners.
10. What are the differences between a C corp and an S corp?
11. What are an LLC and an LLP? Why have they become more popular business entities over the past ten years? What concerns should an investor investigate before forming an LLC or LLP?
12. How has globalization affected sport finance in the past ten years? How might it affect sport financial management in the future?
13. What is your reaction to Phil Mickelson's 2013 comments regarding taxes? What is the potential impact of Mickelson and others' leaving California because of high taxes?
14. What are jock taxes? How was Tennessee's jock tax unique?

Practice Problems

1. If an interest rate is currently 6% and a lending institution announces a 25-basis point increase, what percentage increase does this represent?
2. Calculate the straight-line and sum-of-years'-digits depreciation schedules for a $450 video camera that will have a salvage value of $50 after five years of use.
3. Calculate the double-declining balance depreciation schedule for a $1,000 item that will last four years. What is the estimated salvage value?
4. For a fitness center that is purchasing a $3,000 photocopier expected to produce 30,000 copies, calculate the units-of-production depreciation schedule if the following numbers of copies are expected to be made each year: Year 1, 12,000; Year 2, 8,000; Year 3, 6,000; Year 4, 3,000; Year 5, 1,000.

Case Analysis

Schedule Changes at Darlington Raceway

Darlington Raceway is one of the most important tracks in the history of NASCAR. Opened in 1950, Darlington Raceway became a model for many superspeedway tracks that would be built later in the 1950s and 1960s. For many years, NASCAR held two Sprint Cup Series races at the track—one in the spring and one on Labor Day weekend. In 2003, because of decreased demand for the spring Darlington race and NASCAR's desire to expand its presence to other areas of the United States, Darlington's schedule was reduced to one Sprint Cup race.

Case Questions

1. How might NASCAR's decision to reduce Darlington's races from two to one be received by regular attendees at both events?
2. How might NASCAR's decision affect ticket pricing for the one remaining Darlington race? Explain your answer, referring to the economic and financial principles discussed in this chapter.
3. What would you guess has happened to Darlington's attendance at its one Monster Energy Cup Series race?
4. Did NASCAR make the correct decision in this situation? Explain and justify your answer.

References

67,204-page code confounds taxpayers, yet Congress sits by. (2007, April 4). *USA Today.* Retrieved from http://blogs.usatoday.com/oped/2007/04/post_7.html.

Ackerman, J. (2013). Tiger Woods cites high taxes for leaving California, backing Phil Mickelson's comments. Retrieved from www.policymic.com/articles/23933/tiger-woods-cites-high-taxes-for-leaving-california-backing-phil-mickel-son-s-comments.

Albert Pujols, Angels agree to deal. (2011, December 9). Retrieved from http://espn.go.com/los-angeles/mlb/story/_/id/7330066/st-louis-cardinals-albert-pujols-join-los-angeles-angels.

Allen, T. (2019, April 1). Kansas City NBA team could work out. *The Eyrie.* Retrieved from https://eyrieonline.org/6388/sports/kansas-city-nba-team-could-work-out/.

Alouettes sold to CFL. (2019, May 31). *DownNation.* Retrieved from https://3downnation.com/2019/05/31/alouettes-sold-to-the-cfl/.

Bell, K. (2015, June 9). Pirates pay stub highlights jock taxes. Retrieved from www.bankrate.com/financing/taxes/pirates-pay-stub-highlights-jock-taxes/.

Belson, K. (2015, April 28). After much criticism, N.F.L.'s league office drops tax-exempt status. *The New York Times.* Retrieved from www.nytimes.com/2015/04/29/sports/football/nfls-league-office-to-drop-its-tax-exempt-status.html?_r=0.

Birth of a team and a legend. (n.d.). Retrieved from www.packers.com/history/birth_of_a_team_and_a_legend/.

Boortz, N., & Linder, J. (2008). *Fair tax: The truth. Answering the critics.* New York: HarperCollins.

Branda, M. (2013, February 1). Understanding the business of baseball: Insurance on player contracts. Retrieved from https://metsmerizedonline.com/2013/02/understanding-the-business-of-baseball-insurance-on-player-contracts.html/.

Butler, C. (2013, April 12). Slap shot: TN 'jock tax' applies to hockey, basketball players, but not NFL. Retrieved from http://tennessee.watchdog.org/2013/04/12/slap-shot-tn-jock-tax-applies-to-hockey-basketball-players-but-not-nfl/.

Caldwell, D. (2017, August 21). Kansas City still trying to stay in the conversation for future expansion. *ESPN.com*. Retrieved from www.espn.com/nhl/story/_/id/20312842/nhl-kansas-city-trying-stay-conversation-future-expansion.

Chass, M. (2003, May 16). Baseball: With quick approval, Moreno buys Angels from Disney. *The New York Times*. Retrieved from http://query.nytimes.com/gst/fullpage.html?res=9903E2DA173EF935A25756C0A9659C8B63&sec=&spon=.

Claim game. (2013, January 26). *The Economist*. Retrieved from www.economist.com/finance-and-economics/2013/01/26/claim-game.

Conlin, B. (2008, July 30). Braves not the same without Turner. *Philadelphia Daily News*. Retrieved from www.philly.com/philly/sports/phillies/20080730_Bill_Conlin Braves_not_the_same_without_Ted_Turner.html.

Curtis, B. (2013, March 20). Q&A: Jason Giambi on growing up, the best ballpark taunts, and his Vegas lifestyle. *Grantland*. Retrieved from https://grantland.com/the-triangle/qa-jason-giambi-on-growing-up-the-best-ballpark-taunts-and-his-vegas-lifestyle/.

Dodd, D. (2017, March 23). Jaylon Smith's insurance payout could lead to more players skipping bowl games. Retrieved from www.cbssports.com/college-football/news/jaylon-smiths-insurance-payout-could-lead-to-more-players-skipping-bowl-games/.

Edelman, M. (2018, May 16). Explaining the Supreme Court's recent sports betting decision. *Forbes*. Retrieved from www.forbes.com/sites/marcedelman/2018/05/16/explaining-the-supreme-courts-recent-sports-betting-decision/#54f6396a537c.

Edwards, C. (2006, April). Income tax rife with complexity and inefficiency. Retrieved from www.cato.org/pubs/tbb/tbb-0604-33.pdf.

Eichelberger, C. (1998, September 1). NFL may drop ownership rules. *The Journal Record*. Retrieved from http://findarticles.com/p/articles/mi_qn4182/is_19980901/ai_n10120517/pg_1.

Euchner, C.C. (1994). *Playing the field: Why sports teams move and cities fight to keep them*. Baltimore, MD: Johns Hopkins Press.

Fainaru, S., & Fainaru-Wada, M. (2019, January 17). For the NFL and all of football, a new threat: An evaporating insurance market. *ESPN.com*. Retrieved from www.espn.com/espn/story/_/id/25776964/insurance-market-football-evaporating-causing-major-threat-nfl-pop-warner-colleges-espn.

Fantex invites you to join an NFL player in buying some Jamba Juice stores. (2015, April 21). *Daily News*. Retrieved from www.dailynews724.com/other/fantex-invites-you-to-join-an-nfl-player-in-buying-some-jamba-juicestores-h457720.html.

Fort, R., Gerrard, B., Lockett, A., Humphreys, B., Soebbing, B., Tainsky, S., Winfree, J., & Coulson, E. (2008). Bill Veeck, the IRS, and the Omnibus Tax Act of 2004. *Proceedings of the North American Society for Sport Management Conference*. Toronto, Ontario, Canada.

Friedman, T.L. (2000). *The Lexus and the olive tree*. New York: Anchor Books.

Friedman, T.L. (2005). *The world is flat*. New York: Farrar, Straus and Giroux.

Garcia, A. (2016, July 1). NFL cuts Roger Goodell's pay again. CNN Money. Retrieved from https://money.cnn.com/2016/07/01/news/nfl-roger-goodell-salary/index.html?iid=EL.

Giacopelli, J. (2018, October 8). Understanding the new tax code. *Forbes*. Retrieved from www.forbes.com/sites/forbesnycouncil/2018/10/08/understanding-the-new-tax-code/#672aa6551dc7.

Grossman, A.L. (2014, April 14). Is the tax code really 70,000 pages long? *Slate*. Retrieved from https://slate.com/news-and-politics/2014/04/how-long-is-the-tax-code-it-is-far-shorter-than-70000-pages.html.

Harris, D. (1986). *The rise and decline of the NFL*. New York: Bantam.

How many pages long is the U.S. income tax code in 2013? (2013, February 17). Retrieved from http://finance.town-hall.com/columnists/politicalcalculations/2013/02/17/how-many-pages-long-is-the-us-income-tax-code-in-2013-n1514277.

Joyner, J. (2006, May 24). NFL to move existing team to Los Angeles—eventually. *OTB Sports*. Retrieved from http://sports.outsidethebeltway.com/2006/05/nfl-to-move-exist-ing-team-to-los-angeles/.

Kaplan, D. (2001, August 6–12). Club's financial rise dates to market debut. *Sports Business Journal*, 4(16), 30.

Kaplan, D. (2009, October 26). NFL pares ownership rule. *Sports Business Journal*. Retrieved from www.sportsbusinessdaily.com/Journal/Issues/2009/10/20091026/This-Weeks-News/NFL-Pares-Ownership-Rule.aspx.

Kilgore, A. (2012, November 27). As the Dodgers hit paydirt, the Nationals-MASN talks remain in limbo. *The Washington Post*. Retrieved from www.washingtonpost.com/blogs/nationals-journal/wp/2012/11/27/as-the-dodgers-hit-paydirt-the-nationals-masn-talks-remain-in-limbo/.

King, B. (2003, April 21–27). Angels' reduced price raises questions. *Sports Business Journal*, 5(52), 5.

King, B. (2005, January 31–February 6). Tax change cuts into baseball bonuses. *Sports Business Journal*, 7(38), 10.

Loss-of-value insurance FAQs. (n.d.). Retrieved from www.ncaa.org/about/resources/insurance/loss-value-insurance-faqs.

Lowe, Z. (2013, July 19). Paying to play in Memphis? The strange case of Tennessee's jock tax. Retrieved from www.grantland.com/blog/the-triangle/post/_/id/69059/paying-to-play-in-memphis-the-strange-case-of-tennessees-jock-tax.

Lucas Oil to sponsor Colts stadium. (2006, February 28). Retrieved from www.bizjournals.com/losangeles/stories/2006/02/27/daily12.html.

McClam, E. (2013, July 15). New Jersey wages federal court battle to allow gambling on sports. Retrieved from http://usnews.nbcnews.com/_news/2013/07/15/19437131-new-jersey-wages-federal-court-battle-to-allow-gambling-on-sports?lite.

McCredie, S. (2008, March 27). The best and worst states for taxes. Retrieved from http://articles.moneycentral.msn.com/Taxes/Advice/TheBestAndWorstStatesForTaxes.aspx.

Miceli, A. (2013). Michelson vows drastic changes. Retrieved from http://msn.foxsports.com/golf/story/phil-mickelson-plans-drastic-changes-due-to-tax-situation-012013?ocid=ansfox11.

Moreno keeps promise to Angels fans. (2008, July 29). Retrieved from http://mlb.mlb.com/news/article_perspectives.jsp?ymd=20080729&content_id=3220123&vkey=perspectives&fext=.jsp.

Morris, K.M., & Morris, V.B. (1999). *The Wall Street Journal guide to understanding money and investing*. New York: Lightbulb Press.

Moskal, J. (2002, October 21–27). Devil Rays get win vs. IRS. *Sports Business Journal*, 5(26), 16.

Much, P.J., & Phillips, J.S. (1999). *Inside the ownership of professional sports*. Chicago: Team Marketing Report.

Murphy, E. (2013). 61% tax bite on UK winnings. Retrieved from www.dailyfinance.com/on/price-of-victory-phil-mickelson-hit-with-61-tax-bite-on-uk-win/.

Nagel, M.S., Brown, M.T., McEvoy, C.D., & Rascher, D.A. (2007). Major League Baseball anti-trust immunity: Examining the legal and financial implications of relocation rules. *Entertainment and Sport Law Journal*, 4(3). Retrieved from www2.warwick.ac.uk/fac/soc/law/elj/eslj/issues/volume4/number3/nagel/.

Raunrau, N. (2014, April 7). Tennessee legislature abolishes jock tax. *The Tennessean*. Retrieved from www.tennessean.com/story/money/2014/04/07/tennessee-house-abolishes-jock-tax/7440595/.

Rogers, P. (2007, January 12). Relocating a team to Portland makes sense. Retrieved from http://sports.espn.go.com/mlb/hotstove06/columns/story?columnist=rogers_phil&id=2727901.

Rovell, D. (2003, April 7). Baseball, not players, receive tax break from Puerto Rico. Retrieved from http://espn.go.com/mlb/s/2003/0407/1535207.html.

Rovell, D. (2013, October 18). Fantex to offer Arian Foster stock. Retrieved from http://espn.go.com/nfl/story/_/id/9838351/fantex-brokerage-services-offer-stock-arian-foster-houston-texans.

Schecter, B. (2002, March 25–31). 12.5% tax hits NHL players. *Sports Business Journal*, 4(49), 8.

Shareholder and financial history. (n.d.). Retrieved from www.packers.com/assets/docs/2012shareholder-history.pdf.

Shareholders. (2019). Retrieved from www.packers.com/community/shareholders.

Shipnuck, A. (2014, September 20). Anthony Kim, MIA since 2012, wrestles with whether to tee it up again or reap an eight-figure disability settlement. Retrieved from www.golf.com/tour-and-news/anthony-kim-ryder-cup-breakout-star-2008-nowhere-be-found.

Sibilla, N. (2014, March 28). Over thirty years ago, Maryland tried to seize an NFL team. *Forbes*. Retrieved from www.forbes.com/sites/instituteforjustice/2014/03/28/thirty-years-ago-baltimore-tried-to-use-eminent-domain-to-seize-an-nfl-team/#2deea4a941f5.

Smith, M.C. (2007, April 17). "Jock taxes" mean athletes well fleeced. *OC Register*. Retrieved from www.ocregister.com/ocregister/sports/columns/article_1654569.php.

Spofford, M. (2012, March 1). Stock sale closes; shares top 268,000. Retrieved from www.packers.com/news-and-events/article_spofford/article-1/Stock-sale-closes-shares-top-268000/19d9b0a8-f4ce-497b-b5ae-73f6c72fd973.

Swank, B. (2004). *Baseball in San Diego: From the Padres to Petco*. Charleston, SC: Arcadia Publishing.

Sweet, D. (2002, June 3–9). Monte Carlo beckons tax-weary European pros. *Sports Business Journal*, 4(6), 19.

Tafur, V. (2011, October 9). Davis family will retain ownership of Raiders. *SF Gate*. Retrieved from www.webcitation.org/62JqrJEWp.

Ten years on: What have we learned from quantitative easing? (2018). Retrieved from www.weforum.org/agenda/2018/08/qe-turns-ten.

Tucker, T. (2003, February 16). Chairman or the board? *Atlanta Journal Constitution*. D1, D3.

Unell, J. (2012, October 25). Exclusive: The CEO of AEG, Tim Leiweke, says anchor tenant could "kill" Sprint Center. Retrieved from www.kshb.com/dpp/sports/the-ceo-of-aeg-says-anchor-tenant-could-kill-sprint-center.

Veeck, B. (1996). *The hustler's handbook*. Durham, NC: Baseball America.

Veliotis, S. (2013). Salary equalization for baseball free agents confronting different state tax regimes. *Journal of Sport Management*, 27(3), 247–258.

Wessel, W. (2000). *Economics* (3rd ed.). Hauppauge, NY: Barron's.

Will Charlotte house an MLB team? (2006, January 19). Retrieved from http://journals.aol.com/sportzassassin/SPORTZASSASSINSSPORTSJOURNAL/entries/2006/01/19/will-charlotte-house-an-mlb-team/1375.

Williams, P. (2003, March 17–23). Pay as you go: States make the road taxing for athletes and accountants. *Sports Business Journal*, 5(47), 25.

Wolfley, B. (1997, November 29). Packers stock purchasers are buying for others. *Milwaukee Journal Sentinel*. Retrieved from www2.jsonline.com/sports/sday/sday112997.stm.

Young, E. (2007, November 19). Davis sells minority stake in Raiders for $150M. *San Francisco Business Times*. Retrieved from www.bizjournals.com/sanfrancisco/stories/2007/11/19/daily6.html.

Zimbalist, A. (1992). *Baseball and billions*. New York: Basic Books.

CHAPTER 6

Budgeting

Tom H. Regan and Matthew T. Brown

KEY CONCEPTS

base budget
budget
budget time horizon
business planning horizon
capital expenditure budget
cash budget
decision package
decision unit
expense budget
fixed cost
forecast
going concern
incremental budget
line-item budgeting
mixed cost

modified zero-based
  budgeting (MZBB)
periodic expense
planning
program budget
program planning budgeting
  system (PPBS)
reduced-level budget
revenue budget
sensitivity analysis
step cost
strategic planning
strategic planning horizon
variable cost
zero-based budgeting (ZBB)

INTRODUCTION

Budgeting is an indispensable tool of management and corporate governance. A budget aids management in financial coordination, and because the annual budget of a corporation requires board approval, it also helps ensure the fulfillment of the board's wishes. Beyond these facts, the definition and functions of budgeting vary widely among organizations. Sport organizations regard budgeting mostly as a tool for financial planning. A **budget** is considered to be a set of financial statements based on projections resulting from a particular scenario—generally, the most likely or hoped-for scenario. A budget, therefore, reflects management's opinions about future financial circumstances. Budgets and financial plans are often developed and used similarly, emphasizing the comparison of income and outlay entries—a practice adopted from public corporate bodies. In addition to providing a comparison of income and expenses, a budget can also serve several other functions: to motivate, coordinate, and communicate.

The budget as a means of motivation. Because budgets aid in performance measurement, performance evaluation, and the determination of pay, a carefully considered budget directs managers toward the company's goals. When personal benefits are coupled with business objectives (often expressed in financial form) and when subordinates participate in the planning process, a budget can supply incentive for the workforce to act on behalf of the organization.

The budget as a means of coordination. Because the development of a budget provides an opportunity to consider and plan for the future, the process helps management understand and overcome challenges in earning a profit. Certain budgeting techniques enable managers to uncover production bottlenecks and other problems and to correct any errors in forecasting.

The budget as a means of communication. For management to be effective, subordinates need enough information about organizational goals to be able to act appropriately. Superiors need up-to-date information about progress and results. Budgeting can serve these functions in a formal business setting.

WHAT IS A BUDGET?

A budget quantifies planned revenues and expenses for a period of time. It also includes planned changes to assets, liabilities, and cash flows (Smith, 2007). A budget facilitates the control process and helps with the coordination of an organization's financial activities. Budgets are prepared in advance of the time period they cover. They are based on the objectives of the business and are intended to show how policies are to be pursued in order to achieve objectives.

A budget is a financial plan that sets out a business's financial targets, expressed in monetary terms. It is an agreed-upon plan of action for a given period of time that reflects the policy to be pursued and the anticipated outcomes related to that policy, and it is set out in numerical or financial terms.

RELATION OF PLANNING AND FORECASTING TO BUDGETING

A clear distinction must be made between a plan, a forecast, and a budget.

Planning

Planning is usually a first step, prior to forecasting and budgeting. **Planning** is the establishment of objectives and the formulation, evaluation, and selection of the policies, strategies, tactics, and actions required to achieve those objectives. The planning process produces a *plan* that, along with information about the environment, provides information for the forecasting process.

Forecasting

A **forecast** is a prediction and quantification of future events for the purpose of budgeting. The difference between a forecast and a plan is that a forecast is simply a prediction, whereas a plan defines actions to be taken. (A budget is technically a plan, because it concerns actions to be taken.) A forecast relates to events in the environment, relevant to the implementation of the plan, over which the business has either no control or only very limited control. The environment considered may be internal, external, or personal—all have effects on decision making. A forecast is a prediction of the future as it relates to the organization's plan. The terms *forecast, prediction, projection*, and *prognosis* are typically used interchangeably.

The field of forecasting is concerned with approaches to determining what the future holds and with the proper presentation and use of forecasts. It includes the application of both judgment and quantitative (statistical) methods. Research on forecasting has produced many changes in recommended practice, especially since the 1960s. Many assumptions about the best way to generate forecasts have been found to be wrong. For example, the practice of basing forecasts on regression models that fit historical time-series data has been found to produce inaccurate results. Sometimes the research findings have been upsetting to academics—such as the discovery that in many situations relatively simple models are more accurate than complex ones (Makridakis, Wheelwright, & Hyndman, 1997; Ord, Hibon, & Makridakis, 2000).

Forecasts may be conditional. That is, if policy A is adopted, then X is most likely to occur, but if B is adopted, then Y is most likely. Forecasts of future values are often for a time-series, such as the number of tickets that will be sold in a year or the likely demand for season tickets. A forecast may also predict a one-off event, such as the outcome of free agency or the performance of a new recruit. A forecast may project a distribution, such as the locations of potential security risks or the sales of merchandise among different age cohorts.

The individuals who complete a budget will determine the forecasting tasks to be done. For example, a budget may require estimates of future ticket sales, merchandise sales, concessions, donations, gifts, and licensing fees. Determining the necessary forecasting tasks is part of the planning stage of budgeting.

The forecasting task itself may be complex. In order to estimate sales, for example, a prudent manager will look at past sales histories and various factors that influence sales. Marketing research may reveal that sales are expected to stabilize, because the organization cannot produce enough to sustain growth in sales or because a general economic slowdown is anticipated to result in stagnating sales. In such a case the budget team will need input from administration, managers, and other parties in related cost centers. This is just a sample of the process of developing forecasts.

Forecasting is concerned with what the future *will* look like, whereas budgeting is concerned with what it *should* look like, from management's point of view. If the sport organization does not like the forecasts, it can generate other plans until one is found that leads to acceptable outcomes. Of course, many organizations take a shortcut and merely change the forecasts. This is analogous to a family deciding to change the weather forecast so they can go to a baseball game.

GUIDELINES FOR FORECASTING

The approaches to forecasting described below should be helpful in the budgeting process.

1. Forecasting relies on observing past relationships and making predictions from historical information. However, if these relationships change, forecasts become inaccurate. For example, if a team's star player retires or signs with another team in the off-season, forecasts of attendance for the next season will likely be inaccurate. Hence, forecasters must both extend past trends and make adjustments for known changes.

2. Consider developing several forecasts under different potential scenarios. Assign a probability to each scenario and calculate a weighted average to arrive at an acceptable forecast. This process is often called **sensitivity analysis.**

3. Longer planning periods tend to produce less accurate forecasts. To increase accuracy, consider shortening the planning period. The appropriate length of a planning period will also depend on how often plans must be evaluated, which in turn will depend on sales stability, business risk, financial conditions, and the organization's budgeting approach.

4. Forecasts of large interrelated items are more accurate than forecasts of specific itemized amounts. For example, a forecast for the entire athletic department for one academic year will be more accurate than a forecast for one specific game. The variations in single games will tend to cancel each other out within a group of games. An overall economic forecast will be more accurate than an industry-specific forecast.

We now turn to budgeting, the process of determining what management feels the organization and its activities *should* look like in financial terms.

BUDGET PREPARATION

In a typical organization, each department submits an annual budget recommendation, which, once approved, is incorporated into the organization's annual operating budget. This budget becomes the basis of authority for the financial operation of each department during the fiscal year. The organization should set a general budgeting policy to guide resource allocation on the basis of program justifications.

The budget formulation process should:

1. Define financial objectives, which determine the direction and thrust of each department's operations.
2. Establish goals for achieving these objectives within the budgeted time frame.
3. Identify the activities and quantify the elements needed to achieve established goals.
4. Describe the factors and situations that may affect planned activities.

Each year, the budget formulation process is initiated by the organization's business manager, chief financial officer, or comptroller. Employees with budgetary responsibilities should obtain copies of the previous year's budget, review it carefully, and use it as the basis for budget recommendations for the coming year. Requests for capital expenditures, equipment, and administrative expenditures should be carefully itemized and fully described. Requests for new positions and other increases in the budget may also be made at this time. These recommendations will be reviewed by the appropriate business manager, the CFO, or the comptroller.

The business office typically initiates the planning cycle on or around the end of the second financial quarter of each fiscal year; team coaches and department administrators begin soon after. The schedule and approach to the budgeting process will vary depending on the size of the organization.

Timing and Budgets

Individuals involved in budgeting should consider three distinct time periods: the *budget time horizon*, the *business planning horizon*, and the *strategic planning horizon*. The **budget time horizon** is the immediate future, which can be predicted with a reasonable degree of certainty on the basis of past business decisions and commitments. The budget time horizon is generally considered to be the next 12 months. The **business planning horizon** is the period over which forecasts can be made with a reasonable degree of confidence—generally, three to five years. Individuals who are developing budgets usually gather data to produce short-term and long-term budgets for these two time periods. They might inquire, for example, how ticket sales have changed over the past year, two years, three years, and five years and use the pattern to make forecasts and produce short- and long-term budgets. Finally, the **strategic planning horizon** extends far into the future; planning for this time period focuses on the long-term aspirations of the sport organization and management.

Keys to Successful Budgeting

Successful budgeting depends on the involvement of the entire organization in both the planning and the implementation phases. Hence, two keys to successful budgeting are (1) input from the entire organization and (2) a means of sharing the budget across the organization.

Input from each cost center, department, or management unit is vital to drawing up a budget that realistically reflects revenue and expenses from each unit, department, or sport. A budget arrived at in a "top-down" fashion—that is, with input only from the head office or higher administration—is not likely to be accurate or effective.

To share the budget across the organization, user-friendly software, such as Microsoft Excel, is indispensable. If an organization wants grassroots involvement, managers must have tools they feel comfortable using, and every task must be simplified through software and technology. Online data capture and transparency of data will help coaches, managers, and assistants become involved in the budgeting process, which in turn will result in an efficient process.

Furthermore, a budget must be sustainable. Budgets do not go away, and they must be readily adaptable to changes. The first step toward sustainability is gaining "buy-in" from the administration and department heads. With everyone pulling in the same direction, the organization moves forward together. Involving each department, coach, and employee in developing and maintaining the budget helps ensure buy-in, congruence, and efficiency.

Best Practices in Budgeting

Budgeting should be a value-added activity. To be a value-added activity, these best practices should be followed:

1. Link budgeting to **strategic planning**—the process of defining a vision for your organization and creating goals and objectives to help achieve this vision—since these strategic decisions usually have financial implications.
2. Make budgeting procedures part of strategic planning. Strategic assessments should include identification of historical trends, competitive analysis, and other activities that might otherwise take place within the budgeting process.
3. During the budgeting process, spend less time collecting and gathering data and more time generating information for strategic decision making.
4. Get agreement on summary budgets before you spend time preparing detailed budgets.
5. Automate the collection and consolidation of budgets across the organization. For easy updating, every person with budgeting responsibilities should have access to budgeting software.
6. Set up the budget so that it will accept changes quickly and easily. Budgeting should be a continuous process and one that encourages alternative thinking.
7. Design a budget that will give lower-level managers some form of fiscal control over their own areas of responsibility.
8. Leverage your financial systems by establishing a data warehouse that can be used for both reporting and budgeting.

Not all best practices can be implemented in every sport organization. Time and resources available vary among athletic departments and sport enterprises. Effective budgeting requires that managers understand the resources available and the skills and limitations of the personnel working on the budgeting process.

APPROACHES TO BUDGETING

Several approaches are used in budgeting in the sport industry. Each sport enterprise will need to select the most favorable approach for its business, considering the advantages and disadvantages of each.

Regardless of the approach, budgeting is an easy process when revenues are increasing. In past decades, sport enterprises have enjoyed increasing revenue forecasts, the result of ticket price increases, significant media revenues, luxury and box seating expansion, and lucrative naming rights deals. Budgeting becomes more difficult in an environment where revenues are decreasing and expenses must be cut. During periods of recession or flat revenue streams, the budget becomes a tool for motivation, communication, and, in some cases, job security.

Individuals in all sport job titles are affected by the budgeting process, and all departments—including marketing, operations, ticketing, sales, sports information, and administration—must be involved in it. Budgetary decisions should be made in accord with management's priorities and desired revenue growth to attain the goals of the organization.

For example, suppose the goal of an athletic department is to finish first or second in the Southeastern Conference in every sport. It would behoove every coach, staff member, and administrator to become involved in the budgeting process. If the women's basketball recruiting budget was being reduced—and you were the women's basketball coach—would you still be able to reach the top 10%? A coach who is not involved in the budgeting process might not be aware of an impending reduction. Yet that coach will be evaluated at the end of the year on the team's performance, just the same. If your team needs to be in the top 10% of the conference, you would benefit by becoming involved in the budgeting process to ensure that resources are allocated so that you can meet that goal.

This section discusses in detail the following four approaches to budgeting:

1. Incremental budgeting
2. Program planning budgeting system (PPBS)
3. Zero-based budgeting (ZBB)
4. Modified zero-based budgeting (MZBB)

Within each budgeting approach, there are budgets within budgets. These include revenue budgets, expense budgets, cash budgets, and capital expenditure budgets. Each is briefly summarized at the end of this section.

INCREMENTAL BUDGETING

A form of line-item budgeting often called the object-of-expenditure budget was the earliest type of budget format used in private, public, and non-profit entities. It was considered an innovative development by financial reformers in the early 1900s and remains a popular form of budgeting even today. The line-item budget achieved prominence with the establishment of the executive budget, which assigned responsibility and accountability for spending to the organization's chief executive. This gave the chief executive a powerful instrument for controlling departmental and agency demands for money.

Line-item budgeting is a technique in which *line items* (also known as objects of expenditure) are the main focus of analysis, authorization, and control. Typical line items include supplies, personnel, travel, and operational expenditures. See Exhibit 6.1 for a list of typical expenditures in an athletic department. An **incremental budget** is a form of line-item budgeting in which next year's budget is the result of either decreasing or increasing last year's budget for each line item by the same percentage (as opposed to a zero-based budget, discussed later in this chapter, with which we clear the deck and start all over again). An incremental budget is based on projected changes in operations and conditions. This approach to budgeting tends to lead to budgetary increases over time.

EXHIBIT 6.1 Sample line-item budget for a department of intercollegiate athletics.

The Program University
Department of Intercollegiate Athletics
Budget Projection 2021–2022

REVENUES	2019–2020 BUDGET	2020–2021 BUDGET	2021–2022 INCREMENTAL BUDGET
I. Admissions & Guarantees:			
A. Men's Basketball	$1,000,000	$1,008,000	$1,023,120
B. Football	$7,044,000	$7,874,560	$7,992,678
C. Baseball	$50,000	$50,000	$50,750
D. Women's Basketball	$12,002	$10,000	$10,150
E. Soccer	$15,000	$10,000	$10,150
F. Other	$5,000	$5,000	$5,075
TOTAL	$8,126,002	$8,957,560	$9,091,923
II. Athletic Fees:			
A. Matriculation Fees	$475,000	$475,000	$482,125
B. Debt Service	$610,000	$610,000	$619,150
TOTAL	$1,085,000	$1,085,000	$1,101,275
III. Program Club Revenues:			
A. Contributions	$5,800,000	$5,800,000	$5,887,000
B. Investment Income	$120,020	$150,000	$152,250
C. Endowment Income	$125,000	$125,000	$126,875
D. Non-Cash Gifts in Kind	$160,000	$150,000	$152,250
E. Royalties	$50,000	$50,000	$50,750
F. Jr. Program Club	$10,000	$10,000	$10,150
G. Parking	$4,000	$5,000	$5,075
H. Credit Card Revenue	$5,000	$10,000	$10,150
I. Miscellaneous	$5,000	$5,000	$5,075
TOTAL	$6,279,020	$6,305,000	$6,399,575

(*continued*)

EXHIBIT 6.1   Cont.

REVENUES	2019–2020 BUDGET	2020–2021 BUDGET	2021–2022 INCREMENTAL BUDGET
IV. Other Revenues:			
A. Radio & Television			
1. Basketball	$31,250	$31,250	$31,719
2. Football	$218,750	$218,750	$222,031
3. Talent Reimbursement	$20,020	$20,020	$20,320
4. Miscellaneous	$5,000	$5,000	$5,075
TOTAL RADIO & TV	$275,020	$275,020	$279,145
B. Corporate Sponsorships	$600,000	$600,000	$609,000
C. Mailing & Handling Fees	$45,000	$45,000	$45,675
D. Investment Income	$220,020	$300,000	$304,500
E. Concessions	$435,000	$500,000	$507,500
F. Souvenirs	$15,000	$20,020	$20,320
G. Programs	$75,000	$80,000	$81,200
H. Conference Revenue Sharing	$1,900,000	$1,900,000	$1,928,500
I. Stadium Rental	$0	$25,000	$25,375
J. Miscellaneous	$5,000	$5,000	$5,075
K. NCAA Distribution	$190,000	$190,000	$192,850
TOTAL	$3,485,020	$3,665,020	$3,719,995
V. Subsidy from Non-Restricted Reserve for Debt Service	$125,000	$125,000	$125,000
TOTAL PROJECTED REVENUE	$19,375,062	$20,412,600	$20,716,914

EXHIBIT 6.1   Cont.

EXPENSES	2019–2020 BUDGET	2020–2021 BUDGET	2021–2022 INCREMENTAL BUDGET
EXPENSES			
I. Revenue Sports:			
1. Men's Basketball	$1,283,873	$1,078,823	$1,100,399
2. Football	$4,468,639	$6,033,300	$6,153,966
TOTAL	$5,752,512	$7,112,123	$7,254,365
II. Men's Olympic Sports:			
1. Baseball	$441,725	$335,575	$342,287
2. Golf	$169,010	$146,708	$149,642
3. Soccer	$293,860	$248,871	$253,848
4. Swimming & Diving	$289,427	$214,291	$218,577
5. Tennis	$207,867	$173,751	$177,226
6. Track Indoor/Outdoor & CC	$273,643	$260,555	$265,766
TOTAL	$1,675,532	$1,379,751	$1,407,346
III. Women's Olympic Sports:			
1. Basketball	$461,671	$421,049	$429,470
2. Softball	$243,285	$175,760	$179,275
3. Volleyball	$275,587	$210,307	$214,513
4. Swimming & Diving	$294,496	$198,512	$202,482
5. Tennis	$215,081	$147,661	$150,614
6. Golf	$147,469	$117,612	$119,964
7. Track Indoor/Outdoor & CC	$273,643	$86,567	$88,298
TOTAL	$1,911,232	$1,357,468	$1,384,617

(continued)

EXHIBIT 6.1   Cont.

EXPENSES	2019–2020 BUDGET	2020–2021 BUDGET	2021–2022 INCREMENTAL BUDGET
IV. Cheerleaders:			
TOTAL	$94,017	$87,893	$89,651
V. Support Services:			
1. Sports Information	$447,805	$449,114	$458,096
2. Medical/Training	$626,036	$608,565	$620,736
3. Booster Club	$1,352,586	$1,325,929	$1,352,448
4. Administration	$1,573,484	$2,222,982	$2,267,442
5. Facilities/Grounds/ Projects	$1,105,053	$1,024,196	$1,044,680
6. Business Office	$227,895	$251,791	$256,827
7. Ticket Office	$377,642	$324,354	$330,841
8. Academic Support	$365,089	$355,637	$362,750
9. Strength/ Conditioning	$159,665	$148,256	$151,221
10. Recruiting	$209,264	$203,779	$207,855
11. Compliance	$54,446	$57,645	$58,798
12. Olympic Sports Administration	$349,668	$345,277	$352,183
13. Jr. Booster Club	$15,700	$13,700	$13,974
14. Wellness Program	$126,840	$130,820	$133,436

EXHIBIT 6.1   Cont.

EXPENSES	2019–2020 BUDGET	2020–2021 BUDGET	2021–2022 INCREMENTAL BUDGET
15. Concessions	$74,100	$74,100	$75,582
16. Programs Football/ Basketball	$52,002	$52,002	$53,042
17. Video Support	$191,324	$139,588	$142,380
18. Marketing, Development	$564,057	$385,947	$393,666
19. Student Support Services	$105,347	$103,678	$105,752
20. Stadium	$183,772	$172,388	$175,836
TOTAL	$8,161,775	$8,389,748	$8,557,543
VI. Capital Improvement/ Maintenance and Debt Service:	$2,011,300	$2,011,300	$1,900,000
TOTAL PROJECTED EXPENDITURES	$19,606,368	$20,338,283	$20,593,523
TOTAL PROJECTED REVENUE	$19,375,062	$20,412,600	$20,716,914
PROJECTED INCOME OVER EXPENDITURES	($231,306)	$74,317	$123,391

As Exhibit 6.1 suggests, by using a software spreadsheet we can prepare an incremental budget very quickly. In Exhibit 6.1, the revenues for each line item were increased by 1.5% and the expenses for each line item were increased by 2% for the 2021/2022 budget.

Incremental budgeting is often called the "fair share" approach. It has this name because no one sport program or department is increased or cut at a different level from the others. This form of budgeting is usually associated with a top-down management style, and it has two important characteristics. First, funds are allocated to departments or organizational units, and the managers of these units then allocate funds to activities as they see fit (see Exhibit 6.1). Second, as mentioned previously, an incremental budget develops out of the previous year's budget, and only the incremental change in the budget request is reviewed.

Each of these characteristics creates problems. Incremental budgeting is particularly troublesome when top management seeks to identify inefficiencies and waste. In fact, inefficiencies tend to grow in an organization that uses incremental budgeting, because inefficiencies are easily hidden. In a typical budget of this type, nothing ever gets cut. Because top management looks only at the requests for incremental changes, money may be provided for an activity long after the need has passed.

The incremental budgeting approach is not recommended, as it fails to take into account changing circumstances. Moreover, it encourages managers to "spend up to the budget" to ensure a comparable allocation in the next period. This is a "spend it or lose it" mentality, by which managers are sure to spend all that is allocated to them in fear that if a surplus remains, their request for an incremental increase will be denied. See Exhibit 6.2 for a summary of the advantages and disadvantages of incremental budgeting.

Program Planning Budgeting System

The **program planning budgeting system (PPBS)** is one method used to develop a **program budget**. Whereas traditional budgets, such as line-item budgets, focus on input (e.g., program costs), program budgeting focuses on outputs, or the goals and objectives the organization hopes to achieve. Here, the emphasis is on organizational effectiveness, not spending. Program budgets are based primarily on units of work and secondarily on the character and object of the work. For example, under the heading of the marketing department we would find personnel, office supplies, and advertising. The purpose of program budgeting, as the name suggests, is to highlight the units of activity that the line items support.

In this approach, the organization's policy decisions lead to a specific budget and specific multi-year plans. PPBS, therefore, contributes to the organization's planning process. The goal of PPBS is to link planning with budgeting systematically in the service of clearly identified goals.

PPBS integrates into the planning and budgeting process a number of techniques for

- identifying, costing, and assigning a complexity of resources
- establishing priorities and strategies in a major program
- forecasting costs, expenditures, and achievements in the immediate financial year or over a longer period.

EXHIBIT 6.2   Advantages and disadvantages of incremental budgeting.

ADVANTAGES

- The budget is stable and change is gradual.

- Managers can operate their departments on a consistent basis.

- The budget is relatively simple to prepare and easy to understand.

- Conflicts may be avoided if departments are seen to be treated similarly.

- Coordination between budgets is easier to achieve.

- The impact of changes can be seen quickly, because the budget is relatively easy to prepare and modify.

DISADVANTAGES

- Activities and methods of working are assumed to continue in the same way as before.

- The budget process provides no incentive for developing new ideas.

- The process provides managers no incentives to reduce costs.

- This approach encourages managers to spend up to the budget to ensure that the budget is maintained next year.

- The budget may become out of date and no longer relate to the level of activity or type of work being carried out.

- Changes in the priority for resources may not be reflected in the budget.

- Budgetary slack may be built into the budget, which is never reviewed. Managers may have overestimated their requirements in the past in order to obtain a larger budget allocation, and this situation is never reviewed or remedied.

Planning is the essence of program budgeting, and if a budget is not connected to a plan, it is not a true budget. Many agencies organize the budget into functional categories or sets of activities, but unless a plan gives purpose to these functional categories and activities, it is difficult to identify the purposes the line-item categories are intended to serve. Program expenditures should be related to a set of objectives, which in turn are connected to goals, for a true program budget to exist. The development of goals and objectives for an organization or program unit is fundamental to management planning and PPBS. Together, the goals and objectives plus budgeted resources provide an overall plan. Once a set of long-range goals or general directions has been established, a series of directly related, measurable short-range objectives can be developed. The short-range objectives are the projected or planned achievements for the agency or program during the planning period. Whether these objectives will actually be achieved depends on the resources made available and the ability of management.

Consider as an example a PPBS budget for a summer community tennis camp (see Exhibit 6.3). As stated above, a PPBS budget includes performance objectives, measurement criteria, a productivity measure, and effectiveness measures, unlike the line-item budget presented earlier. The emphasis of this budget is on outcomes: meeting the performance objectives set for the camp. The three performance objectives **A** are matched to the demand **B**, workload **C**, productivity **D**, and effectiveness **E** outcomes to ensure the program is meeting the objectives set for it. In addition, and like the line-item budget, the PPBS budget includes revenue and expenditure information **F**.

As another example, let's return to the collegiate athletic department that has a goal of being in the top 10% of programs within its conference. To achieve this goal, administrative officials and coaches set this objective: build a new state-of-the-art facility in order to recruit the best players. By recruiting the best players, the teams using the new facility and its amenities (e.g., locker rooms, weight rooms, and training room) will improve their chances of moving into the top 10%. If this athletic department uses PPBS for major capital expenditures, it will need to incorporate the planning, programming, and budgeting concepts during the facility's construction phase. In professional sports, an organization's goal might be to increase revenue streams so that the franchise can better compete with larger-market teams. This goal may also lead to the objective of a new facility, which should enhance the revenue streams from the sale of luxury and club seats.

Program budgeting has several advantages. By connecting the budget to a plan, it enables an organization to allocate its scarce resources purposefully. This clarity of purpose in turn enables managers to understand how the work of their particular unit contributes to the work of the organization as a whole. Other advantages pertain to staff involvement in the initial stages of the project. The personnel involved often have significant input, and their needs form the basis of the final budget. For the larger, government-funded sport entity, program budgeting provides a visible and concrete expression to the citizens of how their tax dollars are being spent. Many college athletic departments are state funded and, as a consequence, have a public non-profit mentality. Yet the department must exist in a competitive environment.

The advantages that come from rationally and systematically connecting means to ends and dollars to programs come with disadvantages. One serious disadvantage for managers is that PPBS limits their flexibility in shifting dollars from one program to another. Over time programs build up strong constituency support, which means that any program cuts may attract strong external opposition. Program budgeting has been likened to buying all perfectly matching suits of clothes—it is difficult to treat the parts as interchangeable. In addition to limiting flexibility and increasing the potential for conflict, true program budgeting is quite time-consuming. Staff must be involved, and their input and buy-in are required. The more employees involved in budgeting, the more the timeline expands. Another disadvantage is that the evaluation process is often weak. The length of the budgeting process seems to limit the evaluation process, especially after completion. Finally, a budgeting system like PPBS sometimes allows athletic departments to support irrational objectives, such as moving into NCAA Division I–Football Bowl Subdivision from a lower division (see Chapter 14) and increasing from 20 to 28 sports when the department and its institution do not have the resources to support these changes.

EXHIBIT 6.3 Sample PPBS for a summer community tennis camp.

SUMMER JUNIOR TENNIS CAMPS

Description Designed to introduce tennis, provide recreational opportunities, competitive opportunities

A **Performance Objectives**
1. Provide junior tennis opportunities for the community.
2. Increase the number of programs by 20% over the previous year.
3. Achieve at least a 90% positive satisfaction rating from participants.

MEASUREMENT	PROGRAM	OBJECTIVE	2020 ACTUAL	2021 APPROVED	2021 REVISED	2022 PROJECTED
B Demand						
Estimated Participants	Lil Bits	1	12	16	14	16
	Stars	1	17	20	19	20
	Novice	1	19	20	18	20
	Tournament Play	1	18	20	25	30
Estimated Programs		2	5	5	5	6
C Workload						
Actual Registrations	Lil Bits	1	12		14	
	Stars	1	17		19	
	Novice	1	19		18	
	Tournament Play	1	18		25	
Actual Participants		1	66		76	
Actual Programs		2	5		5	

(continued)

EXHIBIT 6.3   Cont.

	MEASUREMENT	PROGRAM	OBJECTIVE	2020 ACTUAL	2021 APPROVED	2021 REVISED	2022 PROJECTED
D	**Productivity**						
	Average Cost per Participant		1	$173		$180	
E	**Effectiveness**						
	Program Participation Increase (decrease) Over Previous Year		1	7%	15%	15%	13%
	Program Offerings Increase (decrease) Over Previous Year		2	0%	0%	0%	20%
	Percentage Positive Ratings from Participants		3	85%	90%	89%	90%
F	**Fiscal Resources**			**2020 Actual**	**2021 Approved**	**2021 Revised**	**2022 Projected**
	Revenue	Fees		$11,400	$12,880	$13,670	$15,680
	Expenses	Personnel		$6,000	$6,000	$6,000	$7,500
		Maintenance/ Operations		$2,000	$2,000	$2,000	$2,150
		Tennis Balls		$625	$650	$700	$850
		Marketing		$1,500	$1,500	$1,500	$1,500
	Profit (Loss)			$1,275	$2,730	$3,470	$3,680

Source: Adapted from Brayley and McLean (1999).

EXHIBIT 6.4   Advantages and disadvantages of PPBS.

ADVANTAGES

- Enables an organization to allocate its resources purposefully.

- Shows managers how their departments' work relates to the whole organization.

- Provides evidence to citizens of how a department is spending tax dollars.

- Gets staff involved at an early stage and allows them significant input.

DISADVANTAGES

- Limits flexibility to shift dollars between programs.

- Increases the potential for conflict if programs with strong support receive cuts.

- Is time-consuming due to staff involvement and need for staff buy-in.

- Results in a weak evaluation process due to program length.

- May allow support for irrational objectives.

Exhibit 6.4 lists the advantages and disadvantages of PPBS budgeting.

Zero-Based Budgeting

Zero-based budgeting (ZBB) is a budgeting approach and a financial management strategy intended to help decision makers achieve more cost-effective delivery of goods and services. It is well suited to the service industry—of which the sport business is part—and has been a common approach to budgeting in the service industry for over 50 years. ZBB originated with Peter Pyhrr at Texas Instruments in the late 1960s. Pyhrr's 1973 book on the subject remains the most definitive and comprehensive study of this approach to budgeting. His goal was to create a decision-making mechanism that would force an organization to remain competitive in a rapidly changing set of market conditions. He believed this could best be achieved by putting managers in the position of constantly asking why they are doing what they are doing and whether they should be using their resources to do something else.

One of the best ways of putting this question at the center of attention is for managers to begin each budget year with no assumption that they will have what they received last year. What if managers had to start over from scratch each year and justify everything they were doing from the ground up? In short, why not create a level playing field for all managers, and assume that they could stop what they have been doing and use the resources to do something else instead? Wouldn't this generate more innovation and new product lines, thus ensuring the company constant market preeminence? Pyhrr thought so, and he created ZBB to achieve this goal.

ZBB requires building a budget from a "zero base." That is, the budget is not based on the previous year's budget but rather starts all over again from a clean slate. This is the opposite of incremental budgeting, and it is designed to attack the major drawback of incremental budgets—the fact that resource allocation tends to become routine and inefficient. Sport is a fast-changing environment, and ZBB has become a staple budgeting approach for administrators who want to control costs and achieve operational efficiency in this kind of environment. Zero-based budgeting helps to prevent budgets from creeping up each year with inflation, and ZBB also shifts the "burden of proof" to the manager, who must justify why his or her department or sport should receive any budget at all.

ZBB has four requirements:

1. Each budget period starts fresh—budgets are not based on past budgets.
2. Budgets are zero unless managers make the case for resources. The relevant manager must justify the whole of the budget allocation.
3. Every activity is questioned as if it were new, before any resources are allocated to it.
4. Each plan of action must be justified in terms of total expected cost and benefit, with no reference to past activities.

The philosophy of always questioning why we should continue doing what we have been doing is the heart and soul of zero-based budgeting. This philosophy and the system that Pyhrr created have been adopted by for-profit and non-profit organizations and used in government and athletic departments across the country. Through ZBB, budgeting can become a driving force to shape departmental and business policy and force systematic planning.

Key elements of the ZBB system are decision units, base budgets, reduced-level budgets (RLB), and decision packages that are priority ranked. Each part of the organization where budget decisions are made is referred to as a **decision unit**. The **base budget** is first created at the decision unit and contains the expenditure levels necessary to maintain last year's service level at next year's prices. In short, the manager increases the existing budget by the rate of inflation. Next, the decision unit manager creates a **reduced-level budget** that defines a predetermined percentage by which the unit must cut the budget; for example, by 50%. The reduced-level budget includes services considered critical or essential to the unit, and it may include either new or existing programs. Finally, the decision unit manager creates **decision packages**. These are the building blocks of ZBB and are linked to the organization's goals and objectives. Within a decision package are specific additions to the reduced-level budget, ranked in priority order, based on what is viewed to be most critical to the organization. Decision units may be asked to create decision packages beginning with a base budget or reduced-level budget. As the ZBB process begins, managers frequently use cost worksheets like the one given in Exhibit 6.5.

RANKING THE DECISION PACKAGES

An important characteristic of zero-based budgeting is that it forces prioritization. Within the organization, each department and its related activities are ranked. When revenue may be insufficient to meet demand for spending, it is useful for the organization to have a ranking of sports, programs, and activities based on their effectiveness, as well as potential alternatives to expensive or ineffective programs. Despite its virtues, in good revenue years ZBB can accommodate poor decisions, but in years of financial exigency, tough decisions must be made. ZBB requires all managers involved in the budget process to agree to the priority and ranking of their departments and activities. This requirement creates accountability.

In the ZBB process, decision packages are evaluated and ranked in order of importance. On the example cost worksheet (Exhibit 6.5), the decision packages **A** are ranked as Object 01, Object 02, and so forth. Note that subgroups are also ranked. For example, under Position Salaries, we find Object 01: [1] Coaches, [2] Administrative Secretary, and [3] Secretary; see Exhibit 6.5 **B**. Establishing the rankings according to performance measurement tools, including cost/benefit analyses, is clearly very important, but the application of subjective judgment is also appropriate. This is because few activities can be reduced to a manageable number of measures, and some measures may not be practical because of difficulties in real-world application or the expense of data collection. For example, a manager may believe that there would be a "feel good" factor in taking a particular course of action, such as not cutting a team that has been a historical power even though it makes business sense to do so. This could never be accurately quantified and is subjective, but may be valid.

Usually the highest rankings in the decision package for an athletic department are salaries and benefits for the administration, coaches, and staff, as seen in Exhibit 6.5 **B**. For example:

1. Football coach
2. Basketball coach

The athletic director should consider which coach and which sport are most important to the department, and how this sport matches the department's goals and objectives (e.g., to compete on a national level in football and to compete for conference championships in all other sports). The matching of budget priorities with goals is essential for the success of any athletic department, particularly major Division I athletic departments. If football generates 80% of an athletic department's revenue, how does this factor into the allocation of resources in the overall athletic department budget? The football program will likely receive most of the department's resources. But suppose you are the softball coach or the equestrian team coach—what would you say about the hefty allocation of resources to the football program? The reality of the situation is that the department would have no softball or equestrian budget without football, so these coaches cannot effectively question the allocation of resources to football. This brings us to the discussion of allocation of resources.

ALLOCATING RESOURCES

The ranking list results in a priority order for the allocation of resources. The most important items are funded, whether they are existing or new, and in lean years funding for the lower-ranking items can be reduced. Returning to the ZBB cost worksheet (Exhibit 6.5), note that the Coaches and Administrative Secretary positions are fully funded, but funding for the Secretary position has been reduced by half (1.0 position; **C**). The final budget will be made up of the decision packages that have been approved for funding, allocated in the appropriate operational units.

EXHIBIT 6.5   Sample ZBB budgeting cost worksheet for an athletic department.

PROGRAM, FUNCTION, OR ACTIVITY		ATHLETIC DIRECTOR AND COACHES				
A	Position Salaries (Object 01) Position Title	Current FTE	Current $	Grade	Position Code	Request FTE
	Coaches	35.0	$3,055,667	AD	1008	35.0
B	Admin. Sec. I	1.0	48,673	14	4130	1.0
	Secretary	2.0	85,097	12	4120	1.0
	Subtotal	**38.0**	**$3,189,437**			**37.0**
A	Other/Non-position Salaries (Object 02)		Current $	# Hrs.	# Days	Rate
B	Professional Part-time		3,500	100		$35.00
	Supporting Service PT		1,138	67		$16.98
	Subtotal		**4,638**			

Request $	Change $	Change FTE		Justification/ Purpose	Account Number
$3,055,667	—	—		Provide support to underperforming coaches	3-614-1-21
48,673	—	—		Clerical support for the project	2-614-1-40
42,549	$(42,549)	C	(1.0)	Realign 1.0 position to provide more flexible clerical part-time salaries and consultant services	2-614-1-40
$3,146,889	$(42,549)		(1.0)		

# of Persons	Request $	Change $		Justification/ Purpose	Account Number
1.0	3,500	0			2-614-1-82
1.0	7,000	5,862		Flexible part-time assistance needed for peak summer/fall season	2-614-1-90
	$10,500	$5,862			

(*continued*)

EXHIBIT 6.5   Cont.

PROGRAM, FUNCTION, OR ACTIVITY		ATHLETIC DIRECTOR AND COACHES			
A	Consultants/Other Contractual Svcs (Object 03)	Current $	# Hrs.	# Days	Dates of Service
	Consultants/camps	0	40		Nov–Jan
	Subtotal	0			
A	Supplies and Materials (Object 04)	Current $			
	Athletic/program supplies	$41,500			
	Subtotal	$41,500			

A	Other/Including Benefits for Supp. Projects (Object 05)	Current FTE	Current $		Request $	Change $
	Local travel		$114,700		$114,700	0
	Subtotal		$114,700		$114,700	0
	GRAND TOTAL	38.0	$3,350,275		$3,366,827	$16,552

	Employee Benefits from Realignment (Amount to Dept. of Financial Services)	Salary from above	Prof. 20% (.20)	Supp Svc 40% (.40)	Part-time 8% (.08)	Request $
	Reduce for 1.0 secretary		$(42,549)	—	$(17,021)	—
	Add for Support Svcs Part-time		5,862	—	—	$469
	Total Benefits		$(36,687)			0

Rate	Request $	Change$	Justification/ Purpose	Account Number
$53,238	$53,238		Help train trainers/ coaches	5-614-2-01
$53,238	$53,238			

Request $	Change $		Justification/ Purpose	Account Number
41,500	0		Materials for staff to support training activities	4-614-3-03
$41,500	0			

			Justification/ Purpose	Account Number
			Travel from office to schools and out of town games	
$(17,021)				
$469				
$(17,021)	$469			

Under ZBB, previous decisions are not supposed to influence the new budget. Previous outlays for coaches and facilities should, in theory, not be considered. Reality, however, is not theory, and previous budget outlays, especially for coaches and facilities, do matter in preparing the new budget.

ADVANTAGES AND DISADVANTAGES

The zero-based budgeting process of setting priorities provides significant accountability to the administrators, coaches, and staff who develop the criteria. In cases where revenues are flat or decreasing, the lowest-ranked priorities may be eliminated, and conflicts and resistance should be less than under other budgeting systems.

ZBB is no panacea, however. Like incremental budgeting, it has its own set of drawbacks. It increases paperwork and requires time to prepare, managers tend to inflate the benefits of activities that they want funded, and the eventual outcome may not differ much from what would occur with an incremental budget. Exhibit 6.6 summarizes the advantages and disadvantages of ZBB.

EXHIBIT 6.6   Advantages and disadvantages of ZBB.

ADVANTAGES

- Forces budget setters to examine every item.

- Allocates resources based on results and needs.

- Fosters a questioning attitude.

- Eliminates waste and budget slack.

- Prevents creeping budgets (using the previous year's figures with an additional percentage).

- Encourages managers to look for alternatives.

- Has a strong evaluation component.

DISADVANTAGES

- Is a complex, time-consuming process.

- May result in an emphasis on short-term benefits to the detriment of long-term planning.

- Does not officially consider previous money outlays.

- May be unrealistic (it is impossible to eliminate some programs, e.g., sports, although the budget indicates they should be).

- Is affected by internal politics and can lead to annual conflicts over budget allocation.

Modified Zero-Based Budgeting

As service-level budgeting entities, sport organizations are positioned to use a **modified zero-based budgeting (MZBB)** approach. In this approach, spending levels are matched with services to be performed. Under zero-based budgeting, a great deal of effort can be devoted to documenting personnel and expense requirements that are readily accepted as necessary, such as travel expenses for required road games, utility expenses for home games, and staff expenses for home games. MZBB reduces this effort by starting at a base that is higher than zero. An appropriate starting point for a department or program might be 80% or 85% of current spending levels. High-priority requests above this level may be identified in order to restore part or all of the current year's service levels.

ELEMENTS OF MZBB

MZBB has the following characteristics:

- Uses cost identification and behavior techniques
- Begins with a floor of expenses
- Includes decision or add packages
- Requires managers to reduce their budgets by a predetermined percentage
- Puts existing programs in competition with new ones

The use of cost identification and cost behavior techniques (recognizing how costs react to changes in volume) enhances this budgeting approach. Costs are identified as fixed, variable, mixed, or step costs. **Fixed costs** do not vary with volume, whereas **variable costs** change with volume (see Exhibit 6.7). For example, an arena has certain expenses necessary to open the doors for fans for a sport event, regardless of the number of fans. This base is the same for 5,000 or 20,000 fans. These costs include administrative salaries and benefits, property insurance, property taxes, payroll taxes, and depreciation. Other fixed expenses are discretionary and might reflect organizational policies in the form of periodic appropriations for training and development, special promotions, and opponent guarantees, to name a few. Variable expenses for an arena will include cost of goods sold, wages (part-time), and the opponent's share of the gate receipts. **Mixed costs** possess both fixed and variable elements. An example is utilities, which include a flat rate plus a cost for each unit used. For a sport arena, mixed costs include repairs and maintenance, as well as utilities. Finally, **step costs** are constant within a range of use but differ between ranges of use. For example, the cost for security might be fixed under contract, with one rate for event attendance of zero to 2,500 patrons, a higher rate for attendance between 2,501 and 5,000, and a still higher rate for attendance from 5,001 to 7,500. MZBB focuses on variable expenses, and this is why it is a practical approach to budgeting. See Exhibit 6.7 for a comparison of variable and step costs.

Exhibit 6.8 provides an overview of the MZBB focus. The expense floor represents the fixed costs of operations. These costs are the organization's minimal costs needed to stay in business, and they typically represent approximately 70% of total expenses. The top level (approximately 30%) represents mixed and variable expenses. This section is the focus of MZBB.

Zero-based budgeting focuses time and effort on all expenditures. Modified zero-based budgeting is more efficient in focusing time and effort on

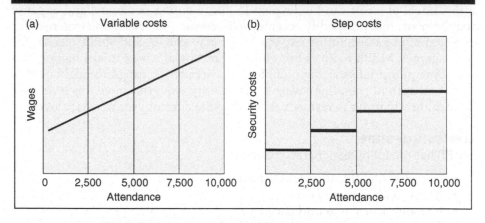

EXHIBIT 6.7   Comparison of the movement of variable costs (in the same direction and at the same rate as their associated activity) to that of step costs (constant within a range of use but different between ranges of use).

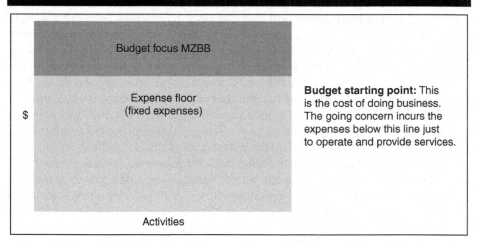

EXHIBIT 6.8   MZBB starting point.

variable expenses and accepting fixed expenses as necessary. All departments and programs will have a base need for expenditures—the minimum necessary for the department or program to operate. MZBB focuses time, energy, and management decision making on the area above this budgetary starting point. Underlying the MZBB process is the concept of the **going concern**—the assumption that the entity will operate indefinitely. A sport entity whose status isn't in question would be prudent to budget for the variable costs, those above the starting point. This will focus effort on areas that pertain to the goals and objectives of the organization and increase the efficiency of the budgeting process.

In general, MZBB asks managers to reduce their budgets to a predetermined level (a percentage of the previous year) and then add back requests for funding. Although this process places some existing programs in competition with new programs, it saves managers the strain of justifying all costs for all programs from the ground up.

In practice, athletic departments and public sector organizations that use MZBB require managers to submit "decision" or "add packages" for discrete activities or programs that need funding above a predetermined reduced level. In the submission stage of the budget process, managers are forced to reduce their appropriation requests to 80% to 90% of the base budget. A manager may then reconfigure existing activities into new decision packages that could bring the total budget request up to 110% to 115% of the previous year's budget.

By this means, new programs may be considered for funding. For example, an athletic department might be presented with the choice of reducing some current operations in favor of adopting a new program, funding the new program out of the savings gained by reducing the existing program. "Service-level budgeting" may be a better description of this budgeting approach, which begins with the minimum costs of providing a given service.

MZBB provides an occasion for managers to try something new and puts them on notice that they cannot assume the status quo. This can be unsettling to employees and managers, who may find their programs part of a "cut" package. Even if their activity is never cut, the employees and managers may feel unappreciated. Because of this potential for demoralization and the extensive time often required for the preparation of decision packages, zero-based budgeting processes, including MZBB, may not be appropriate for use in the public sector, especially where many activities are legally mandated.

STEPS IN MZBB

Step 1. The first step in MZBB is to identify expenses. Mark each expense type as fixed, mixed, or variable. Simply write F, M, or V next to the category (or in another column in a spreadsheet).

Step 2. Next, allocate fixed and mixed expenses. Fixed expenses will probably include the largest expenses, such as debt service and management salaries. Most fixed expenses are probably not negotiable without dramatic business changes or disruptions, so they provide a "hard landscape" around which you will fill in (and prioritize) the variable expenses. By identifying fixed and mixed expenses first you are able then to focus on the smaller, more negotiable amounts that remain.

Some expenses are **periodic expenses**. These are expenses for which we set aside money each month, in order to have sufficient funds when the expense is incurred. Examples are new vehicles, retirement bonuses, certain one-time events, purchases of computer software and equipment, and some insurance payments. Some organizations simply divide these expenses by 12 and set aside that amount each month. However, this approach will not work if the expense is less than a year away. Instead, for each expense, count how many months away it is, and divide the total expense amount by the number of months. For example, if the department plans to purchase a new car in four months with a down payment of $15,000, you would divide $15,000 by four and budget that amount, $3,750, each month. If an additional car will be purchased in the next fiscal year, and the purchase is at least a year away, you would divide the expense by 12 and set aside that amount each month.

This approach may cause strain on the budget at first, but as short-term expenses are paid, the monthly allocations for those expenses will decrease, freeing up cash.

Step 3. Once you have allocated the fixed and mixed expenses, circle back to identify any fixed expenses that could be eliminated. What remains will be the floor of expenses. You will concentrate on the expenses above this starting point line.

Step 4. Next, average the mixed expenses to determine the average amount spent per month over the last six to nine months (some organizations may want to look at a full fiscal year of expenses). Convert the average monthly mixed expenses to a figure for annual expenses. For example, if the average monthly utility expense was $26,500, the annual expense is $318,000. Consider the economic reality that your organization will face during the next budget period. For example, how will the global demand for fuel affect utility rates over the next year? Exact estimates are not necessary; you will make adjustments as the process continues.

Step 5. Now, address and prioritize the variable expenses. The prioritizing of variable expenses is essential to MZBB, and it is the difference between MZBB and ZBB.

Step 6. The variable expenses must be offset against anticipated revenues. Subtract total expenses from total revenues to arrive at the starting point for anticipated profit or loss from operations. Note that the goal of budgeting is not to break even (to make income equal expenses). Although you should conduct break-even analyses to ensure that a net operating loss will not occur, you should budget for a profit or a positive residual, depending on the profit/non-profit status of your organization. By making trade-offs between one category and another, adjust the expense and revenue figures until income equals or exceeds expenses. In this process conflicts often arise among sports, departments, coaches, and administration, because it exposes their conflicting *values*. If a conflict becomes too heated, it may be necessary for the parties to take a break from the process and continue later.

Remember that you will refine the budget as you go. It is a process: Prepare, Compare, Repair.

Budgeting takes time, and it does not end when departments or programs submit their revenue and expense estimates. Many meetings and individual sessions will be necessary to discuss the numbers and the reasoning behind these numbers. Each meeting or session should focus on the goals and objectives of the department and the organization.

The ZBB cost worksheet found in Exhibit 6.5 may be used for MZBB, as well. Recall that whereas under ZBB each program, function, or activity must be justified and placed in a decision packet **A**, MZBB allows a starting point of 80% to 85% of the previous year's budget. Managers use decision or add packages to justify an increase in their unit's allocations above the starting point.

For example, in Exhibit 6.5 **B**, professional part-time salaries are ranked more important than supporting service part-time salaries. Under ZBB, this package would start at zero, and changes to the budget would be based on the priority of the cost-decision package. Under MZBB, however, the package

EXHIBIT 6.9   Advantages and disadvantages of MZBB

ADVANTAGES

- Focuses budget setters on variable costs.

- Allocates resources based on results and variable needs.

- Fosters a questioning attitude.

- Encourages managers to look for alternatives.

- Has a strong evaluation component.

- Is less time-consuming than ZBB.

DISADVANTAGES

- May result in an emphasis on short-term benefits to the detriment of long-term planning.

- Does not consider previous money outlays.

- May be unrealistic, because some programs (e.g., sports) cannot be eliminated.

- Is affected by internal politics and can lead to annual conflicts over budget allocation.

might start at 80% of last year's funds ($3,710.40). To request funds for new activities above the 80%, the manager would submit an add package. The add package would include $5,862 for the new supporting service part-time request.

ADVANTAGES AND DISADVANTAGES

MZBB focuses on the portion of the budget that has flexibility rather than the entire budget. Fixed and mixed costs cannot be eliminated if a service is to be offered, but variable expenses can often be eliminated or reduced—or increased, when warranted. MZBB combines the best advantages of ZBB with the simplification of focusing on the variable costs above the budget starting point. See Exhibit 6.9 summarizing the advantages and disadvantages of MZBB.

Budgets within Budgets

Within each budget type are additional budgets. These budgets track an organization's revenue, expenses, cash, and capital expenditures, and they are some of the most important planning tools an organization can use. They show the impact that the budget will have on future organizational revenues, expenses, cash flows, and capital expenditures.

REVENUE BUDGET

The **revenue budget** is a forecast of revenues based on projections of the organization's sales. For example, to set appropriate ticket prices, athletic directors, general managers, and administrators must consider the strength of their schedule, their conference affiliation, the competition, the advertising budget, their sales force's effectiveness, and other relevant factors, and they must estimate sales volume. Then, based on estimates of demand at various prices, they select the appropriate prices. The result of sales estimates is the revenue budget.

EXPENSE BUDGET

The expense budget is found in all units within a firm and in non-profit and profit-making organizations alike. The **expense budget** for each unit lists its primary activities and allocates a dollar amount to each. Sport managers give particular attention to so-called fixed and semi-fixed expenses—those that remain relatively unchanged regardless of volume. As attendance drops or increases, variable expenses tend to control themselves because they change with volume.

CASH BUDGET

The **cash budget** forecasts how much cash the organization will have on hand and how much it will need to meet expenses. This budget can reveal potential shortages or the availability of surplus cash for short-term investments.

CAPITAL EXPENDITURE BUDGETS

Investments in real estate, stadiums, arenas, buildings, and major equipment are called capital expenditures. These are typically substantial expenditures, in terms of both magnitude and duration. Their magnitude and duration can justify the development of separate budgets for each of these expenditures. **Capital expenditure budgets** allow management to forecast future capital requirements, to keep on top of important capital projects, and to ensure that adequate cash will be available to meet expenses as they become due. Capital budgeting is discussed in detail in Chapter 8.

CONCLUSION

Planning is a controlling activity of decision makers. The "mechanical" (the actual budget on paper) is only part of the planning approach, which involves managerial and motivational elements. Decisions about the future of an athletic department, professional sport organization, or non-profit entity are often made in budgeting meetings. The budgeting process will indicate where next year's growth will focus and what areas will benefit from additional funds. It behooves every manager to take an interest in the budgeting process—and not only because bonuses depend partly on meeting budgetary objectives. Get involved: budgeting affects every department and every individual in the organization.

Concept Check

1. Why is the budgeting process important to the success of a sport organization?
2. How do budgeting and forecasting differ?
3. How does incremental budgeting differ from program planning budgeting? How does it differ from zero-based budgeting?
4. What are the strengths and weaknesses of incremental budgeting?
5. How does program planning budgeting differ from zero-based budgeting?
6. What are the strengths and weaknesses of program planning budgeting?
7. What are the strengths and weaknesses of zero-based budgeting?
8. How does modified zero-based budgeting differ from zero-based budgeting?
9. What are the advantages and disadvantages of modified zero-based budgeting?
10. In team sport (professional or college), which form of budgeting should be used?

Practice Problems

1. The Columbia Arena Company formed in 2021 and uses the accrual basis of accounting. Using the company's 2021 budget, provided in Exhibit 6.10, develop a pro forma operating budget for 2022 based on the following revenue and expense estimates:
   a. It is forecasted that costs and expenditures will change in 2022 as follows:
      - Merchandise COGS, General and Administrative, Event Costs, and Maintenance will increase by 2.5%.
      - Concessions COGS will increase by 4.5%.
      - Utilities will increase by 8.0%.
      - Personnel will increase by 2.5%.
      - Insurance, Contract Services, Marketing, Management Fee, and Reserve are forecasted to remain the same.
   b. The arena is expected to generate cash receipts in 2022 as follows:
      - All rent will increase by 5.5%.
      - Concessions Gross will increase by 4.0%.
      - Merchandise Gross, Suite Revenue, Club Seating Revenue, Advertising Revenue, and Naming Rights are forecasted to remain the same.
      - Box Office, Parking, and Ticket Fee revenues will decrease by 2.3%.
2. After you have calculated the 2022 budget, suppose your boss asks you to revise it so that overall revenues increase by 4% and operating expenses decrease by 1.5%.
   a. Based on current trends in facility management, what revenues do you anticipate can be increased? What expenses can be decreased?
   b. Use the 2022 budget that you created in Problem 1 and create a new 2022 budget based on the revenue increases and expense decreases outlined in Problem 2 and your work on Problem 2a.

EXHIBIT 6.10   Sample budget for Practice Problem 1.

COLUMBIA ARENA COMPANY 2021 OPERATING BUDGET	
Revenues:	
Rent from Sports Teams	$465,000
Rent from Events	$729,000
Equipment Rent	$27,600
Concessions (Gross)	$2,512,000
Merchandise (Gross)	$244,600
Advertising and Sponsorships	$580,400
Naming Rights	$327,000
Box Office	$150,560
Suite Revenue	$781,700
Club Seat Revenue	$549,360
Ticket Fees	$654,000
Parking	$482,010
Total Revenues	$7,503,230
Less COGS:	
Concessions COGS	$1,507,300
Merchandise COGS	$122,300
Total COGS	$1,629,600
Gross Profit	$5,873,630
Operating Expenses:	
Personnel	$981,000
G&A	$218,000
Non-reimbursed Event Costs	$163,500
Utilities	$490,500
Insurance	$272,500
Maintenance	$369,800
Contract Services	$119,900
Marketing and Promotion	$218,000
Management Fee	$109,000
Reserve	$163,500
Total Operating Expenses	$3,105,700
Operating Income (Loss)	$2,767,930

Case Analysis

Coastal Atlantic University

The intercollegiate athletics department at Coastal Atlantic University (CAU) has major budgeting issues. For the 2022 fiscal year, the university's Board of Trustees has approved a $20.4 million budget for the department. The budget projects a $1.4 million shortfall. After CAU's president shifted $1.4 million to athletics to cover the shortfall, groups across campus complained loudly about the role of intercollegiate athletics on CAU's campus.

The CAU athletic program competes as an NCAA Division I–FBS team. The school is a member of a mid-major conference and has 16 varsity teams, the minimum number required by the NCAA for competition at the Division I level. The athletic department's budget is relatively small compared to those of other Division I–FBS teams. The team's football budget was in the bottom half of conference budgets in fiscal year 2020. For the 2021 fiscal year, the budget was cut by 5%. The athletic department employs relatively few staff members, but in 2021 ten positions were cut, saving the department $700,000. In fiscal year 2021, the department spent $20.4 million while generating $4.5 million in revenues. After the athletic department's portion of student fees was transferred to the department, it had a $1.9 million deficit. The department has overspent by a total of approximately $8.2 million over the past few fiscal years.

Beyond its athletics department, the university as a whole faces serious budgeting challenges. Due to the impacts of COVID-19, a slowly recovering economy, and declining state support, CAU will have to cut between $11 million and $24 million in fiscal year 2022. For fiscal year 2023, the cuts may grow higher, to as high as $39.5 million. As the university acts to balance its budget, many are questioning the athletic department's deficit spending. One member of CAU's faculty senate stated, "The athletics department drains resources at a time when academics are being threatened by overall cuts at the university." Other faculty members are asking whether operating the athletic department is worth the expense.

Case Questions

1. If you were advising the athletic director at CAU, what budgeting advice would you provide?
2. What budgeting approach should the athletic department use if it intends to balance its budget in the 2022 fiscal year?
3. For an average athletic department, which budgeting method would most likely keep the program from running a deficit? Why?

References

Brayley, R.E., & McLean, D.D. (1999). *Managing financial resources in sport and leisure service organizations*. Champaign, IL: Sagamore.

Makridakis, S., Wheelwright, S.C., & Hyndman, R.J. (1997). *Forecasting: Methods and applications* (3rd ed.). Hoboken, NJ: Wiley.

Ord, K., Hibon, M., & Makridakis, S. (2000, October). The M3-competition. *International Journal of Forecasting*, 16(4), 433–436.

Pyhrr, P. (1973). *Zero-base budgeting*. New York: Wiley.

Smith, J.A. (2007). *Handbook of management accounting* (4th ed.). London: CIMA.

CHAPTER 7

Debt and Equity Financing

Daniel A. Rascher

KEY CONCEPTS

annual coupon interest payment
bankruptcy
board of directors
bond
bond rating
call premium
call provision
capital gain
capital gains yield
common stock
convertible bond
coupon rate
current yield
default risk

dividends
initial public offering
junk bond
liquidation
liquidity spread
loan
perpetual growth rate
production opportunities
return on equity capital
secured claim stock option
tax abatement
total expected return
trade credit yield curve
yield to maturity (YTM)

INTRODUCTION

Individual people, families, and businesses often have money available that is not being used in their day-to-day lives or businesses. Instead of just keeping this money under the proverbial mattress, they have the opportunity to invest. At the same time, businesses often need capital or financing in order to expand their operation, buy new equipment, launch new products, and so forth. In other words, there are potential suppliers of financial capital and potential purchasers of this capital. The financial markets and intermediaries are where these two sides can connect.

A sport organization in need of financing may decide to raise capital by allowing investors to own part of the company in exchange for the funding or financing (equity financing), or they may decide to borrow money (debt financing). The choice of one or the other (or some of both) depends on the overall cost of each and the related risks. In essence, a financing decision is based on the risk (and creditability) of the company. Typically, companies with lower risk and steady cash flows choose to issue debt. Companies that have higher risk in their cash flows (i.e., they cannot guarantee an interest payment) usually issue equity.

How does a company go about completing a financial transaction to raise capital? The company will probably select one of three methods for doing so. The first is a direct transfer, whereby the business sells its stocks or bonds directly to investors (savers) without using any type of financial institution. When corporate bonds are floated or stock is offered through a secondary stock offering, this is done directly to the market. A second method is to use an investment bank as an intermediary. The business sells its bonds or stocks to the investment bank, which resells them to the market. A third method is that savers invest their money with a financial intermediary, such as a bank, which then issues its own securities. When a person deposits money in a bank, the bank then lends that money out to another person or entity. The saver has no direct connection to the borrower. The bank makes money by paying a lower interest rate to savers than it receives from borrowers. Mutual funds, insurance companies, and pension funds may also act as financial intermediaries.

This chapter discusses equity financing through the sale of shares of stock and its debt counterpart, the sale of corporate bonds and loans. First we will discuss required rate of return, which affects both equity and debt financing.

REQUIRED RATE OF RETURN

The required rate of return is the annual return that an investor would require from a particular investment, whether in stocks or bonds, to account for the riskiness of the investment.

Factors Influencing the Required Rate of Return

An investor purchasing stock (equity) in a company will require a return of at least a certain amount. The amount will depend on (1) production opportunities, (2) time preferences for consumption, (3) risk, and (4) inflation.

Production opportunities. The quality or nature of the **production opportunities** of an investment—that is, the reason the company needs the money in the first place—is a factor in the **return on equity capital**—the combination of dividend payments and capital gains offered by the investment. In other words, the quality of the new product offering or geographic expansion (two examples of production opportunities) will affect the financial return from the project. If the company believes that it can create large returns from the project once it receives the equity capital, it may be willing to pay high returns on that capital. However, competition to invest in a projected high-return business opportunity helps to keep the cost of equity capital down. A competitive market will dampen the production opportunities effect, because multiple equity investors desiring to invest in the project will outbid each other, reducing the expected return on equity capital. As in any market, the final expected return on equity capital is the result of a balance between the supply of possible investments and the demand to invest in these projects.

Time preferences for consumption. Consumers or businesses considering an investment will base their decision partially on their time preferences for consumption. As discussed in Chapter 4, those with a high preference for consuming now will require a higher return on equity capital than those with a low preference for consuming now.

Risk. A potential investor will also consider the risk involved in the investment, in terms of the size of the dividend payments (and when they will be paid) or the expected stock appreciation. With a higher perceived risk, the required rate of return on equity capital will also have to be higher, to entice investors to provide capital for the project.

Inflation. Inflation affects all financial investments, in that gains from the sale of securities will be undercut by the increased costs of goods and services resulting from inflation. Gains must be high enough to outpace inflation and to reward the investors. If expectations for future inflation rise, then the required rate of return will also rise, reflecting the expected future inflation.

Calculating the Required Rate of Return

The required rate of return will be higher if the investor sees a substantial probability of the investment's becoming worthless or worth less than expected. An investor could buy a short-term US Treasury bill (T-bill) and earn its rate without fear of default. Hence, the required rate of return begins at the risk-free or T-bill rate. Then, the investor will add percentage points reflecting default risk (DRP), inflation risk (IP), liquidity risk (LP), and maturity risk (MRP).

You will note that this adding of percentage points is similar to the calculation of the nominal interest rate, as discussed in Chapter 3. See that chapter for definitions of these risk premiums. Exhibit 7.1 gives the formula for the required rate of return (k) as it applies to different types of securities.

From this exhibit, one can see that short-term T-bills will have lower required rates of return (based only on k^* and IP) than other types of securities

EXHIBIT 7.1 Formula for the required rate of return.

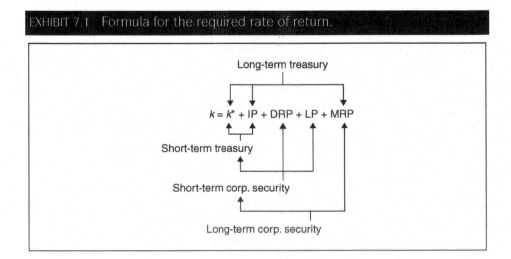

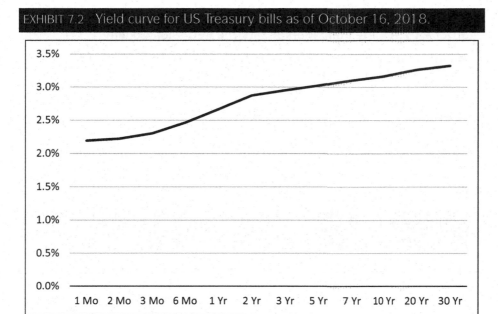

EXHIBIT 7.2   Yield curve for US Treasury bills as of October 16, 2018.

Note: X-axis (Maturity) is not to scale.

Source: www.treasury.gov/resource-center/data-chart-center/interest-rates/Pages/
TextView.aspx?data=yieldYear&year=2018.

because they present the lowest levels of risk; long-term corporate bonds (and other corporate securities) will have higher required rates of return because of various additional risk premiums.

By graphing interest rates against the time to maturity for bonds with equal credit quality, including government bonds, we can create a **yield curve** (or term structure of interest rates). The most frequently reported yield curve is one that plots three-month, two-year, five-year, and 30-year US Treasury debt. Exhibit 7.2 shows a curve for 12 maturities, as of October 16, 2018. Typically, the yield curve slopes upward, with a diminishing slope as maturity increases. (In Exhibit 7.2, the fact that the *X*-axis is not to scale masks this tendency.) Long maturities generally entail greater risk than short maturities because there is more uncertainty in the far future than in the near future. However, the yield curve may be humped or downward sloping. A downward-sloping yield curve is rare and is known as an *inverted yield curve*. It is caused by a market expectation of lower interest rates in the future that outweigh the maturity risk premium. When yield curves are inverted, a recession typically follows.

The **liquidity spread** is the difference between a long-term interest rate (e.g., 30 years) and a short-term interest rate (e.g., three months). This spread will be large if the risk in the distant future of adverse events is high relative to the risks of the near-term future.

SIDEBAR 7.A   The Bond Market Saw The Recession Coming

An inverted yield curve has preceded every recession since World War II, although twice, in 1966 and 1998, the curve inverted but a recession did not follow. The New York Federal Reserve views an inverted yield curve as useful information in forecasting a recession two to six quarters ahead. The yield curve for March 2, 2007, shown in Exhibit 7.3, was inverted or at least flat. The Great Recession began in December 2007, so the inverted yield curve maintained its forecasting accuracy. Again, on August 30, 2019 (and during many days around the same time period), the yield curve was inverted, as it was in late February of 2020. Does this portend a recession?

EXHIBIT 7.3   Yield curves for US Treasury bills as of March 2, 2007 and August 30, 2019.

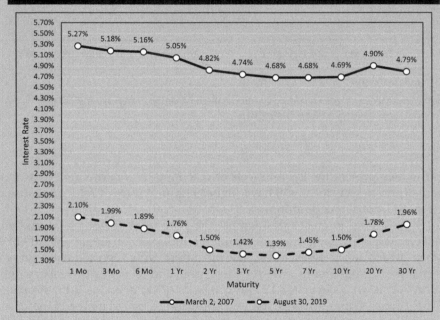

Note: X-axis (Maturity) is not to scale.

EQUITY

As discussed above, equity financing involves the exchange of capital (money) for an ownership stake in a company. This section discusses the various forms of equity financing and stocks (equity ownership).

Types of Equity Financing

Although equity financing is typically considered simply the infusion of equity into a firm in exchange for company shares, this type of financing actually includes three additional funding sources: retained earnings, government funding, and gifts or donations.

SHARES

One way to finance a large project is to issue shares of the company in exchange for money. The buyers of those shares will own stock (typically common stock) in the company, meaning they will own some percentage of the company and will be entitled to a portion of any dividends the company may pay out. **Dividends** are periodic payments made to shareholders of a company as a way of distributing profits to the shareholders. By issuing or selling shares a company obtains financing for a large project (such as a new product line, a new geographic market, or the acquisition of a complementary company).

RETAINED EARNINGS

In another form of equity financing, the firm simply uses cash on hand, or retained earnings, to finance a large project. Technically, the shareholders own the cash on hand—it is their equity. Depending on the board of directors' decision, this cash could be given to the shareholders in the form of a dividend, or it could be reinvested in the company (or some of each).

GOVERNMENT FUNDING

A third form of equity financing is the use of government funding. Chapter 9, "Facility Financing," discusses ways the government has traditionally helped to finance sport stadiums and arenas. This section briefly describes those methods.

Direct financing. Local, regional, state, and federal governments sometimes provide funds directly to sport organizations. For example, the Milwaukee Brewers each year receive $3.85 million from local government as part of the team's agreement to operate Miller Park. These funds are meant for maintenance costs. In 2012 the Nashville Predators received $1.8 million in fees from the City of Nashville to operate their arena, but the team also received an extra nearly $9 million in other local and state money to cover operating losses at the facility. In Indianapolis, the local government owns Lucas Oil Stadium, where the Indianapolis Colts play. As an additional incentive for the team, the government allows the franchise to retain the naming rights revenue, which has amounted to over $6 million per year. The Dallas Cowboys were able to secure a similar deal for Cowboys Stadium. The team sold their stadium naming right to AT&T in 2013 and kept all of the proceeds from the deal despite the fact that the City of Arlington owns the stadium. In cases like these, the income simply becomes part of the organization's cash on hand and is therefore equity (owned by the shareholders). State governments also directly provide financing through their annual budgets to sports at public universities, including intercollegiate athletics, intramurals, and recreation. More information on government financing for stadiums is provided in Chapter 9.

Indirect financing. Other forms of government financing are indirect. One example is the provision of land, or a below-market lease on land, for a sports stadium. Although money does not change hands, the "free" land allows the organization to use its cash on hand for other things. Therefore, the government donation is an indirect form of equity financing. For the Amway Center in Orlando (host of the Orlando Magic), the City of Orlando picked up the costs of the land and infrastructure. Another method of government financing is for a government to forgo the collection of sales or property taxes for a sport organization (known as **tax abatement**). For instance, the Florida Marlins receive a sales tax rebate on tickets and concessions sold in their baseball stadium, which amounts to about $2 million per year in extra cash. Their neighbor, the Miami Heat, also receive about $2 million per year in sales tax rebates. The organizations add this amount to their cash on hand (and owners' equity).

GIFTS

Finally, some sport organizations solicit and receive tax-free donations or gifts. Any non-profit organization set up as a 501(c)(3) can receive donations and provide the donor with a receipt allowing the donor to take a tax deduction. Some intercollegiate athletic departments generate a tenth or more of their annual budget through donations. In 2016, the Ohio State University generated over $33 million in donations to athletics, accounting for about 19% of its athletics budget. Although non-profit organizations and universities do not have equity holders, they do have equity or net assets that management may use in operating the organization, and these donations are added to the cash on hand.

Stocks

All for-profit businesses have equity ownership—someone owns the business, even if it is one person who owns 100% of the equity (or stock) in the business and even if the equity is not traded on a stock market. Sport teams, for instance, are owned either by a single person (such as Terry Pegula, owner of the Buffalo Bills), by multiple owners privately (such as the St. Louis Cardinals), or by multiple owners, with the equity or stock traded on public markets (formerly the case for the Cleveland Indians and Boston Celtics). The latter ownership type is now common in the English Premier League. As mentioned previously, the NFL prohibits the publicly traded ownership model, with the exception of the Green Bay Packers.

   Common stock is held by the owners of a company. State and federal laws govern the specific rights and privileges of ownership, but ownership always implies control of the business. Usually, this means that shareholders (also called stockholders—those owning "shares" of stock) elect a **board of directors** (BoD) whose job is to select the executives and management and to supervise the overall direction of the company. Those executives hire the remaining employees. Thus, shareholders exercise and maintain their control through the BoD, not by directly running the day-to-day operations of the company. Typically, board members own shares or are granted options to buy shares; share ownership ensures that their interests are aligned with those of the stockholders.

PRICE OF EQUITY

Just like other goods, financial goods have prices. The price of borrowing money is the interest rate: the borrower must pay the lender interest, corresponding to the interest rate, in order to borrow the money. Typically, the borrower also pays a transaction fee. The price of obtaining capital by issuing stock takes the form of dividend payments and loss of equity by the company's owners. Any capital gain, or appreciation in the stock price, is now shared with the equity holders who provided the capital.

CALCULATING STOCK VALUES

The value of a share of stock is equal to the present value of its expected dividend stream. See Chapter 4 for the calculation of the present value of a future

EXHIBIT 7.4   Valuation of stock.

NewFangled Sports Products, Inc.
Valuation of Stock

Value of Stock Based on Dividend Payments

			Projected			
	FYE Current Year	FYE CY+1	FYE CY+2	FYE CY+3	FYE CY+4	Terminal Year
① Expected Dividend Payment Per Share	$1.00	$1.10	$1.15	$1.20	$1.30	$1.40
② Discount Period in Years	0.00	1.00	2.00	3.00	4.00	
ⓐ Discount Factor[1]	1.0000	0.8993	0.8087	0.7273	0.6540	0.6540
ⓑ Discount Rate[2]	11.2%					
ⓒ Perpetual Growth Rate[3]	4.0%					
ⓓ Terminal Value[4]						$19.44
③ Present Value - Cash Flow/Terminal Value	$1.00	$0.99	$0.93	$0.87	$0.85	$12.72
④ Net Present Value	$17.36					

Notes:
[1] Reflects end-of-year discounting convention.
[2] Based upon the Cost of Equity Capital as reported in Ibbotson's Cost of Capital Yearbook (data through June 2012) for SIC 3949.
[3] Based upon estimated long term cash flow growth rate of the economy in general.
[4] Terminal Value = Terminal Year Cash Flow / (Discount Rate - Perpetual Growth Rate)

cash flow and Chapter 10 for valuation of a company. As shown in Exhibit 7.4, the present value of a share of NewFangled Sports Products, Inc. (NFSP) is about $17.36, based on the present value of the expected future dividend stream. The first row **1** shows the expected dividend payments. This forecast may be based on what an equity analyst who covers this company (analyzes it for his or her investment bank employer) feels the dividend payments are going to be, or it may be based on guidance from the CEO of NFSP.

The discount period **2** simply reflects how far into the future from the current year the payment is expected to be made. Here the assumption is one dividend payment per year. As discussed in Chapter 4, the discount factor **a** is

$$\frac{1}{(1+i)^n}$$

where i is the discount rate and n is the number of periods.

In other words, the $1.10 dividend is worth only $1.10 × 0.8993 = $0.99 today, because the shareholder will not receive it until one year from today. The discount rate **b** is based on the required rate of return, as discussed above and in Chapters 3 and 4. It reflects the riskiness of the expected dividend payments. The perpetual growth rate **c** is an expected annual growth rate in the dividend payment beyond the four years forecasted, in perpetuity (forever). This rate is projected by the equity analyst and is usually tied to the average US gross domestic product growth rate. The calculation of the terminal value **d** is explained in Chapter 10. Essentially, this is the total value of the stock at the end of Year 4. This value is reflected as a $12.72 present value **3**. The net present value **4** of a share of NFSP with the expected dividends shown is the sum of each year's value in the present value row (i.e., summing $1.00, .99, ...), which equals $17.36.

The concepts of discount rate and present value are fundamental tools of finance. We can use them in many different situations where a cash flow exists over multiple time periods.

SIDEBAR 7.B   The Byte from Apple Continues

Apple Inc. grew quickly in the early 1980s and helped build the personal computer industry. It has been profitable for most years of its existence. Over the years, sales of the iPod, iPhone, and iPad have boosted Apple's income to nearly $60 billion in 2018. That same year, it ended with nearly $66 billion in cash on hand, with $65 billion in other current assets. Since 2003, its revenues have grown by nearly 4,200% and its income has increased from nearly zero to the aforementioned $60 billion. The company finances its R&D with annual expenditures and does not have a lot of capitalized investment in equipment, plants, and so forth, because it outsources manufacturing. Yet it did not pay dividends for decades, until pressure from shareholders (along with low borrowing rates and no immediate need for its excess cash of nearly $100 billion in early 2012) caused it to begin making dividend payments in mid-2012. Thus, a long era of piling up cash with no dividend payments to its owners came to an end and in 2019 the ratio of earnings paid out in dividends was around 25%. Note that Warren Buffett, perhaps the most prescient investor over the past few decades, also does not pay a dividend from his Berkshire Hathaway fund. His role is to buy companies, so he needs the funds to do so.

CHANGES IN STOCK PRICES

In casual conversation, people often talk about a stock being valuable because the price of the stock has risen since they purchased it or because the price is expected to rise. Thus, the person could sell the shares for a **capital gain** (the increase in a stock's price since purchase). Why would the stock price go up? The simple reason is that another person thinks the stock is more valuable than what the owner paid. Why would that person think the stock is more valuable? This line of reasoning will lead eventually to the conclusion that the point of owning a share of stock (or ownership in a company) is to share in any profit that is made. Profits are disbursed to stockholders through the mechanism of dividends. As discussed previously, dividends are payments made to shareholders, usually on a quarterly or annual basis. In other words, shareholders own the company, and they share in the profits of the company.

Many companies pay a consistent dividend each year instead of varying it according to actual profits. This reduces the financial risk of stock ownership in that company. A company might choose to return $1 per share of stock in dividends as a way of giving the owners what is due them. Other companies base the dividends somewhat on the company's profits. For instance, Nike has paid a quarterly dividend since 1984. In the past five years, the company has consistently paid out quarterly dividends, in amounts ranging from $0.16 per share to $0.32 per share.

Though dividends are the fundamental reason for owning stock, other companies, including many listed on the NASDAQ, do not pay dividends but instead opt to invest the money back into the company rather than obtaining financing through debt or some other means. For example, Under Armour has not paid any dividends since going public in 2005, because it is reinvesting its net profits into the growth of the company with the hope of creating even larger profits. The presumption is that Under Armour will pay dividends in the future.

If a company were to state credibly that it was *never* going to distribute a dividend, why would someone want to buy a share of that stock? An investor might hope that someone else would be willing to pay more for the share in the future (the "greater fool" theory). We might ask why that "someone else" would be interested in buying a share of stock that would never provide dividend payments. Logically, no future purchaser would be interested, and the stock's value should be zero. In other words, to extract any money out of owning a share of stock, the owner must receive a dividend payment. For this reason, the value of a stock is based only on expected future dividend payments, not on any capital gain anticipated from selling the stock—because that capital gain itself is based on expected future dividend payments.

Yet stocks do change hands, and that is because expectations differ across investors as to how big or small future dividends are going to be. There are other reasons why investors sell their shares—such as the seller's needing immediate funds or differences in calculated required rates of return. Also, an investor might sell shares of a company because she believes other companies provide better investment opportunities, with higher expected dividend payments and relatively lower stock prices. Proof of this point is in what happens each quarter when a company announces its earnings. If it misses earnings by a few cents per share, its stock price usually drops to reflect the expected drop in the future dividend stream. This is because dividends are, in the long run, tied to earnings. Although companies do not necessarily set the exact dividend amount each year based on that year's earnings, over time earnings will determine how much money is available to be distributed as dividends.

DEBT

Now that we have discussed the sources of equity financing and its pricing, let's consider debt financing. The two major sources of debt financing are corporate bonds and loans. Companies issue **corporate bonds** to raise capital. The investors or buyers of the bonds may range from large institutions to individual people. For reasons discussed below, some investors prefer to own both stocks and bonds. **Loans**, on the other hand, are usually provided by financial intermediaries, such as banks or insurance companies. Loans operate similarly to bonds, except that loans are not originated through a publicly traded market, as bonds are. After discussing bonds and loans in more detail, we will look at what happens when a firm cannot repay or restructure its debt.

Bonds

As mentioned above, bonds are a financial mechanism that organizations use to raise capital through debt (as opposed to equity). A **bond** is a promise to pay back borrowed money plus interest to the investor who has purchased the bond. The par value or face value of a bond is the amount of principal that the bond will be worth at maturity. The face may represent a single investor's total investment (say, $75,000), or the investor may purchase multiple bonds with smaller par values (say, 75 bonds worth $1,000 each). The owner of a bond may sell it to someone else at any time, and the new owner will collect the principal repayment at maturity. The sale price may be higher or lower than the par value, depending on various types of risk. A bond's **coupon rate** is the rate that the organization is paying for use of the money, the equivalent of an interest rate. A bond's maturity is the number of years from issuance until the principal (or par value) will be paid back. Typically, corporate bonds have maturities of six to ten years.

A bond does not provide the investor any ownership privileges, as stock does. The bond holder will receive a fixed payment stream over time. This arrangement has a lower risk than ownership shares of stock, which will rise and fall daily and provide varying dividend payments. An equity (stock) owner, however, has a say in how the company is managed (usually through a vote on the membership of the BoD), whereas a bond holder is not entitled to vote on the management of the company. Bond holders, however, are usually first in line to receive some payment from liquidated assets if the company should go bankrupt. Essentially, stocks and bonds present a trade-off between risk and reward: the bond holder has less risk but usually receives lower expected total returns from ownership (at least historically) compared to equity owners.

CALL PROVISIONS AND PREMIUMS

Sometimes a borrower will obtain sufficient funds and decide to pay off the bonds before the maturity date. Each bond issue usually includes a **call provision**, which allows the borrower to pay the bond off early. Often, a minimum period, called the call protection period, guarantees the lender some interest payments, which should compensate her or him for the costs of the purchase transaction. After the call protection period, the borrower can pay off the bonds by repaying the principal plus a **call premium** (a fee assessed when the borrower pays off the principal prior to the maturity date). Often, the call premium is equal to one year's interest payments, if the call occurs during the first year, and it declines each year thereafter. The typical formula is

$$\text{Call Premium} = \frac{N-t}{N}\text{INT}$$

where N = the full number of years of maturity (e.g., for a 30-year bond, N = 30)
$\quad\quad t$ = the number of years since the issue date
$\quad$ INT = the interest payment

For example, suppose a 30-year bond for $10 million has an interest rate of 8%. The annual interest payment is, therefore,

$$0.08 \times \$10,000,000 = \$800,000$$

If the borrower wishes to pay off the bond in Year 10, then the call premium would be

$$\left(\frac{30-10}{30}\right) \times \$800,000 = \$533,333$$

The borrower would owe $10 million plus $533,333 at the end of Year 10, after having already paid annual interest payments of $800,000 in Years 1 through 10 (since this call premium occurs at the end of Year 10).

Note that the call premium usually declines as time moves forward and maturity approaches. This is not always the case, however. For instance, in January 2009, the Dallas City Council approved the full payment of over $61 million in city government bonds that were initially issued in 1998 as part of the financing of American Airlines Center. The call premium was 1% flat, or about $610,000, so the total payment consisted of $61 million in principal plus $610,000 for the call premium. The city decided to cash in the bonds and reissue new ones, because calculations showed that it would save over $10 million in present value as a result of lower interest rates in 2009 versus 1998. This is similar to refinancing a home mortgage because interest rates have dropped and having to pay an early payoff penalty of 1%. The ability to call a bond and pay it off early provides flexibility to the issuing company. Typically, a borrower will pay a higher interest rate for bonds with a call provision because of the added flexibility.

RATING A BOND

Rating a bond is similar to "scoring" a loan applicant. The rating is intended to convey the likelihood that payments will be made in full and that the borrower will not default. **Default risk** is the risk that a borrower will not pay back the principal of a debt plus interest. Analysts arrive at ratings by studying the financial performance of the corporation issuing the bonds, using indicators such as some of the ratios described in Chapter 2. The company's earnings stability, the regulatory environment, potential product liability, and similar issues affect the **bond rating**.

Rating agencies such as Moody's and Fitch rate bonds as a service to investors. Ratings range from a high of AAA to a low of D. If a bond has a high risk of default, the borrower will have to raise the interest rate in order to interest investors. **Junk bonds** have a bond rating below BBB, such as BB, B, C, or D. These bonds have a significant chance of default and, thus, offer much higher coupon rates.

RETURNS

Investors can make money from a bond in two ways. First, they may receive an annual or periodic payment, called the **annual coupon interest payment**. This is a periodic return from owning the bond and is analogous to a dividend payment. Second, the investor may earn a capital gain upon selling the bond, if it is sold prior to maturity. This one-time gain from the sale of the asset is similar to the capital gain from selling a share of stock.

The **current yield** is the amount that the investor earns annually from the interest payment, compared to the price of the bond. Current yield is expressed as a percentage return and is defined as follows:

$$\text{current yield} = \frac{\text{annual coupon interest payment}}{\text{current price of the bond}}$$

The annual interest payment received from a bond is fixed (the coupon rate), but the price of the bond may vary with changes in interest rates, inflation, required rates of return, and so forth. A bond paying 10% with a par value of $1,000, a ten-year maturity, and a price of $1,000 will have a current yield of 10%. If the price were $887, the current yield would be 11.27%:

$$\frac{0.10 \times \$1,000}{\$887} = 11.27\%$$

The **capital gains yield** of a bond is the annualized percentage change in the price of the bond relative to its current price. Mathematically, it is

$$\text{capital gains yield} = \frac{\text{expected change in bond's price}}{\text{beginning-of-year price}}$$

If the bond was sold for $887, and its sale price a year later was $950, then the capital gains yield is 7.1%:

$$\frac{(950 - 887)}{887} = \frac{63}{887} = 7.1\%$$

The sale price of a bond might rise because of a decrease in the discount rate due to lowered inflation expectations. See below for a discussion of bond valuation.

When we combine the two ways to make money from a bond, we have the **total expected return** from owning the bond. For the bond described above, the total expected return would be:

$$\text{total expected return} = \text{current yield} + \text{capital gains yield}$$
$$= 11.27\% + 7.1\% = 18.36\%$$

(The difference is due to rounding.) This is quite a substantial annual return. The term **yield to maturity (YTM)** is often used for the total annualized return from owning a specific bond. It is the same as the total expected return.

CALCULATING THE VALUE OF A BOND

After purchasing a bond, the investor can either hold it and receive the interest payments plus the principal upon maturity or sell the bond at some time and receive its price at that time. As discussed in Chapter 10, one way of finding the value of an asset is to calculate the present value of its future payment streams, discounted at some discount rate. Recall that the discount rate is based on the required rate of return. Thus, the riskiness of the investment plays a role in determining its discount rate. (An example of calculating a discount rate is provided in Chapter 10.)

If interest rates rise after an investor has purchased a bond, then higher-yielding bonds (those with higher payments because of higher interest rates) will be available to potential buyers, thus driving down the price of the investor's bond. In mathematical terms, higher interest rates cause higher discount rates, which lead to lower valuations for streams of payments. The risk that the price of a bond will go up or down is known as interest rate risk.

The present value of a bond is the price that a buyer would pay for it prior to maturity. On the day of maturity, of course, a buyer would pay the principal amount, because that is what the bond holder will collect on that day. The following formula provides the present value of a bond:

$$PV = \frac{IP}{(1+d)^1} + \frac{IP}{(1+d)^2} + \ldots + \frac{IP}{(1+d)^N} + \frac{M}{(1+d)^N}$$

where IP = interest payment
    d = discount rate or required rate of return
    N = number of annual payments
    M = value at maturity

In other words, the present value equals the sum of the present values of the interest payments, plus the present value of the principal payment (M), which is due at maturity N years in the future.

Consider the present value on the issue date of a ten-year bond with par value $1,000, coupon rate 10%, and a discount rate of 8%. For each of the ten years until maturity, the bond holder will receive a $100 interest payment, and at the end of ten years the principal will be paid back. In nominal terms, $2,000 will be paid out over the ten years. However, the present value on the bond's issue date of that payment stream is:

$$PV = \frac{\$100}{(1+0.08)^1} + \frac{\$100}{(1+0.08)^2} + \ldots + \frac{\$100}{(1+0.08)^{10}} + \frac{\$1,000}{(1+0.08)^{10}} = \$1,134.20$$

Therefore, one could sell the bond for $1,134 on its issue date. After five years, the bond would be worth less, because only five years of payments would remain. If the discount rate were higher (12%)—perhaps because of higher expected inflation or because of default risk or interest rate risk—the present value of the bond would decrease to $887. If the coupon rate were 8% and the discount rate were also 8%, the bond's present value might be surprising:

$$PV = \frac{\$80}{(1+0.08)^1} + \frac{\$80}{(1+0.08)^2} + \ldots + \frac{\$80}{(1+0.08)^{10}} + \frac{\$1,000}{(1+0.08)^{10}} = \$1,000$$

As this example shows, when the discount rate of a bond is the same as the interest rate, the present value is equal to the par value. The explanation illustrates the nature of the discount rate. If an investor is looking for an 8% rate of return on a $1,000 bond, and the bond is paying 8% interest, the investor is getting exactly what he or she is looking for in terms of return. For a ten-year bond, the nominal payments would total $1,800. If the maturity were 20 years, the nominal payments would total $2,600—but the present value would still equal the par value, $1,000, because the annual required rate of return is being met by the interest payments. However, for a bond paying 10% interest, the present value to an investor with a required rate of return of 8% would be greater than the par value.

In 2019, Tottenham Hotspur of the English Premier League opened its new stadium partially financed with loans from a number of international banks.

Yet, those loans (totaling nearly $800 million) were due to be paid off in full by 2022. In order to spread those payments out, the club sold over $650 million in corporate bonds in 2019, whose average maturity is 23 years with an interest rate of 2.66%. This placement allows the club to free up its capital for other endeavors.

SIDEBAR 7.C   When can Debt Transform into Equity?

A convertible bond offers some of the features of both equity and debt. The investor has the option to convert the bond into a fixed number of shares of stock in the company, at a stock price agreed upon at the issuance of the bond—usually 25% to 35% higher than the current stock price at the time of issuance. If the stock price rises, the bond holder sees an increase in the value of the bond, because it can be converted into stock and sold if the stock price is above the conversion price. Effectively, the bond buyer is purchasing a stock option, a contract that allows the bond holder to purchase a specified number of shares of stock for a certain price.

If the stock price drops, the investor still receives interest payments from the bond. Because of the increased upside of convertible bonds, their coupon rates are lower than those of traditional bonds. For the company offering the bonds, convertible bonds offer savings, at least in the short run, because the debt payments will be lower. If the share price rises, the flood of bonds being converted to equity will dilute the equity of existing shareholders—thus keeping the stock price from rising very high. During the uncertainty in financial markets in the fall of 2008, Warren Buffett purchased $5 billion in convertible bonds from Goldman Sachs. He was paid a guaranteed 10% return on the "bond" portion of the investment, with the option to convert it into stock at the price of $115 per share. By 2011, he was paid back the $5 billion loan portion, plus interest and refinancing costs. Then, in March 2013, he exercised his right to convert the convertible bonds into stock. The price that day was about $143 per share, so Buffett could have netted an additional $1.3 billion in profit if he had sold his shares on the day he converted.

Loans

The key aspects of a loan include its maturity, its interest rate, and any prepayment provisions. The economics of a loan are similar to those of a bond, and the two have become even more similar in recent decades as lenders have begun to combine loans into packages or pools (which may include thousands of loans) and buy them from and sell them to other financial companies. This practice enables lenders to diversify their holdings by selling off some loans and purchasing others.

An example of a loan in the sport industry is the NFL's secured loan program called G4. The previous NFL loan facility was called G3 and had a total loan amount of $1.1 billion. Even during the economic downturn of 2008, Fitch gave the G3 loan an A rating (November 18, 2008). This rating was based on large long-term television contracts and the expectation that there would continue to be a hard salary cap, which the 2011–2020 collective bargaining agreement maintains. The new G4 loan (rated A+ by Fitch) provided $200 million each for the San Francisco 49ers', Minnesota Vikings', Las Vegas Raiders', and Los Angeles Rams' and Los Angeles Chargers' new stadiums. The mechanics of the secured loan account allow the lenders to access the television money prior to any distributions to teams or other outflows. The primary risk comes from the uncertain outcomes of collective bargaining.

Trade Credit

Short-term financing often takes the form of trade credit rather than a loan. **Trade credit** is credit granted by a manufacturer to a retailer. By agreement, after the manufacturer ships its product to the retailer for sale, the retailer may delay payment for a period of time, depending on the terms (typically 30, 60, or 90 days). In essence, the manufacturer is providing the retailer short-term financing for the retailer's purchases from the manufacturer. It is in the best interest of manufacturers to help their downstream retailers remain solvent. In the United States, the size of trade credit (as a percentage of total business financing) is only a few percentage points less than the amount that commercial banks lend to businesses. This type of financing cannot be used for any substantial changes to the business, such as expansion, simply because the term is too short.

Nike provides a good example of trade credit. At the end of fiscal year 2019, the company had nearly $4.3 billion in accounts receivable (A/R), meaning that customers (e.g., downstream retailers, such as Foot Locker) owed the company $4.3 billion. Nike also had about $2.6 billion in accounts payable (A/P), meaning that it owed suppliers that amount (for instance, for raw materials for the production of Nike products). Nike has the leverage to pay its suppliers slowly, because they are interested in maintaining a good relationship with the large company. It can also afford to provide trade credit to its downstream retail customers in order to maintain a healthy distribution of its products. On the other hand, Foot Locker had net receivables of $87 million and $387 million in A/P (fiscal year ending January 31, 2019). This is also not surprising, because Foot Locker is being allowed to take its time in paying Nike (and other product suppliers), while collecting directly from customers, who pay in cash or with a credit card, so that Foot Locker receives the income almost immediately.

Bankruptcy

If a company is unable to pay its debts or restructure its debt, it is insolvent. In this situation, the company must enter **bankruptcy**, the process of liquidation or reorganization of an insolvent firm. A bankruptcy court either will order **liquidation** of the company—the sale of its assets piece by piece, effectively removing the company from existence—or will allow the company to reorganize in a way that makes it more valuable than if it were liquidated. The court will choose the method that is likely to provide the highest value to the company's creditors. Note that the selected method will not necessarily provide the highest value to the equity holders—they took on the risk of bankruptcy when they bought into the company. If the company is to be reorganized, the court usually appoints a

EXHIBIT 7.5 The priority of claims on the assets of a company in liquidation.

1. Secured claims

2. Trustee's costs

3. Expenses incurred after bankruptcy was filed

4. Wages due workers (up to a limit, sometimes $2,000 per worker)

5. Claims for unpaid contributions to employee benefit plans

6. Unsecured claims for customer deposits up to some limit (applicable to banks)

7. Federal, state, and local taxes

8. Unfunded pension plan liabilities

9. General unsecured creditors

10. Preferred stockholders, up to the par value of their stock

11. Common stockholders—if anything is left

committee of unsecured creditors to undertake this task. They may decide to restructure the firm's debt by reducing the interest rate on the debt, extending the date to maturity, or exchanging some of the debt for equity. The goal is to reduce the debt payments sufficiently that the company's cash flow can cover them. If this is not possible, liquidation is the best alternative.

When a company is liquidated, its assets are usually divided according to the priority of claims, as shown in Exhibit 7.5. Secured claims take first priority. A **secured claim** is a debt for which the borrower provided collateral—an asset that the creditor has the right to seize if the debt is not paid. For instance, in a home mortgage, the lender (usually a bank) has the right to take ownership of the house and sell it if mortgage payments are not made. This is a secured loan, and the house is collateral. Recall that an unsecured claim is a debt in which the creditor has no right to seize any assets from the company or person who borrowed the money. Credit card debt is an example: the card issuer has no right to seize any products you purchased with the card, even if you do not repay the debt. Consistent with the concepts of risk and interest, secured debt will have a lower interest rate than unsecured debt, because the risk for unsecured debt lenders is higher.

Note that, in general, any debt that is termed *senior* or *subordinated* has higher or lower priority, respectively, than other debt obligations of the company.

One can see why the court-appointed committee that undertakes reorganization of a bankrupt business consists of unsecured creditors—they are so far down the priority list that they will be motivated to make the best decisions, in order to have a chance of getting paid. If the committee were made up of secured creditors, they would have little incentive to ensure payments to parties farther down the priority list. Shareholders would not be the best choice, either: they may prefer to reorganize, in hopes that their shares will become worth something, even if the best move is to liquidate.

TRADE-OFFS OF EQUITY FINANCING

In Europe, especially Britain, dozens of professional soccer teams are publicly traded. One of the main reasons for selling equity has been to raise capital in order to improve the teams' stadiums. Securing funds by selling shares to the public has also allowed some British soccer teams to pursue other ventures, such as running a chain of pubs, selling apparel and leisure products, and building hotel and restaurant facilities. Of course, the teams have also used much of the money to acquire players. This has had the effect of substantially raising soccer players' salaries.

In the United States, in October 1996, the Florida Panthers of the NHL sold shares to the public and were listed on the NASDAQ exchange (and later on the NYSE). For less than half ownership of the team, the public paid $67 million. Independent valuation analysts had pegged the value of the entire team at $45 million only a few months earlier. At first, the Panthers were the primary asset of the company, and fans were targeted to buy shares. However, after only a month of being publicly traded, the entity began to purchase leisure assets, such as resorts and a golf course. Within two years, the hockey team accounted for only about 10% of the company's assets. The Panthers are currently privately owned (not publicly traded).

As discussed earlier, many North American sport leagues either strictly prohibit publicly traded franchises or have rules requiring all owners to approve any transfer of ownership. Outside of spectator sports, the sport industry includes many publicly traded companies, such as Nike (ticker symbol NKE), Callaway Golf (ELY), Under Armour (UA), Madison Square Garden (MSG), and Dick's Sporting Goods (DKS). The remainder of this section will discuss the pros and cons of equity financing, specifically of publicly traded equity financing, where applicable contrasting it with debt financing.

SIDEBAR 7.D   Manchester United Goes Public

On August 10, 2012, Manchester United sold more than 16 million shares to the public (about 10% of its shares) for $14 each, trading on the NYSE under the symbol MANU. The Glazer family (owner of the Tampa Bay Buccaneers) still owns the bulk of the shares, having bought the team for $1.47 billion in 2005, and maintains decision-making power. Through July 2013, the stock had increased about 35% from its IPO price. Revenue grew in the double digits in the first year of public ownership. Half of the proceeds from the sale of stock went to pay off a portion of the $600 million debt that the team had amassed (with long-term debt at over $500 million as of 2019). However, the club is worth over $2.6 billion, according to its market capitalization implied by a stock price of over $16 (as of October 2019), so the team's large debt may not hinder its ability to operate successfully.

Advantages of Publicly Traded Equity Financing

Taking a company public provides many advantages to the owners. First, it provides access to capital or financing that does not require interest payments or even repayment of the principal. However, investors do expect that dividends will be paid once the capital has been used to increase the company's profitability.

Second, once a company becomes a publicly traded entity, it is much easier to issue another round of stock or issue corporate bonds. This is because the financials are now open to the public and in compliance with Securities and Exchange Commission requirements.

A third advantage of going public is that it makes it easier for the owners to carry out an exit strategy. A privately held business does not have a readily available price for its shares. A publicly traded company allows an owner to exit the business with relative ease. If the owner's name is tied to the brand of the business, then selling his or her shares all at once might affect the overall value of the business (and the price at which the owner can sell the shares). Think of how Bill Gates was tied to Microsoft's success or Phil Knight to Nike's success. For this reason, an owner may not be wise to sell his or her shares all at once, but instead would exit gradually by selling a few shares at a time.

In the **initial public offering (IPO)**, the company for the first time offers shares to the public in order to generate cash for the business. When a publicly traded company offers shares for sale to the public, this is called a secondary offering. A secondary offering does not generate cash for the business if it consists solely of an owner's shares, because the cash goes to the stock owner, not the business.

For example, in November 2005 Under Armour offered shares to the public in an IPO. The apparel company had seen quick growth in its short lifespan, increasing sales from $5 million in 2000 to over $240 million in 2005 to over $5 billion in 2018. The offer of 9.5 million shares owned by the company and 2.5 million owned by private investors yielded over $100 million in capital for the company. Shares were offered at $13 and quickly closed over $25. Founder Kevin Plank was able to sell $13 million in shares, piggybacking on the IPO, but then was under a "lockout" period in which he could not legally sell any shares for 180 days. In May 2006, once the lockout was over, he sold about $50 million worth of stock. Lockouts are common after IPOs; they are intended to show the investing public that the "insiders" aren't cashing out and leaving the company but instead are maintaining their leadership roles and navigating the company forward.

The owner of a sports team who wishes to exit will probably find a ready market of billionaires interested in buying the franchise. Given the limited number of teams and the fact that a would-be owner can't just create a new team, there is always demand for franchises. Thus, an IPO is not a necessary exit strategy.

A fourth reason a company benefits from becoming publicly traded is the free publicity generated by the initial public offering process and subsequent coverage of the company's financials. Unfortunately, the publicity can also be bad if the stock price plummets or the company is perceived as weak. When the Arena Football League's Orlando Predators went public, articles in

BusinessWeek and *Slate* were not upbeat about the team's financial future. There were similar warnings about Manchester United's public offering.

The ability to attract and retain key employees, a fifth rationale, is enhanced for a publicly traded company, because the company can offer stock options (an option for an employee to buy stock at a set price in the future, provided the person is still with the company). Stock options can provide incentive for the employee to help make the company more profitable and to stay with the company. Stock options can allow employees at all levels to participate in the growth of the company. Even suppliers and customers of the company may be offered stock options (sometimes at a "friends and family" discount). This helps to align the entire value chain that produces the product or service and gets it to market.

A sixth motivation for going public is that it increases the equity in the company, allowing it to issue debt, if the need arises. With increased equity, the interest rate on debt will be lower than it would otherwise be. This is because offering equity as collateral shows the lender or investor that the company already possesses funds and that owners have an interest in the company's success.

Finally, mergers and acquisitions are more easily arranged for a publicly traded company, because its value is readily determined.

A privately held company may also offer stock options and benefit from some of the advantages discussed above. However, the value of the stock options for these companies is unknown, because the stock is not publicly traded (it has no market price). Offering stock options does not help these companies in the merger and acquisition processes.

Disadvantages of Publicly Traded Equity Financing

The above reasons for going public may give the impression that it is always a good idea, but there are disadvantages. First, the cost of issuing stock is very substantial, often up to 10% or 20% of the value of the company (depending on its size). The fees for lawyers and underwriters (bankers who arrange, finance, and execute a stock offering) may amount to a large portion of the proceeds. When the Cleveland Indians went public in 1998, they paid just above 10% of their proceeds to the lawyers and underwriters (about $6.2 million). Manchester United's public offering in 2012 led to about $14 million in direct fees (6% of the offering). Of course, issuing debt is also costly, but usually less so than issuing stock.

Second, the time required for preparations to go public can be a burden on the operations of a company. Key executives usually travel on a "road show" to inform potential institutional buyers about the IPO. The prospectus can be thought of as a résumé for the company, and the road show is akin to an interview process, where executives meet and answer questions of prospective investors.

Third, if the time is not ripe to go public, the IPO may be postponed or halted altogether. All of the expense and time involved in the process might go for naught. This could happen if the stock market or the economy takes a turn for the worse during the many months between inception of the process (when the confidential IPO prospectus is filed with the Securities and

Exchange Commission) and the actual IPO (up to a year, but generally less than six months).

Fourth, a very important reason that many sport teams and leagues are not publicly traded is the lack of operating confidentiality. The team's prices, margins, salaries, and future plans would be available to competitors, employees, customers, suppliers, and the general public (including fans), because the SEC requires financial disclosure and annual reports. This is a primary factor that sport team owners mention when asked why they do not go public. In fact, it is typically in a sport franchise's interest to appear that it is struggling financially, for the following reasons:

- In negotiating with a players association, a league wants to be able to claim that revenues are low, so money is not available to share with players.
- In bargaining with a city to get a new stadium, a sport franchise benefits from an appearance that it cannot pay for a large portion of the stadium.
- From a publicity perspective, a franchise might want fans to think that it is struggling to break even (or losing money), so that it can justify raising ticket prices.
- To avoid antitrust scrutiny, sport leagues prefer their franchises to appear that they are breaking even at best. This was the case when MLB's commissioner Selig was called into Congress to testify (see the case study in Chapter 10).

It would be difficult for some teams and leagues to show financial hardship and make the above claims if their financials were available to the public.

The SEC's disclosure rules also require public announcements of changes to a company that might "materially" affect the stock, *prior* to those changes being made. This requirement can play havoc with team management and the timing of decisions. For example, a team would have to disclose in advance that it is going to make a trade, sign a player to a free agent contract, or fire its head coach. This could create a bargaining and public relations fiasco.

Fifth, for most publicly traded companies, the original owners do not own 50% or more of the business. This means that the founders of a company could be voted out of management (this happened to Steve Jobs, one of the founders of Apple, in 1985) or even lose their ownership completely through a takeover in which their shares are forcibly sold. The North American major sport leagues all have provisions in their bylaws allowing existing team owners to block the sale or purchase of a franchise if they do not approve the new owner. If a team were publicly traded, this kind of provision could not be legally enforced.

Sixth, public ownership reduces an organization's strategic flexibility. For publicly traded companies, the BoD must approve all major decisions, and each quarter "Wall Street" expects income growth. In contrast, firms with more debt financing typically have greater flexibility to maneuver in changing markets. A company that is debt financed can make a strategic investment that might cause losses for a number of years but that will pay off handsomely down the road. Furthermore, investors may desire annual dividends, even if the company would be better off reinvesting that money. In sport, some owners of a franchise want to maximize profits and other owners want to maximize the chance to win championships. A publicly traded sport team would likely have many owners of both types, resulting in tension over the direction of the business. The Canucks, Celtics, and Panthers each have experienced litigation against the majority shareholders, with the "outside" shareholders claiming that the "insiders" were operating the team to their sole benefit. Traditional publicly traded businesses will almost all be run to maximize profits, so a team with a goal of winning championships may find public ownership counter to its aims.

Seventh, conforming to the SEC's accounting and tax requirements is expensive, certainly more so than the requirements of a private company. These costs have only increased with the advent of the Sarbanes-Oxley Act (2002). Some of the additional costs include the generation of financial reporting documents, audit fees, and setting up an investor relations group and accounting oversight committee(s). When the Boston Celtics went public in 1986, sending annual reports to the many shareholders who owned one share of stock proved very expensive. The costs of printing exceeded the value that the team obtained from these shareholders' purchases of the stock. Sport franchises learned from the Celtics' difficulties and subsequently have required higher minimum purchases of stock. The Florida Panthers required a $1,000 minimum stock purchase.

An eighth reason for a company to avoid going public involves the financial strategy of IPOs. To ensure an initial upward movement and the positive publicity and momentum that can come with it, the underwriters usually set the price artificially below what they believe the market is willing to pay. This artificially low price means that the company is essentially selling part of itself for less than it is worth—buyers are getting the stock for less than the value of the owners' shares. Moreover, the company is exposing itself to the risk that the stock underperforms and further lowers its valuation.

Often, companies with low risk to their future cash flow are easily able to issue debt for their financing needs. A firm with risky future cash flows might be forced to issue equity and share the risk with other investors.

CONCLUSION

This chapter discusses the uses of and methods for debt and equity financing. The ability of firms to raise capital efficiently has allowed developed nations to sustain high economic growth rates for many decades. The financial industry creates efficiency by bringing together those parties with excess capital (investors) and those in need of capital. It allocates capital resources according to expected gains, accounting for risks. The sport industry is no different in its capital needs. In spectator sports, however, the desire to sell equity shares to the public is dampened, compared to most other industries, because of resistance to the transparency of financials.

The economic recession that began in December 2007 brought changes to the structure and regulatory oversight of the financial industry. As of this writing, the changes have not yet been completed and their impacts are not fully understood. However, the fundamental nature of the industry—providing investors with investments and businesses with financing—has not changed.

Concept Check

1. Does higher expected inflation increase, decrease, or have no effect on the required rate of return?
2. What methods can a company use to raise capital?

3. Does a company share its risk by issuing equity or debt?
4. What are some of the advantages of equity financing?
5. What are some of the disadvantages of equity financing, specifically for sport teams?
6. Is the yield curve typically upward or downward sloping? Why?
7. How are the features of a convertible bond similar to both debt and equity?

Practice Problems

1. Using the information in Exhibit 7.4 for NewFangled Sports Products, Inc., calculate the new NPV of a share of stock if the perpetual growth rate doubled from 4% to 8%. Additionally, if the terminal year dividend payment increased from $1.40 to $2.80, what is the new share price?
2. A share of NewFangled Sports stock is expected to provide a $1 per year dividend payment the first year and to grow at 8% thereafter. With a discount rate of 12% and a 15-year horizon, what is the share worth? What is it worth valued into infinity? Compare these results.
3. A minor league professional hockey team embarks on an aggressive facility expansion that requires additional capital. Management decides to finance the expansion by borrowing $40 million and by halting dividend payments to increase retained earnings. The projected free cash flows are $5 million for the current year, $10 million for the following year, and $20 million for the third year. After the third year, free cash flow is projected to grow at a constant 6%. The overall cost of capital is 10%. What is the total value of the organization? If it has 10 million shares of stock and $40 million in total debt, what is the price per share?

Case Analysis

Debt Decisions

Owners of sport franchises face tough decisions related to capital structure when they decide a new facility is needed. The St. Louis Cardinals were faced with these decisions when they decided to finance much of their new stadium privately.

The Cardinals' owners decided that a stadium was needed to replace Busch Stadium II, the team's home from 1966 to 2005. As the plans for the new stadium (Busch Stadium III) were announced, the owners stated that the new facility was needed to generate additional revenues for the franchise. With increased revenues, the franchise would better be able to compete for top players. However, since the facility opened in 2006, the team's debt has limited spending on payroll.

In a presentation to business students at Webster University, Cardinals chairman Bill DeWitt outlined the expenses of the club. Player salaries made up 50% of the team's expenses. Team operations (i.e., travel and coaching salaries) were another 10%, as were player development costs and facility operations expenses. Business operations accounted for 5% to 7% of expenses. The remaining portion of expenses was interest on the team's debt (Strauss, 2009).

The Cardinals are in the 21st largest media market based on households. Thanks to a loyal fan base and high attendance, the team had the sixth highest revenues in MLB as of 2015 (*Forbes*, 2015), generating over $290 million. However, player payroll was at $133 million in 2014. This was the 13th highest in the league. The team plans to continue to maintain a player payroll in this range as long as attendance does not decline.

The owners borrowed approximately $300 million to build Busch Stadium III. The team pays more than $20 million per year in principal and interest on the two instruments that were used to finance the club's portion of the new stadium. The club operates on tight margins and is well managed financially. Further, with annual attendance figures for the last ten years at 3 million plus and very high local television ratings, revenues are close to maximized. Without cutting expenses elsewhere, the team has limited flexibility and cannot increase payroll without losing money.

Case Questions

1. Has the Cardinals' decision to use debt financing hurt the on-field performance of the organization? If so, how?
2. What form of debt financing did the team most likely use to raise its $300 million portion of the stadium construction costs?
3. What equity financing options could the club have considered to raise some of the capital to build the new stadium?

References

Forbes. (2015). St. Louis Cardinals. Retrieved from www.forbes.com/teams/st-louis-cardinals/.

Strauss, J. (2009, December 6). Cardinals say debt limits spending. *St. Louis Post-Dispatch*. Retrieved from www.stltoday.com/stltoday/sports/stories.nsf/cardinals/story/E904AD414CCE59468625768400064FFF?Open Document.

CHAPTER 8

Capital Budgeting

Matthew T. Brown

KEY CONCEPTS

capital
capital budgeting
capital expenditure
current expenditure
discount rate
discounted payback period
incremental cash flow
initial cost

internal rate of return (IRR)
modified internal rate of
   return (MIRR)
net present value (NPV)
payback period
terminal value
weighted average cost of
   capital (WACC)

INTRODUCTION

After the 2019 baseball season ended, Globe Life Park closed its doors as the Texas Rangers prepared to move across the street to their new stadium, Globe Life Field. Globe Life Park opened in 1994, and at 25 years old is a fairly young baseball stadium to face demolition (Hartley, 2019). The venue's original debt issue of $135 million was paid off in 2001, ten years ahead of schedule (City of Arlington, 2016). From a capital budgeting perspective, Globe Life Park created value for the citizens of Arlington. This, however, is not always the case.

In 2010, after 34 years of existence, Giants Stadium was demolished. The former home of the New York Giants and New York Jets, Giants Stadium was the site of Pelé's last game and was the venue for events as diverse as a Mass celebrated by Pope John Paul II in 1995 and Bruce Springsteen and the E Street Band's ten sold-out shows in July and August 2003. The stadium holds the record for the number of NFL games played in one venue. In addition to the Giants and Jets, the stadium also was the home of the New Jersey Generals of the United States Football League (USFL), the New York/New Jersey Knights of the World League of American Football, the New York/New Jersey Hitmen of the XFL, and the New York Sentinels of the United Football League. The Rutgers football team, the New York/New Jersey Metrostars (New York Red

Bulls), and New York Cosmos (North American Soccer League [NASL]) were also tenants at the venue. Further, many international soccer matches and a variety of concerts were held at the stadium. Its initial cost was $75 million (New Jersey Sports & Exposition Authority, 2014).

When Giants Stadium was demolished, $110 million in debt was still owed on the venue (Belson, 2010). In addition to some initial costs, the costs of renovating the facility over time were passed on by politicians to the point that debt is still owed even though the stadium is now a parking lot.

Giants Stadium provides a good illustration of why capital budgeting is important. When it was demolished, each New Jersey resident owed almost $13 for the debt on the former NFL venue. In tangible terms, the facility should be considered to have been a bad investment for the New Jersey citizens, as debt was owed at the time of its demise.

While citizens should hope for outcomes like in Arlington, too many publicly funded venues end up like Giants Stadium. Taxpayers in King County, Washington, owed $80 million when the Kingdome was imploded in 2000 (Belson, 2010). Similar venue debt also remained when stadiums were torn down in Indianapolis and abandoned in Houston. Debt on the RCA Dome (Indianapolis) was $61 million when the building was demolished in 2008 and will not be repaid until 2021. For Houston, debt remains on the Astrodome, which opened in 1965 (Yost, 2011). Today, taxpayers still owe on the building and will be making payments until 2032. Although the building has not been demolished, it lacks a major tenant, as the Houston Astros (MLB) and Houston Oilers (NFL) left the venue in 1999 and 1997, respectively. Further, this type of poor financial planning is not limited to "major league" venues and major metropolitan areas. Vero Beach, Florida, still owed $17 million on a spring training baseball facility when the Dodgers left for Glendale, Arizona, in 2009; taxpayers in Pima County, Arizona, still owed $21.3 million in stadium debt even though the Chicago White Sox and Arizona Diamondbacks moved their spring training facilities from Tucson to Phoenix.

As seen with Globe Life Park, a capital budget can help ensure that any new taxpayer-funded facility will be paid off before the end of its useful life. As you will learn in this chapter, a capital budget can also help a manager evaluate, compare, and select projects to achieve the best long-term financial return on capital investments.

DEFINING CAPITAL BUDGETING

When making investment decisions that involve fixed assets, we need to examine the purchase of **capital**—the long-term, fixed assets that are used in production. In capital budgeting we focus on these purchases and, specifically, analyze them to decide which purchases should be made. More precisely, **capital budgeting** (also known as capital investment appraisal) is the process of evaluating, comparing, and selecting capital projects to achieve the best return on investment over time. Groppelli and Nikbakht (2013) define it as investment decision making that justifies capital expenditures. This process is an important factor in the success or failure of an organization, since investments in capital (or fixed) assets affect the financial health of the organization for many years.

> ### SIDEBAR 8A   Capital Expenditures and the Americans with Disabilities Act
>
> Capital expenditures may include expenditures on mandatory projects required by law. For example, the Americans with Disabilities Act (ADA) of 1990 prohibits discrimination against individuals with disabilities with regard to employment and public accommodation (Public Law 101–336 [S. 933], 42 USCS §§ 12101 et seq.). As a result of this law, the University of Nevada, Reno agreed in 2019 to modify its football venue to make 64 seats compliant after renovations left just under half of the 140 required ADA seats with issues. It was found that for these seats the integrated wheelchair sight lines were not as good as those available to other spectators. Additionally, ADA compliance issues were found in the loge box and suite areas of the stadium (Appleton, 2019). The $3.2 million spent in ADA-related renovations is considered capital expenditure.

A **capital expenditure** is the use of funds to acquire capital assets that will help the organization earn future revenues or reduce future costs. Typically, several different sources of debt and/or equity financing will be used to fund a capital project (see Chapter 7). The cost to obtain capital assets is the weighted average of the cost of each of the funding sources—**weighted average cost of capital (WACC)**. Common and preferred stock, bonds, and any other form of long-term debt are included in the calculation of the project's WACC.[1]

Capital expenditures are long-term expenditures amortized over a period of time (Groppelli & Nikbakht, 2013). Examples of capital expenditures in sport include the purchase of a new artificial turf field for a football stadium, the purchase of a new ice resurfacer for a hockey rink, the building of a new community swimming pool, the installation of a climbing wall in a health club or college recreational center, and the construction of a stadium or arena. These expenditures require a large amount of cash, debt, and other resources that will be committed over a long period of time.

It is important to differentiate between a capital expenditure and a **current expenditure**. Whereas a capital expenditure is long-term and amortized over time, a current expenditure is short-term and is completely written off during the same year as the expense is incurred. Because capital expenses utilize resources over time, they are investments that require a commitment of resources today with the expectation of receiving benefits in the future. For a major Division I institution, this may mean an investment in a new basketball facility with luxury and club seating. A university will decide to invest in the facility with the hope that the facility will return new and additional revenue to the athletic department.

As stated previously, capital budgeting focuses on capital expenditures. Capital budgeting offers several benefits. First, a capital budget helps

---

1   The formula for calculating WACC is $WACC = w_d k_d (1 - T) + w_p k_p + w_c k_c$, where w_d, w_p, and w_c are the weights of debt, preferred stock, and common equity, respectively; k_d, k_p, and k_c are the costs of debt, preferred stock, and common equity, respectively; and T is the corporate tax rate.

management plan the amount and timing of resources that will be needed. For example, a capital budget developed for a stadium renovation might include the timing and amounts of payments for a new $770,000 installation of FieldTurf. A team might put down a large amount at the beginning of the project and pay off the balance through smaller payments over time. A capital budget is also helpful in evaluating alternative capital expenditures. Should FieldTurf, AstroTurf, or a natural grass field be installed? The development of a capital budget will include an evaluation of these alternatives to determine which best utilizes the organization's resources.

A capital budget also focuses management's attention on cash flows. The capital budget allows the manager to identify new cash that will arise from a project and compare that new cash flow to the expenditures the project demands. This information, combined with knowledge of the timing and amount of resources needed, helps management coordinate responsibility centers within the organization to ensure that all financial obligations are met.

THE PROCESS OF CAPITAL BUDGETING

To complete the capital budgeting process, financial managers use a method that comprises four distinct parts:

1. Determine the initial cost of the project or projects.
2. Determine the incremental cash flow of the project.
3. Select the capital budgeting method.
4. Conduct a post-audit analysis.

Most of the methods for completing a capital budget include the evaluation of cash flow risk (based on inflation, interest rates, and project length) and then the determination of an appropriate discount rate for use in analysis of the project. In the case of a capital budget, the **discount rate** is the required rate of return to justify an investment. After the discount rate is calculated, the asset's value to the organization is estimated on a present value basis, and the present value of expected cash inflows is compared to the cost of the project. If the present value of the project exceeds its cost, the project should be accepted and included in the organization's capital budget. Given a choice between two or more projects, managers should select the project that contributes most to the organization's net income.

These steps are outlined in detail below.

Determine the Initial Cost of the Project

The **initial cost** of a project is the actual cost of starting the project, adjusted for any installation, delivery, or packing costs; discounts to the initial price; the sale of existing equipment or machinery; and taxes. For an example of determining the initial cost of a project, let's look at the cost of replacing a natural grass football field with FieldTurf in a university football stadium.

As athletic director of a mid-major university in Ohio, you are overseeing the renovation of the football stadium. The stadium has seating for 25,500. Several prominent boosters have approached you to request the installation of an artificial turf field. They argue that by putting artificial turf in the stadium, the school could attract better recruits and thereby improve its performance on the field. Additionally, the boosters point out that several early-round high school playoff games could be played in the stadium, increasing community goodwill, generating additional revenues for the program, and creating an economic impact for the community from out-of-town spectator spending. After listening to these arguments, you decide to analyze the facts.

Based on your research on synthetic athletic fields, you decide either to install FieldTurf or to leave the natural grass field in place. FieldTurf incorporates the latest innovations in synthetic playing surfaces and has been installed by Michigan, Ohio State, Nebraska, and Notre Dame. If it makes financial sense for the department, you are leaning toward installing the synthetic field, especially since there are problems with the current natural grass field, which was installed last year. Because of these problems, the university will receive a rebate of $250,000 if it chooses to replace the grass field with an artificial surface.

The first step in calculating the initial cost of the FieldTurf installation is to record the invoice price of the investment. The cost to replace the grass field with FieldTurf is $770,000, based on the amount quoted to the university for preparation, materials, and installation.

Next, we calculate additional expenses. As the invoice price includes packing, delivery, and installation, we need not adjust for these costs. However, as mentioned above, because of problems with the current grass field, the university will receive a rebate (a discount from the initial cost) of $250,000 if it chooses to replace the grass field with an artificial surface. Hence, the initial cost of the investment must be reduced by the $250,000 rebate. Therefore, the initial cost of the investment is $520,000.

Often, another adjustment is necessary for the sale of existing machinery or equipment and the tax consequences of that sale. However, in this example, the FieldTurf will replace the damaged sod in the stadium, and nothing will be sold, so no adjustment is necessary. We use the following formulas to calculate the initial cost of a project:

$$IC = IP + ATP - DTP - EQP + TOE$$

$$IC = IP + ATP - DTP - EQP - TCE$$

where

    IC = initial cost of the project
    IP = invoice price of the new investment
    ATP = adjustments to price, such as installation costs, delivery, and packing
    DTP = any discounts to the initial price (IP)
    EQP = revenue from the sale of existing equipment
    TOE = taxes paid on the sale of equipment above book value
    TCE = tax credit on the sale of equipment below book value

For the purchase of FieldTurf, recall that the invoice price of $770,000 includes the price of the new investment and the price for delivery and installation. The university will receive a $250,000 rebate on the installation. In this case, EQP = $0 and TOE = $0. (Note also that there is no tax liability or tax credit when equipment is sold at book value.) Hence,

$$IC = \$770,000 - \$250,000 - \$0 + \$0 = \$520,000$$

Determine the Incremental Cash Flow of the Project

After calculating the initial cost of the project, we compute its incremental cash flow. **Incremental cash flow** is the cash flow created through the implementation of a new project. It consists of any cash flow from the project that is greater than the cash flow that currently exists. The steps to determine incremental cash flow are:

1. Calculate additional net earnings (ANE) from the new project:

$$ANE = ENEPI - ENEWP$$

  where
  ENEPI = estimated net earnings if the new project were included
  ENEWP = estimated net earnings without the new project

2. Calculate the additional tax benefit of the depreciation (ADT) on the new fixed asset:

$$ADT = TAX \times DEP$$

  where
  TAX = tax rate
  DEP = additional depreciation of the new fixed asset

3. Calculate the incremental cash flow (ICF), by using the results of steps 1 and 2:

$$ICF = ANE + ADT$$

  where
  ANE = additional net earnings from the new project
  ADT = additional tax benefit on the new fixed asset

By using these formulas, we can calculate the incremental cash flow of the FieldTurf project. For Step 1, we must first determine the estimated net earnings without the new project (ENEWP) and the estimated net earnings with the new project (ENEPI). If the university were to keep its current natural grass field, it is estimated that the annual net earnings would be $3,300,000. With the change to FieldTurf, it is estimated that earnings would rise to $3,500,000, as additional revenues would be generated from hosting state high school playoff football games.[2] These additional revenues would come from facility rental fees and additional parking and concessions revenue, and they amount to $200,000 after expenses for operations are removed. Therefore, to calculate Step 1:

$$ANE = \$3,500,000 - \$3,300,000 = \$200,000$$

As a university is a not-for-profit entity, there are no tax ramifications resulting from additional depreciation. Hence, for Step 2:

---

2   Because of higher durability and lower maintenance costs, football fields with a FieldTurf installation can be scheduled for use 4.78 times as frequently as fields with a natural grass installation (FieldTurf, 2020).

$$ADT = \$0$$

Thus, the calculation for the incremental cash flow (Step 3) for this project is

$$ICF = \$200,000 + \$0 = \$200,000$$

If, rather than a university, the organization in this example were a professional football team, Step 3 would become important. Suppose estimated net earnings without the new project for Team X are $34.5 million. The team's CFO determines that by installing FieldTurf, the team could host three college games and three state championship football games in addition to the current ten home NFL pre-season and regular season games. This additional revenue would lead to ENEPI of $40.5 million. For Step 1:

$$ANE = \$40,500,000 - \$34,500,000 = \$6,000,000$$

As Team X is a for-profit business, the tax benefit of depreciation must be calculated. According to straight-line depreciation, the additional depreciation (DEP) is $77,000. (The cost for the FieldTurf is $770,000, and it has an estimated useful life of ten years.) At a corporate tax rate (TAX) of 35%, the calculation for Step 2 is

$$ADT = .35 \times \$77,000 = \$26,950$$

For this project, incremental cash flow (Step 3) is

$$ICF = \$6,000,000 + \$26,950 = \$6,026,950$$

Select the Capital Budgeting Method

Once the initial cost of the project and the project's incremental cash flows are calculated, we can complete the capital budgeting process by using any of several methods, including average rate of return, payback period, discounted payback period, net present value, profitability index, internal rate of return, and modified internal rate of return. Each method has advantages and disadvantages; net present value is the method most managers prefer. This chapter focuses on net present value and the two methods that are the foundation of net present value analysis: payback period and discounted payback period. We will also examine internal rate of return and modified internal rate of return.

PAYBACK PERIOD METHOD

The number of years required to recover a capital investment is called the **payback period**. Calculating the payback period of a project is a very basic capital budgeting tool. For any project to be accepted in a capital budget, the project's payback period must be less than the maximum acceptable payback period set by the organization. When a choice must be made between two or more alternative projects, the one with the shortest payback period should be selected.

    Single-project payback period calculation. Suppose a project has an initial cost of $52,700. Incremental cash flows are estimated to be $22,000 in Year

1 and $18,600, $19,250, and $23,000 in subsequent years. Your organization's maximum acceptable payback period is three years. As the finance manager in charge of this project, should you accept it into your department's capital budget?

To determine the answer, it is necessary to calculate the payback period. First, we list the expected cash flows:

YEAR	ICF
0	($52,700)
1	$22,000
2	$18,600
3	$19,250
4	$23,000

By adding the yearly incremental cash flows to the initial cost of the project, we can determine the approximate time needed to recover the project's costs.

YEAR	ICF	CUMULATIVE CASH FLOW
0	($52,700)	($52,700)
1	$22,000	($30,700)
2	$18,600	($12,100)
3	$19,250	$7,150
4	$23,000	$30,150

This analysis shows that the project's costs are recovered between years 2 and 3. As the payback period is less than the three years set by your organization, the project should be accepted as part of the division's capital budget. To determine a more exact payback date, notice that between years 2 and 3 the cumulative return moves from −$12,100 to $7,150, and during Year 3, incremental cash flow is $19,250. We know that by Year 3 the project has reached its payback date. To determine exactly when in Year 2 the payback date is reached, we divide the amount of the last negative cumulative return by the incremental cash flow of the year the cumulative return is positive:

$$-\$12,100 \div \$19,250 = -0.629$$

Hence, the payback period is reached 0.629 years past Year 2, or in 2.629 years. (We disregard the fact that the value is negative.) To convert the fraction of the year to weeks, we multiply 0.629 by 52 weeks:

$$0.629 \times 52 \text{ weeks} = 32.7 \text{ weeks}$$

The payoff period for this project is two years and 33 weeks.

Two-project payback period calculation. When choosing between two projects, we must compare the cash flows of the two projects. For example,

YEAR	PROJECT S ICF	CUMULATIVE CASH FLOW	PROJECT L ICF	CUMULATIVE CASH FLOW
0	($1,000)	($1,000)	($1,000)	($1,000)
1	$500	($500)	$100	($900)
2	$400	($100)	$300	($600)
3	$300	$200	$400	($200)
4	$100	$300	$600	$400

As always, any project must meet the maximum payback period requirement. For this organization, the maximum is three years. If both projects meet the three-year minimum, the project with the shorter payback period is preferred.

A quick analysis of each project's cumulative cash flow reveals that Project S reaches payback faster than Project L, in 2.33 years versus 3.33 years. Project S also meets the payback period maximum. Project S should be accepted into the firm's capital budget.

Advantages and disadvantages of the payback period method. Of all the methods available for capital budgeting, the payback period method is the easiest to use. Few calculations are required to determine how long it will take to recover the initial investment. The payback period method is also the easiest to understand. Most important, the method provides information on how long a firm's funds will be tied up in a project. All else being equal, projects with shorter payback periods provide more liquidity than ones with longer payback periods.

This method also has two major flaws. First, it ignores time value of money concepts (see Chapter 4), as it fails to take into account the cost of capital. It does not recognize the difference between the value of a $1,000 incremental cash flow in the first year and a $1,000 incremental cash flow in the fourth year. Second, this method ignores cash flows produced beyond the payback period. Project A may reach its payback period faster, but over the useful life of the project, Project B might increase the firm's cash flow more.

DISCOUNTED PAYBACK PERIOD METHOD

To improve upon the payback period methodology, we may use the **discounted payback period** method. This method is similar to the payback period, with one major exception: it factors time value of money concepts into the calculation by discounting the expected cash flows at the project's initial cost of capital. (Recall that the discount rate is the rate of return a company must reach in order to justify its investment.) We use this method to determine the number of years necessary to recover the initial cost of a project, by using discounted cash flows (DCFs).

Single-project discounted payback period calculation. Suppose a project has an initial cost of $52,700. Incremental cash flows are estimated to be $22,000 in Year 1 and $18,600, $19,250, and $23,000 in subsequent years. The cost of capital is 10%. Your firm's maximum acceptable discounted payback period is three years. What is the discounted payback period for this project? How does it compare to the payback period? Should the project be accepted?

To determine the answers, we begin by examining the cash flows on a present value basis. By looking at the present value of the future cash flows, we can compare the cost of the initial outlay with those future cash flows, in today's dollars. We use the present value interest factor (see Table A.3 in the Appendix) to discount the cash flows. In Year 0, the initial cost of $52,700 is not discounted, as the value of $52,700 today is $52,700. For Year 1, we apply the discount rate of 10% to the $22,000 cash flow for that year. From Table A.3, we find that the PVIF for one year at 10% is 0.909. We also apply the discount rate to the cash flows for years 2 through 4. By adding the discounted cash flows to the initial cost of the project, we can determine the approximate time needed to recover the project's costs:

YEAR	ICF	PVIF	DCF	CUMULATIVE CASH FLOW
0	($52,700)	—	($52,700)	($52,700)
1	$22,000	0.909	$19,998	($32,702)
2	$18,600	0.826	$15,364	($17,338)
3	$19,250	0.751	$14,457	($2,881)
4	$23,000	0.683	$15,709	$12,828

Analysis of the discounted cash flows shows that the project's initial costs are recovered between years 3 and 4. Additional calculations would find that the exact payback period is 3.18 years, or three years and nine weeks. As the discounted payback period is greater than the firm's maximum payback period, the project would not be included in the capital budget.

By comparing the discounted payback period of this project to the non-discounted payback period, we can see the effect of time on the value of money. Recall that the payback period for this project is two years and 33 weeks when we do not consider this effect; it is 28 weeks later when we do.

Two-project discounted payback period calculation. When choosing between two projects, we compare the cash flows of the two projects. The following projects both have a discount rate of 10%:

PROJECT S YEAR	ICF	PVIF	DCF	CUMULATIVE CASH FLOW
0	($1,000)	—	($1,000)	($1,000)
1	$500	0.909	$455	($545)
2	$400	0.826	$331	($241)
3	$300	0.751	$225	$11
4	$100	0.683	$68	$79

PROJECT L YEAR	ICF	PVIF	DCF	CUMULATIVE CASH FLOW
0	($1,000)	—	($1,000)	($1,000)
1	$100	0.909	$91	($909)
2	$300	0.826	$248	($661)
3	$400	0.751	$301	($360)
4	$600	0.683	$410	$50

The project with the shorter discounted payback period should be selected for inclusion in the company's capital budget. Examining the cumulative returns, we see that Project S reaches discounted payback between years 2 and 3 (in 2.95 years, to be exact). Project L reaches discounted payback between years 3 and 4 (3.88 years). As Project S has a quicker discounted payback, it should be selected for inclusion in the capital budget over Project L.

Advantages and disadvantages of the discounted payback period method. As the discounted payback period method incorporates the time value of money into its calculation, it is a great improvement over the payback period method. It also provides information on the length of time funds will be committed to the project. However, this method, like the payback period method, does not consider the cash flows beyond the discounted payback period.

NET PRESENT VALUE METHOD

As previously stated, net present value is the capital budgeting method managers generally prefer for evaluating a single project or comparing two or more projects. **Net present value** (NPV) is a discounted cash flow method in which the present value of a project's future cash flows is compared to the project's initial cost. Projects are accepted if NPV is positive. Mathematically,

$$NPV = \text{present value of future cash flow} - \text{initial cost}$$

$$NPV = \sum_{t=0}^{n} \frac{CF_t}{(1+k)^t} - \text{initial cost}$$

where CF_t = the expected net cash flow in period t
k = the project's cost of capital
n = the number of periods

By using this formula, we first calculate the present value (PV) of cash flows for each year. Cash outflows are denoted by negative cash flows, and cash inflows are denoted by positive flows. Both the cash inflows and outflows of the project must be included. Up to this point, this process is the same as that for calculating a discounted payback period. Next, we sum the discounted cash flows (i.e., present values) to obtain the project's NPV. If the NPV is positive (i.e., the present value of the project's future cash flows is greater than the initial cost), the project should be accepted. If the present value is less than the initial cost (the NPV is negative), the project should be rejected. In this case, money would be lost if the project were accepted.

Two-project NPV calculation. With two (or more) projects, we calculate each project's NPV. For Project S and Project L above, the NPV of each project is the sum of the discounted cash flows. This will be the same as the final cumulative cash flow figure. The NPV of Project S is $79 and of Project L is $50. If we must choose one, we would select the project with the higher NPV (Project S) for inclusion in the capital budget. If both projects have a negative NPV, neither project would be accepted.

Single-project NPV calculation. Often, NPV analysis focuses on a single project, and the criterion for acceptance in the capital budget is that the NPV must be equal to or greater than zero.

Suppose Project T has an initial cost of $9,000 and a cost of capital of 10%. The expected useful life is four years. In years 1 through 4, the anticipated cash flows are $6,000, $4,000, $3,000, and $2,000, respectively. Should this project be recommended? To answer the question, we first calculate the discounted cash flows by using the PVIF from Table A.3 in the Appendix:

YEAR	ICF	PVIF	DCF	CUMULATIVE CASH FLOW
0	($9,000)	—	($9,000)	($9,000)
1	$6,000	0.909	$5,454	($3,546)
2	$4,000	0.826	$3,304	($242)
3	$3,000	0.751	$2,253	$2,011
4	$2,000	0.683	$1,366	$3,377

After determining the discounted cash flow for each year, we calculate the sum of the discounted cash flows or look at the final cumulative cash flow figure. As the sum of the discounted cash flows is $3,377, Project T would be accepted into the firm's capital budget.

Another proposal, Project Z, would require an initial investment of $40,000. The cost of capital is 8%. The expected cash flows and discounted cash flows are as follows:

YEAR	ICF	PVIF	DCF	CUMULATIVE CASH FLOW
0	($40,000)	—	($40,000)	($40,000)
1	$16,000	0.926	$14,816	($25,184)
2	$12,000	0.857	$10,284	($14,900)
3	$9,000	0.794	$7,146	($7,754)
4	$7,000	0.735	$5,145	($2,609)

Because the total present value of the cash inflows, $37,391, is less than the present value of the cash outflows, $40,000, the NPV for Project Z is negative. Hence, the project is not recommended for inclusion in the organization's capital budget.

If a project has a positive NPV, it will generate cash above its debt service. Therefore, it provides the required return to shareholders, and the excess cash accrues to the shareholders. Because Project Z has a negative NPV, it would remove cash from the firm to service the project's debt. If wealth maximization is the goal, only projects that improve the firm's cash flows should be accepted.

Advantages and disadvantages of NPV. Most managers prefer to use the NPV method for capital budgeting. The method analyzes cash flows rather than net earnings, consistent with modern finance theory. Furthermore, it considers time value of money concepts, discounting cash flows by the project's cost of capital. Most important, it identifies projects with a positive NPV, which will increase the firm's value. Therefore, the owners of the firm will gain wealth.

The NPV method does have some disadvantages. One major disadvantage is that the method requires a detailed prediction of the project's future cash flows. For the hypothetical examples in this section, the useful life of each project is four years. In sport, however, the useful life of a capital investment is often much longer. For example, computing the NPV of a new stadium, such as Globe Life Field in Arlington, Texas, would require forecasting cash flows for the entire useful life of the stadium. Usually, this period is assumed to be 30 years. Hence, the City of Arlington, owners of Globe Life Field, had to calculate the stadium's NPV by using forecasted cash flows from 2020 until 2050. Given that stadium revenue streams have experienced massive changes over time (primarily driven by the addition of luxury suites, club seating, and personal seat licenses; Brown, Nagel, & Rascher, 2003), forecasting these revenues is extremely difficult. A second disadvantage of the NPV method is that it assumes that the discount rate will remain the same over the useful life of the project. In many instances, the cost of capital and, therefore, the discount rate change as firms refinance debt.

Using technology to calculate NPV. The use of either a spreadsheet or a financial calculator can make the calculation of NPV easy. To illustrate, let's return to the example of replacing natural grass with artificial turf in a university football stadium.

As discussed previously, installing FieldTurf would cost $770,000. The initial cost of the investment would be only $520,000, however, as a $250,000 rebate would be applied to the invoice cost of the field. You estimate that with this field you can host three high school playoff dates per year. These games would generate $200,000 in incremental cash flow from parking, rental fees, and concession revenues, after expenses, as demonstrated earlier. The department would have to make payments on the field at an annual rate of 7%. The life of the field is estimated to be ten years.

You are now ready to decide whether to install FieldTurf or keep the stadium's current natural grass field. You will use a spreadsheet to examine the cash flows over the life of the project (see Exhibit 8.1).[3]

NPV can be determined in two ways. First, as discussed earlier, NPV is the sum of the discounted cash flows (see Cell E14 in Exhibit 8.1). Second, NPV can be calculated with the NPV function in Excel (see Cell B16 in Exhibit 8.1). In the NPV function's dialog box, the 7% discount rate is entered as the rate, and the series of incremental cash flows for years 1 to 10 is entered into the Value1 box. The cost of the project must be subtracted "manually" from the formula's result. From the spreadsheet analysis, you see that the NPV for the FieldTurf installation is positive, so you decide to move forward with the project.

---

3   Usually, financial managers use a spreadsheet to conduct capital budgeting analyses. Once a spreadsheet with formulas has been set up, values can easily be changed to show how variations would affect the project's NPV.

EXHIBIT 8.1   Calculating net present value with Excel.

	A	B	C	D	E
1			Analysis of FieldTurf		
2					
3	Time	ICF	PVIF @ 7%	DCF	Sum
4	0	$ (520,000.00)	1.000	$ (520,000.00)	$ (520,000.00)
5	1	$ 200,000.00	0.935	$ 186,915.89	$ (333,084.11)
6	2	$ 200,000.00	0.873	$ 174,687.75	$ (158,396.37)
7	3	$ 200,000.00	0.816	$ 163,259.58	$ 4,863.21
8	4	$ 200,000.00	0.763	$ 152,579.04	$ 157,442.25
9	5	$ 200,000.00	0.713	$ 142,597.24	$ 300,039.49
10	6	$ 200,000.00	0.666	$ 133,268.44	$ 433,307.93
11	7	$ 200,000.00	0.623	$ 124,549.95	$ 557,857.88
12	8	$ 200,000.00	0.582	$ 116,401.82	$ 674,259.70
13	9	$ 200,000.00	0.544	$ 108,786.75	$ 783,046.45
14	10	$ 200,000.00	0.508	$ 101,669.86	$ 884,716.31
15				=B14*C14	=D14+E13
16	NPV =	$884,716.31	=NPV(7%,B5:B14)-520000		

The discounted payback period in this example is found to be two years and 50 weeks. At the end of the second year, the project will begin to create additional cash inflows that can benefit the athletic department's operations.

Finding the NPV of this project with a financial calculator is also easy. We simply enter the cash flows into the cash flow register, along with the value of the discount rate, and press the NPV key.

INTERNAL RATE OF RETURN

Internal rate of return (IRR) is the term for the discount rate at which the present value of estimated cash flows from an investment is equal to the initial cost of the investment. In other words, IRR is the discount rate at which the NPV is equal to zero. The NPV method is a more advantageous capital budgeting method than the internal rate of return. However, IRR is widely used in business, and, therefore, it is important for financial managers to understand how to calculate it (Brigham & Houston, 2019). We calculate IRR as follows:

$$\sum_{t=0}^{n} \frac{CF_t}{(1+IRR)^t} = 0$$

where CF_t = the expected net cash flow in period t
n = the number of periods
IRR = the internal rate of return

The only unknown in this equation is IRR. We simply solve for the value of IRR to find the internal rate of return.

IRR is a measure of a project's rate of profitability. A project with an IRR greater than its cost of capital is advantageous to the organization and should be accepted into the capital budget. When the IRR exceeds the cost of capital, a surplus accrues to the firm's stockholders. By accepting a project whose IRR is greater than the cost of capital, the financial manager increases shareholder wealth.

To calculate IRR with a financial calculator, enter the expected cash flows into the cash flow register and press the IRR key.

Calculating IRR with constant cash flows. If cash flows are constant over the useful life of a project, we can calculate IRR without a financial calculator or a spreadsheet. Dividing the initial cost of the project by its annual cash flow gives the present value interest factor of an annuity (PVIFA). We can look up this value in a PVIFA table (see Appendix, Table A.4) to discover an approximation of IRR.

For example, suppose Project D has an expected useful life of six years and anticipated annual cash flows of $5,000. The initial cost is $20,555. If the cost of capital is 10%, should the project be accepted into the firm's capital budget?

We divide the initial cost of the project by the annual cash flow to find the PVIFA:

$$PVIFA = 20,555 \div 5,000 = 4.111$$

In the PVIFA table (Appendix, Table A.4), we find that for a term of six years a PVIFA of 4.111 results from a rate of 12%; therefore, the project's IRR is 12%. As this value is greater than Project D's cost of capital (10%), the project should be accepted.

Now, suppose Project F has an initial cost of $42,560, an anticipated useful life of eight years, cost of capital of 18%, and expected cash flows of $9,800 per year. Should Project F be accepted into the company's capital budget? The PVIFA for this project is:

$$PVIFA = 42,560 \div 9,800 = 4.343$$

In the PVIFA table, we find that a PVIFA of 4.343 with a term of eight years implies a rate of 16%. Project D's IRR is 16%. As this is less than the project's cost of capital, the project should not be accepted.

SIDEBAR 8.B   Ballpark Villages and Arena Districts

In the National Football League, it has been widely accepted that a new stadium, featuring all of the latest revenue-producing amenities, is an important factor in the financial success of a team (Brown, Nagel, & Rascher, 2003). Revenue accruing from these capital projects provides an important competitive edge for franchises in a league where most of the revenue is shared. In other leagues, the situation is different.

Major League Baseball's St. Louis Cardinals provide an example of the difference between the use of new revenues generated from non-NFL stadiums and NFL stadiums. The Cardinals opened Busch Stadium III in

April 2006. The stadium was built for $388 million, with the team owners paying approximately 77% of the costs. Fans paid $40 million of construction costs through the purchase of seat licenses, and public money was used, as well. The public funds included a $30 million tax abatement (Miklasz, 2005b).

The Cardinals moved into their new stadium at a time when it appeared the club was awash in new revenues. In their last year at Busch II, the club drew 3.5 million fans. When these fans attended games in the new stadium, they paid higher ticket prices, and many sat in a greatly expanded section of premium seats. Additionally, the team had just left long-time radio broadcast partner KMOX for a more lucrative radio arrangement with KTRS. Finally, the Cardinals reportedly expected to receive $23 million from MLB due to the success of MLB.com, the XM Radio league rights fee, and the sale of the Washington Nationals. Despite these new revenues, the club kept its 2006 team payroll at the same level as 2005 (Miklasz, 2005a).

Team officials had claimed that a new stadium was needed to generate the revenues necessary to field a competitive team. They claimed that the revenues from the new luxury and club seating areas would increase significantly and that the team would be in a position to raise payroll significantly (Miklasz, 2005b). In fact, it was reported in *Sports Business Journal* that local revenue would rise between 15% and 20%, to approximately $150 million, during the 2006 season (Fisher, 2005). What was not mentioned was that a large portion of this new revenue—$15 million annually for the next 22 years—would be used to retire the debt on the stadium (Miklasz, 2005b). In all, the new stadium has generated only an additional $5 million to $10 million for the club, after bond payments.

Why would a team like the Cardinals finance a large portion of a new stadium themselves, if it would not lead to a significant improvement in the financial performance of the club? For the owners of the Cardinals and teams in similar situations, the new revenues from a stadium might not alone justify the construction. However, the financial picture changes if the land around the site presents an opportunity for commercial development.

The Cardinals are one of several teams that have built or planned to build a ballpark village or arena district to generate additional revenues. However, the Great Recession delayed many of these projects, and teams that had planned on the projects' additional revenues found these revenues did not materialize. Ground was finally broken for the Cardinals' Ballpark Village development in 2013—eight years after Busch Stadium III opened (Brown, 2013). In the first phase of the project, a $100 million, 100,000-square-foot retail, restaurant, and entertainment space in two buildings was developed. This phase was greatly reduced from the plan's initial blueprints, where the project would have included between 500 and 1,000 residential units to support the area's new restaurants in the off-season and 20,000 to 150,000 square feet of office space, depending on demand for space (Brown, 2005; Fisher, 2005). Only after this phase of the project was completed in 2014 did the Cardinals have additional revenue available to spend on team payroll.

In New York City, three new sport facilities were planned at the time the Cardinals were initially hoping to open their retail space. The public share of funding for each of these facilities was below 25% (Zimbalist, 2005). Most ambitious was the $800 million Atlantic Yards project in Brooklyn. An arena was to be part of a $3.5 billion residential and commercial development and was to be home to the New York Nets (Fish, 2005). After financing delays caused by the recession, the $1 billion Barclays Center opened as the anchor to the Atlantic Yards project in 2012, and is now the home of the Brooklyn Nets and New York Islanders (the Islanders will move to their new venue after the 2020–2021 hockey season). Financial issues related to the commercial (office and residential) development led to a rebranding of the project, now Pacific Park. Eleven years after the project was proposed, Forest City Ratner, the original developer, partnered with Greenland USA, a subsidiary of a Chinese development firm, to help speed the remaining development at the site (Dailey, 2014). The project is expected to be completed in 2035 ("Developer admits," 2018).

Like Pacific Park in Brooklyn, the Ballpark Village in St. Louis is still under development. Phase II of the project is a $261 million investment that includes a 117,000-square-foot office building, a 30,000-square-foot fitness center, a variety of restaurants, a 29-story apartment building, and a new bespoke hotel (Barker, 2020). Funding for the project comes from taxes generated in the Ballpark Village ($72.7 million), equity from the Cardinals and their developer ($28.4 million), and debt issued by the Cardinals and their developer ($160 million) (Barker, 2017).

Colleges are using the development of stadium districts as revenue sources, too. Arizona State University (ASU) plans to turn 300 acres near downtown Tempe, Arizona, into an athletic facilities district that will include office space, apartments, and two hotels, located next to Sun Devil Stadium. Revenues generated in the district will go to pay for building and renovating new athletic facilities on ASU's campus. Ultimately, the district is expected to generate approximately $37.5 million for ASU's athletic department on an annual basis (Reagor, Metcalfe, & Ryman, 2015).

As the costs of new facilities continue to increase, and as organizations are obliged to pay a greater share of funds for facility construction, the trend of packaging stadiums and arenas as a part of larger redevelopment projects will continue. The organization with the most profitable redevelopment—not the most profitable stadium or arena—will gain an advantage. Organizations paying the majority of development costs for a stadium will need to use the facility as an anchor for a larger development.

Calculating IRR with irregular cash flows. When cash flows are not constant, we can find IRR by trial and error with the formula given on p. 257. A financial calculator or spreadsheet software that provides financial analysis formulas is valuable for this type of calculation.

Comparing IRR to NPV. Recall the details of the analysis involving installation of FieldTurf. The initial cost of the project was $520,000, and annual incremental cash flows of $200,000 were anticipated over the ten-year useful life of

EXHIBIT 8.2   Calculating IRR with Excel.

	A	B	C	D	E
1			Analysis of FieldTurf		
2				= B5 * C5	= D5 + B4
3	Time	ICF	PVIF @ 7%	DCF	Sum
4	0	$ (520,000.00)	1.000	$ (520,000.00)	$ (520,000.00)
5	1	$ 200,000.00	0.935	$ 186,915.89	$ (333,084.11)
6	2	$ 200,000.00	0.873	$ 174,687.75	$ (158,396.37)
7	3	$ 200,000.00	0.816	$ 163,259.58	$ 4,863.21
8	4	$ 200,000.00	0.763	$ 152,579.04	$ 157,442.25
9	5	$ 200,000.00	0.713	$ 142,597.24	$ 300,039.49
10	6	$ 200,000.00	0.666	$ 133,268.44	$ 433,307.93
11	7	$ 200,000.00	0.623	$ 124,549.95	$ 557,857.88
12	8	$ 200,000.00	0.582	$ 116,401.82	$ 674,259.70
13	9	$ 200,000.00	0.544	$ 108,786.75	$ 783,046.45
14	10	$ 200,000.00	0.508	$ 101,669.86	$ 884,716.31
15					
16	NPV =	$884,716.31	= NPV(7%,B5:B14)-520000		
17	IRR =	37%	= IRR(B4:B14,0.4)		

the field. The project's cost of capital was 7%. What is the IRR? Does the IRR lead to a different decision than the NPV method?

By using the data entered in Exhibit 8.1, we can quickly calculate the project's IRR with Excel's IRR function (see Exhibit 8.2).

The IRR, 37%, is significantly higher than the project's cost of capital, and both the IRR and NPV methods indicate that the project should be undertaken. When a project is being considered on its own merits, the NPV and IRR methods will give the same accept or reject decision. However, when we are analyzing two or more projects in order to select one, the results of the two methods may conflict—even if both projects have positive NPVs and IRRs greater than their costs of capital. For mutually exclusive projects, the NPV method may indicate Project A should be accepted, and the IRR method may indicate Project B should be accepted. This can occur in two circumstances:

1. The projects differ greatly in financial size.
2. The projects differ greatly in the timing of cash flows.

It is generally accepted that when these conflicts arise, NPV is the method of evaluation that should be used (Brigham & Houston, 2019).

MODIFIED INTERNAL RATE OF RETURN
When a project involves a large cash outflow sometime during or at the end of its useful life, in addition to the cash outflow at the beginning, it is said to have non-normal cash flows. For a project with non-normal cash flows, IRR

may not be usable as a capital budgeting method, because multiple IRRs may exist. Stadiums and arenas often have non-normal cash flows resulting from renovations or improvements. From 1995 to 1999, in the NFL alone, eight franchises, or 27%, played in stadiums that underwent at least $20 million in renovations during that time frame (Brown, Nagel, & Rascher, 2003).

For projects with non-normal cash flows, we recommend the **modified internal rate of return (MIRR)** for finding the rate of return. MIRR is the discount rate where the present value of the project's costs is to equal the present value of the project's terminal value (Brigham & Houston, 2019). Here, terminal value is the future value of the cash inflows compounded at the project's cost of capital. When the present value of the costs equals the present value of the terminal value, we have

$$PV_{costs} = \sum_{t=0}^{n} \frac{COF_t}{(1+K)^t} = \frac{TV}{(1+MIRR)^n}$$

where COF_t = the cash outflow in period t
K = the project's cost of capital
n = the number of periods
MIRR = the modified internal rate of return
PV_{costs} = the present value of costs
TV = the terminal value

In this equation, the first and second terms give the present value of the cash outflows when discounted at the cost of capital. In the rightmost term, the numerator is the compounded value of the inflows (terminal value), with the assumption that the cash inflows are reinvested at the cost of capital.

If the investment costs are all incurred during Year 0, and the first operating cash inflows occur in Year 1, then we can use the following equation for MIRR:

$$PV_{costs} = \frac{TV}{(1+MIRR)^n} = \frac{\sum_{t=1}^{n} CIF(1+K)^{n-t}}{(1+MIRR)^n}$$

Here, CIF refers to the project's cash inflows. Spreadsheet software provides a convenient method for calculating MIRR. Exhibit 8.3 shows such a calculation.

We calculate the terminal value by compounding the cash inflows at the cost of capital (7%). In a spreadsheet, we enter the formulas as shown in Exhibit 8.3. The present value of the project's cost is $520,000. We calculate the terminal value of the project by summing the future values of the expected cash inflows. We then use the RATE function to calculate MIRR (the rate of growth). We enter the present value and terminal value of the project, along with the number of periods (10), into the dialog box for the RATE function, and this gives the value of MIRR. Alternatively, we can use a financial calculator and enter the following data: N = 10, PV = –520,000, PMT = 0, FV = 2,736,400. Press the I key, and the MIRR for the project, 18.18%, will be displayed.

A convenient method for calculating MIRR is to use Excel's MIRR function (see Exhibit 8.4).

EXHIBIT 8.3   Calculating MIRR with the equation for MIRR using Excel.

	A	B	C	D
1			Analysis of FieldTurf	
2				
3	Time	ICF	FVIF @ 7%	Terminal Value
4	0	$ (520,000.00)		
5	1	$ 200,000.00	1.838	$ 367,691.84 ← = B5 * C5
6	2	$ 200,000.00	1.718	$ 343,637.24
7	3	$ 200,000.00	1.606	$ 321,156.30
8	4	$ 200,000.00	1.501	$ 300,146.07
9	5	$ 200,000.00	1.403	$ 280,510.35
10	6	$ 200,000.00	1.311	$ 262,159.20
11	7	$ 200,000.00	1.225	$ 245,008.60
12	8	$ 200,000.00	1.145	$ 228,980.00
13	9	$ 200,000.00	1.070	$ 214,000.00
14	10	$ 200,000.00	1.000	$ 200,000.00
15			Terminal Value =	$ 2,763,289.59 ← = SUM(D5:D14)
16				
17		PV of TV =	$520,000.00	← = -B4
18		NPV =	$0.00	
19				
20		MIRR =	18.18%	← = RATE(A14,0,-C17,D15)

The fact that the MIRR method assumes that cash inflows are reinvested at the cost of capital rather than at the project's IRR makes MIRR a better predictor of profitability. It provides a better estimate of a project's rate of return, and it overcomes multiple problems that arise with the IRR method when cash flows are non-normal. The MIRR method will lead to the same project selection decision as the NPV and IRR methods when we are considering two mutually exclusive projects of equal size and with the same expected useful life.

Conduct a Post-Audit Analysis

The final step in the capital budgeting process is to conduct a post-audit analysis after the project has been completed. This step is often a forgotten element in the capital budgeting process. In the post-audit, we compare the project's actual results with the predicted results and attempt to explain any differences. Post-audit analyses allow managers to make improvements to the firm's forecasting techniques. Generally, the most successful organizations are ones that place great emphasis on post-audits.

Brigham and Houston indicate that several complications can arise in the post-audit analysis. First, because of uncertainty in the forecasting of cash

EXHIBIT 8.4 Calculating MIRR with Excel's MIRR function.

	A	B	C	D	E
1			Analysis of FieldTurf		
2				= B5 + C5	= D5 + E4
3	Time	ICF	PVIF @ 7%	DCF	Sum
4	0	$ (520,000.00)	1.000	$ (520,000.00)	$ (520,000.00)
5	1	$ 200,000.00	0.935	$ 186,915.89	$ (333,084.11)
6	2	$ 200,000.00	0.873	$ 174,687.75	$ (158,396.37)
7	3	$ 200,000.00	0.816	$ 163,259.58	$ 4,863.21
8	4	$ 200,000.00	0.763	$ 152,579.04	$ 157,442.25
9	5	$ 200,000.00	0.713	$ 142,597.24	$ 300,039.49
10	6	$ 200,000.00	0.666	$ 133,268.44	$ 433,307.93
11	7	$ 200,000.00	0.623	$ 124,549.95	$ 557,857.88
12	8	$ 200,000.00	0.582	$ 116,401.82	$ 674,259.70
13	9	$ 200,000.00	0.544	$ 108,786.75	$ 783,046.45
14	10	$ 200,000.00	0.508	$ 101,669.86	$ 884,716.31
15					
16	NPV =	$884,716.31	← = NPV(7%,B5:B14)-520000		
17	IRR =	37%	← = IRR(B4:B14,0.4)		
18	MIRR =	18%	← = MIRR(B4:B14,0.07,0.07)		

SIDEBAR 8.C   Montreal's Olympic Stadium

Olympic Stadium, part of Quebec's $2.6 billion 1976 Summer Olympic construction, was paid off in 2006. Originally, the facilities for the Olympics were to cost $250 million. Many factors led to the increase in costs, including a five-month strike that halted construction in 1975, corrupt contractors, and the government's diversion of tobacco tax dollars from the event to other governmental projects.

Surprisingly, the Montreal Olympic Games ran an operating surplus, but cost overruns at Olympic Stadium left a $1 billion debt from the stadium alone. After hosting the track and field events, as well as the opening and closing ceremonies of the 1976 Olympics, Olympic Stadium was home to the Montreal Expos from 1977 to 2004. Other events held in the venue included trade shows, monster truck rallies, concerts, and Canadian Football League games.

Over its 40-year life, the stadium needed many costly repairs. A retractable roof, called for in the original plans, never worked properly and was replaced by a permanent structure. In 1999, a part of this structure collapsed while a car show was being set up, and it was discovered that the structure could no longer withstand Montreal snowfalls. Therefore, no events could be held in the stadium from December to March. In 1991, a 55-ton concrete beam fell off the side of the stadium, leading to costly repairs and forcing the Expos to play the final month of the season on the road. Engineers determined that the stadium cannot be imploded due to its unique concrete structure. The cost to dismantle the structure would be $500 million, about half of the cost of its construction.

Most recently, in an effort to prepare the stadium to host World Cup games in 2026, the government of Quebec approved $250 million to replace the current roof ("Olympic Stadium", 2019). Also, the stadium's tower was renovated for use as office space with occupation beginning in 2018.

flows, a percentage of projects undertaken will not meet the firm's expectations. Also, projects often fail to meet expectations for reasons beyond the firm's control. See Sidebar 8.C for an example of a stadium project that had unexpected results. At times, these reasons for failure are ones that no one could realistically anticipate, such as Hurricane Katrina's effect on the sport industry along the entire Gulf Coast in the United States. It is also difficult to separate the operating results of one investment, such as a new grass or artificial field, from those of a larger system, such as a stadium. Finally, if disappointments arose because of employees' deficiencies in capital budgeting, discovering this fact will not be helpful if those responsible for entering into a project are no longer with the firm.

CONCLUSION

Capital budgeting is a process for analyzing the capital expenditures of an organization. The process involves identifying the initial cost of a capital project, determining the incremental cash flows resulting from the project's implementation, analyzing the project with one of five capital budgeting methods, and performing a post-audit analysis. All five of the capital budgeting methods discussed in this chapter provide relevant information that will be useful when a manager is selecting a project for inclusion in a firm's capital budget.

The risk and liquidity of a project are indicated by both the payback and the discounted payback method. We found in the FieldTurf case that the project reaches its discounted payback period in two years and 50 weeks. As the project has an expected useful life of ten years, the athletic director is taking a relatively small risk by entering into this fairly liquid project.

The NPV method, which indicates the present value of the dollar benefit of a project to the company, provides the best measure of a project's profitability. In the FieldTurf case, the present value benefit to the athletic department of installing the artificial turf is $884,716. The IRR method also measures profitability but expresses it as a percentage of return, which some decision makers prefer. Stating that the installation of FieldTurf will return at 37% is a convincing argument that the athletic director can present to the university's administration.

The MIRR method offers the same benefits as IRR but improves on the IRR's reinvestment assumption while avoiding the problems that IRR presents with non-normal cash flows. When cash flows are non-normal, MIRR is the best indicator of a project's rate of return. By using the MIRR method, the athletic director will find that the FieldTurf installation would provide an 18% rate of return, rather than the inflated 37% return indicated by the IRR. The MIRR method is preferred in analyses of stadiums and arenas, as these facilities often have non-normal cash flows.

Concept Check

1. What is capital budgeting?
2. What major information (data) do you need for capital budgeting when you want to compare projects?
3. What relevant information is provided in each capital budgeting method?
4. What is the problem with multiple IRRs, and when in sport would they occur?
5. In sport, which method of capital budgeting is superior? Why?
6. What is the purpose of the post-audit in the capital budgeting process?

Practice Problems

1. Project M has a cost of $65,125, expected net cash inflows of $13,000 per year for ten years, and a cost of capital of 11%. What is the project's payback period (to the closest year)?
2. What is the project's NPV?
3. What is the project's IRR?
4. What is the project's discounted payback period?
5. What is the project's MIRR?
6. Based on the answers to questions 1–5, should the project be accepted? Why or why not?
7. Your division is considering two facility investment projects, each of which requires an upfront expenditure of $15 million. You estimate that the investments will produce the following net cash flows:

YEAR	PROJECT A	PROJECT B
1	$5,000,000	$20,000,000
2	$10,000,000	$10,000,000
3	$20,000,000	$6,000,000

What are the projects' net present values, assuming the cost of capital is 10%? 5%? 15%? What does this analysis tell you about the projects?

Case Analysis

Athens City Pool

The residents of the Athens Arts, Parks, and Recreation District suffered from a significant deficiency in swimming opportunities. The Arts, Parks, and Recreation District serves a community of just over 23,800 people in the center of rural southeast Ohio. The original "city pool," which opened in 1972, was declared obsolete in 2002 and was expensive to maintain and upgrade (Morris, 2014). The city pool was a lap pool, though not many people actually swam laps in it.

As a result of the aging pool's condition, the Arts, Parks, and Recreation (APR) Advisory Board, together with APR Department Director Rich Campitelli, recommended that a tax levy set to expire in 2016 be extended to fund construction of a new pool for the city during the summer of 2014. They also decided that a recreation pool should be constructed. Such a pool would offer a superior recreational experience compared to a traditional six- to eight-lane pool. This pool would be able to compete with newer seasonal recreation pools in the neighboring towns of Nelsonville and Marietta. In Nelsonville, a new swimming pool with slides, diving boards, lap lanes, and a gradual-entry shallow end opened in 2004, and soon thereafter Marietta opened an aquatic center with a lazy river, slides, a splash pad, and an interactive pirate ship (Schaller, 2010).The desire for a recreation pool was also economic. Experience with leisure pools in other parts of the country suggested it was probable that revenues from such a facility would at least equal operational costs and probably exceed them. Thus, instead of losing $40,000 a year (as was currently happening), the new pool would likely produce a surplus.

To determine cost and attendance projections, the Athens Arts, Parks, and Recreation District hired a consulting firm that specialized in recreational pool facilities. Their preliminary feasibility study determined that the total development cost of the pool project would be $6.6 million and that the facility would have a 30-year useful life. The consultants estimated initial annual operation and maintenance costs to be $212,000, rising at 3.2% annually. The uniqueness of the facility led the consultants to project substantial local and regional (50-mile radius) demand, with annual attendance ranging from a conservative estimate of 80,000 to an optimistic 250,000 users each year, of which half would be children. The consultants suggested an admission price of $6 for adults and $4.50 for children, with increases of 25% every ten years. The study implied that the pool would be profitable but did not provide a detailed pro forma analysis.

The Athens City Council agreed that changes to the city pool were needed and placed the issue on the ballot for vote. An extension of the 0.1% ARP income tax in the city of Athens was approved by 68% of voters on November 4, 2014. The current rate for a 30-year general obligation bond was 3.5%.

MTB Inc., a South Carolina-based sport consulting firm, was hired to analyze the capital expenses for the new project to determine if the current pool proposal was feasible from an economic standpoint.

Case Questions

1. Based on the facts presented, does the project "make sense"? Be sure to calculate NPV, IRR, or MIRR when answering this question. Assume a 30-year useful life for the facility.
2. Based on your analysis in question 1, would you recommend any changes to the proposed venue? Why or why not?
3. Based on your answers in questions 1 and 2, why do you think the city built the pool (which opened in 2018)?

References

Appleton, A. (2019, September 6). Regents ok $3.2m to bring UNR stadium up to ADA standards. *Las Vegas Review-Journal*. Retrieved from www.reviewjournal.com/local/education/regents-ok-3-2m-to-bring-unr-stadium-up-to-ada-standards-1842455/.

Barker, J. (2017, October 22). Putting the 'village' in Ballpark Village—$261 million will transform the skyline. *St. Louis Post-Dispatch*. Retrieved from www.stltoday.com/business/local/putting-the-village-in-ballpark-village-261-million-will-transform-theskyline/article_b9737d9a-78cb-582e-b7a3-b2fd9c5addb9.html.

Barker, J. (2020, February 20). With bespoke hotel, Ballpark Village finally filling out. *St. Louis Post-Dispatch*. Retrieved from www.stltoday.com/business/local/with-bespoke-hotel-ballpark-village-finally-filling-out/article_76e36622-3b36-5632-82fa-712f0f147e4f.html.

Belson, K. (2010, September 7). As stadiums vanish, their debt lives on. *The New York Times*. Retrieved from www.nytimes.com/2010/09/08/sports/08stadium.html?pagewanted=all&_r=0.

Brigham, E.F., & Houston, J.F. (2019). *Fundamentals of financial management* (15th ed.). New York: Cengage Learning.

Brown, L. (2005, July 18). Cards move forward on Ballpark Village. *Sports Business Journal*. Retrieved from www.sportsbusinessjournal.com.

Brown, L. (2013, February 8). Ground finally broken on Ballpark Village. *St. Louis Post-Dispatch*. Retrieved from www.stltoday.com/business/local/ground-finally-broken-on-ballpark-village/article_65f88bb1-e118-5dc1-bc1f-ad280b7f5872.html.

Brown, M., Nagel, M., & Rascher, D. (2003, May). The impact of stadia on wealth maximization in the national football league: To build or renovate? Paper presented at the meeting of the North American Society for Sport Management, Ithaca, NY.

City of Arlington. (2016, August 12). *Master agreement for a ballpark complex*. Arlington, TX: Author.

Dailey, J. (2014, August 4). Atlantic Yards rebrands as Pacific Park, reveals next building. *Curbed NY*. Retrieved from http://ny.curbed.com/archives/2014/08/04/atlantic_yards_rebrands_as_pacific_park_reveals_next_building.php.

Developer admits Pacific Park project will take until 2035. (2018, August 20). Retrieved from https://thebridgebk.com/developer-admits-pacific-park-project-will-take-until-2035/print/.

FieldTurf (2020). *Cost analysis*. Retrieved from https://fieldturf.com/en/why-fieldturf/cost-analysis/.

Fish, M. (2005, June 20). Tight public money forces teams to get creative with stadium finance plans. *Sports Business Journal*. Retrieved from www.sportsbusinessjournal.com.

Fisher, E. (2005, October 3). Making success a tradition. *Sports Business Journal*. Retrieved from www.sportsbusinessjournal.com.

Groppelli, A.A., & Nikbakht, E. (2013). *Finance* (6th ed.). Hauppauge, NY: Barron's Educational Services, Inc.

Hartley, J. (2019, August 6). Arlington will tax tickets and parking to help Rangers pay for their debt on stadium. *Fort Worth Star-Telegram*. Retrieved from www.star-telegram.com/news/local/arlington/article233592372.html.

Miklasz, B. (2005a, December 7). Owners cash in, make Jocketty pinch pennies. *St. Louis Post-Dispatch*. Retrieved from http://stltoday.com.

Miklasz, B. (2005b, December 10). Cards owners use new park as an excuse to scrimp. *St. Louis Post-Dispatch*. Retrieved from http://stltoday.com.

Morris, C. (2014, May 14). Council favors levy to fund new pool, other park upgrades. *The Athens News*. Retrieved from www.athensnews.com/ohio/article-42429-council-favors-levy-to-fund-new-pool-other-park-upgrades.html.

New Jersey Sports & Exposition Authority. (2014). *Economic development: Facts and figures at a glance*. Retrieved from www.njsea.com/economic.aspx?id=73#stadium.

Olympic Stadium roof replacement delayed until 2024. (2019, February 6). *CBC News*. Retrieved from www.cbc.ca/news/canada/montreal/olympic-stadium-roof-replacement-delayed-1.5007619.

Reagor, C., Metcalfe, J., & Ryman, A. (2015, June 19). ASU creating urban hub to pay for athletics facilities. *The Arizona Republic*. Retrieved from www.azcentral.com/story/money/real-estate/2015/06/19/asu-athletics-facilities-district/28958197/.

Schaller, L. (2010, July 22). The Athens city pool looks to update. *Ohio University Online*. Retrieved from www.hanskmeyer.com/ouonline/?p=657.

Yost, M. (2011, February 3). The price of football that even nonfans pay. *The Wall Street Journal*. Retrieved from www.wsj.com/articles/SB1000142405274870343950457611668 0460638092.

Zimbalist, A. (2005, June 27). Big Apple can take a shine to the new threesome of sports facilities. *Sports Business Journal*. Retrieved from www.sportsbusinessjournal.com.

PART

Application of Financial
Management in Sport

CHAPTER 9

Facility Financing

Daniel A. Rascher

KEY CONCEPTS

asset-backed securities
benefit principle
certificate of participation
contractually obligated income (COI)
efficiency principle
franchise free agency
general obligation bond
horizontal equity
lease revenue bond
naming rights
non-excludable
non-rival
opportunity cost

payments in lieu of taxes (PILOT)
positive externalities
price elasticity of demand
private financing
psychic impact
public financing
public good
revenue bond
securitization
sin tax
tax increment financing (TIF)
tourism tax
vertical equity

INTRODUCTION

This chapter discusses why sport facilities are built with public and/or private money, how much it costs to build them, the different sources for financing them, public/private partnerships for sport facilities, and the role of public policy in their construction.

REASONS FOR BUILDING NEW SPORT FACILITIES

Who benefits from a new stadium? Sport teams and team owners, leagues, fans, and even businesses and the residents of a city or region may benefit from a new sport facility.

Teams and Owners

A team, its athletes, and its owner may benefit from a new stadium in numerous ways. A new facility can generate substantial increases in revenues from tickets, concessions, sponsorship, merchandise, personal seat licenses (PSLs), luxury suites, and other premium seating, because customers demand—and are willing to pay for—better seating and atmosphere, food, restrooms, amenities, and access. When NFL teams move into a new stadium, they witness an increase of about 85% in local revenues that are not shared with other teams, and see an increase in franchise values of 35% (Brown, Nagel, McEvoy, & Rascher, 2004). MLB teams gain an additional 65% in local revenues in the first year of a new stadium (Clapp & Hakes, 2005). The Golden State Warriors moved into the new Chase Center in fall 2019 and are expected to increase their total annual franchise revenues from about $400 million to $700 million, a 75% increase. Another advantage is that a new facility can reduce the incremental effect of winning on franchise revenues, by as much as half in the NFL (Rascher, Brown, Nagel, & McEvoy, 2012). This is because wins and losses are less important in getting fans to attend games at the new stadium. Instead, fans care about the experience that the new stadium offers. Fans attend games in a new facility partly because of the facility and not solely because of the team's performance. This can smooth out overall revenues and budgets for years, lowering financial risk (and borrowing rates).

At the same time, a franchise that moves into a new facility also generally has an incentive to improve its on-the-field performance, because doing so will help it leverage the full value of the facility. Each new fan the team attracts to the facility will spend more money in a new stadium than in an old stadium on concessions, merchandise, and so forth. Thus, the return on an investment in better players is higher, so the franchise has an incentive to increase its investment in talented players. Empirically, of the 14 MLB teams that opened new ballparks from 1991 through 2001, 11 of them increased their team payrolls in the years immediately following the move into the new stadium, with an average increase of about 35% for the first year (Baade, 2003; Mellinger, 2009). Of course, the cause-and-effect might also be that the new stadium provides the financing to increase payrolls (under the assumption that the owners could not finance player payrolls from other sources).

Finally, NFL rules have given owners motivation to build new stadiums for reasons other than those listed above. According to the rules, the league shares most of the revenue that individual teams generate (specifically, national media and licensing revenues and ticket revenues). Certain revenue streams, however, that increase substantially in new stadiums belong to the owner (as long as they are used to help pay for the costs of stadium construction), such as naming rights, sponsorships, concessions, parking, and luxury suite or premium seating revenues. Additionally, the NFL has a large fund, the G-4 fund, that provides low-interest loans to help teams build new stadiums.

A franchise's incentive to build a new stadium is further enhanced if it can obtain partial financing from local, regional, and/or state government. A city can improve its justification for investing public money if other political jurisdictions also invest (surrounding counties, the state, the federal government, or other cities), thereby lowering the direct cost to the city. In Milwaukee, Wisconsin, Miller Park was financed through several different sources, including

EXHIBIT 9.1 Stadium funding sources.

MILLER PARK (2000) PROJECTED FUNDING SOURCES		
Naming rights and upfront concessionaire payments	$30,000,000	(1)
Milwaukee business community loans	14,000,000	
City of Milwaukee loan	15,000,000	
Bradley Foundation loan	20,000,000	
WPBD tax-exempt bonds	160,000,000	(2)
City of Milwaukee	18,000,000	
Milwaukee County	18,000,000	
State of Wisconsin	36,000,000	
MLB letter of credit	10,000,000	
Certificates of participation	45,000,000	(3)
Helfaer Foundation loan	1,000,000	
Total Funding Sources	$367,000,000	

Note: This is a projection. Actual costs were substantially higher. The team receives all revenue and is responsible for operating expenses. The team pays $1.1 million in annual rent but receives $3.85 million per year for maintenance and repairs.

(1) Naming rights revenue from Miller Brewing Co.

(2) The Wisconsin Professional Baseball District owns 64% of the stadium and issued tax-exempt bonds backed by a 1/10 of a cent increase in the sales tax and a 1% increase in the room tax for Milwaukee County and the four surrounding counties.

(3) As explained later in the chapter, COPs were used to purchase a scoreboard and other amenities and were paid back via a sales tax.

the City of Milwaukee, which gave $18 million toward construction and loaned another $15 million. This is less than 5% of the nearly $400 million in total construction costs, including infrastructure costs. For an example of additional funding sources, see Exhibit 9.1, which outlines funding sources and amounts as they were projected for Miller Park prior to construction of the facility. The $30 million in naming rights that Miller Brewing Co. paid could be considered local public financing (discussed later), because the stadium is majority owned by the city's special baseball district. However, if the Brewers were not playing in the stadium, the value of the naming rights would be significantly less, so most of the naming rights funds invested in the stadium could be attributed to the team and not the city.

When cities and other political entities invest in a facility, the team will receive most, if not all, of the additional revenue generated within the stadium but will have to pay only part of the cost. Franchises are able to secure the lion's share of revenue because of the relative leverage they have compared to municipalities. For example, a team can threaten to move, but a city can't, and the leagues purposefully allow fewer teams than there are cities interested in teams, thus creating a shortage of teams. When a team spends money on new players, however, that cost is fully borne by the team and not shared with local government.

Leagues

Leagues, and not just their individual teams, desire new construction, because all members benefit through revenue sharing of increased ticket sales.

Fans

Sport fans gain from new stadiums with enhanced offerings and better amenities, such as restrooms, food, and so forth. Although ticket prices typically increase in new stadiums, more fans attend games in these stadiums, providing evidence that fans consider themselves better off. At the same time, fans are often residents of the communities that are taxed in order to help pay for construction, thus fans weigh this trade-off when deciding whether to support a publicly financed stadium.

Cities and Geographic Regions

Cities and their businesses and residents may or may not be better off with a new stadium, depending on the cost to the city. Reasons commonly cited for investing public money in new sport facilities are that they will

- provide economic impact to the community (see Chapter 12)
- increase national and international awareness of the city and enhance its image, thereby increasing future tourism (and possibly firms and families relocating to the city)
- provide a cornerstone for economic development in a blighted or underutilized area
- generate civic pride among residents, or give the city "major league" status
- provide quality-of-life services similar to public parks and museums
- provide positive externalities, including **psychic impact** (the emotional impact of having a local sports team),[1] discussed below
- generate political capital for local politicians.

Positive Externalities

Generally, businesses pay for their own offices and manufacturing facilities, without government intervention or subsidies. For very large projects, however,

---

1 Psychic impact is also termed *psychic income* or *public consumption benefit* in the academic literature.

such as an automobile manufacturing plant or a sport facility, a company may create competition for the project between political jurisdictions (e.g., cities or states), which can result in government intervention or subsidies. This was the case with a $754 million facility that DaimlerChrysler proposed to build in the southeastern United States. State and local subsidies totaled approximately $320 million after DaimlerChrysler chose Georgia over South Carolina. States engaged in a bidding war for the facility because of the potential increases in jobs, local earnings, and taxes. Georgia officials felt that the plant not only would generate quality jobs but also would foster growth in other automotive businesses (such as auto suppliers and parts manufacturers) in the area, creating a net positive economic gain to the region. DaimlerChrysler later backed out of the deal with Georgia and constructed the facility in South Carolina instead. Recently, Amazon created a formal bidding war to locate its second headquarters that ultimately resulted in billions of dollars in incentives, with the final location being split between Long Island City, NY and Arlington, VA.

These overflow effects, or positive externalities, can help governments justify public investment in private industry. **Positive externalities** are benefits produced by an event that are not captured by the event owners or sport facility. In sport, it is clear that some local businesses, such as restaurants, bars, retail stores, and hotels, benefit from having sporting events in town. Local radio stations and newspapers also benefit from local sports, often dedicating an entire segment or section to them. Even newscasts commit a daily segment to sports. If sports were not important to listeners, viewers, and readers, these media outlets would focus on something else. These are clearly positive externalities from sports, for which the local teams do not collect payments. (Negative externalities, such as traffic congestion caused by sporting events, also occur.)

The fact that the team cannot charge local restaurants for increased customer traffic means that this aspect of a sporting event is a **public good**, a good that is **non-rival** and **non-excludable**—meaning that its consumption by one customer does not prevent another customer from consuming it, and the team cannot prevent someone from enjoying the good (via television, the internet, newspapers, discussions with friends, and so forth). As Allan Sanderson (1999) suggests:

> Sports represent a socially-consumed commodity. Water-cooler conversations and office greetings frequently turn on casual greetings such as, "How 'bout them Redskins?" Even if ardent fans are not present in the stands, they can watch games on television and radio, follow their favorite team or athlete through newspaper accounts, and exchange numbers and notions with friends, neighbors, and colleagues.
>
> p. 189

As a result of positive externalities, a local team may underinvest in a stadium, or a sports league may decide not to launch a new franchise, because it is not financially worth the cost to the team or league. However, it may be worth it to the city and its residents. The issue is that the private business (the team) cannot charge for the full value of its business to the community. As a result, the quality of the stadium or the number of teams in the league will be lower than the public wants—not socially optimal. A public subsidy might be justified on these grounds. Public subsidies for stadium development can help push a league over the threshold to offer more expansion franchises. Baade and Matheson (2006) show that stadium subsidies have evoked expansions in major professional sports in the United States, increasing the number of teams closer to the socially optimal level.

PSYCHIC IMPACT

Similarly, Sanderson discusses the fact that psychic impact, which is an externality, may justify public subsidies. The team is not able to charge residents for being happy about the local team (although it tries, through the sale of novelties, merchandise, and apparel carrying the team's name and logo). Sanderson notes:

> Studies suggest that, on average, recycling is an economic loser because the total collection costs exceed the value of the materials to be recycled. But people, even armed with that information, and knowing that recycling is implicitly taking away from other worthwhile foregone alternatives, such as more police, parks, and street repairs, or even a tax rebate, may still vote to continue recycling their newspapers, cans and bottles because the "feel-good" factor is sufficiently large. The corresponding question here is how large the feel-good factor of a professional franchise or a new stadium is, in terms of civic pride or even some "existence value."
>
> p. 189

The loss of a local team, if it moves to another city, may be so devastating in terms of psychic impact that a public investment is justified to prevent it. A key task for politicians is to find a way for those who benefit to pay for it, and for those who do not care about or benefit from sports to pay nothing.

CONTROVERSY REGARDING BENEFITS TO POLITICAL JURISDICTIONS

Controversy often arises because those who gain the most from the construction of a new sport facility are not always those who pay for the facility's construction and upkeep, and because many of the benefits discussed above may not materialize sufficiently to justify the expense. In fact, most academic studies measuring the economic impact of sport facilities (not teams or sporting events) fail to find enough net gain to a community to justify the often large public outlays (Siegfried & Zimbalist, 2000). Although, many of these studies may not be sensitive enough to detect the economic impact that may be occurring because of the relatively large size of the local economies (see Sidebar 12.B in Chapter 12). However, non-economic reasons, such as psychic impact (or public consumption benefit), may in fact justify public investment. As Owen (2006) notes, "the focus on economic impact misses the true source of value teams have for cities as public goods." Owen finds that for the states of Michigan and Minnesota, psychic impact values of $100 million per major professional sport team (i.e., NFL, MLB, NHL, and NBA) are reasonable estimates, with some going much higher than that. The average public subsidy for a sport facility since 2000 is about $229 million (in 2010 dollars), with adjustments for land acquisition, forgone taxes, and other effects raising that figure to $271 million (Long, 2013, table 2.1 and p. 81). Therefore, the psychic impact value does not typically cover the full cost of a public subsidy, but when combined with the economic impact effect it could justify some public facility investments.

So why do sport teams receive large amounts of public funding? Economic and psychic impact values exist for other businesses as well, such as an open-air mall, but those businesses often do not receive public funding. The fact that a sport league has control over the number of franchises means it can prevent a city from hosting a team even if the city wants one. The threat of relocation to another city, known as **franchise free agency**, often motivates a city to help build a facility for a local team. If the team cannot realistically move, it may not be able to obtain a significant subsidy. Some subsidy may be justified if the quality of the stadium, if it were financed solely by private investment, would be less than what the market demands. Perry (2002) estimates that the Washington Redskins could justify a private investment of only $155 million in a new stadium; however, as discussed below, other estimates suggest that NFL teams could finance nearly the entire cost of a new stadium. The bottom line is that the residents of a city do not want to see their hometown team move to another city, so they are often willing to foot the bill for most of a facility's construction and maintenance costs. For all of these reasons, we have seen unprecedented growth in the construction of sport facilities.

HISTORICAL PHASES OF FACILITY FINANCING: PUBLIC VERSUS PRIVATE FUNDING

The construction of sport facilities in the United States has come in three major waves over the past century and has seen changes in the degree of **private financing**—financing that does not use public dollars—and **public financing**—the use of public funds to finance a project.

Phase 1

Twenty-seven facilities were built from the late 1880s through the end of the Depression. One of these still stands today—Wrigley Field. During the first half of this first wave of construction, stadiums were 100% privately financed. Not until 1923, and the construction of Los Angeles Coliseum, was public money used to build a major professional sport stadium. Overall, during the first wave 31% of the costs of construction were financed with public money (Keating, 1999; Baade, 2003). Of the 27 facilities built prior to World War II, only five received public funding.

Phase 2

During the second phase, from 1960 to 1979, 57 major sport facilities were built, many in the all-purpose mold—able to house a baseball and football team or a basketball and hockey team. The second wave saw a significant increase in the cost of construction and in the amount the public was willing to pay, as Exhibit 9.2 shows.[2] On average, public financing covered 83% of the cost of a new stadium during this phase.

---

2   In fact, the public financing trend began immediately after World War II, but not many facilities were built until 1960.

EXHIBIT 9.2   Public subsidies for sport stadium construction.

PERIOD	NUMBER OF STADIUMS BUILT	PERCENTAGE OF STADIUMS PUBLICLY FINANCED	COST OF STADIUMS ($M, 2000 DOLLARS)	PUBLIC SUBSIDIES ($M, 2000 DOLLARS)	PERCENTAGE OF CONSTRUCTION PUBLICLY FINANCED
1887–1923	14	0%	139	0	0%
1887–1939	27	19%	530	166	31%
1923–1939	13	38%	390	166	43%
1947–1959	8	88%	175	173	99%
1960–1969	25	84%	2,791	1,846	66%
1970–1979	32	91%	4,592	4,280	93%
1980–1986	13	100%	882	820	93%
1987–1999	55	93%	10,180	6,674	71%
2000–2002	18	94%	5,330	3,347	63%
2003–2009	15	93%	5,071	4,581	90%
2010–2020	19	79%	14,702	4,317	29%
Total 1887–2020	212	81%	44,253	26,204	59%

Source: Keating (1999), Baade (2003), Long (2013), and Author for 2010–2020 information.
Note: 2020 CPI is estimated using prior years' growth rate.

Phase 3

Construction was relatively quiet during the early 1980s, but in 1987—with the opening of Dolphins Stadium, quickly renamed Joe Robbie Stadium (now Hard Rock Stadium)—a third building spree began. It continued, netting nearly 90 new facilities over a 20-year period. These buildings are often positioned to look like classic sport stadiums of the past (although more recent ones such as Chase Center and SoFi Stadium have begun to look more modern), but they usually house only one major tenant, not two. In fact, during this wave, over 80% of the major professional sport facilities in the United States have been replaced or substantially upgraded. Between 2000 and 2010, 51 new major sport facilities were opened in North America, at a cost totaling about $21 billion, with the public paying for about $12 billion of that (Long, 2013). From 2010 to 2020, 19 new facilities were built in the Big 4 (hosting 21 Big 4 tenants; the Red Wings and Pistons share an arena, as do the Islanders and Nets), with 15 of them receiving public financing. The total costs (in 2000 dollars) were $14.7 billion, with the public paying for a little over $4.3 billion, or nearly 30% of the costs. The past decade has shown a reverse in the trend of publicly financed stadiums, with much more financing coming from private owners for these decidedly-not-retro stadiums, even though the costs of construction continue to rise. However, if one removes the four 100% privately financed facilities (venues housing Giants/Jets, Rams/Chargers, Warriors, and Golden Knights), the percentage of the cost that is publicly financed is about 48%.

Exhibit 9.3 shows trends in major stadium construction. Just in 2010 alone, seven major pro sport facilities were opened in the United States, with the public paying about 40% of the costs. If the privately financed MetLife Stadium is removed from the analysis, then the public's share rises to about 72%. In 2020, the multi-billion-dollar Raiders and Rams/Chargers stadiums opened in the NFL, and the Texas Rangers replaced their 27-year-old stadium with a new $1.1 billion stadium across the street.

If we drill deeper into the ongoing trends, as Zimbalist and Long have done, we find that the public share of facility costs fell from the 1970s through the 1990s but had flattened out between 2000 and 2013, at around 55% (Long, 2013). Even though the share of funding by the public had decreased, the amount in nominal terms had increased because of the steep increases in stadium construction costs. Continuing after 2013, the share of public financing has continued to decline.

Since 2015, most of the major new stadiums that have been built in the US have tended to be more privately financed than in the past, and yet they are more expensive to build. What explains this? One answer is that team valuations have risen dramatically in the past decade (see Chapter 10), leagues are helping to finance the stadiums, and owners can generate much more revenue from the buildings and in the surrounding district, thus enabling them to justify private financing. Chase Center is essentially 100% privately financed, as is the $5 billion SoFi Stadium district (which includes not only the stadium as home of the NFL's Rams and Chargers, but also offices, residential units, and other entertainment offerings). The $1.5 billion Mercedes-Benz Stadium opened in 2017 to host the Atlanta Falcons and Atlanta United (of MLS). The initial public outlay was about $280 million ($200 million in funding from the State of Georgia and about $80 million in tax rebates, discounted land, and

EXHIBIT 9.3   Major sport facility construction trends, 1997–2020 (nominal dollars).

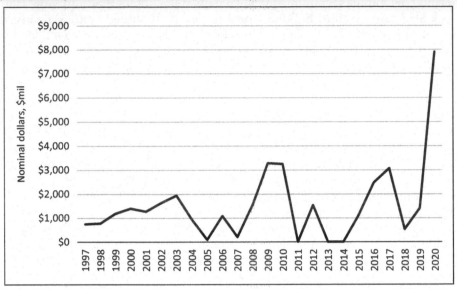

Note: This includes the $5 billion cost of the LA Stadium and Entertainment District at Hollywood Park which includes the football stadium among many other real estate projects. Since it is privately financed, the cost of the stadium alone is not publicly available.

infrastructure), yet future hotel taxes collected would be set aside to maintain, operate, and upgrade the facility and are estimated to have a present value of $700 million (deMause, 2017).

Historical Analysis of Construction Costs

According to the Construction Cost Index (CCI, a measure of inflation in the construction industry), prices in that industry rose by 3.9% annually from 1977 through 2019. In contrast, general inflation (measured by the Consumer Price Index) was 3.5% over the same time period. The difference may seem small, but an item that cost $100 in 1977 and whose price rose at the CCI rate would cost $508 in 2019 and only $430 if it had risen at the CPI rate, an 18% difference.

We can use the CCI to adjust stadium construction costs for inflation in order to compare all stadiums in real dollars. From 1960 to 1994 the real cost of stadiums (data do not include arenas) rose, on average, about 1.76% per year (doubling in price in real terms over nearly 40 years). However, from 1990 to 2014, the real cost of stadium construction rose an average of 3.1% per year, 76% higher than the previous growth rate. According to information compiled by Crompton, Howard, and Var (2003), the average cost of a stadium built from 1995 to 2003 was $339 million in 2003 dollars, whereas the cost of stadiums built during the 1960s was $179 million (in 2003 dollars). Yet, by 2015, the average cost of new stadiums was nearly $800 million (in 2003 dollars). Overall, stadium construction costs have risen significantly faster than inflation in the rest of the economy, and the total dollar amount in real terms (comparable over time) has also risen substantially. (The same can be said for arenas, whose costs have grown at an average annual *real* rate of 3.8% since 1970, from $87 million to $474 million in 2015, on average.)

SIDEBAR 9.A   Choice of an Inflation Index Matters

An important aspect of the analysis of construction costs is that the choice of inflation index matters. If we use the more common CPI, the real cost of sport facilities has risen over time (even recently), but if we use the CCI, that is not the case. All construction costs have risen over time more than costs for consumer products in general (evident in the CPI). Therefore, if a community were to build a museum instead of a sport facility, those costs would also be much higher than in previous decades. Complaints about the rising real costs of stadium construction have little merit if the alternative is another construction project with equally high inflation, such as a library or museum. Of course, the debate over whether public money should be used for a stadium versus another building does have merit.

As shown in Exhibit 9.4, accounting for real costs versus nominal costs has a striking impact on the perception of the rising costs of sport facilities. In nominal terms, the costs of old stadiums were a small fraction (about 10%) of the costs of new stadiums. However, in terms of the real costs, the old stadiums were about 23% as expensive as new ones. It is important to make comparisons over time with real costs, not nominal costs (which, unfortunately, are often the basis of comparisons). Stadiums are of much higher quality than they used to be, with many more amenities, so the quality-adjusted cost may actually be lower than in previous eras.

Given that the average percentage of a stadium's cost that the public pays has shrunk, but the total real cost of stadium construction has risen, we must ask whether the real amount of public dollars spent on stadiums is rising or falling. The answer depends. From 1962 to 1994, total public funding for sport stadiums (not arenas) rose in real terms by about 3.5%, when the CCI is the measure of inflation. During that same period, the public's share of funding remained fairly constant, around 85%. These statistics suggest that the real amount of public dollars spent was rising. However, from 1995 to 2003, total public funding for sport stadiums declined in real terms by about 3.5%, when compared to the cost of all construction projects. In a comparison of eight facilities built between 2010 and 2020 (hosting the 49ers, Falcons, Giants/Jets, Vikings, Raiders, Braves, Marlins, and Texas Rangers), the average annual growth rate in *real* terms of public financing is just less than 1%.

Stadiums and arenas differ in two major ways in terms of public finance. One is that stadiums are much more expensive overall, which is one of the reasons why the percentage that is publicly financed dropped from about 85% during 1961–1994 to 62% during 1995–2003 to 37% during 2010–2020. Arenas are much less expensive to build overall, and they can attract many more events (upwards of 200 events per year can be held in a new arena in a large

EXHIBIT 9.4   Nominal versus real costs of stadiums (1997 dollars).

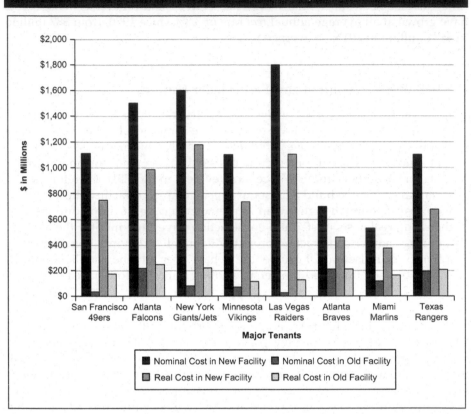

metropolitan area), so private financing is more feasible, yet they are arguably more of a public asset given the larger number of diverse events. From 1961 through 1984, 100% of the cost of arena financing was borne by the public. That figure dropped to about 44% from 1985 through 2003, and to 40% for 2010–2020.

SIDEBAR 9.B   What's in a Name? Money

Twenty-five percent of the 122 major professional sport teams in North America are named after geographic regions different from their host city. For instance, the Minnesota Twins are named for Minnesota and the Twin Cities (Minneapolis and St. Paul), not just Minneapolis, where the stadium is located. The New York Jets and Giants actually play their home games in New Jersey. Yet the geographic moniker chosen by a team does not seem to affect the amount cities are willing to pay in public finance. As of 2012, for Major League Baseball teams, the percentage of stadium construction costs financed by a team's city is 35% for teams whose name includes that of the host city and 44% for teams whose name does *not* include the host city. Thus, cities whose name does not adorn the team actually pay a higher percentage of construction costs. For all major professional sport teams, on average, 32% of the cost of stadium construction is paid by cities whose name is on the team and 30% by cities whose name is not on the team—not much difference. Note that this simple analysis does not account for additional factors that may affect public financing and may vary across these two sets of sport facilities, such as differences in city size.

Exhibit 9.5 lists NBA and NHL facilities built in North America during 2010–2020 and the share of the costs borne by the public. Typically, private sources fund the more expensive facilities in larger markets because the economics of the facilities can justify it (e.g., higher luxury suite, premium seating, sponsorship, and naming rights revenues and more events), and the threat of a team leaving for another market is much less serious—would the Lakers really ever leave Los Angeles?

We must make two important points before leaving this analysis of the costs of stadium construction and how much the public bears. First, as Long (2005) notes, calculations of stadium construction costs typically do not include

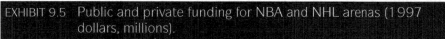

EXHIBIT 9.5   Public and private funding for NBA and NHL arenas (1997 dollars, millions).

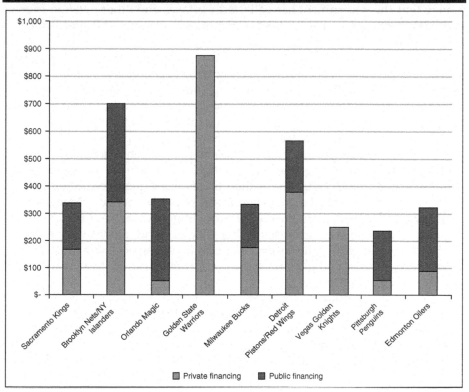

the cost (or opportunity cost) of land acquisition and forgone taxes. As described later, public stadium financing often involves donating the land (or leasing it cheaply) and forgoing various taxes, such as sales tax and property tax, that would normally be collected from the stadium. Long estimates these amounts would add as much as 57% to calculations of construction costs.

Second, lease arrangements with teams have become more beneficial to team owners than they used to be, often allowing the owners to receive all forms of revenue from the stadium (including from non-sport events), with the city collecting a very small annual rent for the stadium's use. For instance, the Baltimore Ravens' football stadium, which opened in 1998, cost approximately $200 million, with the public paying 90% of the costs. The team pays no rent and keeps all revenue streams, while the city authority covers the costs of maintenance and game day staff. It is not hard to understand why Art Modell moved his team from Cleveland to Baltimore.

Changes in Financing Methods

As noted earlier, the types and methods of financing, not just the amount, have changed over the three waves of stadium construction. During the pre-World War II wave, most facilities were privately financed. After the war, the second wave saw growth in public financing of stadiums. Typically, the financing methods of this time were quite simple. These included floating **general obligation bonds (GOBs)**, which last for 20 years or so, with the debt and interest payments paid each year directly out of the general funds of local government(s) coffers. The general fund of a government (city, county, or state) is the pool of money that the government has collected via taxes and other revenue sources and uses to pay for all government programs except those that specifically, by law, require separate funding.

The third wave of construction, which began in 1987 with Joe Robbie Stadium, ushered in a constantly changing array of complex and creative financing methods. Initially, the public funding sources were sales taxes, property taxes, and stadium rent, but funds increasingly came from hotel and rental car taxes and other taxes. Private sources of financing included the capitalization of revenue streams from the facility (e.g., naming rights, premium seating, and sponsorships) and borrowing against those to pay for construction.

Why have financing methods changed so much in recent decades? Beginning in the mid-1970s, the United States has experienced a general tax revolt, with a push toward more privatization of public services. Hence, private industry has had to share in the cost of providing services that the public used to provide through the tax system. This general trend, along with increased public awareness of the true costs of stadium financing and who most directly benefits (i.e., owners and players), has forced team owners to increase their private financing of stadiums.

The Deficit Reduction Act of 1984 prevented tax-exempt bonds from being sold to finance luxury suites. More generally, the 1986 Tax Reform Act (a significant overhaul of the tax system) prohibited tax-exempt bonds from being used to fund sport facilities where a single organization would be responsible for 10% or more of revenues. In other words, a facility that hosted many different events but did not have a major tenant could use tax-exempt bonds, because the facility would be deemed a public use facility, whereas a facility with a single tenant could not use tax-exempt bonds. These laws caused the interest rates on bonds used to pay for sport facilities to increase (in order to give the same competitive return to investors as tax-exempt bonds). Since these bonds cost more to use, other sources of financing began to develop that were not affected by these legal changes, such as sales taxes and hotel and car rental taxes.

General growth in the demand for sports and subsequent revenues enabled owners to justify paying part of stadium costs. City officials, recognizing this growth in demand and revenues, fought harder to convince owners to help pay for construction. In 1987 Joe Robbie discovered new revenues available from leasing luxury suites and used the initial lease payments (and guarantees of future payments) to finance part of construction. Similarly, the Carolina Panthers invented the modern use of personal seat licenses in 1993, generating about $150 million in revenues. More recent developments by sport leagues, including the G-4 fund in the NFL, have helped team owners find cheaper financing options to help pay for stadiums. A recent development is the use of EB-5 funding (a federal government program whereby foreigners invest $500,000 in order to increase jobs in low-income areas, and the foreigner is then able to obtain a Green Card), which generated around $40 million towards the construction of Orlando City's soccer stadium. Additionally, the Golden State Warriors' new arena (Chase Center) was partially financed through PSLs, but instead of keeping the estimated $300 million in revenue generated from them, the franchise will pay back the money to the season ticket holders 30 years after opening the arena (with no interest), enabling the owners to avoid paying income taxes on the $300 million because it is essentially a loan (Ozanian, 2019).

As noted earlier, the trend toward more private financing temporarily slowed in the 2000s, but has recently picked up again. As Zimbalist (2006) notes, sport leagues and their owners still have leverage in negotiating with cities, especially smaller ones, because they can move a franchise to another location if a deal is not to their liking. Also, even though voters are more aware of the true financial costs and benefits of publicly financed sport facilities, they do continue to vote in favor of them. The quality-of-life or psychic impact value of sport teams playing in modern stadiums may be high enough to justify these expenditures. A $250 million public financing package costs about $20 million per year in debt payments, which, when disaggregated into per capita costs, is about $10 per person per year in a region of 2 million people. As voters have learned this, many may have decided that having a sport team is worth the cost of one movie ticket per year. Coates and Humphreys (2005) note that voters who live in close proximity to the facilities are more likely to vote yes for public subsidies.

PUBLIC FINANCING

As we have just discussed, public financing remains a major source of funding for sport facilities. This section will discuss the principles of public financing, sources and techniques of financing, and calculations involved.

Public Financing Principles

Public financing principles determine the financing sources that are appropriate for a given project. Two of these principles are the concepts of equity and efficiency.

EQUITY PRINCIPLES

Equity is a measure of fairness. It includes three major ideas: vertical equity, horizontal equity, and the benefit or user pays principle (Baade & Matheson, 2006). **Vertical equity** is concerned with the taxpayer's ability to pay, typically calling for a tax that does not cause poorer persons to bear a disproportionate share. **Horizontal equity** suggests that individuals with similar incomes should pay similar amounts of a tax. The **benefit principle**, or user pays principle, states that those who benefit from a particular project ought to be the ones taxed. For funding a stadium, a ticket tax on sporting events would satisfy the benefit principle much more than a cigarette tax.

Consider the following examples of how the equity principles apply to public funding for sport facilities. Hotel, rental car, and **sin taxes** (taxes on alcohol and cigarettes) fail the user pays or benefit principle, because the users of a sport facility are not the ones being taxed, except by coincidence. Sin taxes also fail the horizontal equity principle, because people with the same ability to pay (similar income) will pay different amounts of tax, depending on whether they smoke or consume alcohol. If lower-income people smoke more than higher-income people, then a sin tax will fail the vertical equity principle, as well. However, sin taxes are efficient at generating revenues, because their demand is price inelastic (the demand does not change much as a result of a price change). A related effect of taxing specific products or services is that the tax is shared by the consumer and producer (depending on their relative elasticities). Thus, hoteliers will oppose a hotel tax, because it will cut into their profit and make them less competitive with hotels in other destinations. The hotel tax might have the effect of raising the expected amount of revenue for the hotel per guest, but it may also reduce the number of guests. Ticket taxes and personal seat licenses do satisfy the benefit principle, because users of the facility pay them. However, these sources usually cannot fully fund the public's portion of the cost of a stadium. A television tax on sport channels might satisfy the benefit principle and generate substantial funding.

EFFICIENCY PRINCIPLE

The **efficiency principle** calls for a tax to be easy to understand, simple for government to collect, low in compliance costs (meaning that it is not expensive for taxpayers to calculate and pay), and difficult for taxpayers to evade. Moreover, for a tax to be effective in raising tax revenues sufficient to pay for a stadium, it should be applied to products or services with low price elasticity of demand. **Price elasticity of demand** refers to the percentage decrease in the number of units sold compared to the percentage increase in the price of the product. An elasticity of –0.5 means that raising prices by 10% reduces sales by 5%. A product with a high price elasticity of demand would see a substantial decrease in the quantity sold if a tax were imposed, which would offset much of the proposed tax gain.

Public Financing Sources and Techniques

As the costs of facilities have risen, many more sources of financing beyond the general funds of a city, county, or state have been cobbled together to pay for them. Although the use of money from the general fund is on the decline compared to other techniques, it is still popular enough to have helped fund sport facilities for the Milwaukee Brewers (using city, county, and state general fund sources), Philadelphia Phillies, Cincinnati Bengals, Detroit Lions (where Wayne County sold property worth $20 million to raise funds), Houston Texans, and Tampa Bay Lightning, to name a few. This section will examine public sources of financing and how they are implemented. The list in Exhibit 9.6 provides a summary of public financing sources.

SIDEBAR 9.C   If the Public Pays More for the Stadium, will Tickets be Cheaper?

Is there a *quid pro quo* between the public paying more money for a professional football stadium and then paying less for tickets once the stadium is built? In other words, if a franchise is able to save money on construction costs, will it pass some of those savings on to the ticket buyers? Consistent with economic theory, NFL franchises do not appear to set ticket prices based on the amount of public financing they receive for the stadiums in which they play. Economic theory suggests that the franchise will simply pocket any savings from building a football stadium and not pass them on to the public. Pricing decisions are based on the demand to see games and on changes in the variable costs of selling tickets and providing seating. Brown, Rascher, and Ward (2006) have shown that ticket prices are also related to general increases in demand over time, team quality, inflation, consumers' ability to pay in the local market, and the presence of a new stadium (although not how it was financed). Overall, an increase in public funding by 10% reduces ticket prices by only 42 cents, all else being equal. Public financing does seem to reduce ticket prices, but not by much.

GENERAL OBLIGATION BONDS

Historically, general obligation bonds were the most common method of facility financing, besides tapping into the general fund, and they continue to be very common. This is because they spread the cost of the facility over a 20- or 30-year period. The term "general obligation" refers to the fact that the issuer (usually a city, county, or state) has a commitment to repay the principal plus interest (debt payments) through whatever means are necessary, including tapping into the general fund of the city, county, or state. Because the risks of purchasing GOBs for investment are lower than the risks of other bonds, the interest rates are lower (often up to 2% lower), allowing for smaller debt payments. Further, a debt service reserve fund (a separate, or escrow, account that can be tapped into for unforeseen reasons, funded by annual payments) is usually not required, because of the low risk, so the total dollar amount of the bonds necessary to pay

EXHIBIT 9.6   Public financing sources.

- General obligation bonds

- Certificates of participation

- Revenue bonds

- Tax increment financing and property taxes

- Sales tax

- Tourism and food and beverage taxes

- Sin taxes

- Sale of government assets

- State appropriations

- Ticket tax/surcharge or parking revenues/tax

- Lotteries and gaming revenues

- Player income taxes (jock tax)

- Reallocation of existing budget

- Utility tax

- Indirect sources of public financing

  - Land donations

  - Infrastructure improvements

  - Tax abatements

for the stadium or arena is lower. Thus, the total cost of the facility may be less than if higher-interest-rate instruments are used.

A disadvantage of GOBs is that their use may limit the amount of other bonds that the city, county, or state can use for schools, bridges, and other projects. These political jurisdictions are limited in the total amount of bonds (or debt) that can be outstanding or owed, and debt ceilings vary across jurisdictions. Additionally, any voter approval that is needed can raise the total cost of the financing. It is not surprising that the use of GOBs may require a vote, because the funds to pay off GOBs are public dollars, mostly supplied by residents.

To explore the advantages and disadvantages of GOBs further, let's consider whether they satisfy the three equity principles. To do this, we must examine the source of the funds used to pay off GOBs. At the state level, sales taxes or income taxes provide the largest source of funds; for local governments, property taxes are usually the largest source of general funds, although in some situations sales taxes generate more revenue.

Obviously, GOBs do not satisfy the benefit principle, because everyone in a given jurisdiction pays for the facility, not just those who benefit. However, to the extent that property taxes pay off the GOBs and the facility helps to increase property values (this point is debatable and specific to each case), GOBs can come closer to satisfying the benefit principle. GOBs do satisfy the efficiency principle, because they are not burdensome or difficult to understand and cannot be easily avoided. They may or may not satisfy the horizontal and vertical equity principles, depending on whether the largest sources of funding for the general fund follow those principles. Property taxes may satisfy the vertical equity principle, assuming that the individuals who earn more income own higher-valued property and pay higher taxes.

An advantage of GOBs from the bond buyer's perspective is that they are generally tax exempt, meaning that the buyer does not pay taxes on earnings from these bonds. This allows the interest rate on the bonds to be low compared with taxable bonds. For example, the New York City General Obligation series (October 2019) offers a yield of 2.16%. On a taxable equivalent basis, that is the same as 3.32% for someone in the 35% tax bracket. (Earning 3.32% but having to pay 35% of it in taxes results in a 2.16% equivalent [3.32 × (1 − 0.35)]). The City of Minneapolis used GOBs to cover 85% of the purchase of the Target Center in 1995. The construction projects to build facilities for the Jacksonville Jaguars, Nashville Predators, Seattle Mariners, and Tampa Bay Rays over the past few decades all used city, county, or state GOBs as a major financing vehicle. The revenues used to pay off these bonds have included hotel taxes, rental car taxes, food and beverage taxes, sales taxes, and others. If these were to fall short, the general fund would be tapped.

SIDEBAR 9.D   Tax-exempt Auction-rate Bonds can Backfire

A number of recently built or refurbished sport facilities have been financed through tax-exempt auction-rate bonds. For auction rate bonds, the annualized interest rate is set at auctions held every seven to 35 days. Typically, these bonds have lower interest rates than their fixed-rate counterparts because of the risk of the interest rate going up. This is similar to residential housing mortgages, where a borrower can opt for a fixed-rate mortgage at a higher rate than an adjustable-rate mortgage (ARM), which may eventually rise to an even higher rate.

Sport facilities in Louisiana, Indiana, New Jersey, Washington DC, and Cleveland have been financed through auction-rate bonds issued by the respective city or state. Franchise owners have also issued these bonds, including owners of the New York Giants, New England Patriots, and Dallas Cowboys. As the fallout from the sub-prime mortgage crisis reached full swing in the late 2000s, the interest rates (and monthly payments) on these bonds skyrocketed. For instance, debt payments on $238 million of bonds sold for upgrades to the Louisiana Superdome, which totaled about $500,000 during January 2008, more than tripled to $1.8 million in February because the interest rate on the bonds increased from about 4% to 12%. The interest rate increased because, for the first time, the auction lacked bidders; investors were worried about the safety of these investments because bond insurers were suffering and the investors feared they risked failure. The bond insurance companies were stretched as they were forced to pay out on many of the bonds related to sub-prime mortgages.

The rate on $190 million of bonds sold by the New Jersey Sports and Exhibition Authority in November 2007 rose from 4.3% to more than 15% during one week in February 2008. Similar events occurred for Lucas Oil Stadium (Indianapolis Colts) and Cleveland Browns Stadium (now FirstEnergy Stadium).

CERTIFICATES OF PARTICIPATION

A **certificate of participation (COP)** is an instrument that a government agency or non-profit corporation that is set up to build a facility will sell to one or more financial institutions to obtain the initial capital for construction. Then, the agency or non-profit will lease the facility either directly to the tenant(s) or to a facility operator and use the lease payments to pay off the COP.

Because COPs are backed by lease payments, they are riskier than GOBs and, therefore, offer a higher interest rate. However, they do not require a public vote, so they are often used because they circumvent direct decision making by voters. They also typically do not count against the debt ceiling of the political jurisdiction, depending on applicable law. For instance, Miller Park in Milwaukee issued $78 million in COPs that were paid back not by the team or facility operator directly, but through sales taxes.[3] This example highlights the flexibility in the source of payments for COPs. The flexibility was needed to circumvent a cap on public funding for construction. The COPs did not count against the cap.

REVENUE BONDS

Revenue bonds are a form of public financing that is paid off solely from specific, well-defined sources, such as hotel taxes, ticket taxes, or other sources of public funding. If the specific source of funding does not meet expectations, the bonds will not be paid off in full. Thus, when compared to GOBs, the interest rates are higher for revenue bonds, and a debt service reserve is necessary. Revenue bonds require a debt service coverage payment—an annual payment into an escrow account to cushion against the risk of shortfalls in the revenue sources that back the debt. Therefore, the total cost of using revenue bonds is much higher than that of GOBs, because of the added risk. An advantage of revenue bonds is that because the funding is from a narrower source than GOBs, revenue bonds can be tailored to satisfy the benefit principle, especially if a ticket tax is used. For sport-related construction, revenue bonds typically have terms of 15 to 30 years, generally do not require voter approval, and do not count against the debt ceiling of the political entity using them.

If the source of funding for the bonds is expected to grow over time (e.g., hotel tax revenues will increase because of increasing hotel rates and tourism),

---

3   Note that the projected COP funding was for $45 million, but the actual amount needed, due to unexpected major construction delays and costs, was $78 million.

EXHIBIT 9.7 Example of variable interest bonds.

MARLINS PARK (MIAMI MARLINS)		
	Range of Sources	
County bonds—hotel bed taxes (county)	$300,000,000	(1)
County bonds—property taxes (county)	$50,000,000	(2)
City of Miami	$25,000,000	(3)
Team	$120,000,000	(4)
Team borrowed from county	$35,000,000	(4)
Total Funding Sources	$530,000,000	

(1) Three different hotel bed taxes were used.
(2) County bonds being paid off by property taxes.
(3) The city committed $13 million from hotel bed taxes and another $12 million for improvements.
(4) The team paid $120 million, paid an additional $6 million toward construction, and borrowed an additional $35 million from the county.

The team pays rent of $2.3 million (increasing 2% per year) and $10 per parking space. An additional cost of $115 million was incurred for the parking complex and infrastructure, paid for by the city.

then variable interest bonds may be used, which require lower payments initially and higher payments nearer to the maturity of the bonds. An example of this was the funding for the new baseball stadium for the Miami Marlins, outlined in Exhibit 9.7. County revenue bonds of $300 million were sold and are being paid off from hotel bed taxes. These revenue bond payments start out low and rise over time, in conjunction with the expected increase in hotel rates, usage, and taxes collected over time.

A creative method to attempt to achieve the advantages of both GOBs (lower interest rates) and revenue bonds (satisfaction of the benefit or user pays principle) is to arrange that any shortfalls in revenue bonds will be backed by the general fund (thus nearly ensuring their payment). Essentially, this turns the revenue bond into a GOB, but the payments still come from a specific source, such as ticket taxes. Another method of raising the investment grade of revenue bonds is to require an "insurance wrap," whereby the payments are insured. This method can reduce the interest rate of the bonds, but the insurance expense increases the costs.

Other examples of the use of revenue bonds in sport facility construction include the following:

- For Dolphins Stadium, $30 million in revenue bonds (out of $115 million in total financing) were issued and were paid off by the private sector.
- Riverfront Stadium, built in 1970 in Cincinnati, was paid for entirely with $44 million in revenue bonds that were backed by stadium revenues (team rent and parking).

- Jacobs Field (now Progressive Field) in Cleveland was built with stadium-backed revenue bonds that financed just over 10% of its cost.
- For the Nashville Predators' home arena, financing included $77.5 million in revenue bonds backed by a sales tax on tickets and merchandise.

Lease revenue bonds are a version of revenue bonds in which the revenue stream backing the payment of the bonds is a lease. For instance, a 20-year naming rights deal (which is a contract or lease) may be the source of funds to pay off lease revenue bonds, as opposed to a tax on ticket sales (which is not a lease, but an expected or forecasted revenue stream). As stadiums and arenas have become able to generate more revenues through better amenities, financing through lease revenue bonds has become more common. These bonds are often backed by luxury suite or premium seating revenues, concessions contracts, or sponsorship deals, as well as naming rights deals. Normally, these would be considered private financing sources (discussed later). These bonds illustrate how a partnership between public and private sectors can create synergies—the public entity can float a low-interest-rate bond, and the private entity can generate funding for the bond's payment because of demand for its sport team.

An example of lease revenue bond financing in recreation comes from Montgomery County, Maryland, which built a swim center with lease revenue bonds that were paid for through a lease between the county and the financing authority established to manage the facility. The county's lease payments cover the principal plus interest on the bonds. The Baltimore Ravens' football stadium was paid for through state lease revenue bonds backed by proceeds of the Maryland state lottery and personal seat licenses. In 2018, Clermont County Port Authority issued $30 million in lease revenue bonds for a training facility and youth complex for soccer club FC Cincinnati (which joined MLS in 2019) supported by lease payments from the club for use of the facility.

TAX INCREMENT FINANCING AND PROPERTY TAXES

Proponents of tax increment financing often claim that the public does not pay for this source of facility funding. The rationale for this claim is that with **tax increment financing (TIF)**, only "incremental" (additional or new) taxes generated from a certain source (traditionally property taxes) finance the facility, and those incremental tax revenues would not exist without the facility. The original uses of the taxes collected at the base value are still funded—only the additional tax revenues are used to pay the facility costs. One might argue that a second-best use of the property would also be able to generate some of those incremental tax revenues, but it is true that existing public revenues are not used for the financing. That is TIF's main objective.

For this type of financing, a base year and tax-assessed value are determined. After the facility is built, any increases in tax revenues—assumed to result from the improvement of the area—are used to pay off the tax increment bond. This method captures the assessed valuation growth within a certain TIF district (a predefined area that is geographically related to the facility being built). If the area does not witness increased tax revenues, then the TIF bond may fail. That is, essentially, how tax increment financing works. Like revenue bonds, TIF bonds are riskier than GOBs.

Because the surrounding TIF district needs to see increases in property values, tax increment financing was historically used to help revitalize blighted areas within large urban communities. Mixed-use development around the stadium is expected to increase property values and thereby help pay off the TIF financing. The risk is, of course, that property values might decline. The new arena for the Detroit Red Wings was set to be partially funded from TIF property taxes, capped at $12.8 million per year (see Exhibit 9.8). The Milwaukee Bucks' new arena (Fiserv Forum) was partially financed by new incremental property tax collections within a half-mile radius of the parking structure (see Exhibit 9.9).

EXHIBIT 9.8 Example of tax increment financing.

RED WINGS ARENA (DETROIT RED WINGS)

	Range of Sources	
Property taxes	$219,068,541	(1)
Detroit Development Authority	$34,165,202	(1)
Team	$196,766,257	(2)
Total Funding Sources	$450,000,000	

(1) $450 million worth of bonds would be sold and partially paid off by capturing TIF property taxes.
(2) The team is associated with a development company that would develop the surrounding land and pay part of the stadium costs.

EXHIBIT 9.9 Example of tax increment financing.

FISERV FORUM (MILWAUKEE BUCKS)

	Range of Sources	
State of Wisconsin	$80,000,000	(1)
City of Milwaukee	$47,000,000	(2)
Milwaukee County	$80,000,000	(3)
Team sources	$317,000,000	
Total Funding Sources	$524,000,000	

(1) State-issued bonds, a portion of which will be paid off from 50 cents of a $2 ticket surcharge.
(2) Tax increment financing used to collect property taxes within a half-mile radius of the parking structure. A 2.5% hotel tax, 3% car rental tax, and 0.5% on food and beverage for the Wisconsin Center District, which contains the arena.
(3) $2 surcharge for tickets, with $1.50 going to help pay for the arena.
The Bucks will receive all revenues from the arena and surrounding district.

EXHIBIT 9.10   Example of rededication of property taxes.

ROGERS PLACE (EDMONTON OILERS)

	Range of Sources	
City of Edmonton	$316,000,000	(1)
Team sources	$173,000,000	(2)
Ticket surcharge proceeds going to city	$125,000,000	(3)
Total Funding Sources	$614,000,000	

(1) Property taxes redirected to pay for arena along with additional parking revenue and sales tax within the arena.

(2) A portion of this is in the form of rent payments to the city.

(3) A ticket tax (whose rate is set annually to meet financing needs) was 9.5% in 2018.

City of Edmonton will own the building and lease it to the Oilers. Oilers will retain all arena revenue.

While used less often because the funds are already spoken for, the rededication of existing property taxes to help fund a sports facility was used to pay a large portion of Rogers Place in Edmonton, Alberta (see Exhibit 9.10).

An initial proposal for a new sport arena and entertainment district in Sacramento offered an option to rely on TIF. The TIF option was to include the incremental property taxes, utility taxes, sales taxes, and hotel taxes collected in the 240-acre entertainment district. Ziets (2002) states,

> The risks with this kind of a development-based financing plan are two-fold: (i) the market may not bear what is required by the developer, in which case the team may struggle to finance the development and the City may not realize sufficient taxes; and/or (ii) absent a specific requirement to develop, the hoped-for development may never materialize thus resulting in a shortfall in tax revenues. As a result, cities typically will secure any bonds backed by the incremental taxes with a general fund pledge or a more secure stream of revenues.
>
> p. 108

For AT&T Park (originally Pac Bell Park), often cited as being entirely privately financed, financing included $15 million of TIF funded through the Redevelopment Agency in San Francisco, while the rest of the stadium's cost was privately financed. This is an example of stadium construction financed without using existing tax revenues. Because of the substantial property value increases in San Francisco since construction of the stadium began, this TIF project has presented virtually zero risk.

SALES TAX

Sales tax revenues are the most common source of public financing for sport facilities. Some facilities use only sales tax revenues for the public portion

EXHIBIT 9.11 Sales tax funding for facility construction.

COORS FIELD (COLORADO ROCKIES)		
Denver metro area sales tax (0.1% increase)	$72,000,000	(1)
Denver metro area sales tax bond issuance (0.1% increase)	$103,000,000	(2)
District investment earnings	$15,000,000	(3)
Rockies equity	$12,000,000	
Premium seating revenue	$16,000,000	
Concessionaire fees	$7,000,000	
Equipment lease proceeds	$6,000,000	(4)
Total Funding Sources	$231,000,000	

(1) Collected during the period of construction of the facility; spans six counties.
(2) Set to be paid back over the 18-year period of the bonds. Due to growth in sales taxes collected, this was paid off after six years.
(3) The metropolitan baseball district, which owns the facility, invested $15 million.
(4) Equipment purchased by the district and leased to the team.

of financing. Such projects have included facilities built for the Arizona Diamondbacks, Colorado Rockies (see Exhibit 9.11), Phoenix Suns, Tampa Bay Buccaneers, Arizona Coyotes, and Minnesota Wild. A number of methods are available for using sales taxes to pay for facilities. One is to raise the sales tax rate a small amount and "pay as you go." Maricopa County, in Arizona, increased the county sales tax by 0.25% from April 1995 through November 1997, raising $238 million during the construction period. This covered most of the public financing for Bank One Ballpark (now Chase Field).

Another method is to issue government bonds and pay them off through an increase in the sales tax. In this method, the payment period is longer (and more interest is paid), but the cost each year is lower than with the "pay as you go" method. Small increases in sales taxes do not impose a large burden on any one specific person or group, so strong opposition is often less likely—whether or not it is justified. For the baseball stadium built in 1992/1993 in Arlington, Texas, for the Rangers, the public financing package included $135 million in 15- and 20-year bonds. Sales tax revenues grew more quickly than anticipated, and the bonds were paid off after just ten years. A similar result occurred in Denver, where the 18-year bonds took only six years to pay off (see Exhibit 9.11). In another example, more than half of the cost of the 2001–2003 renovations to Lambeau Field was paid for by a one-half-cent sales tax increase in Brown County, Wisconsin, whose proceeds paid off the long-term bonds in 2011, instead of the projected year of 2021.

Still another method is to fund a facility through sales taxes limited to those collected from the facility itself or from a district in the immediate vicinity. This may include a diversion of current sales taxes related to the immediate region or funding through new sales taxes that will be collected at the facility, with or without an increase in the sales tax rate. For the Seattle Seahawks' football stadium, sales taxes collected at the stadium complex are being used to pay off over $100 million in financing.

TOURISM AND FOOD AND BEVERAGE TAXES

As voters have become more adamant in opposing large amounts of public support for sport facilities, proponents have been reducing the use of sales taxes and instead have begun to tax non-residents. **Tourism taxes** include taxes on hotel stays and rental cars, and they may also include food and beverage taxes in certain districts. Under these plans, visitors to the area, not local residents (to the extent that local residents do not rent cars locally), help finance the stadium. The success at the ballot box for these types of financing mechanisms has been relatively high. However, as Baade and Matheson (2006) suggest, residents of one city will be tourists in another city, and they may then face high hotel and car rental taxes. Another drawback is that the number of tourists to a city may decline as the cost of visiting that city increases. Event planners (including those in the sport industry) are especially sensitive to hotel and rental car taxes when they are planning major, heavily attended events.

Nonetheless, these taxes are very popular and have been used to finance facilities for the Houston Astros (2% hotel tax increase and 5% car rental tax increase), Tampa Bay Rays (1% hotel tax increase), St. Louis Rams (3.5% hotel tax increase), Seattle Mariners (2% car rental tax increase), Indianapolis Colts (3% increase in hotel taxes and 2% increase in car rental taxes), Texas Rangers (a 2% hotel tax and 5% car rental tax), and Milwaukee Bucks (2.5% hotel tax rate and 3% car rental tax), to name a few.

King County (Seattle) sold bonds supported by an increase in the food and beverage (F&B) tax of 0.5%. It was the single largest source of financing, providing $150 million for the stadium. Marion County, containing Indianapolis, raised F&B taxes by 1% and expected to generate $274.5 million to pay off debts on Lucas Oil Stadium (see Exhibit 9.12).

These taxes generally fail the benefit principle, because tourists (as well as hoteliers and car rental operators) are not necessarily the users of sport facilities. Although F&B taxes do not satisfy the benefit principle, they do typically fulfill some sense of vertical equity, in that people with higher incomes spend more on food and beverages outside the home and, hence, pay a larger share of the taxes than people with lower incomes.

Mercedes Benz Stadium is using hotel taxes to pay off city bonds sold to fund construction, but after the first $200 million are collected (and used to pay off the bonds), a portion of the ongoing hotel taxes will go toward operations, maintenance, and stadium improvement (see Exhibit 9.13).

SIN TAXES

Sin taxes are another type of financing source that generally receives less opposition than others, presumably because the items being taxed are considered socially undesirable. These taxes are regressive, because people with low incomes tend to spend a higher proportion of their income on cigarettes and alcohol, relative to those with high incomes. The taxation of cigarettes and

EXHIBIT 9.12 Facility funding through tourism and food and beverage taxes.

LUCAS OIL STADIUM (INDIANAPOLIS COLTS)

Team	$50,000,000
City for termination of Colts' lease	$50,000,000
Marion County F&B tax (up 1%)	$274,500,000
County hotel tax (up 3%)	$134,200,000
County car rental tax (up 2%)	$30,500,000
Sports development tax	$85,400,000
Sporting event ticket tax (up 1%)	$36,600,000
Restaurant tax (up 1%)	$36,600,000
Sale of Colts license plates	$6,100,000
Total Funding Sources	$703,900,000

Note: Team will retain $121.5 million naming rights (20-year agreement).

Team retains all game day revenue and half of revenue from non-Colts events. City pays all operating and maintenance costs.

alcohol is sometimes claimed to have a side benefit of reducing smoking and drinking, but this assertion is paradoxical, because if the use of cigarettes and alcohol were to decline significantly, insufficient tax revenues would be generated to make sin taxes a feasible financing mechanism.

For construction of the baseball stadium where the Cleveland Indians play, financing included a 15-year tax on cigarettes and alcohol. Specifically, $3 per gallon was charged on liquor, 16 cents per gallon on beer, and 4.5 cents per pack of cigarettes. Minnesota used a cigarette tax as a small portion of its new NFL stadium financing ($26.5 million). These taxes remain less common than tourism taxes.

SALE OF GOVERNMENT ASSETS

Local, regional, and state governments own a great deal of land, and at times they determine that its best use is in the hands of private industry. Some sport facilities have been partially financed through government sales of land, with the proceeds serving as a direct source of funds. Land may also be an indirect source of financing (as discussed later in the chapter).

The Charlotte Bobcats' arena was financed partially through the local government's sale of land for $50 million and other assets for $25.8 million. Wayne County, Michigan, generated $20 million from the sale of some of its properties, to be used for the financing of Ford Field, where the Detroit Lions play.

EXHIBIT 9.13   Hotel tax funding for facility construction and ongoing operations.

MERCEDES BENZ STADIUM (ATLANTA FALCONS)

	Range of Sources	
City bonds backed by hotel-motel tax	$200,000,000	
Ongoing collection of hotel-motel taxes provided to team	$300,000,000	(1)
Construction sales tax rebates	$30,000,000	
Land costs	$24,000,000	
Team paying off debt on previous stadium (Georgia Dome)	$100,000,000	
Team-provided additional construction costs	$250,000,000	(2)
Team pays for infrastructure upgrades	$50,000,000	
Arthur Blank's foundation for neighborhood development	$15,000,000	
City of Atlanta surrounding neighborhood development	$15,000,000	
State of Georgia spending towards parking garage expansion	$40,000,000	
Naming rights and concessions rights	$128,000,000	
Personal seat license sales	$150,000,000	
NFL G-4 loan program	$200,000,000	
Total Funding Sources	$1,502,000,000	

(1) After the first $200 million in city bonds is paid off, then 39.3% of the 7% hotel-motel tax (2.75% tax) would go toward operations, maintenance, and stadium improvement.
(2) Team is responsible for construction overruns.

STATE APPROPRIATIONS

Many sport facilities receive some funding from their state governments. Local residents might be apt to back a stadium project if they know that some money is coming from the state. For instance, Miller Park received $36 million from the State of Wisconsin, $18 million each from the county and city, and additional funding from other sources (some of which were also public). The recently opened Fiserv Forum (home of the Milwaukee Bucks) received $80 million from the State of Wisconsin which sold bonds (to be partially paid off from a ticket surcharge). The St. Louis Rams' stadium received 50% of its public financing from the State of Missouri. Similarly, the Tennessee Titans' facility received $55 million from the State of Tennessee, through general obligation bonds. In other situations, the state may be willing to pay for related infrastructure and not the facility directly, such as the State of Georgia's $40 million toward a parking garage expansion near Mercedes Benz Stadium.

REVENUES FROM TICKETS AND PARKING

To satisfy the benefit principle, many facility financiers are turning to ticket taxes and parking revenues or taxes to help pay for stadium construction and maintenance costs. Typically, these sources do not cover the bulk of the financing, but they can make an important contribution. Many political jurisdictions (cities, townships, counties, and states) require a vote to raise taxes, but in some situations a "surcharge" does not require a vote. The economics of a tax versus a surcharge are not much different, yet the law in many cases does not require a vote for a surcharge. Facilities for the Mariners, Phillies, Pacers, Browns, Eagles, Bucks, Oilers, and Lightning have been partially financed through ticket taxes at the facility or general admission taxes at all local sporting events. At NRG Stadium in Houston, fans pay a 10% ticket tax (not to exceed $2 per ticket) and a $1 ticket surcharge. In many cases, local sales taxes also apply to the purchase of tickets. For the Arizona Cardinals' football stadium, a $4.50 ticket surcharge is generating $35 million in stadium financing.

Parking taxes or surcharges function in the same way as ticket taxes. City parking revenues generated over $10 million of the $157 million cost for the Amalie Arena, home of the Tampa Bay Lightning. NRG Stadium has a 10% parking tax. At the arena for the Minnesota Wild, game day parking revenues are helping to pay off its $65 million bond from the City of St. Paul. At Ford Field, the local sport authority (set up to build and manage the local sport facilities) sold the rights to parking revenues to the nearby Detroit Tigers for $20 million, even though Ford Field is home to the NFL's Detroit Lions. The Tigers used the revenue for stadium funding. The Seahawks' stadium is expected to generate $4.4 million in parking tax revenues, to fund about 1% of total stadium costs. The City of Sacramento plans to rely on parking revenues from its city-owned parking garages to help pay off a planned $258 million bond sale covering its portion of financing for the new Golden 1 Center. The backup plan, if needed, is to rely on hotel taxes. As shown in Exhibit 9.14, Globe Life Field (opened in 2020 to host MLB's Rangers) is partially paying off construction costs using a 10% ticket tax and a $3 parking tax. These sources continue to be popular, as they satisfy the user benefits principle.

LOTTERIES AND GAMING REVENUES

State-run lotteries and local gaming establishments are creative, non-sport sources of financing. The Baltimore Orioles were one of the first teams to play in a new stadium built during the latest wave of stadium financing. In 1992, the Orioles began play at Camden Yards, for which most of the construction costs were financed through lease revenue bonds and notes backed by special sport-themed state lottery tickets. The Seattle Mariners and Seahawks play in facilities that are funded partially from state lottery revenues. For Safeco Field, home of the Mariners, $50 million in bonds was secured by lottery revenue related to newly created lottery games. Public funding for the Seahawks from sport-related lottery games amounted to nearly $128 million.

The Pittsburgh Penguins flirted with moving to Kansas City but stayed in Pittsburgh because a financing deal was put in place that included approximately $7.5 million per year, for 30 years, in payments from PITG Gaming's casino income. An additional $7.5 million per year comes from the State of Pennsylvania's slot machine economic development fund.

EXHIBIT 9.14 Facility funding through ticket and parking taxes.

GLOBE LIFE FIELD (TEXAS RANGERS)

	Range of Sources	
City bonds backed by taxes	$500,000,000	(1)
Team contribution backed by revenues and taxes	$400,000,000	(2)
Ticket tax and parking revenues	$300,000,000	(3)
Total Funding Sources	$1,200,000,000	

(1) 0.5% sales tax, 2% hotel occupancy tax, 5% vehicle rental tax, Rangers rent payments of $2 million per year.

(2) Team is responsible for construction overruns. Naming rights of $11 million per year (through 2048) goes to the team.

(3) A 10% ticket tax and $3 parking tax will go towards stadium financing.

Lottery and gaming sources of funding are generally considered regressive, failing the horizontal equity principle because people with lower incomes play the lottery or engage in gaming activities more often, and spend a higher proportion of their income or wealth in doing so, than those with higher incomes. Proponents of the use of lottery and gaming revenue often note that these activities are optional.

PLAYER INCOME TAXES

Individuals in favor of charging athletes of visiting teams an income tax draw a parallel to the use of non-resident taxes, such as tourism taxes, to help fund a sport facility. It seems logical that the athletes who benefit from the facility should help to fund it. Many states and cities tax the income of visiting players, usually charging between 1% and 4% of the salary earned during the athlete's time in the state or city. Most of the revenues go into the political jurisdiction's general fund. However, the City of Pittsburgh uses the revenue directly to pay off the bonds on its baseball and football stadiums (PNC Park and Heinz Field). Opponents of these taxes argue that no other visiting entertainers are taxed—only athletes in major professional sports. Because minor league athletes and those outside the "Big 4" are not necessarily taxed, this tax raises questions of fairness, although it satisfies the vertical equity principle.

A public financing proposal in 2003 in Washington DC included a player income tax that was projected to generate approximately $5 million per year in funding, which was to go directly to paying off the public's portion of stadium debt. The financing plan ultimately chosen did not include this tax.

UTILITY AND BUSINESS LICENSE TAXES

Utility taxes are state and local taxes on energy consumed, which are collected along with customers' utility payments. General business taxes include state and local corporate income taxes and sales and use taxes collected from businesses. The Washington Nationals play in a baseball stadium that is

EXHIBIT 9.15 Example of PILOT financing.

YANKEE STADIUM (NEW YORK YANKEES)		
	Range of Sources	
City of New York Bonds (2006)	$942,500,000	(1)
City of New York Bonds (2009)	$259,000,000	(1)
City interest earnings	$46,400,000	(2)
Yankees cash payment	$77,000,000	
Equity contributions (Yankees)	$225,500,000	(3)
Total Funding Sources	$1,550,400,000	

(1) All tax revenues related to Yankee Stadium are used to pay off the bonds, making this a PILOT (payments in lieu of taxes) financing plan.

(2) Interest earned by the city after selling the bonds, during the period of construction.

(3) Yankees equity contributions come from new revenue streams in the new stadium (e.g., suites and sponsorships).

The team retains all revenues (including naming rights), but pays operating costs and PILOTs and makes an annual lease payment to the city of $10 (enabling the team to obtain revenue sharing from MLB).

funded partially by $14 million per year in general business taxes (collected from businesses with more than $3 million in annual revenue) and $15 million per year in utility tax revenues. For the FedExForum, home of the Memphis Grizzlies, financing included $30.4 million in revenues from the city's electric utility. Instead of the utility paying franchise, property, or sales taxes to the City of Memphis, Memphis Light, Gas, and Water (MLGW) provides **payments in lieu of taxes (PILOT)**. Essentially, the city is simply using some of the payments that it receives from MLGW to pay for the stadium. PILOT financing is common when the land used for a stadium does not generate property taxes (because it is owned by the government). The Yankees' new stadium used PILOT financing for most of the cost of the stadium. The tax revenues related directly to the stadium (e.g., sales taxes) have been directed toward paying off the New York City bonds that were sold in 2006 and 2009, as shown in Exhibit 9.15.

REALLOCATION OF EXISTING BUDGET

In a very few cases, cities have funded sport facilities through their existing budgets, either by reallocating budget dollars or by assuming new incremental revenues from a specific source (e.g., hotel taxes). This funding method is uncommon because the public is often not willing to reduce funding for existing government programs in order to build sport facilities. Allegheny County, Pennsylvania, partially funded new stadiums for the Pittsburgh Pirates and Steelers through reallocation of its existing Regional Asset District (RAD) budget (which included local revenues from certain sales taxes). Allegheny County was successful in this approach, in part because the RAD was already funding the existing Three Rivers Stadium. The savings achieved by demolishing Three Rivers Stadium were applied to the new buildings. The same concept was used in Philadelphia, when the city funded Veterans Stadium. This approach may be appropriate in any situation where the public sector funds operating costs of the current facility. In other situations, states have simply budgeted for these projects in their general fund. Pennsylvania, Tennessee, and Ohio are examples of states that have assisted local municipalities in funding sport facilities through budget allocations or through debt as part of the state's capital budget.

INDIRECT SOURCES OF PUBLIC FINANCING

Indirect sources of public financing include non-cash sources (land donations, infrastructure improvements) and exemptions from payments such as property or sales taxes (i.e., tax abatements).

Land donations. The San Francisco 49ers struggled in 2008 to develop a stadium plan for a location in the San Francisco Bay Area. In June 2008, voters in the city approved an advisory measure (a non-binding measure, similar to a survey of residents) to allow a developer to use 720 acres of city-owned land for free to build a football stadium and other structures. A common misperception about arrangements such as this one is that if a city or county provides land for free or at discount for the construction of a sport facility (whether it is given outright to the team owner or is leased), the cost is zero, because no dollars change hands. However, the actual cost to the political jurisdiction includes the **opportunity cost**—the lost opportunity to do something else with the land, such as sell the land to a private entity at a market price. Most stadium financing plans have some form of opportunity cost, although it is rarely mentioned as part of the total cost of the facility. The Islanders supposedly have leased land for their arena at below-market rates (deMause, 2018). Similarly, the Angels may end up purchasing land from the City of Anaheim at a discount (Custodio, 2019).

Perhaps a more important type of "land donation" is the government's use of eminent domain to obtain access to land owned by private citizens. In November 2009, the New York State Court of Appeals ruled that New York City could secure the land needed for the New Jersey Nets' new basketball arena in Brooklyn by forcing current residents and businesses to move and paying them a fair market value for their real estate.

Infrastructure improvements. Infrastructure improvements to accommodate new facilities—such as freeway exits, road expansions, parking lot entrances and exits, and sewer and electrical systems—are most often paid for by local and state governments (or sometimes the federal government, through special transportation grants). These costs are rarely included in the overall cost of financing a facility. One could argue that any new use of land would require some form of infrastructure improvements, so these should not be considered when sport facility construction is compared to other options. However, this would be true only if the developer would not be paying any of these costs and if the cost of infrastructure improvements would be the same for various alternative uses. The City of Orlando paid for the $100 million in land and infrastructure improvements needed for the new arena for the Orlando Magic, as shown in Exhibit 9.16.

Tax abatements. Tax abatements exempt the beneficiary from paying certain taxes, such as property or sales taxes. Thus, the local government is helping to finance the stadium by *not* charging the franchise taxes that would

EXHIBIT 9.16   Examples of land and infrastructure improvements paid for by a city.

AMWAY CENTER (ORLANDO MAGIC)

	Range of Sources	
Team sources	$70,000,000	(1)
County bonds	$310,000,000	(2)
City	$100,000,000	(3)
Total Funding Sources	$480,000,000	

(1) The team can choose how to cover this, but it typically comes from new suites and sponsorships.

(2) This is covered by a Tourist Development Tax increase of 6%. Team has to guarantee $100 million of the bonds.

(3) The city will pick up the cost of land and infrastructure improvements.

City of Orlando keeps non-Magic event ticket revenue. Team covers construction cost overruns. Team will pay $1 million per year in rent for 30 years and an additional $1.75 million per year (increasing at 3% per year) in additional fees.

presumably have been paid by an alternative user of the space. The City of Sandy, Utah, for example, provided a $10 million property tax rebate to the ownership group that built an MLS stadium there.

Most sport facilities are publicly owned and leased to the team that plays there, which exempts the team from paying property taxes altogether. As will be discussed in Chapter 12, many states are reviewing these situations to determine whether these are actually private businesses operating in public buildings. In Florida, sport teams are now required to pay property taxes (although each county can lower the property tax payments or even reduce the assessed value of the facility). The Columbus Blue Jackets pay property taxes that amount to about half of what would normally be paid based on the county assessor's valuation of Nationwide Arena.

The Houston Texans, an NFL team, play in NRG Stadium, whose owners receive a sales tax rebate to cover part of the cost of the stadium. The Jaguars received similar financing in Jacksonville, Florida. The Miami Marlins are also receiving a sales tax rebate, on tickets and concessions in their new facility, which is expected to provide $2 million per year that the team can put toward stadium financing.

Appendix 9.A summarizes some of the more common forms of public financing for stadiums and arenas.

Calculating Public Payments for Stadium Financing

To calculate the annual payment for a general obligation bond—for instance, so that public officials and residents will understand the annual cost—we use a payment schedule table similar to the one for the Minnesota Twins ballpark (shown in Exhibit 9.17). That project has a relatively simple financing

EXHIBIT 9.17   Example payment schedule for a new Minnesota Twins ballpark.

NO.	PAYMENT DATE	BEGINNING BALANCE	INTEREST	PRINCIPAL	ENDING BALANCE	CUMULATIVE INTEREST	TOTAL PERIODIC PAYMENT	PAYMENT PER RESIDENT
1	12/15/2008	$392,000,000.00	$19,521,600.00	$5,920,455.88	$386,079,544.12	$19,521,600.00	$25,442,055.88	$22.67
2	12/15/2009	386,079,544.12	19,226,761.30	6,215,294.59	379,864,249.53	38,748,361.30	25,442,055.88	22.56
3	12/15/2010	379,864,249.53	18,917,239.63	6,524,816.26	373,339,433.28	57,665,600.92	25,442,055.88	22.45
4	12/15/2011	373,339,433.28	18,592,303.78	6,849,752.11	366,489,681.17	76,257,904.70	25,442,055.88	22.34
5	12/15/2012	366,489,681.17	18,251,186.12	7,190,869.76	359,298,811.41	94,509,090.82	25,442,055.88	22.23
6	12/15/2013	359,298,811.41	17,893,080.81	7,548,975.07	351,749,836.34	112,402,171.63	25,442,055.88	22.12
7	12/15/2014	351,749,836.34	17,517,141.85	7,924,914.03	343,824,922.30	129,919,313.48	25,442,055.88	22.01
8	12/15/2015	343,824,922.30	17,122,481.13	8,319,574.75	335,505,347.55	147,041,794.61	25,442,055.88	21.90
9	12/15/2016	335,505,347.55	16,708,166.31	8,733,889.57	326,771,457.98	163,749,960.92	25,442,055.88	21.79
10	12/15/2017	326,771,457.98	16,273,218.61	9,168,837.28	317,602,620.70	180,023,179.53	25,442,055.88	21.68
11	12/15/2018	317,602,620.70	15,816,610.51	9,625,445.37	307,977,175.33	195,839,790.04	25,442,055.88	21.57
12	12/15/2019	307,977,175.33	15,337,263.33	10,104,792.55	297,872,382.78	211,177,053.37	25,442,055.88	21.46
13	12/15/2020	297,872,382.78	14,834,044.66	10,608,011.22	287,264,371.56	226,011,098.03	25,442,055.88	21.36
14	12/15/2021	287,264,371.56	14,305,765.70	11,136,290.18	276,128,081.38	240,316,863.74	25,442,055.88	21.25
15	12/15/2022	276,128,081.38	13,751,178.45	11,690,877.43	264,437,203.95	254,068,042.19	25,442,055.88	21.14

#	Date							
16	12/15/2023	264,437,203.95	13,168,972.76	12,273,083.13	252,164,120.82	267,237,014.94	25,442,055.88	21.04
17	12/15/2024	252,164,120.82	12,557,773.22	12,884,282.67	239,279,838.16	279,794,788.16	25,442,055.88	20.93
18	12/15/2025	239,279,838.16	11,916,135.94	13,525,919.94	225,753,918.22	291,710,924.10	25,442,055.88	20.83
19	12/15/2026	225,753,918.22	11,242,545.13	14,199,510.76	211,554,407.46	302,953,469.23	25,442,055.88	20.73
20	12/15/2027	211,554,407.46	10,535,409.49	14,906,646.39	196,647,761.07	313,488,878.72	25,442,055.88	20.62
21	12/15/2028	196,647,761.07	9,793,058.50	15,648,997.38	180,998,763.69	323,281,937.22	25,442,055.88	20.52
22	12/15/2029	180,998,763.69	9,013,738.43	16,428,317.45	164,570,446.24	332,295,675.65	25,442,055.88	20.42
23	12/15/2030	164,570,446.24	8,195,608.22	17,246,447.66	147,323,998.58	340,491,283.88	25,442,055.88	20.32
24	12/15/2031	147,323,998.58	7,336,735.13	18,105,320.75	129,218,677.82	347,828,019.01	25,442,055.88	20.22
25	12/15/2032	129,218,677.82	6,435,090.16	19,006,965.73	110,211,712.10	354,263,109.16	25,442,055.88	20.12
26	12/15/2033	110,211,712.10	5,488,543.26	19,953,512.62	90,258,199.48	359,751,652.42	25,442,055.88	20.02
27	12/15/2034	90,258,199.48	4,494,858.33	20,947,197.55	69,311,001.93	364,246,510.76	25,442,055.88	19.92
28	12/15/2035	69,311,001.93	3,451,687.90	21,990,367.99	47,320,633.94	367,698,198.65	25,442,055.88	19.82
29	12/15/2036	47,320,633.94	2,356,567.57	23,085,488.31	24,235,145.63	370,054,766.22	25,442,055.88	19.72
30	12/15/2037	24,235,145.63	1,206,910.25	24,235,145.63	0.00	371,261,676.48	25,442,055.88	19.62
							$763,261,676.48	

Notes: Population assumed to grow at an annual rate of 0.5%.

This table shows a payment schedule for a constant payment. The actual payment plan combines variable and fixed interest rates expected to average 4.98%. The average annual payment will differ from year to year but will be slightly lower than that shown in the table.

mechanism. Hennepin County is paying for 75% of the stadium and related infrastructure through a 0.15% sales tax increase. Tax-free county bonds worth a total of $392 million were sold and are being paid back over 30 years. The payment schedule in Exhibit 9.17 shows the annual payments on the 30-year bonds, which are paying an average 4.98% interest rate. Note that the total payments (given at the bottom of the table) far exceed the original cost, because the interest is being paid over a lengthy period of time. To avoid having to pay $392 million during the construction period, the residents paid only $25.4 million per year, but will have to do so for 30 years. The annual payments are constant, but the portion of those payments that goes toward paying off principal (as opposed to interest) increases, until the final year, when the entire project is paid off. As of 2019, due to higher-than-expected ballpark sales tax collections, and lower interest rates than planned, the stadium debt is on schedule to be paid off ten years earlier (in 2027).

To make the payment schedule more meaningful, we can divide the annual payment by the population of the political jurisdiction paying for the venue, to get a sense of what it is costing per person to finance the stadium. Hennepin County had a population of 1,122,093 in 2008. Thus, the payment per person began at over $22 per year and will decrease to under $20 per year, assuming a population growth rate of 0.5%. Given that the actual growth rate of the county's population from 2008 to 2018 was 1.1%, the cost per person was $20.20 in 2018 instead of the estimated $21.57. See the far right column in Exhibit 9.17.

PRIVATE FINANCING

A fair question to ask is: why aren't sport facilities 100% privately financed, like the buildings of other industries? As discussed above, one reason is that private investors may not be willing to build spectacular palaces that lure many high-profile events, because much of the revenue will flow to businesses outside the building. For this reason, the public has to contribute to the construction. But what is the private return on new sport facilities?

Private Return on New Facilities

As discussed at the beginning of this chapter, private returns on new sport facilities can be quite substantial. Put in terms of attendance, Coates and Humphreys (2005) show that the impact is largest in Major League Baseball, with a typical franchise selling about 2.5 million incremental tickets over the eight seasons that follow the opening of a new facility. An NFL team sells only about 138,000 additional tickets over a five-year period (the likely reason for the lower number is that most NFL teams sell out even in old stadiums). In terms of return on investment, Baade (2003) shows that MLB teams earn an ROI of about 20.5% when they build new stadiums. For a new football stadium for the Washington Redskins, analysis showed that the maximum private investment that would break even would be only $155 million. Anything beyond that would create a loss for the investor. To get a $500 million stadium built, the public would have to finance 70% of it.

Private Financing Sources and Techniques

The sources of private financing are unlimited, in the sense that an owner can use whatever money he or she possesses, if he or she so chooses. Billionaire owners can tap their private net wealth. However, many choose to tie the financing sources to the franchise itself, rather than to their own finances. For instance, most stadium financing packages include annual rent payments from the team to the owner of the facility. However, annual rents range from zero to a few million dollars (e.g., the Texas Rangers pay $3.5 million per year). Rents, therefore, cannot cover the entire private facility financing obligation.

CONTRACTUALLY OBLIGATED INCOME

Contractually obligated income (COI) is a revenue stream that a team receives under multi-year contracts. For example, the San Francisco Giants signed luxury suite holders to five- and seven-year contracts and club seat holders to three- and five-year contracts, thus nearly guaranteeing those revenue streams. Other possibilities for COI are multi-year pouring rights sold to concessionaires, naming rights, and sponsorship. Often, it is important that the team secure these revenue streams up front (or sign contracts with terms of five to seven years or more). These revenue sources may serve as collateral for loans. For instance, a team can pledge as collateral the revenues from naming rights, sponsorship rights, pouring or concessionaire's rights, premium seating deposits, or ticket surcharges. In 2000, the San Francisco Giants borrowed $170 million from Chase Manhattan Bank with collateral from naming rights, signage, and other COI. The team also collected charter seat license revenue of approximately $70 million. In 2013, the San Francisco 49ers signed a 20-year naming rights deal with Levi Strauss for $220 million, of which 70% will go to help pay off the government bonds sold to get construction underway (Exhibit 9.18). The 100% privately financed MetLife Stadium, opened in 2010, hosts both the New York Jets and the New York Giants. MetLife is paying $425 million over 25 years for the naming rights.

ASSET-BACKED SECURITIES

Instead of borrowing from a bank, a franchise may package guaranteed COI or expected revenue streams together and sell bonds based on these assets, known as **asset-backed securities (ABS)**. This technique, called **securitization**, is most often used with financial instruments that pay interest, instead of COIs or revenue streams. Because COIs provide known and consistent payments, they can be securitized in this way, as can other predictable revenue streams. Staples Center in Los Angeles was financed partially through securitization. The "security" is derived from the naming rights revenue from Staples, ten corporate founding partners' agreements, two concessions agreements, premium seat revenues, a ticket sales contract with TicketMaster, and the revenues from 101 of 160 luxury suites. The naming rights deal alone is reportedly worth $100 million over 20 years. The $315 million in bonds are taxable, pay an interest rate of 7.653%, and mature in 27 years.

PUBLIC/PRIVATE PARTNERSHIPS

The dominant paradigm over the past few decades in stadium financing has been public/private partnerships, with the major tenant (e.g., the team)

EXHIBIT 9.18   Example of naming rights revenue use in stadium funding.

LEVI'S STADIUM (SAN FRANCISCO 49ERS)		
	Range of Sources	
G-4 loan from the NFL to the 49ers franchise	$200,000,000	(1)
Naming rights revenue	$154,000,000	(2)
Tax increment bonds	$42,000,000	(3)
Parking garage revenue bonds	$17,000,000	(3)
Electric utility contribution	$20,000,000	(3)
Hotel tax increase (2.0%)	$65,000,000	(3)
Team sources such as PSLs, suites, and sponsorships	$613,000,000	
Total Funding Sources	$1,111,000,000	

(1) The NFL has created its fourth loan vehicle (G-4) used to help finance stadium construction.

(2) Levi's agreed to pay $220 million over 20 years for naming rights to the local government. The team gets 30% of that.

(3) These are local government sources of revenue.

Construction and operating cost overruns are paid for by the team. The team will pay $30 million per year in stadium costs but get half of non-NFL event revenue.

generating equity via stadium-related revenues and additional capital provided by a municipal bond that was also backed by stadium revenues. This paradigm does not preclude the use of revenues not directly related to the stadium, such as hotel and car rental taxes, but it places the onus of payment on those who use and benefit from the facility. A public/private partnership is essentially a co-production of a sport facility with the goal of producing surplus value that would not be produced by either partner working alone. For example, a private entity might have difficulty improving the ingress and egress for a new facility without government cooperation. Similarly, a government entity is not likely to be in a position to maximize the revenues within a new facility.

As Ziets (2002) had noted, the trend in funding of new sport facilities began shifting away from tax increases. Public officials have continued to look to alternative sources of capital, including

- taxes generated directly from the facility, the team, players, and other facility users or vendors
- taxes generated from redevelopment surrounding the facility
- special assessments in a uniquely identified sports and entertainment district.

The most compelling justification for a strategy of this type is that, in effect, the users or beneficiaries who frequent the district fund the facility over time through their use of the district. These mega-real estate projects are often developed by partnerships of public and private entities. For instance, the public entity may set up special tax districts to collect revenue to help pay for the district financing and may provide infrastructure for the area (e.g., roads, water, and electricity). The private developer might build the facility and the surrounding district, with the help of many private businesses.

The issue of who pays—along with many others—is a matter of public policy. This section discusses, first, the sometimes congruent but often conflicting goals of public and private parties and, second, the public policy issues that affect public/private partnerships related to facility financing. As noted above, recent facility construction in large metropolitan areas has been more toward private financing (e.g., Chase Center and SoFi Stadium).

Goals of Public versus Private Parties

Public and private parties in partnership focus on different goals. Franchises are concerned with league restrictions, site/design control, facility control/management, revenue control, and cash flow. Most leagues restrict the debt ratio that a team may establish. For instance, an NBA team in 2008 could have at most $175 million in debt. That has been increased to $375 million. An NHL team, on the other hand, can have debt up to half of the franchise's value (Kaplan, 2014).

The financing goals of team owners are to maximize contractually obligated income and minimize debt service payments and coverage requirements. Team owners also desire a strong voice in the design of a facility in order to maximize COI, even if they are paying a minority of the cost of construction. The revenue potential of a sport facility is affected by the number and design of luxury suites, club seats, food venues, and so forth. Often, the owner will advocate a higher total cost, in order to provide better amenities and generate better contracts for luxury seating, than the government counterpart or partner will favor.

In the past, team owners did not manage the publicly owned facilities in which their teams played. In recent decades, team owners have desired complete management of the sport facility. This allows them not only to control scheduling for their teams but also to schedule other events, such as family shows, motorcycle or monster truck events, and professional wrestling. Many leases provide for the team owner to retain most, if not all, of the revenues generated by the facility. Management of the facility and control over revenue are complementary. Team owners have done a much better job of getting the most use out of facilities than have government managers. The management of facilities is currently an issue in Japan, where local government owns and operates most buildings, and there is no strong push to maximize net revenues flowing from the buildings.

The financing goals of government in these partnerships are to maximize the credit quality of pledged revenues, maintain debt service coverage, and maintain a reserve fund. Government agencies tasked with overseeing sport facilities also care about resource allocation, the amount of public financing required, the impact on the government's borrowing credit, the government's share in the upside of a facility (e.g., revenues from naming rights, parking, and rent), and the possibility that the team might relocate if the facility is not built.

The question of resource allocation is always of concern to local and regional governments. Is $200 million of the public's money better spent on a sport facility or on a new library and school? As discussed above, there may or may not be justification for spending millions of dollars from public coffers on a sport facility. Most cities limit how much outstanding debt they will take on. Public financing that is to be paid back from sources other than the general fund, such as sources related to the stadium itself (e.g., ticket taxes and parking revenues), does not typically count against a city's debt limit. Washington DC used revenue bonds rather than general obligation bonds to help finance the Washington Nationals' ballpark. One of the reasons for the use of revenue bonds may be that they do not count against the city's debt limit.

SIDEBAR 9.E   Where Do We Start? The Mayor Knows

In the early stages of a feasibility study to build a new arena for the Sacramento Kings, the mayor of Sacramento noted that the following issues had to be addressed before any type of public/private financing partnership could be determined:

1. Which sources of financing would require voter approval and which could be passed by the local government without a vote?
2. Of the possible financing sources, who would pay for them—would users of the arena pay, or local residents, or tourists, or local businesses?
3. Would the arena be paid for now, or in the distant future with government bonds of 20- or 30-year terms?
4. Who would be responsible for cost overruns or financing shortfalls?
5. Who would pay the costs of selling the various revenue streams at the arena (naming rights, sponsorships, luxury suites, and so forth), given that the city would own the arena, but the team would manage and operate it?
6. Between the city and the team, who would keep which revenue streams, such as parking, concessions, and naming rights?

Public policy analysis of stadium projects focuses on these and other essential questions.

When the Cleveland Browns relocated to Baltimore to become the Baltimore Ravens, the City of Cleveland immediately went to the NFL with a request for an expansion team for the city, which it received a few years later. The cost to the public of building a stadium for the expansion team was approximately $200 million (another $100 million was private money). According to people familiar with the situation, to keep the Browns from moving to Baltimore would have cost approximately $190 million (and this likely would not have resolved the owner's personal desire to move).

Public Policy Issues and Public/Private Partnerships

Before policy makers determine the type of financing sources to be used in a public/private partnership, they must consider some important issues in regard to financing, such as the following:

- Who will own the facility?
- Should the public financing package be put to a vote?
- What should be the payment terms?
- Who will be responsible for cost overruns?
- Who will pay the costs of and keep the revenue from future revenue streams?
- What sources of public financing can be used?

OWNERSHIP

Most likely, the first question that policy makers will consider is who will own the facility: the major tenant (or other private organization) or the city, county, state, or a combination thereof? Most facilities are owned by a public entity, often a joint authority of multiple political jurisdictions. For example, the Oakland Arena in Oakland, California, is owned by the Oakland-Alameda County Coliseum Authority, a joint authority of the City of Oakland and Alameda County.

Why would a public entity own a facility? The most obvious reason relates to property taxes. Public entities (i.e., cities or stadium authorities) do not pay property taxes, but private businesses do. For a $475 million stadium sitting on $25 million worth of land, a 1% property tax would cost about $5 million per year to the stadium owner. The franchise saves $5 million per year in property taxes when the city owns the stadium and leases it to the major tenant. As discussed in Chapter 12, some states are changing these laws to begin charging the major tenant a property tax. Another reason that a city might own a stadium is that it has paid most of the cost of building the structure and can use it for additional events. In the end, however, cities often allow the team to manage the entire facility and all of its events. An example is the new Dallas Cowboys stadium in Arlington, Texas, renamed AT&T Stadium in 2013 after a naming rights deal was arrived at worth a reported $17 million to $19 million per year.

VOTER APPROVAL

A second important decision for policy makers is whether the public financing package should be voted upon by local residents or decided upon by politicians without a popular vote. Some sources of financing, such as raising sales taxes or hotel taxes, require voter approval in most jurisdictions, but reallocation of existing sales tax revenues often does not require voter approval. There have been instances when voters turned down a public financing package, but a version was approved outside the voting process. In Milwaukee, for instance, a statewide vote to create a sports lottery to fund a new Brewers stadium failed, so the state legislature passed a bill that raised the sales tax by 0.1% in the counties surrounding the stadium (see Exhibit 9.1). The decision to hold a public vote opens up many sources of financing, but compliance with a requirement for a public vote can be very costly. It also adds risk to the process: all of the work and effort involved in building a financing package might go for naught if the public votes no. However, if this is the will of the people, so be it.

In Texas, the residents of Arlington voted 55% to 45% in favor of spending over $400 million toward a billion-dollar stadium and associated complex for the Cowboys. Along with a contribution from the county, the city agreed to increase the sales, hotel, and car rental taxes and to add a parking tax and admissions

EXHIBIT 9.19   A public/private finance package with taxes approved by voters.

AT&T STADIUM (DALLAS COWBOYS)

	Range of Sources	
Team rent payments	$20,000,000	(1)
County contribution	$25,000,000	
Admissions tax (10%) and parking tax ($3)	$115,000,000	(2)
City tax increases: sales (0.5%), hotel (2.0%), car rental (5.0%)	$304,000,000	(2)
NFL G-3 loan	$150,000,000	
Team's private sources (usually from sponsorships and premium seating sales)	$580,000,000	(3)
Total Funding Sources	$1,194,000,000	

(1) The team will pay this to the city over the life of the lease.
(2) Financing approved by public vote.
(3) The team sold hundreds of suites and dozens of sponsorships worth hundreds of millions of dollars.

Five years after opening, the team landed a $17–$19 million per year naming rights deal from AT&T.

tax at the stadium. The team pays rent toward the debt service payments, funds the rest of the facility itself (through sponsorship and premium seat sales), and controls the stadium (Exhibit 9.19). This public/private partnership is on pace to pay off the public debt much earlier than expected.

PAYMENT TERMS

A third policy decision to be made prior to choosing financing sources is whether to pay for the facility now or later. Some facilities have been paid for with a current increase in sales taxes, whose revenues pay off the facility within a few years (as in Denver and San Antonio). Many more facilities are financed through the sale of 20- or 30-year bonds paid for through sales tax revenues; the actual payments occur over the 20- or 30-year term of the bonds. This is a fundamental decision for all sorts of public financing, not just sport-related financing. It is essentially the same as deciding whether to buy a house with cash or take out a 30-year mortgage. The total payments will be much higher, but they will occur over a longer period of time, thus pushing most of the cost into the future.

RESPONSIBILITY FOR COST OVERRUNS

As with many complex construction projects, the final actual cost of a stadium or arena often exceeds the expected cost. A study done in the mid-1990s of 14 facilities showed that cost overruns for stadiums averaged about 73% (see Bess, 1995). Policy makers must determine in advance who will be responsible for

EXHIBIT 9.20   Cost overruns in stadium construction.

SAFECO FIELD (SEATTLE MARINERS)

Lottery proceeds	$50,000,000	
Team bank loans	$25,000,000	
Interest income	$5,000,000	
County GO bonds (0.5% F&B tax)	$150,000,000	
County GO bonds (2% rental car tax)	$71,000,000	
County GO bonds (0.017% state tax credit)	$71,000,000	(1)
5% admission tax	$25,000,000	
Personal seat licenses	$20,000,000	
Team owner (covering cost overruns)	$100,000,000	
Total Funding Sources	$517,000,000	

(1) The state has a 6.5% sales tax, of which 0.017% will be returned to the county.

cost overruns—the public entity, the franchise, or some other organization. The Mariners' new stadium cost $517 million, about $100 million over budget. The franchise paid the additional costs, thus protecting the public (see Exhibit 9.20). As part of the negotiation, a city can protect itself from cost overruns, as Arlington did with respect to the Cowboys stadium. The city agreed to pay the lesser of $325 million or 50%—an important consideration given that the facility cost over $1 billion. The Atlanta Falcons ownership was responsible for any cost overruns for Mercedes Benz Stadium.

MANAGEMENT OF FUTURE REVENUE STREAMS

When a new sport facility is created, many revenue streams must be initiated and managed. The sale of **naming rights**—the right to place a firm's name on a facility (a form of sponsorship)—is paramount to the financing and completion of a new stadium. Policy makers must determine who will pay the costs of selling those rights. Similarly, who will pay the costs of selling luxury suites, concessions rights, sponsorship rights, PSLs, and so forth? The overall cost of selling these revenue sources frequently runs into the millions of dollars. Additionally, when it comes time to renegotiate these deals, who will pay *those* costs?

Even more important is the question of who will keep which of the revenue streams. Although the cost of selling those assets is substantial, it is a fraction of the revenue that will flow from them. In the case of naming rights, the purchaser often pledges the payment for them as part of the financing package. As discussed in the section on private sources of financing, naming rights revenue can exceed $100 million (e.g., Philips paid $168 million in a 20-year deal). In some very complicated leases, the public entity shared a small portion of ticket sales (via an admissions tax) and parking (perhaps the first $500,000 after the first $1 million) or even was able to rent out the facility on some non-game days for certain events in which it would share net revenues.

More recently, cities have opted to exit the stadium management business and allow the team or a third party (such as AEG or Service Management Group [SMG]) to manage the facility in exchange for a fee. Often the managing entity receives a portion of net revenues from hosting any events in the facilities, plus a minimum management fee. For example, SMG signed a deal to manage the Liberty Bowl stadium under which it will receive 20% of any revenues above $1.66 million (Masilak, 2008).

FINANCING SOURCES

A key general question about the sources of financing, addressed earlier in this chapter, is what sources of public financing can be used and who, ultimately, will pay for those sources. Just about everyone in a community pays a little when the source is a general sales tax. On the other hand, only attendees of events at the facility pay when the source is a ticket tax. This is probably the most important fundamental factor in facility financing.

CONCLUSION

As the nominal and real costs of sport facilities continue to rise, the sources and methods of financing have become very complex and creative. Moreover, partnerships between political jurisdictions and team owners have increased, as has the public's understanding of the benefits and costs of sport facilities. What will the next wave of stadium financing bring?

Concept Check

1. How can a stadium or arena be built without putting too much financial burden on a local government?
2. How does location affect the costs of a stadium or arena project? What are the pros and cons of locating a stadium downtown versus out near a highway?
3. When the construction ends up costing more than initial projections, should the local government be responsible for paying the additional costs?
4. Of the following list of public financing sources, which ones satisfy the principles of horizontal equity, vertical equity, the benefit principle, and efficiency?

general obligation bonds	certificates of participation
revenue bonds	tax increment financing and property taxes
sales tax	tourism and food and beverage taxes
sin taxes	sale of government assets
state appropriations	ticket and parking revenues
player income taxes	lotteries and gaming revenues

land donations   reallocation of existing budget

infrastructure   tax abatements
  improvements

Practice Problems

Calculate the savings in total construction costs from issuing a $100 million GOB paying out at 5% rather than a revenue bond paying out at 7%, both with a 25-year maturity.

Case Analysis

Financing an MLB Stadium

Develop a public financing plan for a new baseball stadium in Oakland, California, to host the Oakland A's. The stadium will have a total cost of $750 million, and the public will finance 35% of the construction cost. The City of Oakland will be the sole source of public financing. Devise a public financing plan that uses funds from at least three different sources.

Case Questions

1. Determine the total amount that must be financed.
2. Determine which sources will be used and what changes to those sources must be made (e.g., raising hotel taxes 0.5%).
3. Determine the amount of financing that will be generated from each source. These amounts should sum to the total amount that must be financed.
4. Determine the timing: when money will be collected from each source and when it will be paid back. For instance, if a general obligation bond is used and it is paid for with an increase in hotel taxes, what is the annual payment necessary to pay it off?
5. Create a table showing the sources of financing, the total amount financed from each source, the annual payment amounts, and the time period of those payments.
6. Include a brief discussion of how the financing plan fits with the principles of financing described in this chapter (e.g., vertical equity, horizontal equity, benefit principle, efficiency).

References

Baade, R.A. (2003). Evaluating subsidies for professional sports in the United States and Europe: A public-sector primer. *Oxford Review of Economic Policy*, 19(4), 585–597.

Baade, R.A., & Matheson, V. (2006). Have public finance principles been shut out in financing new stadiums for the NFL? *Public Finance and Management*, 6(3), 284–320.

Bess, P. (1995, April 2). Coors Field and the state of the art. *Denver Post*.

Brown, M., Nagel, M., McEvoy, C., & Rascher, D. (2004). Revenue and wealth maximization in the National Football League: The impact of stadia. *Sport Marketing Quarterly*, 13(4), 227–235.

Brown, M., Rascher, D., & Ward, W. (2006). The use of public funds for private benefit: An examination of the relationship between public stadium funding and ticket prices in the National Football League. *International Journal of Sport Finance*, 1(2), 109–118.

Clapp, C.M., & Hakes, J.K. (2005). How long a honeymoon? The effect of new stadiums on attendance in Major League Baseball. *Journal of Sports Economics*, 6(3), 255.

Coates, D., & Humphreys, B.R. (2005, July). Novelty effects of new facilities on attendance at professional sporting events. *Contemporary Economic Policy*, 23(3).

Crompton, J., Howard, D., & Var, T. (2003). Financing major league facilities: Status, evolution, and conflicting forces. *Journal of Sport Management*, 17(2), 156–184.

Custodio, S. (2019, December 18). Is $325 million starting price for Angel Stadium fair? Nearby land sales indicate differently. *Voice of OC*.

deMause, N. (2017, September 29). Why are Georgia taxpayers paying $700m for a new NFL stadium? *The Guardian*.

deMause, N. (2018, March 5). Cuomo's gift to Islanders could be worth nine figures: State agency never assessed value of Belmont Park property before leasing it for new arena. *Village Voice*.

Kaplan, D. (2014, April 14). NHL prepares loan pool that will top $1B: Credit facility would be first for teams. *Sports Business Journal*.

Keating, R. (1999, April 5). Sports pork: The costly relationship between major league sports and government. *Policy Analysis*, 339, 1–33.

Long, J.G. (2005, May). Full count: The real cost of public funding for major league sports facilities. *Journal of Sports Economics*, 6(2), 119–143.

Long, J.G. (2013). *Public/private partnerships for major league sports facilities*. New York: Routledge.

Masilak, J. (2008, June 18). SMG may run Liberty Bowl: City panel OKs hiring consultant to manage stadium. *Memphis Commercial Appeal*.

Mellinger, S. (2009, June 24). How does Royals' salary increase compare to other teams that opened new stadiums? *Kansas City Star*.

Owen, J. (2006). The intangible benefits of sports teams. *Public Finance and Management*, 6(3), 321–345.

Ozanian, M. (2019, May 6). IRS rules Golden State Warriors do not have to pay taxes on $300 million interest-free loan. *Forbes*.

Perry, C. (2002, May). The cheap seats. *Project Finance*.

Rascher, D., Brown, M., Nagel, M., & McEvoy, C. (2012). Financial risk management: The role of a new stadium in minimizing the variation in franchise revenues. *Journal of Sports Economics*, 13(4), 431–450.

Sanderson, A. (1999). In defense of new sports stadiums, ballparks, and arenas. *Marquette Sports Law Journal*, 10.

Siegfried, J., & Zimbalist, A. (2000). The economics of sports facilities and their communities. *Journal of Economic Perspectives*, 14(3), 95–114.

Ziets, M. (2002). Analysis of a new sports and entertainment district in Sacramento. Goal Group LLC, SportsEconomics, and Keyser Marston Associates.

Zimbalist, A. (2006, September 18). Leagues' power, consumers' attitude fuel resurgence of facility financing. *Sports Business Journal*.

APPENDIX 9.A Sources of financing for stadiums and arenas.

LEAGUE	TEAM	General fund	Project generated redevelopment	Gas tax	Sewer & water Revenues	Excise tax	Lottery revenues	Admission tax	Wage tax	Property tax	Parking tax	Sin tax	Entertainment tax	Long-term loan	Food & beverage tax	Rental car tax	Hotel tax	Sales tax
MLB	Astros									✓						✓	✓	
MLB	Braves											✓				✓	✓	
MLB	Brewers	✓																
MLB	Cardinals													✓				
MLB	Diamondbacks																	✓
MLB	Giants									✓								
MLB	Indians											✓						
MLB	Mariners						✓	✓							✓	✓		✓
MLB	Marlins									✓							✓	
MLB	Mets									✓								

(continued)

APPENDIX 9.A Cont.

Funding source	Nationals	Orioles	Padres	Phillies	Pirates	Rangers	Rangers (2020)	Reds	Rockies	Tigers	Twins	White Sox
General fund				✓	✓			✓		✓		✓
Project generated redevelopment		✓										
Gas tax												
Sewer & water Revenues												
Excise tax												
Lottery revenues		✓										
Admission tax	✓			✓			✓					
Wage tax												
Property tax		✓										
Parking tax							✓					
Sin tax												
Entertainment tax												
Long-term loan												
Food & beverage tax	✓											
Rental car tax				✓			✓			✓		
Hotel tax		✓			✓		✓			✓		✓
Sales tax					✓	✓	✓	✓	✓		✓	
LEAGUE	MLB	MLB	MLB	MLB	MLB	MLB	MLB	MLB	MLB	MLB	MLB	MLB

League	Team							
MLB	Yankees							
NBA	Bucks	✓		✓	✓	✓		
NBA	Cavaliers		✓			✓		
NBA	Grizzlies			✓	✓			
NBA	Hawks			✓	✓			
NBA	Heat			✓				
NBA	Kings					✓		
NBA	Magic			✓	✓			✓
NBA	Mavericks			✓				
NBA	Pacers		✓	✓	✓	✓	✓	
NBA	Rockets			✓	✓			
NBA	Spurs			✓	✓			
NBA	Suns			✓				
NBA	Thunder			✓				
NBA	Timberwolves		✓	✓	✓			
NFL	Bears			✓	✓			
NFL	Bengals			✓	✓			✓

(continued)

APPENDIX 9.A Cont.

LEAGUE	TEAM	Sales tax	Hotel tax	Rental car tax	Food & beverage tax	Long-term loan	Entertainment tax	Sin tax	Parking tax	Property tax	Wage tax	Admission tax	Lottery revenues	Excise tax	Sewer & water Revenues	Gas tax	Project generated redevelopment	General fund
NFL	Broncos	✓		✓				✓	✓			✓						
NFL	Browns																	
NFL	Buccaneers	✓																
NFL	Cardinals	✓	✓	✓							✓	✓						
NFL	Colts		✓	✓	✓							✓						
NFL	Cowboys	✓	✓	✓														
NFL	Eagles			✓								✓						
NFL	Falcons		✓															
NFL	49ers		✓															
NFL	Jaguars	✓	✓															
NFL	Lions		✓	✓														✓

NFL	Packers
NFL	Rams
NFL	Ravens
NFL	Seahawks
NFL	Steelers
NFL	Texans
NFL	Titans
NFL	Vikings
NHL	Coyotes
NHL	Devils
NHL	Hurricanes
NHL	Lightning
NHL	Oilers
NHL	Panthers
NHL	Penguins
NHL	Stars
NHL	Wild

Source: Goal Group Estimates, Mark S. Nagel, Daniel A. Rascher.

CHAPTER 10

Valuation

Daniel A. Rascher

KEY CONCEPTS

arm's length	market multiples approach
asset-based approach	market transactions approach
capital structure	marketability
controlling interest	media equivalency
cost approach	mid-year convention
discount factor (DF)	minority discount
discounted cash flow (DCF) analysis	net working capital (NWC)
fair market value	price-to-revenue (P/R) ratio
fair value	related-party transaction
fiduciary duty	residual value
hybrid income and market approach	strategic value
income approach	synergistic premium
liquidation value	transfer pricing
market approach	valuation date

INTRODUCTION

This chapter will discuss general approaches and specific techniques for valuing an enterprise or asset. An *asset* is any item of economic value. Examples include cash, securities, inventory, equipment, property, and intellectual property. An *enterprise* is generally considered to be a legal entity, association, business, corporation or the like, or unit of an organization. Enterprises often hold many assets. Determining the value of individual assets or of an enterprise as a whole is the job of an appraiser or valuation analyst.

It is often easier to value an entire business than a portion of a business, such as a brand or the name of a sport team. One reason for this is that a successful organization creates complementarities or synergies among its assets, which increase the value of the business beyond the sum of the values of the individual assets. For instance, a hockey team without a compelling name, logo, and so forth has a certain value. A name and a logo, although they may be very compelling, have very small values separate from a team. Putting the name and logo together with the team increases the value of the combined entity more than the sum of the individual values. Attempting to value the name and logo is very difficult, because revenues that flow from the name and logo are not easy to separate from revenues that flow from the team itself (whose games create fans who purchase products imprinted with the logo). This obvious example shows that it is easier to value an entire franchise, by using its total revenues, than to try to value a portion of the franchise.

The valuation of assets is a common task in sport finance. Consider the following scenarios:

- A person may wish to purchase a sport franchise. How much should he or she pay for the franchise? At what price should the seller be willing to sell?
- A corporation may be interested in sponsoring a sport organization by paying a fee to place its name on a facility or on signage within the facility. How much should the company pay for this form of marketing? What price should the facility owners charge for the naming rights? This type of valuation is known as *sponsorship valuation*. It is a fundamental aspect of sport marketing, especially for corporations—such as Coca-Cola, Molson Coors, or Visa—that regularly spend in excess of $100 million annually on sport sponsorships.
- A professional golfer may be interested in receiving endorsement income in exchange for wearing clothing or golf shoes, using clubs, or carrying a golf bag that represents a corporation. How much can the golfer charge for the endorsement? Valuation techniques can help her determine a fair endorsement value.

In sport, as in other industries, it is extremely important to understand the context of a valuation. Most financial valuation tasks require a clear description of the industry in which the subject enterprise participates and the future expectations for the industry. For example, let's consider the context of Major League Soccer. An important first step in understanding this context is to determine where the league is headed. A decade ago, the league's expansion plans included the goal of having 16 teams by 2010 (up from 12 in 2006). By 2019, the league had 24 teams with agreements to add more (perhaps growing to 30 teams). Attendance has continued to grow. New soccer-specific stadiums (or other facilities designed to account for soccer) have been built that are enhancing the teams' revenues. MLS's sponsorship and media deals have grown and are expected to continue to grow. Soccer viewership is up in the United States, and the game is played by more American kids than just about any other sport, although participation is declining.

Next, knowing how an entity is organized is another important aspect of its context. MLS is organized as a single entity, meaning that it is a single business or one company. (This structure has been successfully defended in court.) A person who wants to run an MLS team invests in the league as opposed to an individual team, and the league assigns the operation of a team. This method helps control costs, especially player costs.

This is just a snippet of what an analyst would consider in order to understand the context of a valuation. The context is important because valuation is forward looking. For valuation, understanding where the business is headed is actually more important than understanding where it came from. However, aside from plans, expectations, and hopes, the information that is available is necessarily historical: we look into the future by looking backward through a rearview mirror.

Valuation is part science and part art. The result is an estimate of the asset's true underlying value. A valuation is always uncertain, with the uncertainty arising both from the asset being valued and from the valuation methodology.

We will begin this chapter by discussing common standards of value and the adjustments made to valuations for marketability and controlling interest (defined below). Then we will present three important approaches to valuation. When valuing any asset, it is important to consider multiple valuation approaches. If more than one approach can be used, then the findings from each can be compared to arrive at a final estimate of value.

FAIR MARKET VALUE

A final determination of value depends on the standard of value being used. A widely used standard of valuation is **fair market value**—the net price for an asset that would result in a transaction between a willing buyer and a willing seller, neither of whom is under compulsion to buy or sell, both having reasonable knowledge of the relevant facts, and the two parties being at arm's length. A *willing seller* is one who is not being forced to sell the asset. If a person files for bankruptcy and is forced to sell an ownership interest in a local sporting goods store, this is not a willing seller, but a forced seller. Being at **arm's length** means that the buyer and seller (whether they are individuals, businesses, or estates) are not "related" in any way. This means that

- they have no familial relationship
- neither party is a subsidiary of the other
- neither party has an ownership interest in the other
- the parties have no financial relationship.

If any of these statements is not true, then the price of the transaction might not be at fair market value. However, the parties *could* choose to determine the fair market value and use that price for the transaction. Thus, one could show that even though the two entities are not at arm's length, they chose a price as if they were.

Other standards of value include fair value, strategic value, and liquidation value. **Fair value** is based on the transaction price of "two specific parties taking into account the respective advantages or disadvantages that each will gain from the transaction" (International Valuation Standards, 2007). In other words, the parties are not a typical willing buyer and willing seller, but actual specific buyers and sellers. **Strategic value** is the value that a buyer would be willing to pay in order to obtain the assets because it has the ability to use the assets in a way to get more value out of them than a typical buyer would (e.g., Disney buying assets of Fox or adidas buying Reebok). **Liquidation value** is the value of the assets when they are not being used together. In other words, this is the value when the company's assets are sold separately, piece by piece.

ADJUSTMENTS TO VALUE

Once the value of a business has been determined, certain adjustments may be required to arrive at the appropriate value of a specific ownership interest in the business. The two most common adjustments relate to whether the ownership interest effectively controls the business (**controlling interest**) and whether the ownership interest is freely marketable (**marketability** or **liquidity**).

A third type of adjustment is necessary if the business will be purchased for strategic or synergistic reasons. In this case, the purchaser might pay more for it than would someone purchasing it for stand-alone financial reasons. As an example, suppose that a regional brewery purchased an MLB team. One reason for the purchase might be that the brewery would be able to sell beer at the stadium during games. The brewery might be willing to pay a higher price than another investor would because of this synergistic tie with its core business. The incremental or added price is sometimes called the **synergistic premium**. The adjustments for controlling interest, marketability, and synergy are discussed below.

Controlling Interest

A controlling interest is an ownership interest that effectively controls the business. The necessary elements of control must be in place. These include:

- choosing management and their compensation and perquisites
- acquiring or liquidating assets
- setting dividend policies
- controlling company strategy and direction.

To understand the value of control, it is helpful to review the basic principles of corporate governance. The stockholders of a corporation do not directly manage the corporation's affairs; instead, they elect directors who are charged with this responsibility. The majority stockholder controls the corporation by controlling the board of directors. Only if the majority stockholder happens to run the business along with owning a share in it does that stockholder have direct control instead of indirect control. The ability to control the board of directors offers a number of benefits to a majority stockholder. For example, he can cause the corporation to employ himself or family members. Control of the corporation provides a higher degree of job security for the controlling stockholder or family members than is normally available in the current market.

Thus, an individual who owns a majority of stock normally will control the board of directors and, therefore, control selection of management, dividend distribution policy, and his or her own employment. For a sport team, a controlling interest allows an owner to choose the general manager, coaches, and even players. It also allows the owner to control ticket prices, team colors, the team name, logos, and perhaps even location. An investor without controlling interest would not possess these elements of control. However, many companies are set up (and laws and regulations are in place) to provide certain protections for the non-controlling owners, so that not having control of the business does not put them at an undue disadvantage.

A **minority discount** is an adjustment to the value of a share because it is not controlling. A non-controlling interest is also termed a *minority interest.* The key to identifying a controlling versus a minority interest is whether the owner possesses the elements of control listed above. In certain situations, a shareholder may possess these elements of control even though the interest is less than 50% of the voting stock.

As you might expect, a controlling interest in a business is worth more than a non-controlling interest on a per-share basis. In other words, an investor might pay $10 per share to buy into a business without gaining controlling interest. Another investor might be willing to pay $18 per share to buy into that same business if she thereby gained control of the business. If the seller understands this and if there are enough bidders, the fair market value of the controlling interest will be higher than that of the non-controlling interest.

Prior to performing an appraisal (another term for valuation), it is necessary to evaluate the facts and circumstances of the situation to determine whether the asset will provide effective control. The conclusion from the analysis must reflect the appropriate standard of value. That is, if the valuation technique that is used gives a conclusion based on a non-controlling interest, then, if the transaction is for a controlling interest, a controlling interest premium (also called a control premium) may be required. If, on the other hand, the valuation technique gives a conclusion based on a controlling interest, but the asset being valued is not a controlling interest, then the analyst must make an adjustment downward (apply a minority discount) to reflect the fact that the interest is non-controlling.

ESTIMATING A NON-CONTROLLING INTEREST DISCOUNT

The minority discount is the difference in the price that an investor would pay to purchase a non-controlling interest (typically a small ownership stake) versus a controlling interest in a business. The prices of stocks listed on stock exchanges include a minority discount, because these are prices that individuals have paid to purchase shares without acquiring control.

When estimating the appropriate discount for a minority or non-controlling interest, it is important to specify the aspects of control that are not available to the minority block of owners. (If there is nothing different about being a minority shareholder versus a majority shareholder, then control is worth nothing.) The following are a few important general principles:

- Valuation of a minority interest discount is highly dependent on the specific circumstances, such as those listed here.
- Fiduciary duties reduce the value of control. Here, **fiduciary duty** means the responsibility of management to act in the best interests of all shareholders. For example, a majority owner has a duty not to keep an unfair portion of cash flow, compared to what goes to a minority shareholder (e.g., through overpaying herself in her role as manager or expensing items to the company that are not directly related to the

business). In modern corporations, ownership and control do not necessarily go together, and fiduciary duties ensure that those who do have control act in the interests of the owners.

- If the distribution of cash flows is based on ownership percentages, the valuation of control should be reduced.
- An owner of a significant minority interest may possess some aspects of control. This is one area in which a publicly traded company differs significantly from a privately held one, where there are fewer minority owners and each has a larger stake.
- A minority interest that is expected to become a controlling interest at some point in time has elements of control.

ESTIMATING CONTROLLING INTEREST PREMIUMS

When the valuation approach results in a valuation based on a non-controlling interest, the analyst may need to estimate the value of a controlling interest. The following methods provide information for determining the incremental value of control.

Controlling/non-controlling changes in ownership. Perhaps the most direct evidence for the value of control would be changes in ownership that involve both controlling and minority interests at about the same time. Given the prices of these transactions, the analyst could determine the fair market value of the price of one share for a minority interest and for a controlling interest. The equation for controlling interest premium (CP) is

$$CP = \big(\big(\text{price paid for control} / \text{price paid for minority interest}\big) - 1\big)100\%$$

If the price in the minority interest transaction was $10 per share and in the controlling interest transaction was $18 per share, then the control premium would be 80%. The minority discount is given by

$$\text{minority discount} = \frac{CP}{100 + CP}$$

Thus, for the example above, the minority discount is

$$\frac{80\%}{100 + 80\%} = 44.4\%$$

If the analyst does not have the necessary information on recent transactions in the subject company, an alternative is to discover similar businesses for which the control premium (or the minority discount) is known. Suppose the analyst needs to know the control premium for a sport team. One source of information is the stock market, where the price per share for minority interests in similar companies is provided on a second-by-second basis. Bear in mind that if the subject franchise is privately held, there may be important differences between it and publicly traded sport franchises that might make the comparison difficult or inapt.

Sidebar 10.A provides an example of measuring a minority interest stock price and a controlling interest stock price.

SIDEBAR 10.A   Measuring Controlling and Minority Interest Stock Prices

In 2002, the Boston Celtics were publicly traded (the ticker symbol was BOS), meaning that the team's shares were available to the general public to buy and sell. On September 26, 2002, the closing price was $10.60 for one share of BOS. On the next day, it was announced that Lake Carnegie LLC would purchase a controlling interest in the team. The NYSE halted trading in the stock.* Trading resumed nearly two weeks later (on October 9, 2002) at a price of $28. A few months later (on December 31, 2002), the Lake Carnegie transaction was completed, with a final price listed on the stock exchange of $27.50. The non-controlling price (or unaffected price, as it is also known) was $10.60, and the controlling interest price was $27.50. Thus, the controlling interest premium was

$$\frac{\$27.60}{\$10.60} = 159.43\%^{\dagger}$$

* Although it is rare, stock exchanges sometimes prevent trading in certain companies for part of a day or longer if there are irregularities in the company's financials or if significant information about the company is unclear. In addition, stock trading that is done automatically by computers (program trading) can be halted if the market indexes move up or down too much.

† If any shareholders knew or speculated about the acquisition prior to the public announcement, the stock price might have crept up in the days or weeks prior to the announcement. To measure the unaffected price, we must find a price where no knowledge about the announcement was incorporated into the stock price.

When we compare stock prices on different dates, we must keep in mind the possibility that the stock market in general could change substantially between the two dates and that the difference in the stock prices reflects, at least in part, general changes in the market (and economy) instead of a control premium. For the Boston Celtics purchase, it turns out that the S&P 500 did not change much over the time period, so the initial estimate of the net control premium is probably fairly accurate. (Recall that the S&P 500 is simply the aggregation of 500 stocks into an index that Standard & Poor's deems to be reflective of the stock market in general. We can study the S&P 500 and apply the conclusions to the stock market as a whole.) To account for general movement in the stock market between the unaffected price date and the transaction price date, we discount the premium by the growth in the S&P 500 over the same time period. The final adjusted controlling interest premium is 154.80%. Exhibit 10.1 shows that the announcement of the controlling interest transaction caused a substantial increase in the stock price.

The Cleveland Indians, a publicly traded company in the late 1990s, provide another example. On May 12, 1999, the stock traded at $9.94. The next day, Richard Jacobs announced that he intended to sell his controlling interest in the team (although no specific buyer was named at the time). At the end of the

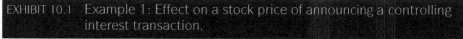

EXHIBIT 10.1   Example 1: Effect on a stock price of announcing a controlling interest transaction.

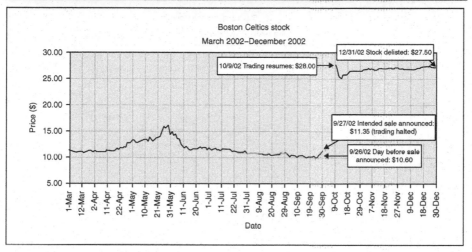

day, the stock price had risen to $16.25. On November 4 of that year, Lawrence Dolan announced his intention to purchase the team. The stock price went up to $20.63. The transaction was completed on February 15, 2000, with the stock price at $22.56. If it can be shown that the unaffected price was $9.94, the controlling interest premium in the Cleveland Indians purchase was 127.04%. When we adjust for movement in the S&P 500 over the same time period (from 1,364 to 1,402), the controlling interest premium becomes 123.5%. The control premium is confirmed in Exhibit 10.2.

The examples described above are two of the few cases in which we can calculate a controlling interest premium in the sale of a sport business, because these teams were publicly traded rather than privately held corporations. Another example involves the soccer club Aston Villa of the English Premier League. In August of 2006, Randy Lerner announced a bid to take over the club and pay $10.36 per share, a price that was 47% higher than the club's price prior to all announcements of possible takeovers that had occurred during the previous nine months (which would have caused the share price to change on the belief that a sale was imminent) and 10% higher than the previous day's closing price. Further, among sports apparel and sporting goods companies we can find many examples of publicly traded companies. For instance, in August 2005, adidas-Salomon offered to buy Reebok for $59 per share, a jump of 34% over Reebok's share price just prior to the announcement. The deal closed at the end of January 2006 at the same price, $59 per share. Thus, the control premium was 34%, assuming Reebok's price prior to the announcement did not reflect any knowledge of the possible takeover.

In 2012, adidas AG purchased Adams Golf Inc. for a 9.5% controlling interest premium over the share price just prior to the announcement, at a price that was over 40% higher than the price just two months earlier. In a case of a declining business (much of it due to Amazon's rise and other ecommerce businesses financially damaging retailers), it was announced on March 26,

EXHIBIT 10.2 Example 2: Effect on a stock price of announcing a controlling interest transaction.

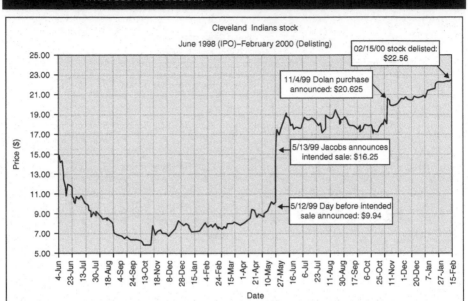

2018 that Finish Line would be sold to JD Sports for $13.50, when the previous trading day had Finish Line at $10.55, for a control premium of 28%. On June 15, 2018, Finish Line ended its final day as a separate publicly traded business. As noted, the announcement date will typically cause the market to react, not just the actual date on which the transaction is finalized.

In fact, for the Boston Celtics and Cleveland Indians purchases, the control premium was much higher than is typical for companies in other industries (e.g., Reebok's control premium of 34%). When we compare the control premiums of the sports apparel/sporting goods companies mentioned above to those of the Celtics and Indians, we should not be surprised that sport franchises may have high control premiums, for reasons discussed later in this chapter.

Mergerstat Review Premiums and Discounts. To determine control premiums, we can also refer to a database of control premium estimates compiled by the company Mergerstat. The median control premium (based on hundreds of company transactions) for 2012 was approximately 44% across all industries. For the Amusement and Recreation Services industry (Standard Industrial Classification 79), the database shows a control premium for 2012 of about 24% across the 13 transactions analyzed. For 2018, it is 41% (across 20 transactions). The control premium has shrunk since nearly two decades ago, when between 2000 and 2005 the control premium for SIC 79 was about 55%.

Bona fide offers. Another source of information on control premiums—and asset valuation in general—is *bona fide* offers on sport-related businesses. A remarkable and rare example was an offer in 2005 to purchase an entire major professional sport league. On March 2, 2005, Game Plan LLC and Bain & Company offered $3.5 billion to purchase the entire NHL. This figure later rose to $4.3 billion (Eichelberger, 2006). A few weeks earlier, on February 16, 2005, the

NHL season had been cancelled, and uncertainty about the future of the NHL was very high. During the time between the cancellation of the season and the Game Plan/Bain offer, the Anaheim Mighty Ducks were sold to Henry Samueli for $70 million, substantially below the $108 million pre-lockout value that *Forbes* had placed on the team. It is understandable that in a time of high uncertainty about the future of the league, the price for a franchise would decrease. These pieces of information provide some evidence as to the controlling interest premium of the NHL. We have a transaction for one team and an offer to buy the entire league during the same time period. Information about the future of the league was likely similar across these two situations. We can calculate a discount on the value of the Mighty Ducks due to the lockout and extrapolate that value to all NHL teams. The result is a league value of $3.176 billion. (The lockout discount is simply the transaction price of $70 million divided by *Forbes*'s estimate of $108 million.) The Game Plan/Bain offer of $4.3 billion for control of the league, during this time of uncertainty, establishes a controlling interest premium of 35.4% (4.3/3.176 – 1). This is a lower bound, because the NHL owners did not accept that offer. A sale of the NHL would have required an offer higher than $4.3 billion; hence, the actual control premium would have been higher.

In this example, a bona fide offer provided some evidence about the value and control premium of the NHL. This example, however, took place during a period of high uncertainty, so although it provides information about the value of league control, we probably do not have reasonable knowledge of the facts, given that the specifics of the future of the league were highly uncertain.

Value of the control premium in sport versus other industries. The control premium is generally higher for sport teams than for many other industries (or even sporting goods, sports retail, and other non-team sport companies) because there are many reasons to own a sport franchise above and beyond annual operating profits. Besides profits, ownership of a sport team can provide

- benefit as a consumption good (meaning that the owner enjoys the role of operating the team)
- associated rights or income streams
- synergies with the owner's other businesses or assets
- shelters from federal income tax
- profit taking from the expense side (e.g., paying oneself an inflated salary or lawfully charging parts of one's personal life on the company's books)
- league revenue sharing and future expansion fees.

As Randy Vataha, co-founder of Game Plan LLC, one of the companies that sought to purchase the NHL, has stated, "In non-sports businesses, the control premium is generally a function of operational control and does not include the notoriety factor that can add significant value to the control premium of a professional sports team" (Rascher, 2006, p. 75). An owner has authority over who coaches the team, who plays on the team, the style of offense and defense, the type of entertainment provided at home games, and so forth. As a result, for many people, control of the management and decision making for a sport team would be far more exciting than, say, controlling an iron-ore extraction company.

Researchers have studied whether "sportsman" owners exist in professional sport. A "sportsman" owner is an owner who purchases and manages a team mostly for its consumption benefits (i.e., the enjoyment of winning games and operating a team) instead of its investment benefits. According to Stefan Késenne (2006), analysis of soccer clubs in Europe shows that some are not managed under a pure profit maximization objective; management includes the desire to win (separate from its effects on profitability) in the decision process. As another example, the major reason the NHL did not accept the Game Plan/ Bain offer was that a number of owners did not want to sell at any price. They liked owning a hockey franchise. Economist Rod Fort finds that "the portion of ownership value not associated with annual operations appears to be significant" (Fort, 2006, p. 9). Explaining why he purchased the Boston Celtics along with Wycliffe Grousbeck, Stephen Pagliuca said, "We both viewed the Celtics as a community asset, a labor of love, really, not as an investment for investors" (Shanahan, 2004). This sportsman owner effect can have a substantial impact on franchise valuation, as discussed below.

Another reason to own a sport franchise, beyond direct net cash flow and enjoyment, is that team ownership may bring associated rights or income streams. For example, team owners in most sport leagues have complete or nearly complete operating rights to the facilities in which their teams play. Thus, owning a team might provide income through the facility operation itself. Wayne Huizenga owned the Florida Marlins and the stadium in which the team played. He earned revenues from premium seating, naming rights, parking, signage, and merchandise through the stadium company, not the team—yet without the team, the stadium would not have provided these revenue sources (Zimbalist, 1998). This is a typical example of a **related-party transaction**, a transaction between two businesses that have some form of pre-existing relationship (more generally defined as **transfer pricing**, the pricing of assets transferred within an organization).

Similarly, an owner's other businesses may benefit. For instance, the late George Steinbrenner, former owner of the New York Yankees, created YES, a regional sports network, reportedly worth $3.5 billion in 2019 (Lafayette, 2019). Rupert Murdoch claimed that his then-ownership of the Dodgers prevented Disney from creating a regional sports network in southern California, and that alone was worth his investment in the team (Zimbalist, 2003). The Atlanta Braves were once owned by Ted Turner, who also owned the Braves' media company, TBS. Reportedly, the media fees paid to the Braves were zero.

Another reason for ownership is that management salaries and payments, an expense item on the franchise's income statement, often go to the owner— who is also an executive of the team. Franchise ownership can also provide shelters from federal taxes through vehicles such as the roster depreciation allowance. The IRS allows the full purchase price of a team to be allocated to player contracts over 15 years. The contracts are considered depreciable assets for tax purposes (Brunner, 2006).

Synergistic Premium

When we calculate a control premium, we must be very careful to account for synergistic premiums—amounts that a buyer might pay over the control premium for reasons of strategy or synergy. The concept of control relates to making decisions regarding the business, such as the direction of the firm, marketing, compensation, and so forth. Often, however, buyers acquire companies for strategic or synergistic reasons (such as a regional brewery purchasing a sport team). Synergistic relationships are often revealed in related-party transactions and transfer pricing.

Where synergies exist, the purchase price may include a synergistic premium. A brewery might pay a price that is higher than the current per-share price for a franchise, not just because it wants control of the franchise but also because it desires the synergy of selling and promoting its beer at the games. The 34% premium that adidas paid to Reebok not only gives adidas control of Reebok, but also—as adidas has stated to its shareholders and the public—offers many synergies for adidas. For instance, adidas's ties and distribution network in Europe can help Reebok sell there (as is the case for Reebok's ties in the United States). Reebok is a sales-driven company, while adidas focuses on technology and performance. Combining these two strengths will enhance the offerings of both brands. Further, the combined size of the business will enable both adidas and Reebok to negotiate better terms from retailers. The 34% premium that adidas paid likely includes both a control premium and a synergistic premium. Separating these is very difficult.

Often the synergies for a franchise transaction can be characterized as either horizontal or vertical. It is becoming more common for an owner of a sport franchise to buy another sport franchise (horizontal purchase), such as Stan Kroenke's ownership of the St. Louis Rams, Arsenal FC, Denver Nuggets, and Colorado Avalanche. Horizontal synergistic value can exist in the potential cost savings in managing the franchises, for instance, or in additional revenues from selling a sponsorship that includes all of the teams. A synergistic vertical relationship is Comcast Spectacor's ownership of Wells Fargo Center, the Philadelphia Flyers, Paciolan (a ticketing company), and Ovations Food Services. In this case the same company owns the facility, the team, the ticketing company, and the food service business. Cost savings and enhanced revenue generation are possible with this arrangement.

On the other hand, there are not likely to be any substantial synergistic reasons for the previously discussed purchases of the Indians and the Celtics, or the offer for the NHL. Zimbalist (2003) discusses synergistic ownerships in MLB. He finds these relationships for approximately half of the teams in MLB, but not for the Cleveland Indians. The press coverage regarding the Celtics purchase does not mention any synergistic reasons (although some may exist). The offer for the NHL by finance-related companies does not suggest any obvious synergistic benefits, although there may have been benefits related to market power from the control of an entire league. Thus, we can assume that the control premium for these transactions did not have a component for synergies.

Marketability Discount

Sometimes we value an equity interest in a closely held (privately held) business based on observations of transactions in a publicly traded stock, by using price-to-earnings or other multiples. In these cases we must apply a *marketability discount*, also known as a liquidity discount, because the sale of stock in publicly traded companies is easier than that of privately held companies. The marketability discount, therefore, is based on the premise that an ownership interest that is readily marketable is worth more than an interest that is not readily marketable. This premise is justified because the owner of an interest in a closely held company cannot sell shares in the public market to achieve liquidity.

If, on the other hand, we estimate the value of a non-marketable asset by reference to appraisals of or transactions in similarly non-marketable assets, no marketability adjustment is necessary. For example, a real estate appraiser could estimate the value of a building by reference to recent sales of similar buildings in similar locations. All of the buildings would have similar relative marketability, and no marketability discount would be needed.

Generally, in a situation involving a controlling interest in a closely held company, any marketability discount is greatly reduced. This is the case because the owner of a controlling interest can market the company without any impediment—the only consideration is the cost of doing so. In addition, a controlling interest generally will be easier to market than a minority interest in a closely held stock.

Information on liquidity discounts can be found in *Valuing a business: The analysis and appraisal of closely held companies* (Pratt, 2008). According to this book, two comprehensive studies of liquidity discounts (conducted by Emory and by Willamette Management Associates) covering 1975–1995 show liquidity discounts ranging to just above 40%. Other, more recent work tends to put these discounts at below 10% due to more controls and adjustments made compared to the earlier studies (Comment, 2012). The median value for liquidity discounts allowed by the courts has been about 20%.

APPROACHES TO VALUING AN ASSET

The adjustments for controlling interest, marketability, and synergistic purchases discussed previously are made after a baseline valuation has been determined. The remainder of this chapter discusses various approaches to making the baseline valuation.

The many methods for valuing an asset, a business, or an interest or equity in a business may be categorized into the following three approaches. The **market approach** relies on prices that similar assets sell for in the marketplace. To account for differences across the assets being compared, such methods use financial ratios, such as price-to-ticket revenue, price-to-revenue, or price-to-earnings. Under the **income approach**, income or cash flow serves as the basis for the value of the business or asset. For the **cost** or **asset-based approach**, we determine what it would cost to re-create the business or asset.

Some businesses or assets lend themselves to certain valuation approaches more readily, whereas others can be valued with all three approaches. As we will see, sport franchises are best valued under the market approach. On the other hand, a golf course can be valued with all three approaches. (What are other, similar golf courses selling for? What income is the golf course generating through greens fees and other revenue sources? What would it cost to build a similar golf course?)

The valuation of sponsorships is an important and growing concern in sport. The methods most commonly used today are based on the market approach (What are similar sponsorships selling for?), but these methods are less than satisfying because the "similar" sponsorships may be under- or over-priced in terms of their true underlying value. Alternatively, some analyses measure the exposure (the number of people seeing the sponsor's ad or signage) and determine what it would cost to achieve the same exposure through some other form of media, often called **media equivalency**. Ultimately, though, we want to understand how a sponsorship leads to sales of the sponsoring company's products or services. Thus, the income approach would make the most sense. However, it is difficult to link a sponsorship directly to sales, because many other pieces of the marketing mix occur concurrently with the sponsorship, and because external factors (such as competitors' actions) and the economy in general affect sales, as well. Regardless of whether you are valuing a golf course or a sponsorship, it is appropriate to review many possible methods for valuing the business, unless you are constrained by time or budget.

Market Approach

Under one type of market approach, often called the **market transactions approach**, we determine the value of a company by reference to the value of comparable firms that have been sold within a reasonably recent period of time, with appropriate adjustments for the time value of money (see Chapter 4). The comparable firms may include closely held corporations, publicly traded firms, divisions or subsidiaries of larger firms, and so forth. Additionally, transactions involving some of the ownership or equity of the subject firm itself can provide excellent evidence as to its value. For instance, if the entire company was sold two years ago, this would provide some evidence for its value today. If one of the owners sold her 5% stake in the business nine months ago, that would also provide useful valuation information. For instance, in March 2012, the owners of the New York Mets sold twelve 4% shares of the team for $20 million each. This put the non-controlling interest of the team at $500 million. However, the sale was under duress—the owners were essentially being forced to sell shares in order to raise money. Using the 2012 SIC 79 control premium average of 24% (see above) would put the team's value at around $620 million. This figure likely underestimates the franchise value because the transactions were under duress. *Forbes* estimated the value of the team at $719 million in its March 21, 2012, issue. This is an example of minority transactions (12 of them at 4%) that provide information on the overall franchise value, albeit likely a lower-bound value.

The choice of comparable firms is the first step in the market transactions approach, and an important one. It may be necessary to make adjustments reflecting the differences between the comparable firms and the subject company. By comparing transaction price-to-revenue ratios or transaction price-to-earnings ratios (discussed later in this chapter), we can establish a basis for applying information about one firm to another. For valuation of sport franchises, it is also common to examine differences in attendance (price-to-ticket revenues) across comparables, the quality of the stadium and the terms of the team's lease, whether a new facility is in the works, and the status of future television and other media revenues.

Another type of market approach, similar to the market transactions approach, is often called the **market multiples approach**. This approach is based on the premise that the value of the business enterprise depends on what investors in a competitive market actually pay to own equity or shares of stock in similar companies. The first step is to select a sample of firms that are comparable to the subject firm. These are typically selected from companies that are traded on organized capital market exchanges (for example, the NYSE, American Stock Exchange, NASDAQ, and over-the-counter market). It is possible, however, to use closely held businesses and their information, assuming that the information is accessible and reliable. In the next step, we perform a financial analysis to select and apply appropriate multiples (for example, price-to-earnings ratio) to estimate the value of the subject company. The resulting estimate represents the fair market value of the subject company.

It is important to realize that market pricing multiples among comparable firms will vary depending on differences in expected growth rates, risk, and capital structure. These factors can vary across businesses in the same industry for many reasons. For instance, a firm with a new patent in place or a new line of products can expect higher growth rates than a firm without new products or patents. A firm with higher volatility in its quarterly earnings is a riskier business than one with stable earnings, and the price of a share of the riskier firm will likely be lower to reflect that risk. A firm's **capital structure** (amount of debt and equity) can affect its returns to shareholders and, in turn, its stock price and valuation.

Sometimes, a large sample of comparable firms is available, and we can employ statistical analyses to determine how observed market multiples correspond to fundamental attributes of the companies in the sample. For example, statistical analysis may reveal a relationship between price-to-sales ratio and gross margin. Then, we can use the statistical relationship to select the multiple for use in valuing the subject firm. The market multiples for a comparable firm may be unusually high or low due to transitory changes in the firm's operating performance. For example, if a comparable firm has temporarily low earnings or stock price, we must account for that in the analysis and choose the appropriate dates on which to compare the firms.

An important difference between the market transactions approach and the market multiples approach is that, whereas the market multiples observed for publicly traded securities provide a value of the subject company's equity on a minority-interest basis (because the observed stock prices reflect transactions in minority interests), the market transactions approach provides an estimate of the value to a control buyer. Observed prices in the market transactions approach will include premiums reflecting expected benefits to a buyer who seeks to benefit from synergies or better utilization of assets.

Let's put the market approach into practice and consider the various methods within this approach for measuring the value of a business: the price-to-revenue ratio, price-to-earnings ratio, and equity shares sold. For the purpose of this discussion, we will use examples from baseball, football, soccer, and auto racing. If we wish to determine the value of Major League Soccer (MLS) on June 30, 2019, we could use the market approach as a starting point. Recall that under this approach, we refer to the value of comparable firms or assets. To find a value for MLS, we could use the value of one team as a basis for valuing the other teams, and then we could determine how to value the activities of the league office itself and any other non-team assets.

In March 2006, Red Bull GmbH, a maker of energy drinks, purchased the operating interests of the MetroStars from Anschutz Entertainment Group and renamed the team the New York Red Bulls. The transaction price was $25 million. Fast-forward six years and, in 2012, the Montreal Impact paid $40 million to join MLS. In 2015, New York City Football Club (NYCFC) paid a $100 million expansion fee to join. One cannot simply compare the Red Bulls and Montreal fees and make a simple conclusion about the growth of expansion fees or team values, because the two markets are vastly different. However, a New York-based MLS franchise is now four times as expensive as it was, and the new franchise has to share the market with the Red Bulls. The conclusion that an MLS franchise is now worth at least four times what it was less than a decade ago is a good starting point in determining the growth in the value of MLS.

Similarly, in 2007 DC United was purchased for about $33 million. Five and a half years later, the owner sold 60% of the team for $30 million (valuing the team at $50 million). Thus, the team's value grew at an annual rate of about 11.5%. The Columbus Crew sold for $68 million in July 2013 (Ozanian, 2013). The Crew were an original MLS club, having paid $5 million to join in 1995. The team also invested $28.5 million to build Crew Stadium. Fast-forward to 2019 and an MLS expansion fee (the right paid to purchase shares of MLS, LLC and Soccer United Marketing, LLC and run a team) price is $200 million, as St. Louis joined MLS (Barrabi, 2019). While an expansion fee is not the same as purchasing an existing franchise, it tends to mirror those fees.

These are important pieces of information for valuing MLS. To value each of the teams in MLS, we could start with the price-to-revenue ratio. Because this ratio relies on market transactions and revenue, it is considered an application of the market approach. Typically, an analyst would have access to the organization's financial information, including a team's total revenues. However, as we have discussed, most sport teams are privately owned and their revenues (and other financials) are not made available to the public. Since we do not have information on the franchises' revenues, we will use an estimate in order to illustrate the principles of valuation. For the San Jose Earthquakes, let us assume a financial transaction of $235 million (for 100% of the shares to operate that club) with annual revenues of $36 million (Smith, 2018). This implies a price-to-revenue ratio of 6.53x. The "x" in 6.53x is a symbol meaning 6.53 is a multiplier that we use on revenue to find price (or financial value). This is up from estimates a decade earlier of P/R ratios of about 3.0 for MLS franchises.

PRICE-TO-REVENUE RATIO

In professional sport, a common starting point for franchise valuation is to examine the transaction price (or some other estimate of franchise value) divided by total annual revenues for the franchise. This is the **price-to-revenue (P/R) ratio**. To develop the popular franchise value estimates found in *Forbes* magazine, analysts begin with price-to-revenue ratios based on actual transactions, apply them to all the teams in a league, and make adjustments for other factors, such as a new stadium under construction, a new local television contract about to begin, or a historical brand (Ozanian, 1999). In an interview, Randy Vataha stated that only the price-to-revenue ratio has any real value in professional sports (Rascher, 2006). As further evidence of the importance of P/R ratios in valuing professional sport teams, in late 2001 Allan "Bud" Selig, commissioner of MLB, in testimony before the US Congress stated his estimates for each team's valuation and total revenues. He had estimated that the average price-to-revenue ratio was 1.96x, with only a very small variation across teams.[1] These estimates indicate that multiplying team revenue by 1.96 provides a very accurate starting point for team values in MLB as of 2001. Academic research concurs. For instance, George Foster discusses the usefulness of market multiples in valuing sport teams, noting that financial statements (and the income estimates presented in them) offer a noisy basis for valuation (Foster, Greyser, & Walsh, 2005).

Returning to the MLS valuation, to estimate the league's value as a whole, we would generate a P/R ratio from an actual transaction (or multiple transactions) and apply this ratio—which accounts for differences in market size, attendance, and other factors that make each team unique, via total revenues—to the other teams in MLS. Exhibit 10.3 shows the application of the San Jose Earthquakes P/R ratio of 6.53x to each of the MLS clubs, using the most recent estimate of annual team revenues from 2018. We then add up the values for all teams and get $5.307 billion **A**. Exhibit 10.3 does not reflect the fact that FC Cincinnati joined in 2019 and four other teams will be joining by 2022 (with an expectation of further expansion up to a total of 30 teams). These expansion teams will be paying expansion fees up to $200 million. These payments increase the value of MLS, LLC, but also lower the percentage of MLS, LLC that each current owner has, which adds more recipients of the existing media and other national revenue streams. Sorting out the overall impact to a share of MLS, LLC would require more information and assumptions. However, one could assume that MLS, LLC would expand in value by adding these clubs or else it would not approve of the expansions in the first place.

With access to data, this could be evaluated, but let's assume that one-quarter of the revenue in the league (25% of $813 million) comes from national sources (media and national sponsorships), and that adding teams won't grow that amount because, for instance, the national media deal won't be showing more games nationally just because more teams have been added. Thus, the 23 teams (as of the end of the 2018 season) would in the near future be splitting current national revenues with a total of 28 teams (FC Cincinnati in 2019 plus the four expansion teams), thus lowering their national revenues by about 18% (or 1 − (23/28)). That would lower their total revenues effectively from $813 million to $777 million (one-quarter of $813 million lowered by 18%). Using $777 million to multiply by the P/R ratio of 6.53x shows a total value of $5.07 billion. Therefore, adding the five teams lowers the value by about $237 million, yet the expansion fees more than make up for that as they total $525 million, for a net gain of $288 million **B**. Hence, the preliminary value for MLS is $5.595 billion **C**.

This does not account for when those various revenue streams and expansion payments take place and thus no time value of money effect is accounted for. This shows the complicated nature of franchise valuation because of the

---

1   The standard deviation was 0.19, which is very small when compared with the mean. The P/R ratio for all but four teams was between 1.89 and 2.15.

EXHIBIT 10.3 Valuation analysis of Major League Soccer as of June 30, 2019—similar transactions methodology.

SIMILAR TRANSACTIONS METHODOLOGY—TOTAL REVENUE

$s in millions FRANCHISE (1)	2018 TOTAL REVENUE (est.) (2)	TEAM VALUE USING PRICE/REV RATIO* 6.53x (3)
Atlanta United	$47	$307
Chicago Fire	27	176
Colorado Rapids	18	118
Columbus Crew	24	157
D.C. United	26	170
FC Dallas	34	222
Houston Dynamo	28	183
Los Angeles Galaxy	63	411
LAFC	50	326
Minnesota United	24	157
Montreal Impact	24	157
New England Revolution	28	183
New York City FC	42	274
New York Red Bulls	38	248
Orlando City SC	44	287
Philadelphia Union	26	170
Portland Timbers	48	313
Real Salt Lake	22	144
San Jose Earthquakes	36	235
Seattle Sounders	52	339
Sporting Kansas City	41	268
Toronto FC	49	320
Vancouver Whitecaps	22	144

(*continued*)

EXHIBIT 10.3   Cont.

SIMILAR TRANSACTIONS METHODOLOGY—TOTAL REVENUE

$s in millions FRANCHISE (1)	2018 TOTAL REVENUE (est.) (2)	TEAM VALUE USING PRICE/REV RATIO* 6.53x (3)
Value Indications	$813	A $5,307
Plus: Adding Expansion Teams (but sharing national revenues)		B $288
Preliminary Team Value Indication (June 30, 2018)		C $5,595
Adjustments for Control		41%
Implied Value of MLS		D $7,889

* San Jose Earthquakes price/revenue multiple based on estimates from *Forbes* (Smith, 2018). LAFC estimates provided by authors.

interconnectedness of clubs (especially in MLS because it is a single entity, but also based on the revenue sharing in other major sports leagues) and the timing of revenue streams.

Selecting the valuation date. Recall that we wished to calculate a valuation of MLS as of June 30, 2019. For any valuation, we must select a specific date, the **valuation date**. Obviously, the value of a business can change from month to month or even day to day. An important principle of valuation is to consider only information that is reasonably known for the valuation date. In litigation, the parties must use an exact date so that they can work on the same issue (e.g., the value of company X on the date on which the contract stipulates that it will be sold). For a merger, the analyst might choose a current date, and if the merger is actually consummated six months later, then an adjustment might be made to reflect any change in value.

A very important aspect of valuation (discussed in Chapter 4) is to incorporate the concept of the time value of money. In our valuation of MLS, we used revenue figures for the year 2018 and various adjustments to national revenues and future expansion fee payments. However, in order to perform time value of money calculations, we need a specific beginning date, not just the year 2019. How do we select a date?

Revenue in MLS is generated and paid throughout the year, with most of it coming in during the season (April through November). Often, when exact details for the flow of revenue over the year are not available, the analyst may choose to use the **mid-year convention**—selecting a date halfway through the year (i.e., June 30), based on the notion that if half of the revenue came in before this date and half after this date, then a good approximation for valuation purposes is to treat the revenue as if all of it came in on June 30. Alternatively, the analyst may choose to be "conservative" and treat the revenue as if it became available on December 31. This approach is considered conservative because it accounts for the revenue later than it was actually generated and, therefore, based on the time value of money, this approach reduces the asset's value. In the MLS valuation, we can use the assumption that all of the revenue came in on June 30. Hence, because we seek a valuation as of June 30, 2019, we do not need to make a mid-year convention adjustment, but instead only annual time value of money adjustments. In fact, this is why the specific valuation date of June 30 was selected.

Adjusting for the controlling interest premium. The final adjustment in Exhibit 10.3 is made to account for the controlling interest premium. The purchase of MLS club operations allows the new owners to run that team. They would own equity in MLS, but not *control* MLS. In fact, a club is just one of 24 teams in the league. Therefore, a transaction provides controlling interest in a team's operation (subject to the restrictions placed on it by MLS), but it does not provide control of MLS as a whole. In fact, if some party were to buy MLS outright, the new owner would be able to choose, among other things, the location of and the number of teams, the salary cap and revenue sharing rules (subject to any collective bargaining agreement with players that may be relevant), the types of players and coaches, the length of the season, and so forth. Given that the comparable transaction that we have used to value MLS (San Jose Earthquakes) is not one that provides controlling interest in MLS, we must make an adjustment to account for control, in order to estimate the full value of MLS as a whole.

To estimate the control premium for MLS, we can use any of the control premiums discussed earlier (for the Celtics, Indians, NHL, and SIC 79), because these are comparable, in that they involve other sport teams and leagues. However, for illustrative purposes, we will choose the 2018 Mergerstat premium of 41% for SIC 79. Applying this control premium of 41% to $5.595 billion gives a value for the control of MLS of $7.889 billion **D** ($5.595 billion × 1.41 = $7.889 billion).

In this example, we assume that the total value of MLS is captured by its franchises/clubs. If the league office has a separate value, then we would need to include this in each owner's revenue estimates or add it as a separate asset with its relevant revenues and ratio. MLS does (mostly via Soccer United Marketing) sell national television and sponsorship rights. A complete analysis would account for these additional sources of revenue, if they are not already included at the franchise level.

Choosing a multiple. In choosing a multiple to apply to a variable such as total revenue, it is important to be able to compare the subject at hand to the comparable assets ("comps") being used. The San Jose Earthquakes example of a transaction is only one transaction. It is often the case that adjustments to the multiple (6.53x) would be applied to each team based on their individual circumstances. As an example, in an older transaction from 2013, the Columbus Crew were purchased for a reported $68 million. Estimates of revenue at the time for the Crew provide a P/R ratio of 4.72x; however, the purchase includes complete ownership of the stadium. It might be that another team is about to move into a new stadium, which will increase its revenues. Thus, use of a backward-looking revenue number for 2013 would not account for the growth in revenue expected with the new stadium. Alternatively, we might look to other similar leagues to see what price-to-revenue multiples are used in those leagues. Key considerations in choosing a revenue multiple for the valuation of MLS include:

- franchise value appreciation
- stability of the league
- cross-marketing and promotional opportunities
- strategic/synergistic benefits with other business interests
- image and public relations benefits
- personal/corporate prestige and recognition
- corporate/personal tax benefits.

In terms of these considerations, MLS compares satisfactorily to the other sport leagues. It has experienced franchise appreciation, as shown above by the high growth in expansion fees. As of 2019, the league was stable, entering its 24th season and on its way to having a full slate of soccer-specific stadiums and nearly 30 teams. The cross-marketing and promotional opportunities are strong—for example, the investment by the Yankees and Manchester City in NYCFC club. The potential synergistic and tax benefits in MLS are the same as in other major sport leagues (perhaps even greater in MLS, with many team operators owning or managing their own stadiums). Although the image and corporate prestige of MLS are not what they are in the NFL, MLS has certainly gained ground with its media deals and expanded coverage.

The median price-to-revenue multiple of MLB, the NHL, the NBA, and the NFL (the Big 4) is 5.63, based on 2019 figures (see Exhibit 10.4). A review of other sport-related properties reveals somewhat similar ratios, although the variation is quite large for these other properties, from 0.80 to 4.16. Historically, the Big 4 had higher P/R multiples than MLS because those franchises were more profitable and the leagues were more stable. Yet in the past few years, MLS valuations have skyrocketed based on an increased demand to operate a top division soccer club. Yet, with negative income the norm in MLS, the relatively high prices are based on anticipated growth in the future leading to profitable clubs.

PRICE-TO-EARNINGS RATIO

As discussed in Chapter 2, investors who are analyzing stocks commonly use a ratio called price-to-earnings (P/E): the cost of purchasing the stock relative to the earnings that it generates. The P/E ratio provides an estimate of how much money an investor will pay for each dollar of a company's earnings and allows for comparisons of the market values of companies of various sizes. Chapter 2 presents an example of the calculation of price-to-earnings for a sport retail organization, Under Armour. For sport teams, earnings are not reflective of value, because many owners are willing to tolerate low earnings or even lose money if it means winning more games, or just for the satisfaction of operating a team. Also, related-party transactions in sport make it difficult to assess actual earnings. Therefore, analysts do not typically use P/E ratios to value sport team properties and instead employ P/R ratios.

EXHIBIT 10.4 Professional sport valuations.

COMPARATIVE TRANSACTIONS METHODOLOGY—PRICE/REVENUE RATIO

$s in millions

SIC CODE		ANNUAL REVENUES	PRICE/REV RATIO
SIC 7941	Churchill Downs (Oct. 1, 2019, minority interest)	$1,180	4.16
	Magna Entertainment	$658	1.10
	Global Entertainment (Central Hockey League)	$14	2.60
	Association of Volleyball Professionals, Inc.	$13	0.80
SIC 7948	Canterbury Park	$55	1.00
	Dover Motorsports	$91	2.20
	International Speedway (Oct. 1, 2019, minority interest)	$673	2.90
	Speedway Motor Sports	$481	3.50
Other	Continental Basketball Association	$10	1.00
	Median NHL Team (2019)	$146	3.51
	NHL Bain final offer in 2005	$2,238	2.15
	Median MLB Team (2019)	$290	5.03
	Median NBA Team (2019)	$257	6.20
	Median NFL Team (2019)	$439	6.26
	Median NFL Team (2001)	$134	3.90
	Median International Soccer Club (2012)	$244	2.23
Average			3.03
Median			2.75
Median of Big 4 2019 estimates			5.63

Source: Research by *Forbes* (2018, 2019) and SportsEconomics (2019).

SIDEBAR 10.B   The Value of Major League Baseball Teams: Take Annual Revenue and Quintuple it!

In December 2001, MLB commissioner Allan "Bud" Selig was called before the House Judiciary Committee to discuss baseball's antitrust exemption and the possible contraction of a number of teams. As part of the proceedings, Selig released financial information about MLB and its franchises. Exhibit 10.5 summarizes the information. At that time, the franchise valuations fell within a tight range around a price-to-revenue multiple of 1.96x. Since then, MLB revenues have increased by about 150% and franchise valuations are more than six times higher, as shown in Exhibit 10.6. Why have franchise valuations increased more than revenues? One answer is that profits are much higher than they were in 2001, and ultimately net income or profit is what owners are after (besides winning). Price-to-revenue multiples serve as a stable proxy to looking directly at income or earnings figures, which are less stable. In 2019 for MLB the price-to-revenue multiple was about 5.03, compared to 1.96 in 2001.

EXHIBIT 10.5   2001 financial information for MLB and its franchises, including estimates of franchise values.

FRANCHISE	2001 REVENUES	SELIG VALUATION	SELIG MULTIPLE
Anaheim Angels	$91,731,000	$193,056,000	2.10
Arizona Diamondbacks	$125,132,000	$243,832,000	1.95
Atlanta Braves	$146,851,000	$283,055,000	1.93
Baltimore Orioles	$128,302,000	$251,257,000	1.96
Boston Red Sox	$176,982,000	$337,526,000	1.91
Chicago Cubs	$129,774,000	$252,980,000	1.95
Chicago White Sox	$111,682,000	$219,163,000	1.96
Cincinnati Reds	$70,887,000	$155,178,000	2.19
Cleveland Indians	$162,242,000	$311,230,000	1.92
Colorado Rockies	$131,813,000	$257,597,000	1.95
Detroit Tigers	$106,791,000	$218,709,000	2.05
Florida Marlins	$60,547,000	$139,655,000	2.31

EXHIBIT 10.5 Cont.

FRANCHISE	2001 REVENUES	SELIG VALUATION	SELIG MULTIPLE
Houston Astros	$124,629,000	$244,073,000	1.96
Kansas City Royals	$63,696,000	$143,389,000	2.25
Los Angeles Dodgers	$143,607,000	$278,107,000	1.94
Milwaukee Brewers	$113,350,000	$228,444,000	2.02
Minnesota Twins	$56,266,000	$131,621,000	2.34
Montreal Expos*	$34,171,000	$96,859,000	2.83
New York Mets	$182,631,000	$349,593,000	1.91
New York Yankees	$242,208,000	$457,876,000	1.89
Oakland Athletics	$75,469,000	$161,458,000	2.14
Philadelphia Phillies	$81,515,000	$174,782,000	2.14
Pittsburgh Pirates	$108,706,000	$219,194,000	2.02
San Diego Padres	$79,722,000	$168,112,200	2.11
San Francisco Giants	$170,295,000	$334,282,000	1.96
Seattle Mariners	$202,434,000	$386,077,000	1.91
St. Louis Cardinals	$132,459,000	$256,689,000	1.94
Tampa Bay Devil Rays	$80,595,000	$173,574,000	2.15
Texas Rangers	$134,910,000	$261,076,000	1.94
Toronto Blue Jays	$78,479,000	$166,788,000	2.13
MEDIAN	$118,989,500	$236,138,000	1.96
AVERAGE	$118,262,533	$236,507,740	2.06
STANDARD DEVIATION	$47,435,620	$82,304,131	0.19

* In 2005, the Montreal Expos relocated to Washington DC, and became the Nationals.

EXHIBIT 10.6   2019 & 2020 (avg.) financial information for MLB and its franchises ($ millions), including estimates of franchise values.*

TEAM	CURRENT VALUE	REVENUE	OPERATING INCOME	PRICE/ REVENUE	PRICE/ INCOME	OPERATING MARGIN
New York Yankees	4,800	676	32	7.1	150.0	0.05
Los Angeles Dodgers	3,350	553	96	6.1	35.1	0.17
Boston Red Sox	3,250	518	87	6.3	37.6	0.17
Chicago Cubs	3,150	462	78	6.8	40.6	0.17
San Francisco Giants	3,050	457	90	6.7	33.9	0.20
New York Mets	2,350	351	19	6.7	127.0	0.05
St. Louis Cardinals	2,150	370	69	5.8	31.4	0.19
Los Angeles Angels	1,938	363	40	5.3	48.4	0.11
Philadelphia Phillies	1,925	367	84	5.3	23.1	0.23
Washington Nationals	1,825	353	26	5.2	71.6	0.07
Houston Astros	1,813	394	83	4.6	22.0	0.21
Atlanta Braves	1,750	363	82	4.8	21.5	0.22
Texas Rangers	1,700	330	50	5.2	34.0	0.15
Chicago White Sox	1,625	279	71	5.8	22.9	0.25
Seattle Mariners	1,588	318	31	5.0	51.2	0.10
Toronto Blue Jays	1,563	265	0	5.9	NA	0.00
San Diego Padres	1,400	288	51	4.9	27.7	0.18
Baltimore Orioles	1,340	254	25	5.3	53.1	0.10

EXHIBIT 10.6   Cont.

TEAM	CURRENT VALUE	REVENUE	OPERATING INCOME	PRICE/ REVENUE	PRICE/ INCOME	OPERATING MARGIN
Arizona Diamond backs	1,290	277	19	4.7	69.7	0.07
Pittsburgh Pirates	1,268	264	53	4.8	24.1	0.20
Colorado Rockies	1,250	298	26	4.2	48.1	0.09
Detroit Tigers	1,250	276	25	4.5	51.0	0.09
Minnesota Twins	1,250	283	29	4.4	43.9	0.10
Milwaukee Brewers	1,188	292	55	4.1	21.8	0.19
Cleveland Indians	1,150	286	30	4.0	39.0	0.10
Oakland Athletics	1,100	222	22	5.0	51.2	0.10
Cincinnati Reds	1,063	267	30	4.0	35.4	0.11
Tampa Bay Rays	1,030	246	48	4.2	21.7	0.19
Kansas City Royals	1,025	248	16	4.1	63.5	0.07
Miami Marlins	990	223	−14	4.4	−71.0	−0.06
Average	1,814	338	45	5.2	42.4	0.13
Median	1,575	295	36	5.0	37.6	0.11
Standard Deviation	890	105	29	0.9	36.6	0.07

* Current value of team based on current stadium deal (unless new stadium is pending) without deductions for debt (other than stadium debt). Debt/value includes stadium debt. Operating income is earnings before interest, taxes, depreciation, and amortization.

Source: Forbes, www.forbes.com/mlb-valuations/list/.

SIDEBAR 10.C   Price-to-earnings Ratios are Volatile for Sport Teams

Stock market investors often use P/E ratios to estimate enterprise or firm values, but for sport team valuations we use P/R ratios, because sport team owners do not always seek maximization of earnings. Also, because of related-party transactions, reported sport franchise earnings do not necessarily reflect a team's true value.

In 2001, MLB commissioner Selig claimed that each franchise was worth about twice its annual revenues. In fact, the standard deviation was so small that only three low-revenue teams (the Marlins, Twins, and Expos) appeared above a 2.30x multiple, and only the Yankees fell below 1.89x. Yet, data provided in the *Forbes* 2001 MLB team valuations yield a P/R multiple of around 2.35x *(Forbes*, 2002). Why would *Forbes* give a significantly higher multiple than Selig? One reason is that it was in MLB's interests to appear small and financially poor before Congress, rather than presenting itself as a highly profitable monopoly.

Similarly, Selig's information shows that MLB had total operating losses of $232 million for 2001, whereas *Forbes* shows an operating profit of about $74 million. Because of related-party transactions and transfer pricing for MLB, it is possible to report differing amounts of revenues and expenses, depending on how the revenues and expenses are assigned.

Based on *Forbes*'s data for 2019 (Exhibit 10.6), MLB's average P/R multiple is 5.19 (and median 5.03). Yet, the standard deviation is quite low at 0.86, meaning that most of the teams are valued at around the 5.19 multiple. Given the changes in the traditional advertising business model of television, sports programming has become very important because it is one of the few types of programming that people want to watch live (and thus will be exposed to commercials); thus franchises in larger markets with more lucrative local media deals tend to produce higher income.

Comparing price-to-revenue to price-to-income ratios shows that the latter ratio is so volatile as not to be of much use as a tool for valuing MLB clubs. Recall from Chapter 2 that another term for earnings is income. While the median price-to-income ratio is about 36, which is reasonable and comparable to the stock market, the standard deviation is over 69. One can easily see in Exhibit 10.6 how much the P/I ratios vary across the clubs. Although this is an improvement over 2015, when the median was similar, but the standard deviation was nearly 150, because only a few teams show low income (and thus an unstably high P/I ratio).

In the NFL, the median P/R ratio had remained stable until recently. For example, according to *Forbes* (Ozanian, 2003), the value of NFL franchises in 2002 was estimated at $20.1 billion with revenues of $4.9 billion. Thus, the median P/R ratio ranged from 4.0 in 2002 to 4.7 in 2015. Between 2002 and 2015, revenues in the NFL nearly doubled, then from 2015 to 2019, they rose by 50%. In the first period, P/R ratios had not changed very much because the average operating margin (operating income divided by revenue) had remained fairly constant, around 16%.

Yet in the past few years (primarily driven by media revenue growth), margins have grown to around 21%. Therefore, the revenue growth had been matched by income growth, but now since the underlying income margin has grown, so has the P/R ratio, since franchises are more valuable even controlling for revenues because more of those revenues are profits now. In addition, to the extent that winning matters to owners, there is no evidence that the desire to win has changed, either. Yet, in this stable environment, the price-to-income ratio also has a lot of volatility associated with it, as the high standard deviation shows in Exhibit 10.7.

EQUITY SHARES OF THE SAME BUSINESS

Within the market approach, another method for measuring the value of a business is to look at market transactions for known equity amounts in the subject business. For example, if an owner sold 1% of a sports league for $5 million, the implied value of the business (on a non-controlling basis) would be $500 million. Exhibit 10.8 shows the adjustment for the time value of money from the actual transaction date of January 1, 2017, up to the valuation date of June 30, 2019. The valuation growth rate used here is 6.5%. Based on this rate, $500 million on January 1, 2017, is equivalent to $585 million on June 30, 2019. Adding the controlling interest premium of 24% puts the value of the sports business at $726 million. (We add the control premium because the 1% stake does not provide control of the league, whereas the value of the league in its entirety includes control.)

A transaction that occurred 2.5 years in the past would be adjusted to reflect changes in the underlying revenue or income. For example, if the league's income grew at 6.5% annually during those 2.5 years, then it stands to reason that the value of the league grew at a similar rate, because the owner will receive a higher income along with the same (assumed) other benefits of owning the league.

Income Approach

The income approach is based on the idea that the fair market value of an asset is equal to the present value of its expected future cash flows. An analysis of this type is often referred to as a discounted cash flow (DCF) analysis. We project cash flows for a number of years into the future and discount them back to the present (or the date of valuation), using a suitable discount rate. To calculate the fair market value of a business, we add the present value of expected future net cash flows to the residual value of the business and subtract outstanding debt. In other words, we discount each year's cash flow (whether positive or negative) and add these figures together. Separately, we estimate and discount the residual value of the business—what the business will be worth at the end of the period for which we have projected cash flows, whether the company will be liquidated or continue operations. Finally, we calculate the discounted value of debt that will remain at that time. The sum of all these amounts provides an estimate of the value of the business.

EXHIBIT 10.7 2019 & 2020 (avg.) financial information for the NFL and its franchises, including estimates of franchise values ($ millions).*

FRANCHISE	CURRENT VALUE	REVENUES	OPERATING INCOME	PRICE/ REVENUE	PRICE/ INCOME	OPERATING MARGIN
Dallas	5,250	907	393	5.8	13.4	0.43
New England	3,950	597	238	6.6	16.6	0.40
New York Giants	3,600	506	146	7.1	24.7	0.29
Los Angeles Rams	3,500	384	49	9.1	71.4	0.13
San Francisco	3,275	481	100	6.8	32.9	0.21
Washington	3,250	492	121	6.6	26.9	0.25
Chicago	3,175	442	81	7.2	39.2	0.18
New York Jets	3,025	459	123	6.6	24.7	0.27
Houston	2,950	481	169	6.1	17.5	0.35
Philadelphia	2,900	470	132	6.2	22.0	0.28
Denver	2,825	437	100	6.5	28.3	0.23
Green Bay	2,740	445	51	6.2	54.3	0.11
Pittsburgh	2,695	427	94	6.3	28.8	0.22
Atlanta	2,678	455	105	5.9	25.5	0.23
Baltimore	2,670	428	119	6.2	22.4	0.28
Miami	2,670	429	62	6.2	43.4	0.14
Seattle	2,668	426	89	6.3	30.1	0.21
Oakland	2,660	346	26	7.7	102.3	0.08
Minnesota	2,550	418	78	6.1	32.9	0.19
Indianapolis	2,515	383	86	6.6	29.4	0.22
Los Angeles Chargers	2,390	361	60	6.6	39.8	0.17
Carolina	2,350	410	70	5.7	33.6	0.17
Jacksonville	2,203	408	70	5.4	31.5	0.17
Arizona	2,200	390	81	5.6	27.3	0.21

EXHIBIT 10.7   Cont.

FRANCHISE	CURRENT VALUE	REVENUES	OPERATING INCOME	PRICE/ REVENUE	PRICE/ INCOME	OPERATING MARGIN
Kansas City	2,200	395	72	5.6	30.8	0.18
New Orleans	2,178	427	121	5.1	18.1	0.28
Tampa Bay	2,100	392	77	5.4	27.3	0.20
Tennessee	2,100	383	51	5.5	41.6	0.13
Cleveland	2,063	387	32	5.3	65.5	0.08
Cincinnati	1,900	370	59	5.1	32.2	0.16
Detroit	1,825	373	39	4.9	47.3	0.10
Buffalo	1,750	375	75	4.7	23.5	0.20
Average	2,713	440	99	6.2	34.5	0.21
Median	2,669	427	81	6.2	29.8	0.20
Standard Deviation	703	99	69	0.9	18.0	0.08

* Current value of team based on current stadium deal (unless new stadium is pending) without deductions for debt (other than stadium debt). Debt/value includes stadium debt. Operating income is earnings before interest, taxes, depreciation, and amortization.
Source: Forbes, www.forbes.com/nfl-valuations/list.

STEPS IN THE INCOME APPROACH

Exhibit 10.9 provides an example of a DCF valuation analysis for NewFangled Sports Products, Inc. (NFSP), a fictitious sports product manufacturing company. Recall that the principle behind the DCF method is that the value of a business or asset is based on the cash that it is expected to generate, as opposed to what an investor would pay for a similar business (as in the market approach) or what it would cost to recreate the business (as in the cost approach, discussed later).

How far out should the analyst project cash flows? The answer is: for the lifetime of the business. Two important qualifications make the application of DCF manageable. First, it is seldom necessary in practice to project cash flows beyond ten or 15 years (and can be uncertain even beyond five years), because a cash flow that far in the future is not worth a significant amount today, when typical discount rates are used (see Chapter 4). Second, once the business reaches a stable, mature growth period, we can calculate a "terminal" value. In fact, analysts typically assume that a company cannot continue to grow faster

EXHIBIT 10.8 Adjustments in the valuation of a sports league reflecting the time value of money.

EQUITY TRANSACTIONS

$ in thousands	1-JAN-17	1-JAN-18	1-JAN-19	30-JUN-19
Interest Purchased	1.00%			
Repurchase Price	$5,000			
Implied Business Valuation on a Minority Basis (a)	$500,000	$532,521	$567,156	$585,310
Annual Income Growth	6.5%			
Adjustments for Control	24.0%			24.0%
Implied League Valuation on a Control Basis				$725,784
Implied Value of Sports League	**$725,784**			

Note: The half-year convention is used for 2019 since the valuation date is June 30, 2019.

SIDEBAR 10.D Sponsorship Valuation ... It's All About the Comps

The valuation of sponsorships or endorsements is difficult because, typically, product sales have many other drivers besides the sponsorship. In other words, suppose a telecom company sponsors an auto racing team and notices that sales increase. Can the company attribute those sales to the sponsorship? Perhaps the sales increase was the result of other factors, such as advertising, public relations, new product features, or the economy. Most current methods of sponsorship valuation rely on understanding what others pay in the marketplace for similar exposure to that of a prospective sponsor.

Information is available from companies such as IEG or Wasserman about the racing teams in each sport and the amounts that other sponsors are paying for their sponsorships. This gives both the property (racing team) and the sponsor an idea of the value of a sponsorship at a given level. Essentially, the information is presented with an approach akin to the market approach, in that other similar sponsorships are the points of reference.

To measure the value that a specific sponsor has received from a sponsorship, we would need to look at the assets that are included in the sponsorship. In a recent racing sponsorship, the sponsor received television exposure, in-person exposure, hospitality, online presence/exposure via the racing team's website and sanctioning body website, the ability to sit in a car and go around the track, and the ability to use the sponsorship in advertising. For measurements of the value of each of those assets within the sponsorship package, we can turn to any of a number of companies that offer this service.

For instance, the TV exposure can be measured and compared (taking a market approach) to what it would cost to buy a corresponding amount of advertising time and create a commercial instead of having the camera show the sponsor's logo. This is often called media equivalency, as stated earlier. The in-person or on-site exposure can be compared to the cost of signage at the event. Similarly, online exposure can be compared to the cost per thousand for getting members of the target market to visit a website. Additionally, we can add up the cost of providing hospitality at an event (taking a cost approach) to measure the value of the hospitality portion of the sponsorship.

Other assets, such as obtaining direct business from a company, are potentially very valuable. For example, Mobil 1 sponsored the Corvette racing team in the American Le Mans. It was also a business partner of General Motors, which owns the Corvette brand. This sponsorship may help Mobil 1 develop or maintain its relationship with GM. The measurement of the value of the direct business is often based on the income (taking an income approach) that the company would earn if it received more business from another company. Indirect business relationships can be developed among sponsors of the same racing team, too.

As an example of a sponsorship that included all of these elements, a racing team in the American Le Mans was shown to have provided about $6 million of value to its primary sponsor, most of that coming from television exposure (*Vici Racing v. T-Mobile*, 2014).

EXHIBIT 10.9 Discounted cash flow valuation analysis.

NEWFANGLED SPORTS PRODUCTS, INC.	PROJECTED					
$s in thousands	FYE CURRENT YEAR	FYE CY+1	FYE CY+2	FYE CY+3	FYE CY+4	TERMINAL YEAR
Revenue	$7,600	$8,000	$8,400	$8,900	$9,300	$9,800
Growth		5.3%	5.0%	6.0%	4.5%	5.4%
Cost of goods sold	3,700	3,895	4,089	4,333	4,528	4,771
Gross profit	3,900	4,105	4,311	4,567	4,772	5,029
SG&A	3,000	3,158	3,316	3,513	3,671	3,868
R&D	500	400	300	300	300	300
EBITDA	400	547	695	754	801	861
Depreciation & amortization	300	300	300	300	300	300

(continued)

EXHIBIT 10.9 Cont.

NEWFANGLED SPORTS PRODUCTS, INC.				PROJECTED		
$s in thousands	FYE CURRENT YEAR	FYE CY+1	FYE CY+2	FYE CY+3	FYE CY+4	TERMINAL YEAR
EBIT	100	247	395	454	501	561
Interest expense	5	6	7	8	9	10
EBT	95	241	388	446	492	551
Effective tax rate	40.0%	40.0%	40.0%	40.0%	40.0%	40.0%
Income tax expense	38	97	155	178	197	220
Net income	$57	$145	$233	$268	$295	$330
Debt-free net income	57	145	233	268	295	330
Depreciation/ amortization	300	300	300	300	300	300
Gross cash flow	357	445	533	568	595	630
Capital expenditures	400	350	200	100	100	100
Increase in net working capital	75	60	60	75	60	75
Net cash flow	($118)	$35	$273	$393	$435	$455
Discount period in years	0.50	1.50	2.50	3.50	4.50	5.50
Discount factor[a]	0.9506	0.8588	0.7758	0.7008	0.6329	0.5717
Discount rate[b]	10.7%					
Perpetual growth rate[c]	3.0%					
Terminal value[d]						$5,913
Present value—cash flow/terminal value[e]	($112)	$30	$212	$275	$276	$3,381
Net present value	$4,061					

Notes:

a Reflects mid-year discounting convention. Discount factor (the number that is multiplied by the net cash flow to make it discounted cash flow) is $(1/(1+d))$ for one year into the future, $(1/(1+d)^2)$ for two years into the future, and so on, where d is the discount rate.

b Based on the median weighted average cost of capital as reported in Valuation Handbook 2019 U.S. Industry Cost of Capital (Duff & Phelps) for SIC 59.

c Based on estimated long-term cash flow growth rate of the economy in general.

d Terminal value = terminal year cash flow/(discount rate – perpetual growth rate).

e Present value to mid-current year.

than the economy forever into the future, so its growth rate is constrained by the growth rate of the economy.

In Exhibit 10.9, we value NFSP from the current year (CY) to CY+4 at a higher than average growth rate. Then, we project that it will settle into a 3% annual growth rate in perpetuity (going forward forever). The revenues forecasted for a five-year period typically have the most impact on the final value: revenue growth drives income growth, which drives cash flow growth. To forecast revenue growth, we must consider

1. Whether the industry in which the company operates is growing or shrinking, and at what rate.
2. How the company is doing in terms of market share compared with its competitors.
3. Expectations for new product offerings.
4. Expected price changes.
5. Any other factors that would affect demand for the company's product(s).

The revenue growth projected for NFSP is between 4.5% and 6.0%, based on business forecasts. To calculate net cash flow for CY, we start with revenue and then

1. Subtract variable costs, such as the cost of goods sold (COGS), to obtain gross profit.
2. Subtract other expenses, such as selling, general, and administrative costs (SG&A) and research and development (R&D), to obtain earnings before interest, taxes, depreciation, and amortization (EBITDA).
3. Subtract depreciation and amortization (D&A) to obtain earnings before interest and taxes (EBIT).
4. Subtract interest expenses to obtain earnings before taxes (EBT).
5. Subtract income taxes to obtain net income (a 40% corporate income tax rate is assumed).
6. Add back depreciation and amortization (D&A) to determine gross cash flow.
7. Subtract capital expenditures and increases in net working capital to obtain net cash flow (NCF).

This information is typically drawn from audited financial statements and business forecasts.

In Step 6, we add back depreciation and amortization after calculating income taxes to determine gross cash flow. This is because D&A expenses reduce the company's income tax liability, but they do not actually lower the real cash flow that is available to the company's owners—so we add them back after calculating income tax.

In Step 7, we subtract increases in net working capital and capital expenditures from gross cash flow to determine net cash flow. **Net working capital (NWC)** refers to the cash needed to run the business on a daily basis (measured in annual dollars needed), which is not available to be given to the owners of the business because it is needed for operations. We calculate it simply by subtracting current liabilities from current assets. The change in working capital is its difference from year to year. We subtract increases in net working capital because these increases in net working capital are needed to run the business; therefore, that cash is not available as a cash flow to the owners of the company. We add decreases in net working capital because a decrease in net working capital means it is less expensive to run the business throughout the year, so that extra cash is now available to the owners of the business. Thus, we add it to cash flow. In other words, if more working capital is required each year, more cash is needed for operations, and that cash is not available to the owners; the converse is also true.

VALUATION CALCULATIONS IN THE INCOME APPROACH

Exhibit 10.9 shows that NCF for NFSP is negative during CY (even though net income is positive), but it becomes positive thereafter. Once we have estimated NCF, we discount it back to the middle of CY (June 30 of CY). For NFSP, at the end of CY, NCF is –$118,000, but when this figure is multiplied by the discount factor (DF, defined in note (a) in Exhibit 10.9) it becomes –$111,000 (noted as present value in Exhibit 10.9). We calculate the discount factor as follows:

$$DF = \frac{1}{(1+i)^n}$$

where i = the discount rate
n = the number of years in the period

For the current year, we are discounting the December CY value back to June CY, so $n = 0.5$. For CY+1, the estimate is for December of the year following CY, which is 1.5 years ahead of June CY, so $n = 1.5$, and so on for CY+2 through CY+4. We select a discount rate of 10.7%, which Duff & Phelps (2019) reports for SIC 59 (Miscellaneous Retail). We would normally use the *actual* weighted average cost of capital (WACC) that NFSP faces. The rate of 10.7% is simply the median that Duff & Phelps reports for this industry, and we have selected it for illustrative purposes.

The perpetual growth rate—the implied growth rate of NCF year after year beyond CY+4—impacts the expected NCF only beyond the terminal year. To obtain the terminal year PV, we subtract the perpetual growth rate from the discount rate and divide the terminal year NCF, $455,000, by this number.[2] The capitalized value of the company in CY+5 and beyond is $5.9 million. To bring that back to mid-year CY, we multiply it by the discount factor (0.5717). The resulting present value of the terminal value of the company is $3.381 million. Finally, we add all present values to obtain the net present value (NPV) of expected future net cash flows, $4.061 million. In this example, there is no residual value, because the business is expected to continue operations indefinitely.[3] Assuming the present value of outstanding debt is $500,000, a fair market value for NFSP is $3.561 million.

2   See Appendix 10.A for a proof that the discount factor's infinite geometric series converges such that NPV = NCF/($r - g$), where r is the discount rate and g is the perpetual growth rate.
3   Suppose a business's sole income is a patent that is expected to run out in a certain number of years, and the business will cease operations at that time. In such a situation, the analyst would determine the residual value of the assets (perhaps an office building, land, and cash), add that to the NPV of NCF, and subtract the NPV of any debt.

SIDEBAR 10.E What Discount Rate would Provide NFSP Investors with their Required Return?

As discussed in Chapter 4, if $100 to be received in one year is worth $90 today (implying a discount rate of 11.1%), then an investor with $90 today would invest in a company only if that investment could grow from $90 to $100 in one year, or at a rate of 11.1%. Otherwise, the investor might go elsewhere to invest the $90. Thus, the discount rate comes from the opportunity cost that the investor faces when making an investment decision. If the investor requires an 11.1% return, then the cost of capital for the company (the price it must pay in order to return $100 to the investor at the end of one year) is 11.1%. NFSP is anticipating $273,000 in cash flow for CY+2. If this cash flow is required by the investors of the company, and they put $202,000 in during mid-year CY, then, essentially, those investors are asking for a 12.8% return. Therefore, 12.8% is the discount rate needed to provide the investors' required return.

THE INCOME APPROACH AND SPORT FRANCHISES

The DCF method does not apply well to sport franchises because of the non-financial reasons for franchise ownership and related-party transactions. As further evidence that the DCF approach is not applicable to—or at a minimum understates the value of—sport franchises and leagues, *Forbes*'s estimates of team values for MLB for 2019 show that some teams valued at over $1 billion report negative income (the Blue Jays, Orioles, and Marlins; see Exhibit 10.6). Thus, the DCF approach (assuming continued expected negative income and net cash flow) would find a negative value for these franchises, even though they clearly have positive value (i.e., someone would pay a positive amount to buy the franchise).

SIDEBAR 10.F Valuing Highly Profitable Sports Franchises—A Hybrid Income and Market Approach

In recent years, there have been some sports franchises that have reportedly begun to produce extraordinary net income (e.g., Manchester United, Real Madrid, Dallas Cowboys, Los Angeles Lakers). Simply relying on a multiple of revenue would miss the real differences in net income of these franchises compared to the comparables in their leagues.

Imagine a franchise with $200 million in annual revenue, but zero income. Imagine another franchise with $200 million in annual revenue, but with $50 million in income. A price/revenue valuation method might mistakenly value both franchises equally, when the latter would be worth much more. Similarly, consider a franchise that generates $100 million in revenues, has $0 income, and is worth about $320 million (implying a simplified P/R ratio of 3.2x). Consider a franchise that generates $260 million in revenue and $50 million in profit. The application of the 3.2x P/R ratio from the former franchise to the latter would imply a valuation of $832 million. That valuation accounts for revenue differences, but not necessarily income differences.

What if a zero-income NBA franchise only had sportsman owner-ship value (utility or fun value) because it consistently produced zero profit? If so, then a hybrid income and market approach method that adjusts for the weaknesses in the comparables would take the $320 million as the zero-profit value of owning an NBA franchise (because of the utility value of owning it) and *add* to it the capitalization of earnings value of the $50 million in income (which is just a purely financial value of owning a franchise, the same as owning a black box that produces $50 million each year). At a discount rate of 9% and annual growth rate in earnings of 3%, this implies an "income-driven" value of $833 million which would be added to the utility value of $320 million to get $1.15 billion in value (this is a simplification given that no other adjustments have been made). The capitalization of earnings is the same as valuing the terminal value (see Exhibit 10.9).

This hybrid approach separates the fun part of owning an NBA team from the financial part, allowing one to value highly profitable franchises for which the P/R ratio simply undervalues because it doesn't account for the differences in income across the comparables (only revenue). This can be seen by noting that in the NBA, according to *Forbes*, the average P/R ratio is 9.4x for the highly profitable Knicks, Lakers, Warriors, Bulls, and Celtics, while the rest of the NBA has an average P/R ratio of 6.3x. This is clearly because the P/R ratio misses out on valuing the high income of those franchises. In fact, the correlation is over 0.75 between the P/R ratio and operating income of the NBA franchises. If one were to use 6.3x to measure the value of the Lakers, for instance, the estimate of value would be more than $1 billion short of what a 9.4x P/R ratio implies. Thus, a typ-ical NBA P/R ratio alone does not work to value highly profitable sports franchises. The hybrid approach accounts for this.

An accurate DCF analysis requires information about all of the net cash flows available to the team's owner, not just those that are accounted for on the team's financial statements. The analyst will need to know each team's net cash flow; each owner's salary, if any; the net cash flows from national sponsorships, licensing, and media; the net cash flow of the facility in which the team plays; and any revenues from other sources. For instance, a team owner might generate substantial net cash flow through local sponsorships, parking, and concessions but might "book" that information on a facility management company that he or she also owns. Without all of this information, DCF analysis of a sport team will likely show a value that is lower than the team's true value.

SIDEBAR 10.G What's Amalie Arena Worth? The Cost Approach in Action

Most sport arenas are publicly owned or situated on public land and, therefore, are not subject to property taxes; also, they are not frequently bought and sold. Thus, it is rarely necessary to determine the value of a sport arena. However, in 2001, the Florida State Supreme Court determined that private organizations that lease space at public facilities are not necessarily exempt from paying property taxes (*Sebring Airport Authority v. McIntyre*, 1993). This judgment quickly became an important concern for the state's sport teams. Essentially, each team was going to be asked to pay property taxes for the sport arena in which it played.

A sport arena, such as Amalie Arena in Florida (formerly known as the St. Pete Times Forum, Tampa Bay Times Forum, and Ice Palace), has a different value to a private buyer than to a public buyer. This is because the private buyer does not fully internalize the benefit of the arena to the community. Sport arenas often create positive externalities that overflow into the community. In the case of Amalie Arena, these benefits include, but are not limited to, an increase in sales to nearby businesses (at least partially driven by spending from visitors to the community who attend arena events), an increase in value to nearby properties, a positive psychic impact on the community, additional tax revenues, and advertisement for the Tampa Bay region. The value of each of these aspects is difficult to measure. (See Chapter 12 on economic impact.)

The arena, of course, also has a positive value to the owner of the Tampa Bay Lightning (an NHL team), which plays in the arena. The arena, therefore, would have a positive internality to a private buyer, and it has a positive externality to the surrounding community and county (counties in Florida assess and collect property taxes). Whenever a particular entity has these characteristics, without public intervention the free market will produce an arena of less than the socially optimal size and quality. This is one of the reasons why the public often chooses to finance all or part of sport arena construction, notwithstanding whether the public actually receives the full value of the arena. The other reason for the public's willingness to finance arena construction is that the market for sport teams is competitive. If a team can credibly threaten to locate elsewhere, then it can extract more public financing for an arena than if there were plenty of alternative teams (see Chapter 9). As a result, when valuing Amalie Arena, we must account for the private and public value.

The arena originally cost $166 million to build, with the franchise (the Lightning's first ownership group) paying about $73 million of the costs. The day the arena opened, it would not have been worth $166 million to a private buyer, because that buyer would not have been able to capture the arena's full value, especially the overflow value that accrued to local businesses from arena attendees who spent money in local restaurants, hotels, and retail stores. Thus, from a private perspective, we could estimate that the arena is worth, say, $73 million (a reasonable figure because this is the price the franchise paid to gain access to the arena's cash flows).

The public receives about $93 million in additional value from the arena ($166 million less $73 million). Under the cost approach to valuation, the arena was worth $166 million on opening day—the replacement cost. Under the income or market approach, the value is only about $73 million (as a rough estimate, not accounting for negotiating leverage and other factors)—what a private buyer would pay. So, which is it?

The appeals court in Florida sided with the Tampa Bay Lightning franchise, claiming that an arena's value is what a willing buyer would pay for the facility. The Lightning's second ownership group paid $25 million for the facility when it bought the team for $100 million ($25 million was allocated to the facility). Originally, the county assessed the building at $110 million, based on the construction cost (cost approach) and depreciation of approximately $50 million. The decrease from $110 million to $25 million reduces the franchise's property tax burden by 77%.

This example shows that even under an apparently simple approach, the cost approach, the valuation of an asset depends on the standard of value that is accepted. One could argue that the county was actually already collecting property taxes that related to the cost of the arena, because the arena's construction raised property values for those restaurants and other businesses that benefit from it, thus increasing the property taxes of those businesses.

Cost Approach

Under the cost approach to determining the value of a business, the analyst discreetly determines the replacement costs of all of the firm's assets. This approach requires a discreet appraisal of current assets, tangible personal property, real property, and, occasionally, intangible assets. The sum of the asset values serves as an estimate of the business's fair market value. This approach is appropriate for valuing assets for which substitutes could reasonably be bought or built.

The cost approach has never been an accepted approach for measuring sport franchise or league values. The cost approach can be an effective tool for measuring the value of certain assets, such as equipment or a training facility, but it is not helpful for estimating the values of intangible assets that make up a substantial part of enterprise value in sport. Much of the value of a sport franchise, for instance, is in its ability to schedule games with other teams in the league as part of a championship season. This is not something that can be re-created in the marketplace. Consider, for example, the Kentucky Derby horse race. A competitor could host another race, but the value of the competing derby would not be as high as the Kentucky Derby, simply because the Derby has a brand and history that will garner larger revenues.

As the sidebar illustrates, the valuation of sport arenas is complex, because of the difference between the value of the arena to a private business owner and the value to the public in general.

Another example of a valuation in which the market and income approaches were not helpful for valuing the key asset, but the cost approach was useful, involved the valuation of a sponsorship in auto racing. A marketing agent was hired to seek sponsorships for a racing team in Champ Car (now part of IndyCar Racing). The agent was able to secure Toyota as a sponsor. In the agreement, Toyota was to provide $2 million in cash; approximately 50 racing engines; the use of three fully loaded trucks for use to transport equipment, the crew, and so forth; and two engineers from Toyota who were experts on the racing engines.

The marketing agent was due a 15% commission based on the value of the sponsorship. The valuation of the cash was simple ($2 million in cash is worth $2 million)—although, since payments were to occur over three years, the time value of money needed to be accounted for. The analyst valued the use of the three trucks by looking elsewhere for what it would cost to lease similar trucks from a dealer (essentially, the market approach). Similarly, the engineers' time was valued based on how much they were being paid by Toyota. The racing engines, which generate 800 horsepower, were more difficult to value.

To use the income approach, the analyst would need to determine how much more income the racing team earned by using those engines, compared with the next best alternative. Given that winning races and prize money involves many different factors, the income approach was not applicable. The market approach involves understanding what similar engines sell for in the "marketplace." Yet, these engines are generally not sold, but are used in racing as part of these sponsorships in exchange for the sponsor's signage on the car, hospitality, and all of the other benefits from sponsorship. Finally, the analyst employed the cost approach and worked with Toyota Racing Development to determine the incremental cost of making one engine (including parts, labor, and so forth). It turned out that the engines were worth about $50,000 each.

CONCLUSION

Valuation is both a science and an art. For any valuation, the analyst should undertake to use all three approaches: market, income, and cost. If more than one approach may be used, the analyst's second task will be to integrate the findings into a single estimate of value. For some assets, it is possible to use all three approaches. A golf course, for example, could be valued based on the cash flow it generates from greens fees and the like (income approach), the price that buyers are paying for similar golf courses (market approach), and the cost of building a course from scratch (cost approach). For the valuation of sponsorships in sport, analysts should employ the income approach along with the market and cost approach methods that are currently used. All three methods are valid, and the analyst should compare their results to determine the final estimate of value.

Concept Check

1. In Exhibit 10.5, which shows 2001 valuations, why did the Montreal Expos have the highest price-to-revenue multiple under Selig's valuation?
2. Give examples of ways in which the majority owner of a sport team could violate fiduciary duties and financially harm the minority shareholders.
3. In a discounted cash flow analysis, what happens to the NPV if, all else being equal, the discount rate goes up? What happens to the NPV if the growth rate for the terminal value (perpetual growth rate) rises?

4. Give examples of how a sport franchise can use related-party transactions to reduce its net income. For each example, how does it reduce net income?
5. When an analyst determines the value of a private company owned 100% by a single investor by analyzing the share prices of publicly traded companies, what adjustments must he or she make in order to arrive at a final value?

Practice Problems

1. If the minority price for a single share of stock of a company is $20, there are 500,000 shares of stock, and a person offers to buy the entire company for $14.5 million, what is the controlling interest premium being offered?
2. Based on the same information, what is the minority or non-controlling interest discount for this company?

Case Analysis

Net Present Value Calculated under the Discounted Cash Flow Income Approach

As described in Sidebar 4.C, the Silna family had a contract to receive 1/7th of the television revenue of four NBA teams (Denver Nuggets, San Antonio Spurs, Brooklyn Nets, and Indiana Pacers) in perpetuity. The NBA's television deal running from the 2008–2009 season through the 2015–2016 season paid the family $18.9 million annually.

Use the above information and the following parameters to calculate the NPV of the contract.

- The valuation date is January 1, 2009.
- Assume that the Silnas received their first payment on January 1, 2009, and that the payments will continue annually thereafter.
- Assume that the Silnas are taxed at 35% for their income on this deal.
- Assume that their payments from this NBA deal will grow at 2% per year in perpetuity after the final year of this contract. (Although the Silnas' deal has ended in reality, for purposes of this exercise we will assume that the deal will continue forever.)
- Assume a discount rate of 8%.
- Create a table that shows the results you found and gives a brief description of your steps, assumptions, and so forth.
- What would the value be if the discount rate were 10% and the NCF growth rate were 4%?

ADVANCED CASE ANALYSIS

Fair Market Valuation: Market Approach, Income Approach, and Liquidation Value

VALUATION CASE STUDY: THE DUKE'S SPORTING GOODS STORE
OBJECTIVE

The goal of this analysis is to determine a financial valuation of the fair market value of 100% of the Duke's Sporting Goods Store ("Duke's"), by using two of the three approaches to valuation (income and market approaches, but not the cost approach). The valuation date is December 31 of the current year.

Your instructor will provide you with an Excel file containing two spreadsheets: Duke's Discounted Cash Flow Analysis and Market Approach. Data have been entered in these spreadsheets that will allow you to calculate valuations for Duke's under the income and market approaches.

FACTS

1. The company's assets are cash ($100,000), inventory (worth $400,000 based on cost), and accounts receivable ($25,000).
   a. Inventory can be sold back to manufacturers for 50% of its cost.
   b. Accounts receivable can be sold to a collections agency for 40% of its current level.
2. The company's liabilities are accounts payable of $75,000 and accrued expenses of $75,000.
3. The Discounted Cash Flow Analysis spreadsheet shows the most recent three years' income statements in simplified form.
4. Assume the company pays a corporate tax rate of 40%.
5. For the current year, depreciation and amortization is $25,000. The company is using straight-line depreciation. Thus, D&A is expected to be $25,000 going forward.
6. The physical depreciation and/or amortization of fixed assets is allowed to be booked as an expense, thus lowering the taxable income. Yet, it is not an actual decrease in dollars so it is not a decrease in cash flow. That is why it is added back in to net income on the way to calculating net cash flow. Net cash flow is actual physical dollars coming out of the business during the time period.
7. There is no interest expense.
8. For the current year, capital expenditure (CAPEX) is $50,000. CAPEX refers to the current expenditure of money by the company to purchase equipment and other assets that will help the company earn more money in the future. It directly affects net cash flow because it is spent in the current year instead of being passed through to the owners (as NCF).

ASSUMPTIONS

1. Assume the discount rate is 16% (based on comparables collected from a suitable database and other adjustments for risk).
2. Assume that the perpetual growth rate of net cash flow is 3.5% for the terminal year and beyond (the terminal year is the fourth year out from the current year, and it represents every year thereafter, adjusted for the perpetual growth rate).
3. Assume CAPEX is constant over the relevant time periods because the company is consistently and constantly investing in its future.
4. Assume D&A will continue to be $25,000 per year, given that the equipment and capital expenditures are being used to obtain fixed assets that are depreciable.

INCOME APPROACH (worth 45 points)

1. **Forecast.** Use the Discounted Cash Flow Analysis spreadsheet provided by your instructor and forecast revenues and expenses for current year + 1 (CY+1), CY+2, CY+3, and terminal year. For this case study, use only the previous years' revenues and expenses as a guide. (Normally, you would also use other information about the economy, the industry, the company, and so forth.) Come up with your own reasonable forecast.

2. **Net income.** Calculate the net income for CY+1, CY+2, CY+3, and terminal year.

3. **Net cash flow.** Calculate the net cash flow for CY+1, CY+2, CY+3, and terminal year.

   a. As described in the text and illustrated in Exhibit 10.9, calculate NCF from net income.

   b. Start with net income and add back depreciation and amortization to find gross cash flow.

   c. Subtract CAPEX from gross cash flow.

   d. Subtract any increase (or add any decrease) in net working capital. To calculate changes in NWC, subtract current liabilities from current assets (not including inventory, since, even though inventory is technically a current asset, a manager would not want to rely on inventory to pay workers). Make a reasonable assumption for changes in NWC for future years.

   e. The result is net cash flow.

4. **Net present value.** Calculate the NPV of Duke's.

   a. Determine the discount period for each year (CY and going forward).

   b. Determine the discount factor for each year, including the terminal year.

   c. Enter the discount rate and perpetual growth rate in the spreadsheet.

   d. Calculate the terminal value.

   e. Calculate the present value of the NCF for each year, including the terminal year.

   f. Add up each year's present value to find the net present value of the entire business, based on cash flow.

MARKET APPROACH (worth 45 points)

After an exhaustive search, three businesses that appear to be comparable to Duke's are found. The Market Approach spreadsheet gives basic financial information about the businesses and recent transactions involving them and provides space for the calculations. The comparable businesses are the following:

- **Charlie's Sporting Goods.** Charlie's is located in a neighboring town and has a similar clientele to Duke's. It has been in operation for seven years and over the past three years has generated steady revenues and net income. The current majority owner, Bill, purchased Charlie's from the founder two years ago for $1.5 million. He sold a small piece of it recently for $60,000.

- **Mary's Sporting Goods.** Mary's is located a few towns away and has existed for over a decade. It specializes in women's and girls' sporting goods and draws from a larger market area than Duke's. Mary's offers free training on its equipment, which adds to its expenses, but Sally (the current owner) feels that this policy grows its customer base and leads to more sales. Sally, who is quite risk averse (like Mary), purchased the business outright in the current year.

- **Jamie's Sporting Goods.** Jamie's is a three-store chain located on the north and south sides of the nearest large city. It has been operating for over two decades. It recently added its third store and financed this expansion with a loan from a local bank. It is paying substantial interest on that loan. While it produces a high net income, it is also more leveraged than Mary's or Charlie's. Jamie, the current majority owner, sold 8% of the business for $500,000 in the current year.

  1. **Ratio calculations.** Calculate the relevant ratios for the comparables.
  2. **Valuation of subject company based on comparables.** Use the market approach to determine a financial value for Duke's.
  3. **Adjustments.** Adjust the financial value of Duke's for a controlling interest premium and marketability discount, if needed.

LIQUIDATION VALUE (worth 10 points)

What is the liquidation value (as opposed to the fair market value) of Duke's? Look at the present value of all assets that could be liquidated and account for all debts (at their present value). Determine the sum of those values. In other words, if the company were to be liquidated, how much cash would be left over?

APPENDIX 10.A PROOF OF THE CALCULATION OF THE NPV OF THE TERMINAL VALUE

Following is proof that the net present value of the terminal value is equal to the net cash flow divided by the difference between the discount rate and the growth rate of the business's NCF. Since $\infty-1$ does not exist, but reduces to ∞, the last component of Eq. (1) has the same exponent in the numerator and denominator. Eq. (3) recognizes that the right-hand side of Eq. (2) is equal to NPV, as written in Eq. (1), plus NCF/(1 + g).

$$\text{NPV} = \frac{\text{NCF}}{(1+r)} + \frac{\text{NCF}(1+g)^1}{(1+r)^2} + \cdots + \frac{\text{NCF}(1+g)^\infty}{(1+r)^\infty} \tag{1}$$

$$\frac{(1+r)}{(1+g)}\text{NPV} = \frac{\text{NCF}}{(1+g)} + \frac{\text{NCF}}{(1+r)^1} + \frac{\text{NCF}(1+g)}{(1+r)^2} + \cdots + \frac{\text{NCF}(1+g)^\infty}{(1+r)^\infty} \tag{2}$$

$$\frac{(1+r)}{1+g}\text{NPV} = \frac{\text{NCF}}{(1+g)} + \text{NPV} \tag{3}$$

$$\text{NPV} = \frac{\text{NCF}}{(r-g)} \tag{4}$$

References

Barrabi, T. (2019, August 20). MLS expands to St. Louis: Why $200M startup fee may soon seem like a bargain. *FOXBusiness*.

Brunner, J. (2006, April 5). Tax write-off may help ease owners' losses. *Seattle Times*.

Comment, R. (2012). Revisiting the illiquidity discount for private companies: A new (and "skeptical") restricted-stock study. *Journal of Applied Corporate Finance*, 24(1), 80–91.

Eichelberger, C. (2006, January 11). Hockey teams gain investment luster as NHL refutes obituaries. *Bloomberg News*.

Forbes. (2002, April 15). MLB team values.

Fort, R. (2006). The value of Major League Baseball ownership. *International Journal of Sport Finance*, 1(1), 9–20.

Foster, G., Greyser, S., & Walsh, B. (2005). *The business of sports: Text and cases on strategy and management*. Oklahoma City: Southwestern.

International Valuation Standards Council. (2007). *International valuation standards* (8th ed.). London: Author.

Késenne, S. (2006). Competitive balance in team sports and the impact of revenue sharing. *Journal of Sport Management*, 20(1), 39–51.

Lafayette, J. (2019, August 29). Disney sells YES network to group including Sinclair. *Broadcasting and Cable*.

Ozanian, M. (1999, September 20). What's your team worth? *Forbes*.

Ozanian, M. (2003, September 15). Showing you the money. *Forbes*. Retrieved from www.forbes.com/free_forbes/2003/ 0915/081tab.html.

Ozanian, M. (2013, August 1). Columbus Crew sold by Hunt Sports Group for record $68 million. *Forbes*. Retrieved from www.forbes.com/sites/mikeozanian/2013/08/01/columbus-crew-sold-by-hunt-sports-group-for-record-68-million/.

Ozanian, M. (2014, January 24). Murdoch buys control of New York Yankees channel for $3.9 billion. *Forbes*. Retrieved from www.forbes.com/sites/mikeozanian/2014/01/24/murdoch-buys-control-of-yes-network-for-3-9-billion/.

Ozanian, M., & Badenhausen, K. (2006, April 20). The business of baseball. *Forbes*.

Pratt, S. (2008). *Valuing a business: The analysis and appraisal of closely held companies* (5th ed.). New York: McGraw-Hill.

Rascher, D. (2006). Executive interview with Randy Vataha. *International Journal of Sport Finance*, 1(2), 71–76.

Sebring Airport Authority v. McIntyre, 623 So. 2d 541 (Fla. 2d DCA 1993).

Shanahan, M. (2004, December 28). Wyc Grousbeck would jump through hoops to make Celtics a winner again. *Boston Globe*.

Smith, C. (2018, November 14). Major League Soccer's most valuable teams 2018: Atlanta United debuts on top. *Forbes*.

Valuation Handbook. (2019). U.S. industry cost of capital. Duff & Phelps.

Vici Racing LLC v. T-Mobile USA Inc., 13–1615 (2014).

Zimbalist, A. (1998, October 18). Just another fish story. *New York Times*.

Zimbalist, A. (2003). *May the best team win: Baseball economics and public policy*. Washington, DC: Brookings Institution Press.

CHAPTER 11

Feasibility Studies

Daniel A. Rascher

KEY CONCEPTS

comparables analysis
competitive analysis
corporate depth
cost-benefit analysis
feasibility study

financing analysis
market demand
primary research
secondary research

INTRODUCTION

When the construction of a new stadium or arena is under consideration, many questions must be answered: What would it cost to build? Where would it be located? How would it be paid for? Does it make sense for local government to help fund it? Would events at the facility generate enough revenue to justify building it? Feasibility studies help answer these questions.

FEASIBILITY STUDIES DEFINED

In general, a **feasibility study** is a study conducted to determine whether a project is likely to be sensible and successful, considering such items as engineering, land use, financing, demand, and economic impact. Feasibility studies in sport are undertaken to determine the practicality and likely success of large projects. They can answer such questions as

- whether a city should build a community recreation center, a professional sport stadium or arena, or a public pool
- whether a metropolitan area should lure a sport team to town, and how it could be done
- whether a city should bid to host a major sporting event
- whether an athletic director should build a new facility or renovate an existing one

- whether a university should add a locker room to the campus recreation center
- whether an entrepreneur should open a new health club
- whether a small town should build a new soccer field.

A feasibility study incorporates many **cost-benefit analyses**—analyses of the cost of a project in relation to its potential benefits. For a sport facility, a cost-benefit analysis assesses whether there is likely to be enough demand for events at the new facility and enough corporate support for sponsorship of the facility. Together, these two assessments determine whether there is a *market* for the project. Additionally, a feasibility study analyzes how to fund a project, where it should be located, its cost, and its scale. It may also include information on the operation of the facility once it is in place or methods to secure a major tenant.

Phases of a Feasibility Study

Feasibility studies are often broken into two phases. The initial phase, or a Phase I feasibility study, tests whether a more in-depth analysis should be undertaken. It is typically based on secondary sources of information, including comparisons with other sport facilities and other similar cities or communities. Phase I is quicker to complete and is significantly less costly than a more in-depth study. The general purpose is to present the information that the parties need in order to proceed with project development discussions. If the project passes muster, then often a Phase II, or more in-depth, study is completed, based on primary data that are generated specifically for the study. A Phase II feasibility study for a sport facility lays out a specific financing plan (whereas a Phase I financing analysis will present a number of possible financing sources), actual site selection (not just possibilities), facility design details and renderings, a market demand analysis based on primary research about location (not just comparisons to other facilities and cities), and primary research on economic impact.

Parts of a Feasibility Study

A feasibility study typically consists of four main parts, which provide analyses of

1. Market demand
2. Location, construction cost, and engineering
3. Financing
4. Economic and fiscal impact.

The findings in each of these sections will affect or be affected by the findings of the other sections. As Exhibit 11.1 illustrates, the analysis of market demand will help determine the suggested size of the facility, including the number of seats, luxury suites, premium food areas, and so forth (see arrow 1). The location, construction cost, and engineering analysis suggests a suitable location for the facility and determines the overall cost of construction, based on the size suggested by the market demand analysis. That cost will be an input into the **financing analysis**—an assessment of how much money will be needed to build the facility and from which sources (arrow 2). The information about the

EXHIBIT 11.1 The parts of a feasibility study.

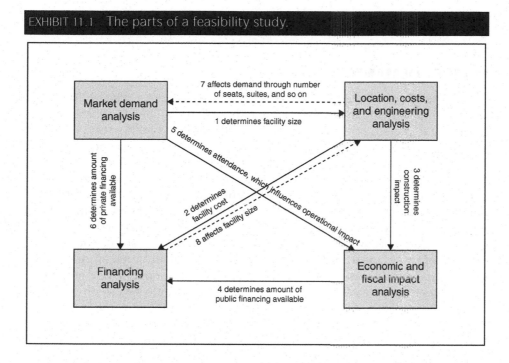

cost and process of construction will help determine the economic and fiscal impact of the facility during the construction period (arrow 3).

The fiscal impact portion of the economic impact analysis provides information on how much government revenue the construction and operation of the facility will generate. That revenue will be considered in the evaluation of possible financing sources, and it will also be a factor in the determination of how much public money will be used to finance the construction (arrow 4). The market demand findings provide information on expected attendance for events at the facility. That information will factor into the analysis of the facility's economic and fiscal impact (arrow 5). Market demand findings will also help in the determination of how much net private revenue the facility and its events will generate. These private revenue sources and amounts (especially the possible naming rights sponsorship) will be listed as possible private financing sources (arrow 6).

Feedback loops in the process will cause readjustments in the original estimates. Once the location, costs, and engineering analysis determines the size of the facility and related costs, the facility size may change from the original estimate, which was based solely on market demand (arrow 7). The change in the number of seats and luxury suites will, for instance, affect the overall estimate of the number of customers. This estimate will then affect all of the other sections of the feasibility study. Another feedback loop links financing with the overall cost and size of the facility. The financing costs, largely determined by interest rates, will affect the overall cost of construction and can limit the size of the facility (arrow 8).

A detailed examination of market demand analysis follows, making up the bulk of this chapter. Because economic impact is an important and diverse topic, it has its own chapter (Chapter 12). Similarly, facility financing, briefly mentioned here, is discussed in detail in Chapter 9. A thorough examination of construction costs and engineering is beyond the scope of this text, but at the end of this chapter we summarize the elements of this part of a feasibility study.

MARKET DEMAND

The market demand analysis often drives much of the rest of a feasibility study, and it is typically the major portion of a Phase I study. For a sport facility, it is necessary to measure the **market demand**—the demand in the marketplace for a facility—in order to determine whether the facility will attract enough events, patrons, and corporate dollars to justify its construction. The likely demand is also important for establishing the specifications of the facility in terms of seats, luxury suites, club seats,[1] parking spaces, and square footage.

The researchers who are conducting a feasibility study use both primary and secondary methods to estimate market demand. **Primary research** is the generation of information specifically for the purpose of the study. For instance, a survey of fans or local businesses to determine their likely attendance at events is a form of primary research. The interpretation of survey results about intent to purchase requires caution. The old adage that people vote with their feet and not their mouth suggests that respondents may say one thing, but when it comes time to part with their money, they may do another. Therefore, it is best to rely on both secondary and primary research, whenever possible.

Secondary research typically involves the analysis of data that have already been generated for other purposes but might provide information for the question at hand. For instance, an analysis of attendance at other new sport facilities around the country, with adjustments for differences in the locations, might provide useful information on expected attendance at the facility that is the subject of the feasibility study. The use of information from comparable markets is similar to the use of comparables for valuation, discussed in Chapter 10. This type of secondary research is known as **comparables analysis**. In the case of a sport facility feasibility study, comparables analysis is based on the idea that if sport facilities are successful in comparable cities, then a facility will be successful in the city that is the subject of the study. The researchers of a feasibility study are trying to measure the expected value of various revenue streams (e.g., tickets) in order to predict the financial health of the proposed facility. An assessment of comparable markets and their facilities can provide insight about what to expect if a facility is built.

The market demand analysis for a sport facility feasibility study can be divided into the following subsections:

- individual ticket demand **A**
- corporate demand (club seats, luxury suites, and sponsorships) **B**
- event activity **C**
- facility specifications and operating estimates **D**.

Exhibit 11.2 shows how these subsections (labeled **A** through **D**) fit into the overall feasibility study.

---

1 A club seat is an individual seat that is usually closer to the action than most seats in the facility and also often comes with exclusive amenities, such as special parking privileges and access to a club eatery. Typically, only season or multi-game ticket holders may purchase club seats.

EXHIBIT 11.2   The parts and subsections of a feasibility study.

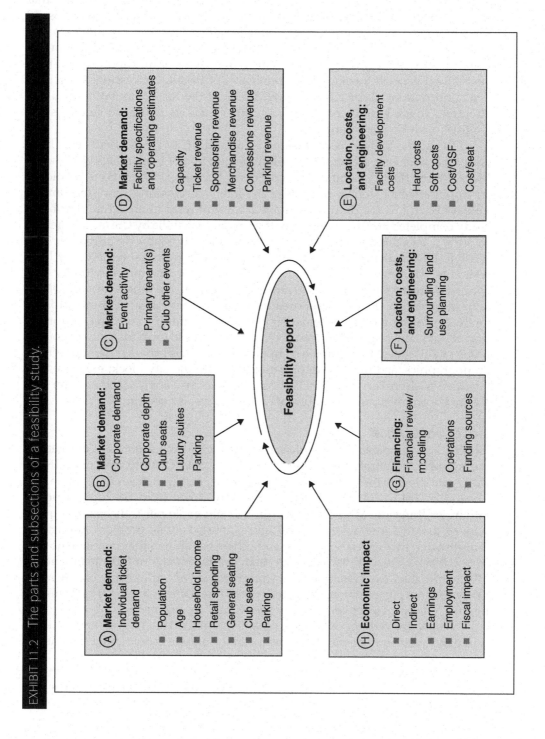

Individual Ticket Demand

To estimate ticket demand, we may use comparables analysis. Consider that a sport arena may host 150 events annually or a football stadium may host 12 to 25 major events (with newer stadiums designed to host many more smaller events that don't utilize the full playing surface, but perhaps one of the on-site restaurants and a sports museum built within the stadium footprint). These events will generate revenue from purchases of tickets, concessions, merchandise, and parking. Typically, we would look at the local population of likely attendees to see how it compares with other markets that have similar sport facilities with similar tenants.

To use the United Soccer League's Louisville City FC (football club) franchise as an example, a comparison of the population of Louisville's Designated Market Area (DMA) to other United Soccer League (USL) markets would be an important first step in predicting the likely success of a new stadium for Louisville FC.[2] Throughout this chapter we will refer to an actual feasibility study completed in 2016 on behalf of the City of Louisville by CSL and Legends. In such a feasibility study, the researchers typically study demographic and lifestyle information, such as the age, income, and purchasing habits of local residents. The US Census Bureau provides some of this information by city, county, or metropolitan statistical area, while Nielsen and others provide DMA-level information.[3] The Census Bureau's American Factfinder program (https://factfinder.census.gov/faces/nav/jsf/pages/index.xhtml) provides information about gender, age, education level, income, and so forth for a city or county name or ZIP code. Many private companies also provide market demographics, ethnographics, and lifestyle information down to the city block; examples are Claritas, Nielsen, Esri, and NPD. The researchers also analyze the number and size of corporations and revenues of comparable sport stadiums.

SIZE OF POPULATION

Exhibit 11.3 compares the populations of the 26 (at the time) USL markets as measured by the number of people living in each DMA in 2015. When we divide the population by the number of professional sports franchises in the area, the Louisville DMA falls approximately one-third down from the highest population per franchise. Measuring the number of people per franchise is a quick way of looking at relative demand across markets. One problem, though, is that research by Andrew Zimbalist and others has shown that people who live in one market are often fans of more than one team (say, an NBA team and an NFL team); thus, two franchises that share a market of 4 million people are more likely to have higher demand per team than one team in a market of 2 million people. Yet, this is a convenient way for estimation of a market.

Purely based on population, Louisville is in the 19th largest market listed (out of 26); yet, once the number of teams in the market is accounted for, it is the

---

2 A Designated Market Area is a group of counties that form an area in which the home market television stations hold a dominance of total hours viewed, (www.nielsen.com/us/en/intl-campaigns/dma-maps/). It is typically larger than a metropolitan statistical area.

3 A metropolitan statistical area "comprises the central county or counties containing the core, plus adjacent outlying counties having a high degree of social and economic integration with the central county as measured through commuting" (Office of Management and Budget, 2010).

EXHIBIT 11.3 Comparison of the populations and number of franchises of USL markets.

RANK	DESIGNATED MARKET AREA (DMA)	POPULATION (2015, EST.)	NUMBER OF PROFESSIONAL FRANCHISES	POPULATION PER FRANCHISE (2015)	POP. PER FRANCHISE INDEX
1	New York City	21,297,405	13	1,639,681	188%
2	Los Angeles	18,036,490	11	1,638,262	188%
3	Bethlehem, PA	8,100,260	5	1,620,052	186%
4	Sacramento	4,147,424	3	1,382,475	159%
5	Orlando	3,902,970	3	1,300,990	150%
6	Seattle	5,017,340	5	1,003,468	115%
7	Phoenix	5,273,888	6	878,981	101%
8	Louisville	1,740,041	2	870,021	100%
9	Portland	3,233,915	4	808,479	93%
10	St. Louis	3,197,498	4	799,375	92%
11	Richmond	1,511,923	2	755,962	87%
12	Pittsburgh	2,844,927	4	711,232	82%
13	Austin	2,068,620	3	689,540	79%
14	McAllen, TX	1,355,570	2	677,785	78%
15	Harrisburg	2,011,536	3	670,512	77%
16	San Antonio	2,646,959	4	661,740	76%
17	Salt Lake City	3,138,595	5	627,719	72%
18	Cincinnati	2,360,486	4	590,122	68%
19	Charlotte	3,114,296	6	519,049	60%
20	Kansas City	2,479,540	5	495,908	57%
21	Colorado Springs	952,989	2	476,495	55%
22	Charleston, SC	848,927	2	424,464	49%
23	Tulsa	1,426,509	4	356,627	41%
24	Oklahoma City	1,904,790	6	317,465	36%

(continued)

EXHIBIT 11.3   Cont.

RANK	DESIGNATED MARKET AREA (DMA)	POPULATION (2015, EST.)	NUMBER OF PROFESSIONAL FRANCHISES	POPULATION PER FRANCHISE (2015)	POP. PER FRANCHISE INDEX
25	Rochester	1,041,053	6	173,509	20%
26	Wilmington, NC	484,631	3	161,544	19%
	Average (excl. Louisville)	4,040,971	4.4	789,296	91%
	Median (excl. Louisville)	2,479,540	4.0	689,540	79%

Includes US-based USL markets only.

Source: CSL and Legends.

eighth largest. When referencing this type of information, we commonly speak in terms of an index where the market of interest is set at 100 and the other markets are above or below this number, according to how they compare to the market of interest. For instance, Seattle's population per team is 15% higher than Louisville's, so its index is 115%. Given that sport facilities are useful for a number of decades, it may also be important to consider the expected population growth of the area surrounding the facility. For instance, Louisville's DMA has an expected compounded annual growth rate (CAGR) from 2015 to 2020 of 0.6% compared to 0.8% for the US overall.

AGE

In addition to the size of the population, the age distribution of the population is another factor to consider when analyzing ticket demand in comparable markets. The target market of many USL clubs is people between the ages of 18 and 44, because these are likely ticket buyers (based on research by the USL). For the USL, Exhibit 11.4 shows that Louisville skews slightly older than a typical USL market (reflected in its rank of 20 out of the 26 USL markets).

INCOME AND UNEMPLOYMENT

The income of the local population is an indicator of its ability to purchase tickets for facility events. In Exhibit 11.4, we see that Louisville's median household income is relatively low compared with the rest of the USL. Households with larger incomes are more likely to purchase season tickets (as opposed to single game tickets) and club seats.

Sport facilities offer tiered pricing and quality. At the bottom of the scale are the "cheap seats," which are often sold on an individual-event basis.

EXHIBIT 11.4 Louisville–USL market comparison (in 2015 dollars).

RANK (BY POP.)	DESIGNATED MARKET AREA (DMA)	MEDIAN AGE	AGE INDEX	HOUSEHOLD INCOME	INCOME INDEX	SOCCER PARTICIPATION	PARTICIPATION INDEX	UNEMPLOYMENT	UNEMPLOYMENT INDEX
1	Los Angeles	35.0	89%	$58,861	121%	3.8%	158%	7.5%	167%
2	New York City	38.5	98%	$66,274	137%	3.5%	146%	6.1%	136%
3	Rochester	40.2	103%	$53,827	111%	2.7%	113%	6.9%	153%
4	Bethlehem, PA	39.1	100%	$59,877	123%	3.2%	133%	5.4%	120%
5	Sacramento	36.1	92%	$56,241	116%	3.1%	129%	6.0%	133%
6	Harrisburg	40.7	104%	$56,172	116%	2.5%	104%	6.6%	147%
7	St. Louis	39.2	100%	$52,726	109%	2.6%	108%	6.8%	151%
8	Kansas City	37.0	94%	$54,273	112%	2.8%	117%	6.3%	140%
9	Richmond	39.5	101%	$54,842	113%	2.8%	117%	5.4%	120%
10	Seattle	38.5	98%	$63,585	131%	3.3%	138%	3.3%	73%
11	Portland	38.3	98%	$55,746	115%	3.0%	125%	4.4%	98%
12	Phoenix	36.4	93%	$50,998	105%	3.0%	125%	5.0%	111%
13	Colorado Springs	37.0	94%	$51,733	107%	2.8%	117%	5.1%	113%
14	Orlando	41.5	106%	$46,784	96%	2.8%	117%	4.5%	100%

(continued)

EXHIBIT 11.4 Cont.

RANK (BY POP.)	DESIGNATED MARKET AREA (DMA)	MEDIAN AGE	AGE INDEX	HOUSEHOLD INCOME	INCOME INDEX	SOCCER PARTICIPATION	PARTICIPATION INDEX	UNEMPLOYMENT	UNEMPLOYMENT INDEX
15	Pittsburgh	43.1	110%	$50,914	105%	2.4%	100%	4.6%	102%
16	Cincinnati	38.1	97%	$54,074	111%	2.6%	108%	4.5%	100%
17	Charleston, SC	37.4	95%	$49,613	102%	2.8%	117%	4.5%	100%
18	Austin	34.4	88%	$61,619	127%	3.4%	142%	2.6%	58%
19	Wilmington, NC	42.0	107%	$45,901	95%	2.5%	104%	4.7%	104%
20	Charlotte	38.0	97%	$49,544	102%	2.6%	108%	4.5%	100%
21	Louisville	39.2	100%	$48,498	100%	2.4%	100%	4.5%	100%
22	San Antonio	35.1	90%	$51,433	106%	3.0%	125%	3.2%	71%
23	McAllen, TX	29.5	75%	$32,608	67%	3.4%	142%	4.5%	100%
24	Salt Lake City	30.3	77%	$60,137	124%	2.8%	117%	2.9%	64%
25	Oklahoma City	36.0	92%	$47,786	99%	2.6%	108%	3.2%	71%
26	Tulsa	38.3	98%	$46,661	96%	2.3%	96%	3.4%	76%
	Average (excl. Louisville)	37.6	96%	$53,289	110%	2.9%	121%	4.9%	108%
	Median (excl. Louisville)	38.1	97%	$53,827	111%	2.8%	117%	4.6%	102%

Includes US-based USL markets only.

Source: CSL and Legends.

Season ticket seats are closer to the playing surface, and even better seats—club seats—are very close to the action and provide other amenities. At the top of the pricing tier are luxury suites, which are small rooms that overlook the playing surface and provide tables, food, TVs, restrooms, and more, in addition to seating. The fact that the typical (median) household income of the Louisville region is relatively low suggests that it may be more difficult to sell season tickets and club seats in Louisville than in the average market, all else being equal.

Adjusting income to reflect the cost of living can provide a more realistic measure of disposable income, or income left over after paying for necessities. For instance, the Council for Community and Economic Research (C2ER) offers cost of living indices (COLI). Alternatively, or in addition, we might want to look at income after taxes, or effective buying income (EBI). For example, if one were to look at the Oakland market (compared to other NFL markets), it is above average in terms of income, yet once the COLI is accounted for, it is about average, and then once taxes are included, it is actually below the average for NFL markets.

Unemployment, like income, can provide insight into whether or not local residents will likely purchase tickets, merchandise, concessions, etc. related to a local sports franchise. On this factor, Louisville is better than the average or median USL franchise (see Exhibit 11.4), meaning that is has a slightly lower (better) unemployment rate.

SPORT-SPECIFIC FACTORS

Other possible predictors of whether many fans would attend USL games in a new stadium might be the local television ratings of soccer matches, the per-person purchases of soccer balls, and/or the soccer participation rate, as shown in Exhibit 11.4. These can indicate whether the local population is generally interested in soccer. Louisville fares rather poorly in this latter factor, with the average USL market (excluding Louisville) having a greater than 20% higher rate of soccer participation.

ANNUAL REVENUES

For additional useful information in a ticket demand analysis, we might look at the annual revenues of the sport facilities in comparable markets (and also the number of seats and prices of the different seating sections). These revenues would suggest how successful these facilities are. If half of the facilities are struggling financially, this would indicate that a facility in Louisville could be expected to struggle, as well. Unfortunately, revenue information is generally not available, as sports franchises are almost always privately held businesses that are not required to disclose their financial data to the public. Additionally, each tenant has its own method of accounting for facility revenues, making comparisons difficult. See the discussion of transfer pricing and related-party transactions in Chapter 10, where it looks at how revenues for certain facility events may be captured on a different set of financials, representing a different company. A separate company may secure and host events in a facility outside of the main sports team tenant and show high profits from those events, while the financial statements of the facility itself might show losses. Yet, the overall combined enterprise might be profitable.

Moreover, the winning prospects of the tenant(s) of a sport facility certainly affect ticket sales. However, reliance on a winning team over a few decades is not reasonable, given the tenuous and temporary nature of winning in team sports. Typically, an analyst assumes an average-quality team when conducting a feasibility study. This is one of the many assumptions that are necessary to conduct a feasibility analysis.

USING THE DATA TO CALCULATE TICKET DEMAND

Estimating ticket demand for an existing team (as opposed to a future expansion team or franchise relocated from another market), like Louisville FC, is driven by historical attendance and adjusted to reflect the effects of a new stadium. For instance, Louisville FC's average attendance in 2015 was over 7,000. However, moving into a new stadium often invokes the "honeymoon effect," which has been shown to bump up attendance for a number of years. For instance, in two studies focused on Major League Soccer, DeSchriver, Rascher, and Shapiro (2016) and Shapiro, DeSchriver, and Rascher (2017) found that a new stadium would have about 10% higher attendance, and other research has shown that this higher attendance comes with higher revenues per attendee (because prices are typically higher and attendees tend to spend more money in new stadiums on the often-improved food and beverage offerings), in some cases raising stadium revenues by 20% or more. If the data is available, one would want to look at other new USL stadiums and what the changes in revenues are.

Based on historical average paid attendance for Louisville City FC (LCFC) games (5,747) and information on league attendance and effects of new stadiums, CSL and Legends estimated a jump in paid attendance of about 14% to 6,553 for LCFC games in a new stadium, with larger jumps in sponsorship, concessions, and other revenues. A full financial pro forma will be discussed at the end of this chapter.

SIDEBAR 11.A   Luxury Suite Prices: What Drives Them?

Luxury suites are an increasingly important source of revenue for sport franchises and form part of the revenue forecast in feasibility studies. In 2007, on average, American sport facilities generated nearly $10 million per facility in luxury suite revenues. Suite prices in 2008 ranged from about $60,000 to $250,000, and in 2010 MetLife Stadium, home to the New York Jets and the New York Giants, opened with some of its suites priced at $1 million for the year. Not only are suite revenues significant, but they are often more consistent over time than ticket revenues (which vary more as teams win and lose).

Shapiro, DeSchriver, and Rascher (2012) analyzed the factors that drive luxury suite prices in North American facilities and found them to include population, number of mid-sized corporations, per capita income, number of games that can be watched by suite holders, the type of facility (indoor or outdoor), league (NFL, MLB, NBA, NHL, or MLS), winning percentage of the major tenants in the facility, and competition with other facilities in the area that offer suites.

For example, an increase in market population of 10% (about 480,000 people) increases annual suite prices by about 3.5% (or $6,000). Per capita income that is 10% higher is associated with a 10% jump, approximately, in suite prices. Each additional game adds about $2,000 to suite prices, which is not surprising. A 10% increase in average winning percentage points over the most recent five years (e.g., from 0.500 to 0.600) generates an extra $15,000 per suite, or a 9% increase. Finally, each additional competing facility in a marketplace lowers prices by about 15%, thus providing some evidence that facilities compete with one another for corporate dollars.

Corporate Demand

An important factor in sport facility market demand is corporate demand for season tickets, club seats, luxury suites, and sponsorships, which directly affects facility revenues. In the NBA, for example, over 50% of season ticket holders are corporations. The USL tends to have a higher percentage of fans at its games who are simply fans of the team or sport, but revenue derived from corporate demand is expected to increase relative to fan demand as a sport becomes established and stable. Accordingly, assessment of corporate demand is an important component of the market demand analysis in a feasibility study. We will use a comparables analysis to estimate corporate demand for Louisville City FC.

CORPORATE DEPTH ANALYSIS

As suggested above, corporations are often potential purchasers of season tickets, club seats, luxury suites, and sponsorships. **Corporate depth**, or the depth of a market's corporate base, provides information for predicting corporate-related revenues. One measure of corporate depth is the number of headquarters of Fortune 500 companies in the local area. We can also compile more detailed measures of the number of companies of certain sizes in an area.

Exhibit 11.5 gives the number of companies with annual sales of at least $2.5 million and at least ten employees in markets that are comparable to Louisville. Louisville is about in the middle of the group (15th) when measured by the total number of corporations, but once the number of teams are accounted for, LCFC ranks fifth, because of the relative lack of competition with professional sports teams. An even deeper analysis might incorporate competition with local college sports, as the University of Louisville has a very popular men's basketball program, as well as substantial demand for its other sports.

SUITE AND SEAT REVENUE POTENTIAL

We can estimate the amount of revenue that can be generated by luxury suites by studying the results in comparable markets. Exhibit 11.6 shows the wide range of the number of club seats and luxury suites available across comparable USL markets (this information is typically available from the Association of Luxury Suite Directors or team representatives). As shown, there is a relatively

EXHIBIT 11.5 Corporate depth of markets comparable to Louisville.

RANK (BY POP.)	DESIGNATED MARKET AREA (DMA)	CORPORATE DEPTH	NUMBER OF PROFESSIONAL FRANCHISES	CORPORATIONS PER FRANCHISE	CORPORATE DEPTH PER FRANCHISE INDEX
1	New York City	14,456	13	1,112	179%
2	Los Angeles	9,684	11	880	142%
3	St. Louis	2,913	4	728	118%
4	Pittsburgh	2,558	4	640	103%
5	Louisville	1,239	2	620	100%
6	Phoenix	3,303	6	551	89%
7	Cincinnati	2,181	4	545	88%
8	Richmond	1,032	2	516	83%
9	Austin	1,463	3	488	79%
10	Seattle	2,339	5	468	76%
11	Sacramento	1,320	3	440	71%
12	Orlando	1,234	3	411	66%
13	Portland	1,630	4	408	66%
14	San Antonio	1,491	4	373	60%
15	Charlotte	2,066	6	344	56%
16	Kansas City	1,518	5	304	49%
17	Tulsa	1,067	4	267	43%
18	Charleston, SC	483	2	242	39%
19	Colorado Springs	392	2	196	32%
20	Salt Lake City	957	5	191	31%
21	Harrisburg	565	3	188	30%
22	Rochester	1,075	6	179	29%
23	Oklahoma City	1,049	6	175	28%
24	McAllen, TX	287	2	144	23%

EXHIBIT 11.5   Cont.

RANK (BY POP.)	DESIGNATED MARKET AREA (DMA)	CORPORATE DEPTH	NUMBER OF PROFESSIONAL FRANCHISES	CORPORATIONS PER FRANCHISE	CORPORATE DEPTH PER FRANCHISE INDEX
25	Bethlehem, PA	641	5	128	21%
26	Wilmington, NC	185	3	62	10%
	Average (excl. Louisville)	2,269	5	416	67%
	Median (excl. Louisville)	1,320	4	408	66%

Includes US-based USL markets only.

Source: CSL and Legends.

EXHIBIT 11.6   Number of suites across select USL markets.

TEAM	TOTAL CORPORATE INVENTORY	CLUB SEAT INVENTORY	CORPORATIONS PER CLUB SEAT	SUITE INVENTORY	CORPORATIONS PER SUITE
Highmark Stadium (Pittsburgh)	2,558	200	12.8	15	171
Bonney Field (Sacramento)	1,320	200	6.6	--	--
WakeMed Park (Cary, NC)	906	--	--	6	151
Rhinos Stadium (Rochester)	1,075	250	4.3	14	77
Toyota Field (San Antonio)	1,491	864	1.7	16	93
RGVFC Stadium (Edinburg, TX)	287	600	0.5	24	12
Median	1,198	250	4.3	15.0	93.2
Average	1,273	423	5.2	15.0	100.7
Estimated Louisville Demand	1,239	**288**	4.3	**13**	93.2

Note: McAllen DMA includes Edinburg, TX.

large supply of club seats at RGVFC Stadium compared with the other markets shown. However, in Pittsburgh (at Highmark Stadium), there is a large contingent of suitable companies to sell club seats and luxury suites to. Yet, there is more competition across venues in Pittsburgh because of the large number of other professional teams. It is often important to account for the club seats or suites in the marketplace overall.

This is further explored in Exhibit 11.7, which focuses on a comparison of comparable NFL markets to Oakland to assess the relative demand and supply of club seats. This is taken from a feasibility study involving the Oakland Raiders (authored by CSL and JMI Sports), who were in the market for a new stadium and ultimately opted to go to Las Vegas. The table includes corporate depth (the number of corporations) and the number of high-income households. Both corporations and high-income households (defined as earning at least $100,000) are potential customers for club seats. The list is sorted by the number of corporations divided by the number of club seats available, and the Oakland market ranks eighth out of the 30 NFL markets. It would be seventh if ranked by the number of high-income households divided by the number of club seats available. Dividing the number of potential buyers by the supply of club seats indicates the relative demand and supply for the product compared with other markets (similar to the ratio analyses across companies discussed in Chapter 2). Compared to most of the rest of the NFL markets, the Raiders should be able to sell club seats in the Oakland market more easily. However, compared to the other markets that are similar in size, the Oakland market is just below average in number of corporations per club seat, but just above average in high-income households per club seat.

Comparing the number of club seats for major professional teams in Pittsburgh, over 13,000, to the 200 shown in Exhibit 11.6, reveals a very important issue that feasibility analysis requires one to resolve. Namely, determining the extent to which another venue competes with the subject venue. Does a potential buyer of a USL club seat in Pittsburgh (at a cost of $560 for the season) consider the purchase of an NFL club seat for thousands of dollars a substitute? If so, then those thousands of additional club seats make it more difficult to sell a club seat at Highmark Stadium for USL games.

Primary Research on Corporate Demand

In a Phase II feasibility study, rather than undertaking a comparables analysis, we may conduct primary research on corporate demand as an alternative or additional method. Surveys of corporations to investigate their likelihood of buying premium seating and sponsorships would provide some direct evidence. Bear in mind that caution is necessary in interpreting survey results about intent to purchase. We recommend relying on both secondary and primary research whenever possible.

NAMING RIGHTS AND OTHER SPONSORSHIP REVENUE

Naming rights are the largest single sponsorship revenue source for a sport facility. To estimate the naming rights values for specific facilities, many sport marketing firms have developed naming rights models that use existing naming

EXHIBIT 11.7 Club seats, corporate depth, and high-income households in NFL markets.

RANK	MARKET	COMPARABLE MARKETS (X: CORPORATIONS; Y: INCOME)	CLUB SEATS				TOTAL CLUB SEATS	TOTAL CORPORATIONS[1]	CORP. PER CLUB SEAT	TOTAL HIGH-INCOME HOUSEHOLDS[2]	HIGH-INCOME HOUSEHOLDS PER CLUB SEAT
			NBA	NHL	MLB	NFL					
1	Boston	xy	1,068	1,068	688	6,460	9,284	5,540	0.60	541,352	58.3
2	Minneapolis	-	352	2,800	3,400	242	6,794	3,820	0.56	322,928	47.5
3	Detroit	x	1,000	-	1,039	7,312	9,351	4,970	0.53	337,326	36.1
4	Chicago	xy	3,000	3,000	5,443	8,376	19,819	9,610	0.48	843,302	42.6
5	Atlanta	xy	1,800	1,800	5,400	6,180	15,180	5,190	0.34	444,716	29.3
6	Houston	xy	2,900	-	4,776	8,464	16,140	5,320	0.33	457,248	28.3
7	Philadelphia	xy	1,810	1,810	3,571	8,447	15,638	5,110	0.33	559,081	35.8
8	Oakland/San Francisco/San Jose	-	2,726	3,300	9,221	5,552	20,799	6,740	0.32	844,796	40.6
9	New York	xy	2,860	6,508	11,000	19,277	39,645	12,120	0.31	1,997,162	50.4
10	Green Bay/Milwaukee	-	250	-	4,150	6,089	10,489	3,050	0.29	168,646	16.1

(continued)

EXHIBIT 11.7 Cont.

| RANK | MARKET | COMPARABLE MARKETS (X: CORPORATIONS; Y: INCOME | CLUB SEATS | | | | TOTAL CLUB SEATS | TOTAL CORPORATIONS[1] | CORP. PER CLUB SEAT | TOTAL HIGH-INCOME HOUSEHOLDS[2] | HIGH-INCOME HOUSEHOLDS PER CLUB SEAT |
			NBA	NHL	MLB	NFL					
11	Seattle	-	-	-	5,059	7,826	12,885	3,590	0.28	348,459	27.0
12	Dallas	xy	2,025	2,025	5,500	14,102	23,652	6,340	0.27	511,836	21.6
13	Washington DC	xy	2,200	2,200	1,999	17,263	23,662	6,200	0.26	803,433	34.0
14	St. Louis	-	-	1,200	3,707	6,692	11,599	2,830	0.24	207,328	17.9
15	Phoenix	-	2,228	400	4,400	7,356	14,384	3,450	0.24	323,613	22.5
16	Cleveland	-	2,400	-	2,063	8,345	12,808	3,050	0.24	141,545	11.1
17	Baltimore	-	-	-	3,800	8,108	11,908	2,650	0.22	284,763	23.9
18	Kansas City	-	-	-	2,575	7,715	10,290	2,250	0.22	152,962	14.9
19	Indianapolis	-	2,648	-	-	7,264	9,912	2,030	0.20	132,582	13.4
20	San Diego	-	-	-	6,760	7,668	14,428	2,940	0.20	289,845	20.1
21	Cincinnati	-	-	-	3,380	7,793	11,173	2,230	0.20	163,311	14.6
22	Denver	-	1,900	1,900	4,526	7,749	16,075	3,200	0.20	232,919	14.5

#											
23	Pittsburgh		-	2,200	2,975	8,100	13,275	2,490	0.19	150,491	11.3
24	Charlotte		2,300	-	-	11,223	13,523	2,110	0.16	129,858	9.6
25	Miami	y	1,800	2,300	10,209	10,470	24,779	3,740	0.15	409,233	16.5
26	Tampa Bay		-	3,222	3,000	12,053	18,275	2,530	0.14	181,838	10.0
27	Nashville		-	1,100	-	11,682	12,782	1,650	0.13	109,445	8.6
28	Jacksonville		-	-	-	11,692	11,692	1,340	0.11	98,941	8.5
29	Buffalo		-	2,500	-	8,831	11,331	1,180	0.10	69,259	6.1
30	New Orleans		3,320	-	-	8,593	11,913	1,120	0.09	76,449	6.4
	Average (excluding Oakland)						14,920	3,850	0.26	361,720	22.6
	Average in Comparable Markets (excluding Oakland)						19,152	6,711	0.38	729,707	35.2

Ranked by corporations per club seat.

1 Includes corporations with at least 25 employees and $25 million in annual sales.

2 Includes households with annual household income greater than $100,000.

x Comparable markets are defined as having more than 4,000 companies.

y Comparable markets are defined as having more than 400,000 high-income households.

Source: CSL & JMI Sports Study (2010).

rights deals as comparables. Some academic publications, such as DeSchriver and Jensen (2003), also provide models. Recent deals have continued to escalate in annual price, with Social Financial, Inc. (SoFi) paying more than $30 million per year to be the name of the home stadium for the Los Angeles Rams and Los Angeles Chargers, and JP Morgan Chase paying $15 million per year for the host arena of the Golden State Warriors. The aforementioned Highmark Stadium reportedly has a deal worth $100,000 per year for naming rights. Other USL stadiums have higher six-figure deals.

Event Activity

Another element in determining market demand or penetration for a feasibility study is a competitive analysis regarding the supply of facilities, incorporating primary research on potential events. This is different from a comparables analysis, where we are trying to find similar situations from which to learn. In a **competitive analysis**, we directly investigate existing facilities (stadiums, arenas, and amphitheaters) that might compete with the subject facility for hosting events. A sport facility essentially has three major types of clients: attendees who show up for events, event property owners (or team owners) who decide where to hold their events or games, and sponsors who are trying to use fans' avidity for the teams/events in order to market their products to them. A particular market may have high incomes, a large population, and a lot of corporate depth, but it also may already have a lot of competition for shows or events, in the form of other arenas, stadiums, or concert halls. For instance, in Louisville there is a college soccer stadium (Dr. Mark & Cindy Lynn Stadium) that can seat about 5,000 people, Cardinal Stadium (hosting the University of Louisville football team), the KFC Yum! Center (hosting the schools' basketball teams), and other smaller and older indoor and outdoor venues. As shown in Exhibit 11.8, a new stadium for LCFC could plan to host ten non-LCFC events and would need to determine how much competition it would face in securing those events from other Louisville-based facilities.

In order to estimate facility usage and the number of expected events, it is common to conduct primary research in the form of discussions with event owners, including Live Nation Entertainment, AEG, and IMG. These discussions should result in an estimate of the number and type of events that might be held at a new sport facility. Exhibit 11.8 provides an estimate for the proposed new soccer stadium in Louisville. This estimate is meant to be conservative. As with all feasibility analyses, it is important that the analysis be somewhat conservative, providing room for error without jeopardizing the facility's future financial health. Interestingly, a few years after the feasibility study was written, Louisville was awarded an expansion franchise in the National Women's Soccer League (NWSL), with games to be played at the stadium for which the feasibility study was written. This would amount to an additional 12 home games. Average NWSL attendance in 2019 was over 7,000. These additional events help cover the annual operating costs and possibly pay down the capital costs of the facility.

EXHIBIT 11.8   Estimate of the number and types of events for the proposed new soccer stadium in Louisville.

	ANNUAL EVENTS	AVERAGE PAID ATTENDANCE	ANNUAL PAID ATTENDANCE
Louisville City FC			
Regular Season	15	6,500	97,500
Exhibition Games	2	6,000	12,000
US Open Cup	1	7,500	7,500
Playoffs	1	7,500	7,500
Subtotal	19	6,553	124,500
Other Events			
National/International Soccer	1	7,500	7,500
Concerts	2	10,000	20,000
Other Events	7	2,000	14,000
Subtotal	10	4,150	41,500
Total—All Events	29	5,724	166,000

SIDEBAR 11.B   Kansas City … BBQ, Jazz, and Basketball?

A Statistical Approach to Feasibility

One limitation of the use of information like that given in Exhibits 11.3 through 11.7 is that we do not know the relative importance of each piece of information. Relying on each of the variables equally implies, for instance, that the age of a population is exactly equally important to the population number. What if the local market has a relatively high population but a relatively low income or age? Does that bode well for the market, or not? Rascher and Rascher (2004) attempted to answer this question by analyzing markets for their viability as hosts for an NBA team. By using regression analysis, the researchers created weights for some of the variables discussed thus far, along with many more. The measures of success used in the study were attendance, ticket revenues, and total team revenues. In other words, markets with high attendance and revenues were deemed to be successful, and the statistical analysis combined the variables into a single estimate of what attendance or revenues could be expected if a team were to move into a market that did not already have an NBA team.

Exhibit 11.9 shows the study's results. The cities were ranked by estimated gate receipts. Boldfaced cities did not have NBA teams during the period of the study, 1997–1999.

This type of research provides another method for measuring the feasibility of bringing a team to a particular city. It incorporates the type of information given in Exhibits 11.3 through 11.7 into a single financial estimate of team success. The researchers predicted that a team in Memphis would fare well in terms of gate receipts but only passably in terms of total revenues (as it has), and that a team in New Orleans would struggle financially—as it has. The analysis was conducted concurrently with a feasibility study done for the Sacramento Kings in the early 2000s. The analysis's estimate of attendance for Sacramento, 17,138, is close to the Kings' historical average.

For another example of using this research to determine the feasibility of a facility project, consider the events in Kansas City surrounding the construction of the Sprint Center. In July 2004, the city was in the midst of a debate about the feasibility of building a new downtown sport arena. A referendum was placed on the ballot for a special election in August 2004. Without the benefit of results of a feasibility study, and without a major tenant in place, the public was being asked to vote to spend about $143 million in public money to build the arena. The hope seemed to be that "if you build it, they will come." However, we can conduct a quick assessment of the market by using results from Rascher and Rascher's research.

Kansas City was lower down the list than 11 other markets that do not have an NBA franchise. Expansions and relocations in the NBA are rare, but if an owner were to move or the league were to expand, one of many other markets would likely be chosen instead of Kansas City.* Also, a simple measure of the ability to host a new team—population divided by the current number of major professional sport teams—put Kansas City second to last, just ahead of Milwaukee, out of 48 cities. It already has an NFL and an MLB team—getting an NBA team would spread its population and corporate support thin. Support for the Kansas City Chiefs is slightly above the NFL average in terms of locally generated revenues (according to data from 1999–2000). At the time, support for the Kansas City Royals was substantially below average for MLB. In fact, the Royals were estimated to be fourth from the bottom in terms of gate receipts and sixth from the bottom in terms of attendance. Of course, the Royals' on-field success in 2014 and 2015 (along with recent facility upgrades) has increased demand and revenues.

When a city is trying to lure a team to town, projected facility costs rise, because the team has the leverage of competition among multiple cities. Moreover, if the team is not included in the construction design process, then once an owner does decide to move into the arena, millions of dollars' worth of upgrades and changes will have to be made and paid for by the public. For example, in 1990 the Suncoast Dome was opened in St. Petersburg, Florida, at a cost of $138 million, with the hopes of luring an

EXHIBIT 11.9 Results of study analyzing markets for hosting an NBA team.

CITY/TEAM (RANKED BY GATE RECEIPTS)	FORECASTED ATTENDANCE	FORECASTED GATE RECEIPTS	FORECASTED TOTAL REVENUES
Chicago Bulls	20,108	$45,283,019	$103,944,723
New Jersey Nets	19,667	$44,609,289	$103,666,295
New York Knicks	18,717	$41,543,980	$96,906,295
Washington Wizards	19,704	$41,358,306	$83,281,956
Los Angeles Clippers	17,899	$38,422,655	$97,575,067
Los Angeles Lakers	17,899	$38,422,655	$97,575,067
Seattle SuperSonics	19,757	$38,312,641	$71,904,303
Detroit Pistons	18,249	$34,583,135	$77,497,291
Houston Rockets	18,325	$34,298,557	$69,692,269
Boston Celtics	18,218	$33,924,509	$68,763,022
Indiana Pacers	19,235	$32,993,512	$66,299,117
Philadelphia 76ers	17,729	$32,781,592	$75,895,337
Portland Trail Blazers	18,715	$32,330,039	$64,190,119
Memphis	18,796	$31,596,200	$59,847,117
Utah Jazz	18,622	$31,209,019	$62,109,120
Hartford	18,134	$30,943,166	$56,251,917
Phoenix Suns	18,286	$30,498,141	$72,479,118
Minnesota Timberwolves	17,526	$30,384,199	$67,701,633
Miami Heat	18,315	$29,977,964	$67,583,986
Baltimore	17,560	$29,429,689	$64,518,291
Louisville	18,311	$28,911,371	$59,396,878
San Diego	17,372	$28,460,087	$66,524,446
Las Vegas	17,545	$27,242,661	$59,699,671
Nashville	17,528	$26,882,101	$58,132,275
Milwaukee Bucks	16,978	$26,290,903	$58,624,142
Sacramento Kings	17,138	$26,101,881	$52,459,725

EXHIBIT 11.9   Cont.

CITY/TEAM (RANKED BY GATE RECEIPTS)	FORECASTED ATTENDANCE	FORECASTED GATE RECEIPTS	FORECASTED TOTAL REVENUES
Golden State Warriors	15,762	$26,011,957	$63,966,882
Honolulu	16,467	$25,830,914	$50,552,504
San Antonio Spurs	17,354	$25,604,283	$54,161,323
Norfolk, Virginia Beach, Newport News	17,058	$24,720,174	$59,816,386
Dallas Mavericks	15,907	$24,685,943	$60,500,450
Charlotte Hornets	16,516	$23,644,230	$51,580,247
St. Louis	16,074	$23,606,227	$62,257,248
Atlanta Hawks	15,625	$23,464,312	$62,783,478
Orlando Magic	16,506	$23,263,533	$55,287,320
New Orleans	16,314	$22,026,250	$59,897,920
Jacksonville	16,085	$21,331,308	$54,111,519
Cincinnati	15,644	$20,361,607	$53,771,644
Cleveland Cavaliers	15,119	$20,272,483	$56,035,523
Austin–San Marcos	15,931	$19,766,609	$49,390,583
Denver Nuggets	14,939	$19,541,896	$51,326,220
Kansas City	15,280	$19,503,955	$54,329,534
Albuquerque	15,394	$17,362,572	$45,547,891
Columbus	13,879	$13,684,159	$45,976,470
Pittsburgh	13,357	$12,543,029	$48,788,601
Omaha	13,553	$12,345,181	$39,255,986
Buffalo-Niagara Falls	13,659	$11,974,656	$46,414,481
Oklahoma City	11,432	$11,114,854	$33,726,430
Tucson	11,071	$10,608,078	$31,618,100
El Paso	9,311	$10,178,875	$19,506,282

Note: Boldface cities are those without an NBA team in 1999.

MLB team. In 1998 the Tampa Bay Rays finally began play in the facility. The upgrades required cost $70 million, 50% of the arena's original cost. Not only were there significant public costs above and beyond the original construction costs, but also the public paid for many years for a facility that did not have a major tenant. We can find similar examples in New Orleans and San Antonio, where the NBA owners required publicly financed upgrades of approximately 20% of each arena's original cost.

In summary, an assessment of Kansas City as a viable market for a third major sport franchise shows that the franchise would likely struggle. An updated version of these models utilizing data from 2012–2015 shows that Austin, Louisville, and Las Vegas would be the best markets for an NBA expansion team (or relocation). Interestingly, compared to a decade-and-a-half earlier, Austin has really climbed the ranks as a viable host of major sports teams. This has been driven by its increase in population and average incomes. Notably, MLS recently allowed an expansion team in Austin (after the owners of the Columbus Crew tried to relocate there).

* When the NBA's Grizzlies left Vancouver, British Columbia, for Memphis, the league shopped around and seriously considered moving the team to San Diego, Las Vegas, St. Louis, Louisville, Memphis, or New Orleans, but not Kansas City. When the Charlotte Hornets moved in 2002, Louisville and Norfolk were considered before the league finally settled on New Orleans. When the NHL expanded in 1998–2000, the four expansion cities were chosen from a pared-down list of six cities. Oklahoma City and Houston were the final cities eliminated prior to the league choosing Nashville, Atlanta, Minneapolis–St. Paul, and Columbus. Again, Kansas City was not even considered.

Facility Specifications and Operating Estimates

The previous discussion focused on the analysis of market demand and likely attendance. Market demand analysis forms the basis for estimates of facility revenues. Exhibit 11.10 gives an example of a revenue and expense estimate for Louisville City FC. It does not include media revenues (as those are not directly tied to the feasibility of a new stadium). Many of the numbers are based on the findings in the rest of the feasibility study on the viability of the Louisville market and how other USL stadiums have performed. The projected financials show a profit margin (before debt) of about 5%, with about 60% of revenue coming from ticketing and seating. Often, a new stadium would operate at break-even as opposed to seeing large losses or profits. This presumption is simply based on the leverage that the franchise has to negotiate for these revenues.

As mentioned, facility revenues are typically split between the facility and the major tenant or tenants. (There may be more than one major tenant, especially in the case of a facility that hosts both an NHL and an NBA team or an NFL and MLB team.) An estimate of facility revenue is necessary to determine whether market demand is sufficient to generate revenues for the major tenant(s) and to pay facility financing costs (both construction and operation costs). Negotiations for how the facility owner and major tenant will split

EXHIBIT 11.10   Estimate of facility financials for LCFC.

	2019	2020	2021	2022	2023
Revenues					
Ticket Sales	$2,330,598	$2,400,516	$2,472,531	$2,546,707	$2,623,109
Sponsorship & Advertising	$742,500	$764,775	$787,718	$811,350	$835,690
Suites	$288,400	$297,052	$305,964	$315,142	$324,597
Club Seats	$101,250	$104,288	$107,416	$110,639	$113,958
General Concessions	$492,530	$507,306	$522,525	$538,201	$554,347
Premium Concessions	$57,364	$59,085	$60,857	$62,683	$64,564
Event Rent	$180,000	$185,400	$190,962	$196,691	$202,592
Merchandise	$149,707	$154,198	$158,824	$163,589	$168,497
Parking	$199,651	$205,641	$211,810	$218,164	$224,709
Youth Development	$100,000	$103,000	$106,090	$109,273	$112,551
Ticket Rebates	$128,531	$132,387	$136,359	$140,449	$144,663
Total Revenues:	**$4,770,531**	**$4,913,647**	**$5,061,056**	**$5,212,888**	**$5,369,275**
Expenses					
Team Operations	$2,825,000	$2,909,750	$2,997,043	$3,086,954	$3,179,562
Stadium Operations	$1,715,000	$1,766,450	$1,819,444	$1,874,027	$1,930,248
Total Expenses:	**$4,540,000**	**$4,676,200**	**$4,816,486**	**$4,960,981**	**$5,109,810**
Net Income Before Debt	**$230,531**	**$237,447**	**$244,570**	**$251,907**	**$259,465**

revenues and construction/operation expenses often take place after the feasibility study is complete.

Switching to a discussion of basketball, an NBA franchise might begin with information on market demand from a feasibility study and add its non-arena revenues (e.g., revenues from the league and from local TV and radio) to obtain total estimated franchise revenues, which it could compare to its estimated expenses. If the net profits are high enough, then the team could

EXHIBIT 11.11   Estimating the optimal size of an arena based on comparable markets.

Average 30-Mile Population of the Comparable Markets	1,650,000
Average Capacity of the Comparable Markets for 41 Home Games	750,000
Ratio of Population to Capacity	2.20
Naismithville's 30-Mile Population	1,900,000
Naismithville's Capacity Based on the Population to Capacity Ratio	863,636
Estimated Capacity at 100% Sold Out (41 Home Games)	21,064
Estimated Capacity at 90% Sold Out (41 Home Games)	18,958

feasibly contribute to financing the facility construction. Similarly, if facility revenues will be high enough, then the facility owner could contribute to the construction. Often, the total revenues generated by the facility do not appear to be adequate to cover the operating costs of the facility, the major tenant's portion of revenues, and construction costs. In these cases, proponents will argue that the facility will benefit the local community economically by attracting visitors and tourism to the region. If it can be shown that the extra spending in the community will be sufficient to cover the facility's construction, then the local government may help to finance the construction.

The following sections present the steps in determining a feasible NBA arena size, including the number of seats, club seats, and luxury suites and their respective prices and revenues, based on an analysis of the hypothetical city Naismithville for an NBA franchise in a 30-year-old arena.[4] It also discusses the method for determining the expected ongoing revenues and expenses for the facility. Often, much of the information upon which a facility study is based is not publicly available, because sport teams and arena operating companies are private businesses. Obtaining access to this type of information is one of the challenges of conducting a feasibility study.

FACILITY SIZE AND TICKET RETURN

One method for estimating the optimal size of an arena is, once again, to look at comparable markets. As Exhibit 11.11 shows, we first divide the average population within 30 miles of the comparable markets (1,650,000) by the total number of seats available in those comparable markets (750,000) to obtain the ratio of population to capacity (2.20). The number of seats is based on 41 home games at the average capacity of the comparable markets. Second, we divide Naismithville's population (1,900,000) by that ratio (2.20) and then by the number of home games (41). This results in a seating capacity of 21,064. This figure assumes 100% sellout. To be conservative, we use a 90% sellout rate, which gives a seating capacity of 18,958. This is closer to the feasible capacity of a new arena based on historical NBA averages.

---

4   Dr. James Naismith invented basketball in late 1891 in Springfield, MA.

EXHIBIT 11.12 Estimates of facility revenues resulting from the market demand analysis for Naismithville.

REVENUE SOURCE	AMOUNT	NUMBER OF SEATS	AVERAGE PRICE
General Tickets (NBA events only)	$34,756,848	11,774	$80 per game
Luxury Suites (incl. event tickets & other events)	$12,800,000	1,224 in 64 suites	$200,000 per suite
Club Seats Fees (all arena events)	$11,920,000	5,960	$2,000 for seat rights
Club Seats Tickets (NBA events only)	$48,872,000	--	$200 per event for tickets
Other Arena Events Net Tickets and Rent	$10,000,000	--	--
Sponsorship (all arena events)	$20,000,000	--	--
Naming Rights (all arena events)	$5,000,000	--	--
Merchandise (all arena events)	$1,875,000	--	$5 average per capita spending
Concessions (all arena events)	$8,100,000	--	$12 average per capita spending
Parking (all arena events)	$4,500,000	--	$9 average per auto spending
Total Arena-Related Revenues	$157,823,848		

Using research similar to that discussed earlier for LCFC, we find that about $12 million in club seat revenues can be generated from a new arena. The estimates in Exhibit 11.12 suggest that 5,960 club seats should be built and that they should have an average price of $2,000, not including event tickets. NBA tickets, based on comparables, would cost about $200 per event, generating over $48 million in club seat event ticket revenue. Luxury suite revenue was estimated at about $13 million per year, with prices, including event tickets, at approximately $200,000. This suggests that the arena should have about 64 luxury suites, with an average of 19 seats per luxury suite.

The ticket price for general seating is typically based on prices in comparable markets, which average around $80. To calculate the number of general seats, we subtract the number of club seats (5,960) and luxury suite seats (1,224) from total capacity (18,958). This works out to general seating of about 11,774. A sellout rate of 90% would lead to 10,597 general seat tickets sold per game, netting nearly $35 million in general seating revenue. For other events in the arena, the facility owner will receive rent and/or a share of ticket revenues, depending on negotiations with the event owner. Based on comparables the arena can be expected to receive approximately $10 million in rent and other event ticket revenue.

OTHER FACILITY REVENUES

The primary revenue sources for a facility other than ticket revenues and rent are concessions, merchandise, and parking. We base an estimate of concessions revenue on average per capita concessions sales for events in comparable markets. Typically this figure is about $12 per person. If we use this number and assume that 1.5 million people attend arena events each year and that the facility earns a 45% gross profit (55% of retail price being cost of goods sold and staffing costs), concessions net revenue would total approximately $6 million.

Merchandise net revenue would be smaller, at about $1.875 million annually. We calculate this figure by assuming that each attendee spends $5, with 1.5 million attendees and a profit margin of 25%.

Parking revenue estimates are based on a long history of data on the number of cars per event attendee. Generally we expect that one parking space is utilized for every 4.5 attendees. (This does not mean that each car contains 4.5 passengers on average, because some attendees will take other forms of transportation.) Gross profit margins for parking are quite high, around 75%. Thus, the 1.5 million attendees will purchase about 400,000 parking spaces; at approximately $15 per space, this yields about $4.5 million in parking net revenue. Thus, total arena revenues amount to nearly $160 million.

Results of Market Demand Analyses

The end result of a market demand analysis is an estimate of expected quantities sold and prices for tickets, luxury suites, concessions, merchandise, sponsorships, and any other revenue streams, and the revenues generated from each one. This information will be used in the economic impact analysis, the analysis of financing, and the engineering analysis. For example, the calculation of economic impact depends partly on the number of people attending events at a facility. In the analysis of financing, concessions revenues and naming rights (a form of sponsorship) are often capitalized, and their value helps pay for the cost of construction (see Chapter 9). This affects the overall assessment of financing sources. The size of the facility is, of course, a significant factor in engineering and land-use decisions. If a larger facility is built, not only might location be affected, but the overall cost will be higher and financing will be affected. The type and quality of the facility also affect demand, especially with respect to luxury suite sales and sponsorships. Higher-quality suites, which are more expensive to build, might elicit higher demand. Once again, the feasibility study is an iterative process, with many layers of adjustment and readjustment.

FINANCING

Another crucial analysis in a feasibility study is an assessment of the cost of financing the facility and the potential sources of that financing (see Chapter 9). To determine what sources of financing are available, we ask questions such as:

is it possible to institute or raise a car rental tax and use the proceeds to help fund the construction?

This analysis is another iterative process (look back to Exhibit 11.1). The money that is available for construction affects the type of facility that can be built, and vice versa. The initial driver for money decisions is the number and types of expected events and the expected market demand. This basic information helps determine the appropriate number of seats and suites, which in turn allows us to calculate initial project cost estimates.

The economic and fiscal impact estimates provide information about the amount of incremental money that will flow into the local economy, including sales taxes (see Chapter 12). For instance, if the economic impact analysis shows that a facility will generate $3 million per year in incremental hotel taxes, then that $3 million might be earmarked to help finance the facility. Chapter 9 discusses sport facility financing in full detail.

LOCATION, CONSTRUCTION COSTS, AND ENGINEERING

A discussion of the location, construction costs, and engineering sections of a feasibility study is beyond the scope of this text. Briefly, these analyses focus on the hard costs (construction costs, improvements to the actual building) and soft costs (fees, engineering, consulting, movable items such as furniture) of facility construction, architectural and engineering renderings, infrastructure issues (such as roadway or exit ramp construction, widening of streets, and traffic flow), environmental impacts, water and sewage needs, and so forth. This section of a feasibility study provides a project cost estimate, which is needed to determine the economic and fiscal impacts of construction and is the most important input in the financing section.

FEASIBILITY STUDIES FOR RECREATION FACILITIES

Most of the feasibility analyses conducted in North America pertain to local recreational facilities such as swimming pools, baseball fields, soccer complexes, and so forth. The principles are the same as with spectator-driven facilities—we generate an estimate of the size and finances of the facility. Typically, the analyst uses comparable facilities in other markets as benchmarks. For instance, a study for an ice center in Pennsylvania determined the number of people who were not served by other ice skating centers in the region and who would be closer geographically to the proposed new facility (Pashek Associates, 2006). This provided the basis for estimates of the potential market and demand for the building. Analyses and tables comparing age, income, population, and entry price, similar to those found in this chapter, were used to determine the likely number of patrons and revenues. The number of events, besides general usage, was also determined based on other facilities. Finally, a very detailed financial projection was created that showed total revenues and expenses. After a few years of ramping up, the facility was projected to show a net profit. Similarly, a swimming center feasibility study completed in 2016 investigated competitive facilities in order to help determine demand (TSE Consulting, 2016).

CONCLUSION

The feasibility study is a very important component of any major facility construction project, because it specifies the size and cost of the facility, the expected revenues to be generated, the types and sources of financing, and the facility's likely economic impact. The feasibility study involves a complex analysis that includes surveying people and businesses, gathering data from other facility projects, and synthesizing the results into a report that decision makers can use to develop the facility. It requires the application of many of the sport finance tools described in this book.

Concept Check

1. What factor or variable is the most important in forecasting market demand for a new MLB stadium? Provide evidence for your answer.
2. What factor or variable is the most important in forecasting market demand for a new minor league baseball stadium? Provide evidence for your answer.
3. Is a comparables analysis a type of secondary research or primary research? Explain your answer.
4. Suppose a community is considering constructing a large pool facility for use by community residents. How might it go about conducting a feasibility study for the pool?
   a. Describe possible methods for determining annual usage at the pool.
   b. Describe possible methods for determining prices to be charged (if any) for entry, concessions, and any other services or items to be sold.
   c. Describe possible methods for determining costs of construction, operations, and maintenance.
5. Why do analysts sometimes use retail spending as a factor in measuring market demand for a sport facility? What are the pros and cons of using it?

Case Analysis

Preliminary Feasibility Questions

As discussed in this chapter, a feasibility study for a sport stadium requires forecasting annual attendance and total revenues at the facility. Consider the following hypothetical situation: A small group of men and women in Ventura, California, are interested in building a minor league baseball stadium and moving an existing Single A franchise to the stadium. They plan to locate the stadium on the edge of Ventura's central business district. They would like you to answer a few key questions, given your expertise in sport management. For each response, give the reasons for your answer and the methods you used to arrive at it.

Case Questions

1. Assuming that the club is average in terms of performance on the field, what would be the expected attendance per season during a typical year (once the "honeymoon effect" has worn off)?

2. What revenue would you expect to be generated from tickets, concessions, parking, and merchandise?
3. What revenues would you expect from naming rights and sponsorship?

References

CSL and JMI Sports. (2010). Feasibility analysis for a new NFL stadium in Oakland. Retrieved from assets.bizjournals.com/cms_media/sanfrancisco/pdf/Oakland-Public-Presentation- 1 0-1-10.pdf.

CSL and Legends. (2016). Feasibility study: Professional soccer stadium, Louisville. Retrieved from https://louisvilleky.gov/sites/default/files/louisville_forward/csl_report_louisville_professional_soccer_stadium_-_media.pdf.

DeSchriver, T.D., & Jensen, P.E. (2003). What's in a name? Price variation in sport facility naming rights. *Eastern Economic Journal*, 29(3), 359–376.

DeSchriver, T.D., Rascher, D.A., & Shapiro, S.L. (2016). If we build it, will they come? Examining the effect of expansion teams and soccer-specific stadiums on Major League Soccer attendance. *Sport, Business and Management: An International Journal*, 6(2), 205–227.

Office of Management and Budget. (2010, June 28). *Federal Register*, 75(123), 3724 6–52. Retrieved from www.whitehouse.gov/sites/default/files/omb/assets/fedreg_2010/06282010_metro_standards-Complete.pdf.

Pashek Associates. (2006). Indiana ice center feasibility study. Retrieved from www.dcnr.state.pa.us/cs/groups/public/documents/document/dcnr_004973.pdf.

Rascher, D.A., & Rascher, H.V. (2004). NBA expansion and relocation: A viability study of various cities. *Journal of Sport Management*, 18(3), 274–295.

Shapiro, S.L., DeSchriver, T.D., & Rascher, D.A. (2012). Factors affecting the price of luxury suites in major North American sports facilities. *Journal of Sport Management*, 26(3), 246–257.

Shapiro, S.L., DeSchriver, T.D., & Rascher, D.A. (2017). The Beckham effect: Examining the longitudinal impact of a star performer on league marketing, novelty, and scarcity. *European Sport Management Quarterly*, 17(5), 610–634.

TSE Consulting. Aquatic feasibility study: Bandon Community Swimming Pool Development Corporation. Retrieved from http://bandonpool.com/wp-content/uploads/2018/01/FINAL-AQUATIC-FEASIBILITY-STUDY-BA...-5.pdf.

CHAPTER 12

Economic Impact Analysis

Daniel A. Rascher

KEY CONCEPTS

capture rate	indirect economic impact
casual visitor	induced economic impact
construction impact	leakage
direct impact	multiplier
displaced spending	multiplier effect
economic impact	operations impact
incremental spending	reverse time-switcher
incremental visitor	time-switcher

INTRODUCTION

Economic impact is the net economic change in a host community resulting from spending attributed to an event or facility. An economic impact analysis is a type of cost-benefit analysis (an analysis or study of the cost of a project in relation to its potential benefits). It is based on the theory that a dollar flowing into a local economy from outside is a benefit to the locality. An economic impact analysis may be part of a feasibility study, or it may be a stand-alone source of information. Often, an economic impact analysis provides the public with important information regarding the return on an investment in a development project. Such an analysis makes it possible to compare a project to other possible public investment projects. An economic impact analysis may be performed for proposed events or projects (such as facility construction) or for events that have already occurred.

The most important principle in evaluating economic impact is to measure new economic benefits that accrue to the region *that would not occur, or would not have occurred*, without the project or event. This may sound simple, but once a facility has been constructed or a game has been played, the difficulty lies in measuring what would have happened in the region without the event having taken place.

Economic impact analyses are conducted for sporting events, teams, and sport facilities, among other things. An event, such as the Super Bowl, can have an impact on a community. A team may be thought of as a series of events (e.g., 41 regular season home games for NBA basketball teams); impacts may also result from the location of team headquarters in a local community. A sport facility can have an impact in the construction phase, during which millions of dollars change hands. It can also have an impact after it is opened, as hundreds of events may take place in the facility each year.

The financial return for residents in a community comes in the form of new jobs, new earnings or income, and new tax revenues.[1] Some of the new earnings go to local residents who work for the event, team, or facility. However, most of the earnings are generated for residents who are not directly associated with the sporting event, team, or facility, but who benefit from positive externalities. As stated previously, positive externalities, or overflow benefits, are those benefits that are produced by an event or facility but that are not captured by the event owners or sport facility. For instance, when visitors go to New Orleans to attend the Sugar Bowl college football game, they will probably spend money at local food establishments, gas stations, retail stores, and hotels. This spending benefits the owners and employees of those establishments, as a positive direct economic impact.

In this chapter, we first discuss setting the parameters for the analysis. The next section discusses the methodologies we can use in conducting an economic impact analysis. The extension of these techniques to team and facility impacts is described next, and this is followed by a discussion of common mistakes made in economic impact analyses.

SETTING THE PARAMETERS

Two important parameters of events must be determined in the beginning stages of an analysis: the geographic area of impact and the type of spending.

Geographic Area of Impact

The geographic area of impact is an important characteristic of the analysis and should be determined early in the study. Generally, the geographic region selected is the region that is considering funding the event or facility. This definition of the impact region allows for a proper cost-benefit analysis. If a county government contributes funding for a sport facility, then the residents and businesses of that county are paying for the investment, and it is appropriate to determine the benefits that the county receives—not some other county or area—and compare the benefits to the costs. In reality, any major sporting event has an area of impact that is a continuous region, not divided by city or county boundaries, and the impacts decrease with distance from the event location. Additionally, there may be more than one public funding source (e.g., a city, a county, and a state); thus, the economic impact analysis might measure the impact on each of these three areas.

---

1 Additionally, local major sporting events enhance community and civic pride. This effect, known as *psychic impact*, is discussed later.

Different definitions of the geographic area of impact will affect the amount of economic impact that is measured. For example, imagine a resident of Oakland, California, who would typically spend his entertainment dollars attending a movie near home, but who decides to attend a baseball game in San Francisco, 15 miles away. If he spends money at the event and in a restaurant next to the stadium, this spending may not be new spending in the San Francisco/Oakland/San Jose Consolidated Metropolitan Statistical Area (CMSA), because he would have spent the money in Oakland anyway. Instead, it is considered substituted, displaced, or redirected spending.

In a conservative estimate, most local spending is considered to be **displaced spending**—spending by local residents on an event that would have been spent elsewhere in the local economy if the event had not occurred. For this reason it is not counted as part of economic impact. In general, it is improper to count this spending in the economic impact totals, because while more spending is occurring in San Francisco because of the baseball game, less spending is taking place in Oakland. If, however, the chosen geographic area of impact is just the city of San Francisco, then an Oakland resident who attends the game provides a positive direct economic impact on San Francisco. In contrast, a resident of Fresno, California (almost 200 miles away), who attends a baseball game in San Francisco would provide a positive economic impact regardless of whether the geographic area of impact was the entire CMSA or just the city of San Francisco.

Spending

Because spending by local residents typically should not be counted in an economic impact study, it is very important that the analyst differentiate between event attendees who are visitors (those who live outside the geographic impact area) and those who are local residents (those who live inside the area). We can also describe visitors as

- **Casual visitors**—visitors who were already in town for another reason and decided to attend the event.
- **Time-switchers**—visitors who would have come to town at another time, but opted to come to town during this time instead, in order to attend the event.
- **Incremental visitors**—visitors who came to town because of the event and would not have come to town otherwise. The direct spending of this group is fully counted in economic impact.

Exhibit 12.1 is a sample breakdown of attendees at an event. The spending of casual visitors and time-switchers should not be fully counted as new spending; only their **incremental spending**—the spending above and beyond what they would have spent if the event had not occurred—should be counted. For example, suppose a person on a business trip spends $200 per day on a hotel room, food, and local transportation, and decides to stay an additional half-day in order to attend a local NBA game, spending an additional $30 on a meal. The incremental spending is $30, and only this amount should be counted toward the economic impact of the NBA team. The other $200 is economic impact coming from the business portion of the trip. The cost of the NBA ticket

EXHIBIT 12.1   Sample breakdown of attendees at an event.

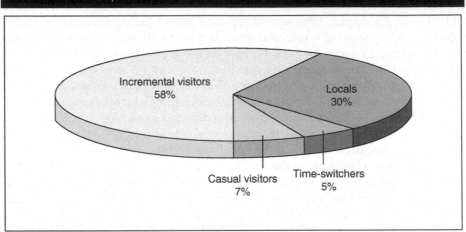

is typically not counted as part of the economic impact, but instead how much is spent in the local community by the franchise in order to run its organization.

It is typically not practical to measure the incremental spending of time-switchers and casual visitors. It is difficult to know how much these individuals spent because of the event, beyond what they would have spent on their visit had the event not taken place. Since we usually cannot measure the incremental spending of casual visitors and time-switchers, we might use an estimate from some other source or simply state that this spending was not measured and the final estimate should be considered a lower bound for the economic impact.

A first step in measuring the economic benefit is to analyze direct spending, which has two components. The first component is incremental visitor spending. As opposed to the spending of time-switchers and casual visitors, direct spending by incremental visitors is fully counted in economic impact. The goal is to measure the amount of spending in the geographic area of impact that goes to local businesses. For example, how much are incremental visitors spending at sporting events? How much are they spending at restaurants and for retail purchases, transportation, and so forth? Whether to count the spending that takes place inside the sport facility is debatable. It is in the geographic area of impact, but how much of it goes to local businesses? To answer this question we might look at how much money from the event is spent locally, or we might find out what happens to the revenue spent inside the facility. Where does it go? Does the local government (often the owner of the facility) receive a percentage of it?

The second component of direct spending is organizational spending. How much do the event host committee, the event management company, corporate sponsors, media, and other related entities spend in the geographic area?

METHODOLOGIES FOR MEASURING ECONOMIC BENEFITS OF AN EVENT

This discussion focuses on spending methodologies and fiscal or tax impact methodology.

Spending Methodologies

Economic impacts are often subdivided into direct, indirect, and induced impacts—the three stages of economic impact. Each of these stages is further subdivided into effects on total output, earnings or income, employment, and public finances. We use different methodologies for studying the spending at each of the stages.

DIRECT SPENDING METHODOLOGY

The analysis of **direct impact**—expenditures on a project or event that contribute to economic impact, also called direct spending—may involve secondary or primary research.

Secondary research. The market demand analysis discussed in Chapter 11 provides an estimate of the number of events that will take place at a facility and the expected attendance at those events. An economic impact study that uses secondary research begins with attendance estimates from the market demand analysis and adds other information about the expected patrons, such as what percentage are visitors and how much money they will spend. Often, this information is gathered from comparable events in other locations, as described in the previous chapter. For a feasibility study, secondary research methods are employed that are similar to the techniques for determining market demand. One method is to evaluate primary studies that have been conducted in other cities for similar projects, with adjustments to account for the differences in circumstances between the primary studies and the subject study.

Primary research: spectator surveys. To determine direct spending, we often create a survey instrument (a questionnaire) to guide interviews with event patrons in order to determine whether they are local residents or visitors, how much money they are spending because of the event, and other information that may be helpful. Exhibit 12.2 is a simple survey for measuring direct spending for an event. The data provide an estimate of the amount of spending per capita per day for incremental visitors for the different spending categories. It allows the researcher to identify casual visitors and time-switchers (see questions 9, 10, and 11) and to account for the number of days a visitor is in town and for the size of groups.

When enough spectators are surveyed, the analyst can estimate how much the typical visitor spends and how long he or she stays.[2] Given the percentage of survey respondents who are local residents versus visitors and an estimate of total attendance, we can estimate the total population of visitors at the event. Similarly, we can extrapolate the findings for the sample related to spending to represent the spending of the entire population of spectators. Exhibit 12.3 shows some intermediate calculations that were initial steps in measuring the economic impact of X Games Minneapolis 2019 (ESPN's annual summer action sports event) in Minneapolis, MN. The total number of spectators at the event was multiplied by the percentage of survey respondents who were visitors, in this case approximately 80%,[3] to obtain the estimate of total visitors (40,000).

---

2 Calculation of the necessary sample size is beyond the scope of this text. Consult a business research or marketing research methods text.

3 Best efforts are made to survey a random sample of people attending the event. The numbers provided here are based on an actual study, but sanitized to protect their confidentiality.

Sometimes the total number of spectators is available from the facility managers if it is a one-day event, otherwise it is common to include questions about which days of the multi-day event the spectator is attending to avoid double-counting the same person on multiple days. An analysis of ticket sales and ZIP codes can also provide this type of information. Based on survey questions such as 9, 10, and 11 in Exhibit 12.2, we can make similar adjustments to account for casual visitors and time-switchers, to obtain the number of relevant ("incremental") visitors. In Exhibit 12.3, we first subtract people who are *only* time-switchers *or* casual visitors from the number of visitors and then subtract the visitors who are *both* casual visitors *and* time-switchers to calculate the number of incremental visitors.

In addition, the surveys can help us develop a typical visitor profile. In Exhibit 12.3, the typical visitor spent $225 per day outside of the official events (mostly in U.S. Bank Stadium) and stayed 2.5 days, resulting in an average of $563 spent outside of the official events for the entire trip. Multiplying the number of incremental visitors by the amount that the typical incremental visitor spent provides an estimate of the spectator portion of direct spending.

Typically, direct spending by visitors attending an event occurs in several geographic categories simultaneously. X Games Minneapolis 2019 has taken place in Minneapolis a number of times. Direct spending occurs in the city of Minneapolis, in Hennepin County, in the Minneapolis-St. Paul-Bloomington, MN-WI MSA, and in the states of Minnesota and Wisconsin. The area of impact defined for an economic impact study will depend on how the results are to be used. If the county is investing in hosting the event, then county decision makers need to know the economic benefits and costs of the event for the county. If the state is going to help fund the event, then state decision makers need to know the impact on the entire state. It is possible, but complicated, to measure the economic impact on more than one area. The direct spending measurement will be derived from the spending of visiting spectators and participants on entertainment, food and beverage, transportation, retail, lodging, and other miscellaneous items, plus event-related spending by non-local businesses (such as the event owner).

Primary research: corporate spending surveys. In addition to the visitor survey, the researcher might survey or interview the event management group or owner (e.g., ESPN for the X Games), host committee, sponsors, and so forth to determine local corporate spending that is related to the event *that would not have occurred otherwise.* As with visitor spending, it is important to distinguish between corporate spending that would have taken place anyway and corporate spending that would *not* have occurred otherwise. A local restaurant chain may spend money to sponsor a local college football bowl game. It may also spend money with local advertising agencies and printers to promote or activate its sponsorship with a television commercial or billboard advertising. The money spent locally is counted toward the economic impact of the bowl game *if* the restaurant chain would not have made those purchases otherwise. If the bowl game had not taken place, and the restaurant chain would have advertised on television with a more typical restaurant ad, then the bowl game did not provide an economic impact to the local community in this case. It simply affected exactly how and why the money was being spent. The same amount would have been spent locally with or without the game; hence, there was no net economic impact.

EXHIBIT 12.2 Example survey for measuring direct spending at an event.

X GAMES 2019 (MINNEAPOLIS, MN) ECONOMIC IMPACT SURVEY

1. Are you attending the X Games? ☑ Yes ☐ No

2. Your age: ☐ 18–24 ☑ 25–34 ☐ 35–44 ☐ 45–54 ☐ 55+

3. What is your gender? ☐ Female ☑ Male

4. Your annual household income: ☐ <$25,000 ☐ $25,000–$49,999 ☑ $50,000–$74,999
   ☐ $75,000–$99,999 ☐ $100,000–$124,999 ☐ $125,000 +

5. What is your residential zip code? __08055__

6. How long will you be visiting Minneapolis? __4__ day(s) __3__ night(s)

7. While visiting Minneapolis, how many people in your party will you be paying for, including yourself? __3__

(continued)

EXHIBIT 12.2   Cont.

8. While in Minneapolis during the X Games, how much do you plan to spend DAILY for the above group on the following?

Lodging $180

Transportation in Minneapolis (rental car, gas, parking, taxi, bus, etc.) $65

Event-related (tickets, concession, merchandise at X Games) $125

Food/beverage (not at X Games) $160

Entertainment (not at X Games) $75

Shopping (not at X Games) $120

Other (not at X Games) $20

9. Would you have visited Minneapolis this weekend if the X Games were not in town?   ☐ Yes   ☑ No

10. Does this visit to Minneapolis replace any other past/future visit to this area?   ☐ Yes   ☑ No

11. Primary reason for trip to Minneapolis:

Attend this event ✓   Business _____   Pleasure/Vacation _____   Other _____

EXHIBIT 12.3 Visitor profile created from the results of a visitor survey.

KEY FINDINGS FROM THE VISITOR SURVEY	
CATEGORY	**ESTIMATE**
Total Attendance	90,000
Total Number of Unique Attendees (individual people attending)	50,000
Number of Local Residents	10,000
Total Number of Visitors	40,000
Number of "Time-switchers" Only	–4,000
Number of "Casual" Visitors Only	–3,000
Number of Visitors who came because of the X Games, but did not attend the official events[1]	500
Number of "Incremental" Visitors Counting Towards Economic Impact[2]	33,500
Average Expenditure Estimates	
Average Daily Expenditure per "Incremental" Visitor Outside of Official Events	$225
Average Number of Days Stayed per "Incremental" Visitor	2.50
Average Expenditure for Entire Trip per "Incremental" Visitor Outside of Official Events	$563
Total Direct Spending of "Incremental" Visitors Outside of Official Events[3]	$18,843,750

1 A number of people (typically children and spouses) came to Minneapolis because of the event, but did not attend any of the official events.
2 Spending by "time-switchers" and "casual" visitors was not used in the impact analysis.
3 Spending is only within Minneapolis.

When a non-local business sponsors a bowl game, this is considered to be net new spending (unless the company would have spent the same money locally without the game). For practical reasons, and to develop a conservative estimate of economic impact, we do not consider spending by local companies to be new spending unless it can be specifically identified as new spending. Thus, spending by local companies is not typically counted toward economic impact. In other words, the researcher starts with the assumption that local spending is displaced spending and is not new incremental spending. If a company specifically states that its spending is new and would not have occurred otherwise, then that spending may be considered part of economic impact.

INDIRECT AND INDUCED SPENDING METHODOLOGY

The economic output that results from direct spending during an event subsequently affects many other industries and workers. For instance, when visitors attend the Men's Final Four, they may eat in a local restaurant before the event. With the money the visitors spend, the restaurant will pay employees, purchase food, pay for utilities, and so on. The food wholesaler will pay the farmer, who (if it is a small, local farm) will purchase clothing at the local retail store. These expenditures continue through successive rounds until the money ceases to circulate locally, when either it leaks out of the local economy or a resident or local company saves it for a significant period of time.

The spending described in the previous paragraph illustrates **indirect economic impacts**: impacts that occur in the area of impact that represent the circulation of initial visitor expenditures (direct impacts). The total of the successive rounds of spending constitutes the indirect impact estimate, which will be explained below.

The **induced economic impact** is the effect of direct and indirect economic impacts on earnings and employment. As the initial spending and subsequent spending occur, a portion goes to local residents and to the local government in the form of taxes. Increases in demand resulting from the economic impact lead to increases in employment, which will affect earnings. When we report these impacts, we describe employment impacts in terms of full-time equivalent (FTE) jobs and earnings impacts in terms of dollars of personal income. A more detailed discussion of induced economic impact occurs later in this chapter.

Multiplier effect to measure indirect and induced impacts. A **multiplier** is a number that helps researchers quantify indirect and induced economic impacts, by measuring the change in output for each and every industry as a result of the injection of one dollar of direct impact into any of those industries.

To derive a multiplier, we begin by categorizing the spending that represents indirect and induced economic impacts. The recipients of initial direct spending generally re-spend it in five ways:

1. With other private-sector businesses in the same local economy—on inventory, maintenance, and so forth.
2. With employees who reside in the same local economy—as wages, tips, and so on.
3. With local government—as sales taxes or property taxes.
4. With non-local governments—as sales taxes or taxes on profits.
5. With employees, businesses, or organizations who reside outside the local economy.

The first three types of spending recirculate money through the local economy. The last two categories of spending are considered **leakages**— movement of money out of the geographic region. They reflect the degree to which a region is not economically isolated but engages in commerce with other regions. The larger and more diverse the geographic region, the less leakage, all else being equal, because a large region is usually relatively self-sufficient.

For the above five scenarios, we create input/output tables that disaggregate the economy into industries and quantify the flow of goods and services among them. We then mathematically derive multipliers that describe changes in output that result from changes in input. We apply a separate multiplier to each of the 432 industry groups (as defined by the US Bureau of Economic Analysis [BEA]).

Typically, the researcher does not actually create the multipliers for the 432 industry groups but instead purchases a regional multiplier model based on the USDA Forest Service IMPLAN (IMpact Analysis for PLANning) and data from the US Bureau of Economic Analysis. Many vendors supply these multiplier tables, including MIG, Inc. and Regional Economic Models, Inc. The researcher either purchases the multiplier information for a county, city, MSA, or state from one of these vendors or, in some cases, gathers information from the BEA and derives the multipliers him- or herself.

For an example of the multiplier in action, consider a group of spectators from outside Minneapolis who visit the city to attend the X Games and spend $1,000 total in the community. This initial direct expenditure stimulates economic activity and creates additional business spending, employment, household income, and government revenue in Minneapolis. The initial spending (the direct impact) results in a ripple effect, termed the **multiplier effect**. The multiplier effect consists of indirect and induced impacts.

The local hotels, restaurants, retail stores, transportation providers, and others who receive portions of the initial $1,000 will spend the money in the five ways listed previously. The recipients of *those* expenditures will again spend the money in one of the five ways, and the chain of purchases continues. Exhibit 12.4 charts the direct and indirect effects of the original $1,000 of spending.

The manner in which the local economy is defined—especially its size—affects the values of the multipliers. In a small local geographic region, many game attendees will probably be visitors. This is an advantage to the local economy. However, small geographic areas suffer from a high degree of leakage, because a small geographic region is less self-sufficient than a large region.

There are a number of different types of multipliers, and each has a specific purpose. The first type of multiplier is an output multiplier (also called a sales or transaction multiplier). It measures the indirect and induced effects of an extra unit of direct spending on *economic activity* within the local economy. This multiplier relates direct expenditures to the increase in economic activity that results from the spending and re-spending of the initial direct spending.

An income multiplier, the second type, measures the indirect and induced effects of an extra unit of spending on the level of *household income* in the local economy. It is the ratio of change in income to the initial change in expenditure. It is the clearest indicator of the effect of economic impact on the residents of the host community.

The third type of multiplier is an employment multiplier, which measures the direct, indirect, and induced effects of an extra unit of spending on *employment* in the local economy. It measures the number of full-time equivalent jobs supported in the local economy as a result of visitor expenditures.

Exhibit 12.5 is a multiplier table listing the output, earnings, and employment multipliers for industrial categories in Hennepin County, whose major city is Minneapolis (followed closely by St. Paul).

Example of indirect and induced event spending analysis. To illustrate the analysis of indirect and induced spending, we refer to Exhibit 12.5. If a visitor to Minneapolis spends $100 on lodging, this will create an extra $56 in indirect spending (for total spending of $156). Of that, $52 will be retained as income or

EXHIBIT 12.4   Direct and indirect effects of initial spending.

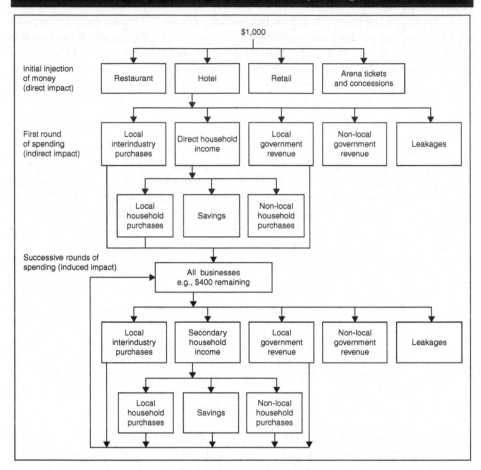

EXHIBIT 12.5   Example output, income, and employment multipliers.

HENNEPIN COUNTY MULTIPLIERS			
	OUTPUT	EARNINGS	EMPLOYMENT*
Transportation	1.70	0.78	16.86
Retail	1.68	0.68	17.23
Lodging	1.56	0.52	11.81
Entertainment	1.65	0.54	20.04
Food and Beverage	1.62	0.62	21.85
Miscellaneous	1.70	0.61	9.76

* The employment multiplier is measured on the basis of a $1 million change in output.
Source: Data from IMPLAN, 2017.

earnings to residents of Hennepin County. Given the employment multiplier for the lodging industry, 11.81, we can expect that for every $1 million spent in Hennepin County on lodging, approximately 12 FTE jobs will be created. Another way to think about this is as follows: in order to create or support one job, the lodging industry has to take in a certain amount of money. We can calculate this amount by dividing the basis change in output ($1 million) by the employment multiplier:

$$\text{money necessary to support one job} = \frac{\text{basis change in output}}{\text{employment multiplier}}$$

$$= \frac{\$1,000,000}{11.81}$$

$$= \$84,659$$

This is the average total cost of employing a worker in the lodging industry, including benefits (e.g., health or retirement benefits), payroll costs (e.g., social security taxes), and assorted overhead.

The results from a survey like the one shown in Exhibit 12.2 allow us to calculate total spending for the X Games by category.[4] The results, given in Exhibit 12.6, show that Lodging, Food & Beverage, and Retail were the three categories with the highest spending for visiting spectators at the X Games and related activities, which included multiple events within U.S. Bank Stadium. Further, included in the Transportation category was about $400,000 spent on rental cars. The survey showed that the average incremental visitor spent about $124 on lodging. Given that there were 33,500 incremental visitors (see Exhibit 12.3), the direct economic impact for lodging is $4.2 million.

To calculate the total economic impact of X Games Minneapolis 2019, we multiply each of the direct spending categories in Exhibit 12.6 by the appropriate multiplier given in Exhibit 12.5 and then total these amounts. In this example, spending inside U.S. Bank Stadium is not included in the economic impact measurement. The measurement does include, under corporate spending, expenditures by ESPN, non-local media, visiting athletes, and corporate sponsors that hosted parties and event-related activities (dozens of such events took place during the multi-day event). We can easily calculate the indirect economic impact by subtracting the direct economic impact from the total economic impact.

$$\text{total economic impact} - \text{direct economic impact}$$
$$= \text{indirect economic impact}$$

$$\$45,359,175 - \$28,141,100 = \$17,218,075$$

---

4   A more expanded survey similar to that in Exhibit 12.2 was used by Dr. Tiffany Richardson (University of Minnesota) and Dr. Daniel Rascher (one of the co-authors of this text, University of San Francisco) to measure the economic impact of X Games Minnesota 2019 on the city of Minneapolis.

EXHIBIT 12.6 Calculating total economic impact.

CATEGORY	DIRECT SPENDING*	MULTIPLIER	TOTAL
Transportation	$1,632,000	1.70	$2,774,400
Retail	$1,972,000	1.68	$3,312,960
Lodging	$4,155,000	1.56	$6,481,800
Entertainment	$975,100	1.65	$1,608,915
Food & Beverage	$4,385,000	1.62	$7,103,700
Miscellaneous	$422,000	1.70	$717,400
Inside U.S. Bank Stadium	—	—	—
Corporate/Team/Media	$14,600,000	1.60	$23,360,000
Total Direct Spending	$28,141,100	Total Economic Impact	$45,359,175

* Does not include spending within U.S. Bank Stadium.

EXHIBIT 12.7 Induced economic impacts from X Games Minneapolis 2019.

TYPE OF IMPACT	
Earnings	$17,708,794
Employment	480

Note: Figures do not include spending within U.S. Bank Stadium.

Exhibit 12.7 gives the induced impacts from the X Games. These portions of direct spending are retained as income or earnings for local residents. The multiplier pertaining to income for each of the spending categories is shown in Exhibit 12.5 in the Earnings column. The indirect spending resulting from the events *also* contributes to increases in income. However, as discussed above, it is practically impossible to track indirect spending. For this reason, we use a general aggregate multiplier to estimate induced earnings impacts from indirect spending. We can determine this aggregate multiplier by calculating the weighted average multiplier for the city across all 432 industry categories. The employment impact from indirect spending is calculated in the same fashion.

Fiscal (or Tax) Impact Methodology

An analysis of the fiscal or tax implications of economic impact is often complex. First, the analyst must understand the tax code for the city, county, or state—a daunting requirement. Second, the task of separating tax revenue according to recipient, such as city, county, or state government, can be difficult. Third, accounting for tax-exempt spending by visitors and relevant local organizations can be time-consuming, and it often results only in estimates of those exemptions. Fourth, accounting for the tax effects of indirect and induced impacts requires information that is not always readily available.

Continuing with the X Games as an example, let's look at the fiscal impact of a sporting event. During the event, sales, lodging, entertainment, liquor, and restaurant taxes are collected from direct spending. In 2019 in Minneapolis, these taxes were:

- *Sales:* The sales tax collected in Minneapolis is 8.025 percent, of which 0.5 percentage points goes to the City of Minneapolis, and the remainder to other jurisdictions. Since the area of impact is defined as the City, only taxes flowing to that entity are included in this analysis.
- *Lodging:* In addition to sales tax, Minneapolis levies a 3.0% lodging tax on hotel room sales in addition to the sales tax being applied to those room rentals.
- *Entertainment:* Minneapolis charges a 3.0% entertainment tax also in addition to the sales tax being applied for admission fees, the use of amusement devices and games, food, drinks and merchandise sold in public places during live performances, and short-term lodging within the City limits.
- *Liquor:* The Minneapolis liquor tax is 3% and is applied in addition to the sales tax.
- *Restaurant*: The restaurant tax is also 3% and is applied in addition to the sales tax.

We calculate direct fiscal impacts by multiplying the tax rates for each category by the direct spending for each category. (See Exhibit 12.8.) For example,

$$\text{fiscal impact for restaurant tax} = \text{food and beverage direct spending}$$
$$\times \text{Minneapolis restaurant tax rate}$$
$$= \$4,385,000 \times 3\%$$
$$= \$131,550$$

Additionally, a significant portion of the $15 million in corporate spending consisted of spending on food.

The calculation of fiscal impacts is complicated by tax exemptions. Not every item in a grocery store is subject to sales tax; in some states, sales taxes must be paid for food at a restaurant if a customer eats in, but not for takeout; and, often, a different tax rate is imposed on cigarettes than other grocery store items. To sort out these issues, we gather information from a variety of sources. For instance, based on information from a number of state restaurant associations, it is estimated that 20% of a typical restaurant bill for tourists is made up of alcoholic beverages. Alternatively, we could adjust our survey to ask specific questions about expenditures on alcoholic beverages.

We measure *indirect* fiscal impacts by applying recent historical aggregate average tax rates to the indirect spending estimate. Given that indirect spending is disbursed throughout many sectors of the local and state economies—some

TAX CATEGORY	
EXHIBIT 12.8 Calculation of fiscal impacts for X Games Minneapolis 2019 (Minneapolis only).	
Sales	$67,706
Lodging	$124,650
Entertainment	$153,903
Liquor	$26,310
Restaurant	$131,550
Subtotal	$504,119
Indirect Taxation	$349,583
Total Fiscal Impact	$853,701

Note: Figures do not include spending within U.S. Bank Stadium, nor any rent paid by ESPN to the government-owned stadium.

of those sectors being subject to certain taxes and others not—one way to estimate the fiscal impact of indirect spending is to analyze the total spending that takes place in a county relative to total taxes collected. In some states, the gross state product (GSP), an estimate of total spending in the state, is disaggregated by city and county. By combining that information with the total taxes collected in the city or county, we can obtain an estimate of the indirect spending tax rate. For instance, if total spending in a town during one year is $100 million, and the total of taxes collected in that town from all relevant sources for that year is $5 million, then, on average, for every dollar spent, five cents is collected in local taxes. This type of calculation provides an estimate of the fiscal impact of indirect spending. From Exhibit 12.6, indirect spending at the X Games can be calculated as the difference between total economic impact and direct spending ($45,359,175 − 28,141,100 = $17,218,075). From historical information, we know that the average tax collected in Hennepin County was about 2.03 cents per dollar (2.0303 to be exact). We can now calculate the fiscal impact of indirect spending pertaining to the X Games.

$$\text{fiscal impact of indirect spending} = \text{indirect spending} \times \text{average tax rate}$$

$$= \$17,218,075 \times 2.03\%$$

$$= \$349,583$$

MEASURING EVENT COSTS

We have explained techniques for measuring the economic benefits of an event. Now we turn to the costs of hosting the event. Many economic impact studies do not provide estimates of the costs of generating economic impacts. It can sometimes be difficult to determine the full costs of hosting an event and the entities responsible for paying these costs. For instance, if a host committee spent $4 million to bid for and host an event, and 75% of that money was spent locally, the analyst might be tempted to count the $3 million as positive economic impact. However, if the source of the money is the local government, then the impact generally does not count. If the event had not taken place, the money would likely have been spent in town on something else. If the source of funds was outside the community—perhaps the state government or non-local corporate sponsors—then the spending could be considered an economic benefit and counted as part of economic impact.

Although many economic impact studies do not address costs, a complete study does include an analysis of event costs. In addition to local government funding, these often include costs of security, ticket sales, printing, advertising, transportation, communication, travel, and lodging.

ECONOMIC IMPACT OF A LOCAL TEAM

Measuring the economic impact of an event is a formidable task, but measuring the economic impact of a team is even more complex. A team may be thought of as a series of events—for example, 81 home games for an MLB team. Typically, the analyst will gather data on one or two games and extrapolate the results to an entire season. Based on discussions with team officials, the researcher might choose to study a weekday game and a weekend game, because the mix of patrons probably varies the most across those two types of games. Additionally, the analyst must measure the impact of the team as a local business, including organizational spending in the area and direct employment of the franchise. NFL teams often employ more than 200 people, including players.

Similarly, an NFL team may spend more than $200 million annually. The percentage that is spent locally is called the **capture rate**. Typically, a significant portion of organizational spending takes place outside the local city. In fact, a conservative estimate may be that only 10% is spent locally.[5] The largest single expense item is player salaries. For a proper estimate of organizational spending, the researcher must account for where players reside and—for an even more conservative estimate—must assume that players do not spend all their money but rather save a significant portion of it. To estimate the capture rate of franchise spending, we can audit a team's spending patterns. This is not often done because of the high labor costs required to do so. Aside from organizational spending and employment, measuring the economic impact of a team is similar to measuring that of an event.

A feasibility study is often conducted prior to a team's moving to town. In this case, the analysts employ secondary research methods similar to the techniques used in determining market demand. One method is to evaluate primary studies that have been conducted in other cities for similar projects, making adjustments to account for the differences in circumstances between the primary studies and the subject study. An assessment of common denominators,

---

5   A self-audit by two major professional sports teams found a capture rate of 20% of the team's total budget (averaging the two numbers that were quite close to each other).

such as both cities having an NBA team, can also be helpful. For example, a feasibility study for Orange County, Florida, to host an NFL team might include the analysis of a primary economic impact study of the Indianapolis Colts. In adjusting the findings to fit Orange County, the analyst might look at existing primary economic impact studies for the two relevant NBA teams, the Indiana Pacers and Orlando Magic.

SIDEBAR 12.A   Where Do Visitors Spend Their Money?

In order for an event to generate substantial economic impacts, it needs visitors to stay overnight, causing them to spend money on lodging and a number of meals. Those are the big-ticket items when it comes to economic impact. Many events, however, are single-day events. Yet, some event owners, such as IRONMAN Group (owned by Wanda Sports Holdings), have managed to turn a one-day event into a three-day event. The Rock 'n' Roll Marathon series occurs in multiple countries, stages an expo the day before the marathon and requires runners to register at the expo—that's two days. Then, after the marathon is a musical event that continues late into the evening, making it hard for participants to board a plane and leave the city until the next day. That's three days.

SportsEconomics, a firm that provides financial and marketing research analysis to clients in a wide variety of sport-related fields, has

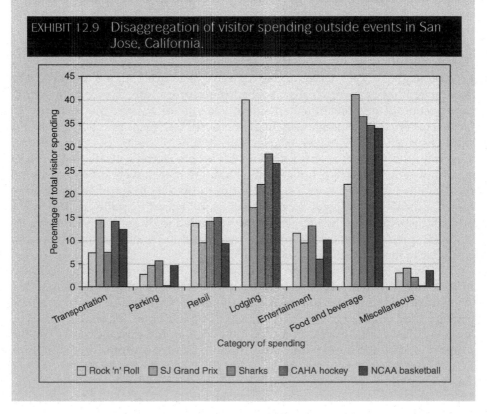

EXHIBIT 12.9   Disaggregation of visitor spending outside events in San Jose, California.

measured the economic impact of three Rock 'n' Roll Marathons in two locations, and the economic impact is quite large.* Not only do marathon runners spend a lot per day when they travel to an event (they generally have relatively high incomes), but they make a mini-vacation out of it and often bring along a friend or two.

Where do they spend their money? Exhibit 12.9 shows where visitors spend their money for a variety of events in the City of San Jose. Three of the events are mostly spectator driven (San Jose Grand Prix, San Jose Sharks game, and NCAA Men's Basketball Regionals), and two of them are more participant driven (the Rock 'n' Roll Marathon and the CAHA Youth Hockey Tournament). Lodging and food and beverages account for over 50% of the spending by visitors to these events. Transportation, retail, and entertainment account for just over 10% each.

* Two of the studies were conducted in conjunction with Dr. Richard Irwin.

ECONOMIC IMPACT OF A SPORT FACILITY

The measurement of a sport facility's economic impact can be controversial because the results are often cited as evidence in debates over how much public funding the facility should receive (see Chapter 9 for more on this topic). A sport facility can provide economic impact both during the construction phase and during the operational phase, when it hosts hundreds of events. As already described, a facility will provide **operations impact** (impact generated through daily operation) from games and other events. A facility will also provide direct spending impacts, like those of a team. The methodology for measuring a facility's operational economic impacts is similar to that for events and teams.

The measurement of **construction impact**—the amount of money that comes into the community during the construction phase that would not otherwise have entered the community—has been perhaps the most controversial aspect of sport economic impact analysis. In general, if a city government spends money to construct a building, the net economic impact must be measured in terms of the forgone alternative uses of the same funding and land, i.e., the opportunity cost. Would other uses have had a greater or lesser economic impact? Typically, government spending is not considered to generate economic impact for a specific project, because that money could have been spent on another project. This is similar to the reason why spending by local residents is not generally considered to add to operational economic impact, as discussed previously. If a resident spends money at a football game, then he or she will not spend that money at the movies or for other local entertainment.

In terms of a facility, if a local government uses $20 million of its annual budget to build a sport arena instead of upgrading the facilities of the local school district, then the arena construction provides a construction impact only to the extent that it results in more private money being spent locally. If a team owner spends $300 million in conjunction with the local government to build a $500 million arena, then the $300 million in private funding would be a construction impact, but the $200 million in public funding would not. See also Sidebar 12.C.

COMMON MISTAKES IN ESTIMATING ECONOMIC IMPACT

As with all business research, economic impact analysis provides an *estimate* of the true impact. Analysts cannot avoid making assumptions, and they are well advised to minimize the number of assumptions and to test the validity of the assumptions. Controversy surrounds sport economic impact analyses, partly because, frankly, many researchers do not do a very good job of avoiding common mistakes. Such mistakes will cause the analysis to either over- or underestimate the true economic impact.

Causes of Underestimating

One of the main causes of estimates being too low is the fact that it is impossible to account for all local corporate spending that relates to an event. For instance, for events that are televised, expenditures by the media (e.g., ESPN) with local businesses to produce coverage of the event are not likely to be accounted for in the economic impact study. Most media organizations do not release the relevant information. Of course, we can make estimates, but this step is often skipped.

> ### SIDEBAR 12.B   Smaller Teams, Smaller Communities = Greater Economic Impact
>
> Academic research conducted by economists to measure the economic impact of sport facilities often shows that these facilities have little or no economic impact on the community, primarily because of the high construction costs that the public usually pays. Certainly, the facilities do generate new revenues, because they draw people from out of town for events, but those incremental revenues do not cover the public's portion of the construction cost. Also, research into sales taxes collected in a county hosting a professional sport facility shows that often the impact from the facility is too small to measure. Robert Baade, Victor Matheson, Brad Humphreys, and Dennis Coates, among others, have conducted numerous studies of this type (see Coates & Humphreys, 2003, and Baade & Matheson, 2006). Researchers have hypothesized that smaller teams in smaller communities may have a greater possibility of producing positive economic impacts (Seaman, 2004; Matheson, 2006).
>
> It may be difficult to discern the impact of a single business such as a sport facility on a county or metropolitan area over a period of time as long as a year or even a month, but the general belief is that events at these facilities crowd out regular visitors to a community if the events are large, or cause visitors to substitute event attendance for another visit to the community, so the net effect is zero or small. However, the findings

from surveys of visitors are contrary, in that even after accounting for time-switchers and casual visitors, these studies find there are incremental visitors who spend money in the community that they would not have spent otherwise. Reconciliation of these two opposed findings is fodder for future research.

Nola Agha (2013) conducted a comprehensive study of all 238 metropolitan areas hosting minor league baseball teams from 1985 through 2006 and found that communities hosting AAA and A+ teams, and AA and rookie stadiums, have statistically significantly positive gains in local per capita income, when other possible reasons for the growth are controlled for. Why the difference between major and minor professional teams? Agha and Rascher (2016) scanned the evidence and found nine reasons, taken as a whole, why minor league baseball teams might be more likely to provide net positive economic impacts than major league teams: (1) relatively more new visitors attend, (2) geographic isolation means fewer substitutes, (3) local residents alter spending patterns, (4) more vacationing at home occurs, (5) leakages, (6) government spending, (7) new stadiums, (8) venue utilization, and (9) crowding out.

Additionally, Rascher, Hyun, and Nagel (2020), using multiple years of data, have created an experiment where a random set of metro areas (experimental group) received an injection of various levels of economic impact to their gross domestic product or GDP (treatments range from $25 million per year to $1 billion). Standard panel regression techniques utilized in the sports economics literature to measure economic impact are then tested on both the baseline model (all areas with their actual GDPs) and the experimental model (containing all metro areas with the experimental group having received the treatment) and a comparison of the resulting impacts is made. The findings show that the methods often used in the literature fail to be able to detect the built-in-by-design injections of economic activity for the experimental group until very high levels of treatment of at least $300 million to $1 billion are present. The issue is that the economies where sports franchises locate are so large that the impact of the sports team is just too small compared to the general variation over time in economic activity. Hence, Agha and Rascher's (2016) finding that smaller markets might receive discernible impacts from sports teams could be simply because those markets are small enough for franchises and their operations to be detectable.

Some events produce economic impact from visitors who come to town because of the event but do not attend the event itself. For the NCAA Men's Final Four basketball tournament held in San Antonio in 2004, approximately 7,000 visitors came to town for the event, but, for a variety of reasons, did not attend any of the games. Many studies will fail to measure impacts like this. About 5% of visitors for a recent X Games event came, but did not attend the event. Nearly 100% of them came with someone who did.

How the researchers treat blank survey responses can affect the final results. Counting a blank response as zero lowers the overall estimate of economic impact. Counting it as the average of other responses on the same question can result in a more accurate estimate, unless the respondent meant for the answer to be zero. Sometimes looking at the raw surveys will suggest the best way to treat the response. If the respondent answered some of the spending categories but left others blank, he or she probably intended the blank responses to mean zero.

As described above, to produce a conservative estimate, we do not count spending by local residents and by casual visitors and time-switchers toward economic impact, because we assume that the spending would have occurred even if the event had not taken place. However, research shows that this may not always be the case. For example, after the 2004 MasterCard Alamo Bowl, local residents indicated that they spent, on average, just under $40 per person *more* in town than they would have if the event had not been held in San Antonio. Perhaps even more important is the notion of "vacationing at home," when a local resident stays in town because of an event instead of leaving and spending money outside town (see Sidebar 12.C).

SIDEBAR 12.C   Vacationing at Home

It is typical in economic impact studies that the spending by local residents is not counted toward economic impact. This is done to be conservative—to have a measurement of economic impact that is likely to be lower than the true amount (not higher than the true amount and, thus, subject to legitimate scrutiny). However, this concept often feels at odds with the instincts of event owners, who note that many local residents "vacation at home" and spend their money locally instead of leaving town to spend it on some other external vacation.

This concept of "vacationing at home" was analyzed in depth by Cobb and Olberding (2007). In a study of the Cincinnati Flying Pig Marathon, they found that many local runners—who account for a significant percentage of race participants in many marathons—actually use their home-city marathon as a substitute for a race out of town. They found that economic impact was actually more than 20% higher than previous estimates when spending by these local residents was included.

A key element of this type of analysis is that the researcher should count the amount of money the local resident *would have spent* had he or she traveled to another location and run a marathon, not how much the person actually did spend locally related to the hometown marathon. The reason for this is that the amount the individual would have spent abroad was not spent and is available to be spent locally, whether it be during that same few days or within a reasonable time period. In other words, the money stayed home and likely will eventually be spent at various local businesses. Using the same methodology, Irwin and Rascher (Irwin & Rascher, 2005, 2007a, 2007b; Rascher & Irwin, 2004) have found that many events seem to draw a substantial number of local residents who vacation at home, and the numbers may be greater for participatory events (than for spectator events).

EXHIBIT 12.10   Percentages of local residents attending selected events who would have attended the event if held outside the area.

EVENT	RESIDENTS OF...	% THAT WOULD HAVE ATTENDED THE EVENT...	HAD IT BEEN HELD OUTSIDE OF...
US Figure Skating Championships (San Jose, 2012)	city	12%	county
USA Gymnastics Championships (San Jose, 2012)	city	17%	county
Nike Women's Marathon (San Francisco, 2011)	city, city, state	39%, 19%, 22%	city, state, state
AAU Junior Olympic Games (Houston, 2012)	county	79%	state
Dr Pepper Big 12 Championship (San Antonio, 2007)	county, state	27%, 44%	state, state
Alamo Bowl (San Antonio, 2007)	county, state	26%, 33%	state, state
Alamo Bowl (San Antonio, 2012)	city	13%	state
Alamo Bowl (San Antonio, 2011)	city, state	4%, 33%	state, state
Alamo Bowl (San Antonio, 2010)	city, city	15%, 4%	city, state

Exhibit 12.10 lists the percentages of local residents attending selected events who would have attended the event if held outside the area, according to surveys. For example, an economic impact study for the 2007 Dr Pepper Big 12 Championship (a college football game) found that "[a]pproximately 5 percent of San Antonio residents, 27 percent of Bexar County residents, and 44 percent of in-state respondents indicated they would have attended the event if it were hosted outside of the State of Texas. This is highly correlated with those fans who said that they were a fan of one of the two teams playing." Almost half of the spectators from within the state of Texas (but outside of Bexar County, where the game was played) indicated that they would have traveled to a nearby state to watch the championship if it had not been held in Texas. The money stayed home: the football game helped keep residents of the state from taking their money outside the state. Thus, that money is incremental in that it would not be in the state to be spent at some point had the football game not occurred. That money should be counted toward economic impact.

Often, fiscal impacts are not fully accounted for. This is especially true of business or personal income taxes collected on the earnings or income type of economic impact. User fees related to energy usage and airport taxes levied per person using the local airport are examples of other fiscal impacts that are often not accounted for.

Another shortcoming of standard economic impact analysis is that most measurements account only for current new spending, ignoring the possibility that an event might cause an increase in the number of *future* visitors to the community. For instance, the economic impact analysis for the 2004 NCAA Men's Final Four basketball tournament reported that approximately 20% of visitors said that after coming to San Antonio for the Final Four, they are likely to visit again. These future visits should be attributed at least partially to a particular event, yet they are often ignored. Media coverage of an event can also inspire viewers to visit the host city in the future; this is termed the media impact. For example, 5.5 million spectators viewed the 2019 Valero Alamo Bowl, held in San Antonio, Texas, on the ESPN national coverage of the game. During the game, the announcers often mentioned the name of the city, increasing viewers' awareness of it. Other media outlets, such as newspapers, radio stations, and websites, provided free coverage of San Antonio during the game. It is extremely difficult to measure the way media coverage translates into actual new visitor expenditures. Notwithstanding, it is possible to calculate the expense that the local convention and visitors bureau would have had to incur to obtain a similar amount of media coverage, based on standard advertising rates. Findings from studies for the 2004 version of the game suggest that San Antonio received nearly $1.8 million in media coverage from the telecast itself, not including other forms of media coverage. This area is ripe for future economic impact research.

Further, most economic impact analyses do not account for psychic impact, even though it could be an important factor in some cases (see Sidebar 12.D). Researchers have estimated that the Pittsburgh Penguins of the NHL are worth approximately $16 million per year to the residents of Pittsburgh solely in terms of emotional or psychic impact. This works out to an average of about $7.27 per person in the Pittsburgh MSA (Johnson, Groothuis, & Whitehead, 2001). The Indiana Pacers have an annual psychic impact on the Indianapolis community worth about $35 million per year (Alexander, Kern, & Neill, 2000). The Minnesota Vikings are worth approximately $10 per resident of the state in psychic impact (Fenn & Crooker, 2004). A more recent study of University of North Carolina athletics showed that residents of Chapel Hill would be willing to pay hundreds of dollars each to prevent the closure of the athletic department (Zagorin, 2017).

How does one quantify happiness? Researchers using the contingent valuation method (CVM) ask respondents how much they would be willing to pay for hypothetical projects. Researchers studying environmental impact often use CVM to measure the public's valuation of new parks, species preservation, pollution cleanup, and so forth. In sports, we might ask respondents to name the highest amount that they would be willing to pay, out of their own household budget, each year to make a new arena possible or host a major sport event in town. For example, if asked to contribute to a fund for a new arena or a major sport event, would you contribute $0, $5, $10, $15, $20, or more than $20? How

EXHIBIT 12.11 Example of an economic impact analysis where psychic impact matters.

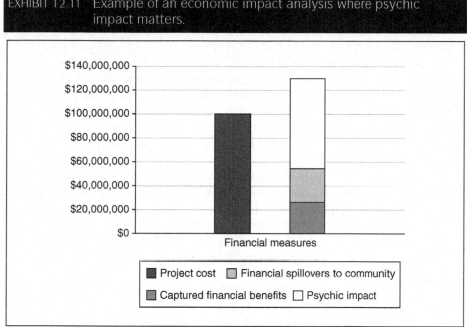

much would you pay to bring a professional sport team to your town or to help sponsor a national sport event?

The sport industry, more than most other industries, is about fanaticism, emotion, and community; to leave these impacts out of an analysis is to miss an important part of the picture. The reason the public funds museums, zoos, and orchestras is that these institutions enhance the community. Similarly, sport teams, events, and facilities are also public goods, enhancing the quality of life of the areas in which they locate. Analysts should measure these positive externalities in order to assess fully the impact that a sport team or facility brings to a locality. As Exhibit 12.11 illustrates, it may cost $100 million to build a local baseball park, but the private financial gain by the facility operator or team might be approximately $22 million. In this situation, private investors will not build the facility. If businesses located around the facility, such as restaurants and retail stores, receive economic impact worth about $25 million, this still is not enough to justify expending private and public funds to build the facility. However, if the psychic impact is worth enough to push the total impact over $100 million, then construction financed through a public/private partnership may be worthwhile.

SIDEBAR 12.D   Psychic Impact

One role of government is to provide cultural, civic, and entertainment goods and services that residents enjoy but that no private firm is willing to provide. These goods, whose consumption is non-excludable and non-rival, are termed public goods, discussed in Chapter 9. In general, public goods are funded by governments in the appropriate jurisdiction (e.g., state parks, national defense) because private industry is not willing to offer them.

Major professional sport teams, entertainment districts, and sport and cultural events enhance the quality of life in a region, as do zoos, museums, aquariums, parks, the arts, and other public goods. Sporting events provide an entertainment option, especially for individuals who value attending or viewing spectator sports or attending related events, such as fan festivals. They also provide benefits that are public goods, including psychic impact.

Psychic impact is the emotional impact on a community that results when the community hosts prestigious events or major sport teams. Cultural events often are part of the fabric of a community, increasing civic pride and community spirit. Psychic impact includes emotional benefits received by members of a community who are not directly involved with managing an event but who still strongly identify with the event. Sport's psychic impact includes the pleasure and camaraderie that individuals feel when they attend or discuss games or teams. Most other industries do not provide the same degree of emotional impact.

For example, when Atlanta was awarded the 1996 Summer Olympics, local residents were moved by the announcement. Many people cried with joy. They felt that Atlanta had now proved itself as a "real" international city. Newspaper reports described the city as a sea of honking horns and cheers as people were swept up in jubilation. Is it possible to quantify in financial terms the collective emotional upswing of Atlantans? Another example comes from Minnesota, where a former governor, Arne Carlson, said that "If you were to make a list of 10 or 15 of the most prized possessions of the state, [the Twins] would probably be one of them, and you never want to lose one of your prized possessions. Never" (Meryhew, 1997).

Psychic impact techniques focus on measuring the value of psychic impact.* Event owners capture part of the value of psychic impact through ticket sales, merchandise sales, and so forth. However, much psychic impact is provided free to local residents simply through their knowledge of the event. This is one of the reasons for the public/private partnerships that build sport venues. Proper decisions about the spending of public dollars require knowledge of both economic impact and psychic impact.

* Economist Bruce Johnson pioneered the application of research in psychic impact, also called psychic income or public consumption benefit, in sport. See Johnson and Whitehead (2000); Johnson, Groothuis, and Whitehead (2001); and Groothuis, Johnson, and Whitehead (2004).

Causes of Overestimating

Overestimations of economic impact occur because most analyses do not account for **reverse time-switchers**, those local residents who leave town during an event period because of the event. Expenditures that reverse time-switchers would have spent in town are instead spent outside the local area. Only mega-events, when local residents expect traffic congestion or anticipate the possibility of renting their home out to visitors for a profit, typically have reverse time-switchers.

Economic impact analyses often neglect to account for important opportunity costs. For instance, if U.S. Bank Stadium had to turn down a major event because of a time conflict with X Games Minneapolis 2019, then calculation of the net incremental gain from hosting the event must account for the lost economic impact of the other event.

Another potentially important opportunity cost is the lost impact from visitors who would have come to town under normal circumstances but were unable to because the event filled all of the hotels to capacity. If these would-be visitors came at some time anyway and lodged within the geographic area, then there is no loss in revenue. However, if any individuals did not come to town at all because of the event, then the economic impact analysis for the event should account for that loss.

In the parlance of economic impact analysis, what is often called economic impact is really gross economic benefit, because it includes all spending, even by local residents, and it does not account for the costs of hosting the event. When the analyst properly accounts for spending, costs, and other similar items, then economic benefit becomes economic impact, although it is sometimes called incremental economic impact. When we account for opportunity costs, such as those arising from capacity constraints at the sport facility or at local hotels, then we have what is often called the net incremental economic impact. A true economic impact analysis accounts for all of these adjustments; it nets out all effects to measure the true incremental impacts. When we read economic impact studies, we must know how these terms are being defined and used.

Perhaps the most egregious cause of overestimating economic impact is that the analyst has some incentive to find a very large impact. Often, these studies are paid for by advocates (such as franchise owners or politicians) for building the facility or bringing the event to town, especially if part of the funding will come from public sources. When we read these studies it may be difficult to follow the methodological details given (if any), but "reverse engineering" the study (e.g., looking for logical missteps or interim calculations and results that aren't believable) can show if the analyst missed or misused steps discussed in this chapter.

For an unethical analyst, the easiest way to obtain a large economic impact estimate is to count all attendees at an event toward economic impact, not just relevant or incremental visitors. Sometimes an analyst will even count a person who attends three days of an event as three individual people (simply adding up the stated attendance for each day of the three-day event, rather than determining the number of individual attendees). Another method is to count total spending by organizations, corporations, and local government related to the event as benefit rather than cost. Of course, all of these methods result in bogus estimates. If local government spends $1 million to help bring an event to town, that is a cost, not a benefit. If visitors attending a game spend $10 million buying tickets, merchandise, and concessions inside the game, and the owner spends $9 million of those revenues to produce it, the real economic impact would be

EXHIBIT 12.12 Factors in analyzing the methodology of an economic impact study.

CONSIDER WHETHER:
Local spending is not counted.
Only incremental spending by casual visitors and time-switchers is counted.
Incremental visitor spending is fully counted.
Spending within a facility is not counted.
Spending that comes out of the event, team, or facility is counted.
Only the organizational spending by the event host committee, event management company, and corporate sponsors in the geographic area of impact is counted.
Only corporate spending in the geographic area of impact that would not have occurred otherwise is counted.
Spending by organizations, corporations, and local governments related to bringing the event to town is counted as a cost rather than a benefit.
Leakages outside the geographic area of impact (sales and income taxes of non-local governments and spending with non-local employees, businesses, and organizations) are not counted.
Only the capture rate portion of franchise spending is counted.
Opportunity costs are accounted for.

$9 million (or $10 million, perhaps, if the owner's business is a local business)—not $19 million. When you read economic impact studies, consider the source and carefully review the methodology. See Exhibit 12.12 for guidelines for analyzing the methodology of an economic impact study.

SIDEBAR 12.E The Further They Travel, The More They Spend

In 2007, Brown, Rascher, McEvoy, and Nagel published an article in the *International Journal of Sport Finance* that examined whether the distance golfers traveled to play golf affected how much they spent once they arrived. In economics, the Alchian-Allen Theorem (sometimes referred to as the Third Law of Demand) posits that as a fixed cost is added to the price of two products, the more expensive product becomes relatively cheaper compared to the less expensive product, and consumers will then be more likely to purchase the more expensive product. This raises the question, with respect to tourism, will consumers ignore the sunk costs of travel when making their choices about dining, hotels, and so forth?

Sports tourism is an excellent setting for a study of this phenomenon. The researchers concluded:

> The analysis of spending by golf tourists in Ohio is not just about the support for the Alchian-Allen theorem. It is also about whether golf consumers bundle decisions together or separate them out sequentially. Here, the customer has a choice regarding whether to bundle costs or not. The data from this study indicates that most golfers, especially golf tourists, do bundle the quality costs with the intermediate costs of transportation, lodging, and food.

An online survey of 376 golfers traveling within or to the state of Ohio showed very high correlations between distance traveled and greens fees of 0.55 for all golfers and 0.98 for golf tourists. These findings are consistent across other events, whether participatory (as with the golfers in Ohio) or spectator events. The 2007 Valero Alamo Bowl pitted Penn State University against Texas A&M University. An examination of the data from the economic impact study reveals a positive and statistically significant correlation between miles traveled and the amount of money spent on concessions and merchandise at the event. Without further analysis, it is not possible to know whether the fans who traveled farther to attend the Valero Alamo Bowl are more fanatical about the event or the teams and, therefore, are willing to spend more on concessions and merchandise at the event. In other words, do these fans simply have higher demand for better or more concessions and merchandise than fans who live closer to San Antonio?

A study of fans at the 2006 Busch Series motorsports event at O'Reilly Raceway Park also showed a positive correlation between spending on food and whether the fan was from out of state (conducted by SportsEconomics, LLC). Similarly, data from the 2008 Rock 'n' Roll Marathon in San Antonio exhibited statistically significant and positive correlations between whether participants came from out of state and how much they spent on food, beverages, and entertainment while in San Antonio.

Event marketers would be wise to address where their patrons are coming from when they develop marketing tactics. Packages can be designed and marketed to appeal specifically to potential customers who have traveled a long distance and, therefore, might be willing to spend more than local fans.

CONCLUSION

Economic impact analysis is a widely used decision-making tool for private businesses and governments. Essentially, it is a form of cost-benefit analysis, where the analyst measures true costs and benefits to assess net effect or impact. The fundamental principle in economic impact analysis is to measure the spending that resulted (or can be expected to result) from the event, versus the spending that would have occurred otherwise. The analyst must ask, "but for the event, what would spending in the community have been?" This "but for" analysis is similar to economic damages calculations in litigation, where analysts try to determine what financial harm occurred, for example, from patent infringement or malfunctioning equipment, by estimating what would have happened without ("but for") the infringement or malfunction. Analysts conducting economic impact studies should continually ask themselves whether a specific set of spending measurements is truly new or is incremental compared to what would have happened otherwise.

Concept Check

1. What is the difference between induced and indirect economic impact?
2. Can a person be both a casual visitor and a time-switcher for the same event?
3. Under what conditions should spending by local residents be counted in a calculation of economic impact?
4. In measuring the economic impact of a sport team, is it correct to count both the spending by fans inside the stadium and the spending by the team (in running its operations) in the community?
5. All else being equal, does increasing the size of the geographic area of impact raise, lower, or have no effect on the capture rate?
6. How would one determine the extent to which locals are reverse time-switchers for a particular event?
7. What are some of the causes of overestimating the economic impact of a sport event? Of underestimating?

Case Analysis

Economic Impact Study Simulation

Review the following description of an economic impact study and answer the questions that follow. When you have finished, you will have measured the economic impact of a large sport event.

You have been commissioned to analyze the economic impact on the city of Cincinnati of the MLB All-Star Game. Specifically, the community wants to know the direct spending impact, the indirect spending impact, and the fiscal/tax impact. Cincinnati officials want to know whether it would be profitable to fund and bid for similar future events for the city. This event cost the city about $8 million to host.

You created a survey (Exhibit 12.13) and administered it to 342 people around Great American Ball Park during the game, making an effort to obtain a random sample. Only 325 of the surveys were usable because of various errors by the respondents. You entered the data into a spreadsheet and are now ready to analyze the economic impact. To allow you to do this analysis, your instructor will provide you with an Excel file containing two spreadsheets: Survey 1 and Key. Survey 1 is the spreadsheet in which the data have been entered, and the Key spreadsheet describes and explains each column of data. Be sure to measure economic impact for all visitors, not just those who responded to the survey. (A survey is a sample of the target population.)

EXHIBIT 12.13 Sample completed survey for economic impact case analysis.

MAJOR LEAGUE BASEBALL ALL-STAR GAME ECONOMIC IMPACT SURVEY

1. Are you attending the All-Star Game? ☑ Yes ☐ No

2. Your age: ☐ 18–24 ☑ 25–34 ☐ 35–44 ☐ 45–54 ☐ 55+

3. What is your gender? ☑ Female ☐ Male

4. Your annual household income: ☐ <$25,000 ☐ $25,000–$49,999 ☑ $50,000–$74,999
    ☐ $75,000–$99,999 ☐ $100,000–$124,999 ☐ $125,000 +

5. What is your residential zip code? <u>08055</u>

6. How long will you be visiting Cincinnati? <u>4</u> day(s) <u>3</u> night(s)

7. While visiting Cincinnati, how many people in your party will you be paying for, including yourself? <u>3</u>

(continued)

EXHIBIT 12.13   Cont.

MAJOR LEAGUE BASEBALL ALL-STAR GAME ECONOMIC IMPACT SURVEY

8. While in Cincinnati during the All-Star Game, how much do you plan to spend DAILY for the above group on the following?

    Lodging $140

    Transportation in Cincinnati (rental car, gas, parking, taxi, bus, etc.) $55

    Event-related (tickets, concessions, merchandise at All-Star Game) $125

    Food/beverage (not at All-Star Game) $130

    Entertainment (not at All-Star Game) $75

    Shopping (not at All-Star Game) $120

    Other (not at All-Star Game) $20

9. Would you have visited Cincinnati this weekend if the All-Star Game were not in town?   ☐Yes   ☒ No

10. Does this visit to Cincinnati replace any other past/future visit to this area?   ☐Yes   ☒ No

11. Primary reason for trip to Cincinnati:

    Attend this event ___✓___ Business _____ Pleasure/Vacation_____ Other _____

Based on discussions with the local organizing committee and Cincinnati government officials, you determine that:

- Great American Ball Park seats 42,059.
- The game was sold out.
- The city sales tax is 6.5% and is collected on all goods and services except hotels.
- The city hotel occupancy tax is 10.5%.
- Hotel capacity in the city is 35,000 rooms. The typical occupancy rate is 83%.
- The average number of persons per room for large events such as this is 2.4.
- Total spending by the local organizing committee was $4.5 million, with 60% of that amount coming from organizations outside of the city. This is in addition to the amount the city itself spent. Sponsors spent $1 million in town activating their sponsorships.
- The spending multiplier for the city of Cincinnati is 1.6 (based on information from MIG, Inc.).
- Of spending inside Great American Ball Park (including tickets) for this event, 20% went to the city government (fiscal impact).

Case Questions

Note: A few data entry or survey respondent errors have been included in the spreadsheet.

1. How many people attended the All-Star Game in total?
2. How many visitors (people who are not local residents) attended the All-Star Game?
3. How many visitors who attended the game were time-switchers?
4. How many visitors who attended the game were casual visitors?
5. How many visitors should be used in the calculation of the economic impact estimates?
6. What is the per-person spending per day by the "incremental" visitors for everything but lodging? (Use your result from Question 5.) What is the per-person spending for lodging per night stayed?
7. What is the average length of stay for incremental visitors in terms of days and nights?
8. What is the per-person spending per stay by the incremental visitors?
9. What direct economic impact, *not* accounting for any hotel capacity constraints, may exist? (Be sure to account for the new/incremental spending by the event organizer and the costs of hosting the event.) Those capacity constraints are addressed in Question 11.
10. What is the total economic impact?
11. Based on hotel capacity information, how many typical visitors did the event visitors crowd out?
12. What is the new direct and total economic impact, accounting for the crowding out?
13. What is the fiscal or tax impact of the event on the city?

References

Agha, N. (2013). The economic impact of stadia and teams: The case of minor league baseball. *Journal of Sports Economics*, 14(3), 227–252.

Agha, N., & Rascher, D.A. (2016). An explanation of economic impact: Why positive impacts can exist for smaller sports. *Sport, Business, and Management*, 6(2), 182–204.

Alexander, D.L., Kern, W., & Neill, J. (2000, September). Valuing the consumption benefits from professional sports franchises. *Journal of Urban Economics*, 48(2), 321–337.

Baade, R., & Matheson, V.A. (2006). Have public finance principles been shut out in financing new stadiums for the NFL? *Public Finance and Management*, 6, 284–320.

Brown, M., Rascher, D., McEvoy, C., & Nagel, M. (2007). Treatment of travel expenses by golf course patrons: Sunk or bundled costs and the first and third laws of demand. *International Journal of Sport Finance*, 2, 45–53.

Coates, D., & Humphreys, B. (2003). The effect of professional sports on earnings and employment in the services and retail sectors in U.S. cities. *Regional Science and Urban Economics*, 33, 175–198.

Cobb, S., & Olberding, D. (2007). The importance of import substitution in marathon economic impact analysis. *International Journal of Sport Finance*, 2, 108–118.

Fenn, A., & Crooker, J.R. (2004). The willingness to pay for a new Vikings stadium under threat of relocation or sale. Unpublished document.

Groothuis, P.A., Johnson, B.K., & Whitehead, J.C. (2004, Fall). Public funding of professional sports stadiums: Public choice or civic pride? *Eastern Economic Journal*, 30(4), 515–526.

Irwin, R.L., & Rascher, D.A. (2005, February 4). 2004 Alamo Bowl: Economic and fiscal impact analysis.

Irwin, D., & Rascher, D. (2007a). 2007 Dr Pepper Big 12 Championship economic & fiscal impact analysis: A primary study.

Irwin, D., & Rascher, D. (2007b). 2007 Valero Alamo Bowl economic & fiscal impact analysis: A primary study.

Johnson, B.K., Groothuis, P.A., & Whitehead, J.C. (2001, February). The value of public goods generated by a major league sports team: The CVM approach. *Journal of Sports Economics*, 2(1), 6–21.

Johnson, B.K., & Whitehead, J.C. (2000, January). Value of public goods from sports stadiums: The CVM approach. *Contemporary Economic Policy*, 18(1), 48–58.

Matheson, V.A. (2006). Is smaller better? A comment on 'Comparative Economic Impact Analyses' by Michael Mondello and Patrick Rishe. *Economic Development Quarterly*, 20(2), 192–195.

Meryhew, R. (1997). How important are the Twins to Minneapolis? *Minneapolis Star Tribune*.

Rascher, D.A., Hyun, G., & Nagel, M. (2020). Is there a consensus?: An experimental trial to test the sufficiency of methodologies used to measure economic impact. *Journal of Applied Business and Economics*, 22(12).

Rascher, D.A., & Irwin, R.L. (2004, May 13). 2004 NCAA Men's Final Four: Economic and fiscal impact analysis.

Seaman, B. (2004). The supply constraint problem in economic impact analysis: An arts/sports disparity. Paper presented at Lasting Effects: Assessing the Future of Economic Impact Analysis of the Arts Conference, Tarrytown, NY.

Zagorin, L.J. (2017). Beyond economic impact: The psychic income received by the Chapel Hill community from Carolina Athletics. Unpublished document.

PART IV

Financial Attributes of Select Sport Industry Segments

CHAPTER 13

Public Sector Sport

Matthew T. Brown

KEY CONCEPTS

assessed value

assessment ratio

competitive issue

excise tax

grant

joint use agreement

local option sales tax

mill

millage

millage rate

municipal bond

negotiated issue

net assessed value

pay-as-you-go approach

property tax

public facility authority (PFA) bond

public sector sport

public/private partnership

sales tax

serial bond

sponsorship

tax rate

tax receipts

tax subsidy

term bond

use tax

INTRODUCTION

Public sector sport is offered to serve societal need rather than profit potential (Brayley & McLean, 2008). Hence, indicators of social benefits, not solely financial indicators, are commonly used to determine success in public sector sport. For the public sector, we measure success by comparing achievement to goals. Here, goals are based not solely on financial measures but on social outcomes, as well. We measure success by comparing the social benefits derived from the programs to the expenses of achieving those outcomes. For example, numerous studies have shown that participation in high school sport is good not only for students' health but also for improving students' academic performance (Cook, 2012). For reasons such as this, we measure health and academic performance outcomes against the expenses of participatory sports.

When we think of the public sector in sport, our first thought is probably of state university athletic programs. However, in this chapter we focus on less-often considered segments: park and recreation agencies and public high school sports. In general, these agencies provide sport that benefits a broad segment of the local community rather than the more elite set of athletes participating in collegiate sport. This sport sector meets the social needs of the community, and, because sport is being provided for members of the community, the agencies responsible for it generally have the power to levy taxes to fund their operations and facility construction. Because public funds are being used, managers in this sector are accountable to taxpayers, and they operate based on the perceived needs of the electorate (Brayley & McLean, 2008). The 2017 *Annual survey of state and local government finances* shows that a considerable number of taxpayer dollars are spent on parks and recreation. The US Census Bureau report for 2017 indicates that state and local governments spent $45.2 billion that year (US Census Bureau, 2017). High school sport spending is big, too. For example, in McKinney, Texas, voters approved spending 63 million taxpayer dollars to build a 12,000-seat high school football stadium. Naming rights deals, television broadcasting revenues, and multimillion-dollar venues being built for high school athletics are becoming commonplace (McPhate, 2016). Hence, an understanding of this sector is important for a complete grasp of financial principles in the sport industry.

FINANCIAL MANAGEMENT TRENDS IN PUBLIC SECTOR SPORT

Several trends over the past ten years have affected the financial operation of public sector sport facilities ("Trends in," 2020). Budget tightening and cuts that began during the Great Recession, coupled with a change in culture to focus on competition and elite performance, have caused park and recreation agencies to depend on innovative programming. The types of facilities and varieties of programming have increased to meet consumer desire. Parks used to be fields of grass and woods; now they include interactive playgrounds, sporting courts, game fields, and advanced trail systems. Community centers, once offering little more than gym space and meeting rooms, have evolved into large multipurpose facilities. These venues frequently offer aquatics facilities, climbing walls, open gym space, running tracks, fitness centers, multipurpose rooms, esport facilities, and childcare areas.

Over the past 20 years, park and recreation agencies have returned to partnerships between cities and local school districts to provide programming and optimal facilities. For example, in 2001 the high school and community in Mason, Ohio, built a $72 million recreation center that features weight rooms, fitness rooms, a leisure pool, a competition pool, an auditorium, and a gym (Huddleston, 2001). In Anne Arundel County, Maryland, a partnership of the public high schools and county officials has led to shared usage of athletic fields, reducing the cost per field for the county and schools. Similar joint use agreements exist in San Marcos, California, Broomfield, Colorado, and other cities across the United States (Brown, 2008b). The Kansas City, Missouri Parks and Recreation Department has established some of the most extensive partnerships in the nation. These partnerships exist to allow the district to leverage its resources while generating city-wide interest in its programming, facilities, and events. In total, the district participates in more than 50 partnerships with school districts, non-profit organizations, neighborhoods, and businesses (Kansas City Parks and Recreation, 2015). Sidebar 13.A examines how Frisco, Texas, has used public/private partnerships to benefit the local community and school district with the construction of world-class facilities.

High school athletic facilities provide a place for physical education curricula, but they are primarily built to benefit those athletes participating in interscholastic sport. On the other hand, community parks and recreation centers are intended for the use of all. Park and recreation agencies have a mandate to provide services that benefit the public health and welfare of the local community; therefore, the agencies have developed facilities and programs that appeal to a broad demographic. However, this approach can result in controversies over pricing. For example, in one community an annual membership in the publicly owned and operated recreation center was $820. In addition to the annual fee, members were charged for fitness classes. A private health club in the same community required a $600 annual fee, which included fitness classes. The public recreation center's vast array of programming and amenities, designed to appeal to a broad population base, resulted in a pricing structure that was higher than that of the single-purpose private health club (Berg, 2020). Community members might question the use of public finances, when membership in a private health club is more affordable than joining a recreation facility funded in part by taxpayer dollars.

Trends over the past 50 years have resulted in this pricing paradox. During the 1970s, discussions of pricing centered on keeping public recreation activities affordable for the broadest possible segment of the population. Activities and memberships were nominally priced, and some residents paid nothing at all. The philosophy was that every member of the community should be able to afford the programs and services offered. Since then, the size and scope of recreational complexes have grown and changed, while the demand for public dollars from other agencies for a variety of local purposes has increased. Meanwhile, communities have reduced state and local taxes. As a result, community sport and recreation departments are now expected (1) to provide a multitude of sport and recreation services to the community, while keeping them affordable, and (2) to provide programs and facilities that are financially self-sufficient or that generate enough revenue to offset any expenses not covered by an established subsidy. These conflicting expectations have led to the pricing situation described earlier.

The Boulder, Colorado, Parks and Recreation Department proposed to meet these challenges by implementing service-based pricing, in which fees are set based on the cost of the program being offered. Programs would be divided into four classifications. At the most basic programming level, for introductory or general programming offered to all age levels, program costs would be offset by the department's tax subsidy. At the highest level, including competitive adult sports and advanced classes, fees would be set to cover administrative overhead, instructor pay, and facility time (Popke, 2010).

SIDEBAR 13.A   Frisco, Texas: School District, Community, and Professional Sport Partnerships

Toyota Stadium and the Toyota Soccer Center opened in Frisco, Texas, on August 6, 2005. Built on 145 acres, the multipurpose sport and entertainment facility includes the home stadium for MLS's FC Dallas. In addition to the 25,000-seat stadium, the complex—used by adult and youth soccer leagues and for high school sports—includes 17 tournament-sized soccer fields. It has become one of the top complexes for professional and amateur soccer in the United States, attracting more than one million visitors per year. The $105 million complex is owned by the City of Frisco in a partnership with FC Dallas owner Hunt Sports Group (HSG), the Frisco Independent School District (ISD), and Collin County ("About Toyota Stadium," 2020). The City of Frisco and Collin County each paid $20 million, backed through municipal bonds. The Frisco ISD paid $15 million, with the money raised as a part of a school bond referendum backed by a property tax increase. The remainder of the cost was paid for by HSG.

Because of the success of this partnership with HSG and FC Dallas, the City of Frisco and the Frisco ISD once again entered into a public/private partnership to construct new athletic facilities. This time, the two partnered with the Dallas Cowboys to build a 91-acre mixed-use development to include the team's headquarters. The centerpiece of the development is a 12,000-seat indoor stadium and two outdoor football fields that are used by the Cowboys, the City of Frisco, and Frisco ISD. The school district contributed $30 million to the project, with the money coming from revenue generated through a TIF district. The City of Frisco contributed another $30 million, and two economic development corporations contributed a combined total of $55 million. The Cowboys were responsible for any cost overruns (Frisco Independent School District, 2013). The Frisco ISD uses the complex for football and soccer games, as well as for entertainment events and other competitions. The district needed to build another football stadium (its third at the time) because of its growth. It opened its seventh and eighth high schools in 2014 and 2015. The cost of a stand-alone stadium was estimated to be between $27 million and $30 million; however, through the partnership, the district estimated that it would obtain a much better facility at the same cost. When the facility was completed, the Frisco ISD became the only school district in Texas with an indoor stadium. The city and economic development corporations reap long-term benefits, as the economic impact of the development is expected to be $23.4 billion over the next 30 years.

As with park and recreation agencies, the public funding available for high school sports has also decreased. According to the National Federation of State High School Associations (NFHS), in 2019 the number of participants in high school sports decreased for the first time in 30 years, with more than 7.9 million students participating. The decline was attributed to a decrease in the number of participants in youth sports and the decline in the overall number of students in high school. Nationally, the impact of pay-for-play fees seemed to have little effect on participation ("Participation in," 2019).

Pay-for-play is often implemented after a school district faces a reduction in state funding or fails to pass a new tax levy. For example, in Ohio public schools saw a $1.8 billion cut in state education funding in 2011 and 2012. As a result, schools sought to reduce the numbers of teachers and programs while raising money from fees, including pay-for-play athletic fees. A May 2012 survey showed that 82% of schools in southwest Ohio had instituted these fees. In one district the fee was $550 per child per sport; in another, cross country cost $521 per athlete and tennis $933. Despite numbers from the NFHS that suggest the third highest participation level ever in high school sports, pay-for-play is impacting the number of participants negatively in Ohio and a 30-year growth streak in participation has ended. One district, after implementing pay-for-play, saw its sports participation decrease 14%. Another district dropped its freshman football team because of decreased numbers of participants. Nationwide, it is estimated that 54% of high school athletes have to pay a fee to participate; the average fee in 2019 was $161 (Mostafavi, 2019).

SOURCES OF FUNDS

Park and recreation agencies, and to a great extent high school sport, exist to meet the social needs of the communities they serve (Brayley & McLean, 2008; Mostafavi, 2019). For this reason, they receive funding from the public sector for both facility construction and facility/program operations. Their goal is to provide sport facilities and programs that enhance quality of life for members of the community while serving the common good. To achieve this goal, the programs and services have traditionally been subsidized through tax revenues, because fees charged do not fully cover operational costs. **Tax subsidies**—in which tax receipts are used to fund programs or businesses—enable the agencies and school districts to offer programs for free or at a reduced cost. Typically, municipalities have funded public sport facility construction through the sale of tax-supported municipal bonds, and local tax receipts have provided a majority of operational funds. **Tax receipts** are tax revenues from all sources received by a municipality.

However, with shrinking local and state revenues, public sector sport has increasingly turned to new sources of revenue to fund programming. Municipal bonds and tax receipts are still commonly used to fund construction costs and provide operational revenues (Wall, 2015), but public sport agencies are increasingly relying on other revenue sources, including revenues from advertising and corporate sponsorships (Mostafavi, 2019).

Public Sources of Funds

In an older study, but one of the most thorough studies on park and recreation center and program finance, Sherman (1998) detailed how these facilities were funded. Sherman found that 69% of construction funding came from taxes. For operations, 52% of funding came from tax revenues. Although no similar study on high school sport exists, it is known that taxes do pay for much of the cost of facility construction and programming. Although the percentage of public funding today is likely lower than it was in 1998, tax revenue and municipal bonds remain important sources of revenue. For example, in Lexington County, South Carolina, the Lexington County Recreation and Aging Commission (LCRAC) issued $23 million in bonds to improve recreation facilities in the county and build new ones. The LCRAC bonds were issued in 2013 and used for several major projects over the next six years. A large portion, $3 million, was used to convert a former football stadium into a multipurpose baseball facility to be used by the Lexington County Blowfish, a summer wood bat baseball team competing in the Coastal Plain League. The facility also is rented for baseball tournaments and concerts. Another $5 million was used for youth sports. The refurbished Midlands Sports Complex has one football field and six baseball and softball fields. Overall, the funding was used to improve recreation facilities for 9,000 children in seven sports (Grant, 2019). Two large additional projects are still underway. The $5 million Lexington Soccer Complex will include three new full-size soccer fields and a new gym housing two full-size basketball courts. The Gilbert Sports Complex includes six new baseball fields and allows girls' softball to expand from three fields to eight. In another example, the operational budget of the Texas state parks system is partially funded by revenues from an excise tax on sporting goods sales. In 2019, $205.2 million of the system's $345.6 million budget (59%) was from this source.

For high school sport, tax revenue comes from a variety of state and local sources. In Saline, Michigan, about 56% of the $1.1 million high school athletic budget comes from the district's general fund (Biolchini, 2014). Within the general fund, 23% of revenues come from property taxes, 49% are allocated to the district from the state, 18% come from operating grants and contributions, and 10% come from charges for services and other sources. The rest of the athletic department's revenue comes from participant fees (32%) and gate receipts (12%). Saline is just one example of school sport funding. There is considerable variability in the ways districts fund sports.

Below we discuss the major sources of public funding, including property taxes, sales taxes, excise taxes, pay-as-you-go financing, and bonds.

PROPERTY TAX

The tax source most often used to fund the construction or operation of public sector sport facilities is the **property tax**, a government levy based on the value of property (Sherman, 1998; Brayley & McLean, 2008). Property taxes generated 31.8% of all state and county tax revenue in 2017 and 72.1% of all local tax revenue (US Census Bureau, 2017). Sherman reported that 73% of recreation construction and operation funding involved property taxes. Although this percentage is likely lower today for recreation projects, we can assume that property taxes still provide a majority of funding here. For high school sport construction, property tax revenues are still likely to fund almost all of a project's cost. For example, in the Richland 2 School District in Columbia, South Carolina, an $86.5 million bond referendum was passed in 2018 to improve the district's arts and athletic facilities. In addition to minor projects like expansion of arts areas and athletic training facilities, installing artificial turf on practice facilities, and adding lights to practice fields, the project included $23.4 million for a new performing arts center, and $25.6 million for two new football stadiums (Richland 2 School District, 2020).

In many states, two types of property are taxed: real property and personal property. *Real property* includes land and all structures built on or improvements made to the land. *Personal property* includes everything else that has value. Typically, automobiles, watercraft, motorcycles, trucks, and airplanes are taxed as personal property. Businesses often pay personal property taxes on furniture, fixtures, and equipment.

A wide variety of public entities establish a municipality's property tax rates. In general, city or town councils, school boards, and special purpose districts (such as park and recreation departments) determine their budgetary needs and the percentage of revenues they require from property tax sources. In essence, these public bodies determine the rate of tax, or **millage**, necessary to meet their budgets. The specific **millage rate** for a particular resident in a tax district is the total of the levies by the city, county, school district, and any special districts in which that resident lives. One **mill** is equal to 1/1,000 of a dollar (or 1/10 of a penny). Therefore, if a resident's **tax rate** (millage rate) is 315 mills, that resident would multiply the assessed value of his or her property by 0.315 to determine the amount of tax owed. Returning to the example of Lexington County, South Carolina, the county is divided into 28 tax districts. The tax rates of these districts vary based on school district, whether the property is within a municipality, and whether the property is within a tax increment financing district. As a result, Lexington County residents pay 28 different property tax rates.

Assessing property value and tax due. The determination of the assessed value of a property is a complex operation usually undertaken by a city or county auditor or assessor. The taxes are collected by city and county treasurers or tax collectors. The city or county auditor will prepare a list of the owners of all taxable real and personal property. The city or county assessor then appraises the value of this property and determines each property's **assessed value**, the product of its fair market value and its assessment ratio.

assessed value = fair market value x assessment ratio

The fair market value of a property is the value for which the property can reasonably be expected to sell on the open market with a willing buyer and a willing seller. The **assessment ratio** is the percentage of the property that is subject to taxation. Assessment ratios are set by elected officials. Exhibit 13.1 lists the assessment ratios for residents of Lexington County, South Carolina. We can determine the assessed value of an individual's primary residence by multiplying the assessment ratio for residential property by the fair market value of the residence. Let's assume the fair market value of a primary residence is $250,000. Then,

assessed value = fair market value × assessment ratio for primary residence

$$= \$250,000 \times 0.04$$

$$= \$10,000$$

For this piece of property, $10,000 of its value would be subject to taxation. To find the amount of tax due, we multiply the assessed value by the millage rate.

property tax due = assessed value × millage rate

Recall that the millage rate is the tax rate approved by the city council, school board, special purpose district, and county council to meet the budgetary needs of each entity. In Lexington County, the total county operating millage in 2020 was 77.178 (County of Lexington, 2020). For a $250,000 property with an

EXHIBIT 13.1 Assessment ratios by property type for Lexington County, South Carolina.	
Primary residence	4.0%
Second residence	6.0%
Other real property	6.0%
Commercial real property	6.0%
Agricultural real property—privately owned	4.0%
Agricultural real property—corporate owned	6.0%
Aircraft	10.5%
Business personal property	10.5%
Camper[a]	10.5%
Manufacturing, real and personal	10.5%
Motor home[a]	10.5%
Railroads, airlines, pipelines, real and personal	9.5%
Utility, real and personal	10.5%
Vehicle, personal	6.0%
Vehicle, personal[b]	10.5%
Watercraft/boat[a]	10.5%

a May qualify as primary or second residence.
b Vehicle, personal @ 10.5% if gross vehicle weight is in excess of 11,000 pounds and net vehicle weight is in excess of 9,000 pounds.
Source: https://lex-co.sc.gov/departments/assessor/tax-faqs/property-tax-amounts.

assessed value of $10,000, the property tax owed to Lexington County would be calculated as follows:

$$\text{property tax due} = \text{assessed value} \times \text{millage rate}$$
$$= \$10,000 \times 0.077178$$
$$= \$771.78$$

Calculating new property tax needs. As property taxes are one of the main sources of revenue for building and operating public recreation facilities, it is important to understand the impact of increased funding needs on the tax rate of residents of a community. Returning to Lexington County, South Carolina, let's assume that the board of the LCRAC has proposed a new multipurpose recreational facility with a cost of $12.5 million and an annual operating budget of $1.8 million.

A municipal bond will be issued to pay for the construction cost. Because Lexington County has a credit rating from Moody's of Aa1 and Standard & Poor's of AA, the LCRAC can issue a $12.5 million, 30-year municipal bond at a rate of 4.00%. Assuming that the county will annually set aside the principal portion of the bond while making interest payments to bondholders, the county would need to budget roughly 30 equal payments of $916,667.[1] Regarding the financing of operational costs, the LCRAC assumes that 52% of the $1.8 million annual budget ($936,000 per year) will be paid from an increase in the current millage rate for the district, with annual operating cost increases based on changes in the consumer price index. Therefore, the millage rate for those living within the LCRAC district will need to increase to provide funds for the operating costs and the cost of construction.

To calculate the new millage required for the operating costs, we must know the **net assessed value** of property in the LCRAC district, that is, the total assessed value of property in the district, less tax-exempt property.

$$\text{net assessed value} = \text{total assessed value} - \text{tax-exempt property}$$

Typically, property owned by non-profit and governmental entities is exempt from taxes. In 2020, the net assessed value of property in the LCRAC district was $807,772,000, according to Lexington County records. Next, we divide the required tax revenues by the net assessed value of property to obtain the tax rate.

$$\text{tax rate} = \frac{\text{required tax revenues}}{\text{net assessed value}}$$

The required tax revenue amount is the annual operating cost of $936,000. So,

$$\text{tax rate} = \frac{\$936,0000}{\$807,772,000}$$

$$= 0.001159$$

The tax rate of 0.001159 is the same as the millage rate; therefore, the millage rate must be increased by 1.159 mills.

To calculate the rate increase needed for the project's debt service, we will use the same process. However, the rate increase will be in effect only for the 30-year life of the project. To service the debt, $916,667 is needed annually. Hence,

$$\text{tax rate} = \frac{\text{required tax revenues}}{\text{net assessed value}}$$

$$= \frac{\$916,667}{\$807,772,000}$$

$$= .001134$$

For the next 30 years, the millage rate must be increased by 1.134 mills.

The combined annual increase for the next 30 years is 2.293 mills. In 2020, the LCRAC millage rate was 12.315. With the new project, the overall rate would

---

1   $500,000 in annual interest costs plus $416,667 set aside to pay the principal amount in 30 years.

increase to 14.608. This is an 18.6% increase over the current rate. The LCRAC, now that it knows the overall millage required for the project, may need voter approval through a tax referendum to increase the millage rate.

A property owner can calculate the impact of the proposed tax as follows. If the total assessed value of the property is $10,000,

$$\text{property tax increase} = \text{assessed value of property} \times \text{millage rate increase}$$

$$= \$10,000 \times 0.002293$$

$$= \$22.93$$

SALES TAX

To fund the construction or operation of recreational sport facilities, the second most common tax source after property tax is the **sales tax** (Sherman, 1998; Brayley & McLean, 2008), a tax on the sale of certain goods and services. Sales taxes generated 17.5% of all local tax revenues in 2017 and 48.3% of all state tax revenues, according to the US Census Bureau (2017). Sherman reported that only 26% of all recreational sport construction or operational funding involved sales taxes. This is quite low compared to the 73% funded through property taxes.

The rules and regulations regarding sales tax vary by state. These regulations can directly affect the sources of funds available at the local level for recreational programming and services. For example, South Carolina collects a 6% state sales and use tax. Nearly all retail sales are subject to a sales tax. A **use tax** is a levy imposed on certain goods and services that are purchased outside the state and brought into the state. A use tax may also be imposed on certain goods and services for which no sales tax is paid. Under South Carolina law, counties may collect only an additional 1% in a local sales tax, and only if the county's voters approve the tax. This tax may be used for county-defined purposes. Lexington County, South Carolina, collects an additional 1% school district sales tax that supplements K–12 funding within the county. Hence, sales tax revenue is not an option to fund recreational sport facilities or programs in the county, as the residents chose to fund K–12 education instead. However, residents of neighboring Richland County chose to impose a 1% local option sales tax. **Local option sales taxes** may be used for a wide variety of purposes. The Richland County Council could choose to use funds generated through this tax to fund recreation programs and facilities.

As an example of the differences among states, in Missouri sales taxes are used at three levels of government to fund park and recreation programs and projects. A resident of Fenton, for example, will pay a sales tax of 8.238% for non-food sales. The sales tax in Fenton is the total of the state sales tax (4.225%), St. Louis County sales tax (3.513%), and the city's 0.5% sales tax (used to fund parks and storm water projects). When a Fenton resident makes a non-food purchase in its transportation development district (TDD) located within the city limits, the sales tax is 9.238%, as an additional 1% sales tax is levied in this district. Whether a consumer in Fenton pays 8.238% or 9.238% on a purchase, a portion of the sales tax will support parks and recreation. At the state level, 0.1% of the 4.225% state sales tax is designated for state parks and soil conservation. In St. Louis County, 0.288% of the 3.513% county sales tax is designated for the county's park and recreation programs. As stated above, at the city level, all of the tax (0.5%) is designated for parks, recreation, and storm water removal. Overall, an individual who makes a non-food purchase in Fenton pays 0.888% in sales tax to fund state, county, and city parks and recreation services ("Welcome to Fenton," 2020).

The City of Fenton combines storm water removal, parks-related police services, and parks and recreation in one fund. For these services, total operating revenues in FY 2020 were expected to be $5.9 million (City of Fenton, 2020). Sales tax revenue was expected to contribute $4.15 million during 2020, or approximately 70% of overall revenue. Additionally, 26% of revenue was to come from the operation of the city's recreation center, and 4% of revenue was to come from park and recreation programs (see Exhibit 13.2). The city will be using sales tax revenue to pay for park and recreation-related capital projects and storm water improvements; and to meet a portion of the operational needs of the parks and storm water systems (see Exhibit 13.3). Exhibit 13.4 provides an overview of the 2020 budget for the city's storm water/parks fund.

EXCISE TAXES

Whereas sales taxes are levied on items we purchase every day, including goods and services, **excise taxes** are sales taxes that apply to particular

EXHIBIT 13.2 Proposed FY 2020 revenue for the City of Fenton storm water/parks fund.

REVENUE SOURCE	AMOUNT
Sales tax	$4,150,000
RiverChase	$1,509,975
Parks and recreation	$231,550
All other revenue	$30,000
Total revenues	$5,921,525

Source: www.fentonmo.org/DocumentCenter/View/8057/2020-Approved-Budget.

EXHIBIT 13.3 Storm water/parks fund sales tax use by the City of Fenton.

REVENUE USE	AMOUNT
Transfer to Capital Projects Fund	$596,308
Storm water/parks/RiverChase operations	$3,553,692
Total	$4,150,000

Source: www.fentonmo.org/DocumentCenter/View/8057/2020-Approved-Budget.

EXHIBIT 13.4   Budget for the Fenton storm water/parks fund, FY 2020.

	AMOUNT	PERCENT
Revenues		
Operating revenues		
Parks operations	$231,550.00	3.91%
RiverChase operations	$1,509,975.00	25.50%
Sales tax revenues	$4,150,000.00	70.08%
Other revenues	$30,000.00	0.51%
Total revenues	**$5,921,525.00**	**100.00%**
Expenditures		
Operating expenditures		
Parks and recreation operations	$826,780.00	14.89%
RiverChase operations	$2,212,302.00	39.83%
Parks-related police services	$394,610.00	7.11%
Storm water maintenance	$120,000.00	2.16%
Subtotal—operating revenues	$3,553,692.00	63.99%
Capital Projects Fund		
Transfer to Capital Projects Fund	$2,000,000.00	36.01%
Subtotal—Capital Projects	$2,000,000.00	36.01%
Total expenditures	**$5,553,692.00**	**100.00%**
Profit (Loss)	**$367,833.00**	

Source: City of Fenton (2020).

products. Excise taxes may benefit park and recreation services and facilities, too. For example, Orange County, Florida, used an excise tax to fund a variety of sport, entertainment, and recreation venues (Brown, 2008a). The county imposed a 6% hotel tax to generate revenue for a $1.1 billion project, including funding for renovation of the Citrus Bowl ($175 million), construction of a new performing arts center ($375 million), construction of a new sport and entertainment arena ($480 million)—which became the home of the Orlando Magic—and construction of five new recreation centers ($25 million) to be run by the county.

In Orlando the excise tax on hotel rooms was used to fund a wide array of projects, but excise taxes are often designed to impose the costs of specific services on those who actually use the services (Crompton, 2009). In Texas, as mentioned previously, the excise tax on sporting goods sales is designed to tax those who use the state parks system. Former governor Rick Perry remarked in a State of the State address, "Let's spend the sporting goods tax on what it was collected for: to create first-class parks that give our people open spaces and fresh air for needed recreation" (Bynum, 2007a, p. 2).

PAY-AS-YOU-GO FINANCING

Rarely do municipalities adopt a **pay-as-you-go approach**—that is, an approach of paying for costs as they arise, without incurring debt—when constructing new facilities (Crompton, 2009). One of the few examples is the City of San Antonio, Texas. For construction of the Alamodome, the city raised almost all of the $174 million needed through a voter-approved sales tax increase of a half cent on every dollar spent for five years. It was estimated that if a long-term bond had been used to build the facility, the total cost of the debt service would have been $435 million, or $17 million per year for 25 years. The City of Fenton, Missouri, is using this method to fund smaller capital improvements for its parks and recreation program. Exhibit 13.4 shows that $2 million from the storm water/parks fund was transferred to the city's capital projects fund in 2020. The city adopted this capital budgeting approach after paying off its debt obligations for its RiverChase recreation facility.

Municipalities, however, typically choose not to use the pay-as-you-go approach. For one, there is a delay between the decision to build a new facility and the collection of all the monies needed to construct that facility. In rapidly growing communities, this delay could lead to the overcrowding of existing facilities (see Sidebar 13.B). Another reason this approach is seldom used is that, from an equity perspective, the method is inequitable and inefficient (Crompton, 2009). Given the frequency with which people move in and out of communities, some residents may pay the full cost of a facility and never get to use it, because they have moved from the community. Others may benefit fully without making any financial contribution at all, if they move into the community after others have paid for the facility.

SIDEBAR 13.B   Pay-as-you-go Financing for the Blythewood Baseball and Softball League Fields

In Blythewood, South Carolina, the 550 members of the Blythewood Baseball and Softball League currently use three fields. The league has difficulty scheduling games and practices due to the large number of participants and teams. In many cases, games must be rescheduled because of rain, and, in turn, teams lose their practice times. T-ball teams must practice in nearby open spaces and can use the league's fields only for games on Saturdays between 9:00 and 11:00 a.m.

Further, the league is located in one of the fastest-growing communities in South Carolina. It is expected that the number of participants will soon increase to more than 600. The league has been unable to arrange financing to build two new fields. As a result, the league has had to adopt a pay-as-you-go approach to building the fields and, meanwhile, limit the number of league participants to 550. The league is currently raising funds for construction of new fields and has also been working with the City of Blythewood to arrange financing for immediate construction.

BONDS

Most public capital projects are funded through either short-term or long-term debt rather than a pay-as-you-go arrangement because this debt places less of an immediate financial burden on taxpayers. Bonds are the traditional source of capital improvement revenue for governmental entities. As discussed in earlier chapters, simply stated, a bond is a promise by a borrower to pay back one or more lenders a certain amount of money plus interest over a certain period of time. Here, the borrower is the city, county, state, school district, or recreation district. The lenders are the bondholders—the individuals and institutions that have purchased the bonds. A **municipal bond** is simply a bond for which the borrower is a municipality. Bonds are classified by their method of retirement. A **term bond** is paid in a single payment at the end of the loan period. A **serial bond** requires regular payments on principal and interest over the life of the bond.

In order to issue bonds, a municipality or district has to receive approval to borrow money, from either the voters or the appropriate legislative entity. The process will vary in each jurisdiction depending on state and local laws. Once the borrower obtains legal authority to issue bonds, usually an underwriter issues the bonds on the municipality's behalf. The underwriter is typically a national or regional investment bank. The bank then sells the bonds on the municipality's behalf through either a competitive or negotiated sale.

Competitive versus negotiated issue. In a **competitive issue**, the municipality publishes a notice of sale, seeking bids from underwriters. The underwriter that submits the lowest bid, or lowest interest rate, will be selected to underwrite the bonds. For a **negotiated issue**, the municipality selects one underwriter, and the parties negotiate the terms of the sale. In either case, the parties will prepare the bond issue's official statement and obtain the bond's rating.

Typically, municipal bonds are negotiated issues, as this type of issue provides more flexible interest-rate schedules and is sold by the underwriter on the open market. Approximately 70% of all bond issues are negotiated sales. Once the underwriter issues and sells the bonds, revenue is available to the borrower. Exhibit 13.5 illustrates this process.

Revenue versus general obligation bonds. To fund capital projects for public sector sport, one of two types of municipal bonds will typically be issued: either revenue bonds or general obligation bonds. Recall that revenue bonds are secured by future revenues generated by the project being funded, whereas general obligation bonds are secured by tax revenues and the issuing

EXHIBIT 13.5   Negotiated issue of municipal bonds.

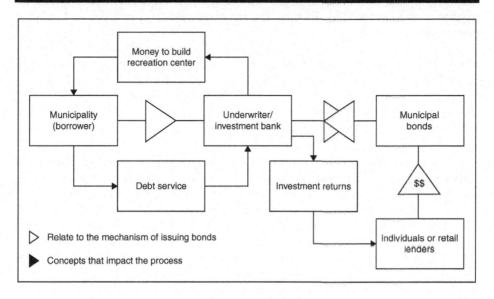

entity's ability to impose new taxes. General obligation bonds must have voter approval prior to their issue.

To select the type of bond, the municipality or recreation agency must first determine whether the project will generate enough revenue both to retire debt and to operate and maintain the facility. If not, the municipality must determine whether supplemental revenue from an existing general fund or another revenue source could pay for the project. If either of these options is available, then the agency may elect to use a revenue bond. If none of these options exists, a general obligation bond backed by a tax source will have to be used. In this case, the municipality must determine the tax source that will secure the bond. Frequently, this source is an increase in real property taxes. However, increases in sales tax are also common.

To see how bonds impact the financial operations of a parks and recreation department, we will look again at the City of Fenton. While the city currently uses pay-as-you-go financing for smaller capital projects in its recreation department, historically it has used bond financing for larger capital projects. For example, in 1997 the city purchased a piece of land called the Fabick property and later turned it into a nature preserve. To purchase the land, the City of Fenton initially issued **public facility authority (PFA) bonds**. PFA bonds are similar to revenue bonds, discussed previously, but PFA bonds are issued by a public facility authority, a non-profit corporation established by the borrower according to Internal Revenue Service ruling 63–20. The PFA can hold title to a project, secure financing for the project, and later hand over the project to the city. For the Fabick property, the Fenton PFA issued bonds to finance the purchase of the land, and it is holding title to the land and receiving payments from the City of Fenton for use of the land through a long-term lease agreement. Eventually, once the project's debt obligations have been discharged, the Fenton

PFA will give the land to the city. The city paid for the project with the operating revenues of the storm water/parks fund. Payments were made directly to the trustee of the Fenton PFA. In turn, the trustee made the principal and interest payments on the bond.

In 2011, the city refinanced the PFA bonds, using certificates of participation to finance the remaining $2.23 million owed for the property (the project's initial cost was $5.99 million). The debt was refinanced to reduce the cost of borrowing, as annual interest rates had declined since the bonds were originally issued. From 2012 to 2015, the city would have paid rates ranging from 3.75% to 4.35%, but under the refinancing, the city was able to lock in an annual interest rate of 2.00% (see Exhibit 13.6).

PFAs are often used to fund parks and recreation projects in Missouri because, under state statute, no public referendum is needed to issue bonds via a PFA. The PFA has no taxing authority, and the municipality is under no obligation to levy any form of tax to pay for the bonds.

For its RiverChase recreation center, the City of Fenton issued certificates of participation. The certificates of participation were issued by a lending institution to a trustee overseeing the recreation center. The city paid lease fees to the trustee, who then made payments on the bond. As Crompton (2009) notes, the use of certificates of participation is growing. This is true especially in states that place strict limits on borrowing. For example, Missouri's Hancock Amendment sets tax and expenditure limitations in the state. According to this amendment to the state's constitution, state and local budgets cannot grow faster than residents' ability to pay for the growth. In essence, the amendment prevents state and local governments from increasing taxes for state and local revenues without voter approval. Twenty-three additional states have some form of tax and expenditure limitation similar to Missouri's Hancock Amendment.

The city formed a corporation to handle the financing of the RiverChase project. In situations such as these, the corporation acts as a public trustee and issues certificates of participation to finance the project. Through the certificates of participation, a lending institution provides funds to the corporation/trustee for the project's construction. The trustee holds the title to the project for the benefit of the investors (certificate holders). The city then pays lease fees to the trustee, who in turn pays back to the financial institution the principal plus interest (Crompton, 2009). Exhibit 13.7 provides the debt service schedule for the RiverChase certificates of participation. Note that these bonds were refinanced, too.

Both the initial PFA bonds and the certificates of participation that the City of Fenton used to fund the Fabick property and RiverChase projects were non-guaranteed. They were backed not by the full faith and credit of the city but by operating revenues generated from the storm water/parks fund.

EXHIBIT 13.6 Debt service schedule for the Fabick property.

City of Fenton, Missouri
COPS Notes—Series 2011
Fabick Property Purchase
Debt Service Schedule

DATE	INTEREST RATE	PRINCIPAL	INTEREST	NET PAYMENT	ANNUAL DEBT SERVICE	OUTSTANDING BONDS
						$2,225,000
1/1/12	2.00%	$540,000.00	$30,408.33	$570,408.33	$570,408.33	$1,685,000
7/1/12			$16,850.00	$16,850.00		$1,685,000
1/1/13	2.00%	$565,000.00	$16,850.00	$581,850.00	$598,700.00	$1,120,000
7/1/13			$11,200.00	$11,200.00		$1,120,000
1/1/14	2.00%	$585,000.00	$11,200.00	$596,200.00	$607,400.00	$535,000
7/1/14			$5,350.00	$5,350.00		$535,000
1/1/15	2.00%	$535,000.00	$5,350.00	$540,350.00	$545,700.00	
Totals		$2,225,000.00	$97,208.33	$2,322,208.33	$2,322,208.33	

January 1 payments considered part of the preceding year, actually made in December.
Source: City of Fenton (2020).

EXHIBIT 13.7 Debt service schedule for the RiverChase.

REFUNDING CERTIFICATES OF PARTICIPATION—SERIES 2013 DEBT SERVICE SCHEDULE

DATE	INTEREST RATE	INTEREST	PRINCIPAL	TOTAL PAYMENT	ANNUAL DEBT SERVICE	OUTSTANDING BONDS
9/10/13						$4,240,000
4/1/14	2.00%	$70,573.33	$1,425,000.00	$1,495,573.33		$2,815,000
10/1/14		$48,950.00		$48,950.00	$1,544,523.33	$2,815,000
4/1/15	3.00%	$48,950.00	$1,470,000.00	$1,518,950.00		$1,345,000
10/1/15		$26,900.00		$26,900.00	$1,545,850.00	$1,345,000
4/1/16	4.00%	$26,900.00	$1,345,000.00	$1,371,900.00	$1,371,900.00	
Totals		$222,273.33	$4,240,000.00	$4,462,273.33	$4,462,273.33	

Source: City of Fenton (2020).

SIDEBAR 13.C Bond Financing for the City of Fenton, Missouri

The City of Fenton, Missouri, used two types of bonds to finance the two capital projects (see Exhibit 13.8 for debt payments by project). The first capital project, the Fabick property, consisted of land purchased for future park and recreation use. The total payment for the project in 2014 was $325,766. This was the project's final bond payment. The second capital project was for the city's RiverChase recreation center. For the recreation center, the final payment of $1.37 million was made in 2016.

EXHIBIT 13.8 Debt service for the Fenton storm water/parks fund by project.

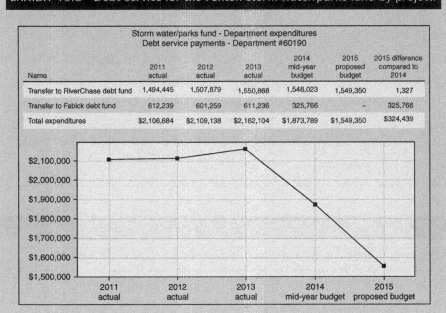

Storm water/parks fund - Department expenditures
Debt service payments - Department #60190

Name	2011 actual	2012 actual	2013 actual	2014 mid-year budget	2015 proposed budget	2015 difference compared to 2014
Transfer to RiverChase debt fund	1,494,445	1,507,879	1,550,868	1,548,023	1,549,350	1,327
Transfer to Fabick debt fund	612,239	601,259	611,236	325,766	–	325,766
Total expenditures	$2,106,684	$2,109,138	$2,162,104	$1,873,789	$1,549,350	$324,439

Private Sources of Funds

The City of Fenton was fortunate that it had sufficient operating revenues to fund the two major capital projects (see Sidebar 13.C). Without those revenues and the funding mechanisms used, the city would have had to turn to the voters to raise taxes to fund the projects or turn to private sources for the funds to purchase park property and build the new recreation facility. A growing number of sport programs in the public sector have to seek funding from private sources of revenue to meet budget shortfalls (Sherman, 1998). In fact, the City of Fenton received between $80,500 and $442,000 of its storm water/parks fund revenues from private grants from 2016 through 2019 (City of Fenton, 2020). Other municipalities have turned to fundraising, advertising, and sponsorships to supplement construction and operating revenues for agencies in this sector.

FUNDRAISING AND GRANTS

As stated, facilities and programs typically rely on tax revenues and user fees to fund their operations; however, public construction projects have begun to rely more on funding from private sources. These sources include gifts, grants, and other private sources of income. For example, the $750,000 Shorewood Community Fitness Center in Milwaukee, Wisconsin, was built with funds generated in a decade-long fundraising campaign. In contrast, the Stacy Multi-Purpose Center in Princeton, Missouri, was funded through a single gift from Festus Stacy, a multimillionaire who had been born in the community. The center includes a swimming pool, a gym, a weight room, and offices. Both the Shorewood Community Fitness Center and the Stacy Center are reserved for use by their respective local school districts during the school day and are open to the community after school hours and on non-school days.

These two facilities may be exceptions, because few facilities—mostly those in smaller rural communities—rely on fundraising to generate revenue for construction. More frequently, communities seek grant revenue. A grant is a financial award typically given by a governmental entity (federal, state, or local) or a non-profit foundation or organization. In California, the City of Thousand Oaks has a Sports Facilities Endowment Fund, which provide grants for the construction, expansion, or upgrading of area recreation facilities. The endowment grants approximately $100,000 in gifts each year ("City sponsored," 2020).

One of the most aggressive grant-seeking recreation departments is the Sapulpa Parks and Recreation Department in Oklahoma. Since it began its grant-seeking efforts in 1991, the department has received more than 50 grants from federal, state, and private funding sources to repair, renovate, and expand the city's recreation facilities and to construct new parks and recreation facilities. For example, the department received grant revenues in 2003 from the Oklahoma Tourism and Recreation Department and the Fishing Access Development Grant for work at a lake in one of its larger parks. The department has also received significant funding from the National Park Service's Land and Water Conservation Fund (Land and Water Conservation Fund, 2010). Grants from the fund helped construct a new swimming complex, which opened in 2010. In total, 34,000 people used the public swimming facilities during the summer the pool opened. Since 1970, five of Sapulpa's nine parks have been constructed or improved with support from the Land and Water Conservation Fund. These funds have been used for sports fields, trails, park restrooms, and even golf course improvements.

ADVERTISING AND SPONSORSHIPS

To fill gaps in appropriations from governmental entities, public sector sport organizations have increasingly turned to advertising and sponsorship revenues. In fact, as mentioned previously, municipal recreation facilities nationwide are increasingly expected to be self-sufficient. According to IEG, sponsors are looking for new and meaningful ways to engage with consumers. Parks and recreation venues provide a non-traditional, but growing approach to sport sponsorship. For emerging brands, naming rights for recreation facilities are more cost-effective than in professional sport venues. Further, recreation facilities offer access to family and community focused programs where brands can position their sponsorship to align with family-friendly programming. Brands which have already signed naming rights agreements with parks and recreation complexes include Kaiser Permanente, the Chicago Blackhawks, Glenview State Bank, Coca-Cola, Jet Blue, Walmart, and Charter (Kithcart, 2018).

The State of Michigan's Parks and Recreation Division (PRD) of the Department of Natural Resources is required under state law (Section 706 of 2007 PA 122) to report on its plan to generate sponsorship revenues to support state park and recreation operations. Its report to the state shows that the PRD has gone beyond pure sponsorship in an effort to obtain funds from private sources: it takes a blended advertising/sponsorship and fundraising/grants approach. The PRD has received funds through a variety of funding methods, including gifts, grants, and donations. For example, the W.K. Kellogg Foundation provided $3 million in funding to construct universally accessible features in state parks and recreation areas. The Friends of the White Pine Trail donated $242,000 to match a Michigan Department of Transportation Grant to extend paving on that trail. The department also received donations to pay for two new playgrounds and sponsorship funding for new events held in the state's parks (Schafer, 2008).

The PRD also developed a naming rights policy and a sponsorship/partnership policy, each of which received approval from the state's National Resources Commission. In addition, the PRD pursued the development of new events to be held in state parks (e.g., car shows), the development of a gift (donation) guide, and the redevelopment of the non-profit Michigan State Parks Foundation. Further, the PRD is working with the Citizens Committee for Michigan State Parks, whose charge includes studying options for long-term, sustainable funding (Schafer, 2008).

For the Pleasant Prairie Parks and Recreation Department in Wisconsin, advertising revenue is one of its main sources of non-membership revenue. Companies can advertise inside two facilities with signage, sponsor a team, and purchase commercial time on the facilities' television monitors (Bynum, 2005). The department operates without tax proceeds and employs three staff members to operate the advertising program.

School districts are likely to turn to naming rights, in addition to sponsorship and advertising revenues, to help fund construction of athletic complexes and provide revenues for operational expenses. Fourteen football stadiums in northeast Ohio have naming rights deals, as well as extensive corporate sponsorship presences in the venues (Zurick, 2014). Naming rights deals for these schools range from a $150,000, five-year deal to a $750,000, ten-year naming rights contract for a stadium.

Some school districts have also received grants. In Chicago, Riverside Brookfield High School received an $8.9 million grant from the State of Illinois to renovate its football stadium. The school district is hoping to sell naming rights to offset some of the renovation costs, which might allow them to use leftover grant money to pay for roof repairs at the school (Ruzich, 2015).

COLLABORATIVE FINANCING

Collaboration among organizations for the financing of new sport facilities has become an economic necessity. As mentioned briefly in the chapter introduction, this is true in the public sector, as well. Whether the collaboration is a joint use agreement between two public entities, such as a recreation district and a school system, or a public/private partnership between, for example, a nonprofit organization and a municipal recreation department or school district, cooperation—usually in the form of joint use agreements and public/private partnerships—is becoming increasingly common.

Joint Use Agreements

We can find many examples of joint use agreements—formal agreements outlining how facilities will be shared—between public school districts and municipal park and recreation programs. In addition to field and/or facility usage, these agreements may cover the responsibility for construction costs, operational costs, maintenance, and management. For example, a joint use agreement allows a high school in San Marcos, California, to use a public park as a private facility. The 32-acre park includes a skate park, softball fields, and a soccer field. In Broomfield, Colorado, city revenues from new construction impact fees have been funneled from the city to the school district for construction of gymnasiums and athletic fields, which are shared by the school district and community members (Brown, 2008b).

A joint use agreement must be clear in specifying

- who has access to each facility or field
- who maintains each facility or field
- when each party will have access to facilities and fields.

The parties must ensure that the term of the joint use agreement is sufficient to offset the costs of the capital investments. The joint use agreement between county and school officials in Anne Arundel County, Maryland, provides an ideal example (Brown, 2008b). The project involved the installation of three new synthetic turf fields each year at county high school stadiums for four years, at a total cost of $10.7 million. The county's recreation department provided 75% of the funding for the new fields. The department was able to secure a portion of this funding through a grant from Program Open Space, a Maryland Department of Natural Resources initiative. Program Open Space provides funds for the development of parks, conservation areas, and recreation areas. The county provided the funding to the schools because it would not have been able to construct new fields on its own. Through the partnership with the school district and a long-term use agreement, the recreation department was able to develop new fields at less than $1 million per field.

The joint use agreement grants school programs exclusive use of the fields on weekdays until 7:00 p.m. (later on football Fridays) and until noon on Saturdays. The recreation department uses the fields for three to four hours during the week, ten hours on Saturday, and all day Sunday. This access alleviates overcrowding at existing recreation district facilities. In lacrosse alone, county recreation leagues fielded more than 400 teams. Field maintenance is the responsibility of the school district, as is operation of the concessions stands (Brown, 2008b).

Public/Private Partnerships

Joint use agreements work well in some instances, and public/private partnerships work well in others. These partnerships are simply collaborations between the public and private sectors.

Altamonte Springs, Florida, has successfully used public/private partnerships over the past 15 years (Bynum, 2007b). In 2007, the State of Florida reformed its property tax system, resulting in a tax freeze. The changes in tax law forced cities and counties to reduce their 2007 expenses by $2 billion. For fiscal year 2008, they were required to reduce expenses by another 3% to 9%. Park and recreation programs were targeted for cuts and had to develop alternative sources of revenue to save programs and facilities.

Park departments have often entered into partnerships with private entities to manage publicly owned stadiums, golf courses, and skating rinks, but Altamonte Springs was one of the first departments to outsource the operation of its recreation leagues and events, in an effort to cut expenses and generate additional revenue (Bynum, 2007a). Through a bid process, the Altamonte Springs leisure services department contracts with private companies for sport instruction and league and tournament play. The leisure services department provides facilities and marketing for recreation events and tournaments. For municipal sport programs, the city receives a percentage of registration fees. For events, the city receives 15% of registration fees and ticket sales. Sporting events are held on an average of 45 weekends each year, and the department bids for Amateur Athletic Union (AAU) tournaments, American Softball Association (ASA) regional and national tournaments, and the like. In addition to the previously mentioned revenue sources, the city may also receive a percentage of merchandise sold at events.

The YMCA often partners with school districts in building facilities and operating programs. According to the YMCA, 33% of all of its facilities are built in partnership with local school districts. Further, over half of YMCAs share facilities, field space, and/or programs with local school districts. In total, there are nearly 2,700 YMCAs nationwide, so the public/private partnerships are numerous. For example, in Tampa, Florida, the YMCA raised money to build the $16.4 million Spurlino Family YMCA. The land on which the facility sits is owned by Hillsborough County and is governed by a joint-use lease agreement with the Tampa Metropolitan Area YMCA (Quesada, 2019).

CONCLUSION

As in other sectors of the sport industry, the financial management of public sector sport is challenging. Although annual government spending on parks and recreation exceeds $45.3 billion (US Census Bureau, 2017) and spending on high school sport is growing rapidly (with the total amount of spending unknown), managers face many financial challenges. Crompton (2009) notes that competition from non-profits and the private sector creates pricing pressures for public sector agencies charged with providing services across a diverse demographic. Further, these public agencies are seeing the erosion of their traditional tax-based sources of operating and construction revenue. As a result, the agencies are developing new revenue models to meet the demand for sport in the public sector.

Property and sales taxes still provide the majority of revenues for the construction and operation of facilities in this sector, but many states and municipalities restrict the use of tax revenue to fund new projects and programs. Therefore, public agencies are now less likely to rely on general obligation bonds to finance new capital projects. Today, revenue bonds and certificates of participation are common means to circumvent the voter approval needed to finance a project through a general obligation bond. Further, public agencies are adopting some of the funding approaches that we associate with other sectors of the sport industry. Agency heads now focus on fundraising, grant seeking, sponsorships, and advertising as means to generate revenues. They are also increasingly entering into joint use agreements or public/private partnerships in their efforts to reduce expenses and generate revenue.

Concept Check

1. What factors will affect the type of bond that a city will choose to issue for construction of a new recreation facility?
2. What factors will affect the type of bond that a school district will choose to issue for construction of new athletic facilities?
3. What differences, if any, are there when selecting a bond to construct a community recreation facility versus a high school athletics facility?
4. In your hometown, how have local recreation facilities and high school athletic facilities been financed?
5. What are the main sources of revenue for your hometown's recreation center?
6. What pricing paradox do the managers of public recreation centers face?
7. How should the manager of a public recreation center measure financial success?
8. Over the past 30 years, how has the funding of park and recreation agencies and high school athletic programs changed?
9. Explain the process of calculating the millage needed to fund a new recreation center or high school facility.

10. The debt service schedules for Fenton, Missouri, are found in Exhibits 13.6 and 13.7. In Exhibit 13.7, why does the rate of interest that the city pays increase over time? Why does the city make two interest payments and one principal payment, in most years?
11. How does state tax law affect the financing of parks and recreation facilities and programs?
12. For the funding of projects, why are municipalities moving from the use of general obligation bonds to revenue bonds, PFA bonds, and certificates of participation?
13. How can an individual's experiences working in professional sport finance benefit a park and recreation agency? What problems might arise in the negotiation of a joint use agreement?

Practice Problems

You are tasked with calculating the property tax needed to fund construction and operation of a $22.5 million complex. The facility's annual operating budget is forecast at $3.6 million, to be covered by revenues from programs offered at the facility. A 30-year general obligation bond with a rate of 5.5% will be issued to pay for the facility's construction costs. The net assessed value of property in the municipality is $725 million.

1. Calculate the amount that must be set aside each year to meet the bond's principal and interest obligations over 30 years.
2. Calculate the additional millage required to cover the project's debt service.
3. For an owner of property with a total assessed value of $15,000, by how much will his/her property tax increase?

Case Analysis

Billie Jean King National Tennis Center

Perhaps one of the most successful public/private partnerships between a municipality and a private entity is the USTA Billie Jean King National Tennis Center. The National Tennis Center, located in Flushing Meadows, New York, is the world's largest public tennis facility. The partnership between New York City and the United States Tennis Association (USTA) is classified as a private-sector takeover. In a private-sector takeover, a private organization assumes responsibility for operation of a publicly owned facility. (See Chapter 9 for a discussion of public/private partnerships.)

THE PROBLEM

The partnership between the USTA and New York City began in the late 1970s (Specter, 1997). Prior to its move to the National Tennis Center, the US Open was played at the West Side Tennis Club. As its popularity increased, the tournament began to outgrow the site. At the same time, the relationship between the USTA and the West Side Tennis Club was deteriorating. During negotiations for a lease extension in 1976, the USTA was presented with a take-it-or-leave-it option of paying $7 million for needed renovations at the club and ceding much of its control over the tournament and its revenues. The general attitude of the membership was that the tournament's success depended on the club. Then USTA President Slew Hester summed up their attitude thus: "The members of West Side do not need the US Open as much as the US Open needs the West Side Tennis Club" (p. 10).

THE PLAN

Faced with the club's unfavorable offer, Hester began to look for new sites in the New York area. While flying over New York City, he noticed the Singer Bowl, sitting vacant on the grounds of Flushing Meadows Park (the site of two World's Fairs). Thinking that the site would be perfect for the US Open, he began to talk to city officials. Fortunately for the USTA, the city had been trying to sell the Singer Bowl for five years (Specter, 1997).

THE OFFER

In exchange for taking over the Singer Bowl and the land surrounding the stadium, the USTA offered to spend a minimum of $5 million to renovate the site and facility. The USTA sought a 15-year lease agreement giving them exclusive use of the facility for 60 days each year. Further, the USTA offered to maintain the site and operate it as a public municipal tennis facility. As rent, the USTA offered to pay the city 10% of court rental fees or an annual minimum of $125,000, whichever was higher. The city agreed, and the partnership between New York City and the USTA began in 1977 (Specter, 1997).

THE RESULTS

The USTA spent $10 million renovating the Singer Bowl and developing the land into a world-class tennis facility. Out of the shell of the Singer Bowl, the USTA created Louis Armstrong Stadium and the Grandstand Court for tournament use. Outdoor courts were built for tournament and public use, as well as an indoor tennis complex with nine courts. Within ten months of renovations beginning, the first US Open was played at the site. New York City had a new public tennis facility, and the USTA had created a facility to promote the game of tennis. The US Open soon was generating over $10 million per year for the USTA (Specter, 1997).

TODAY

The USTA and New York City extended their initial 15-year agreement, as the partnership has been beneficial to both parties. In 1995, the USTA began a four-year, $285 million construction project to build Arthur Ashe Stadium and to renovate Louis Armstrong Stadium and the grounds of the National Tennis Center (United States Tennis Association, 2020). The USTA provided all funds for the renovations, which were completed with no costs to the city or its taxpayers. Its next upgrade began in 2014 and was completed in 2018. A new practice area, courts, and a tournament gallery were completed in 2014. By 2016 a roof on Arthur Ashe Stadium was completed and a new grandstand stadium opened. Finally, by 2018 a renovated Louis Armstrong Stadium was complete. The total cost of the project was $600 million, including $100 million for a retractable roof on Arthur Ashe Stadium. No public funds have been used for the project.

Today, the center remains completely public and is open for use 11 months of each year. The USTA now pays $400,000 per year plus 1% of the US Open's revenue in rent (United States Tennis Association, 2020). The current lease began in 1994 and had a term of 25 years. The USTA then has six ten-year renewal options and a final 14-year renewal option on the property.

The quality of the facility has improved since its opening. In addition to the stadium courts and grandstand court, 20 outdoor tennis courts are available for public use. The Indoor Tennis Center has 12 courts, classroom space, fitness facilities, a pro shop, and a café. For the fans of the US Open, Arthur Ashe Stadium seats more than 22,000; it is the largest tennis stadium in the world (United States Tennis Association, 2020). Revenues for the USTA have increased dramatically. According to *Forbes*, the US Open is the top stand-alone sporting event in the world (Minassian, 2018). In 2018, the tournament generated over $350 million in revenues.

Case Questions

1. What benefits did the USTA receive when it entered the partnership with the city?
2. What benefits did the city receive?
3. Do the benefits to both parties seem equal? Why or why not?

References

About Toyota Stadium. (2020). Retrieved from www.fcdallas.com/stadium/about.

Attwood, E. (2012, June). Increasing participation in recreation programs. *Athletic Business*. Retrieved from www.athleticbusiness.com/Recreation/increasing-participation-in-recreation-programs.html.

Berg, A. (2020, July). Public parks and rec resumes serving diverse populations. *Athletic Business*. Retrieved from www.athleticbusiness.com/recreation/public-parks-and-rec-resumes-serving-diverse-populations.html.

Biolchini, A. (2014, January 29). Self-sustaining high school sports? Saline continues quest to cut district purse strings. *MLive.com*. Retrieved from www.mlive.com/news/ann-arbor/index.ssf/2014/01/self-sustaining_high_school_sp.html.

Brayley, R.E., & McLean, D.D. (2008). *Financial resource management: Sport, tourism, and leisure services* (2nd ed.). Champaign, IL: Sagamore Publishing.

Brown, N. (2008a, January). Appearing act. *Athletic Business.* Retrieved from http://athleticbusiness.com/articles/default.aspx?a=1692.

Brown, N. (2008b, May). Rec departments get new fields through partnerships with schools. *Athletic Business.* Retrieved from www.athleticbusiness.com/recreation/rec-departments-get-new-fields-through-partnerships-with-schools.html.

Bynum, M. (2005, December). Commercial success. *Athletic Business.* Retrieved from http://athleticbusiness.com/articles/default.aspx?a=1117.

Bynum, M. (2007a, April). A Texas U-turn. *Athletic Business.* Retrieved from http://athleticbusiness.com/articles/default.aspx?a=1488.

Bynum, M. (2007b, September). Outside help. *Athletic Business.* Retrieved from http://athleticbusiness.com/articles/default.aspx?a=1627.

City of Fenton (2020). Approved budget. Retrieved from www.fentonmo.org/DocumentCenter/View/8057/2020-Approved-Budget.

City sponsored grants. (2020). City of Thousand Oaks. Retrieved from www.toaks.org/departments/city-manager-s-office/grant-opportunities.

Cook, B. (2012, August 22). Will 'pay for play' become a permanent part of school sports? *Forbes.* Retrieved from www.forbes.com/sites/bobcook/2012/08/22/will-pay-to-play-become-a-permanent-part-of-school-sports/.

County of Lexington. (2020, April 14). *Annual budget overview.* Lexington, SC: Author.

Crompton, J.L. (2009). *Financing and acquiring park and recreation resources.* Champaign, IL: Human Kinetics.

Frisco Independent School District. (2013, August 13). FSID students to play in new Cowboys practice facility. Retrieved from www.friscoisd.org/news/2013/08/13/cowboys-partnership.

Grant, T. (2019, February 4). $23 million bond boosts recreational facilities in Lexington County. *Cola Daily.* Retrieved from www.coladaily.com/communities/lexington/archive/23-million-bond-boosts-recreational-facilities-in-lexingtoncounty/article_3cdfa9fa-b8e4-5202-947e-d1c2d60d7118.html.

Huddleston, E. (2001, September). Partnerships between municipalities, schools providing better facilities, programs. *Athletic Business.* Retrieved from www.athleticbusiness.com/partnerships-between-municipalities-schools-providing-better-facilities-programs.html.

Kansas City Parks and Recreation. (2015). Partners. Retrieved from http://kcparks.org/partners/.

Kithcart, M. (2018, August 29). Parks & rec: The next big naming rights opportunity. *Carvel Marketing.* Retrieved from www.caravelmarketing.com/parks-rec-the-next-big-naming-rights-opportunity/.

Land and Water Conservation Fund. (2010). State and local assistance program: 2010 annual report. Washington, DC: National Park Service.

McPhate, M. (2016, May 11). That's right, $63 million for a football stadium ... for high schoolers. *The New York Times.* Retrieved from www.nytimes.com/2016/05/12/sports/high-school-football-stadium-texas-63-million.html.

Minassian, G. (2018, August 10). How the U.S. Open became a $350 million business. *Forbes.* Retrieved from www.forbes.com/feature/usopen/#33177d6913d8.

Mostafavi, B. (2019, March 18). Does "Pay-to-Play" put sports, extracurriculars out of reach? *Michigan Health.* Retrieved from https://healthblog.uofmhealth.org/lifestyle/does-pay-to-play-put-sports-extracurriculars-out-of-reach.

Participation in high school sports registers first decline in 30 years. (2019, September 5). National Federation of State High School Associations. Retrieved from www.nfhs.org/articles/participation-in-high-school-sports-registers-first-decline-in-30-years/#:~:text=The%202018%2D19%20total%20of,time%20record%20high%20of%207%2C980%2C886.

Popke, M. (2010). Rec department wants to operate more like a business. *Athletic Business*. Retrieved from www.athleticbusiness.com/rec-department-wants-to-oper-ate-more-like-a-business.html.

Quesada, K. (2019, January 3). Spurlino Family YMCA now accepting members in Riverview. *Osprey Observer*. Retrieved from www.ospreyobserver.com/2019/01/spurlino-family-ymca-now-accepting-members-in-riverview/.

Richland 2 School District. (2020). Pathway to premier: Bond projects. Retrieved from www.richland2.org/About/Facilities.

Ruzich, J. (2015, February 12). Riverside Brookfield High School selling naming rights for stadium. *The Chicago Tribune*. Retrieved from www.chicagotribune.com/ suburbs/ oak-park/news/ct-riverside-brookfield-naming-rights-met-20150215-story.html.

Schafer, S.M. (2008, February 22). Dear Senator McManus and Representative Lahti. Retrieved from www.michigan.gov/documents/dnr/Parkscorpsponsorshipmemo_226381_7.pdf.

Sherman, R.M. (1998, September). The numbers game. *Athletic Business*, 37–44.

Specter, D.K. (1997, February 20). A stadium is born. *Tennis Week*, 10–15.

Trends in Parks & Recreation. (2020). Recreation management. Retrieved from https://recmanagement.com/feature/202006FE03.

US Census Bureau. (2017). *Annual Survey of State and Local Government Finances*. Retrieved from www.census.gov/programs-surveys/gov-finances.html.

United States Tennis Association. (2020). Strategic transformation. *USOPEN.org*. Retrieved from www.usopen.org/Event_Guide/strategic_transformation/?intloc=headernavsub.

Wall, S. (2015, April). $848M bond funds four high school district stadiums. *Athletic Business*. Retrieved from www.athleticbusiness.com/stadium-arena/848m-bond-funds-stadiums-for-four-district-high-schools.html.

Welcome to Fenton. (2020). Retrieved from www.fentonmo.org/DocumentCenter/View/7959/Sales-Tax-Rates-as-of-4-01-2019.

Zurick, M. (2014, September 5). 9 Northeast Ohio high school football stadiums with sponsors: Fields of green. *Cleveland.com*. Retrieved from www.cleveland.com/lyndhurst-south-euclid/index.ssf/2014/09/9_northeast_ohio_high_school_f.html.

CHAPTER 14

College Athletics

Matthew T. Brown

KEY CONCEPTS

80/20 rule
90/10 rule
allocated revenues
arms race
athletic support group (ASG)
campaign case statement
capital campaign
department-generated revenues
endowed gift
major gift
National Association of
    Intercollegiate Athletics (NAIA)
National Collegiate Athletic
    Association (NCAA)

National Junior College Athletic
    Association (NJCAA)
NCAA Division I–Football Bowl
    Subdivision (FBS)
NCAA Division I–Football
    Championship Subdivision (FCS)
NCAA Division I-Other
NCAA Division II
NCAA Division III
NIL cap
point system
prospect
rule of thirds
self-sustaining
traditional gifts table

INTRODUCTION

On June 8, 2019, the Yale crew team beat Harvard in the teams' annual regatta. Although this annual event goes unnoticed by most fans of college athletics, it is significant for its history. Yale and Harvard held their first crew competition in 1852. This regatta is generally considered to have been the first intercollegiate sporting event in the United States (Powers, 2014). As an interesting side note, the first event was sponsored by the Boston, Concord & Montreal railroad company (Barr, 2012).

From this first race, college sport quickly grew. By 1905, the Intercollegiate Athletic Association of the United States (IAAUS) had been formed to govern college sport. In 1912, the IAAUS changed its name to the **National Collegiate Athletic Association (NCAA)**. Today, the NCAA, **National Association of**

Intercollegiate Athletics (NAIA), and **National Junior College Athletic Association (NJCAA)** are the three main governing bodies overseeing college sport in the United States. As college sport grew, so did the business of college sport. From the sponsorship of the inaugural Harvard-Yale race, college sport has grown to a $40 billion-plus business.

FINANCIAL STATUS OF INTERCOLLEGIATE ATHLETICS

Data from the US Department of Education (2019) provide an inside look at the financial operation of one of the most successful college athletic programs, the Ohio State University Buckeyes. For the 2018/2019 academic year, the Ohio State University athletic department had $210.5 million in revenues, 150 coaches, 36 teams, and 1,054 athletes. The department was one of only a few self-sufficient athletic departments nationwide. For example, Ohio State's athletic department receives no subsidy from the university (one of 15 departments to receive no allocated revenues out of the 227 public NCAA Division I universities examined by *USA Today*; "NCAA finances," 2019); however, it lost $10 million with expenses at $220.6 million in 2018/2019. This loss was mainly caused by changes to the way the athletic department recorded donations. Without these bookkeeping changes, the loss would be $624,000 (Kaufman, 2020). The deficit was covered by the athletic department's $8.9 million reserve fund. While the department receives no subsidies from the university, it transferred back $3.1 million for use by the school. Also, the athletic department paid $25.5 million on debt payments (up $4.6 million from the previous year) and saw its football ticket revenue drop $8.8 million.

The University of Florida's athletic department is similarly sized. With a budget of approximately $159.6 million for the 2018/2019 academic year, it had an operating profit of $17.9 million ("How Florida," 2020). The department has sufficient financial strength to build new facilities and expand existing ones. In 2020, for example, the new $65 million baseball stadium will be complete. It was built as a part of an athletic district that includes softball, lacrosse, and soccer. Florida will also break ground on a new football facility once the baseball stadium project is complete. Further, the school is planning to build a clubhouse for soccer and is beginning to plan for renovations to its football stadium (Dosh, 2020).

The Florida athletic department is fortunate to have a strong development foundation. Gator Boosters, Inc. contributed $38.0 million during the 2019 fiscal year to Florida's University Athletic Association, Inc. (UAA). Contributions came from three primary areas: football-related ($30.8 million), basketball-related ($2.9 million), and capital improvement contributions ($6.4 million; Gator Boosters, Inc., 2019).

The Race to Build New Athletic Facilities

The construction of new athletic facilities at schools like the Ohio State University and the University of Florida has contributed to a phenomenon commonly referred to as the **arms race** in college athletics: the continuous building of bigger and better facilities for the sole purpose of landing key recruits. Ohio State is able to pay the debt service on its new facilities through funds set aside in its operating budget. As the athletic department is fully self-sufficient—meaning it receives no funds from the university's general budget or student fees—the department must generate revenue to offset the cost of the building projects over the life of the financing for those projects. Florida was fortunate in that individual gifts generated enough revenue to cover the costs of building the new football complex, so no debt financing was needed. Both athletic departments are fortunate in being able to afford these facilities. Athletic departments that are not so financially sound face difficult decisions about the construction or upgrading of facilities in order to create their own recruiting "wow" moments on campus.

An illustration of the impact of the arms race on college athletic departments can be seen at the University of South Carolina. Founders Park, a $40 million baseball stadium with a capacity of 8,242, opened in 2009. In the ten years prior to its opening, the baseball team made regular trips to the NCAA Super Regionals and three trips to the College World Series. To elevate the baseball program even further and attract even better recruits, the head baseball coach and the university's athletic director felt a new stadium was needed Founders Park houses offices for coaches, indoor batting cages, chair-back seats for fans, and other modern amenities. Given average construction costs at the time for Triple-A minor league baseball stadiums of $40 million to $50 million and for Double-A stadiums of $25 million to $35 million, the baseball stadium at the University of South Carolina was the equivalent of a high-end Double-A or low-end Triple-A facility. In fact, when it opened, the new stadium was the most expensive baseball stadium ever built for a college team. For comparison, Alex Box Stadium at Louisiana State University, completed in 2009, had a final cost of $37.8 million. Texas spent almost $27 million and the University of North Carolina spent $25.5 million to rebuild their on-campus facilities completely. Even with new revenue-generating stadiums, not all of these traditional baseball powers will turn profits (Morris, 2008).

Eric Hyman, then athletic director at the University of South Carolina, stated in an interview that the $40 million baseball stadium made little business sense (Morris, 2008). Hyman was responsible for finding the revenue needed to pay the stadium's debt service of $1.9 million per year for 30 years. Fans had to pay higher ticket prices, saw increases in concessions prices, and had to pay for seat licenses. Despite the additional revenue generated at the facility, Hyman noted that the department might not earn enough new revenue to offset the expenses of the team and facility. For the 2008 season, its last at Sarge Frye Field, the team had an operating budget of $1.2 million and revenues of $700,000—a deficit of $500,000.

Regardless of whether the Carolina baseball team turns a profit and generates enough revenue to cover its debt service, the athletic department is obligated to pay Founder Park's annual $1.9 million debt obligation. Despite making "little business sense," the new stadium arguably did in fact help the school attract better recruits and, therefore, elevate the team's performance. From 2009 through 2014, the Carolina baseball team played in the post-season each season, losing in the NCAA Regionals twice and the Super Regionals once. The team made the College World Series from 2010 to 2012. In 2010 and 2011 the team won the national championship, and it finished second in 2012. From 2010 to 2012, Carolina baseball won 22 consecutive post-season games, including 12 straight at the College World Series, both NCAA records (Gamecock Athletics, 2015). The team's success in the new venue, however, was not sustained as it has only made post-season play twice since 2014 (2016 and 2018).

The initial success of Carolina baseball after the opening of its new facility fuels the desire of others to build in order to win. This desire is not limited to Division I programs, as it has spread to Division III institutions, as well. Athletes competing at NCAA Division III institutions attend school without the benefit of athletic scholarships. New England College (NEC) received a $5 million gift to use towards its $12 million goal to build a new state-of-the-art athletic complex for its teams. NEC has athletics and fitness as central parts of its mission as more than half of the college's residential undergraduate students participate in intercollegiate athletics. The venue will have a 25,000-square-foot gym for use by basketball, volleyball, and wrestling. Further, its 1,300 seating capacity will allow NEC to host NCAA-sanctioned tournaments and competitions ("New England," 2020).

In Wisconsin, three Division III schools are investing in their facilities to help with recruiting and "filling beds" at the colleges. St. Norbert College is spending $26 million on athletic facilities and Ripon College will spend $20 million. Lawrence University started the local arms race after spending $5 million to upgrade its football facility with plans for further expenditures in athletics (Moser, 2016). Funding sources for these new Division III facilities are similar to those used at the Division I level. The St. Norbert project was made possible by a $13 million gift from one alumnus. In 2018, colleges in the Autonomous 5 athletic conferences in Division I have spent or plan to spend $1.5 billion for new athletics facilities or renovations to existing venues (Broughton, 2018).[1] In 2021 alone, new campus arena openings will top $1 billion (Broughton, 2020). At all levels, the race continues to be on to build improved athletic facilities.

The Race to Change NCAA Divisions

The arms race affects more than facilities; it also affects an institution's choice of NCAA division. For smaller Division I–FCS football schools, the transition to Division I–FBS from Division I–FCS can be difficult. Even more so may be the move to Division I from Division II; however, the lure of being a Division I institution was so great that the NCAA issued a four-year moratorium on new Division I applications in 2007. As of this writing, three universities are in the process of transitioning from Division II to Division I: California Baptist, Merrimack, and North Alabama. Another three are moving from Division III to Division II: Staten Island, Frostburg State, and Texas at Tyler (NCAA, 2020).

Presbyterian College provides one example of this challenge. The school, located in Clinton, South Carolina, has 1,200 students, and the Carnegie Foundation has classified it among the most selective liberal arts colleges in the United States. Athletics is an important part of student life at Presbyterian. The school fields 16 teams—seven men's and nine women's. Presbyterian decided to move from Division II to Division I in 2007, and the school was fortunate that

1   The Autonomous 5 conferences include the Big 10, Big XII, the ACC, the Pac 12, and the SEC.

its application was accepted prior to the NCAA's temporary moratorium. One reason the school gave for the move up in classification was that similar-sized schools, such as Wofford College, Elon University, and Gardner-Webb University, had recently moved to Division I, and these moves had affected recruiting at Presbyterian. Potential recruits living within a one-hour drive of Presbyterian College were deciding to go to similar schools two or three hours away, solely because those schools were Division I. Presbyterian's head men's basketball coach at the time felt that missing the chance to play in the NCAA Division I men's basketball tournament was too big a recruiting obstacle (Darcy, 2007).

Presbyterian was fortunate that it was accepted into a conference, the Big South, two days after announcing its move to Division I, although the school would play without an affiliation the first year. Beginning in the 2008/2009 academic year, the school's teams competed in the conference, although they were ineligible for conference championships and NCAA post-season play until they earned full NCAA Division I certification, which occurred prior to the start of the 2012/2013 academic year.

The financial impact of a move from Division II to Division I is staggering. Presbyterian College's move demonstrates how both revenues and expenses are altered dramatically when a school makes this transition. During the initial transition year (2007–2008), Presbyterian had to play as an independent, meaning the school had no conference affiliation. Darcy chronicled the impact of the move during the year on one of Presbyterian's programs, the men's basketball team. As a result of joining the Big South conference a year later, in the 2008–2009 season, the men's basketball team played only five home games but 25 road games. On its longest road trip, the team was away 11 nights, leaving in December on the day final exams ended. The team played in 12 states and traveled more than 13,000 miles by bus and plane. To generate revenue to pay for the trip, the team's road games, and the greater operating expenses at the Division I level, the coach scheduled games with four Atlantic Coast Conference (ACC) teams, three SEC teams, Ohio State, and Nebraska. Playing these major conference schools generated $650,000 in guaranteed money for Presbyterian. However, the school still did not have the funds to pay for administrative support, such as a coordinator of basketball operations (a position found in almost all Division I basketball programs). Instead, an assistant basketball coach had to take on those duties in that first season along with his regular coaching responsibilities. As of 2014, seven years after its transition to Division I began, the athletic department's budget had grown to $11 million per year. However, revenues generated by the program totaled only $2 million (Moss, 2014).

Other Races to Be Won

After US District Judge Claudia Wilken ruled in *O'Bannon v. NCAA* (2014) that prohibiting football and men's basketball athletes from being paid for the use of their names, images, and likenesses (NIL) violated antitrust law, changes in NCAA policy began to impact athletic departments' budgets. New arms races began. Shortly after this ruling, the NCAA Division I Board of Directors enacted a new governance model allowing the Autonomous 5 conferences to create their own legislation to benefit athletes. Now, coaches can compete for recruits by offering four-year scholarships (previously scholarships were restricted to one-year, renewable contracts), which cover the full cost of attending a university (Solomon, 2014a). The market will now dictate what men's basketball and football recruits receive. The judge's rules went into effect on July 1, 2016, so those recruited during the 2015/2016 school year were the first to be affected (Solomon, 2014b). It was estimated that these new regulations will cost athletic departments an additional $7,500 per athlete per year (Solomon, 2015). *USA Today Sports* (Berkowitz & Kreighbaum, 2015) estimated the projected additional spending on athletes related to the addition of full cost-of-attendance scholarships—including tuition, travel, and personal expenses—at more than 90 schools. For example, the authors estimated that Auburn will spend an additional $2.1 million and the Ohio State University an additional $1.65 million.

Further change was made in 2019 with *In Re: NCAA Grant-in-Aid Cap Antitrust Litigation*. US District Judge Claudia Wilken again ruled against the NCAA and ordered the association to revise its grant-in-aid rules to be more competitive and to be set at the conference level. Schools can now compete for recruits by offering scholarships of higher value, beyond tuition, books, fees, room, board, and other expenses related to the cost of attendance. Scholarships can include monies for computers, lab equipment, musical instruments, or other tangible things related to the student's area of study (McCann, 2019). While the NCAA appealed this decision, the appellate court upheld Judge Wilken's ruling (Murphy, 2020). It is estimated that this ruling will lead to an additional $100 million going to college athletes on an annual basis.

SIDEBAR 14.A   University of Alabama-Birmingham Football: The Cost of On-field Success

In 1996, the University of Alabama-Birmingham (UAB) moved its athletic department and football program from Division I–FCS to Division I–FBS. As with many programs that have made this move recently, the hope was to use the football program to help meet the university's mission and to create a new identity for the university. However, by 2014 UAB decided to terminate its football program—the first Division I–FBS program to drop its football team since the University of the Pacific dropped its program in 1995. The same year that UAB decided to terminate it, the UAB football program had its best on-field success in ten years, becoming bowl eligible for the first time since 2004. Despite this on-field success, the financial costs were too high for UAB, as approximately 67% of the athletic department's budget was subsidized by the university (Strauss & Schonbrun, 2014).

A comprehensive review by UAB of its athletic program cited increases in costs due to new NCAA legislation relating to cost-of-attendance payments to players, increasing facility costs, and increasing coaching costs as reasons for the program's termination. The review estimated that the university would have had to provide over $100 million in subsidies to the athletic department from 2015 through 2020. The review indicated that to remain competitive in Conference USA (C-USA), the football program would need another $49 million plus over $22 million in facility improvements. UAB planned to funnel its football savings into supporting its remaining "priority" sports in the hopes of competing for conference and national championships in those sports (Greer, 2014).

However, in less than a year, the administrators at UAB changed their minds. Despite acknowledged programmatic losses and heavy subsidies from the university and students through their fees, UAB President Ray Watts announced on June 1, 2015, that the school would not drop its football program. The university commissioned a second study on the football program and found that it would need only $17.2 million in additional revenues over the next five years to remain competitive, plus $12 million for a new football practice facility (Nocera, 2015). The new study stated that the first study underestimated what the school would receive in revenues from the first College Football Playoff payment. Also, the first study failed to consider that the school, without a football team, would no longer be a member of C-USA (Dufresne, 2015).

In announcing the return of the program, President Watts said that monies would need to be raised to cover the expenses required to remain competitive, as the university would not be increasing its current $20 million subsidy of athletics. Just prior to the June 1 announcement, corporate leaders in Birmingham had pledged enough money to cover the additional $17.2 million five-year costs and had also raised significant amounts of money to build the new practice facility (Nocera, 2015). The team returned to the field in 2017.

The Autonomous 5 conferences and their member schools have made additional changes besides full cost-of-attendance scholarships, guaranteed four-year scholarships, and scholarship changes related to the student's academic pursuits. One change involves dining (Myerberg, 2015). New legislation allows college athletes to receive unlimited access to food and snacks. Before this rule was enacted, athletes were limited to meal plans that provided three meals a day. Now all athletes, both those on scholarship and those who are not, are receiving significant dining upgrades on campuses across the United States.

At Wisconsin, the athletic department upgraded athletes' breakfast options and provided an enhanced training table and refueling stations for its athletes. Oregon now has a breakfast and brunch station that is open until noon each day. Schools are adding nutritionists, too, to monitor the athletes' food options. At Nebraska, it is estimated that the new dining regulations will cost an additional $1.2 million per year. The school's total budget for sports nutrition is now $3.2 million, with $2.1 million for food and supplements and $1 million for payroll expenses, new kitchen equipment, and operating costs. Southern California expects new costs to be $1 million, while Wisconsin will spend an additional $1.2 million ($842,000 for its new breakfast alone).

These changes suggest that the way athletic departments feed their athletes could become a recruiting advantage. Wisconsin athletic director Barry Alvarez stated that the recruiting benefit was not the intent of the unlimited food legislation, but it might lead to an arms race in dining like the ones that exist for practice fields and weight rooms. According to Alvarez, "If we have it and someone else doesn't have it, then we have an advantage" (Myerberg, 2015, para. 25).

Overall, the size and complexity of athletic department budgets have grown dramatically as the arms race continues into the 2020s. Whether it is construction of new athletic facilities, a move to a higher division, or the adaptation to new NCAA legislation, the impact on the athletic department's finances can be dramatic.

FINANCIAL OPERATIONS

This section focuses on the financial operation of the NCAA—the national governing body most responsible for shaping and controlling intercollegiate athletics in the United States (Covell & Walker, 2019)—and its member conferences and schools. Discussions of financial issues in college sport focus primarily on NCAA Division I programs, usually those in the Football Bowl Subdivision (FBS). To gain a thorough understanding of the financial operations of college sport, however, we must undertake a broader examination. The NCAA has 1,115 member schools. Of its active membership, 130 are Division I–FBS members, 124 are Division I–Football Championship Subdivision (FCS) members, 96 are Division I members (without a football program or with a non-scholarship football program), 310 are Division II members, and 438 are Division III members. The lower a school's classification, the smaller and less complicated are the athletic department's revenues and expenses.

National Collegiate Athletic Association

The NCAA has a net worth of $450 million (see Exhibit 14.1). Revenues for FY 2019 were $1.1 billion (see Exhibit 14.1), an increase of 1.9% from 2018. (The NCAA fiscal year, September 1 to August 31, coincides with the academic year.)

The primary sources of revenue (approximately 78%) were television and marketing rights fees. Television revenue—specifically, the NCAA's contracts with CBS, Turner Broadcasting, and ESPN—provides most of the $867.5 million in fees. The NCAA sold the television broadcast rights for the Division I Men's Basketball Championship, along with other championship and marketing rights, to CBS and Turner Broadcasting for $10.8 billion in 2010. The agreement had a term of 14 years, covering the 2011 through 2024 academic years. All parties agreed to extend this agreement for an additional eight years in 2016 (through 2032) for $8.8 billion more. In 2020, the NCAA was to receive $827 million from CBS and Turner; however, the coronavirus pandemic, which led to the cancellation of the Division I men's and women's basketball tournaments, will lead to a lesser amount received. Exhibit 14.2 lists payments the NCAA will receive for the remaining years of the contract (National Collegiate Athletic Association, 2019).

Exhibit 14.2 also lists the payments the NCAA will receive from ESPN for television rights for certain fall, winter, and spring championships; the NIT tournaments; and the international distribution of the Division I Men's Basketball Championship. The agreement between the NCAA and ESPN, reached in 2011, guaranteed the NCAA $500 million over 14 years, from 2010 to 2024 (National Collegiate Athletic Association, 2019).

NCAA BALANCE SHEET
CONSOLIDATED STATEMENT OF FINANCIAL POSITION
FISCAL YEAR ENDED AUGUST 31, 2019

Assets	
Cash and cash equivalents	$15,150,504
Prepaid expenses	$4,920,944
Accounts receivable, net	$61,465,921
Investments	$473,713,892
Goodwill	$6,300,000
Intangible assets, net	$780,000
Properties, net	$43,478,741
Other assets	$5,083,949
Total Assets	$610,893,951
Liabilities	
Accounts payable and accrued liabilities	$100,682,159
Deferred revenue and deposits	$48,147,363
Bonds payable, net	$11,922,422
Total Liabilities	$160,751,944
Net Assets	
Without donor restrictions	$447,799,739
With donor restrictions	$2,342,268
Total Net Assets	$450,142,007
Total Liabilities and Net Assets	$610,893,951

(continued)

EXHIBIT 14.1   Cont.

NCAA INCOME STATEMENT
CONSOLIDATED STATEMENT OF ACTIVITIES
FISCAL YEAR ENDED AUGUST 31, 2019

Revenues	
Television and marketing rights fees	$867,527,070
Championships and NIT tournaments	$177,872,026
Investment income, net	$14,566,001
Sales, services, and other	$55,395,739
Contributions—facilities	$3,134,709
Total Revenues	$1,118,495,545
Expenses	
Distribution to Division I members	$610,911,851
Division I championships, programs, and NIT tournaments	$153,777,866
Division II championships, distribution, and programs	$53,313,095
Division III championships and programs	$35,179,996
Association-wide programs	$149,966,362
Management and general	$44,808,669
Total Expenses	$1,047,957,839
Change in Net Assets	$70,537,706
Net Assets—Beginning of Year	$379,604,301
Net Assets—End of Year	$450,142,007

Source: National Collegiate Athletic Association (2019).

EXHIBIT 14.2   NCAA television broadcast payments from CBS, Turner Broadcasting, and ESPN.

FISCAL YEAR ENDING	CBS/TURNER	ESPN
2020	$827,000,000	$40,214,000
2021	$850,000,000	$41,823,000
2022	$870,000,000	$43,469,000
2023	$873,000,000	$45,235,000
2024	$873,000,000	$47,045,000
Thereafter	$8,800,000,000	
2020–2032 Total Payments	$13,093,000,000	$271,813,000

The NCAA's expenses in 2019 were $1.05 billion, a decrease of 2.3% from 2018. The main expenses are the distribution of revenues to member institutions, association-wide programs, and costs associated with conducting championships (see Exhibit 14.1). The $610.9 million distribution to Division I members accounted for 58% of expenses in 2019 and represents an increase of $1.7 million, or 0.03%, from 2018. Revenue is distributed to Division I and Division II members annually.

The amount of money that each school receives is determined from a formula created by the NCAA. For Division I members, funds are distributed based on eight criteria. The basketball fund distribution is based on a school's historical performance in the Division I Men's Basketball Championship. Schools also receive funds based on the number of sports they sponsor and scholarships they give. Funds are also granted to institutions for the academic enhancement of student-athletes and provision of student-athlete opportunities. The NCAA also provides conference grants, a conference fund, and maintains a special assistance fund to assist student-athletes in emergency situations (see Exhibit 14.3). Division II members receive a distribution based on the school's historic performance in the Division II Men's and Women's Basketball Championships and the number of sports sponsored, plus an equal amount given to all active members. The total of Division II distributions in 2019 was approximately $7.3 million (National Collegiate Athletic Association, 2019).

The NCAA spent $153.8 million conducting championships and running the NIT Tournament during the 2019 fiscal year, a decrease of almost 3% compared to 2018. The amounts spent running Division II and Division III championships and programs were $45.4 and $35.2 million respectively.

EXHIBIT 14.3 NCAA's 2019 Division I revenue distribution fund.

FUND SOURCE	AMOUNT
Basketball Performance Fund	$168,500,833
Grants-in-Aid Fund	$146,932,780
Sports Sponsorship Fund	$75,118,234
Equal Conference Fund	$53,550,181
Academic Enhancement Fund	$49,219,502
Special Assistance Fund	$18,630,621
Conference Grants	$9,965,217
Student Athlete Opportunity Fund	$67,958
2019 Revenue Distribution Total	$589,875,809

Source: National Collegiate Athletic Association (2019).

Conferences

The $589.9 million in revenue distributed to member schools in 2019 flows from the NCAA primarily through the conferences. Each conference sets policy determining the amount of revenue that an individual school receives. The Big XII, an Autonomous 5 conference, has a fairly straightforward revenue distribution plan. Revenues received by the conference are first used to pay for conference operating expenses and fund any established reserves. Next, any NCAA subsidies received or member participation subsidies awarded for participation in post-season competition are paid directly to the member institution. All remaining revenues are then divided among members in equal portions, with the only adjustments made being related to broadcasts of games on permitted member institution outlets (e.g., Longhorn Network).

DIVISION I–FBS, AUTONOMOUS 5 CONFERENCES

The financial strength of the major conferences can be seen when examining the amount of revenues received from the NCAA. From 1997 through 2018, the Big 10 received a combined $340.4 million, while the Pac 12 received $247.7 million. On average, over that period Autonomous 5 conferences received $295.6 million in revenues from the NCAA. The five remaining Division I–FBS conferences, or the Group of 5 (American Athletic, C-USA, MAC, Sunbelt, and Mountain West), received less, with the American Athletic Conference earning $106.4 during that same time frame ("What's an NCAA," 2019). It must be noted that the 2020 NCAA revenue distribution plan was impacted with the cancellation of winter and spring championships. The NCAA was scheduled to distribute approximately $600 million that year. The shutdown due to the coronavirus pandemic resulted in loss of revenue related to the cancellation of the Division I Men's Basketball Championships. As a result, the NCAA planned to distribute only $225 million to its member institutions, of which $50 million came from its reserves ("NCAA presidents," 2020). A large portion of this revenue, $53.6 million, was split equally among the 36 Division I basketball-playing conferences and was distributed through the Equal Conference Fund. The rest was proportionally distributed through the remaining NCAA distribution funds.

By reviewing conference tax filings (Form 990, Return of Organization Exempt from Income Tax), we can examine the non-COVID-impacted differences among conference revenues in Division I. First, we must note the difficulty of making direct comparisons in collegiate sport between two similar organizations, as there is no standard for reporting financials. Exhibits 14.4 through 14.6 do, however, provide a basis for comparison. Exhibit 14.4 gives revenues and expenses for 2017 for two major conferences, the SEC and Big XII. From the conferences' tax returns, we can see that the Big XII reported its revenue in much greater detail than the SEC, although we can directly compare revenue from media rights and post-season events. The Big XII earned $194.9 million less from media rights than the SEC. It also earned $35.0 million less than the SEC from bowl game, NCAA, and ticket sales revenue (the SEC lumps these revenues under "Post-season events"). Clearly, the SEC was in the stronger financial position, as the conference's revenue was $286.0 million more than that of the Big XII.

In the SEC, schools on average received $43.1 million in revenue from the conference in 2017. This amount has doubled since 2014. The growth of

EXHIBIT 14.4 2017 revenues and expenses of two Division I–FBS Autonomous 5 conferences.

SOUTHEASTERN CONFERENCE		BIG XII	
REVENUE		**REVENUE**	
TV/radio rights fees	$432,075,960	Television contracts	$237,151,436
Post-season events	$168,237,426	Bowl games	$83,204,041
Royalties	$35,833,667	NCAA revenue	$38,256,898
Contributions, gifts, grants received	$19,356,640	Ticket sales	$11,776,213
Investment income	$3,438,319	Other revenue	$2,714,021
Gain on sale of assets	$996,580	Contributions, gifts, grants received	$288,784
		Royalties	$329,430
		Investment income	$153,675
		Digital	$50,000
Total Revenue	$659,938,592	Total Revenue	$373,924,498
Expenses		**Expenses**	
Payments to members		Payments to members	
Florida	$45,553,083	Baylor	$33,284,658
Arkansas	$45,507,137	Iowa State	$34,886,507
Tennessee	$45,228,598	Kansas	$33,595,866
Missouri	$44,687,788	Kansas State	$34,612,071
Mississippi State	$43,921,438	Oklahoma	$36,611,074
Kentucky	$43,106,558	Oklahoma State	$34,865,519
Texas A&M	$43,099,160	TCU	$34,485,243
Vanderbilt	$43,093,310	Texas	$34,978,575
Auburn	$42,949,228	Texas Tech	$34,291,201
Alabama	$42,892,843	West Virginia	$34,457,354
Georgia	$42,756,439	Salaries	$7,476,109
LSU	$42,756,438	Miscellaneous	$70,505

(continued)

EXHIBIT 14.4   Cont.

SOUTHEASTERN CONFERENCE		BIG XII	
South Carolina	$42,756,438	Other	$7,524,331
Mississippi	$35,832,364	Employee benefits and pension contributions	$1,082,335
Post-season events	$34,113,720	Rent	$173,711
Salaries	$7,268,928	Legal fees	$5,989,311
Grants, scholarships, fellowships	$8,810,593	Travel	$976,553
Production and game management	$4,176,321	Advertising and promotion	$884,029
Conferences, conventions, meetings	$1,669,720	Office expenses	$395,099
Employee benefits and pension contributions	$1,255,479	Depreciation and amortization	$523,018
Marketing	$478,669	Payroll taxes	$284,661
Travel	$851,565	Information technology	$285,349
Legal fees	$2,253,662	Insurance	$437,282
Rent	$312,225	Accounting expenses	$31,617
SECU	$459,758	Championship facility fee	$1,921,680
Office expenses	$415,187		
Advertising and promotions	$2,622,430		
Payroll taxes	$302,843		
Insurance	$234,580		
Other	$1,286,044		
Accounting expenses	$59,000		
Total Expenses	$670,711,546	Total Expenses	$374,123,658

Note: Figures based on each conference's 2017 IRS Form 990.

revenues in the SEC has mirrored growth in the popularity of college football and the resulting creation of conference broadcast networks. Revenues from television rights fees accounted for 65.5% of SEC member institution revenues. In the Big XII, television contracts accounted for 63.4% of member institution revenues. Because of the strength of their media property, the SEC Network, the SEC received $720.6 million in revenue during the 2018/2019 fiscal year. Each member institution received $45.3 million on average, an increase of $2.2 million over the previous year. Only the Big 10 received more, almost $759 million in total. Each school in the Big 10 received roughly $54 million (Berkowitz, 2020).

Prior to 1984, the NCAA controlled the television rights for college football. In that year, the University of Georgia and University of Oklahoma sued the NCAA, claiming that the NCAA's control over broadcasting violated the Sherman Act. The US Supreme Court agreed that the NCAA's actions violated Section 1 of the Act *(NCAA v. Board of Regents*, 1984). After the ruling, most of the major football conferences and football independents (Penn State and Notre Dame) joined together as the College Football Association (CFA) to negotiate a collective television package for members. The Pac 12 and Big 10 negotiated their own television contracts. By 1991, Penn State and Notre Dame had left the CFA in order to negotiate on their own. The CFA was disbanded after the SEC left in 1995 to pursue an opportunity to increase its revenues through an exclusive contract with CBS. (CBS had just lost its NFL television package to Fox.) After its television contract was signed, total SEC disbursements to member schools increased from $45.5 million to $58.9 million. In 2008, the SEC considered following the Big 10 model with the launch of its own television network; however, the league opted to sign an agreement with both CBS and ESPN. Its partnership with ESPN and CBS brought the league $205 million per year in media rights revenues (Smith & Ourand, 2008).

The Big 10 created its own network in 2007 with partner News Corp. The conference's 51% ownership stake in the network resulted in $66 million in new revenues during FY 2007. Over the lifetime of the agreement, the Big 10 could average $112 million annually, with the fees paid to the conference expected to rise over the lifetime of the deal. At the same time that the Big 10 was launching its network, it signed a ten-year, $1 billion national rights contract with ABC/ESPN. The Big 10 received $83 million during the first year of the agreement (2008), with the rights fees expected to increase over the life of the contract. As a result of these television agreements, total Big 10 revenue increased 39.8% between 2006 and 2008, and distributions to member schools increased 30.9% (Broughton, 2008). Although the partnership with News Corp for the Big Ten Network (BTN) goes through 2032, its football and basketball agreements with ABC/ESPN and CBS expired after the 2017 season (Sherman, 2015). That year, the Big 10 announced a six-year partnership with ESPN and Fox Sports for $2.4 billion (Greenstein, 2017). As noted previously, the Big 10 had NCAA record conference revenues in its 2018 fiscal year ($759 million). Revenues increased 48% from the 2017 fiscal year. This increase coincided with the new Big 10 television agreements that began at the start of the 2017–2018 school year (Berkowitz, 2019).

SEC Network was created in partnership with ESPN and grew out of its 2008 media rights deal with the network. Following the Big 10's lead, the ESPN-owned SEC Network launched in 2014 and will generate revenues for the conference through 2034 (McMurphy, 2015). The SEC also began negotiating for a new rights deal for its Saturday afternoon television package of 15 to 17 games. Currently the conference receives $55 million from CBS. That contract ends after the 2023 football season. The SEC is reportedly receiving offers in excess of $300 million per year for these rights (Ourand, 2019).

As the Big 10 and SEC illustrate, the earning power of a conference has a positive impact on its member schools. Most of a conference's revenue is distributed to its member schools (see Exhibit 14.4). In the SEC, payments to member schools range from $35.8 million to $45.5 million. Mississippi received about $7 million less than other SEC schools due to its football bowl ban. The Big XII earned less as a conference in overall revenues in 2017, and its member schools received less revenue too, ranging from $33.2 million to $35.6 million.

DIVISION I–FBS, GROUP OF 5 CONFERENCES

Exhibit 14.5 highlights the revenues and expenses of two Division I–FBS Group of 5 conferences: C-USA and the American Athletic Conference (AAC). By comparing the revenues of the conferences in Exhibits 14.4 and 14.5, we can see the importance of media rights in generating conference revenue. All four conferences compete at the same level, but not having their own networks or large media rights agreements for the broadcast of football, basketball, and other sports affects overall conference revenue and, in turn, that of member schools. Whereas C-USA received $3.7 million in television and marketing revenues and the AAC reported $21.5 million in media revenues, the SEC received $432.1 million and the Big XII received $237.2 million. These figures make it clear that the leveraging of games—primarily football and conference basketball games—through a media rights deal is critical to conference revenue generation.

Exhibit 14.5 also illustrates the benefits of having a conference championship in football. The AAC clearly identifies revenues from its conference championships in its federal filing, at $3.2 million in 2017. Further, we can see the importance of quality basketball programs. Without a guaranteed annual participant in a College Football Playoff game or a bowl affiliated with the College Football Playoff, conferences must rely on teams from schools like Western Kentucky or Memphis to generate revenues in the NCAA Men's Basketball Championship tournament. C-USA generated $3.2 million in 2017 in basketball revenue. While the AAC does not break out types of post-season revenues in its filing, the conference generated $45.0 million during the post-season for all of its sports combined. In 2017, the AAC received $21.5 million in television revenue, which is just over half the *total* revenues received by C-USA—although it is a small fraction of the $432.1 million in television revenue the SEC received.

Exhibit 14.5 reveals an impact of the arm's race. UAB's decision to stop and then restart its football program affected its conference distribution in 2017, receiving about a third as much as the next lowest school. Wichita State joined the AAC as a non-football member in 2017, while Navy is a football only member since 2015.

Exhibit 14.6 lists the revenues and expenses of the Atlantic 10 (A10) Conference. The schools of the A10 are Division I members, and the conference's main sources of revenue are related to basketball, as Exhibit 14.6 shows. The conference received $22.5 million from the NCAA for its men's basketball

CONFERENCE USA		AMERICAN ATHLETIC CONFERENCE	
REVENUE		**REVENUE**	
Television and marketing	$3,672,618	Post-season tournaments	$44,998,023
Contributions, gifts, grants received	$446,943	Television and radio rights	$21,464,200
Other	$4,773,994	NCAA sponsorships and grants	$6,391,593
Membership dues	$4,841,385	Conference championships	$3,164,769
College Football Playoff revenue	$15,441,232	Corporate sponsors	$1,234,381
NCAA/NIT tournament revenue	$3,227,568	Contributions, gifts, grants received	$288,784
Investment income	$205,564	Other services revenue	$146,541
Royalties	$14,821	Investment income	$94,806
Bowl revenue	$3,301,159	Miscellaneous income	$10,653
Student athlete opportunity	$2,824,566		
Total Revenue	$38,749,850	Total Revenue	$77,793,750
Expenses		**Expenses**	
Payments to members		Payments to members	
Middle Tennessee	$2,921,341	Connecticut	$9,159,706
Western Kentucky	$2,271,255	South Florida	$8,914,679
Louisiana Tech	$2,179,172	Cincinnati	$7,610,012
ODU	$2,168,452	Central Florida	$7,429,397
Texas San Antonio	$1,768,276	Houston	$5,433,315
Southern Mississippi	$1,637,810	Memphis	$5,184,811
North Texas	$1,515,577	Temple	$4,987,876
UNC Charlotte	$1,360,622	Southern Methodist	$4,553,210
Marshall	$1,355,324	East Carolina	$3,885,640

(continued)

EXHIBIT 14.5 Cont.

CONFERENCE USA		AMERICAN ATHLETIC CONFERENCE	
Rice	$1,328,386	Tulsa	$3,852,990
Texas El Paso	$1,316,861	Tulane	$3,742,756
Florida International	$1,161,941	Naval Academy	$3,156,071
Florida Atlantic	$1,142,433	Wichita State	$11,691
UAB	$483,597	Officiating	$5,648,777
Post-season events	$7,894,105	Salaries	$5,187,699
Other disbursements	$4,520,058	Championships	$3,229,943
Salaries	$2,102,815	Advertising and promotion	$1,110,087
Production and game management	$712,365	Employee benefits and pension	$855,999
Employee benefits and pension	$527,471	Rent	$756,442
Legal fees	$334,265	Uninsured losses	$625,717
Conferences, conventions, meetings	$285,347	Other	$599,330
Rent	$248,064	Conferences, conventions, and meetings	$381,059
Insurance	$235,610	Insurance	$346,834
Other	$222,363	Information technology	$298,629
Office expenses	$220,106	Travel	$253,739
Advertising and promotions	$150,694	Payroll taxes	$242,806
Payroll taxes	$135,723	Office expenses	$150,801
Grants, scholarships, fellowships	$56,000	Legal fees	$109,674
Depreciation and amortization	$49,669	Depreciation and amortization	$37,612
Travel	$41,610	Accounting expenses	$34,215
Accounting expenses	$31,018		
Total Expenses	$40,378,330	Total Expenses	$87,791,517

Note: Figures based on each conference's 2017 IRS Form 990.

ATLANTIC 10	
Revenue	
NCAA/NIT tournament revenue	$22,581,351
Television and marketing	$4,797,260
Investment income	$1,058,612
Grants, gifts, and contributions	$590,727
Other	$265,463
Licensing	$130,675
Total Revenue	$29,424,088
Expenses	
Payments to members	$19,949,300
Salaries	$2,462,076
Production and game management	$1,310,113
Other	$710,715
Employee benefits and pension	$344,527
Conferences, conventions, meetings	$277,808
Travel	$240,756
Rent	$187,751
Office expenses	$154,280
Advertising and promotions	$137,450
Payroll taxes	$108,171
Information technology	$98,627
Insurance	$91,300
Grants and assistance	$37,250
Depreciation and amortization	$35,824
Accounting expenses	$31,066
Legal fees	$20,290
Investment management fees	$472
Total Expenses	$26,197,776

Note: Figures based on the conference's 2017 IRS Form 990.

tournament appearances, more than C-USA received. As the A10 receives no football revenues compared to schools in Division I–FBS conferences, distributions to A10 member schools are considerably less than the distributions to Division I–FBS member schools. The A10 lists only the total distribution to its membership—$19.9 million in FY 2017. With 14 member institutions in 2017, that averages to $1.36 million per institution.

Schools

The revenues that member schools receive from conference distributions are important, but they are a small percentage of overall departmental revenues, according to the Knight Commission on Intercollegiate Athletics (2018). On average, distributions from the NCAA and conferences account for only 21.8% of a Division I–FBS program's general revenues. For schools in major conferences, the largest portion of the athletic program's revenues comes from football (see Exhibit 14.7). However, even with large revenues coming from the NCAA and

EXHIBIT 14.7 Michigan athletic department budget.

FISCAL YEAR 2020 OPERATING BUDGET (IN THOUSANDS)		
REVENUES	**BUDGETED AMOUNT**	**% OF TOTAL**
Spectator admissions		
Football	$49,500	25%
Basketball	$4,675	2%
Hockey	$1,775	1%
Other	$658	0%
Conference distributions	$55,924	28%
Priority seating		
Football	$28,300	14%
Basketball	$2,001	1%
Hockey	$460	0%
Gifts and scholarship fund	$6,500	3%
Corporate sponsorship	$18,481	9%
Licensing royalties	$9,854	5%
Facilities	$4,898	2%
Concessions/parking	$3,941	2%

EXHIBIT 14.7   Cont.

FISCAL YEAR 2020 OPERATING BUDGET (IN THOUSANDS)

REVENUES	BUDGETED AMOUNT	% OF TOTAL
Other	$2,843	1%
Investment income	$6,450	3%
Current Revenues	$196,260	100%
Expenses		
Salaries	$75,083	36%
Student financial aid	$28,310	14%
Team and game expense	$38,269	16%
Transfer to university	$7,978	1%
Facilities	$10,276	7%
Deferred maintenance fund transfer	$4,000	3%
Other operating and administrative expenses	$14,985	11%
Debt service transfer	$17,359	10%
Current Expenses	$196,260	100%
Net Operating Surplus	$0.00	

Source: University of Michigan (2019).

conferences, and football revenues supporting the overall athletic programs at major schools, it can still be difficult for these programs to earn a profit. For an example of the financial difficulties that athletic departments face, read Sidebar 14.B, which discusses the situation at the University of South Carolina.

The financial difficulties at the University of South Carolina described in Sidebar 14.B are not uncommon. The NCAA noted that only 29 Division I athletic departments had revenues that exceeded expenses in 2018 ("Finances of," 2019). The average surplus for these 29 schools was $9.3 million. For the 65 universities in the Autonomous 5, the median expense exceeded revenues by 2.6 million. For the remainder of Division I, median expenses were $22 million greater than revenues. Compounding the financial difficulties for schools is the fact that, although revenues are growing each year, expenses are growing faster, due to increases in scholarship costs, escalating costs for football and men's basketball coaches, and the costs of building new or renovating old athletic facilities.

SIDEBAR 14.B   Financial Turnaround for an Intercollegiate Athletic Program

When Eric Hyman was hired as the athletic director at the University of South Carolina in 2005, he inherited a program that had lost $2.65 million in the previous year. In his first year as athletic director, the program lost another $2.46 million. Fortunately, the department had a reserve fund that covered some of the losses (Person, 2006a). However, the department eventually needed a $2.74 million subsidy from the university (Person, 2008). One reason for the department's poor financial shape was a change to the football coaching staff. The department owed buyouts to several members of former coach Lou Holtz's staff, and for a few months paid salaries to both Holtz's staff and coach Steve Spurrier's staff (Person, 2006a).

Upon arriving on campus, Hyman recognized the department's financial issues and set out to increase revenues and control costs. To increase revenues, Hyman turned to the department's strength. By raising ticket prices to football games by $10 per ticket, the program raised an additional $4.5 million (Person, 2006a). The department also began planning to overhaul its ticket distribution system for football games, in an effort to increase revenues from members of the Gamecock Club, the South Carolina athletic department's athletic support group. Under the existing system, to qualify for a season ticket package, an individual first had to make a donation to the Gamecock Club. Then, based on the amount of the person's giving and the number of years the individual had given, the department determined the person's season ticket package eligibility. Packages ranged from a full package (all seven home games) to a partial, four-game package featuring the team's lesser opponents. Donors were rewarded for longevity, not the total amount they had given to the booster organization. To increase revenues, Hyman instituted a premium seating system.

South Carolina's premium seating system is referred to as yearly equitable seating (YES). The system was created to honor the loyalty of past donors while balancing donors' giving level and history of donations. To keep their seats for Gamecock football games during the 2009 season, members had to maintain their 2008 Gamecock Club membership status through annual giving to the club. The Gamecock Club members were also required to make a YES donation ranging from $50 to $395 per seat, based on seat location.

As a comparison, Auburn University initiated a premium seating system at the same time that was expected to generate an additional $3.5 million in revenues annually. To keep a seat located between the 30-yard lines and in the lower bowl, Auburn season ticket holders were required to make an additional donation of $400 per ticket. In other sections, season ticket holders were required to donate an additional $200 or $300 per seat (Person, 2006b).

The South Carolina athletic department's changes enabled the department to reverse its financial position by the end of 2007. Exhibit

14.8 gives the department's pre-pandemic fiscal year 2021 budget. Seat fees added $7.9 million in revenue on top of the $13.0 million collected through membership in the Gamecock Club. The department has run a surplus since 2007.

Since FY 2007, the South Carolina athletic department has been able to replenish its reserve fund through departmental surpluses. Revenues have grown from $48.1 million in 2007 to what was a pre-COVID forecast of $127.1 million in 2021. In addition to increasing its football ticket revenues, the department extended its partnership with IMG. The ten-year agreement began in 2017 and included enhanced signage in its basketball arena, baseball stadium, and football stadium in addition to $110 million for multimedia rights (Del Bianco, 2016). Increases resulting from the SEC's lucrative media rights deals, the YES program, and a new sales program have led to a 153% increase in revenues over 14 years.

FINANCIAL PROFITABILITY

To examine an athletic department's profitability is a challenging task. As mentioned earlier, the reporting of financial data is not standardized. One institution's method of recording revenues and expenses is likely different from another institution's. As a result, institutions often have difficulty comparing their financial performance to benchmarks published by the NCAA. Another source of difficulty is that individuals analyzing athletic department performance frequently treat revenues allocated to the department in varying ways. For example, *USA Today* publishes on its website revenues and expenses of 227 Division I public colleges and universities (see http://sports.usatoday.com/ncaa/finances/).[2] The data for FY 2019 show that 81 athletic departments lost money; 146 schools reported a profit or broke even. These results contrast with the NCAA's statement that in FY 2018, only 29 Division I institutions (all FBS schools) were self-sustaining.

Without examining the financial data, we would probably expect that a school affiliated with a major conference would be in better financial standing than one that is not. An examination of only the net operating surplus or net operating deficit (expense to revenue difference), however, would also be superficial. To understand the financial strength of an athletic department, we must examine revenue closely.

A quick glance at the revenues and expenses in the *USA Today* database shows that 81 schools lost money in 2019. When we do this, however, we are looking only at the expenses to revenue differences for each athletic department, while ignoring significant variations in the way departmental revenues were reported at many of the schools in the study. Revenues are reported to the NCAA in two categories: **department-generated revenues** are those revenues

2   Data were obtained through freedom of information (FOI) requests. *USA Today* sent requests to the public schools that have an obligation to release their data through FOI requests. Private institutions have no legal obligation to comply with such requests, and none has done so. Also, state law in Pennsylvania and Delaware exempts schools in those states from complying.

EXHIBIT 14.8   University of South Carolina athletic department budget.

FISCAL YEAR 2021	
Revenues	
Ticket sales	$19,528,000
Guarantees	$0
Premium seating	$7,877,500
Student fees	$2,875,000
Gamecock Club revenues	$12,970,400
Gifts and donations	$9,950,000
NCAA/SEC distributions	$47,415,000
Sponsorships, media rights, royalties	$17,555,000
Ancillary sales	$5,080,000
Other revenue	$3,885,500
Total Revenues from Departmental Operations	$127,136,400
Expenses	
Salaries	$54,236,300
Grants-in-aid	$12,731,200
Team travel	$6,999,400
General travel	$369,100
Recruiting	$1,966,100
Team and department functions	$2,394,800
Game services	$7,696,300
General services	$3,189,500
Marketing services	$1,278,400
Uniforms, supplies & equipment	$7,235,900
Facilities	$8,811,800
General and administrative	$4,511,300
Guarantees	$2,776,600
Total Expenditures from Department Operations	$114,196,700

EXHIBIT 14.8 Cont.

FISCAL YEAR 2021	
Operating Revenue over Expenditures	
Before transfers	$12,939,700
Transfers	
Transfer to university (net)	$1,097,000
Transfer to university scholarships	$4,094,500
Transfer to university auxiliary	$180,000
Transfer to university R&R/capital projects	$1,500,000
Transfer to debt service	$4,602,200
Total Transfers (net)	$11,473,700
Revenue over Expenditures and Transfers	$1,466,000

Source: University of South Carolina (2020).

generated independently by the athletic department and its programs; **allocated revenues** are revenues that the school transfers to the athletic department. These revenues are not generated by the athletic department but given to the department by the institution or a governmental entity. As Brady, Berkowitz, and Schnaars (2015) note, allocated revenues are bailouts by universities that enable their athletic departments to balance their books. When the NCAA reported that 29 schools were **self-sustaining** in 2019, it meant that the revenues generated by these athletic departments alone covered each department's operating expenses. These institutions did not need to allocate revenues to offset revenue shortfalls in their athletic departments.

To understand the importance of allocated revenue versus department-generated revenues better, let's compare revenue and expense data submitted to *USA Today* for two athletic departments. Exhibit 14.9 lists the revenues and expenditures for FY 2019 of the University of Memphis and Iowa State University, as reported by *USA Today*. Memphis, a member of the American Athletic Conference, had a net operating surplus of $320,784. Iowa State, a member of the Big XII, had net operating income of $96,508. According to *USA Today*, 36.9% of Memphis's revenues were allocated revenues, while only 2.2% of Iowa State's revenues were allocated revenues. If we remove allocated revenues from the analysis, Memphis had $35.2 million of operating revenues and $55.5 million in operating expenses, for an operating expense to revenue difference of –$20.3 million. For Iowa State, the expense to revenue difference is –$2.0 million. Hence, although the raw data contained in the *USA Today* reports make it appear that the Memphis athletic department was in the stronger financial position, in reality the athletic department at Iowa State was

EXHIBIT 14.9   2019 revenues and expenses of two Division I–FBS universities.

	MEMPHIS		IOWA STATE	
	AMOUNT	% OF TOTAL	AMOUNT	% OF TOTAL
Revenues				
Department Generated Revenues				
Total ticket sales	$10,755,844	19.3%	$16,474,938	17.3%
Rights/licensing/NCAA & conference distributions	$10,648,541	19.1%	$52,016,490	54.5%
Cash contributions from alumni and others	$13,063,202	23.4%	$18,206,649	19.1%
Other	$772,010	1.4%	$6,659,493	7.0%
Total Generated Revenues	$35,239,597	63.1%	$93,357,570	97.8%
Allocated Revenues				
Institutional support	$13,624,357	24.4%	$0	0.0%
Student fees	$6,951,155	12.5%	$2,054,314	2.2%
Total Allocated Revenues	$20,575,512	36.9%	$2,054,314	2.2%
Total All Revenues	$55,815,109	100.0%	$95,411,884	100.0%
Expenses				
Grants-in-aid	$9,503,874	32.9%	$9,518,283	14.0%
Salaries and benefits	$19,102,707	37.1%	$31,430,716	40.2%
Building/grounds	$3,834,748	0.7%	$20,975,219	10.5%
Other	$23,052,996	29.3%	$33,391,158	35.2%
Total Operating Expenses	$55,494,325	100.0%	$95,315,376	100.0%
Expense to Revenue Difference	$320,784		$96,508	

Source: Data compiled from NCAA Financial Reports Database. Available at http://sports.usatoday.com/ncaa/finances/.

much stronger, as it could nearly cover its operating expenses with its operating revenues, whereas Memphis relied heavily on institutional support and student fees to operate its department.

Moreover, both the *USA Today* revenue and expense reports and NCAA's statement regarding self-sufficiency neglect a significant expense: debt service on athletic facilities. Both Memphis and Iowa State report only operating expenses and fail to include debt service and costs for replacement of facilities in expenses. The athletic department budget given in Exhibit 14.8 shows the impact of these expenditures on profitability. South Carolina shows a net operating surplus of $12.9 million. When non-operating expenses are subtracted, South Carolina has a net increase of $1.5 million in its operating surplus. Considering debt service and transfers to the university reduces profit further and at times turns a profit into a loss. Based on analysis of these two budgets, we can conjecture that the number of self-supporting Division I athletic departments is fewer than the NCAA's estimate.

SIDEBAR 14.C   A Deeper Look at Athletic Department Budgets

An argument has been made—and was used in the *O'Bannon* case—that the NCAA intentionally provides inaccurate data when reporting on the financial health of athletic departments (Goff & Wilson, 2013). The main tenets of this argument are that data presented in the NCAA reports on revenue and expenses in its divisions include one-way adjustments that reduce revenue, while adjustments for items that would increase revenue or reduce expenses are not made. Next, as athletic departments operate in a non-profit setting, there is not an incentive to show a profit. Without equity holders in the "business" closely monitoring revenues and expenses in order to produce profits and generate dividend payments, a use-it-or-lose-it budget management process may develop (see Chapter 6 on budgeting). Finally, on college campuses, significant related-party transactions often occur, which hide the true size and scope of the athletic department by understating substantial sources of profits. These related-party transactions primarily include business done between the parent company (the university) and its subsidiary (the athletic department) and business done between two subsidiaries (e.g., the athletic department and university housing) of a common parent (the university). See Exhibit 14.10 for examples.

Several studies support the notion that profit and loss statements for athletic departments understate profits. Borland, Goff, and Pulsinelli (1992) found that a reported $1.5 million loss for Western Kentucky University athletics was only a $330,000 loss when it was adjusted for several related-party transactions. For example, concessions revenues were understated, and the costs of providing food and grants-in-aid to athletes were overstated. When the researchers also accounted for the enrollment impact of athletics on the university as a whole, a $5 million gain was seen. Regarding the impact on enrollment (positive in this case), the statement is often made that "athletics are the front porch of the university." However, the athletic department receives no credit for its marketing and public relations work on behalf of the institution. Other studies with similar findings include those by Skousen and Condie (1988), Goff (2000), and Rascher and Howell (2011).

EXHIBIT 14.10   Examples of possible related-party transactions in collegiate athletics.

Revenues undervalued
- Concessions
- Sport camps
- Licensing
- Merchandise (bookstore)
- Parking

Revenues not listed
- Athletic donations directly to tuition
- The marketing arm of the university
- Increase in applicants due to the "Flutie Effect" (athletic success yields more applications)
- Enrollment of non-tuition athletes
- Increases in quality of freshmen applicants
- Increases in retention rates and graduation rates
- Higher tuition at capacity constrained schools
- Increases in diversity
- Increases in overall university donations
- Increases in media coverage of the university

Expenses overvalued
- Gifts-in-kind
- Food (40% of listed cost)
- Books (80% of wholesale)
- Room (may be very low cost if not excess demand)
- Tuition (no out-of-pocket cost unless the non-paying student-athlete blocks a full-paying non-athlete from taking course)
- Gold-plating (use-it-or-lose-it)

Expenses not listed
- Cleaning and security for events
- Capital costs
- Student services and compliance costs for specific athletic-related work (Registrar's Office, Admissions, Financial Aid, Data Services)

DIVISION I: SCHOOL TRENDS AND PERFORMANCE

Exhibit 14.11 gives a breakdown of median revenues and expenses for Division I athletic departments by subdivision. The median revenues are based on data collected for the 2009–2018 *NCAA Financial Database* (NCAA, 2019). For FBS Autonomous 5 schools, the median revenue was $113.6 million, while the medians for FBS Group of 5, FCS and non-football Division I programs were $37.6 million, $19.2 million, and $17.5 million, respectively. It is important to note that there was not much difference among the median values within allocated revenues, direct and indirect institutional support across all subdivisions except FBS Autonomous 5. The FBS Autonomous 5 group median was significantly lower in direct and indirect institutional support. Student fees were highest among the FBS Group of 5. The primary difference in total revenue

EXHIBIT 14.11   Median operating revenues and expenses for Division I athletic departments by subdivision.

FY 2018	FBS AUTONOMOUS 5	FBS GROUP OF 5	FCS	NON-FOOTBALL SUBDIVISION
Revenues				
Department-generated revenues				
Total ticket sales	$18,700	$2,000	$500	$300
NCAA and conference distributions	$11,900	$3,100	$1,000	$600
Bowl games	$1,200	$200	$ -	$ -
Guarantees and options	$500	$1,500	$700	$200
Contributions from alumni and others	$23,900	$3,800	$1,100	$800
Other:				
Concessions/ programs/novelties	$2,000	$200	$100	$ -
Media rights	$25,600	$100	$ -	$ -
Royalties/licensing/ advertising/ sponsorship	$9,600	$1,400	$300	$400
Sports camps	$100	$ -	$ -	$ -
Endowment/ Investment income	$1,600	$100	$ -	$100
Miscellaneous	$2,200	$600	$200	$200
Total Generated Revenues	$106,340	$13,910	$4,940	$3,320

(*continued*)

EXHIBIT 14.11   Cont.

FY 2018	FBS AUTONOMOUS 5	FBS GROUP OF 5	FCS	NON-FOOTBALL SUBDIVISION
Allocated revenues				
Direct institutional support	$1,500	$9,500	$9,000	$10,100
Indirect institutional support	$ -	$1,300	$1,200	$1,100
Student fees	$300	$6,000	$1,000	$300
Total All Revenues	$113,640	$37,590	$19,180	$17,470
Expenses				
Grants-in-aid	$14,500	$7,800	$5,200	$5,100
Guarantees and options	$2,100	$700	$100	$100
Administrative compensation	$19,200	$5,000	$2,400	$2,500
Coaching compensation	$21,300	$6,900	$3,500	$3,000
Severance pay	$700	$ -	$ -	$ -
Team travel	$6,600	$2,800	$1,700	$1,400
Student-athlete meals (non-travel)	$1,700	$400	$100	$100
Recruiting	$1,800	$600	$300	$300
Fundraising	$2,300	$800	$200	$300

EXHIBIT 14.11   Cont.

FY 2018	FBS AUTONOMOUS 5	FBS GROUP OF 5	FCS	NON-FOOTBALL SUBDIVISION
Game expenses	$4,600	$1,200	$400	$400
Bowl expenses	$1,700	$300	$ -	$ -
Medical and insurance	$1,300	$600	$300	$200
Membership dues	$100	$300	$100	$100
Sports camps	$ -	$ -	$ -	$ -
Spirit groups	$400	$100	$ -	$ -
Facilities maintenance and rental	$22,100	$3,500	$800	$700
Indirect facilities and support	$ -	$600	$900	$900
Other	$6,800	$2,000	$700	$500
Total Operating Expenses	$115,240	$37,530	$ 18,820	$17,460
Net Generated Revenues (Generated revenues – total expenses)	$(2,610)	$(22,160)	$13,900	$(13,300)
Net Revenue (Total revenue – total expenses)	$2,730	$ -	$ -	$ -

Note: Revenues and expenses were reported in median dollars. Median values cannot be added; therefore, the total amounts are the median totals for the data collected. They are not the summations of data presented in this table.

Source: NCAA (2019).

results from revenues generated by the athletic department. The median was $106.3 million for FBS Autonomy 5 schools, $13.9 million for FBS Group of 5 schools, $4.9 million for FCS schools, and $3.2 million for the non-football schools. Large differences in median values among subdivisions are found in ticket sales, NCAA and conference distributions, contributions, media rights, and game day revenues (concessions/programs/novelties).

The median operating expense for an FBS Autonomous 5 school was $115.2 million; it was $37.5 million for FBS Group of 5 schools, $18.8 million for FCS schools, and $17.5 million for non-football schools (see Exhibit 14.11). Likely, the differences in expenses are tied to costs associated with running FBS Autonomous 5 football programs. For example, the varying costs for scholarship football players affected median values for scholarships across the three subdivisions. For the FBS Autonomous 5, the median cost was $14.5 million; for FBS Group of 5, $7.8; for FCS schools, $5.2 million; and for the non-basketball subdivision, $5.1 million.

Guarantees, a fixture of FBS programs with seven home football games per season, have a median cost of $2.1 million for FBS Autonomous 5 programs, compared to $700,000 for FBS Group of 5 schools, $100,000 for FCS schools, and $100,000 for non-football schools. The cost of operating major programs, both football and basketball, is reflected in the median values of university-paid coaching salaries and benefits; we see a large difference in median values among subdivisions: $21.3 million for FBS Autonomous 5 schools, $6.9 million for FBS Group of 5 schools, $3.5 million for FCS schools, and $3.0 million for non-basketball schools. The same can be said for major differences in median expenses between FBS schools and the rest of Division I schools for team travel, recruiting, game expenses, and facility maintenance and rental.

The NCAA also analyzed trends during a 14-year span (2004–2018). The association noted that from 2004 to 2018, median generated revenues rose 140% for FBS Autonomous 5 schools, 44% for FBS Group of 5 schools, 123% for FCS schools, and 105% for non-football schools. Expenses grew on par with revenues for FBS Autonomous 5 schools during the same time frame. They were up 87% in FBS Group of 5 schools, 116% for FCS schools, and 120% for non-football schools. As a result, median losses remained constant or grew across all three subdivisions.

The major sources of revenue during each of the 14 years of the study were ticket sales and contributions from alumni and others. This was true across all three subdivisions. Similarly, two items were the major expenses across the three subdivisions: grants-in-aid (or scholarships), and salaries and benefits. The NCAA noted that these two expenses make it difficult for athletic departments to control costs. As the cost of tuition increases nationwide, the cost for providing scholarships correspondingly increases for all schools. In the case of salaries and benefits, market demand for top coaches drives these costs.

The NCAA also discussed programmatic trends. For FBS schools, total athletic expenditures as a percentage of the total university budget grew from 4.5% in 2005 to 6.0% in 2018. For FCS schools, growth was greater: 6% to over 8%. For the schools in the non-basketball category, expenditures have fluctuated as a percentage of overall budgets, ranging from 5% to 6.7% over the same time frame. These trends indicate that it is becoming increasingly difficult for most athletic departments to maintain a high ratio of generated revenue to expenses—a measure of self-sufficiency. This is referred to by the NCAA as Positive Generated Net Revenue (PNR). The number of schools across Division I with PNR ranged from 16 to 29 from 2005 to 2018. In 2018, the average PNR for schools reporting PNR was $9.1 million.

DIVISION II: SCHOOL TRENDS AND PERFORMANCE

Exhibit 14.12 gives revenues and expenses for the average Division II program. Division II programs are classified as either football or non-football. Like the Division I reports, the Division II reports provide information on median revenues and expenses in each classification. For Division II programs with football, the average generated revenues were $860,000, with allocated revenues bringing the total to $7.6 million. Non-football program generated revenues averaged $390,400, with allocated revenues bringing total revenue to $5.5 million. We can see major generated-revenue differences between the two classifications. Under allocated revenues, approximately $1.4 million more institutional support was provided for football programs than for non-football programs.

As with revenues, expenses were greater for Division II programs with football. Although scholarship costs were only $200,000 higher for football programs, coaching salaries were $600,000 higher for these programs.

The NCAA (2019) discussed trends in Division II athletic department financial operations. The benchmarks cover the 2018 fiscal year. Between 2004 and 2018, negative net generated revenue (generated revenues minus total expenses) grew from –$2.7 million in 2005 to –$6.1 million in 2018 for programs with football. For those without football, negative net generated revenue grew from –$2.0 million to –$5.2 million over the same period. Universities are, therefore, making up the increases in Division II budgets through increases in allocated revenues. The impact on revenue growth of increases in institutional support is evident, as 62% of revenue received by programs with football is direct institutional support, while the figure is 69% for programs without football. As with Division I programs, the two largest expense categories were grants-in-aid and salaries.

DIVISION III—SCHOOL TRENDS AND PERFORMANCE

Exhibit 14.12 also provides median expenses for Division III athletic departments, also classified as football or non-football. As with the benchmark data for Division II programs, the most recent publicly available Division III data cover the 2018 fiscal year (NCAA, 2019). For programs with football, operating expenses increased 130% from 2004. The increase was 171% for programs without football. As Division III schools offer no grants-in-aid for athletes, major expenses were slightly different than for Division I and II programs. Still, salaries were major expenses.

ATHLETIC DEPARTMENT FUNDRAISING

Analysis of NCAA revenues and expenses shows that for most programs operating expenses are increasing faster than operating revenues. In fact, the desire of some university administrators and alumni to win, coupled with rising salary and scholarship costs, caused growth in athletic department spending

EXHIBIT 14.12 Median operating revenues and expenses for Division II and Division III athletic departments by classification.

FY 2018	DIVISION II		DIVISION III	
	FOOTBALL	NON-FOOTBALL	FOOTBALL	NON-FOOTBALL
Revenues				
Department-generated revenues				
Total ticket sales	$100	$ -	$ -	$ -
Contributions from alumni and others	$300	$100	$200	$100
Other:				
Sports camps	$100	$ -	$ -	$ -
Total Generated Revenues	$860	$390	$390	$170
Allocated revenues				
Direct institutional support	$4,400	$3,800	$2,900	$1,200
Indirect institutional support	$600	$400	$600	$200
Student fees	$400	$ -	$ -	$ -
Total All Revenues	$7,060	$5,490	$4,210	$2,250
Expenses				
Grants-in-aid	$2,200	$2,000	$ -	$ -
Compensation—administration	$800	$700	$690	$550

EXHIBIT 14.12   Cont.

FY 2018	DIVISION II		DIVISION III	
	FOOTBALL	**NON-FOOTBALL**	**FOOTBALL**	**NON-FOOTBALL**
Compensation—coaches	$1,600	$1,000	$1,390	$690
Team travel	$500	$500	$500	$290
Student-athlete meals (non-travel)	$20	$ -	$ -	$ -
Recruiting	$70	$40	$70	$30
Fundraising	$40	$20	$10	$10
Game expenses	$100	$100	$110	$90
Medical and insurance	$120	$70	$70	$20
Membership dues	$40	$30	$30	$30
Sports camps	$20	$ -	$ -	$ -
Spirit groups	$10	$ -	$ -	$ -
Facilities maintenance and rental	$140	$90	$90	$40
Indirect facilities and administrative support	$490	$380	$380	$130
Other	$120	$110	$130	$40
Total Operating Expenses	$7,180	$5,610	$4,140	$2,320
Net Generated Revenues (Generated revenues – total expenses)	$(6,060)	$(5,180)	$(3,540)	$(2,070)
Net Revenue (Total revenue – total expenses)	$ -	$ -	$ -	$ -

Note: Revenues and expenses were reported in median dollars. Median values cannot be added; therefore, the total amounts are the median totals for the data collected. They are not the summations of data presented in this table.
Source: NCAA (2019).

to outpace overall university growth. From 2009 to 2018, athletic expenses as a proportion of institutional expenses grew from 22.2% to 27.8% across NCAA Division I institutions (NCAA, 2019). For Division II, the growth was from 10.9% of institutional expenses to 16.0%. Division III grew as well, from 6.9% to 8.8%. This growth led schools, with the exception of Autonomous 5 athletics departments, to become increasingly reliant on allocated revenues, especially direct and indirect institutional support and student fees.

However, with many public universities facing cuts in state appropriations, athletic departments are being pressured to reduce their reliance on allocated resources. This is especially true in fiscal years 2020 and 2021. Due to the coronavirus pandemic's impact on universities and sport, both university and athletic department revenues were severely impacted. Fortunately for post-pandemic athletic program finances, organizations such as the Knight Commission on Intercollegiate Athletics have been examining ways to reform college sport, including finances. The financing of college athletics and the commercialization of many athletic programs are issues that unite university administrators, faculty, and students (Lewin, 2014).

On campuses where pressure is growing to reduce the athletic department's allocated resources, the development staff must find ways to generate greater amounts of revenue through giving. These development officers must raise increasing amounts of revenue not only for the operating budget but also to fund new athletic facilities on campus. Athletic fundraising, therefore, is crucial, as monies generated through the development office will offset the rising expenses of operating an athletic department and help to reduce the department's reliance on allocated revenues. Across the NCAA, athletic departments and their affiliated booster clubs raised $2.9 billion (15.9% of overall revenues) during 2018 (NCAA, 2019). The majority of this money was raised through such initiatives as capital campaigns and annual giving programs.

The Capital Campaign

Much of the money that athletic departments raise goes to offset the costs of new facilities and other capital projects. Usually, when an athletic department needs to begin replacing its older facilities, the department will initiate a **capital campaign**, an intensive effort to raise funds in a defined time frame through gifts and pledges for a specific purpose. When infrastructure built with public funds needs replacing, athletic departments increasingly turn to fundraising. From 2009 to 2018, the amount of revenue generated by athletic departments through fundraising nearly doubled (NCAA, 2019). For example, Texas A&M raised $85.4 million in 2019, with a majority of the funding going towards athletic facilities. As another example, Michigan State University raised $286 million as part of the university's $1.8 billion Empower Extraordinary campaign. Of the money raised, 35% is earmarked for facility projects and 19% for endowments. Texas Tech University Athletics wrapped up its Campaign for Fearless Champions in 2020. The goal of the campaign was to raise $185 million, of which $160 million would go toward capital support, $15 million toward endowment support, and $10 million toward ongoing support through planned giving (Texas Tech University Athletics, 2020). In 2019, the University of Maryland announced a $36 million campaign to fund a new basketball performance center. The center will feature two full-size practice courts, a strength and conditioning area tailored to basketball players, and new meeting and office spaces for coaches and staff.

MAKING A CASE

One of the most important elements of a capital campaign is the **campaign case statement**. The case statement answers all the critical questions regarding the campaign and presents arguments for why an individual should support the campaign. The case statement also lets potential donors know how they can give to the campaign. According to Kihlstedt (2009), a typical case statement includes six sections:

1. Institutional mission
2. Record of accomplishment
3. Directions for the future
4. Urgent and continuing development objectives
5. Plan of action to accomplish future objectives
6. The institution's sponsorship.

For a better understanding of each of these sections, examine the case statement presented in Exhibit 14.13 for the Texas Tech University athletic department's "Fearless Champions" campaign.

MAJOR GIFTS PLANNING

To reach a capital campaign goal, a development department needs to receive major gifts from program supporters. Most development departments define a **major gift** as a donation worth $25,000 or more. The number, size, and types of major gifts needed to reach a campaign goal are determined through various mathematical formulas based on national giving patterns. A major gifts table is developed from these formulas. Dove (2000) notes that a major gifts table demonstrates the importance of major gifts to a campaign. Not only does the table provide an outline of the number and size of gifts needed to reach a campaign goal, it also serves as a reality test for the organization. After the table is developed, the organization can determine whether it indeed has enough prospective donors to reach the campaign goal.

Gift table rules. There are three major mathematical ways to create a major gifts table (Dove, 2000). The first applies the **80/20 rule**. This rule states that, based on past giving patterns, 80% of the needed funds will come from 20% of the donors. Hence, for Texas Tech, $148 million of the $185 million total would come from 20% of the campaign's donors. Trends in giving seem to be shifting, however. Some development officers now rely on the **90/10 rule**, which states that 90% of the total money needed for a campaign will come from 10% of the campaign's donors. On this basis, for the Texas Tech campaign, $166.5 million would come from 10% of those giving to the campaign.

The third model uses the **rule of thirds**. According to this rule, the top ten gifts to the campaign will account for 33% of the campaign's total goal; the next 100 gifts will account for an additional 33%, and the remaining gifts will account for the final third. For Texas Tech, $61.05 million would come from the top ten donors, $61.05 million would come from the next 100 donors, and the remaining funds would come from the rest of the campaign's donors.

EXHIBIT 14.13 Example case statement for Texas Tech University's Campaign for Fearless Champions, titled *For Our Fearless Champions.*

Institutional mission. The TTU athletic department's document contained the following statements regarding the department's mission:

- *Preparing our student-athletes for life after graduation is a key part of our mission at Texas Tech.*
- *We want to make access to a first-rate college education available for even more student-athletes.*

Record of accomplishment. In speaking of the department's record of accomplishment, the document contained the following:

- *Two national titles in individual sports*
- *First College World Series appearance and NCAA Super Regional Championship*
- *Fifteen NCAA All-America Honorees and one Academic All-America Honoree*
- *102 First Team All-Big 12 Selections and 72 Academic All-Big 12 Selections*

Future directions. The case statement should discuss the department's directions for the future. Texas Tech's case statement stated:

- *Such substantial upgrades will improve team facilities, modernize sports medicine areas and provide new fan amenities, setting the stage for the next decade of athletic accomplishments.*
- *Establishing an endowment guarantees the Fearless Champions Leadership Academy will become an integral and lasting component of Texas Tech Athletics.*

Development objectives. Texas Tech's urgent and continuing development objectives, which include the campaign's priorities and costs as well as the master plan, are expressed in the following statements:

- *Our competition and training facilities give us an advantage when recruiting prospective student-athletes … We have some of the best stadiums, arenas and fields in the Big 12, and we plan to keep them that way.*
- *Surpass $20 million in student-athlete scholarship endowments.*
- *Complete 25 facility projects that upgrade every sporting venue for our student-athletes and fans.*

Plan of action. In outlining its plan of action, TTU stated:

- *Unwavering in their loyalty to Texas Tech, [the student-athletes] deserve an equal commitment from each of us.*
- *Reaching our campaign goals will take a new level of support from our alumni and fans. Every gift counts, and each gift brings us closer to realizing our vision for the future of Texas Tech Athletics.*

Institution's sponsorship. Finally, the institution's sponsorship of the campaign is stated as follows:

- *Announcing The Campaign for Fearless Champions, Texas Tech University's effort to enhance our athletic facilities, invest in our scholarships endowments and grow the Fearless Champions Leadership Academy …*

Source: Texas Tech University Athletics (2020).

EXHIBIT 14.14   Traditional gifts table for a $185 million campaign.

GIFT AMOUNT	PROSPECTS NEEDED	GIFTS NEEDED	CUMULATIVE TOTAL	% OF GOAL
$18,500,000	4	1	$18,500,000	10%
$9,250,000	7	2	$37,000,000	20%
$4,625,000	12	4	$55,500,000	30%
$2,312,500	24	8	$74,000,000	40%
$1,156,250	48	16	$92,500,000	50%
$578,125	96	32	$111,000,000	60%
$289,063	192	64	$129,500,000	70%
$144,531	384	128	$148,000,000	80%
$72,266	768	256	$166,500,000	90%
> $31,250	Many	Many	$185,000,000	100%

Traditional gifts table. All of these rules lead to campaigns developing similar major gifts tables, known as **traditional gifts tables.**

For the $185 million Campaign for Fearless Champions, we would develop a traditional gifts table as follows (see Exhibit 14.14):

- The lead gift, or the largest single campaign gift, is set at 10% of the campaign goal—$18.5 million.
- The amount of the next largest gift is set to half of the lead gift, or $9.25 million, and we double the number of donors needed—i.e., we double one to get two.
- The value of the next largest gift is half of the previous gift amount ($4.625 million), and the number of needed donors is double the last number (four).
- We continue this process until the campaign goal is reached.

It must be noted that the table does not always work, especially as giving trends appear to be changing. In some instances, 10 to 15 donors have given 50% to 70% of the campaign totals. For some campaigns, the lead gift is set at an amount less than 10% of the campaign goal because an analysis of potential donors reveals little potential for a large lead gift. If the lead gift is set at a level less than 10% of the goal amount, there is a good chance that the campaign's goal will not be reached, as the mathematical standards that were developed based on actual past giving to campaigns will not have been met (Dove, 2000).

When finalizing the gift table, we must factor all known information regarding major gift possibilities into its formulation. For example, if it is known that a donor plans to give a large portion of the campaign total at the launch of the campaign, this gift must be factored into the table. Also, the number of gifts that the program is seeking must be specified. Many athletic departments have conducted capital campaigns in part to endow athletic scholarships. If a goal of a campaign is to endow twenty scholarships, there must be twenty $500,000 spots on the gift table. (This assumes that an average scholarship costs an athletic department $25,000. Endowments generally pay at a 5% rate; therefore, $500,000 must be raised to endow each scholarship.)

Pre-campaign research. The goal of a campaign should be based on pre-campaign research to determine the level of giving that alumni and friends of the athletic program can provide. Once the potential for giving is determined, the campaign amount can be set and the gift table can be created. When setting a campaign goal and creating the gift table, it is important to remember that it takes many donors to reach each level of giving. Also, at each level of giving the gift table must match the donors' potential for giving at those levels.

Development officers have observed that three or four legitimate prospective donors are required per gift at each level of giving. For the Texas Tech campaign, three or four potential donors must have the ability to give at least $18.5 million, or it is unlikely that Texas Tech will receive its lead gift. Six to eight must have the potential to give $9.25 million, and so on. As we move down the chart, fewer prospects are required per gift. The table in Exhibit 14.14 is based on this fact. At the lower levels of giving, we assume three prospects per gift, rather than making the more conservative assumption of four per gift. This reflects a potential spillover effect of donors from higher to lower giving levels. For example, if Texas Tech identified three potential donors to give at the $18.5 million level, one of those donors might decide to give, but to give $14 million rather than $18.5 million. This gift would be recorded at the $9.25 million level. Spillover from higher categories into lower giving categories often occurs, so that fewer potential donors are needed at lower levels of giving.

IDENTIFYING MAJOR DONORS AND PROSPECTS

In order to obtain major gifts, an organization must actively identify, cultivate, and solicit major donors. Major donors have the following traits:

- They often desire to provide opportunities that they did not have, to help the less fortunate, to improve quality of life, and to help solve problems in society.
- They tend to be very religious, have a strong belief in free enterprise, and be basically conservative.
- They know someone in the athletic department or know something about the department, and they believe in someone who is working for the department or believe in something that the academic institution or athletic department represents.
- They view giving as an investment and will want to see, or at least understand, the return on their investment.
- They have the resources to make a major gift. (Kihlstedt, 2009)

Knowing these characteristics of major donors, the athletic department can identify giving prospects. Kihlstedt defines a **prospect** as "any individual, foundation, corporation, or organization that has the potential to give and is likely to do so" (p. 189). When a donor has potential to give but little probability to give, the development office must cultivate the donor and move him or her toward becoming a probable giver.

To identify and rate prospects, the research department will evaluate individuals who are affiliated with the athletic department and determine who is capable of making a commitment to the capital campaign. The researcher might begin with those who have previously given to the department. According to one development officer, among all donors who give above $25,000, 75% first gave a gift of $250 or less to an annual giving initiative. Further, 83% had made annual fund donations for at least five years, and almost 60% had made annual fund donations for 11 years or more.

Kihlstedt summarizes the objectives and expected outcomes of the prospect research process. First, beyond simply identifying prospects, research must determine these individuals' relationships with other prospects and with athletic department constituents. It must determine each prospect's association with the department, his or her previous levels of giving, and his or her interests in the department. It must also identify the prospect's wealth, ownership interests, control, and influence. Finally, the research staff must reduce this information into reports that pertain to the current capital campaign.

The development staff use these reports to rate potential donors and implement a strategy for action for each—that is, a strategy for cultivating the prospect. The staff will determine which campaign items the prospect will probably support and decide which department member is best suited to cultivate the prospect. For example, suppose it is determined that a certain prospect is able and likely to give at the $2 million level. The prospect played tennis at the institution and currently holds basketball season tickets. Also, the prospect was an Academic All-American. Based on preliminary research and information gathered through the cultivation process, the development staff will determine at what level the prospect is likely to give and target solicitation of a gift based on that information. The staff might target this individual to give to a new academic enrichment center. A staff member overseeing academics would then be assigned to cultivate the prospect. The staff will determine a timeline for cultivating the prospect. According to one development officer, major gifts are usually closed after about nine meaningful contacts over a period of six months to two years.

ASKING FOR DONATIONS

After the prospect has been identified, researched, rated, and cultivated, he or she must be asked to give the gift. Development officials hold varying opinions regarding when a prospect has been cultivated enough to be likely to respond positively to an "ask." A few officials feel it is best to ask for a gift right away, as the donor probably knows that you intend to do so at some time. Others feel that a predetermined number of contacts should be made prior to the request. Most state that you should ask when the time feels right.

Kihlstedt provides guidelines for asking for a major gift. First, the amount of money solicited must be sufficiently large. Often, development officers will ask for gifts two to four times larger than the prospect's giving rating. It is easier to move down to an amount that is acceptable for the prospect than to discover later that a prospect could have given more and try to obtain a higher commitment. Second, development officials should listen during conversations.

Suppose that in conversations, the prospect described previously mentions over and over an affinity for basketball and asks questions relating to the basketball program's needs. That prospect would probably be more receptive to giving to basketball than to an academic center. The development officer must be flexible in presenting alternatives if the conversation indicates that the prospect may be more likely to give in an unexpected area.

Annual Giving Programs

Capital campaigns are important to the long-term plans of athletic programs, but annual giving programs are necessary to sustain operating revenues. For Division I institutions, contributions from alumni and others—the third largest source of department revenue for the average Autonomous 5 FBS program and the largest for the Group of 5 (see Exhibit 14.11)—are the fastest-growing source of athletic department revenues. In 1965, contributions from alumni and others accounted for 5% of the average Division I budget. Today, contributions make up 17.4%.

ATHLETIC SUPPORT GROUPS

In most athletic departments, the **athletic support group (ASG)** or booster club is responsible for the annual giving program. ASGs are usually operated as non-profit organizations, which are tax-exempt, and they are separate legal entities from the college or university. They may also be operated as athletic department clubs. The Gamecock Club, for example, is the University of South Carolina's ASG. It is incorporated as a 501(c)(3) public charitable organization. According to the club's 2018 Form 990, the purpose of the Gamecock Club is "to support the University of South Carolina's Athletic Department by providing the necessary financial resources for scholarships and other educational services." Other successful ASGs, organized similarly, include North Carolina State's Wolfpack Club and the University of North Carolina's Rams Club.

An individual's level of giving to an ASG results in his or her club membership classification. The level required for membership ranges from $100 to over $10,000. Members receive differing benefits based on their giving level. For the most part, ASGs offer six to ten levels of membership, including student memberships. For the Wolfpack Club, current students can join for $30 per year, or $100 for four years, and enjoy benefits including a club T-shirt, the opportunity to purchase priority student seating at basketball and football games, meetings with coaches and athletes, and a car decal. Non-students must pay a minimum of $120 to join at the base level, called the Teammate Club. The highest level of membership, the Alpha Wolf level, requires a donation of at least $50,000. At this level, members receive a football and basketball preview magazine, a membership package and card, a car decal, season ticket applications for football and basketball, an option to purchase parking passes for athletic department events, and an invitation to the "Pride of the Pack" celebration. In between are 13 additional levels of membership, each with differing benefits.

The University of North Carolina's Rams Club is structured similarly. Students can join for $25. Non-students must pay $100 to become Tar Heel members of the club. The highest level is the Champion level, for which members contribute at least $25,000. Again, benefits increase as giving increases. For Rams Club members, one category is tied to endowed giving: the Scholarship level. To reach the Scholarship level and receive two basketball season tickets, a member must give $250,000 within five years to partially endow an athletic scholarship. The member then must make an annual contribution at the Coaches Circle level ($6,000) to maintain benefits.

Schools with smaller enrollments have succeeded in increasing departmental donations by focusing on the wealthiest donors. At Wake Forest University, the Moricle Society was created for donors who contribute at least $60,000 per year. These members of the Deacon Club, Wake Forest's ASG, receive free flights on team charters and may meet with coaches before games for private overviews of game strategy. The Moricle Society has obtained over $1 million per year in additional revenue for the ASG.

RELATION BETWEEN ANNUAL GIVING AND TICKET SALES

Most Division I–FBS athletic departments link the purchase of tickets to football and men's basketball events with annual giving. In Chapel Hill, season tickets to North Carolina men's basketball are in high demand. The only way a donor can be sure to be able to purchase a season ticket is by giving at either the Coaches Circle level ($6,000), the All-American level ($12,000), the Champion level ($25,000), or the Scholarship level. At the Coaches Circle and All-American level, a donor may purchase two basketball season tickets, while a donor at the Champion or Scholarship level may purchase four. The ability to purchase tickets for high-demand events and the location of seats are based on a point system.

Point systems. Athletic departments have developed **point systems** to assign tickets to donors in an objective way. These systems vary slightly from institution to institution, but they generally award points based on the donor's amount of annual giving, the number of years or consecutive years the donor has given, and the number of years or consecutive years the donor has purchased season tickets. The more points earned, the higher priority the donor has to purchase tickets. The location of the donor's seat is also based on points earned.

The Wolfpack Club's website (www.wolfpackclub.com) provides an example calculation of a donor's points. A donor can earn points in four ways:

1. The donor receives 1 point for each consecutive year he or she has contributed to the club. For long-time donors, 2 bonus points per year are earned for donations made in years 6 to 10, 3 points are earned each year for years 11 to 20, and 1 additional point is earned each ten-year period for donations made in years 21 and prior.
2. The donor's cumulative gift total includes both annual giving and giving to capital campaigns. The donor earns 0.008 point for each dollar of the cumulative gift total.
3. The donor receives 0.012 point for each dollar of current annual pledge. Further, a donor can earn bonus points for increasing the pledge from year to year. The donor receives 0.012 bonus point for each dollar given over the previous year's total.
4. Donors earn 1 point per year for ordering season tickets for football and 1 point per year for ordering season tickets for men's basketball.

Points are totaled, and the donor receives a ranking based on the total points. This ranking determines the donor's priority when ordering tickets and selecting seat location.

Suppose a member gives $720 for her annual membership. She has donated $6,600 in total, including payments toward one of the club's capital campaigns and her membership fees over the past five years. She has not ordered season tickets for football or men's basketball. The calculation for determining this club member's points is as follows:

- Five consecutive years of membership earns five points: $5 \times 1 = 5$ points.
- With $6,600 of cumulative giving, she earns 52.8 points: $6,600 \times 0.008 = 52.8$ points.
- The $720 donation this year earns 8.64 points: $720 \times 0.012 = 8.64$ points.
- As she has not purchased season tickets to either men's basketball or football, no additional points are earned: $(0 \times 1) + (0 \times 1) = 0$ points.
- Total points earned for this donor are 66.44: $5 + 52.8 + 8.64 + 0 = 66.44$ points.

Her rank, or priority, is based on the 66.44 points earned and where her points fall compared to the points of all other Wolfpack Club members.

For many athletic department donors, their only donation to the department is the fee to purchase football or men's basketball tickets. Some universities now include donations to other school departments in the calculation of a donor's points. For example, the Tiger Athletic Foundation at Louisiana State University includes academic contributions in the calculation of points that earn premium seating rights and other athletic department-related benefits. One priority point can be earned for every $1,000 donated to the LSU Foundation or LSU Alumni Association.

Seating policy restructuring. Because the ability to purchase tickets to high-demand games drives donations to ASGs, over time schools reassign seats and overhaul their point systems both to generate additional revenue and to make the system more equitable for long-time and newer donors alike. Some schools, such as the University of Maryland and the Ohio State University, reassign seats each season based on their point systems. Other institutions, such as Iowa State University and the University of Missouri, only reassign seats periodically based on their point systems.

SIDEBAR 14.D   Intra-university Development Issues

When donations go to an athletic department, many faculty members complain about the emphasis placed on athletics. At Oklahoma State University, T. Boone Pickens donated $165 million to the athletic department. Fourteen years later, this donation was still the largest single donation in the history of college athletics. All of the money went toward athletic facilities. Football received $120 million for new offices, training rooms, and additional seating in the stadium, and $54 million went to a new multipurpose indoor practice facility. The tennis program received $15 million for a new, modern facility. A former chairman of Oklahoma State's Faculty Council was publicly critical of the gift and cited the donation as an example of the university's overemphasis on college athletics. Pickens countered that you give the money to the programs you choose (Wieberg, 2006).

Some are concerned that the increases in giving to athletics will impact the giving of gifts to the university as a whole. At the University of Connecticut, giving to athletics rose from $900,000 in 1989 to $4.29 million in 1993. Over that same period, all other university giving fell from $7.5 million to $4.29 million. The net result, therefore, was a $180,000 increase in giving to the university (Zimbalist, 2007). For Division I–FBS schools, athletic donations were 15% of an average university's total donations in 1998. By 2003, athletic donations accounted for 26% of the total (Stinson & Howard, 2007). This trend has aroused fear on campuses about the limited pool of money donors are willing to give.

As an example, Clemson University restructured its football seating policy after the 2007 season (Strelow, 2008). The restructured policy, according to Clemson officials, rewarded donors' loyalty, as well as their giving. A reseating usually assigns seats to the donors who gave the most or who earned the most priority points, but the Clemson policy gave current ticket holders the right to keep their premium seats (seating between the 30-yard lines) if they met the new monetary standards set for those seats. The resulting change affected membership in the highest categories of IPTAY, Clemson's ASG, as 70% of members seated in the newly designated premium seating area increased their giving level in order to retain their seats or to improve their seat location. For example, the Heisman level ($10,000) increased from 200 members to 316 members, and the McFadden level ($5,600) increased from 103 members to 459 members. In all, for the five highest membership categories ($2,100-plus), membership increased 54%. The increase in giving exceeded expectations, and demand for premium seats outpaced supply. Demand was so great that some donors who significantly increased their giving had to remain in their current seat location or even had to move to slightly less desirable premium seats.

Seat licenses. In restructuring their seating policy, some schools have added a second layer of giving for a donor to qualify for premium seats. These schools require a seat license, similar to the PSLs that have been sold in professional sport over the last two decades, on top of annual giving minimums for access to seating purchases. To purchase season tickets in its baseball stadium, a fan at the University of South Carolina must be a member of the Gamecock Club and pay a seat license fee (see Exhibit 14.15). The cost of each season ticket, then, is the $260 ticket price, plus the seat donation required to purchase the particular seat, plus the required donation to the Gamecock Club. Annual donations to the Gamecock Club bring privileges across sports, so one donation made during the year can fulfill the season ticket requirements for both football and baseball.

ENDOWMENT FUNDAMENTALS

Endowed giving has been mentioned already, but it merits a deeper discussion. Establishing and raising funds for endowments may be included in a capital

EXHIBIT 14.15   Seats and seat giving requirements for Carolina Stadium.

SEAT TYPE	NUMBER AVAILABLE	MINIMUM GAMECOCK CLUB MEMBERSHIP	SEAT LICENSE FEE
Black	1,746	Roost ($100)	$25
Garnet	1,807	Roost ($100)	$50
Gold	1,250	Roost ($100)	$75
Box	113	Roost ($100)	$115
The Perch	150	Silver Spur ($3,500)	$1,250
Club	128	Silver Spur ($3,500)	$1,500
Suite	80	Silver Spur ($3,500)	$37,500

Note: There are five suites with 16 tickets per suite. Fees are on a per suite basis.

campaign or an annual giving program. For an athletic department, an endowed fund is a fund made up of **endowed gifts**. These gifts, held by the department or its ASG in perpetuity, are invested, and only a portion of the fund's annual investment return is used for the fund's specific purposes. To protect against inflation, the remaining investment return is added to the fund's principal amount. The goal of the reinvestment is to maintain the value of the principal. Typically, athletic departments use endowed funds for scholarships, coaching salaries, or program-specific support. An endowment may be created through gifts of cash, publicly traded securities, stock in closely held corporations, real estate, or bequests. The donor may receive tax advantages including savings on income taxes, capital gains taxes, and transfer taxes, depending on the asset given and the gift arrangement.

CONCLUSION

Though it appears that college athletics is awash in money—from the NCAA's $800 million annual television contract with CBS and Turner Sports to the profile of high-powered athletic programs—it is very difficult for an athletic department to generate more operating revenues than operating expenses, let alone be self-sustaining. This is especially true for Division I–FCS, Division I–Other, Division II, Division III, and non-NCAA schools. As allocated revenues are the foundation of many programs' revenues, financial pressures on campuses across the country are resulting in an increasing emphasis on athletic department development programs. At all levels, programs are implementing capital campaigns, creating detailed annual giving programs, and creating endowments to support the ongoing mission of athletics on campus in an effort to secure the financial future of intercollegiate athletics.

Case Analysis

Endowing Tobacco Road

The University of North Carolina and Duke University have two of the more developed athletic department endowment programs in the NCAA. The main endowed fund at North Carolina is the Scholarship Endowment Trust, with about $235 million in assets. From this principal, 5% ($11.74 million) is used to pay annual scholarship costs. The trust is being built through endowed giving and the fund's investment returns. Donors may endow a scholarship with a gift of $500,000, payable over a five-year period. The Scholarship Endowment Trust only covers 65% of the costs of all of North Carolina's athletic scholarships. The goal is to raise over $130 million for this endowment to fully cover the $18.2 million (which would be 5% of the endowment total) cost of providing approximately 500 scholarships to athletes in 2020. North Carolina hopes to fund athletic scholarships fully through this endowment, but with the cost of education rising faster than inflation (North Carolina scholarship costs have doubled over the past ten years)—and, more important, rising faster than the return rate of the endowment—North Carolina has had to continue to raise money for the fund.

In addition to raising funds to offset scholarship costs, North Carolina has begun to create endowments for each of its teams. The funds for the Sports Operating Endowments are invested, providing an annual yield of 5%, which is the same yield provided by the Scholarship Endowment Trust. Sports Operating Endowments provide supplemental income to each team's individual budget, and the money may be used at the coach's discretion. Typically, this fund provides monies to enhance recruiting, team travel, and assistant coaches' salaries.

Duke University, through its ASG, the Iron Dukes, responded to North Carolina's endowment efforts with two major programs. First, Duke created an endowment fund for scholarships. According to the Iron Dukes website, approximately 30% of Duke scholarships are now covered by endowment income.

As Duke is a private institution, the cost of providing an athletic scholarship is considerably higher than the cost at North Carolina, a public institution. To endow a full scholarship at Duke requires a gift of $1.5 million. At North Carolina, the amount is $500,000.

A second major endowment initiative at Duke was its Basketball Legacy Fund, created in 2000 to fund Duke University men's basketball perpetually. The fund's yield is used for player scholarship costs, coaching salaries, and the operating costs of its team. The Legacy Fund was fully endowed in 2012. It pays for the costs of 13 scholarships, 2.5 managers' scholarships, the head coach's salary, and salaries of two assistant coaches, an intern, and an academic advisor (Beaton & Kyle, 2012). Today, Duke is beginning to replicate its men's basketball fundraising success and has launched endowments for the remaining 26 of its sports teams through its Iron Dukes Varsity Club.

Case Questions

1. How are development efforts used to fund athletics at your institution?
2. How do these development activities at your institution compare to North Carolina's and Duke's activities?

3. What risks are involved when an athletic department relies on the interest earned from an endowment to fund its program?
4. What are the benefits of using endowments?

Concept Check

1. How does money flow from the NCAA to its member institutions?
2. What differences in structure lead to financial differences among NCAA member institutions?
3. What financial role does college football play at NCAA Division I–FBS institutions? How does this compare to Division I–FCS institutions?
4. Why are athletic departments' development efforts so critical?
5. What problems may exist in the relationship between donations and ticketing for college athletic events?

Practice Problems

1. As director of development for Southern Ohio State University (SOSU), you have been charged with developing a plan to endow 12 men's basketball scholarships. The current cost of a scholarship athlete is $45,000. With tuition expenses expected to increase at a 5.5% rate annually and the endowment's return expected to average 7% over time, calculate the total amount that will have to be raised to endow the 12 scholarships fully.
2. Based on your work in Problem 1, develop a major gifts table for the capital campaign. Explain the method you used to construct the table.

References

Barr, C.A. (2012). Collegiate sport. In L.P Masteralexis, C.A. Barr, & M.A. Hums (Eds.), *Principles and practice of sport management* (4th ed.) (pp. 145–169). Gaithersburg, MD: Aspen.

Beaton, A., & Kyle, N. (2012, October 12). Duke basketball completes its Legacy Fund endowment. *The Chronicle.* Retrieved from www.dukechronicle.com/articles/2012/10/01/duke-basketball-completes-its-legacy-fund-endowment#.VYMfZPlViko.

Berkowitz, S. (2019, May 15). Big Ten Conference had nearly $759 million in revenue in fiscal 2018, new records show. *USA Today.* Retrieved from www.usatoday.com/story/sports/2019/05/15/big-ten-revenue-hit-nearly-759-million-fiscal-2018/3686089002/.

Berkowitz, S. (2020, January 30). Southeastern Conference generated $721 million in revenue for 2019 fiscal year. *USA Today.* Retrieved from www.usatoday.com/story/sports/ncaaf/sec/2020/01/30/sec-generated-721-million-revenue-still-trails-big-ten/2856234001/.

Berkowitz, S., & Kreighbaum, A. (2015, August 19). College athletes cashing in with millions in new benefits. *USA Today.* Retrieved from www.usatoday.com/story/sports/college/2015/08/18/ncaa-cost--attendance-meals-2015/31904839/.

Borland, M.V., Goff, B.L., & Pulsinelli, R.W. (1992). College athletics: Financial burden or boom? *Advances in the Economics of Sports*, 1, 215–235.

Brady, E., Berkowitz, S., & Schnaars, C. (2015, May 15). College athletics finance report: Non-Power 5 schools face huge money pressure. *USA Today.* Retrieved from www.usatoday.com/story/sports/college/2015/05/26/ncaa-athletic-finances-revenue-expense-division-i/27971457/.

Broughton, D. (2008, June 23). Big Ten posts record revenue. *Sports Business Journal*, 11(10), 35.

Broughton, D. (2018, January 8). A reset, then a reboot: Record run ends, but construction spending to take off again in '19. *Sports Business Journal*. Retrieved from www.sportsbusinessdaily.com/Journal/Issues/2018/01/08/Facilities/New-facilities.aspx.

Broughton, D. (2020, January 26). Facilities: Record year ahead. *Sports Business Journal*. Retrieved from www.sportsbusinessdaily.com/Journal/Issues/2020/01/06/In-Depth/Facilities-2020.aspx.

Covell, D., & Walker, S. (2019). *Managing intercollegiate athletics* (2nd ed.). London: Routledge.

Darcy, K. (2007, December 20). The schedule is from hell, but Presbyterian is loving life in DI. *ESPN.com*. Retrieved from http://sports.espn.go.com/espn/priont?id=3162742&type=story.

Del Bianco, J. (2016, September 16). Gamecock Sports Properties gets new contract. *The Big Spur*. Retrieved from https://247sports.com/college/south-carolina/Article/Gamecock-Sports-Properties-gets-new-contract--47506068/.

Dosh, K. (2020, February 29). Scott Stricklin's approach to prioritizing athletic facilities projects at Florida. *Forbes*. Retrieved from www.forbes.com/sites/kristidosh/2020/02/29/scott-stricklins-approach-to-prioritizing-athletic-facilities-projects-at-florida/#3aed2b55b112.

Dove, K.E. (2000). *Conducting a successful capital campaign*. San Francisco: Jossey-Bass.

Dufresne, C. (2015, June 15). UAB football drama shows deep love of the game in Alabama. *Los Angeles Times*. Retrieved from www.latimes.com/sports/la-sp-uab-football-20150615-column.html.

Finances of intercollegiate athletics. (2019). *NCAA.org*. Retrieved from www.ncaa.org/about/resources/research/finances-intercollegiate-athletics.

Gamecock Athletics. (2015). *2015 Baseball Media Guide*. Retrieved from http://grfx.cstv.com/photos/schools/scar/sports/m-basebl/auto_pdf/2014–15/misc_non_event/15-bb-mg-sec-1.pdf.

Gator Boosters, Inc. (2019, June 30). Financial Statements. Retrieved from http://d811do19jx3e0.cloudfront.net/gatorboosters/img/about-us/financials/2018-19-Gator-Boosters-Inc-Financial-Statement-v2.pdf.

Goff, B. (2000). Effects of university athletics on the university: A review and extension of empirical assessment. *Journal of Sport Management*, 14, 87–99.

Goff, B., & Wilson, D. (2013, March). Estimating the MRP of college athletics from professional factor shares. Paper presented at the Southern Economics Association.

Greenstein, T. (2017, July 24). Big Ten announces six-year deal with ESPN, Fox Sports worth $2.64 billion. *Chicago Tribune*. Retrieved from www.chicagotribune.com/sports/college/ct-big-ten-espn-fox-sports-20170724-story.html.

Greer, T. (2014, December 2). University of Alabama at Birmingham announces results of athletic department strategic review. *UAB News*. Retrieved from www.uab.edu/news/updates/item/5595-university-of-alabama-at-birmingham-announces-results-of-athletic-department-strategic-review.

How Florida athletic departments rank in revenue, expenses for 2019 fiscal year. (2020, July 16). Naples Daily News. Retrieved from www.naplesnews.com/story/sports/college/2020/07/16/florida-fsu-athletics-rank-revenue-expenses-2019/5447692002/.

In Re NCAA Ath. Grant-In-Aid Cap Antitrust Litigation. 375 F. Supp. 3d 1058 (N.D. Cal. 2019).

Kaufman, J. (2020, February 14). Ohio State athletic department lost money despite $210 million in revenue. *The Columbus Dispatch*. Retrieved from www.usatoday.com/story/sports/ncaaf/bigten/2020/02/14/ohio-state-athletic-revenue-210-million-but-department-lost-money/4760028002/.

Kihlstedt, A. (2009). *Capital campaigns: Strategies that work.* Burlington, MA: Jones & Bartlett Learning.

Knight Commission on Intercollegiate Athletics. (2018). College athletics financial information (CAFI) database. Retrieved from http://cafidatabase.knightcommission.org/

Lewin, T. (2014, April 7). Colleges increasing spending on sports faster than on academics, report finds. *The New York Times.* Retrieved from www.nytimes.com/2014/04/07/education/colleges-increasing-spending-on-sports-faster-than-on-academics-report-finds.html?_r=2.

McCann, M. (2019, March 8). Why the NCAA lost its latest landmark case in the battle over what schools can offer athletes. *Sports Illustrated.* Retrieved from www.si.com/college/2019/03/09/ncaa-antitrust-lawsuit-claudia-wilken-alston-jenkins.

McMurphy, B. (2015, May 29). SEC schools to each receive record $31.2 million payout. *ESPN.com.* Retrieved from http://espn.go.com/college-sports/story/_/id/12974161/southeastern-conference-distribute-record-435m-revenue-member-schools.

Morris, R. (2008, May 1). Fans will pay for elite aspirations. *TheState.com.* Retrieved from www.thestate.com/sports/v-print/story/391806.html.

Moser, J. (2016, July 22). Local Division III schools investing big. *Fox 11 News.* Retrieved from https://fox11online.com/sports/college/local-division-iii-schools-investing-big.

Moss, R. (2014, December 5). Paid to play? Money circulation in PC athletics. *The Blue Stocking.* Retrieved from www.presby.edu/bluestocking/2014/12/05/paid-to-play-money-circulation-in-pc-athletics/.

Murphy, D. (2020, May 18). Appeals court upholds ruling that colleges can pay for all NCAA athletes' education expenses. *ESPN.com.* Retrieved from www.espn.com/college-sports/story/_/id/29191519/appeals-court-upholds-ruling-colleges-pay-all-ncaa-athletes-education-expenses.

Myerberg, P. (2015, April 26). NCAA schools put money where athletes' mouths are. *USA Today.* Retrieved from www.usatoday.com/story/sports/college/2015/04/26/unlimited-food-snacks-wisconsin-oregon-ncaa-student-athletes/26405105/.

National Collegiate Athletic Association. (2019). *Consolidated financial statements: August 31, 2019 and 2018.* Indianapolis, IN: Author.

NCAA. (2019). *NCAA financial database.* Retrieved from www.ncaa.org/about/resources/research/finances-intercollegiate-athletics-database.

NCAA. (2020). *Reclassifying members.* Indianapolis, IN: Author.

NCAA finances. (2019). *USA Today.* Retrieved from http://sports.usatoday.com/ncaa/finances.

NCAA presidents set revised financial distribution to support college athletes. (2020, March 26). *NCAA.org.* Retrieved from www.ncaa.org/about/resources/media-center/news/ncaa-presidents-set-revised-financial-distribution-support-college-athletes.

NCAA v. Board of Regents, 468 U.S. 85 (1984).

New England College receives $5 million gift to create a state-of-the-art athletic complex. (2020). *New England College.* Retrieved from www.nec.edu/new-england-college-receives-5-million-gift-to-create-a-state-of-the-art-athletic-complex/.

Nocera, J. (2015, June 9). Alabama football follies. *The New York Times.* Retrieved from www.nytimes.com/2015/06/09/opinion/joe-nocera-alabama-football-follies.html.

O'Bannon v. NCAA, 724 F.3d 1268 (2014).

Ourand, J. (2019, December 20). SEC football leaving CBA after 2023, likely for ESPN/ABC. *Sports Business Daily.* Retrieved from www.sportsbusinessdaily.com/SB-Blogs/Breaking-News/2019/12/SEC.aspx.

Person, J. (2006a, May 14). In the red—$2,656,084. *TheState.com.* Retrieved from www.thestate.com/mld/thestate/sports/colleges/university_of_south_carolina.html.

Person, J. (2006b, May 14). Ticket distribution for football under scrutiny. *TheState.com.* Retrieved from www.thestate.com/mld/thestate/sports/colleges/university_of_south_carolina.html.

Person, J. (2008, June 19). Athletics firmly in the black. *TheState.com.* Retrieved from www.thestate.com/gogamecocks/v-print/story/438098.html.

Powers, J. (2014, June 7). Harvard defeats Yale in 149th regatta. *The Boston Globe.* Retrieved from www.bostonglobe.com/sports/2014/06/07/harvard-defeats-yale-regatta/3rOYuj0kIgEkZbud84Zb4K/story.html.

Rascher, D.A., & Howell, J. (2011). *An analysis and assessment of intercollegiate athletics at the University of San Francisco.* San Francisco: University of San Francisco.

Sherman, E. (2015, March 11). Big Ten facing crucial decisions about its TV future. *Chicago Tribune.* Retrieved from www.chicagotribune.com/sports/columnists/ct-sherman-media-big-ten-spt-0312-20150311-column.html.

Skousen, C.R., & Condie, F.A. (1988). Evaluating a sports program: Goalposts vs. test tubes. *Management Accounting,* 70(5), 43–49.

Smith, M., & Ourand, J. (2008, August 25). ESPN pays $2.25B for SEC rights. *Sports Business Daily.* Retrieved from www.sportsbusinessdaily.com/Journal/Issues/2008/08/20080825/This-Weeks-News/ESPN-Pays-$225B-For-SEC-Rights.aspx.

Solomon, J. (2014a, August 8). O'Bannon judge rules NCAA violates antitrust law. *CBSSports.com.* Retrieved from www.cbssports.com/collegefootball/writer/jon-solomon/24653743/obannon-judge-rules-ncaa-violates-antitrust-law.

Solomon, J. (2014b, August 9). Q&A: What the O'Bannon ruling means for NCAA, schools, and athletes. *CBSSports.com.* Retrieved from www.cbssports.com/collegefootball/writer/jon-solomon/24654805/qa-what-the-obannon-ruling-means-for-the-ncaa-schools-and-athletes.

Solomon, J. (2015, March 13). O'Bannon v. NVAA: A cheat sheet for NCAA's appeal of paying players. *CBSSports.com.* Retrieved from www.cbssports.com/collegefootball/writer/jon-solomon/25106422/obannon-vs-ncaa-a-cheat-sheet-for-ncaas-appeal-of-paying-players.

Stinson, J.L., & Howard, D.R. (2007). Athletic success and private giving to athletic and academic programs at NCAA institutions. *Journal of Sport Management,* 21, 235–264.

Strauss, B., & Schonbrun, Z. (2014, December 2). It's a game of spiraling costs, so a college tosses out football. *The New York Times.* Retrieved from www.nytimes.com/2014/12/03/sports/ncaafootball/uab-cancels-football-program-citing-fiscal-realities.html.

Strelow, P. (2008, July 17). Clemson football tickets: Money can't solve everything. *The State.* Retrieved from www.thestate.com/sports/v-print/story/463115.html.

Texas Tech University Athletics. (2020). *The Campaign for Fearless Champions.* Lubbock, TX: Author.

University of Michigan. (2019, June 20). *Proposed fiscal year 2020 operating budget.* Ann Arbor, MI: Author.

University of South Carolina. (2020, June). *The University of South Carolina Department of Intercollegiate Athletics proposed budget fiscal year 2020–2021.* Columbia, SC: Author.

US Department of Education. (2019). The equity in athletics data analysis cutting tool. Retrieved from http://ope.ed.gov/athletics/.

What's an NCAA tournament unit worth? Millions. Here's how. (2019, March 26). *USA Today.* Retrieved from www.usatoday.com/story/sports/ncaab/2019/03/26/whats-an-ncaa-tournament-unit-worth-millions-heres-how/39256149/.

Wieberg, S. (2006, August 16). Tycoon's $165m gift to Oklahoma State raises both hopes and questions. *USA Today.* Retrieved from www.usatoday.com/money/2006-08-15-pickens-oklahoma-state-donation_x.html.

Zimbalist, A. (2007, June 18). College athletic budgets are bulging but their profits are slim to none. *Sports Business Journal,* 10(10), 26.

CHAPTER 15

Professional Sport

Mark S. Nagel

KEY CONCEPTS

collective bargaining

collusion

competitive balance

cord cutting

draft lottery

dynamic ticket pricing

esports

expansion fee

franchise ownership model

free ride

inheritance (death) tax

Larry Bird exception

League Think

local market

lockout

luxury tax

monopoly

offset language

OTT—over-the-top

permanent seat license

personal seat license

player draft

pooled debt

profit maximization

relegation system

reserve clause

salary arbitration

salary cap

salary slotting

scalping

secondary ticket market

Sports Broadcasting Act (SBA)

stadium-related revenue sources

territorial rights

transfer

value over replacement
    player (VORP)

variable ticket pricing

win maximization

wins above replacement (WAR)

INTRODUCTION

Professional sport leagues operate differently from other businesses. Whereas most companies would like to dominate and even eliminate their competitors, individual franchises in professional sport leagues need other franchises to exist so that competitive games can be scheduled. Without competitors, a franchise is unlikely to attract many customers. Owners of professional sport teams must consider the impact of their financial decisions on the other owners in the league. Former Cleveland Browns and Baltimore Ravens owner Art Modell noted the unique nature of professional sports ownership where competition and cooperation were critical when he said that NFL owners are "a bunch of fat-cat Republicans who vote socialist on football" (Berrett, 2018, para. 3).

Cooperation rather than pure competition is just one aspect of the fact that professional sport franchise owners often have different motivations in purchasing and operating a team than owners in non-sport industries. Certainly, one goal of every business is to generate revenues that exceed costs and expenses, and consistent generation of profits will maximize the value of the organization (Groppelli & Nikbakht, 2000). In most cases, shareholders will insist that management pursue the continual generation of profits. Although all professional sport owners certainly desire to generate profits, for some, **profit maximization**—the pursuit of the highest profits possible—is a secondary goal. In the early 1900s, the majority of professional sport owners operated their team as their primary income source, but today most professional sport owners have already established highly successful non-sport organizations that have earned millions or billions of dollars in profits. For some of these owners, ownership of a professional sport franchise is primarily about competition, the opportunity to be a key figure within a community, and ego gratification (Rascher, Nagel, McEvoy, & Brown, 2011). These owners may be more interested in **win maximization**—the pursuit of winning as a primary goal.

Owners for whom profit maximization is not the primary goal typically focus their financial resources on their team's on-field success. The pursuit of winning may or may not increase the overall value of the firm. For example, in MLB throughout the 2000s, the New York Yankees had the highest player payroll in the league. The Yankees' spending attracted numerous high-quality players, who led the team to on-field success and higher profits. On the other hand, in the early 2000s Jerry Colangelo, owner of the Arizona Diamondbacks, spent lavishly in an attempt to sign players to win a championship. Though the Diamondbacks beat the Yankees in the 2001 World Series, Colangelo eventually experienced financial hardship, as the team did not generate enough additional revenues to offset expenses. The Diamondbacks had to decrease salaries, as well as other expenses, a few years after the World Series victory, and in 2004 Colangelo sold his interest in the franchise.

Within a league, the various team owners possess different financial resources that accrue from the team and other business ventures. The "excessive" pursuit of on-field excellence by one franchise or a small group of franchises could have an adverse financial impact on other owners. If an owner who has large financial resources elects to diminish or eliminate potential franchise profits in the pursuit of winning, other owners may not be able to compete in signing the best players. If many teams in a league do not have an opportunity to acquire or retain top players, the league's **competitive balance** is disrupted. Competitive balance may be defined or measured by various specific metrics, but generally it is held that each franchise, if its management executes a sound strategy, should have a reasonable opportunity to compete for a playoff spot at least every couple of seasons. When competitive imbalance—or merely the perception of competitive imbalance—occurs, fans may lose interest not only in their local team but also in the entire league.

Because of the unique financial nature of professional sports, where owners have divergent goals regarding win maximization versus profit maximization, league offices establish rules and regulations to ensure that individual teams, as well as the entire league, can succeed financially. Complicating this effort is the fact that each franchise operates in a **local market** that has distinct differences in population, economic activity, and passion for sport. League offices attempt to balance franchises' financial and competitive goals with the overall goal of increasing the financial viability of the league.

LEAGUE STRUCTURES

The most popular professional sport leagues in North America—MLB, the NBA, the NHL, and the NFL—began as regional enterprises with limited financial resources. During their early existence, financial survival was typically their most pressing concern. However, as these leagues became financially stable and began to expand, concern for the league's structure and operating procedures became more important. Leagues that have been established more recently, such as Major League Soccer, Major League Lacrosse (MLL), and the National Lacrosse League (NLL), have been able to learn from the experiences of the Big 4 professional leagues.

SIDEBAR 15.A   NFL Value Skyrockets as the League Turns 100 Years Old

In 2019, the NFL celebrated its 100-year birthday with a number of special on- and off-field activities. As the dominant professional sport league in North America, the NFL has experienced tremendous financial growth from its humble beginnings as a collection of owners who met in a car dealership in Canton, Ohio, on August 20, 1920 to establish the American Professional Football Association (APFA). By 1922, the league had changed its name to its current moniker, but a number of the original teams experienced financial difficulty. Among the original teams, many, such as the Akron Pros, Muncie Flyers, and Racine Legion, became defunct shortly after their founding. To some observers, investing in the NFL was a foolish idea. However, there were a few owners who were able to see the league grow from its humble beginnings to an established league. Among the original owners was George Halas, the owner of the Decatur Staleys, which would later move to Chicago and change their nickname to the Bears. Halas initially paid $100.00 for the Staleys. Halas not only owned the team but also coached it until 1967. By the time of his death in 1983, Halas's modest investment had increased to be worth tens of millions of dollars. However, his heirs enjoyed even greater increases in team value as, by 2019, the Bears were estimated to be worth $3.45 billion (Moskowitz, 2019)! Though Halas had to endure many years of financial concern as many teams over the first 30 years experienced business hardship, his commitment to professional football made him a wealthy man and his heirs ultra-wealthy. His initial $100 investment returned 19.26% over the first 100 years of the NFL. Conversely, $100 invested in the S&P 500 in 1920 would have generated a 10.382 annualized return (with dividends reinvested) by 2019.

Franchisee/Franchisor Structure

North American professional sport leagues usually operate as quasi-socialist franchisee/franchisor cartels (Scully, 1995). Under the **franchise ownership model**, owners purchase individual franchises from the league and then sign players, arrange for a facility in which to play games, conduct marketing activities, and control all other aspects of the team's operation. While operating their individual franchises, owners work with the owners of other franchises to set policies that affect the entire league.

SIDEBAR 15.B Beyond the Big 4

In addition to the Big 4, a number of additional North American professional sport leagues have been established or are emerging. Numerous minor league baseball leagues have operated for over 100 years, and many of their teams continue to set yearly attendance records. Sports such as lacrosse now have professional leagues that attract thousands of fans each year. Leagues for individual sports such as golf (Ladies Professional Golf Association, Professional Golfers Association), tennis (Association of Tennis Professionals, Women's Tennis Association), and bowling (Professional Bowlers Association) have for many years operated popular events.

Every professional sport league or organization, regardless of its history or current operation, faces similar financial challenges. This chapter focuses primarily on the Big 4 North American professional sport leagues, as well as NASCAR and MLS, because these leagues tend to have the highest revenues and the greatest diversity of revenue sources. In most cases, their considerable financial reserves ensure that they will remain in existence for many years into the future. Among the "emerging" leagues, the Arena Football League (AFL) had one of the more stable financial foundations. Despite this, the league folded operations in 2009 with dwindling revenues and a stalling economy. The league was able to re-form in 2010 but by 2019 had ceased operations for a second time. Certainly, a variety of professional sport leagues are worthy of study and employment, and readers are encouraged to study the establishment, growth, and financial operations of other professional sport leagues.

ROLE OF THE COMMISSIONER

Typically, owners in a league hire a commissioner and establish a league office. The commissioner's office, in consultation with the owners, will negotiate national television contracts, establish relationships with vendors for league-wide licensed merchandise sales, hire and supervise game officials, and negotiate a collective bargaining agreement (CBA) with the players' union. The commissioner is the "leader" of the league, but he or she remains the employee of the owners. Kennesaw Mountain Landis, former federal judge and the first MLB commissioner, worked under a "lifetime" contract, but today most commissioners do not enjoy such job security. Many fans believe that the commissioner's role is to do what is best for the sport, but in reality it is to do what is best for the owners. Former MLB commissioner Fay Vincent displeased the owners to such an extent that they gave him a vote of no confidence after he had served less than three years on the job. The vote effectively ended his commissionership, and he resigned on September 7, 1992.

SIDEBAR 15.C   Pete Rozelle and "League Think"

The National Football League has been the dominant North American professional sport league for over 30 years. The NFL's tremendous financial success can in large part be directly attributed to commissioner Pete Rozelle and his idea of "**league think**." When Rozelle became NFL commissioner in 1960, the 12-team league had low attendance figures for many of its games, and much of its television coverage occurred at the local level. Rozelle immediately began to lobby the NFL owners to think of the overall financial health of the league as their first priority and individual franchise profits as a secondary concern. His "league think" philosophy was intended to pull the disparate NFL owners together in their efforts. Although financially "stronger" franchises, such as the Cleveland Browns, New York Giants, and Washington Redskins, appeared to have power and financial status to lose in a "league first" environment, their willingness to pool television revenue was a critical factor in the rapid growth of the NFL's popularity in the 1960s. Without Rozelle's prodding and the willingness of NFL owners such as Wellington Mara to relinquish some of their short-term profits, the NFL likely would not be the most popular professional sport league in the United States today.

In addition to convincing the NFL owners that it would be in their best interests to collectivize some of their efforts, Rozelle lobbied Congress for a special antitrust exemption for professional sport leagues. The pooling and selling of television rights by leagues was against the law until passage of the **Sports Broadcasting Act (SBA)** in 1961, which provided the exemption Rozelle sought. Once Rozelle had convinced the US Congress that the SBA would not cause significant hardship to consumers, he negotiated a television contract with CBS that dramatically increased the revenues of every NFL owner. The NFL's television contracts continued to increase, in some cases dramatically, throughout Rozelle's tenure and after his retirement in 1989. Although every professional sport league has financially benefited from pooling television rights, the NFL has especially benefited, since it pools and sells every regular season and playoff game.

Rozelle's efforts to strengthen the league through collective action were not limited to television revenues. While owners in other leagues often voiced public disagreements over league operations, Rozelle kept the owners (except for Al Davis) primarily working toward the league's financial goals. The NFL's ability to maximize league revenues through shared ticketing and licensed merchandise revenues has enabled "small market" franchises, such as the Green Bay Packers and Pittsburgh Steelers, not only to exist but to prosper competitively and financially. NFL franchises are now by far the most valuable among the North American professional leagues, and much of that value is directly attributable to Rozelle's vision.

ROLE OF THE LEAGUE OWNERS

The commissioner's office will handle routine activities, but a major responsibility of league owners (or their representatives) is to meet regularly to vote on various league policies. Each league establishes rules and voting procedures for decision making. In some cases, a majority vote is all that is required to approve a change in policy, while in other cases a larger majority, such as two-thirds or three-fourths, is needed. League votes on certain issues can have a tremendous impact on the finances of the league and individual franchises. On occasion, individual owners, despite having agreed to operate under the league bylaws when they entered the league, have rejected league decisions and sought legal recourse.

The most famous example of an owner suing his own league took place in the 1980s and involved the NFL's Oakland Raiders. Despite sellout crowds in Oakland throughout the 1970s, by 1980 Raiders owner Al Davis desired to move his team to Los Angeles, where it could play in the Los Angeles Memorial Coliseum (which was much larger than the Oakland–Alameda County Coliseum). The move required yes votes from three-fourths of the owners— but in fact they voted 22–0 (with some abstentions) against the move, partially because they felt it would send a bad message to every NFL fan if a team that had attracted sellout crowds simply abandoned its home marketplace (Harris, 1986; Shropshire, 1995). The Los Angeles Memorial Coliseum Commission (LAMCC) and the Raiders sued the NFL for restricting franchise movement. The LAMCC and the Raiders claimed that restricting movement was an unfair restraint of trade and a violation of antitrust law (*Los Angeles Memorial Coliseum Commission v. National Football League*, 1984, 1986).

The Raiders and the LAMCC eventually won the case, despite the negative public relations that the case created in the Bay Area and the efforts of the City of Oakland to retain the franchise (Harris, 1986). Numerous subsequent legal decisions established that professional sport leagues could require relocating teams to compensate the other league owners financially if the move had a negative effect on overall league revenue (Shropshire, 1995). The NFL's St. Louis Cardinals did provide compensation to the rest of the league's owners when they moved to Arizona in 1987, as did the Los Angeles Rams when they moved to St. Louis in 1995. Ironically, despite the extensive litigation the Raiders endured for their move to Los Angeles, Al Davis decided to move the franchise back to Oakland in 1995 due to the changing economic environment in the NFL (which placed greater emphasis on luxury suite revenues rather than general ticket sales) and promises of considerable upgrades to the Oakland–Alameda County Coliseum. The second itineration of the Oakland Raiders lasted until 2020, when the team moved to Las Vegas to play in a new state-of-the-art facility.

Single-Entity Structure

Despite occasional contentious battles with maverick owners, most North American professional sport leagues operate effectively with a franchisor/ franchisee structure. However, some leagues have now attempted to adopt a single-entity structure, in which owners purchase shares in the league rather than purchase an individual franchise. With a single-entity structure, the league office handles all player transactions, such as negotiating contracts and assigning players to teams. This structure is designed to distribute players throughout the league in a manner that encourages competitive balance, which should increase fans' interest. Under a single-entity structure, the league office will also negotiate sponsorship and media contracts for the entire league and will ensure that revenues are generated and used in a manner that maintains the league's financial solvency.

As discussed in Chapter 1, a single-entity structure will typically reduce league costs, as individual owners cannot sign players to salaries that do not conform to the overall goals of the league. In addition, the league office can ensure cost containment for travel, equipment, and team staff. Although a single-entity structure provides some financial benefits, critics have argued that it reduces individual franchises' incentives to maximize their revenues (Mickle & Lefton, 2008). Most professional sport franchises generate a substantial portion of their revenues from local sources. Though the league office may be effective in negotiating national media contracts and sponsorship agreements, local sponsorships are difficult to identify and foster. In addition, if individual teams do not have incentive to increase revenues, creative marketing activities that would attract additional customers are less likely to occur, which negatively affects the entire league. The Women's National Basketball Association initially operated under a single-entity structure but soon switched to a franchisee/franchisor model to encourage the maximization of local revenues. The WNBA commissioner at the time, Donna Orender, noted, "While the launch model was successful, it became evident that owners wanted more control" (Mickle & Lefton, 2008, para. 10). However, as individual owners exert marketing and financial control in a franchisee/franchisor model, large revenue discrepancies can occur, which can hurt the league's overall competitive balance.

Major League Soccer began play as a single-entity league in 1996. Though the single-entity model enabled the league to build its fan base slowly and consistently, some of the players argued that the league's structure unfairly and illegally held down player salaries. Because just two men, Lamar Hunt and Philip Anschutz, were the league's primary investors and the "operators" of multiple franchises, the players felt that there was no incentive for these owners to compete for player services. In *Fraser v. Major League Soccer* (2000), a group of players filed an antitrust suit against MLS claiming that the league's structure unfairly restrained trade, since players could not offer their services among the different MLS teams. The league countered that the single-entity structure instead prevented any unfair restraint of trade, because one individual entity cannot conspire with itself to hurt the marketplace ("Court accepts," 2000). In addition, the league argued that competition for player services had increased since MLS was founded, because before 1996 there was no viable Division I professional soccer league in the United States. The court eventually ruled in favor of MLS, determining that its single-entity structure, though unusual in North American professional sport at the time, was legal under antitrust laws. The players lost the case, but the attention that the lawsuit drew led to negotiations between the league and the players that increased player benefits. In addition, as MLS became profitable, new investors were attracted, and the league began to incorporate elements of a franchisee/franchisor model (Wagman, 2008).

SIDEBAR 15.D   Esports Attract Attention in Traditional Sports

Since 2011, competitive video games, or esports, have grown dramatically in stature and influence. While some still visualize video games being played solely on home consoles such as Atari and Nintendo systems, the industry has morphed tremendously into a billion-dollar worldwide enterprise. The massive growth in esports has attracted a number of players and owners from the traditional sports world. Mark Cuban, Shaquille O'Neal, Jerry Jones, Robert Kraft, Rich Fox, Alex Rodriguez, and a number of other prominent athletes have invested in some sort of esports entity. In addition, professional sports leagues such as the NBA and FIFA have partnered with game designers to create their own tournaments and leagues. Perhaps the most interesting indicator of the future influence of esports is the investment that a number of current professional sport owners made in the Overwatch League (OWL). When first launched in 2018, franchise fees for the initial 12 franchises were $20 million. Teams were in Europe, North America, and Asia. By the second year, eight additional franchises were added, with the expansion fees exceeding the initial $20 million price. By the 2020 season, the league was firmly established, and teams began to play a home-and-away schedule, with many matches being played in esports-specific venues built and operated by the franchises. The long-term goal of the league is to become one of the world's first yearly, league-based global competitions.

OWNERSHIP RULES AND POLICIES AND LEAGUE FINANCES

Every professional sport league has an interest in maintaining financially successful teams. Because a successful league depends on competent and well-financed owners, leagues establish ownership rules and policies to protect the solvency of every league member. If one or more of the league's franchises experience significant financial hardship, then the league itself might suffer.

Each of the major North American professional sport leagues experienced numerous franchise problems during its early history. Some teams, such as the Akron Pros of the NFL, Louisville Grays of MLB, Pittsburgh Pirates of the NHL, and Toronto Huskies of the NBA, failed and no longer exist. Other teams, such as the NFL's Decatur Staleys (Bears) and the NBA's Fort Wayne Pistons, moved from their initial location shortly after being created in an effort to establish a viable fan base. Given these early franchise problems, it is no wonder that leagues sought to put rules and policies in place to protect the financial well-being of the league. This section discusses league rules and policies regarding new ownership, debt, expansion, and territorial rights.

New Ownership

Each of the professional sport leagues has established rules regarding who may become an owner and join the "club." In many cases, the potential new owner must convince the current owners that he or she will work well within the established league structure. In 2009 Jim Balsillie met with resistance to his attempt to purchase the NHL's financially struggling Phoenix Coyotes. Much of the resistance was not related to Balsillie's offered purchase price, financial reserves, or mental acumen, but rather to his earlier attempts to purchase NHL teams. In particular, other NHL owners were not happy with Balsillie when he attempted to purchase and relocate the Nashville Predators in 2007. Balsillie announced the purchase and move of the franchise before the league owners approved the sale, which caused consternation among the owners and in the commissioner's office. As another example, the NBA has fined Dallas Mavericks owner Mark Cuban over $1 million for his actions and criticisms of the league since he purchased the team in 2000. Observers have speculated that if the NBA owners had anticipated Cuban's behavior, they would have rejected his purchase. Although many owners may agree with some of Cuban's observations and opinions, the way he has voiced his displeasure regarding certain league activities has caused internal strife.

SIDEBAR 15.E   NASCAR

The National Association for Stock Car Auto Racing (NASCAR) has a unique ownership structure in North American professional sports. Founded by William France, Sr. in Daytona Beach, Florida, in 1948, NASCAR is a sanctioning body of automobile racing. The racing teams are owned and operated by other individuals. These racing teams hire drivers and all of the other employees necessary to prepare for competition. NASCAR's early years were focused on organizing stock car races, primarily in the southern portion of the United States. Since the early 1980s, the popularity of NASCAR events has grown tremendously. NASCAR currently organizes multiple racing series, the Cup Series being the most popular. Each year, millions of fans attend NASCAR events, and millions more watch the races on television. Though William France, Sr. retired as chairman in 1972, NASCAR has remained largely a family-operated business, with William France, Jr. succeeding his father, and grandson Brian France succeeding William Jr. in 2003. In 2018, Jim France, the son of William France, Sr. and uncle of Brian France, became NASCAR CEO and chairman.

Though NASCAR is certainly the dominant force in North American automobile racing, it only owns some, not all, of the tracks on which its events are held. Until 2019, the France family was the majority shareholder of International Speedway Corporation (ISC), an organization that owned and operated 12 racetracks that hosted NASCAR events. William France, Sr. founded ISC in 1953 as the organization that would build and operate the Daytona International Speedway. Despite opening the Talladega Superspeedway in 1969, ISC experienced slow growth during its first 40 years of existence, until in 1999 it merged with Penske Motorsports, which gave it control of four additional tracks. After that merger, ISC continued to open new racetracks, most of which were awarded races in NASCAR's popular Cup Series. In 2019, NASCAR decided to merge its operations with ISC. The decision streamlined operations and resulted in ISC being delisted from the NASDAQ Stock Exchange (Weaver, 2019).

The France family's "dual ownership" of NASCAR and selected racetracks has generated criticism of the family and legal challenges to NASCAR's structure. In 2005, Kentucky Speedway filed an antitrust lawsuit against NASCAR and ISC claiming that they had conspired to prevent eligible racetracks from submitting bids to host NASCAR events. Though Kentucky Speedway had hosted NASCAR Nationwide Series and Camping World Truck Series events, it had not been successful in its attempts to host a Cup Series event. A Cup Series event would have generated millions of dollars in additional revenue for the racetrack and the surrounding community. Kentucky Speedway argued that NASCAR could have made more money by running a Cup Series race at its venue than at some of the other venues that currently hosted Cup Series races. Kentucky Speedway further argued that the France family had illegally conspired to keep the top NASCAR events out of Kentucky's newest and "superior" track in favor of other "less desirable" venues (some of which ISC controlled). The case generated considerable publicity in the sport business world, but it was thrown out of court in January 2008. Kentucky Speedway filed an appeal in July 2009, but in December 2009 it decided to drop litigation against NASCAR. In 2011, NASCAR began holding a Sprint Cup Series race at the Kentucky Speedway. Each year since, the Quaker State 400 has run in late June or early July.

The current owner of the Kentucky Speedway, Speedway Motorsports, Inc. (SMI), has developed positive relationships with NASCAR, even though some of their activities would be seen as competitive. SMI owns eight racetracks that host NASCAR events. Some of those tracks were acquired by SMI in a bidding war with ISC. Though there is certainly the potential for real or perceived slights to occur, over the past ten years, there has been relative business "peace" between NASCAR and SMI, which has helped expand the sport and provided a better experience for racing fans.

Potential personality conflicts are important considerations, but of greater importance is a potential owner's ability to operate a franchise without incurring significant financial losses. Each of the leagues requires that potential owners provide information regarding their finances. If a prospective owner does not have sufficient financial resources, the league is likely to reject the ownership bid in fear that a financial problem for an individual franchise could prove detrimental to the entire league.

SIDEBAR 15.F   Japanese Professional Baseball Problems Beginning to Change?

Professional baseball has been popular in Japan since the game's founding in 1936. Nippon Professional Baseball (NPB) operates with teams in two separate leagues (Central and Pacific) and uses rules similar to those of MLB, but it has a very different business model. Whereas most MLB owners are individuals who desire to achieve some combination of on-field and financial success, the owners of NPB franchises have traditionally been corporations. In most cases, the owners of the NPB teams have not been motivated primarily by direct profits. Instead, corporate owners have viewed their teams as marketing vehicles for enhancing the brand recognition and sales of the parent company (Whiting, 1989, 2004). Previously, teams rarely considered implementing marketing initiatives to attract and retain customers or revenue-generating ideas that are commonplace in professional sport in the United States.

This financial and operating structure was adequate for many years, but it has recently created problems, as many prominent Japanese players have sought to leave Japan to play in MLB. With several of the top Japanese stars leaving—and access to MLB games in Japan growing because of new television distribution opportunities and the prevalence of the internet—many baseball fans in Japan have decreased their consumption of NPB games and ancillary products. For years, the Japanese have taken great pride in developing some of the world's top baseball players through the country's unique baseball system. Unfortunately, the traditions and cultural expectations that have helped to develop top players have also hindered change to NPB's business activities.

However, this may finally be changing. Former MLB managers, such as Bobby Valentine, Trey Hillman, and Terry Collins, have taken jobs in Japan and attempted to incorporate revenue-generating ideas into the Japanese system. Changes have also come from young Japanese baseball executives who were educated or previously employed in the United States. Marketing and promotion activities that were once perceived as inappropriate in the 1980s and 1990s have become more commonplace in Japanese baseball. Although change has met with considerable resistance in the past, the understanding that the high-quality on-field Japanese baseball product may fade if changes to the business model are not implemented is slowly but steadily beginning to permeate some of the franchises and the league office (Nagel & Brown, 2009).

The NFL has the strictest ownership requirements of all the North American professional sport leagues, including a steep cash down payment requirement. Potential owners who cannot meet this requirement may find their bids rejected. In 2005, Reggie Fowler agreed to purchase the Minnesota Vikings from Red McCombs for $625 million (Casacchia, 2005). McCombs and Fowler announced the sale prior to the other NFL owners' granting final approval. The sale was to be historic, as Fowler would have been the first African American owner in the NFL and only the second African American owner in the Big 4 leagues. However, the other owners rejected Fowler's bid because he was unable to meet the NFL's mandated 25% cash down payment (in this case over $150 million). Fowler's net worth was well over the purchase price, but his lack of liquidity forced the owners to reject his bid. The team was later sold to Zygmunt Wilf.

In addition to a cash down payment, the NFL also requires that an individual owner, rather than a corporation, operate the team. (As discussed in Chapter 5, the Green Bay Packers' current ownership is permitted because it was established prior to the current ownership rules.) For much of the NFL's history, the league required the primary owner to own at least 51% of the franchise, but due to escalating value of franchises, the league lowered that amount to 30% and then lowered it again in 2004 to 20% for one individual if at least another 10% was controlled by a family member (Kaplan, 2015). The loosening of the equity rules was driven by the desire to permit families to continue to own and operate NFL teams if an owner died. In 2009, four of the five brothers who had inherited 80% of the Pittsburgh Steelers from their father, Art Rooney, Sr., sold some or all of their shares in order to meet the NFL's requirement (Prine, 2009). Prior to the sale that provided Dan Rooney with enough shares to meet the NFL's mandate, the five brothers each owned 16% of the team ("Art Rooney Jr.," 2008).

Other professional leagues have some ownership requirements. Major League Soccer requires the majority owner to have at least a 35% stake in the franchise. The NBA requires the controlling owner to possess at least 15% of the franchise. In addition, the NBA enacted rules to require minimum minority ownership thresholds in 2015. A number of franchises had sold small stakes in their teams to celebrities to boost their brand image (Hanlon, 2015). Perhaps the most well-known minority owner transaction involved the New Jersey Nets selling less than 1/15 of 1% of their team to Jay Z (Hanlon, 2015). Though Jay Z later divested his minority ownership stake when he founded his sports agency, Roc Nation Sports, he was a catalyst for creating excitement for the team and its new venue, the Barclays Center, which opened in 2012. Despite the popularity of celebrity minority owners, the NBA altered its rule to mandate no more than 25 total owners of a team and that no owner could own less than 1% of the franchise (Kaplan, 2015).

In 2013, the NBA was involved in "choosing" a new owner. In 2008 commissioner David Stern and the other owners allowed the Seattle Supersonics to move to Oklahoma City to become the Thunder, leaving Seattle without an NBA franchise. When, in 2013, the owners of the Sacramento Kings experienced significant financial difficulty and desired to sell their franchise, a Seattle ownership group headed by Chris Hansen and then-Microsoft CEO Steve Ballmer offered $625 million for the team. However, the NBA "encouraged" the Kings' owners, George, Joe, and Gavin Maloof, to seek a new ownership group that would keep the team in Sacramento (Richter & Hurt, 2013). In 2013, the Kings were sold to an investment group headed by Vivek Ranadive for $534 million ("Done deal," 2013).

Though the NBA experienced some public backlash from fans in Seattle who were annoyed that the league permitted the Sonics to leave and prohibited the Kings from later taking their place in the Evergreen State, few could have anticipated the public furor over the comments made by Los Angeles Clippers owner Donald Sterling in 2014. Sterling, long unpopular with fans because of his unwillingness to spend money to retain players or maximize the fans' game day experience, was recorded making blatantly racist remarks to his long-time female companion, V. Stiviano. Though Sterling had committed worse actions in his dealings with various minority groups as a prominent landlord, the recorded comments became international news and the backlash was extensive. In one of his first acts as NBA commissioner, Adam Silver announced that Sterling was permanently suspended and would be required to sell his stake in the Clippers franchise. Eventually, Steve Ballmer paid a record $2 billion for Sterling's interest.

SIDEBAR 15.G   Long-term Family Ownership to End in Professional Sports?

With the recent rapid increase in the value of North American professional sport leagues, some concerns have been raised regarding the future ownership of franchises—particularly those in the NFL. The United States (as well as many individual states) applies an **inheritance** (or **death**) **tax** to wealthy estates when a person dies. In 2009, a 45% tax applied to any inheritances exceeding $3.5 million. In the case of an estate worth $5 million, the heirs would have had to pay $675,000 (45% of $1.5 million) in taxes. The President and the US Congress often alter the inheritance tax—sometimes in an apparently haphazard manner—for political gain. In 2010, there was no scheduled federal inheritance tax, so an estate could pass directly to the heirs without a federal tax consequence (though many individual states retained inheritance taxes). This situation inspired morbid jokes about it being wise to pick 2010 to die in rather than 2011, if a person were given the choice. New York Yankees owner George Steinbrenner did die in 2010, "saving" his family an estimated $500 million in death taxes that would have been due had he died in 2009 ("How Steinbrenner saved," 2010). The 2011 laws scheduled a 35% inheritance tax on estates larger than $5 million, with small increases scheduled in the estate-size exclusion amount in future years. However, the estate tax laws were altered as part of President Donald Trump's Tax Cuts and Jobs Act in 2017. The estate tax rate was lowered to 40% and the threshold for estate taxes to apply was increased dramatically to $11.4 million in 2019 (Garber, 2019).

Inheritance taxes are a contentious political topic. Some argue that it is unfair to tax the assets of deceased individuals, as the money that person earned has already been taxed (in some cases multiple times). Others counter that considerable accrued wealth should not be permitted to be passed down from one generation to the next. Since many professional sport franchises are worth hundreds of millions or even billions of dollars, the cash necessary to pay potential inheritance taxes may be overwhelming, and the heirs might be forced to seek loans or even sell the team. Former Cleveland Browns owner Art Modell sold the team partially because of his concern regarding inheritance taxes. Former Jacksonville Jaguars owner Wayne Weaver sold his majority interest to Shahid Khan for $760 million, having earlier expressed a desire to avoid inheritance tax issues (Clayton, 2008).

Recognizing the massive increases in values and their potential impact on long-time family ownership, in 2015 the NFL voted for the first time to permit owners to place all or a portion of their ownership stake in an irrevocable family trust (Kaplan, 2015). Such a tax-sheltering mechanism has a variety of short- and long-term financial repercussions, but it typically assists in passing assets to heirs with fewer headaches … and significantly lower estate taxes. The NFL had previously granted a special exemption for the Kansas City Chiefs to utilize an irrevocable trust to more easily permit Clark Hunt to inherit the team from his father Lamar. The NFL's decision to formally permit irrevocable trusts caused some to speculate that Carol Davis, the widow of the late Al Davis who bought part of his stake in the Raiders for "only" a few million dollars in the 1960s, might utilize such a mechanism to more easily pass her shares in the Raiders to son Marc upon her eventual death (Kaplan, 2015).

Debt

In addition to scrutinizing prospective owners' financial standing, leagues also establish ownership rules regarding the debt levels that a team may carry. For example, the NBA required teams to have no more than $175 million in debt until that was increased to $250 million in 2014 and then again to $325 million in 2018 (Lombardo & Kaplan, 2014; Wojnarowski, 2018). Prior to 2005, MLB teams could carry debt equal to 40% of their franchise value (Kaplan, 2003). In 2005, MLB changed the debt limit to a maximum of ten times the team's earnings before interest, taxes, depreciation, and amortization. Up to 15 times was acceptable if the franchise had recently borrowed money to build a new stadium. Later, MLB required debt to be no more than 12 times annual revenue minus expenses in most cases (Shaikin, 2016). In addition, MLB raised the required principal payments when teams paid back loans on the league's established credit lines. These rules are intended to prevent franchise owners from reckless borrowing.

The MLB debt rules were applied in 2009 when Joseph Ricketts and his family purchased the Chicago Cubs out of bankruptcy. In perhaps the most complicated sport franchise sale in history, the Tribune Company sold the Cubs, Wrigley Field, and other broadcast assets for $845 million (Sachdev, 2009). Once the Ricketts family established how they would fund and finance the purchase, MLB became concerned about their proposed debt levels. As a result, the Ricketts family had to agree to provide an additional $35 million in cash as an extra reserve in the event that projected cash flows did not meet expectations (Sachdev, 2009).

Once the Ricketts family established their ownership of the Cubs and began to increase revenues, they embarked on an aggressive $850 million plan to renovate Wrigley Field and to acquire and remodel a number of properties on Sheffield and Waveland avenues … by utilizing a variety of debt instruments. Many of the acquired buildings were remodeled to provide new rooftop seating options which offered excellent views of the facility. By 2017, the Cubs had acquired and renovated 11 rooftop properties and consolidated the various debts from that aspect of the overall plan into one loan worth $65 million with

Wintrust Bank (Ori, 2017). The debt agreement was designed to allow the Cubs to access additional cash from Wintrust over the ten-year loan agreement.

Leagues establish debt rules to prevent owners from experiencing significant financial problems, but in some cases a league must provide financial assistance when an owner does experience financial hardship. In rare cases, the rest of the owners in a league may elect to purchase the troubled team. Major League Baseball purchased the Montreal Expos in 2002 and owned the team until the league moved the club to Washington DC and sold it to Theodore Lerner. When the Phoenix Coyotes declared bankruptcy in 2009, it was revealed that for some time prior to the bankruptcy filing the team had largely been funded and operated by the NHL (Sunnucks, 2009).

Professional sport leagues do not want to see any of their franchises experience bankruptcy. This has been a rare occurrence in the Big 4 North American professional leagues since 1950, but teams such as MLB's Seattle Pilots (1969) and the NHL's Buffalo Sabres (2003) and Pittsburgh Penguins (1975 and 1998), in addition to the Coyotes, have filed for bankruptcy. When a team enters bankruptcy, potential problems may arise for the league, because of the financial uncertainty—particularly if the team cannot adequately reorganize its debt or if a new owner is not immediately found to purchase the financially troubled franchise. As mentioned earlier, the NHL worked to avoid the sale of the Phoenix Coyotes to Jim Balsillie once the team went into bankruptcy (Morris, 2009). Balsillie's plan to move the team to Hamilton, Ontario, Canada, might have generated increased revenues, but the NHL desired to keep the team in Arizona, and current owners opposed Balsillie's purchase for the additional reasons described earlier. Eventually the team was sold to Ice Edge Holdings, which agreed to keep the team in Phoenix (though it did plan to play a few games in Canada to increase potential revenue). Most of the recent bankruptcies in the Big 4 have involved hockey franchises, but the Chicago Cubs, one of the most storied teams in all of sports, declared bankruptcy in 2009, indicating that even a rabid fan base and a strong media presence (the Cubs were owned by the Tribune Company) cannot shield a professional sport franchise from poor financial decisions and the impact of a slowing economy.

More recently, the Los Angeles Dodgers experienced a financial disaster, which some observers viewed as actually the least pressing of the team's problems. Despite MLB rules requiring owners to maintain 60% equity and league scrutiny of any team purchase, Frank McCourt and his wife, Jamie, purchased the Dodgers in 2004, largely through debt that clearly violated MLB rules. It was later determined that their financial position was not as strong as initially believed. However, despite their extensive use of debt, the McCourts likely could have operated the Dodgers successfully if the antics in their personal lives had not caused so much controversy—and expenditure of cash. In October 2009, after nearly 30 years of marriage, the McCourts announced they were separating. As the divorce proceeded, tabloid stories of marital infidelity, general nastiness between the separating couple, and an IRS investigation, as well as tales of massive expenditures of money on luxury items—all financed through debt primarily backed by the Dodgers—dominated much of the Los Angeles media landscape. A variety of websites tracked the sometimes daily developments. As the divorce proceeded, it became apparent to observers, and MLB, that the Dodgers were in danger of experiencing significant financial difficulty. Adding to the team's misfortunes, in the first week of the 2011 season a San Francisco Giants fan, Brian Stow, was attacked outside Dodger Stadium. Stow suffered extensive injuries that resulted in long-term cognitive difficulties. The attack on Stow shocked the baseball world.

When the Dodgers needed special loans from Fox Broadcasting against a not-yet-MLB-approved future television deal to make payroll in April 2011, the reality that McCourt could no longer successfully operate the Dodgers became apparent to everyone. Major League Baseball stepped in and appointed a trustee to oversee the club on April 21, 2011. When the Dodgers requested that MLB sign a proposed $3 billion media contract with Fox, the league declined. Commissioner Bud Selig perceived the contract to be below market value and to be designed to provide Frank McCourt with enough money in the short term to retain the team while sacrificing long-term revenue opportunities (Wojciechowski, 2011). After a year of contentious negotiations—which included various interventions by different courts—the Dodgers, Dodger Stadium, and some adjacent real estate were sold in March 2012 to investment group Guggenheim Baseball Management (in which Magic Johnson was a minority partner) for $2.15 billion. This figure shocked many because less than two years earlier the team had been believed to be worth less than $1 billion (Egan, 2012).

The new Dodger ownership group immediately invested significant sums of money to acquire talented players, expand its scouting department, and make improvements to Dodger Stadium. The results on the field were impressive as the Dodgers were in first place in the National League West every year from 2013 to 2020. However, their large payrolls were of concern to MLB since the ownership group utilized a large amount of debt to acquire cash in the short term. MLB rules permit teams to violate their debt rules during the first five years after an ownership acquisition, but after that grace period greater scrutiny is to occur (Shaikin, 2016). While the Dodgers led the league in payroll from 2013 to 2017, in 2018 and 2019 they made some difficult player salary decisions and were passed by a few other teams for the highest payroll in the league. Though the Dodgers denied their financial changes were related to the MLB debt rules, the decrease from the top payroll spot coincided with the completion of Guggenheim's fifth year of ownership (Shaikin, 2016; "MLB Team Payroll Tracker," 2018).

In the NFL, team debt limits have long been set at conservative levels (relative to the franchise values). However, as previously mentioned, the dramatic increase in NFL franchise values has caused the league to re-evaluate a few of its long-standing rules so that owners who do desire to sell can find capable buyers. In 2018, the NFL elected to increase its franchise debt limit from $250 million to $350 million (Ozanian, 2018). The increase was thought to provide greater opportunities for Jerry Richardson to sell the Carolina Panthers as a potential owner could bid a higher price knowing he or she could use more debt to secure the transaction. Despite the large debt level increase, Fitch Ratings still evaluated the NFL's debt rating as excellent because of its large and ever-expanding revenue sources.

A league's purchase or direct assumption of control of a troubled team is a dramatic move and one that happens rarely. However, leagues often will provide various types of financial support for franchises. One is **pooled debt**. When a lender evaluates a loan applicant, it investigates the applicant's ability to repay the loan. Since the combined financial stature of an entire league is much stronger than that of an individual team, the league can borrow money more readily and often at a slightly lower interest rate than a team. During the Great Recession in 2008–2009, a number of professional sport leagues froze their debt limits due to the uncertainty about the short-term financial future. As the economy slowly improved, leagues sought greater pooled debt instruments and increased their teams' debt limits (Kaplan, 2013). The NFL's G-3 and G-4 funds (discussed in Chapter 7), established to assist teams building new stadiums, are examples of pooled debt instruments. Recently, the NFL's strong desire to return to the Los Angeles market and have a state-of-the-art facility resulted in the league permitting the Rams to access $400 million in G-4 stadium financing, with $200 million technically being allocated to the Chargers who became tenants after the facility opened in 2020. The G-4 funding was granted in combination with the league permitting the Rams to secure a debt-rule waiver that permitted the club to increase its total debt to more than $2.6 billion (Kaplan, 2018).

In 2009, the NBA created a pooled-debt instrument to assist financially struggling franchises. The league borrowed $200 million to distribute to teams in need of cash. The loan was backed by the projected revenues of the entire league, resulting in a lower interest rate and a larger loan amount than any team could have secured individually. NBA commissioner David Stern noted, "This was a show of strength in the creditworthiness of the NBA's teams" ("NBA lines up," 2009, para. 4). Some teams were criticized for utilizing the fund. The Orlando Magic and Utah Jazz were believed to be interested in tapping into the league's available credit due to cash-flow concerns. However, despite experiencing (apparent) financial difficulty, the teams signed players to high-priced contracts soon after the NBA announced the new financing. The Magic signed backup center Marcin Gortat to a five-year, $34 million contract, and the Utah Jazz signed backup power forward Paul Millsap to a four-year, $32 million contract. These contract signings suggested that the financial problems some NBA franchises were experiencing may have resulted from their own decision making rather than a slumping economy.

Expansion

A critical element in any professional sport league's success is the ability to expand into new territories at appropriate times. When a league expands, current owners are likely to see their portion of shared revenue from media contracts and licensed merchandise decrease in the short term, as more teams are splitting the revenue. To compensate the current owners, the league typically charges a new owner an **expansion fee**, which is distributed to the other owners. Prospective owners have typically been willing to pay expansion fees to join a league, as professional sport ownership is certainly an exclusive club. Though the initial financial return on an expansion team is often small or even negative, many wealthy individuals are motivated by the non-financial ownership benefits already discussed; they view sport franchise ownership as a new challenge that cannot be duplicated elsewhere. In addition, an expansion franchise presents an owner with the opportunity to enhance his or her personal brand while providing a metropolitan area its first opportunity to have a "new" team—an exciting prospect, even if the team's on-field success in the first few years is limited. During the past 20 years, the expansion fees charged to new league owners have grown tremendously. Exhibit 15.1 lists expansion fees paid in the Big 4 leagues from 1991 through 2021. Of interest is the expansion fees paid by the new entrants from Las Vegas and Seattle. During the early 2000s, some NHL franchises experienced financial hardship and a few clubs were sold with little profit made by the owners. In some cases, new owners essentially assumed debt obligations that the teams had accrued (Bernstein, 2002). The $500 million expansion fee paid for the Las Vegas Golden Knights was thought by some to be exorbitant, but their immediate success on and off the ice—combined with a solid financial footing for the rest of the NHL—led to an increased price for future expansion teams. In 2018, investors paid NHL owners $650 million for the expansion Seattle Kraken.

For most professional sport leagues, expansion is a critical component of their strategic plan. In the late 1950s, the NFL failed to recognize that it should expand to emerging metropolitan markets such as Denver, Boston, and Houston, which allowed the upstart American Football League to establish a presence in these areas. The leagues desire to expand at a rate that prevents rival upstart leagues from entering untapped metropolitan areas, but they typically will leave at least one or two viable cities unoccupied. This "failure" to meet potential demand is designed to preserve sufficient scarcity to motivate established markets to spend money to retain established teams. If the leagues allowed the supply of teams to equal or exceed the number of viable markets, this would reduce teams' ability to use the threat of relocating to force municipalities to build new stadiums or remodel existing ones. In addition, under most of the collective bargaining agreements in North American professional sport leagues, expansion revenues are not considered in yearly league revenues and therefore are not directly shared with the players.

Territorial Rights

Ownership of a professional sport franchise confers a variety of benefits. One of the most important involves **territorial rights**—exclusive control of a predetermined area (typically a city's entire metropolitan area). In theory, the establishment of specific territories enables a professional sport team to market exclusively in that area without fear that another team in the same sport will enter the area and "steal" customers. Every professional sport franchise vehemently protects its territory, as the limitation of direct competitors increases ticket prices and the value of media contracts. In the rare cases when teams have "invaded" another team's territory (after receiving permission from the league to relocate)—as the NHL's Anaheim Ducks and New Jersey Devils did—they paid compensation to the existing team.

EXHIBIT 15.1 Expansion fees paid to the Big 4 leagues, 1991–2021.

NHL	YEAR	TEAM	FEE
	1991	San Jose Sharks	$50 million
	1992	Ottawa Senators	$50 million
	1992	Tampa Bay Lightning	$50 million
	1993	Florida Panthers	$50 million
	1993	Anaheim Mighty Ducks	$50 million
	1998	Nashville Predators	$80 million
	1999	Atlanta Thrashers	$80 million
	2000	Minnesota Wild	$80 million
	2000	Columbus Blue Jackets	$80 million
	2017	Las Vegas Golden Knights	$500 million
	2021	Seattle Kraken	$650 million
MLB	**YEAR**	**TEAM**	**FEE**
	1993	Colorado Rockies	$95 million
	1993	Florida Marlins	$95 million
	1998	Arizona Diamondbacks	$130 million
	1998	Tampa Bay Rays	$130 million
NFL	**YEAR**	**TEAM**	**FEE**
	1995	Carolina Panthers	$140 million
	1995	Jacksonville Jaguars	$140 million
	1999	Cleveland Browns	$530 million
	2002	Houston Texans	$700 million
NBA	**YEAR**	**TEAM**	**FEE**
	1995	Vancouver Grizzlies	$125 million
	1995	Toronto Raptors	$125 million
	2006	Charlotte Bobcats	$300 million

SIDEBAR 15.H   The Future of Women's Professional Basketball in the United States

Since its founding in 1996, the Women's National Basketball Association has attempted to build its brand and attract a stable fan base. From 2007 through 2014, the league averaged between 7,500 and 8,100 fans at each game, with consistent television ratings that roughly equaled those of MLS (Cardillo, 2013). The league's attendance dipped slightly in 2017–2019, but much of that was due to the New York Liberty and Washington Mystics moving their home games from expansive NBA arenas to more intimate facilities. By playing games in the summer, the WNBA has enabled its players to also play overseas in leagues that often offer far greater financial compensation. In particular, franchises in the Russian Premier League, which are usually owned and supported by tycoons who primarily desire to win games, have begun to offer salaries that can exceed $1 million a year—much larger than the WNBA's 2019 maximum of $115,500 (Lee, 2019a). In 2015, the Russian team UMMC Ekaterinburg paid star guard Diana Taurasi $1.5 million and asked her to skip the WNBA season. Taurasi agreed to forgo playing the 2015 season with the defending WNBA champion Phoenix Mercury when UMMC Ekaterinburg offered her much more money to rest than her WNBA team did to play (Fagan, 2015). Most of the best players in the world have been offered lucrative incentives to skip the WNBA season; Taurasi was the first one to accept. Though there has not been a mass player exodus from the WNBA, there have been other prominent players who have skipped a season, even when healthy. All-Star Maya Moore skipped the 2019 and 2020 seasons to focus on personal and religious matters. Other players have discussed the wear and tear that comes with playing competitive basketball for most of the year without significant time to mentally and physically rest (Lee, 2019b). Moore's decision to skip the 2019 season came at a volatile time for the WNBA as players and owners negotiated a new eight-year collective bargaining agreement (CBA) that began in the 2020 season. Despite developing revenue sources, the WNBA players repeatedly remarked that they were underpaid and treated with little respect given their stature (Townes, 2019). To address the salary concerns, the new deal increased the base pay of the top players to $215,000 and provided mechanisms for bonuses that could increase total compensation for some players to over $500,000 (Cwik, 2020). In addition, the entire salary pool for all of the players was dramatically enhanced. The WNBA also committed to allocating increased marketing dollars to promote players, enhanced the health benefits available to players, and established that players would be given their own room on road trips. Though the WNBA would not permit charter flights to become commonplace for league travel due to concerns about expenses, they did relent on providing better seating on commercial flights. The hope is the 2020 CBA not only provides financial stability, but also creates an environment where the league and the players can build their fan base and better compensate players compared to what is often offered in some international leagues.

Since territorial rules reduce competition, fans of professional sport must pay a premium, especially in large cities. For instance, the New York City metropolitan market could likely support additional teams in the NFL, NBA, NHL, and MLB, but territorial restrictions limit entry to the market. Certainly, New York offers a larger population base and much greater potential corporate support for a third NFL or NBA team than a city such as Kansas City or Indianapolis would provide. However, most professional sport team owners purchased their teams with the expectation of control of an entire metropolitan territory, and they paid for that benefit. Therefore, territorial rules are likely to remain in force, particularly since North American professional sport leagues have successfully eliminated their direct competitors.

In the last several decades, Major League Baseball has experienced two significant territorial disputes. When MLB purchased the Montreal Expos and decided to move the team to Washington DC, it infringed upon the Baltimore Orioles' territory. After extensive discussion and numerous legal threats from Baltimore Orioles owner Peter Angelos, MLB agreed to guarantee Angelos $365 million if he ever decided to sell the team (Heath, 2005). In addition, the Orioles were to share ownership of the Mid-Atlantic Sports Network (MASN). The Nationals (as the Expos were renamed) were to own 10% of the regional sports network, but their stake was to increase by 1% each year until it reached a cap of 33% in 2032 (Barker, 2019). The yearly profits of the network were to be distributed according to each team's ownership percentage. In addition, MASN was supposed to pay a "fair market" fee to each team for the rights to broadcast their games. The rights fees would be determined every five years. Unfortunately, the Orioles and Nationals were unable to determine what rights fees were appropriate for each club and what the resulting profits MASN would generate after paying those rights fees. Over a number of years and through a variety of legal proceedings (arbitration, court cases, appeals, etc.), the teams fought each other for "adequate compensation." In one court proceeding, documents revealed that from 2012 to 2016 the Nationals received $41.5 million in MASN profits while the Orioles received $234.8 million (Barker, 2019). In one court judgment, the Nationals were deemed to have been shortchanged $296.8 million in rights fees and MASN profits over the years in question (Schmuck, 2019). Much of the litigation occurred during the 2019 season, one in which the Orioles played terribly, and the Nationals won the World Series. This caused an already contentious relationship to become even more strained as both parties fought to win the various rounds of arbitration and court proceedings. The final decision regarding exact compensation was still being litigated as this book went to press.

In the early 1990s, the San Francisco Giants, frustrated with antiquated Candlestick Park, requested access to unclaimed territories in Santa Clara and Monterey counties, California. After the Oakland Athletics and MLB voted to allow the team to move to either of the new territories, the Giants were unable to secure financing for a new facility in either county. The Giants eventually built a new facility in San Francisco. Meanwhile, the A's have been enduring an untenable stadium situation ever since the city remodeled the Oakland–Alameda County Coliseum in 1995/1996, shortly after the Raiders returned. Although the A's supported the Giants' potential move to Santa Clara County, the Giants have countered any potential A's move to San Jose or any other Santa Clara County location. The Giants have steadfastly demanded that the territories they acquired when they considered moving should remain exclusively theirs. The A's, unable to pursue a Santa Clara County destination, have experienced financial hardship compared to other MLB franchises where revenues are skyrocketing. Their dwindling fan base and lowered generated revenue may affect every other team in Major League Baseball, but other franchise owners have been unwilling to rescind the Giants' rights to a portion of their territory (Nagel, Brown, Rascher, & McEvoy, 2007). For many years MLB did not choose to act to resolve the problem, despite the willingness of San Jose officials to finance a new stadium. In 2013, in an effort to move the process closer to resolution, San Jose sued MLB for violating antitrust laws ("San Jose officials explain," 2013). A San Francisco-based federal judge dismissed the lawsuit in October 2013, and the City, in turn, advanced an appeal that was heard in March 2014 (Woolfolk, 2014). In January 2015, the Ninth US Circuit Court of Appeals unanimously rejected San Jose's claims (Mintz, 2015). Despite this legal setback, the City of San Jose elected to file an appeal to the US Supreme Court, but the court did not hear the case (Louie, 2015). Despite playing in an antiquated and substandard MLB facility, the A's have fielded some high-quality teams under the leadership of executive vice president for baseball operations Billy Beane. With the option to move to San Jose blocked, the A's hoped to secure a new facility within their Alameda County territory to avoid having to leave the Bay Area.

COMPETITIVE BALANCE

The numerous rules described previously are intended to maintain a financially viable league, but more critical to a league's long-term success—and more likely to attract media and fan attention—are the league's efforts to maintain competitive balance, so that every team has a financial opportunity to field a competitive team. Determining the optimal level of competitive balance and then achieving that level is difficult, because each franchise operates in a unique local market. Teams located in the largest metropolitan areas, such as New York, Los Angeles, and Chicago, have an inherent financial advantage, because these cities have more people to purchase tickets and other game-related products (such as parking and concessions), a greater number of corporations to lease luxury suites and buy expensive club seating, and many local media outlets bidding for the rights to broadcast the teams' games. Since many **stadium-related revenue sources**, such as the sale of luxury suites, are not shared with the rest of the league's teams, a perfectly fair revenue-sharing system is an impossibility. However, leagues work to ensure that fans of each franchise can legitimately hope their team will be successful. The leagues have enacted a variety of "competition" rules and policies to create an environment that fosters competitive balance. This section discusses the financial implications of the rules and policies designed to ensure competitive balance, including those related to player drafts, salary slotting, free agency, player salary negotiations, luxury taxes, and revenue sharing.

SIDEBAR 15.I   Competing Leagues

The NFL, NBA, NHL, and MLB currently enjoy monopolies in their respective sports, as there are no viable competitors offering similar professional football, basketball, hockey, or baseball contests. However, each of these leagues has had to fight potential competitors. Major League Baseball has had the strongest monopoly among the four leagues. The last serious attempt to establish a viable competitor professional baseball league occurred when the Federal League formed in 1914. The Federal League was able to sign some established Major League players, but others were reluctant to sign for fear of being blackballed by current MLB teams if the Federal League failed.

The Federal League experienced financial difficulty during the 1914 season, partially (the owners felt) due to the actions of MLB. During the off-season, the owners filed an antitrust lawsuit against MLB arguing that MLB owners had established an illegal monopoly for the operation of professional baseball. In US federal court, Judge Kennesaw Mountain Landis, who would later become MLB commissioner, urged the parties to settle the dispute, so the case was not immediately deliberated. After the 1915 season, all of the remaining Federal League owners (the Kansas City franchise had declared bankruptcy and been taken over by the league) settled with the MLB owners, except for the Baltimore franchise, which elected to continue to pursue litigation. Eventually, the US Supreme Court ruled that MLB was a legal monopoly immune from antitrust laws (*Federal Baseball Club v. National League*, 1922). No other serious attempt has been made to compete with MLB. Perhaps the most noteworthy accomplishment of the Federal League, besides the antitrust ruling, was the construction of historic Wrigley Field, which was built for the Federal League's Chicago Whales.

MLB has experienced nearly 100 years of "peace" from potential direct competitors, but the other three major North American professional sport leagues have faced much more competition. The NFL first encountered a viable competitor when the All-American Football Conference (AAFC) was formed in 1946. Though the NFL initially scoffed at the new rival, by 1949 the AAFC's Cleveland Browns, Baltimore Colts, and San Francisco 49ers had been admitted to the NFL through a merger agreement. The Browns were such a powerful team that they won the NFL title in the first year after the merger.

The NFL would later experience competition from the AFL. Multimillionaire Lamar Hunt had sought to purchase an NFL team in the late 1950s. When he was unable to procure a team, he solicited other wealthy people to start a rival league. The league was able to achieve success partially because of the commitment on the part of Hunt and other wealthy owners and partially because the NFL had sold coverage of its games exclusively to CBS. The American Broadcasting Company (ABC) and the National Broadcasting Company (NBC), being shut out of broadcasting NFL football, were eager to sign a deal with the upstart AFL. ABC signed an initial deal in 1960, and in 1964 NBC secured the AFL's television rights. The AFL experienced enough success that by 1969 it had merged with the NFL. Lamar Hunt not only helped build the AFL, but he also became one of the NFL's most influential owners as owner of the Kansas City Chiefs.

The popularity of professional football prompted additional rival leagues to form. In 1974 the World Football League (WFL) was founded as a summertime and fall league. It signed a few established NFL stars but was largely unsuccessful. However, it did help to increase NFL salaries, which had been stagnant despite the growth in the NFL's popularity.

The United States Football League (USFL), which began play in 1983 as a springtime professional league, had some financially powerful owners and immediately signed television contracts with ABC and Entertainment and Sports Programming Network (ESPN). The league also signed some high-caliber NFL players and college stars, such as Herschel Walker, and promised to remain a viable enterprise. However, in addition to the typical problems that start-up leagues endure, numerous USFL owners—such as flamboyant Donald Trump of the New Jersey Generals—refused to adhere to the league's spending guidelines. With some owners signing players to exorbitant contracts and others unable to match that level of spending, the league began to unravel.

In 1986, the league made the critical decision to move to a fall schedule. The league had signed venue and media contracts to play football in the spring, but the NFL had already secured venues and television deals for Sundays in the fall. With the USFL in turmoil—primarily due to certain owners' desire to force a merger with the NFL rather than work to keep the league in operation—and no viable way to conduct a fall league, the owners elected to file an antitrust lawsuit against the NFL. The suit claimed that the NFL was a professional football monopoly that had illegally conspired to force the USFL out of business. The USFL named every NFL owner as a defendant, except for Oakland Raiders owner Al Davis, who testified on behalf of the USFL. The circuit court ruled in favor of the USFL but awarded the league only $1, which was trebled under antitrust laws to $3. When the case decision and awarded damages were affirmed under appeal (*USFL v. NFL*, 1988), the USFL became a footnote in the history of professional sports.

The NBA and NHL encountered rival leagues in the 1960s and 1970s. The American Basketball Association (ABA) was formed in 1967. To build excitement, the free-wheeling league used a red, white, and blue basketball, wide-open play, and a three-point shot. The league was able to sign many of the top amateur players, including Julius Erving, Moses Malone, Spencer Haywood, and David Thompson. Some of the league's teams were financially stable, but others experienced financial hardship. Far too often, teams had difficulty making their payroll, and numerous franchises relocated. At the conclusion of the 1976 season, the Indiana Pacers, San Antonio Spurs, New Jersey Nets, and Denver Nuggets were merged into the NBA.

In 1972 the World Hockey Association (WHA) was formed as a rival to the NHL. The WHA established some of its franchises in "open" hockey cities and, to attract players, attempted to pay higher salaries than those offered in the NHL. The WHA was involved in numerous legal battles with the NHL, most of which did not result in any financial advantage to the WHA. In 1979, four of the remaining six WHA teams were admitted to the NHL, but they each had to pay a $6 million franchise fee. The two WHA franchises that were not absorbed into the NHL were paid $1.5 million in compensation. Although the WHA was not tremendously successful, it was the first professional league in which superstars Wayne Gretzky and Mark Messier played.

Perhaps one of the more interesting side notes to the creation of the WFL, ABA, and WHA is that one man was involved in all three ventures. Attorney Gary Davidson founded or co-founded all three leagues. His tireless efforts to promote the leagues made him one of the most successful sport entrepreneurs of the 20th century. His leagues are estimated to have provided at least $500 million in direct economic impact—a considerable sum in the late 1960s and 1970s (Crowe, 2008). Although Davidson was approached on multiple occasions to begin other leagues, he left the fast-paced world of professional sports to remain close to his family in southern California. He will be remembered as one of the more important figures in North American professional sport history.

One of the enduring lessons we learn from the attempts to establish professional leagues, whether as rivals to an established league or as new operations, is that owners have to be committed to the new venture and have to be willing to spend money—in most cases, lots of it. In addition to following a slow-growth plan, one of the reasons MLS has been successful is that Philip Anschutz and Lamar Hunt were committed to seeing MLS survive long enough to build a fan base capable of supporting soccer-specific stadiums across the country. Hunt (who died in 2006) had a legendary dedication to his sport-business endeavors, as well as a nearly bottomless supply of money to spend. During the first years of the AFL in the early 1960s, it was reported that Hunt was losing over a million dollars a year. When told of this, Lamar Hunt's father, H.L. Hunt, noted that "At that rate, he will last only a hundred years" (Harvey, 1979, para. 3). Hunt's commitment not only enabled the AFL to achieve equal status with the NFL and an eventual merger, but it also resulted in Major League Soccer's achieving a level of success few envisioned when it began competition in 1996. As of 2015, 17 of the 24 MLS facilities were soccer-specific, with plans for future MLS expansion to include soccer-specific facilities as a core element of any bid.

Player Drafts

The player draft is the process by which the leagues assign incoming high school and/or college players to teams. Some leagues, such as MLB, also utilize other drafts to distribute current minor league players throughout the league. First conducted by the NFL in 1936 ("Pro football draft," n.d.) and later implemented by each of the other major North American professional sport leagues, player drafts "reward" poorly performing teams by awarding them higher draft picks. Typically, the worst performing team during each season will "earn" the first pick in every round of the upcoming draft, and the league champion will be awarded the last pick in each round. Other teams will draft between the highest- and lowest-performing teams in inverse order of their success during the past season. Drafted players may negotiate only with the team that selected them. In theory, this system allows the teams with the greatest "need" for an infusion of new players the best opportunity to acquire them. Although selected players have occasionally refused to sign, in most cases drafted players begin their career with the team that selected them in the draft, as soon as possible after the draft. Of course, each team is responsible for determining the best players to pick, and there is no guarantee that they will make "correct" selections.

SIDEBAR 15.J   NBA Draft Lottery

A basketball team has only five players on the court at one time, and the best players will usually play over three-quarters of every game. Hence, unlike teams in the other major North American professional sport leagues, franchises in the National Basketball Association can be instantly and dramatically changed with the addition or subtraction of one superstar player. Some teams perceived that their best opportunity to achieve long-term success was to acquire the highest draft pick possible by losing games—so "unsuccessful" teams with poor records often decided to "tank" games by limiting their best players' minutes or by sitting "injured" players late in the season, once a playoff berth was not a possibility (McCann, 2007).

During the 1983/1984 NBA season, the Houston Rockets attracted attention from the NBA, the media, and fans as it made a series of questionable playing-time decisions during the second half of the season ("Coin flip," 2008). Many suspected that the Rockets worked to lose games in order to have a chance to pick University of Houston center Akeem Olajuwon with the draft's first selection. At the time, the NBA awarded the first pick in the draft to the winner of a coin flip between the teams with the worst record in the Western and Eastern Conferences. After the Rockets won the coin flip and selected Olajuwon, the NBA announced that the 1985 draft order for the seven non-playoff teams would be determined by a **draft lottery**, a lottery used to determine the draft order of the non-playoff teams.

The 1985 lottery created considerable excitement, as the winner would likely select Georgetown University center Patrick Ewing. The team with the worst record in the league, the Golden State Warriors, "lost" the lottery and selected seventh in the 1985 draft. The New York Knicks, who had a better 1984/1985 record than the Warriors, won the lottery and eventually did select Ewing. The 1985 lottery aroused controversy, as some pundits claimed that the NBA had a vested interest in seeing its signature franchise in New York draft the best player (Simmons, 2007).

While denying any conspiracy, the NBA has made numerous changes to its lottery process. In 1987, the lottery identified only those teams selecting in the first three positions. The other teams would draft according to the inverse order of their record, starting with the fourth selection. In 1990, the lottery was altered to allow the 11 teams that did not make the playoffs to have a number of chances related to their record. The worst team received 11 chances out of 66 (16.67%), and the best non-playoff team received one chance out of 66 (1.52%). This format was changed in 1994 after the Orlando Magic won the lottery two years in a row—the second time after earning the best record among the non-playoff teams. The next system provided the team with the worst record a 25% chance to win and the team with the best non-playoff record a 0.5% chance to win, with all other non-playoff teams receiving a percentage between those two "anchors" based upon their position in the overall standings.

NBA officials and observers noticed that despite the lottery changes, several teams appeared to tank to receive a greater chance to win the lottery. Even if a tanking team did not win the lottery, the fact that only the first three picks were allocated by lottery and the rest were assigned based upon record caused many teams to deem the potential rewards from a higher draft pick to be more valuable than the negative attention continued losing would yield. In March of 2012, the Golden State Warriors traded starter Monta Ellis to the Milwaukee Bucks for an injured Andrew Bogut, shut down guard Stephen Curry, and then made several "questionable" game decisions in an effort to drop from the tenth worst record to the seventh. Having already made a trade a year earlier that would convey their 2012 first round pick to the Utah Jazz if it was outside the top seven selections, the Warriors desired to keep their pick and increase their chances of "winning" the lottery. Instead of sending their pick to the Jazz in 2012, the Warriors instead selected Harrison Barnes with the seventh pick and then conveyed their 2013 first round pick to the Jazz after the Warriors completed a successful season. A number of observers speculated that the Warriors were tanking, and their former assistant general manager Travis Schlenk later verified this claim (Feldman, 2017). Barnes and Bogut became key contributors on the Warriors 2014–2015 championship team, though many fans did not appreciate the Warriors "trying" to lose 17 of their last 20 games in 2012.

Sensing that their system needed alterations, the NBA discussed a few changes, most notably the possibility of implementing a "wheel" proposal where all team's picks would be predetermined (Lowe, 2013). Over the course of 30 years, every one of the 30 NBA teams would pick in the 30 different draft slots. The pick would not be based upon a team's record in the previous year. To offer a balanced outcome, every team would be guaranteed a top-six pick every five seasons and at least one top-12 pick over every four-year period. Though the wheel offered some intrigue, it was not embraced by most NBA personnel when it was initially discussed. The NBA did make draft lottery changes in 2019 as it altered the format to offer the top (worst) three teams from the previous year an equal chance to win the lottery.

Salary Slotting

In an effort to control costs and assist franchises in salary negotiations, some professional sport leagues have established official or unofficial **salary slotting** (rules or recommendations regarding initial compensation to be provided to players based on draft positioning) for selected players. The NBA has negotiated salary slots for first-round draft picks. Prior to 2012, Major League Baseball unofficially suggested salaries for each draft "slot"; however, many players and agents insisted that their salaries be negotiated outside the commissioner's suggestions. In 2009, overall number one MLB selection Stephen Strasburg signed a four-year, $15.1 million contract, which eclipsed the previous record— a five-year, $10.5 million contract given to Mark Prior in 2001 ("Nats, Strasburg beat deadline," 2009).

SIDEBAR 15.K   Houston Astros Exploit the MLB Draft Slotting System and Lead Others to Massive Losses

Major League Baseball's latest collective bargaining agreement mandates salary maximums for amateur players selected through the draft. However, the assigned slots are not symmetrical in their decreases after the first pick. For example, though the difference between the 20th and 21st picks in the 2011 MLB amateur draft was $25,000, the difference between the seventh and eighth picks was $100,000 and the difference between the first and second picks was $1 million (Jazayerli, 2013). In addition, the first pick was allocated $7.2 million while the fifth pick was allocated $3.5 million, a difference of $3.7 million. In 2019, the difference between the first ($16,093,700) and second ($13,821,300) picks in the draft had increased to $2,272,400 (Collazo, 2019). The MLB slotting system "rewards" poorly performing teams with more money to sign draft picks, but there is a special incentive not only to be bad, but to finish with the worst record in the league.

Given this set of incentives—and the fact that most baseball prospects take multiple years to develop—after having losing records in 2009 and 2010, and facing limited prospects for success in 2011 due to an aging and significantly substandard roster, the Houston Astros decided that it would behoove the franchise to be not only bad but terrible for a few years. In 2011, the Astros began to trade nearly every veteran player for minor league prospects. Over a four-year period, the Astros finished with the worst record in MLB while fielding some of the most abysmal teams in recent MLB history. However, their poor records translated into higher allocations for signing top amateur prospects under the MLB slotting system—which they did after each draft in 2011, 2012, 2013, and 2014. Though attendance decreased dramatically and the team became a running joke locally and nationally, the Astros were buoyed by a lucrative local television contract that extended through 2022. By the end of the 2014 season, many of the drafted players made it to the MLB roster and began to play well. In 2015, the team enjoyed its first successful season in many years, and most of the best players were young and under team control for many future seasons. In 2017, the Astros won the World Series for the first time in their team history. In 2019, the team lost the World Series to the Washington Nationals in a thrilling seven-game series.

Though some other teams initially questioned the Astros' plans, within a few years of the team's 2015 success, several other general managers began pursuing the same strategy. By 2019, several teams entered the season with little apparent desire to win games (Snyder, 2019). By the end of the season, ten franchises had lost 90 or more games and a record four had lost 100, long a mark of extreme ineptitude. The Royals lost 103 games and had to settle for "only" the fourth pick in the draft. Conversely, a record four clubs won 100 games and there was a feeling within baseball that only roughly half of the clubs were truly trying to advance to the playoffs. The willingness of so many teams to "tank" has a variety of implications for the entire industry. Certainly, having so many teams with terrible rosters lowers attendance and viewership. In addition, teams that plan to lose do not typically invest much money in free agents, meaning veteran players have fewer suitors for their services. A number of baseball executives have indicated that continued "gutting" of teams may need to be addressed with different incentives in the future.

To attempt to create a more "fair" environment, MLB altered its rules beginning with the 2012 amateur player draft. In the 2000s, MLB had instituted "suggested" player salary slots for each of its clubs. The "suggestions" were designed to restrain costs and permit a greater number of talented players to be drafted and signed to lower-revenue-producing franchises. As of 2012, however, these salary slots were no longer "suggestions" that some clubs could conveniently ignore. Instead, each team was allocated a specific amount of money for signing drafted players, based on the total number and order of the team's picks. Every pick in the first ten rounds (of 40 total) was assigned a value. A team could not spend more than its allocation in the top ten rounds. If a team did not sign a draft pick in the first ten rounds, that pick's value would be subtracted from the team's overall draft allocation (Thomas, 2012). Players selected after round ten could be signed for no more than $100,000; amounts in excess would be deducted from the team's overall pool. MLB enacted tough penalties to restrict teams from violating their draft allocations.

NFL owners long discussed including a salary slotting system in the collective bargaining agreement negotiated with the NFL Players Association. The owners became particularly concerned when first-round picks JaMarcus Russell (2007) and Jake Long (2008) signed contracts that guaranteed them more than $25 million—more money than many established veterans would make over their entire career. Under the CBA signed in 2011, NFL rookie salaries were decreased dramatically in a new slotting system. For example, in 2010 Sam Bradford was selected first overall by the St. Louis Rams. He signed a six-year, $78 million contract. In 2011, first overall pick Cam Newton signed a four-year, $22 million contract with the Carolina Panthers (Kostora, 2013). The owners convinced the current players that a more restrictive salary slotting system would allow established players to receive more money because most

NFL clubs operate near the upper salary cap limit and money they *cannot* spend on rookies will then be spent on veterans. The new salary slotting system also minimized contract disputes, such as those that occurred in 2009 after the San Francisco 49ers selected Michael Crabtree with the tenth selection of the first round. Crabtree's agent argued that Crabtree was the best wide receiver in the draft and should have been paid more than Darrius Heyward-Bey, whom the Oakland Raiders selected with the seventh selection. Crabtree missed the first half of the season in the contract dispute.

The NFL's slotting system has created an environment where the most important player a franchise can acquire is a high-quality quarterback on a rookie contract. Given the cost certainly of the slotting system, a quarterback who would be worth $15 million or more on the open market being forced to play for "only" a few million dollars or, in some cases, even less, provides a franchise the opportunity to invest in high-performing players throughout their roster. As the first pick of the 2012 draft, Indianapolis Colts quarterback Andrew Luck would be paid no more than $7.5 million in any of his first four seasons. That presented the Colts with a bargain considering he played very well and led the team to the playoffs his first three years. However, he was not the best "bargain" of the 2012 draft. That distinction went to third-round pick Russell Wilson who was paid less than $2.5 million *total* in his first three years. During that time, the Seahawks were able to surround the highly efficient Wilson with talented players and the team went to the playoffs all three years, won the Super Bowl in the 2013 season, and appeared in the Super Bowl in the 2014 season.

Not every team that has a highly proficient quarterback with a low salary has been able to capitalize on their good fortune. Since he was a 2016 fourth-round selection, the Dallas Cowboys "only" had to pay quarterback Dak Prescott about $5 million total for his first four years in the league. The Cowboys mostly squandered this tremendous financial opportunity as, unlike the Seahawks who managed their cap effectively, the Cowboys used most of the "extra" money they did not have to pay Prescott to cover "dead money" they owed to past players who were no longer on their roster (Barnwell, 2018). The Cowboys did have some limited success in those first four years, but they were unable to advance far in the playoffs when they had Prescott on a very cheap contract.

SIDEBAR 15.L   Is there a Need to Negotiate a Slotted Contract?

Historically, one of the most contentious issues among professional team sport athletes has been the salaries of rookie players. For many years in several sports, highly drafted players may have been paid more than effective veterans. To make the distribution of salaries more representative of what players have accomplished in the professional ranks, a number of recent collective bargaining agreements have "slotted" rookie salaries and bonuses for being picked in various areas of the draft. Slotting systems have reduced the number of rookie holdouts as the salary is essentially predetermined on draft night. However, despite this, a few rookie players have still held out their services until their contracts were structured in a manner that met their demands. In 2016, Joey Bosa was the third pick in the NFL draft by the San Diego Chargers. He was the last first-round selection to sign that year as he held out for over a month. NFL fans familiar with the draft slotting system were puzzled why a salary system that assigns the length, total value, and bonus money in rookie deals would become so time-consuming and contentious (Hoyle, 2016). Bosa demanded that a significant portion of his salary bonus be paid immediately and not spread over time. In addition, he desired for offset language to be removed from his contract so that if the Chargers were to cut him, he could receive the full amount owed and not have any of that money "offset" if he signed with another team (Thomas, 2016). Many observers wondered why the negotiation over these points became so acrimonious since Bosa was a top player and the chances of the Chargers cutting him were extremely small unless he was so terrible that it was unlikely any other team would want his services. In addition, though the $17 million signing bonus was a large amount of money to Bosa, it was not a huge amount for the Chargers, especially since the negotiations were not being contested over a number of years, but rather over a number of months, meaning the potential interest at stake from the Chargers' perspective was likely not worth the trouble of annoying their top draft pick and appearing petty among other NFL owners, most of whom provided their first-round picks in the top five of the draft with demands Bosa was making (Hoyle, 2016).

Though the Bosa situation was quickly forgotten among most fans after he eventually signed, concerns regarding rookie contracts resurfaced in 2019 after Cleveland Browns defensive end Myles Garrett was involved in one of the NFL's ugliest on-field incidents. After grabbing Pittsburgh Steelers quarterback Mason Rudolph's helmet, Garrett then slammed the headgear onto Rudolph's unprotected head. After the game, the NFL acted quickly and suspended Garrett indefinitely without pay. Though the loss of his salary for the remaining 2019 games was substantial, concerns regarding the suspension being extended into the 2020 season demonstrated the importance of contract structure. Though Garrett's suspension was lifted before the 2020 season, if it had remained in effect and Garrett did not play at least six games in 2020, his fourth NFL season would not accrue or "count" for free agency purposes. He would receive a prorated portion of his $4.6 million salary as part of his rookie contract he signed after he was drafted as the number one pick in the 2017 NFL draft, but his fifth season—one in which he would likely have earned roughly $15 million under his rookie contact—would be delayed another year (Graziano, 2019). Garrett's suspension brought scrutiny to how his contract was structured. Other top picks such as Baker Mayfield (2018) and Kyler Murray (2019) had a larger portion of their rookie contract paid as roster bonuses rather than salary. Since fines are based upon a player's salary, the six games Garrett missed in 2019 cost him 6/17 of his $3.230 million salary, which was $1.14 million. Conversely, if Mayfield was suspended for six games, it would cost him 6/17 of $660,000 (his 2019 salary), which is $232,941, while the $2,791,180 Mayfield earned as a 2019 roster bonus would not be affected (Graziano, 2019).

Free Agency

For many years, players in each professional sport league had few rights regarding their conditions of employment. Leagues used **reserve clauses** that tied each player to his team in perpetuity. Fortunately for the players, starting in the 1960s, players associations began to exert more pressure on the owners through **collective bargaining**—the process that occurs when workers in a company or industry agree to negotiate as one unit with management. In 1966, Marvin Miller became executive director of the Major League Baseball Players Association (MLBPA). By the time he retired in 1982, the MLBPA had become the most powerful sports union in North America. Miller's initial demands from the owners concerned "minor" issues involving working conditions, pension payments, and the right of players to profit from their likenesses. However, after achieving initial success, Miller took a series of actions that would lead to the greatest change in salary structure in the history of North American professional sport: the elimination of the reserve clause. This created the right of players to become free agents.

Miller's first attempt to remove the MLB reserve clause involved Curt Flood, an outstanding outfielder for the St. Louis Cardinals in the 1960s (see Sidebar 15.M). Despite the failure of this attempt, Miller was convinced that the players were gaining momentum in their fight for greater rights.

SIDEBAR 15.M   Curt Flood Versus MLB

Curt Flood was a key member of the 1964 and 1967 St. Louis Cardinals World Series Champion teams; he also appeared in three All-Star Games and won seven Gold Glove Awards. At the end of the 1969 season, the Cardinals traded Flood and other players to the Philadelphia Phillies. Flood refused to report to the Phillies, despite his $100,000 playing contract, and demanded that he be declared a free agent—in direct opposition to MLB's established reserve clause, which bound a player to a team forever, even after the player's contract had been fulfilled. Baseball commissioner Bowie Kuhn denied Flood's request, citing the provisions of the MLB standard playing contract.

MLBPA executive director Marvin Miller and the union supported Flood's refusal to report and provided financial assistance for Flood's lawsuit. The suit claimed that MLB's reserve rules were a violation of antitrust law, because they unfairly restricted the ability of players to bargain for their services (*Flood v. Kuhn*, 1972). Commissioner Kuhn and the owners fought the lawsuit all the way to the United States Supreme Court, where, in a 5–3 decision, the owners prevailed, as the court upheld the 1922 ruling declaring MLB immune from antitrust scrutiny (*Federal Baseball Club v. National League*).

Flood returned to play in 1971—with the Washington Senators—but his one-year hiatus and the time devoted to the lawsuit had diminished his skills. After playing poorly in 1971, he retired. Although Flood was unsuccessful in his lawsuit, he is remembered as an important figure in professional sports history. Flood's stance began to alter many fans' perceptions of baseball's employment rules. In 1998—one year after Flood died—the US Congress passed the Curt Flood Act, which eliminated MLB's antitrust exemption with regard to labor issues.

MLB owners had long contended that the reserve clause bound a player to his team for life, but the language in the MLB operating agreement noted that teams controlled players only until they completed their contract and then played out their option (i.e., played another year without a contract). Players rarely played out their option, because they always signed contracts at the beginning of each year. However, in 1975, Andy Messersmith and Dave McNally played a season without signing a contract. Miller believed they had become free agents once the season concluded, and the dispute was submitted for arbitration. Arbitrator Peter Seitz encouraged the owners and players to settle the dispute rather than let him make the final determination, but he eventually ruled that Andy Messersmith and Dave McNally had indeed become free agents after playing a season without a contract (Miller, 1991).

The Seitz decision dramatically altered MLB. Other players began to play out their options and become free agents. Eventually, the owners and players clarified free agent rules through the collective bargaining process. Other leagues have since enacted free agency rules. Players become eligible for free agency after achieving the required service time (typically four to seven years in North American professional leagues). Before players become free agents, most earn salaries that are artificially depressed because the players have little leverage (beyond retiring prematurely) in salary negotiations.

SIDEBAR 15.N   Maverick Owner Charlie Finely Proven Correct … 40 Years Later

Once Peter Seitz ruled that MLB players could become free agents, the owners panicked about losing significant sums of money and their players. However, the answer to their potential financial problems was mentioned in a few meetings, but no one listened because the messenger was often seen as an eccentric character. During his 20 years of ownership of the Oakland A's, Charlie Finley had built a dynasty and had upset most baseball purists with his unorthodox marketing strategies. When the players were granted free agency, Finley advocated for every player to become a free agent … every year (Vaccaro, 2013). He reasoned that with every player available to be employed, many of them would not be paid very much money. Essentially, the stars of the game would be paid handsomely but the vast majority of players who were largely interchangeable would not have the ability to maximize their incomes. Finley's proposal failed and, for the next four decades, the system where only a few established players at each position became free agents each year resulted in rapidly escalating salaries for stars *and* those who might offer varying amounts of extra on-field value than most of the other players who were not eligible for free agency that season.

However, in the Moneyball era since Michael Lewis published his seminal book regarding performance and contribution of baseball players in 2003, many teams have slowly adapted to the idea that paying large salaries for players who provide only a modicum of value over replacement player (VORP) is not a wise decision. For a growing number of baseball general managers, players available through their farm system who could produce at replacement level and be compensated at the league minimum were better options than paying large amounts of money for just a little more production than could be acquired for "free." Despite years of MLB free agents signing lucrative contracts in the off-season, after the 2017 season the number of big-money deals dropped significantly. Players who normally would have been signed before Christmas had to wait, often until after spring training had begun (Lindbergh, 2019). Though big-name stars such as Yu Darvish (2017), Bryce Harper (2018), Manny Machado (2018), Gerrit Cole (2019), Stephen Strasburg (2019), and Anthony Rendon (2019) did sign nine-figure contracts in the winters following the 2017, 2018, and 2019 seasons, a considerable number of players had to not only wait months to find employment, but noted that offers tended to be limited in dollars and number of years (Brink, 2019). The decision to offer higher salaries only to stars rather than all the players concerned the MLBPA and was an important component of future CBA negotiations. Though Finley has been dead since 1996, he would likely be proud to learn that his fellow owners eventually better understood the value of players and the free agency marketplace.

SIDEBAR 15.0   Jean-Marc Bosman – The Curt Flood of Professional Soccer

For most of the history of professional soccer, there was not complete free agency across the various leagues around the world. In Europe, where soccer is extremely popular and profitable in a number of countries, players desiring to move teams often had to negotiate with their present and future clubs for a transfer. The transfer could involve one club paying another club to acquire the player's services. If the present club did not want to transfer the player or did not feel the provided compensation was adequate, the player may not have been transferred. In the 1980s, the transfer market became complex as more and more players attempted to play for clubs in various European countries. In the cases where a player wanted to move from one country to another country, the current club could often block the transfer, even if the player's employment contract had expired. In 1990, Jean-Marc Bosman sued his Belgian club RFC Liège when it refused to grant his request to play for Dunkerque in the French league. Though Bosman had completed his contract, RFC Liège desired more compensation from Dunkerque than they were willing to pay. Eventually, the European Court of Justice ruled in Bosman's favor as restricting European Union (EU) citizens' movement in the EU was illegal under a treaty that involved its member countries (Brand, 2015). In addition to "freeing" Bosman and other players who had completed their contracts, the court ruled that player quotas in EU football leagues were no longer permitted unless the rules restricted players who were not citizens of an EU country. The Bosman ruling has had a tremendous impact upon the entire soccer industry.

Player Salary Negotiations

When evaluating job opportunities, players are like anyone else in that they consider a variety of factors, such as location, work environment, and relationships with colleagues and supervisors. Potential salary is almost always a primary concern. In professional sports, salary is especially important, because the average playing career lasts only a few years. Since players' salaries are paid by individual franchises, the leagues must create an environment where each team has adequate financial resources to scout future players, re-sign their own players, and potentially bid for free agents. The leagues achieve this through two mechanisms: salary caps and, in MLB, salary arbitration.

SALARY CAPS

A **salary cap** limits the compensation an employer may provide to its employees. In sports, a salary cap is designed to restrict salaries for teams across an entire league—ideally, creating an economic environment where every team can be assured of both cost containment and the opportunity to compete for player services. Professional sport team owners can no longer unilaterally implement a salary cap; they must negotiate with the players through the collective bargaining process. Each league has negotiated a variety of compensation systems.

NBA salary cap. Unofficial and official salary caps existed in professional baseball before the 1930s, but the first modern salary cap was implemented in 1983 by the NBA. Numerous NBA teams struggled financially in the late 1970s and early 1980s, and some observers were concerned that teams in larger markets would be able to outspend teams in smaller markets (such as Utah, Indiana, and Cleveland) to the point that small-market teams would suffer considerably diminished on-court performances—which might, in turn, cause some franchises to declare bankruptcy and even cease operations. The NBA owners and players agreed to a salary cap to reduce the possibility that a small group of teams could sign all of the best players. Each year, the owners and players calculate the league salary cap based on overall league revenues. The cap has typically increased each year, but in 2009 the cap decreased due to a reduction of overall league revenues—partially related to the global economic recession (Abrams, 2009).

The NBA salary cap was designed to maintain a level salary field for every team in the league. However, given the nature of the sport of basketball, the loss of one or two players from a 15-player roster could radically alter the quality of a team's performance. For this reason, as part of the initial agreement the NBA instituted a variety of rules that allowed individual teams to circumvent the cap. The most prominent rule, the **Larry Bird exception**—so named because the Boston Celtics were concerned that the loss of Larry Bird to free agency would devastate their team—allows teams, in most cases, to re-sign their "own" potential free agents for salaries that would otherwise cause the team to exceed the designated yearly salary cap. This has created an environment where teams that have drafted quality players tend to have an advantage in free agency salary negotiations, as free agents can usually re-sign with their current team for greater compensation than they could receive from other franchises.

More than ten years after the Larry Bird exception was instituted, the 1998/1999 NBA season was condensed because of a **lockout** (a decision by management to suspend operations while it negotiates with workers—in this case, players). One of the owners' concerns was the escalating salaries of the league's top players. For instance, during the 1997/1998 season, Michael Jordan's salary was $36 million, although the Chicago Bulls' team salary cap was $26.9 million. The lockout resulted in the NBA and the players agreeing to limit individual player salaries in addition to team salaries. For certain players whose current salaries exceeded the individual cap, the excessive salaries were grandfathered into the CBA.

Under the NBA collective bargaining agreement signed in 1999, the NBA experienced financial success. When that agreement expired in 2005, the owners and players quickly ratified a new agreement, with the goal to maintain labor peace and not duplicate the previous failures of the previous negotiations. From 2000 to 2009, the NBA experienced a period of relative financial stability, until the Great Recession caused financial issues for nearly every sport organization in the world. The NBA certainly maintained its presence as a successful league during the 2000s, but there was a sense among the owners that the league was not growing as it had in prior years and the players were earning too great of a percentage of overall revenues. Most franchises sold during the decade were bought for between $250 and $400 million (Cato, 2017). A number of teams were purchased by investors who had previous experience in managing hedge funds rather than professional sport franchises. These owners believed NBA franchises were undervalued, but some observers noted the franchise sales could not be justified without a change in the next CBA or dramatically changing revenue sources being developed. When the 2005 agreement expired in 2011, the NBA owners locked out the players. After cancelling the first part of the season, the players and owners agreed to a new CBA, with some pundits noting that the players were ill prepared for a sustained lockout which resulted in the players granting the owners significant concessions. The players agreed to a guarantee of 51% of the NBA basketball-related income (BRI), a much lower figure than the players had desired at the start of negotiations.

The new CBA, combined with several new revenue sources such as those from international games, expanding media contracts, and other activities, dramatically altered the NBA financial landscape. Owners who had purchased franchises just a few years prior saw their team valuations skyrocket. The Golden

State Warriors were sold for "only" $450 million in 2010, but the Sacramento Kings, a franchise with much lower brand identity playing in one of the NBA's smallest markets, were sold for $534 million in 2013 (Cato, 2017). Within a few years of the 2011 CBA agreement, some NBA teams were valued at more than a billion dollars.

With NBA revenues expanding rapidly, concern about the future application of the NBA salary cap became an important component of collective bargaining negotiations. In 2015, the NBA announced that salary caps were likely to increase in the future—dramatically. One projection pegged the 2015/2016 cap to be $68 million, with the 2016/2017 cap increasing to $90 million, due primarily to the revenues from the league's new nine-year, $24 billion television contract (Aschburner, 2015). Such a rapid increase after many years of small (3% to 7%) increases would provide nearly every NBA franchise with significant cap space to sign free agents. To maintain some semblance of roster stability and to prevent large-market teams from being able to "outspend" other franchises, the NBA owners proposed a "smoothing" plan that would gradually introduce the increased revenues across multiple years. The NBA Players Association rejected the proposal. Eventually, the 2016/2017 cap was set at $94.14 million, a $24 million increase from the previous year. During that off-season, nearly every NBA free agent was flooded with lucrative offers as almost every franchise had significant cap space. It was estimated that NBA teams committed over $1 billion to free agents in the first 24 hours of free agency (Windhorst & Marks, 2018). Many of those contracts were signed for four years (the maximum length for most player contracts) and when subsequent caps "only" increased by roughly $5 million (to $99 million) in 2017–2018, $2.8 million (to $101.8 million) in 2018–2019, and $7.3 million (to $109.1 million) in 2019–2020, a number of players who became free agents in those subsequent seasons were not able to secure lucrative contracts like their colleagues who were "lucky' to be a free agent in the summer of 2016. One NBA general manager noted, "Picture the spending on salaries as a large tank of water ... The last several years, the tank has been getting bigger, and so we've been filling it with more water. But this year the tank is staying about the same size. There's no place for the water to go" (Windhorst & Marks, 2018, para. 14). The summer of 2020 was to offer greater flexibility for teams to sign free agents as the four-year contracts signed in 2016 had then expired, but financial concerns from Covid resulted in a dramatically altered NBA financial marketplace.

The complexity of the NBA's salary cap often causes confusion among journalists and fans. To mitigate this confusion, the NBA has released detailed salary cap information (Coon, 2020).

NFL salary cap. The NFL implemented a salary cap system in 1993 in an effort to maintain competitive balance among its franchises. Under the NFL cap system, similar to the NBA's, a maximum team salary is established each year based on overall league revenues. The NFL's system also sets a team salary floor (a minimum amount to be paid in salaries per team), created to appease players' concerns regarding the unwillingness of some NFL owners to participate in the bidding for player services. Unlike the NBA's salary system, which provides numerous loopholes for exceeding the cap, the NFL's cap has a "hard" ceiling that must be maintained each year.

However, teams can manipulate the NFL salary cap through the use of signing bonuses. If an NFL player signs a four-year, $4 million contract, each year his salary will count $1 million against the team's salary cap, and the player will receive $1 million during each season. Since NFL contracts are usually not guaranteed, the player risks not receiving all the money if he is released (due to injury or ineffectiveness, for example) before the full term of the contract is fulfilled. For this reason, players often negotiate bonuses that are paid immediately upon the contract's signing. Although the player receives the total signing bonus in the first year, for the purpose of the salary cap the league allows the team to allocate the bonus over the years of the contract.

Suppose a player negotiates a $4 million signing bonus in addition to a $4 million, four-year contract. The player receives $5 million in the first year of the contract, and the team must allocate only $2 million each year to its salary cap total. If this player were to be cut after playing two years, he would "lose" only $2 million. Although the team will not have to pay the remaining years of salary on the contract, it will have to account for the remaining $2 million from the signing bonus on its salary cap. This is often called "dead" salary cap money because it must be allocated, but it does not get paid to an active player who can contribute on the field.

NFL teams relied on the continuing escalation of the salary cap to provide additional space for "dead" salary cap amounts, but this strategy was more difficult to implement from 2011 to 2013, as the NFL salary cap remained relatively stagnant over those years (see Exhibit 15.2). As a result of this stagnation, it became untenable for some NFL teams to retain many of their long-term contracts as long as initially planned. In some cases, productive NFL veterans were cut or encouraged to restructure their contracts long before anyone would have expected. Contracts signed during this three-year period were adjusted to the "slow growth" model, but many NFL veterans were not pleased, since they had anticipated much more lucrative contracts being available after they completed their rookie contracts (Barnwell, 2013). Though it was anticipated that the salary cap would grow minimally in 2014, as in the previous three years, NFL revenues increased at a rate that resulted in the 2014 salary cap increasing $10 million (8%) (Barnwell, 2014). The dramatic change in the 2014 cap figure allowed many teams to retain certain players previously expected to become "cap casualties" or to sign prominent free agents at higher salaries than expected. The cap has continued to grow steadily since 2014, which has enabled teams to be more aggressive in paying players as the impact of "mistakes" is not as harsh in an increasing cap environment.

The use of signing bonuses to circumvent the NFL cap in the short term is not without repercussions, even when done "successfully." In the 1990s, the Dallas Cowboys and other teams used signing bonuses to pay numerous players large salaries in the hopes of winning championships. The Cowboys were able to field Super Bowl-winning teams in the short term, but as players retired, became injured, and so forth, the team was unable to sign other players under the cap, as they had used up their budget with past signing bonuses (Nagel, 2005). When the strategy of using signing bonuses to sign players to long-term deals is not executed well, on-field and financial disasters can occur. Numerous NFL teams have been forced to field rosters with glaring weaknesses after the release of veteran players who could only be replaced by lower-cost and lower-performing players. The Oakland Raiders mismanaged their salary cap through long-term contracts so badly that in 2013 they had over $50 million allocated to

EXHIBIT 15.2   Year-by-year history of the NFL salary cap.

YEAR	MAXIMUM TEAM SALARY (MILLIONS)	INCREASE FROM PREVIOUS YEAR (MILLIONS)	PERCENT INCREASE/ DECREASE
2019	$188.20	$11.00	6.21%
2018	$177.20	$10.20	6.11%
2017	$167.00	$11.73	7.55%
2016	$155.27	$11.99	8.37%
2015	$143.28	$10.28	7.73%
2014	$133.00	$9.10	7.34%
2013	$123.90	$3.30	2.74%
2012	$120.60	$0.22	0.19%
2011	$120.38	($2.63)	–2.13%
2010	Uncapped		
2009	$123.00	$7.00	6.03%
2008	$116.00	$7.00	6.42%
2007	$109.00	$7.00	6.86%
2006	$102.00	$16.50	19.30%
2005	$85.50	$4.92	6.10%
2004	$80.58	$5.57	7.43%
2003	$75.01	$3.91	5.49%
2002	$71.10	$3.70	5.48%
2001	$67.41	$5.23	8.42%
2000	$62.17	$4.88	8.53%
1999	$57.29	$4.90	9.35%
1998	$52.39	$10.93	26.38%
1997	$41.45	$0.70	1.72%
1996	$40.75	$3.65	9.85%
1995	$37.10	$2.49	7.20%
1994	$34.61		

Sources: "Year by year" (2010), Farrar (2012), Wesseling (2013), Hanzus (2014), Patra (2015), Benjamin (2019).

"dead" salary money for players no longer on their roster ("Oakland Raiders 2013," 2013). Unfortunately, the Raiders and their fans could not look back fondly on (recent) on-field success, as the team did not have a winning record in any season from 2003 through 2014. The Cleveland Browns were another team that mismanaged their cap. From 2015 to 2019, the Cleveland Browns had over $140 million total in dead money on their books, but in none of those seasons did they finish with a winning record and from 2015 to 2017 they were by far the worst team in the league ("Salary cap space," n.d.)

NHL salary cap. For many years, the National Hockey League's owners desired a salary cap, which the players resisted during collective bargaining negotiations. The 1994/1995 season was nearly cancelled when the owners locked out the players, but a partial season was played after the owners reluctantly agreed to abandon their demand for a salary cap. However, the 2004/2005 season was cancelled when the owners demanded a salary cap and the players refused to acquiesce. After the owners cancelled an entire season for the first time in major North American professional sport history, the players reluctantly agreed to return for the 2005/2006 season with a salary cap in place. In addition, the players allowed the value of every contract to be reduced by 24% (Fitzpatrick, 2005). Owners, players, and fans alike hoped that the highly contentious collective bargaining sessions would yield a salary system that would ensure labor peace in the NHL for a considerable time. However, this was not the case.

The NHL's salary cap implemented in 2005 was designed to be similar to the NFL's, as it had a floor and a ceiling that were based on league revenues. However, even though the NHL's cap was designed to offer few "creative accounting" loopholes, teams quickly realized how to circumvent the cap. One loophole was the use of long-term contracts front-loaded with large yearly salaries, with very small salaries in the final years. Unofficially dubbed the "Luongo Rule" after the Vancouver Canucks signed goaltender Roberto Luongo to a 12-year, $64 million contract, the loophole violated the spirit of the salary cap while adhering to the terms of the CBA. Luongo's contract counted $5.33 million against the Canucks' yearly cap but called for the goaltender to earn $10 million in 2010, roughly $6.7 million each year from 2011 to 2017, $3.3 million in 2018, $1.6 million in 2019 and 2020, and finally $1 million each year in 2021 and 2022. Since the NHL's salary cap allocated the annual average of a contract to the team's yearly salary cap figure, the Canucks' use of the extended "final" years on Luongo's contract, when he would be over 40 years old and unlikely to be playing, allowed the franchise to lower the annual salary average.

Use of this loophole, combined with concerns regarding the rapid growth in revenues and, therefore, the NHL salary caps and floors among the highest-earning teams in the league, led the NHL once again to lock out the players in 2012. Fortunately, the league was able to avoid another cancelled season, as it reached an agreement with the players to begin a condensed season in January 2013. Among the numerous provisions in the new ten-year CBA was the elimination of the "Luongo Rule" and stricter penalties for attempts to circumvent the salary cap. However, despite the new CBA, concerns remained about how the very long-term contracts signed by some clubs under the previous CBA would affect teams as those contracts came closer to expiration (The Neutral, 2013).

Among the numerous salary cap rules, perhaps the most interesting is that teams may choose to retain part of a player's "cap hit" when trading the player to another team. In essence, a team could extract "value" in a trade with another club by retaining a portion of the salary cap allocation that would normally be transferred to the other club. Although a variety of stipulations limit the potential trades, this new wrinkle certainly presents an additional set of strategic decisions for NHL teams (Mirtle, 2013). It will be interesting to see if other leagues copy or adapt this unique salary cap provision.

MLB salary cap. Despite baseball's having been the first professional sport to institute salary caps, which it did during the early part of MLB's history in the 19th century, the Major League Baseball Players Association has adamantly opposed any salary cap system. On August 12, 1994, the MLB players went on strike to protest a potential salary cap. The strike eventually resulted in the cancellation of the World Series for the first time since 1904. Although the players "won" the dispute—they avoided a salary cap—the cancellation of the World Series and the perceived greed on the part of both the players and the owners caused outrage among fans. Major League Baseball players are adamant that they will continue to oppose the implementation of a salary cap (Bloom, 2009).

MLS salary cap. Major League Soccer—which operates as a single entity, with all player salaries paid from a league pool—approved a new salary structure in November 2006. Under this structure, each team had a $2 million salary cap, but individual franchises could sign one player outside the cap limit as a "designated player." The first $400,000 of this "marquee" player's contract would be paid by the league, but the team would be responsible for the remainder. Each team could trade its marquee "slot" to another team, enabling that other team to sign up to two marquee players, whose salaries did not fully count against the team's cap. That rule was unofficially called the "Beckham Rule," because many anticipated that English star David Beckham might be attracted to the MLS if he could earn a salary comparable to what he was making in Europe ("MLS oks 'Beckham,'" 2006). It did not take Beckham long to fulfill the prediction: in 2007, he signed a multimillion-dollar deal with the Los Angeles Galaxy.

In 2013 MLS increased its salary cap to $2.95 million per team and $368,750 per player and then, in 2014, it increased those figures again to $3.1 million and $387,500. In 2015, the league and the players signed a new collective bargaining agreement that increased the overall cap to $3.3 million, with projected increases of 7% per year (Oshan, 2015). By 2019, the salary cap had reached $4.24 million (Smith, 2019). In addition, the new CBA permits each team to sign two players whose salaries do not apply to the individual or team salary caps and permits a team to sign a third star player if the team pays a $250,000 luxury tax to the league. Increases in the salary cap and the ability to sign more designated players have enabled MLS to retain and attract more top-level players, particularly those Americans who in past years would likely have played professionally in Europe (McIntyre, 2013).

SIDEBAR 15.P   Salary Caps in the Age of COVID-19

The havoc caused by the coronavirus in 2020 extended through all areas of life, including the sport industry. Though the primary concern for professional sport leagues was returning to play in an environment that was safe for players, coaches, staff, and then fans, there were also considerable financial concerns to negotiate. Each professional league that returned to competition had to make specific choices about their events. Some, like the NBA and NHL, chose to return in a "bubble format" where players would be quarantined, team travel would be restricted, and no fans would attend games. Major League Baseball did not institute a player bubble but they did limit the normally 162-game schedule to 60 games and had teams play mostly a regional, rather than traditional league schedule. The NFL decided to have games at home team sites with fan attendance being determined primarily by local laws and regulations rather than league edict.

Each league had to determine how diminished revenues would be distributed, made complicated in some cases due to players being under contract. Some of the negotiations between the players and the owners became contentious. In particular, MLB proposed a limited, 82-game schedule with a dramatic decrease in pay for those established players with mega-contracts. At one point, MLB owners offered a plan that would have paid superstar Los Angeles Angels outfielder Mike Trout "only" $7.84 million out of his scheduled $37.7 million 2020 salary (Dougherty, 2020). MLB and the MLB Players Association eventually agreed to a 60-game schedule with more favorable contract concessions remaining in place for the players. Other leagues had to negotiate return-to-play agreements given full schedules in most leagues were not able to be completed as planned. In addition, players and owners had to determine the repercussions for players "opting out" from their contracts. By not playing, players would lose their salaries but also their opportunity to earn a year of service time toward free agency. In most cases, players were permitted to roll over their contracts if they did not want to play but were not allowed to have their "sit" year count for service time.

Though MLB does not have a salary cap, other North American professional sport leagues do. With dramatic decreases in revenues in 2020, the steady revenue growth that most North American professional sport leagues had experienced in the 2010s stalled. Since salary caps are typically determined by overall sport-related revenues, the decreased revenues resulted in future caps decreasing, which caused concerns among players, particularly those planning to be free agents in 2021. Though the long-term effects of the coronavirus on the overall health of professional sports are unknown, a number of pundits predicted it could take years for many elements of the industry, including overall revenues and salary cap figures, to recover to pre-coronavirus levels.

SIDEBAR 15.Q   MLB Collusion

The efforts of MLBPA executive director Marvin Miller and his successor, Donald Fehr, resulted in increased salaries for Major League Baseball players. With MLB's increased popularity during the early 1980s, the owners also saw their overall profits increase. However, many owners were not pleased that they could no longer artificially control players' salaries. In a series of acts that were eventually deemed illegal, the owners, under the direction of MLB commissioner Peter Ueberroth, refused to offer contracts to other teams' free agents during the 1985 through 1987 off-seasons. Prominent players were forced to return to their former MLB teams, as they received no viable contract offers. In perhaps the most shocking example of the owners' conspiracy to reduce salaries, Montreal Expos' Andre Dawson essentially had to ask the Chicago Cubs to sign him for any price. Dawson played for the Cubs in 1987, winning the National League Most Valuable Player Award while earning a salary well below market value.

Eventually, the owners' three years of collusion resulted in a court award to the MLBPA of $280 million in damages. Though this episode is unknown to many younger fans and forgotten by most who followed baseball in the 1980s, it was one of the most important financial disputes in MLB history, and the MLBPA often cites it as a reason to distrust owners' comments regarding the financial health of the league.

SALARY ARBITRATION

Unlike other professional sports, Major League Baseball gives players the right to **salary arbitration**, a process whereby an independent judge determines whether the team's submitted salary or the player's requested salary will be paid. The MLBPA initially negotiated the right to arbitration in 1973 and has consistently insisted that arbitration remain a key component of the MLB's CBA (Haupert, 2007). Players with at least three years of MLB service time, as well as the top 22% of players (by service days in MLB) with at least two years of experience (known as "Super Twos"), are eligible for salary arbitration if they are unable to reach a salary agreement with their team (Ray, 2008). Most players come to an agreement with their club, and only a limited number of cases proceed to arbitration. Both the players and the owners closely monitor these cases to detect any arbitration "trends."

The rule allowing Super Two players to participate in salary arbitration has resulted in some player personnel decisions that are more likely driven by monetary concerns than players' level of preparation. Some teams, particularly those with limited budgets compared to other franchises, have left players in the minors who were likely "ready" to play in the majors to delay their service time clock and keep the players under team control longer. In 2013, the Tampa Bay Rays kept top-rated outfielder Wil Myers in the minors until June 18, likely ensuring he would not qualify for arbitration until after his third season. In 2015, the Chicago Cubs kept highly touted third baseman Kris Bryant in the minor leagues for the first two weeks of the season despite his hitting nine home runs in 14 pre-season games. The move assured the Cubs greater control of Bryant's future earning potential. However, after having several highly productive seasons, Bryant filed a grievance regarding his situation in 2019. Bryant, who had been critical of the Cubs' 2015 decision regarding his status, desired to have that initial season count toward his service time, meaning he could be a free agent in 2020 rather than 2021. Bryant lost his grievance, which was seen as the likely outcome given the language of the MLB collective bargaining agreement (Calcaterra, 2020). The outcome likely solidified the players' resolve to "fix" this manipulation of player service time in the next CBA negotiations.

SIDEBAR 15.R   What is the Cost of a Win?

Every professional sport franchise desires to win games through cost-efficient methods. If a team can generate a profit of $10 million and win a division championship, these accomplishments reflect more effective management than if the team generates a profit of $10 million and finishes with a record below .500. In baseball, one of the recent points of emphasis among front office personnel is analyzing how much each player contributes to on-field success. Analysts calculate a figure called **wins above replacement (WAR)**, which involves a variety of factors (such as batting, fielding, and base running proficiency for position players and, for pitchers, pitching proficiency across the number of innings pitched) that contribute to a team's success. WAR is intended to indicate the number of runs that a player either created or prevented over a season. Typically, ten runs created or prevented are considered to equal one win. A great player will typically produce five or more WAR, solid players produce three or four WAR, and mediocre players generate one or two WAR. Players who do not produce any WAR or produce negative WAR should probably be replaced with readily available alternative options.

As the evaluation of players has evolved—particularly with the success of the small-market Oakland Athletics under General Manager Billy Beane—and as owners of MLB teams have become more concerned with efficiency of expenditures, WAR has been applied to player salaries. Successful teams are those that efficiently allocate resources to acquire players whose performance can exceed what is readily available for little investment. That is, if a player who is called up from the minor leagues and paid the league's minimum salary can contribute a certain level of on-field performance, then a team should not spend any additional resources (either in trade value or in player salary) to acquire a more expensive player, unless that player can perform at a correspondingly higher level. In 2013, the average cost of one WAR was roughly $6 million—meaning that a player who was paid $18 million a year should produce three WAR. If the player did not, he was overpaid (Keri, 2013). In 2019, the cost of acquiring one WAR on the free agent market was estimated at $8.1 million (Kinzy, 2019). Certainly, a player's performance will fluctuate over time, and each player should be evaluated on his WAR over the period of his contract.

Obviously, teams will seek to sign players who will "overproduce" their contracts. As an example, in 2013 the Los Angeles Angels had a payroll of $142 million and finished with a losing record (78–84), while the Oakland Athletics won 96 games and made the playoffs while spending $68.6 million. The inefficiency of the Angels was particularly shocking given that All-Star Mike Trout produced 8.9 WAR (tied for the highest in MLB) while being paid "only" $510,000, the best "bargain" in the league. The rest of the Angels were largely overpaid given their lack of ability to produce wins above what the Angels could have acquired at minimal cost. Unfortunately for the Angels, their "wasting" of Mike Trout's immense talents continued for much of the decade. In 2019, the Los Angeles Angels had a payroll of $177 million and finished with a losing record (72–90), while the Oakland Athletics won 97 games and made the playoffs while spending $102 million.

Administrators in other sports have attempted to created WAR or WAR-like metrics to evaluate players to varying degrees of success. Baseball offers individual performance outcomes that can be graded fairly easily while other sports involve players performing in concert with teammates. Despite these obstacles, a number of new WAR metrics have been developed across leagues such as the NBA, NFL, and NHL.

Luxury Tax

In addition to individual player and team salary caps, in its efforts to promote competitive balance the NBA also imposes a **luxury tax** on high-spending teams to encourage teams to limit their player salaries. The salary cap and luxury tax limits are based on a percentage of the association's basketball-related income (BRI). In the 2019–2020 season, the salary cap was set at $109.1 million and the luxury tax was set at $132.6 million. Prior to 2011, teams that paid salaries in excess of the threshold were assessed a dollar-for-dollar tax, and the collected amounts were distributed equally to all of the teams in conformance with the threshold. However, under the CBA negotiated in 2011, beginning in the 2013/2014 season luxury tax rates increased depending on a team's level of spending above the luxury tax threshold. Also, for the first time, the NBA established a "repeater" tax rate, which in the 2014/2015 season applied to teams that spent above the luxury tax limit the previous three seasons (see Exhibit 15.3). The repeater tax rate applied in 2015/2016 and beyond to those teams that exceeded the threshold in three of the previous four seasons (Coon, 2020). These rates were renewed under the 2017 NBA collective bargaining agreement.

Teams that are close to or at the luxury tax level often avoid paying any additional salaries, since the tax essentially means amounts paid in excess of the threshold actually cost the team a multiple higher than one. For example, for a non-repeating team that spends $1 million above the tax level, that additional $1 million salary will cost them $1.5 million in tax. For a repeater, the extra

EXHIBIT 15.3 NBA repeater and non-repeater luxury tax rates beginning in the 2013/2014 season.

TEAM SALARY ABOVE TAX LEVEL		NON-REPEATER		REPEATER	
BETWEEN	AND	TAX RATE	INCREMENTAL MAXIMUM	TAX RATE	INCREMENTAL MAXIMUM
$0	$4,999,999	$1.50	$7.5 million	$2.50	$12.5 million
$5,000,000	$9,999,999	$1.75	$8.75 million	$2.75	$13.75 million
$10,000,000	$14,999,999	$2.50	$12.5 million	$3.50	$17.5 million
$15,000,000	$19,999,999	$3.25	$16.25 million	$4.25	$21.5 million
$20,000,000	N/A	$3.75 plus $0.50 for each additional $5 million	N/A	$4.75 plus $0.50 for each additional $5 million	N/A

Source: Coon (2020).

$1 million in salary would cost $2.5 million in tax. In addition, teams that exceed the luxury tax limit cannot receive any luxury tax revenues. The luxury tax has helped to restrict some franchises' team salaries to a level that is above the salary cap and below the luxury tax limit, but a handful of teams have surpassed the luxury tax, with various on-court outcomes (see Exhibit 15.4). Teams such as the New York Knicks and New Jersey Nets have paid large amounts of taxes but have not played well in most seasons. Conversely, the Cleveland Cavaliers and Golden State Warriors have recently paid a large amount of luxury taxes but have had tremendous on-court success.

Although the MLBPA has adamantly opposed a salary cap, it has permitted the owners to implement a luxury tax. The luxury tax was first employed in the 1997 through 1999 seasons, was phased out, and then was implemented once again, starting in 2003. Under the 2003–2006 MLB collective bargaining agreement, the tax penalized a first-time offender 22.5% of the amount over the tax limit. When a team exceeded the limit a second time, the penalty rate increased to 30%. For the third and any succeeding violation, the rate was 40% (Brown, 2007). Those rates have since been changed to 20% for first-time offenders, 30% for second-time offenders, and 50% for third-time offenders. In addition, there is now an additional 12% surtax on clubs who exceed the threshold by $20–$40 million and an additional surtax if the luxury tax rate is exceeded by more than $40 million ("Competitive balance tax," n.d.). Teams that drop below the luxury tax threshold for one season have their rate "reset" for the next season. The Dodgers paid luxury taxes each of the first five years under Guggenheim Baseball Management but decreased their payroll below

EXHIBIT 15.4   Comprehensive history of NBA luxury tax payments, 2001–2019 (in millions).

	2002–2003	2003–2004	2005–2006	2006–2007	2007–2008	2008–2009	2009–2010	2010–2011
Atlanta	$3.70							
Boston		$1.60			$8.20	$8.30	$15.00	$5.70
Brooklyn/New Jersey	$5.70	$9.40						
Charlotte								
Chicago								
Cleveland					$14.00	$13.70	$15.40	
Dallas	$18.50	$25.00	$17.30	$7.20	$19.60	$23.60	$17.60.	$19.00
Denver				$2.20	$13.60		$5.60	
Detroit		$0.80						
Golden State								
Houston								$0.80
Indiana	$0.90	$3.30	$4.70					
L.A. Clippers								
L.A. Lakers	$9.70	$8.40			$5.10	$7.20	$21.40	$19.90
Memphis	$7.50		$3.70					
Miami	$5.20				$8.30		$3.00	
Milwaukee	$4.70							
Minnesota	$6.00	$17.60		$1.00				
New Orleans								
New York	$24.40	$40.00	$37.20	$45.00	$19.70	$23.70	$5.20	
Oklahoma City/Seattle								
Orlando			$7.80				$11.00	$20.10
Philadelphia	$12.80	$5.10						
Phoenix	$1.90				$3.90	$4.90	$5.00	

2011–2012	2012–2013	2013–2014	2014–2015	2015–2016	2016–2017	2017–2018	2018–2019	TOTAL
$0.70								**$4.40**
$7.40	$1.20						$3.90	**$51.30**
	$12.90	$90.60	$20.00					**$138.60**
								$0.00
	$3.90			$4.20				**$8.10**
			$7.00	$54.00	$24.80	$50.70		**$179.60**
$2.70								**$150.50**
								$21.40
								$0.80
				$14.80		$32.30	$51.50	**$98.60**
				$4.90				**$5.70**
								$8.90
		$1.30	$4.80	$19.90	$3.60			**$29.60**
$12.60	$29.30	$9.00						**$122.60**
								$11.20
$6.10	$13.30	$14.40						**$50.30**
								$4.70
								$24.60
								$0.00
	$10.00	$36.30	$7.00					**$248.50**
			$2.80	$14.50		$25.40	$61.60	**$104.30**
								$38.90
								$17.90
								$15.70

(continued)

EXHIBIT 15.4   Cont.

	2002–2003	2003–2004	2005–2006	2006–2007	2007–2008	2008–2009	2009–2010	2010–2011
Portland	$52.00	$28.80				$5.90		$2.30
Sacramento	$17.40	$13.10						
San Antonio	$0.20		$0.90	$0.20			$8.80	
Toronto	$2.70	$4.10						
Utah							$3.10	$5.00
Washington								
Total	**$173.30**	**$157.20**	**$71.60**	**$55.60**	**$92.40**	**$87.30**	**$111.10**	**$72.80**

Note: No luxury tax was implemented in the 2001/2002 and 2004/2005 seasons due to insufficient BRI.
Sources: Mark Deeds, Shamsports.com (2015); retrieved from www.shamsports.com/2015/07/complete-history-of-nba-luxury-tax.html. Luke Adams (2019, April 18), Hoops rumors. Retrieved from www.hoopsrumors.com/2019/04/recent-history-of-nba-taxpaying-teams.html.

the tax rate in 2018, their sixth year of ownership. Despite paying the luxury tax every season it was in existence, in 2018 the Yankees dropped their payroll below the threshold to reset their tax payments (Miller, 2019). For many years, Yankee general manager Brian Cashman noted that the opportunity to "reset" the Yankees' luxury tax rate "affects my decision-making process, my communication about the pressure points we have" ("Report: Yanks," 2012, para. 6). See Exhibit 15.5 for MLB luxury tax payments from 2003 to 2019 and Exhibit 15.6 for the luxury tax thresholds.

Though the luxury tax is not a salary cap, it has created a "cap-like" effect on many teams, particularly those who desire to not pay luxury taxes more than one year in a row. Many also believe that the more stringent luxury tax levels have contributed to a decreasing share of the rapidly expanding MLB revenues going to players (Grow, 2015; Brown, 2019). In 2017, the league spent roughly 54% of overall revenues on players, a nearly 4% decrease from 2017 (Bradbury, 2019; Brown, 2019). This continued an overall trend since 2002 of a decreasing share of revenues going to players (Grow, 2015).

Revenue Sharing

Another important policy that professional sport leagues have implemented for competitive balance is revenue sharing. Whereas a salary cap is intended to balance teams' spending on players, revenue sharing is designed to narrow the gaps in the financial resources of the participating teams. Individual owners

2011–2012	2012–2013	2013–2014	2014–2015	2015–2016	2016–2017	2017–2018	2018–2019	TOTAL
							$15.10	**$104.10**
								$30.50
$2.50				$4.90				**$17.50**
							$21.40	**$28.20**
								$8.10
						$7.00		**$7.00**
$32.00	**$70.60**	**$151.60**	**$41.60**	**$117.20**	**$28.40**	**$115.40**	**$153.50**	**$1,531.60**

SIDEBAR 15.S   Golden State Warriors' Dynasty Nearly Costs a Fortune

During the summer of 2016, the Golden State Warriors were able to add Kevin Durant to their already impressive roster. The team won the next two NBA championships, and many consider the 2017–2018 Golden State Warriors to be one of the greatest teams in NBA history. With surefire hall-of-fame players Kevin Durant, Stephen Curry, and Klay Thompson and other prominent players such as Andre Iguodala and Draymond Green, the Warriors won their third NBA title over a four-year span. Though the Warriors lost the 2019 finals to the Toronto Raptors, they appeared set to continue their greatness … and spend more money in tax than many teams spend on salaries. If Kevin Durant had elected to stay at the league salary maximum, while Thompson and Green were afforded extensions that also met the individual maximum contract values, and other role players were retained, the team could have faced a 2019–2020 tax bill of $225 million in addition to $178 million in salary (Marks, 2017)! The $225 million in tax would have exceeded every other NBA team's salary by at least $75 million. Though the Warriors owners were excited about continuing the team's recent run of success in a new, state-of-the-art facility that opened in San Francisco in 2019, Kevin Durant elected to sign with the New Jersey Nets, meaning the Warriors avoided having to pay the largest tax amount in NBA history.

EXHIBIT 15.5   MLB luxury tax payments, 2003–2019 (in millions).

	2003	2004	2005	2006	2007	2008	2009	2010
Los Angeles Dodgers								
New York Yankees	$11.80	$30.64	$34.05	$26.00	$23.88	$26.86	$25.69	$18.03
Boston Red Sox		$3.15	$4.15	$0.50	$6.06			$1.49
Los Angeles Angels		$0.93						
Detroit Tigers						$1.31		
Chicago Cubs								
Washington Nationals								
San Francisco Giants								
Total	**$11.80**	**$34.72**	**$38.20**	**$26.50**	**$29.94**	**$28.17**	**$25.69**	**$19.52**

EXHIBIT 15.6   MLB luxury tax limits and tax rates.

TAX LIMITS	TAX RATES
2012: $178 million	20% first-time offenders
2013: $178 million	30% second-year offenders
2014: $189 million	50% third-year offenders*
2015: $189 million	
2016: $189 million	*Beginning in 2017.
2017: $195 million	
2018: $197 million	
2019: $206 million	
2020: $208 million	
2021: $210 million	

2011	2012	2013	2014	2015	2016	2017	2018	2019	TOTAL
		$11.42	$26.60	$43.60	$31.80	$36.20			**$149.62**
$13.90	$18.90	$28.11	$18.33	$26.10	$27.20	$15.70		$5.65	**$350.84**
$3.43				$1.80	$4.50		$11.95	$12.62	**$49.65**
									$0.93
					$4.00	$3.70			**$9.01**
					$2.96			$6.80	**$9.76**
						$1.45	$2.39		**$3.84**
				$1.30	$3.40	$4.10			**$8.80**
$17.33	**$18.90**	**$28.11**	**$18.33**	**$29.20**	**$42.06**	**$24.95**	**$14.34**	**$25.07**	**$582.45**

may earn revenues from various sources other than the teams they own, and the inequality of these non-league revenue sources can become a concern. Some owners may be able to accept a lower profit margin from their team or even take a yearly financial loss, while other owners may not be able to afford such losses. For instance, since Robert Sarver bought the Phoenix Suns in 2004, the team has sold two first-round draft picks to the Portland Trailblazers and has practically "given away" players such as Kurt Thomas and other first-round draft picks, in order to save money (Coro, 2007; Haller, 2007). Many fans have long been disenchanted with Sarver's skinflint ways (Maynes, 2018). Unlike former Trailblazers owner Paul Allen, co-founder of Microsoft, and a few other owners, Sarver operates his team with the financial bottom line as his primary concern. This certainly can be frustrating for fans who want to see their team consistently strive to win championships (Simmons, 2008). Although it is difficult for leagues to maintain a financial environment of total equality, they pursue competitive balance by establishing rules and policies to govern revenue sharing and mitigate potential discrepancies.

MEDIA REVENUE
North American professional sport leagues share revenues from national media contracts equally. The sharing of national television revenue permits every team to generate the same television revenue regardless of the number of their national

television appearances. Every league shares national television revenues, but their sharing mechanisms have varying impacts. Each of the 16 games in the NFL's once-a-week schedule is broadcast under a national television contract, resulting in a much greater percentage of overall league revenues being shared than in other leagues. With the NBA and NHL's 82-game schedules and MLB's 162-game schedule, these leagues offer many games each week of the season and many opportunities for individual franchises to generate disparate local revenue. Some games are broadcast under an equally shared national television agreement, but most of the games are broadcast under local television agreements, the revenues from which will likely not be shared with other clubs. Since the teams' local television markets vary in size, the potential for generating revenue can vary considerably. For instance, the large population difference between the New York metropolitan area and the Minneapolis-St. Paul metropolitan area means that the New York teams in MLB, the NBA, and the NHL receive potentially millions of additional media dollars.

The proliferation of regional sport networks has exacerbated market-size differences. These cable stations generate money through advertising and subscription fees, and, unlike traditional over-the-air television stations, they typically elect to broadcast as many games as the local team(s) will permit. Regional sport networks have provided large-market franchises with a tremendous financial advantage over their small-market competitors.

In 2013, the Los Angeles Dodgers formally announced a 25-year, $7 billion deal with Time Warner Cable to create a new regional cable station (Nakashima & Blum, 2013). The Dodgers' deal dramatically exceeded its previous cable deal (which paid $39 million in 2013) and all other recently signed deals, including ones that were previously thought to be quite lucrative, such as those of the Los Angeles Angels (17 years, $2.5 billion) and the Texas Rangers (20 years, $1.7 billion; Ozanian, 2012; Thurm, 2012). The Dodgers' deal increased the imbalance in overall revenue for teams. Some "traditional" low-revenue teams, such as the Oakland A's, Kansas City Royals, and Pittsburgh Pirates, are stuck in cable deals that provide less than $20 million a year in local cable revenue, and even teams that typically have generated much more local revenue have local television deals that are dwarfed by the Dodgers' deal and some other recent deals, such as a 20-year, $1.2 billion contract signed by the San Diego Padres in 2012 (Thurm, 2012). In the case of the Atlanta Braves, the team made a poor decision in 2007 to lock in its local television deal for 25 years. Though the deal includes "cost of living" increases, it does not permit renegotiation (Tucker, 2012).

Continuing a trend across MLB, the Dodgers' television deal gives them an equity stake in the newly created cable station. For revenue-sharing purposes, MLB accounts for this equity position differently than it does many other revenue sources (Thurm, 2012). For instance, in MLB 34% of most other local revenue sources (such as ticket sales, concessions, and local television deals) is shared, but equity positions in entrepreneurial media ventures are exempt. The league wants to encourage franchises to expand opportunities in new media ventures, so it allows the clubs to retain profits generated from monies they specifically invest. However, in the case of the Dodgers, their initial structuring of the deal had to be modified multiple times to meet MLB rules, since the other owners felt the Dodgers' deal to be partially motivated by avoiding payments the team would otherwise have been required to make to the revenue-sharing pool. At one point a proposed deal had Time Warner Cable paying the Dodgers for the right to name the new station, which had never been done before. It would have been interesting if this unique idea had been approved, since MLB's 34% revenue-sharing requirement includes money from stadium naming rights deals (Ozanian, 2013). The initial cable deal was announced in December 2012; however, the final approval did not occur until June 2013 (Shaikin, 2013). Though the Dodgers were not permitted to shelter as much money from the revenue-sharing plan as they had initially hoped, the television deal nevertheless dramatically improved their financial position and likely secured their place as one of the top three MLB revenue producers for many years into the future.

Continuing growth of all things online has provided North American professional sport leagues with the opportunity to share revenue streams from online media sources, and the use of the internet to generate revenues is still developing. In 2000, MLB created Major League Baseball Advanced Media (MLBAM) to investigate and manage new media opportunities in areas such as online game streaming. MLBAM became one of the most effective sport business enterprises, generating nearly $500 million in revenue in 2010 (Fisher, 2011) and $800 million in 2014 (Brown, 2014). Majority control of MLBAM was sold to Disney for $1.58 billion in 2017, resulting in every MLB owner receiving over $50 million from the transaction (Yellon, 2017).

Professional sports teams and leagues are uniquely positioned to not only survive but thrive in an ever-increasing streaming media environment. While a large portion of programming is accessed by consumers on demand through **over-the-top (OTT)** methods, sport continues to attract live audiences, which means that regardless of the delivery mechanism, live sporting events will continue to be of importance to media companies. Some teams and leagues have also begun to offer consumers unique content, such as access to practices and press conferences, through their own OTT platforms.

SIDEBAR 15.T   What is the Future for Delivery of "Televised" Sport?

Since 1984, when Congress passed the Cable Communications Policy Act, cable companies have been permitted to "bundle" their cable station offerings. Cable channels such as ESPN, TNT, Fox News, TBS, and dozens more are typically offered to consumers in various packages, but consumers usually are not permitted to purchase individual stations à la carte (Weiner, 2012). This has forced consumers, most of whom typically watch no more than 8 to 12 channels regularly, to pay for content they never view. Though this fact of life applies to every cable subscriber, the sport industry has benefited. As of 2017, ESPN charges cable subscribers $7.21* per month and ESPN2 $0.90, even though in a typical month very few cable TV subscribers will tune in to an ESPN station (Wile, 2017). For many years, the sport industry directly benefited from this arrangement as a large portion of cable subscribers subsidized the cable channels, which in turn payed large rights fees to a variety of sporting events and leagues. In the early 2000s, a variety of disparate factions—including economists worried about market inefficiencies, parents (many of whom are religious) concerned about children's access to inappropriate content, and liberal groups concerned about escalating cable costs and company profits— began to challenge the legitimacy of cable bundling. A number of analysts for both "sides" declared their option (bundling or à la carte) to be better for consumers.

Though the à la carte battle continues, technological advancements and consumer preferences are having a much greater impact upon cable television than Congress. Several customers have been **cord cutting** by stopping their subscriptions to traditional cable providers in favor of internet-based alternatives. Since reaching their peak in 2010, the numbers of overall cable subscribers have steadily declined (James, 2016). This has altered the way many media companies have done business. In 2017, as several internet-based options became more available, ESPN laid off over 150 of its employees—roughly 2% of its workforce—to cut costs (Draper, 2017). ESPN and other sports-oriented channels also introduced streaming alternatives to appeal to a growing set of customers who no longer view cable as the best option. Though the future of sport consumption is likely to remain strong, the primary mechanism through which customers access content will likely change. Professional sport franchises must remain aware of the impact of these changes.

* For comparison, in 2017 most cable channels cost less than $1 per month, with channels such as AMC ($0.50), HGTV ($0.23), The History Channel ($0.30), and TLC ($0.25) being the norm and expensive sport-related channels being the exception (Bouma, 2017).

GATE RECEIPTS

The NBA and NHL do not share revenues generated from gate receipts. MLB teams in the National League used to share 5% and in the American League 20% with the visiting team (Zimbalist, 1992; Dobson & Goddard, 2001). These policies were replaced by MLB's 34% revenue-sharing mandate which involved a primary and secondary pool of money.[1] MLB then altered its sharing formula under the 2016 CBA to one based upon 48% of local revenues being shared, with some specific caveats included (Edwards, 2019).[2] NFL teams share 40% of their gate revenues with visiting teams, but the league allocates the revenues across the entire league, so a visiting team that may attract additional fans does not

---

1 MLB's revenue-sharing formula is complex in regard to who pays and how the funds are distributed. Most reporters discussing MLB revenue sharing simply cite the 34% sharing percentage and do not go into details. For more information, see Wendy Thurm's November 14, 2012 article, "The Marlins and the MLB revenue sharing system," available at www.fangraphs.com/blogs/marlins-mlb-revenuesharing-syste/.

2 Perhaps the most interesting aspect of the 2016 agreement was that the Oakland A's would receive a shrinking share of local revenue-sharing dollars. Though successful on the field, the A's poor stadium has led to the team having relatively low payrolls to maintain desired profit levels. The elimination of some revenue-sharing dollars was designed to help spur the team to pursue a new facility and increase their payroll.

necessarily collect any additional revenue (Brown, Nagel, McEvoy, & Rascher, 2004). Hence, although the Dallas Cowboys are heavily marketed and are one of the more popular teams, owner Jerry Jones does not realize any added financial benefit when the Cowboys play a road game in front of capacity crowds. The 40% share of the ticket sales is distributed throughout the league.

MERCHANDISE SALES

The four major North American sport leagues all share revenues from licensed merchandise sales equally among their teams (Grusd, 2004). The only money that teams retain is from sales of products in the team's facility or in local team stores. The NFL permits a franchise to opt out of the league-wide merchandising deal and keep a portion of their generated licensed merchandise revenues if the team agrees to pay a guaranteed amount back to the league. The Dallas Cowboys are the only NFL team that has opted out of the league-wide sharing agreement (Kaplan & Mullen, 2009) and have generated tremendous amounts of revenue that they retain as a result of that decision (Rovell, 2017).

SPONSORSHIP AGREEMENTS

Revenues from league sponsorship deals are also shared equally. In addition, league rules that are designed to increase the overall value of the league's brand affect individual franchises' marketing arrangements. For example, in 1995, the Dallas Cowboys violated the NFL's exclusive sponsorship agreement with Reebok when they signed an agreement with Nike. The NFL sued the Cowboys, the Cowboys countersued, and eventually the team was permitted to keep its agreements, as the parties settled out of court—possibly because the Nike deal (and others that violated NFL exclusivity arrangements) was with Texas Stadium (which Jones owned) and not actually with the Cowboys. Former Baltimore Ravens owner Art Modell noted the conflict that Jones's (and other owners') individual agreements could create for the NFL: "His marketing deals have been astonishing ... He just has to remember that this is a great league because we share our revenue. It's important that he not forget that in his quest to improve the Dallas Cowboys' balance sheet" (Eichelberger, 1999, para. 28).

REVENUE-SHARING METHODS

Each league, regardless of its financial resources, must establish a revenue-sharing percentage and develop a revenue-sharing plan that fits the unique situation of the league. Revenue sharing has become a critical aspect of collective bargaining agreements, and it will likely increase in importance in the future.

In the NHL, for example, the players and owners agreed to a complex revenue-sharing plan that augmented the salary cap implemented after the cancelled 2004/2005 season. The bottom 15 revenue-producing clubs received additional revenue-sharing dollars beyond the equally shared sources, such as national television contracts (Bernstein, 2005). However, lower-revenue-producing clubs in metropolitan markets that have at least 2.5 million households were ineligible to receive revenue-sharing dollars. In addition, clubs had to achieve predetermined attendance levels to be eligible to receive these revenue-sharing dollars. NHL deputy commissioner Bill Daly noted, "You don't want a revenue-sharing program that doesn't incentivize performance" (Bernstein,

2005, para. 18). The NHL's complex revenue-sharing formula worked to stabilize the league, but some were concerned that too much money was being shared with teams in untenable positions. The majority of revenue-sharing dollars have been directed to teams in the southern portion of the United States (such as in the states of Florida, Tennessee, and Arizona), causing many Canadian owners to question why they are subsidizing teams in areas that have traditionally not been interested in hockey ("NHL owners," 2008). As previously mentioned, in 2009 the NHL had to take over financial control of the Phoenix Coyotes as a result of the team's mismanagement and failure to attract a sufficient fan base to generate revenues to cover costs, despite receiving revenue-sharing dollars (Sunnucks, 2009). In the case of the Atlanta Thrashers, low attendance and minimal community interest led to the team's relocation to Winnipeg in 2011 to become the second version of the Winnipeg Jets.

Under the NHL CBA signed in 2013, the league made some changes to its former revenue-sharing model. The 2013 plan requires the top ten grossing teams to contribute based on how much more revenue they generated than the 11th-ranked team. Under this plan, the top revenue-producing team contributes more—possibly much more—than the 10th highest producing team. Playoff teams also allocate 35% of their gate receipts to the revenue-sharing pool. In contrast to the previous CBA, which prevented any "large market" teams or teams that did not reach certain attendance targets from receiving revenue-sharing monies, the new plan has removed some of those restrictions. The plan is designed to help low-revenue teams to be able to pay players salaries that are closer to the midpoint between the salary floor and the salary cap (Hoag, 2013).

SIDEBAR 15.U   Fixing Free Riding with a Relegation System in European Soccer

Every professional sport league is concerned about the potential of free riding by its franchises, but many of the professional leagues outside North America do not have the same problems that the NFL or MLB may experience. Many European soccer leagues have a **relegation system**, in which, after each season, a certain number of the worst-performing clubs will be sent down or relegated to a lower division, while a certain number of the top-performing clubs from the lower division will be elevated to the higher division. Since the potential operating revenues are typically lower in a less desirable division, each year every franchise must attempt to maximize its on-field performance in order to remain in or earn a place in the higher division. The relegation system provides an effective incentive for clubs playing in a low- or middle-level division to work to achieve success that will translate to a better division, higher revenues, and greater profits. Relegated teams will have decreased revenues, but most of the leagues provide some sort of phase-in or phase-out of shared revenues to minimize the immediate impact. In addition, some leagues may offer relegated teams a "parachute payment" if it appears that relegation could lead to bankruptcy. In England, Arsenal has not been relegated since 1913, and it is also one of six teams that have not been relegated since the Premier League was established as the country's top league in 1992.

Although establishment of a relegation system is occasionally discussed as a means to improve motivation and strategic management of certain North American professional teams, media and sponsorship contracts, as well as other logistical issues, make this highly unlikely in the near future, if ever. For instance, if a relegation system were to be implemented in MLB, national and regional television contracts could be devalued if larger-market teams were replaced by teams with much smaller markets. In addition, since the United States is geographically much larger than European countries, team substitutions could create scheduling difficulties and dramatically increase travel costs.

Major League Baseball's 48% revenue-sharing model and luxury tax payments are designed to help teams improve their on-field product. Some observers are concerned that a few MLB clubs may simply be pocketing their revenue-sharing dollars as profits. Teams such as the Miami Marlins and Milwaukee Brewers have been accused of putting profits over team performance. The Milwaukee Brewers, formerly owned by Bud Selig and his family, received tens of millions of dollars in revenue sharing while fielding low-payroll teams in the early 2000s. This situation aroused speculation that Selig, who was commissioner at the time, would not fine the team for pocketing revenue-sharing dollars rather than spending them to improve the team ("HBO's Real Sports examines," 2004). The Miami Marlins have long been one of MLB's largest revenue-sharing recipients. In 2010, the Marlins were forced to increase their payroll after the MLBPA complained that the team was not spending its money on players but instead was pocketing much of the money ("Marlins pay heed," 2010). The agreement the Marlins reached expired in 2013, which was also the year the team traded many of its better players for inexpensive minor league prospects. It was also the year after the Marlins opened a new $634 million stadium, which was largely financed by the public. Despite their history, in 2014 the Marlins signed superstar outfielder Giancarlo Stanton to a 13-year, $325 million contract. Many pundits wondered if Stanton had made a mistake, as in order to be competitive the Marlins would need additional money to sign other quality players. Though the roster looked to be improving, in 2017 Stanton was traded to the Yankees. In addition, the team soon after also traded Christian Yelich and some of their other best players. Interestingly, many of the trades designed to lower payroll and acquire prospects for the future were executed by former Yankee great Derek Jeter who had led a new ownership group that bought the Marlins in 2017.

One of the concerns of owners and league administrators is the potential for teams receiving large revenue-sharing dollars to **free ride**—to benefit at another's expense without expending usual cost or effort, in this case by electing to minimize their marketing efforts while receiving financial benefits from the "extra" efforts of more successful teams. Jerry Jones has been critical of other NFL owners who he feels have failed to maximize their revenue opportunities (Helyar, 2006). Whereas Jones invests heavily in marketing endeavors to advance the Dallas Cowboys brand, other owners appear content to maintain a smaller marketing staff and a lower advertising budget while they benefit from Jones's efforts. The Cowboys are certainly not the only "large-market" team in the major professional sport leagues to complain about the detriments of revenue sharing, but their complaints are certainly the loudest, since the NFL shares much more of its revenues than other leagues.

SIDEBAR 15.V   Does the Global Game Need More Revenue Sharing?

Soccer is by far the most popular sport in the world. Though nearly every country has thousands or millions of people who play, and though talented players are developed in both large and small countries, a growing concern is that too many professional soccer leagues can no longer retain their best players. Professional soccer franchises have long sold or "transferred" their players to other teams, sometimes in other leagues, and free agent players have often moved to new teams for better opportunities to play and/or to earn a higher salary. However, over the past ten years, the revenue disparities among various soccer leagues and among individual teams have grown dramatically. Where there used to be a significant difference in revenue for leagues in Europe versus those in South America, Africa, and Asia, now even some European leagues are unable to retain their best players. Franchises at the top of the English Premier League and the German Bundesliga, as well as Real Madrid and FC Barcelona, have developed extensive revenue sources that dwarf those of other franchises throughout the rest of the world, and the rest of their leagues. Former FIFA presidential advisor Jerome Champagne noted, "The majority of football (soccer) is today facing this crisis [sic] while the wealthy are becoming wealthier ... the reality is that for two percent of privileged clubs or competitions, you have 98 percent in the opposite situation" (Homewood, 2013, paras. 6 & 8).

The massive increase in television dollars for sports that has affected North American leagues such as the NFL, MLB, and NBA has also impacted top European soccer leagues in England, Italy, Spain, and other traditional powers. Unfortunately, the continued growth of television revenues is not likely to affect each league and country in a similar manner. As some leagues generate more and more dollars, their ability to develop their youth teams will increase. To complete those rosters, teams will likely mimic what FC Barcelona has done over the past 20 years. In an effort to build their youth academy, FC Barcelona signs young players from around the world. Top player Lionel Messi was signed from Argentina at the age of 11. As teams attempt to sign top youth players earlier and earlier, South American, African, and Asian soccer prodigies will likely grow up like Lionel Messi, playing in another country even before they turn 18.

There is no perfect system to ensure competitive balance—particularly since every professional sport owner has a unique rationale for operating a franchise. "Perfect" competitive balance, in fact, is not necessarily a desirable situation, since it would mean all teams finish with nearly the same number of wins as losses—a situation that would likely discourage most fans. Whether they are casual or deeply committed, fans enjoy watching superior players from highly successful teams compete for championships. If the highly successful teams are always the same, problems also arise. The key for each league is to develop a system whereby great players are not all playing for a small number of the league's teams.

REVENUE CONSIDERATIONS

Every professional sport league and individual franchise is constantly investigating and developing new revenue sources that address its unique financial issues. For example, over the past 20 years, the importance of a team's facility has grown. Most of the urban sport facilities built in the early part of the 20th century have been replaced, first, in the 1960s, by "cookie cutter" facilities that were primarily designed to offer large seating capacities and expansive parking areas, and then, starting in the 1990s, by more "intimate" facilities. In the case of every new facility and the remaining historic facilities, such as Wrigley Field in Chicago and Fenway Park in Boston, the emphasis in construction and renovation has been revenue maximization.

An investigation and discussion of professional sport revenue sources could fill its own book. In the remainder of this chapter, we describe some interesting revenue developments that are now influencing the financial management of professional sport organizations.

Luxury Seating

Franchises have always desired to sell a large number of season tickets. These tickets provide revenue, facilitate game management, and earn interest, as the money is typically received prior to the season (and many of the season's expenses). Thus, luxury seating has become an important revenue source for many teams. In addition to "traditional" luxury suites and club seats, some facilities, such as the Palace at Auburn Hills, where the NBA's Detroit Pistons play, are offering luxury suites that do not have a direct view of the field of play. These luxury suites are part of a growing trend to attract higher-end customers, who can afford to pay for exclusive access to certain areas of the facility. Whereas most teams 25 years ago worried primarily about the total number of attendees, now many teams pay significant attention to attracting a small number of affluent customers, whether they are individuals or businesses. This development has even reached soccer leagues in Europe, a place where many teams have been reluctant (or unable) to move from their long-standing homes. In Italy, Juventus F.C. built the 41,000-seat Allianz Stadium in 2011. The facility offers several high-end seating options and the team also controls real estate adjacent to the facility which it has now developed to generate additional revenues. In England, Arsenal, Tottenham, and West Ham all compete in state-of-the-art facilities that have a myriad of luxury seating options.

Seat Licenses

Another indication of the trend toward high-priced seating is the use of **personal seat licenses** (discussed in Chapter 9) and **permanent seat licenses**. A PSL is the right to purchase tickets for a specific seat, for which a customer pays a one-time fee. PSLs can generate a tremendous amount of money for a professional sport franchise, if they are designed and marketed properly. Typically, a personal seat license has a limited time frame, and a permanent seat license is valid for the life of the facility.

The rights that are conferred to the PSL holder vary. Often, a PSL holder will desire to bequeath, transfer, or even sell the PSL to another party. The specific language of the PSL determines whether a customer may confer ownership to another party and whether that transfer may be made in exchange for cash. In numerous instances, PSL holders have believed that the licenses were "theirs" to sell or transfer as they wished. In some cases, litigation resulted (Reese, Nagel, & Southall, 2004). Currently, teams typically allow PSL holders to transfer their rights to another party, as long as they pay a handling fee to the team. Some teams have established websites where PSL holders can solicit bids for their ticket rights.

Some purchasers of PSLs may wish to discontinue their relationship with the facility or team. If the purchasers paid their entire fee up front, the failure of the patron to continue to purchase season tickets (which is usually a mandate of the PSL rights agreement) simply results in the team removing that patron from the list. However, in some cases, teams allowed customers to finance PSLs, meaning they could pay the large up-front fee over time. When those customers choose to default, it can put the team in an awkward situation. In early 2019, several PSL holders in Atlanta who had financed their purchase stopped paying their annual fees and/or stopped buying Falcons season tickets. The defaults likely involved about $30 million of lost revenue, although the team did report that it had successfully resold much of the inventory. Though the team could have pursued legal action for the failure to pay on the financed portion of the PSLs, Falcons CFO Greg Beadles indicated, "We typically try to avoid that … I won't say that we would not do that, depending on the circumstances, but typically that is not our approach" (Tucker, 2019, para. 10). The Falcons were faced with further defections as the team recorded another subpar season in 2019 (Glier, 2019).

Secondary Ticket Market

Season tickets and individual game tickets are increasingly being bought and sold on the **secondary ticket market**. Ticket reselling or **scalping** has surely occurred since the first ticketed event in human history, but over the past 15 years the prevailing view of reselling tickets has largely changed. No longer is ticket reselling done primarily by shadowy characters lurking on dark street corners or in back alleys. Most municipalities have rescinded anti-scalping laws, and ticket reselling has become a multimillion-dollar enterprise. Teams and leagues have recognized the importance of acquiring this growing revenue source. In 2007, StubHub signed a contract to be Major League Baseball's exclusive secondary ticket provider (Branch, 2007), and other leagues have also formalized their secondary ticket resale operations. Many teams offer their fans direct access to the secondary ticket marketplace through their websites.

The secondary ticket market is driven partially by the discrepancy between a ticket's initial price and its market price. For many years, teams set ticket prices without thoroughly researching the optimal price, often setting prices based on the previous year's prices, with some adjustment for the team's performance. Most teams did not consider individual games to have different potential demands, even though the airline and hotel industries had long since determined that the same seat or room can be priced differently based on, for example, the day of the week or month of the year. As research and technology in sports have improved, more franchises are employing **variable ticket pricing (VTP)** to capture added revenues by increasing initial ticket prices for highly demanded games and decreasing ticket prices for lower-demanded games, in an effort to attract customers who would not attend at the "typical" price. VTP has proved profitable for many sport franchises, who are now replacing it in some cases with **dynamic ticket pricing**, in which the ticket price is altered instantly (like a stock on a stock exchange) as demand increases or decreases. In most dynamic ticket environments, the team will establish a ticket "floor" or lowest price to maintain price integrity for tickets they sold on the primary market. To unload highly discounted tickets, many teams clandestinely use a third party rather than their own website. If a person is able to buy a ticket for a very low price (such as $5 for a seat that normally costs $30), that transaction will occur away from the team's direct control so as to avoid any fan backlash. Some teams and events also establish a price ceiling (below that which extremely high demand might warrant) on their website so they do not appear to be engaging in gauging customers for the most desired tickets. The complexity and prevalence of dynamic pricing are likely to increase as teams continue to study their ticket prices and as more advanced software becomes available.

Fantasy Sports and Gambling

The modern era of fantasy sports began in 1979 when writer Daniel Okrent invented rotisserie league baseball and invited a variety of his literary and media colleagues to participate. When members of the league began to write about their exploits, the quirky pastime slowly grew, until it reached the mainstream in the late 1980s and early 1990s. Subsequently, during the internet boom of the late 1990s and early 2000s, fantasy sports became a multibillion-dollar industry. Millions of participants join season-long leagues where individuals draft a "team" and compete against other league participants. The industry has continued to expand and is now credited with attracting millions of viewers for games in a variety of sports, particularly in the NFL.

For a number of years, many observers and skeptics of fantasy sports believed that it was merely a form of gambling. Despite this concern, under the Unlawful Internet Gambling Enforcement Act of 2006, fantasy sports were specifically exempt from potential prosecution. However, the introduction and rapid growth of daily fantasy sport sites such as FanDuel and DraftKings had many contemplating whether the government would begin to perceive these games as a form of gambling (Heitner, 2014). FanDuel and DraftKings had attracted hundreds of millions of dollars in entry fees since 2012, but there were still some unknowns about its future until the United States Supreme Court ruled that the federal government could no longer bar individual states from permitting sport gambling (*Murphy v National Collegiate Athletic Association*, 2018).

The Supreme Court ruling opened the door for many states to establish sport gambling activities. A variety of state laws have been established and, as a result, several professional sport leagues and teams are becoming more closely tied to fantasy sport and other sport gambling organizations. Major League Baseball had acquired a small equity stake in DraftKings in 2013 (Fisher, 2015). Ironically, though DraftKings fought for years to establish daily fantasy as a non-gambling activity, since the ruling in *Murphy*, DraftKings has actively expanded its fantasy and non-fantasy activities and is now one of the most dominant sport gambling companies in the world (Marcelo, 2019). The company has partnerships with the NBA, NFL, and several other sport entities. FanDuel has also partnered with several sport organizations in the new legal gambling environment. Given the expanding gambling opportunities, professional sport teams and leagues will need to balance their desire to pursue new revenue sources with the need to maintain strict integrity of their competitions.

CONCLUSION

Every professional sport franchise and league will continue to develop financial tools to enhance its profitability. Leagues attempt to foster competitive balance among teams, but since each franchise owner has a unique rationale for owning and operating a franchise, achieving competitive balance among the teams will always be difficult, and "perfect" balance may not be desirable. Professional sport franchises share some of the characteristics of other businesses, but their financial management has unique aspects. As revenues, expenses, and potential profits continue to increase in the future, financial planning will become even more critical. No longer can a person expect to become a key member of a professional sport franchise without a thorough understanding of the numbers that drive the business.

Concept Check

1. What is the difference between win maximization and profit maximization? How can these differing philosophies cause problems in professional sport leagues?
2. How does a commissioner interact with owners and players in a professional sport league? What are a commissioner's main responsibilities?
3. How do professional sport leagues such as the NBA, NHL, NFL, and MLB differ in structure from entities such as NASCAR, the PGA Tour, and the PBA Tour?
4. Why do professional leagues establish rules governing the financial operation of individual franchises?
5. Explain the concept of pooled debt instruments.
6. Why have so many rival professional sport leagues failed in the United States?
7. How do you see traditional sport organizations becoming involved with esports in the future? How can established traditional sports leagues create new fans through esports ventures?

8. Explain the concept of competitive balance. How have leagues attempted to achieve competitive balance?
9. Discuss the differences among the salary caps in the NBA, NHL, NFL, and MLS.
10. Explain how the NBA's luxury tax system operates. Research and explain an example where the new tax rates affected (or may have affected) a team's decision to sign players for its roster.
11. What is WAR and VORP (in the context of sport finance)? Conduct research to determine the ten most efficient players during the last MLB season. Then compare their salaries to determine which player offered the best performance value for his salary.
12. What will be the impact of cord cutting on the overall sport industry and professional sports in general? What concerns should league and team administrators evaluate for the future?
13. How do you feel the new gambling environment will benefit North American professional sport leagues and individual teams? Are there any issues organizations should consider in the future? How do other professional sport leagues operate in other countries in which sport gambling has been legal?
14. Explain why a relegation system would be difficult to implement in North American professional sport leagues.

Practice Problems

1. If the federal inheritance tax is set at 40% of all assets above $5 million at the time of death, and a state's inheritance tax is set at 5% of all assets above $1 million at the time of death, what does an individual who dies owning a professional sport franchise that is worth $420 million owe in total tax liability? (Assume no other assets at time of death.)
2. If a 30-team league is contemplating expanding by two teams, how much money should it charge each new franchise to ensure that during the first year of the new 32-team league, each of the existing 30 owners will receive the same amount of revenue as they would have without the expansion? (Assume each owner earns $40 million per year from media contracts and $10 million per year from licensed merchandise sales, that the league will continue to share these revenues equally after the expansion, and that the media contracts are not scheduled to be renegotiated until a year after the expansion is completed.)
3. Suppose that last season, the top pick in a 30-team league's amateur draft signed a contract for $2 million per year. In the upcoming season, the league will implement a salary slotting system under which each pick will be compensated based on his draft selection. If the compensation plan will be based on a 5% increase of the top selection's compensation from last year and a 1% decreasing scale for every pick after the first selection (second pick will earn 99% of what the first pick earns, and so forth), how much will the top selection in next year's draft earn? How much will the ninth pick earn?

Case Analysis

Structuring a League

You have been asked to consult for an entrepreneur who is assembling investors for a new professional sport league. A critical decision for the league will be whether to organize under a single-entity structure or a franchisor/franchisee model.

Case Questions

1. Briefly describe how each structure works and explain the financial advantages and disadvantages of each structure.
2. How have these structures helped or hindered leagues in the past and present? Cite specific examples from existing leagues to support your answer.

References

Abrams, J. (2009, July 8). N.B.A.'s shrinking salary cap could shake up 2010 free agency. *New York Times*. Retrieved from www.nytimes.com/2009/07/09/sports/basketball/09nba.html.

Adams, L. (2019, April 18). Hoops rumors. Retrieved from www.hoopsrumors.com/2019/04/recent-history-of-nba-taxpaying-teams.html.

Allen, J.C. (1998, October 19). Using the future to pay for the present. *Sports Business Journal*. Retrieved from www.sportsbusinessjournal.com/article/19056.

Art Rooney Jr. could decide future of Steelers' ownership. (2008, July 10). *ESPN.com*. Retrieved from http://sports.espn.go.com/nfl/news/story?id=3482116.

Aschburner, S. (2015, February 13). Players union rejects salary cap 'smoothing' proposal. Retrieved from wwwnba.com/2015/news/features/steve_aschburner/02/13/nba-players-union-meeting/.

Barker, J. (2019, September 27). After big court decision in TV rights dispute, Orioles and Nationals disagree on how much MASN ordered to pay. *The Baltimore Sun*. Retrieved from www.baltimoresun.com/sports/orioles/bs-sp-orioles-masn-nationals-2019 0927-flft33bsdrekzft56mkfr3viie-story.html.

Barnwell, B. (2013, March 11). Pawn stars. *Grantland*. Retrieved from www.grantland.com/story/_/id/9039158/bill-barnwell-changes-nfl-free-agent-landscape.

Barnwell, B. (2014, March 4). The money pit. *Grantland*. Retrieved from http://grantland.com/features/the-money-pit/.

Barnwell, B. (2018, September 13). The Cowboys' salary-cap mismanagement is wasting Dak Prescott. Retrieved from www.espn.com/nfl/story/_/id/24653201/how-dallas-cowboys-wasting-dak-prescott-rookie-deal-salary-cap-nfl-2018.

Benjamin, C. (2019, March 1). NFL salary cap rises to $188.2 million for 2019, the sixth straight year with a $10 million increase. Retrieved from www.cbssports.com/nfl/news/nfl-salary-cap-rises-to-188-2-million-for-2019-the-sixth-straight-year-with-a-10-million-increase/.

Bernstein, A. (2002, June 3–9). Sabres carrying $150M in debt, SEC filing says. *Sports Business Journal*, 5(6), 1 & 34.

Bernstein, A. (2005, August 1). Inside the complex NHL deal. *Sports Business Journal*. Retrieved from www.sportsbusinessdaily.com/Journal/Issues/2005/08/20050801/Labor-Agents/Inside-The-Complex-NHL-Deal.aspx.

Berrett, J. (2018, February 2). The NFL: America's socialist utopia. *The Washington Post*. Retrieved from www.washingtonpost.com/news/made-by-history/wp/2018/02/02/the-nfl-americas-socialist-utopia/.

Bloom, B.M. (2009, March 10). Fehr does not foresee a salary cap. *MLB.com*. Retrieved from http://mlb.mlb.com/news/article.jsp?ymd=20090310&content_id=3961482& vkey=news_mlb&fext=jsp&c_id=mlb&partnerId=rss_mlb.

Bouma, L. (2017, September 16). Here is what a la carte TV would really cost (Yes, it will be less expensive than cable). *Cord Cutters News*. Retrieved from www.cordcuttersnews. com/la-carte-tv-really-cost-yes-will-less-expensive-cable/.

Bradbury, J.C. (2019, January 15). What explains labor's declining share of revenue in Major League Baseball? Retrieved from https://papers.ssrn.com/sol3/papers. cfm?abstract_id=3092381.

Branch, A. (2007, August 2). StubHub! and MLB strike precedent-setting secondary ticketing deal. *TicketNews*. Retrieved from www.ticketnews.com/StubHub-and-MLB-Strike-Precedent-Setting-Secondary-Ticketing-Deal8227.

Brand, G. (2015, December 15). How the Bosman rule changed football—20 years on. *Sky Sports*. Retrieved from www.skysports.com/football/news/11095/10100134/ how-the-bosman-rule-changed-football-20-years-on.

Brink, B. (2019, March 19). MLBPA remains concerned about teams' winning intentions. *Pittsburgh Post-Gazette*. Retrieved from www.post-gazette.com/sports/pirates/ 2019/03/19/MLBPA-remains-concerned-about-teams-winning-intentions/stories/ 201903190092.

Brown, M. (2007, December 25). Breaking down MLB's luxury tax: 2003–2007. *The biz of baseball*. Retrieved from www.bizofbaseball.com/index.php?option=com_content&t ask=view&id=1805&Itemid=41.

Brown, M. (2014, July 7). The biggest media company you've never heard of. *Forbes*. Retrieved from www.forbes.com/sites/maurybrown/2014/07/07/the-biggest-media-company-youve-never-heard-of/.

Brown, M. (2019, January 11). MLB spend less on player salaries despite record revenues in 2018. *Forbes*. Retrieved from www.forbes.com/sites/maurybrown/2019/01/11/ economic-data-shows-mlb-spent-less-on-player-salaries-compared-to-revenues-in-2018/#53f3123639d7.

Brown, M., Nagel, M.S., McEvoy, C.D., & Rascher, D.A. (2004). Revenue and wealth maximization in the NFL: The impact of stadia. *Sport Marketing Quarterly*, 13(4), 227–235.

Calcaterra, C. (2020, January 29). Kris Bryant loses service time grievance, remains under Cubs' control through 2021. Retrieved from https://mlb.nbcsports.com/2020/01/ 29/kris-bryant-loses-service-time-grievance-remains-under-cubs-control-through-2021/.

Cardillo, M. (2013, November 12). MLS TV ratings are lower than the WNBA's, can the league do anything to improve them? *USA Today*. Retrieved from http://thebiglead. com/2013/11/12/mls-tv-ratings-are-lower-than-the-wnbas-can-the-league-do-anything-to-improve-them/.

Casacchia, C. (2005, May 26). Fowler's rile reduced in finalized Vikings sale. *Phoenix Business Journal*. Retrieved from http://phoenix.bizjournals.com/phoenix/stories/ 2005/05/23/daily38.html.

Cato, T. (2017, September 5). How much did each NBA owner pay to buy their teams? *SB Nation*. Retrieved from www.sbnation.com/nba/2017/9/5/16255168/ nba-teams-sold-highest-record-price-all-30.

Clayton, J. (2008, July 15). NFL ownership growing increasingly complicated. *ESPN.com*. Retrieved from http://sports.espn.go.com/nfl/columns/story?columnist=clayton_ john& id=3485962.

Coin flip to lottery: Did the Rockets tank to get Olajuwon? (2008, January 19). Retrieved from http://reclinergm.wordpress.com/2008/01/19/coin-flip-to-lottery-did-the-rockets-tank-to-get-olajuwon/.

Collazo, C. (2019, June 1). 2019 MLB draft: Order, slot values & team bonus pool amounts. *Baseball America*. Retrieved from www.baseballamerica.com/stories/2019-mlb-draft-order-slot-values-team-bonus-pool-amounts/.

Competitive balance tax. (n.d.). Retrieved from http://m.mlb.com/glossary/transactions/competitive-balance-tax.

Complete history of luxury tax payments, updated for 2012/13. (2013, July 10). *Shamsports.com.* Retrieved from www.shamsports.com/2013/07/complete-history-of-luxury-tax-payments.html.

Coon, L. (2020). Larry Coon's NBA salary cap FAQ. Retrieved from www.cbafaq.com/salarycap.htm.

Coro, P. (2007, June 29). Suns sell pick, choose Tucker. *The Arizona Republic.* Retrieved from www.azcentral.com/arizonarepublic/sports/articles/0629suns0629.html.

Court accepts Major League Soccer's single entity defense in players' antitrust suit. (2000, Summer). Retrieved from http://law.marquette.edu/cgi-bin/site.pl?2130&pageID=494#5.

Crowe, J. (2008, April 14). Start-ups or upstarts, Gary Davidson was there at creation. *Los Angeles Times.* Retrieved from http://articles.latimes.com/2008/apr/14/sports/sp-crowe14.

Cwik, C. (2020, January 14). WNBA players win better pay, increased marketing and more family benefits with new CBA. *Yahoo Sports.* Retrieved from https://sports.yahoo.com/wnba-players-win-better-pay-increased-marketing-and-more-family-benefits-with-new-cba-151309427.html.

Dobson, S., & Goddard, J.A. (2001). *The economics of football.* Cambridge, UK: Cambridge University Press.

"Done deal": Sacramento Kings sold by Maloof family. (2013, January 11). Retrieved from http://mynorthwest.com/11/2172714/Done-Deal-New-report-says-Sacramento-Kings-sold-to-Seattle-Maloofs-out.

Draper, K. (2017, November 29). ESPN is laying off 150 more employees. *The New York Times.* Retrieved from www.nytimes.com/2017/11/29/sports/espn-layoffs.html.

Dougherty, J. (2020, May 27). Mike Trout would lose $29 million under MLB's embarrassing salary cut proposal. Retrieved from www.sportscasting.com/mike-trout-would-lose-29-million-under-mlbs-embarrassing-salary-cut-proposal/.

Edwards, C. (2019, January 9). A's revenue sharing money heads back to the Yankees. *FanGraphs.* Retrieved from https://blogs.fangraphs.com/as-revenue-sharing-money-heads-back-to-the-yankees/.

Egan, M. (2012, March 28). La La land math: Are the Dodgers really worth $2.15 billion? *Foxbusiness.com.* Retrieved from www.foxbusiness.com/industries/2012/03/28/are-dodgers-really-worth-215-billion/.

Eichelberger, C. (1999, August 12). Major gamble pays big rewards for Cowboys owner Jerry Jones. *The Journal Record.* Retrieved from http://findarticles.eom/p/articles/mi_qn4182/is_19990812/ai_n10131411/.

Fagan, K. (2015, February 4). Diana Taurasi's decision to sit out should spark WNBA salary changes. *ESPNw.com.* Retrieved from http://espn.go.com/wnba/story/_/id/12272036/diana-taurasi-decision-sit-spark-wnba-salary-changes.

Farrar, D. (2012). 2012 salary cap set at $120.6 million. *Yahoo Sports.* Retrieved from http://sports.yahoo.com/blogs/nfl-shutdown-corner/2012-nfl-salary-cap-set-120-6-million-211140326.html.

Federal Baseball Club v. National League, 259 U.S. 200 (1922).

Feldman, D. (2017, October 27). Former Warriors executive: Golden State tanked to get Harrison Barnes. *NBC Sports.* Retrieved from https://nba.nbcsports.com/2017/10/27/former-warriors-executive-golden-state-tanked-to-get-harrison-barnes/.

Fisher, E. (2011, March 21). Ten years later, MLBAM still evolving. *Sports Business Journal.* Retrieved from www.sportsbusinessdaily.com/Journal/Issues/2011/03/21/Media/MLBAM.aspx.

Fisher, E. (2015, April 20). A look into DraftKings MLB deal. *Sports Business Journal.* Retrieved from www.sportsbusinessdaily.com/Journal/Issues/2015/04/20/Media/Draft Kings-MLB.aspx.

Fitzpatrick, J. (2005, July 13). NHL and players make a deal. *About sports.* Retrieved from http://proicehockey.about.com/od/thelatestonthelockout/a/cba_agreement. htm.

Flood v. Kuhn, 407 U.S. 258 (1972).

Fraser v. Major League Soccer, 97 F.Supp.2d 130 (D. Mass. April 19, 2000).

Garber, J. (2019, July 25). Federal estate tax exemptions 1997 through 2019. *The Balance.* Retrieved from www.thebalance.com/exemption-from-federal-estate-taxes-3505630.

Glier, R. (2019, November 25). Poor season could lead to more PSL defaults for Falcons. *Forbes.* Retrieved from www.forbes.com/sites/rayglier/2019/11/25/poor-season-could-lead-to-more-psl-defaults-for-falcons/#6377d71c4c19.

Graziano, D. (2019, November 22). How Garrett's suspension affects his contract. Retrieved from www.espn.com/nfl/story/_/id/28131532/the-cowboys-playing-cowboy-way-offense-good-bad.

Groppelli, A.A., & Nikbakht, E. (2000). *Finance* (4th ed.). Hauppauge, NY: Barrons.

Grow, N. (2015, May 1). MLB's evolving luxury tax. *FanGraphs.* Retrieved from https://blogs.fangraphs.com/mlbs-evolving-luxury-tax/.

Grusd, B.L. (2004). The antitrust implications of professional sports' leaguewide licensing and merchandising arrangements. In S.R. Rosner & K.L. Shropshire (Eds.), *The business of sports.* Boston: Jones and Bartlett Publishers.

Haller, D. (2007, July 20). Kurt Thomas traded to Seattle. *The Arizona Republic.* Retrieved from www.azcentral.com/sports/suns/articles/0720kurttraded-CR.html.

Hanlon, G. (2015, April 9). The perks and perils of owning a small share of a sports team. *Observer.* Retrieved from https://observer.com/2015/04/the-perks-and-perils-of-owning-a-small-share-of-a-sports-team/.

Hanzus, D. (2014, February 28). NFL salary cap makes nearly 10M jump to 133 million. *NFL.com.* Retrieved from www.nfl.com/news/story/0ap2000000329753/article/nfl-salary-cap-makes-nearly-10m-jump-to-133-million.

Harris, D. (1986). *The league: The rise and decline of the NFL.* New York: Bantam.

Harvey, R. (1979, February). Talking football with Lamar Hunt. *Football Digest.* Retrieved from http://prod.static.chiefs.clubs.nfl.com/assets/docs/6_talking_football_with_lamar_hunt.pdf.

Haupert, M.J. (2007, December 3). The economic history of Major League Baseball. *EH. net encyclopedia.* Retrieved from http://eh.net/encyclopedia/article/haupert.mlb.

HBO's Real Sports examines plight of the Brewers. (2004, February 25). *Sports Business Daily.* Retrieved from www.sportsbusinessdaily.com/article/83052.

Heath, T. (2005, April 1). O's get majority of TV deal. *The Washington Post.* Retrieved from www.washingtonpost.com/wp-dyn/articles/A15731-2005Mar31.html.

Heitner, D. (2014, March 13). Major storm brewing between fantasy sports giants: FanDuel vs. DraftKings. *Forbes.* Retrieved from www.forbes.com/sites/darrenheitner/2014/03/13/major-storm-brewing-between-fantasy-sports-giants-fanduel-vs-draftkings/.

Helyar, J. (2006, March 6). Labor peace threatened by rift between owners. *ESPN.com.* Retrieved from http://sports.espn.go.com/nfl/news/story?id=2354095.

Hoag, D. (2013, June 7). 2013 NHL CBA: New revenue sharing program could help the Nashville Predators. *SB Nation.* Retrieved from www.ontheforecheck.com/2013/6/7/4406482/2013-nhl-cba-revenue-sharing-program-explaine.

Homewood, B. (2013, March 20). Overhaul needed to stop talent drain, says Champagne. *Reuters.* Retrieved from www.reuters.com/article/2013/03/21/us-soccer-fifa-champagne-idUSBRE92K01Q20130321.

How Steinbrenner saved his heirs a $600 million tax bill. (2010, July 13). *The Wall Street Journal.* Retrieved from http://blogs.wsj.com/metropolis/2010/07/13/how-steinbrenner-saved-his-heirs-a-600-million-tax-bill/.

Hoyle, J. (2016, August 2). On the Joey Bosa holdout, I call bullsh*t. *SB Nation.* Retrieved from www.boltsfromtheblue.com/2016/8/2/12346564/the-truth-about-the-bosa-holdout-according-to-hoyle.

James, M. (2016, December 5). The rise of sports TV costs and why your cable bill keeps going up. *Los Angeles Times.* Retrieved from www.latimes.com/business/hollywood/la-fi-ct-sports-channels-20161128-story.html.

Jazayerli, R. (2013, May 14). The joy of tanking. *Grantland.* Retrieved from www.grantland.com/story/_/id/9273233/hoarding-prospects-being-horrible-houston-astros.

Kaplan, D. (2000a, September 11). Tigers' finance plan uses a unique twist. *Sports Business Journal.* Retrieved from www.sportsbusinessjournal.com/article/10815.

Kaplan, D. (2000b, September 25). Tigers shelve $250M financing. *Sports Business Journal.* Retrieved from www.sportsbusinessjournal.com/article/10851.

Kaplan, D. (2003, November 3). MLB moves to tighten loan rules. *Sports Business Journal.* Retrieved from www.sportsbusinessjournal.com/article/34677.

Kaplan, D. (2013, April 8–14). MLB will expand loan pool. *Sports Business Journal,* 15(49), 1 & 5.

Kaplan, D. (2015, May 25). NFL votes to allow trust ownership of teams. *Sports Business Daily.* Retrieved from www.sportsbusinessdaily.com/Journal/Issues/2015/05/25/Leagues-and-Governing-Bodies/NFL-trust.aspx.

Kaplan, D. (2018, April 23). Giant debt limit for L.A. surprises NFL insiders. *Sports Business Journal.* Retrieved from www.sportsbusinessdaily.com/Journal/Issues/2018/04/23/Leagues-and-Governing-Bodies/NFL-debt-limit.aspx.

Kaplan, D., & Mullen, L. (2009, June 8). Upshaw payout contributes to rare drop in NFLPA assets. *Sports Business Journal.* Retrieved from www.sportsbusinessjournal.com/article/62723.

Keri, J. (2013, July 29). The 30: Tipping point. *Grantland.* Retrieved from www.grantland.com/story/_Zid/9517904/jonah-keri-ranks-mlb-teams.

Kinzy, T. (2019, June 11). How much does a win cost? Retrieved from www.vivaelbirdos.com/2019/6/11/18660989/how-much-does-a-win-cost-mlb-free-agency-trade-deadline-price-war.

Kostora, N. (2013, April 8). Everything you need to know about the NFL's rookie wage scale. *Bleacher Report.* Retrieved from http://bleacherreport.com/articles/1595987-everything-you-need-to-know-about-the-nfls-rookie-wage-scale.

Lee, A. (2019a, April 27). A WNBA 'supermax' salary can help protect its stars from injury—here's how it would work. Retrieved from www.swishappeal.com/wnba/2019/4/27/18518428/wnba-supermax-salary-superstars-overseas-play-collective-bargaining-agreement-breanna-stewart.

Lee, A. (2019b, May 17). To limit injuries, the WNBA must address overseas play and it short pre-draft period. Retrieved from www.swishappeal.com/wnba/2019/5/17/18624761/wnba-injuries-candace-parker-lindsay-allen-kiara-leslie-overseas-play-pre-draft-workouts.

Lindbergh, B. (2019, January 8). Long, cold winter: MLB free agency is still disturbingly slow. *The Ringer.* Retrieved from www.theringer.com/mlb/2019/1/8/18173625/free-agency-slow-signing-pace-manny-machado-bryce-harper.

Lombardo, J., & Kaplan, D. (2014, April 28–May 4). NBA's global value plays role in sale of Bucks. *Sports Business Journal,* 17(3), 4.

Los Angeles Memorial Coliseum Commission v. National Football League, 726 F. 2d 138 (1984).

Los Angeles Memorial Coliseum Commission v. National Football League, 791 F. 2d. 1356 (1986).

Louie, D. (2015, April 15). Papers filed for Supreme Court to hear Oakland A's relocation case. *ABC 7 News.* Retrieved from http://abc7news.com/sports/papers-filed-for-supreme-court-to-hear-oakland-as-relocation-case/663003/.

Lowe, Z. (2013, December 23). The NBA's possible solution for tanking: Good-bye to the lottery, hello to the wheel. *Grantland.* Retrieved from https://grantland.com/the-triangle/the-nbas-possible-solution-for-tanking-good-bye-to-the-lottery-hello-to-the-wheel/.

Madison Square Garden sues NHL over promotion terms. (2007, September 28). *USA Today*. Retrieved from www.usatoday.com/sports/hockey/nhl/2007-09-28-msg-suit_N.htm.

Marcelo, P. (2019, December 23). Will Wall Street gamble on DraftKings? Sports betting giant plans to go public, close two mergers. *USA Today*. Retrieved from www.usatoday.com/story/money/2019/12/23/draftkings-sports-betting-giant-gambling-mergers-ipo/2738558001/.

Marks, B. (2017, December 6). Can the Warriors afford a dynasty? The price will be unprecedented. Retrieved from www.espn.com/nba/insider/story/_/id/21652258/can-golden-state-warriors-afford-dynasty-price-unprecedented-nba.

Marlins pay heed, will increase payroll. (2010, January 12). *ESPN.com*. Retrieved from http://sports.espn.go.cm/mlb/news/story?id=4819982.

Maynes, A. (2018, December 5). Robert Sarver does not understand that the Phoenix Suns are not his alone. Retrieved from https://valleyofthesuns.com/2018/12/05/robert-sarver-does-not-understand-that-the-phoenix-suns-are-not-his-alone/.

McCann, M. (2007, April 9). Why does tanking occur in the NBA but seemingly not in other leagues? *Sports Law Blog*. Retrieved from http://sports-law.blogspot.com/2007/04/why-does-tanking-occur-in-nba-but.html.

McIntyre, D. (2013, August 23). MLS keeps US players close to home with cap-exempt pay. Retrieved from http://espnfc.com/news/story/_/id/1530917/mls-keeps-us-players-close-home-cap-exempt-pay-espn-magazine?cc=5901.

Mickle, T., & Lefton, T. (2008, August 4). Several leagues later, debate on single-entity model still lively. *Sports Business Journal*. Retrieved from www.sportsbusinessjournal.com/article/59720.

Miller, M. (1991). *A whole different ball game*. New York: Birch Lane Press.

Miller, R. (2019, November 12). Yankees paying luxury tax again: How it could affect Hal Seinbrenner's spending moving forward. Retrieved from www.nj.com/yankees/2019/11/yankees-paying-luxury-tax-again-what-it-means.html.

Mintz, H. (2015, January 15). Federal appeals court rejects San Jose's antitrust case against Major League Baseball. *San Jose Mercury News*. Retrieved from www.mercurynews.com/crime-courts/ci_27326240/san-jose-v-mlb-appeals-court-rejects-citys.

Mirtle, J. (2013, January 8). How the NHL's new salary trading system works. *The Globe and Mail*. Retrieved from www.theglobeandmail.com/sports/hockey/globe-on-hockey/how-the-nhls-new-salary-trading-system-works/article7033878/.

MLB team payroll tracker. (n.d.). *Spotrac*. Retrieved from www.spotrac.com/mlb/payroll/2018/.

MLS oks "Beckham Rule" to attract superstar players. (2006, November 11). *ESPN.com*. Retrieved from http://soccernet.espn.go.com/news/story?id=391320&cc=5901.

Morris, J. (2009, August 20). Fight over ownership of Coyotes could have impact on other sport leagues. *Canadian Press*. Retrieved from www.sportingnews.com/nba/article/2009-08-20/fight-over-coyotes-ownership-could-impact-other-leagues.

Moskeowitz, D. (2019, October 6). 10 most valuable NFL teams 2019: Cowboys lead the pack. *Investopedia*. Retrieved from www.investopedia.com/articles/personal-finance/022315/5-mostvaluable-nfl-franchises.asp.

Murphy v. National Collegiate Athletic Association, 584 U.S. 138 S. Ct. 1461; 200 L. Ed. 2d 854 (2018).

Nagel, M.S. (2005). Salary caps. In *Encyclopedia of world sport* (Vol. 3). Great Barrington, MA: Berkshire Publishing, pp. 1322–1323.

Nagel, M.S., & Brown, M.T. (2009). The business of Japanese baseball. *Asian Sport Management Review*, 3(1), 2–25.

Nagel, M.S., Brown, M.T., Rascher, D.A., & McEvoy, C.D. (2007, Spring). Major League Baseball anti-trust immunity: Examining the legal and financial implications of relocation rules. *Entertainment and Sport Law Journal*, 4(3). Retrieved from www2.warwick.ac.uk/fac/soc/law/elj/eslj/issues/volume4/number3/nagel.

Nakashima, R., & Blum, R. (2013, January 28). Dodgers TV deal: L.A. club inks $7 billion Time Warner Cable, MLB to determine revenue-sharing impact. *The Huffington Post.* Retrieved from www.huffingtonpost.com/2013/01/28/dodgers-tv-deal-time-warner-mlb_n_2570677.html.

Nats, Strasburg beat deadline. (2009, August 18). *ESPN.com.* Retrieved from http://sports.espn.go.com/mlb/news/story?id=4403920.

NBA lines up $200 million for teams. (2009, February 27). *ESPN.com.* Retrieved from http://sports.espn.go.com/nba/news/story?id=3936991.

The Neutral (2013, January 8). Why the Luongo rule makes no sense. *SB Nation.* Retrieved from www.fearthe-fin.com/2013/1/8/3849986/why-the-luongo-rule-makes-no-sense.

NHL owners growing wary of league's revenue sharing system. (2008, October 13). *Sports Business Daily.* Retrieved from www.sportsbusinessdaily.com/article/124637.

Oakland Raiders 2013 salary cap. (2013). *Spotrac.* Retrieved from www.spotrac.com/nfl/oakland-raiders/cap-hit/.

Ori, R. (2017, June 30). Cubs owners borrow more than $65 million on Wrigley rooftops. *Chicago Tribune.* Retrieved from www.chicagotribune.com/business/ct-wrigley-rooftops-ryan-ori-0630-biz-20170629-column.html.

Oshan, J. (2015, March 5). MLS CBA details: Salary cap will go up slowly. *SB Nation.* Retrieved from www.sounderatheart.com/2015/3/5/8156205/mls-cba-details-salary-cap.

Ozanian, M. (2012, December 12). Rangers TV deal may come back to haunt Dodgers. *Forbes.* Retrieved from www.forbes.com/sites/mikeozanian/2012/12/12/rangers-tv-deal-may-come-back-to-haunt-dodgers/.

Ozanian, M. (2013, January 28). Dodgers hope to avoid millions in taxes with TV naming rights scheme. *Forbes.* Retrieved from www.forbes.com/sites/mikeozanian/2013/01/28/dodgers-hope-to-avoid-millions-in-taxes-with-tv-naming-rights-scheme/.

Ozanian, M. (2018, March 30). Increase in NFL debt limit will help sale of Carolina Panthers. *Forbes.* Retrieved from www.forbes.com/sites/mikeozanian/2018/03/30/increase-in-nfl-debt-limit-will-help-sale-of-carolina-panthers/#4bb9fce7db67.

Patra, K. (2015, March 2). NFL salary cap will be 143.28 million in 2015. *NFL.com.* Retrieved from www.nfl.com/news/story/0ap3000000475775/article/nfl-salary-cap-will-be-14328-million-in-2015.

Prine, C. (2009, July 23). Four of five Rooney brothers sign off on deal to sell Steelers' shares. *Pittsburgh Tribune-Review.* Retrieved from www.pittsburghlive.com/x/pittsburghtrib/news/pittsburgh/s_634902.html.

Pro football draft history: 1936. (n.d.). *Pro football hall of fame.* Retrieved from www.profootballhof.com/history/general/draft/1936.aspx.

Rascher, D.A., Nagel, M.S., Brown, M.T., & McEvoy, C.D. (2011). Free ride, take it easy: An empirical analysis of adverse incentives caused by revenue sharing. *Journal of Sport Management,* 25(5), 373–390.

Ray, J.L. (2008, February 23). How baseball arbitration works. *Suite101.com.* Retrieved from http://baseball.suite101.com/article.cfm/how_baseball_arbitration_works.

Reese, J.T., Nagel, M.S., & Southall, R.M. (2004). National Football League ticket transfer policies: Legal and policy issues. *Journal of the Legal Aspects of Sport,* 14(2), 163–190.

Report: Yanks hit with luxury tax. (2012, December 14). *ESPN.com.* Retrieved from http://espn.go.com/new-york/mlb/story/_/id/8748326/report-new-york-yankees-hit-luxury-tax-10th-straight-year.

Richter, M., & Hurt, S. (2013, May 16). NBA denies bid to move Sacramento Kings basketball team to Seattle. *Reuters.* www.reuters.com/article/2013/05/16/us-nba-kings-sacramento-idUSBRE94E1CP20130516.

Rovell, D. (2017, August 4). The business of Jerry: 25 moves made by NFL's top power broker. Retrieved from www.espn.com/nfl/story/_/id/20238460/the-business-jerry-jones-dallas-cowboys-25-moves-biggest-nfl-power-broker.

Sachdev, A. (2009, August 27). Chicago Cubs sale: Ricketts family agrees to $35 million reserve fund. *Chicago Tribune*. Retrieved from www.chicagotribune.com/business/chi-thu-cubs-cushionaug27,0,399238.story.

Salary cap space. (n.d.). Retrieved from https://overthecap.com/salary-cap-space/.

San Jose officials explain decision to sue MLB. (2013, June 18). *San Jose Mercury News*. Retrieved from www.mercurynews.com/oakland-as-move/ci_23488223/san-jose-officials-explain-decision-sue-mlb.

Schmuck, P. (2019, August 23). Judge upholds arbitration ruling that Orioles owe Nationals about $100 million in MASN TV dispute. *The Baltimore Sun*. Retrieved from www.baltimoresun.com/sports/orioles/bs-sp-orioles-lose-latest-round-in-masn-lawsuit-20190823-ww6a53a7nraipgwuypgxef2gt4-story.html.

Scully, G.W. (1995). *The market structure of sports*. Chicago: University of Chicago Press.

Shaikin, B. (2013, June 13). Dodgers to keep more than $6 billion from TV contract in tentative pact. *Los Angeles Times*. Retrieved from http://articles.latimes.com/2013/jun/13/sports/la-sp-0614-dodgers-tv-20130614.

Shaikin, B. (2016, November 26). After $1 billion in player spending, Dodgers under MLB mandate to cut debt. *Los Angeles Times*. Retrieved from www.latimes.com/sports/dodgers/la-sp-dodgers-debt-payroll-20161126-story.html.

Shropshire, K.L. (1995). *The sports franchise game*. Philadelphia: University of Pennsylvania Press.

Simmons, B. (2007, April 19). Links while tossing around conspiracy theories. *ESPN Page 2*. Retrieved from http://sports.espn.go.com/espn/page2/blog/index?name=simmons&entryDate=20070419.

Simmons, B. (2008, May 5). A requiem for the S.S.O.L. era in Phoenix. *ESPN Page 2*. Retrieved from http://sports.espn.go.com/espn/page2/story?page=simmons%2F080501.

Smith, C.C. (2019, April 23). MLS considering "significantly altering the salary budgets." *The Blue Testament*. Retrieved from www.thebluetestament.com/2019/4/23/18512131/mls-considering-significantly-altering-the-salary-budgets-don-garber-cba-negotiations.

Snyder, M. (2019, September 29). There were a record number of 100-win and 100-loss MLB teams in 2019, and it was bad for baseball. Retrieved from www.cbssports.com/mlb/news/there-were-a-record-number-of-100-win-and-100-loss-mlb-teams-in-2019-and-it-was-bad-for-baseball/.

Stark, J. (2012, January 13). Looking for a lower tax bracket. *ESPN.com*. Retrieved from http://espn.go.com/mlb/story/_Zpage/rumblings120113/why-yankees-red-sox-spending-big.

Sunnucks, M. (2009, May 6). NHL takes over Coyotes web site. *Phoenix Business Journal*. Retrieved from http://phoenix.bizjournals.com/phoenix/stories/2009/05/04/daily46.html.

Thomas, J. (2016, August 24). Let's try to make sense of Joey Bosa's holdout with the Chargers. *SB Nation*. Retrieved from www.sbnation.com/2016/8/8/12402198/joey-bosa-contract-holdout-san-diego-chargers-why.

Thomas, K. (2012, June 3). Dollars for draftees: New rules limit what a big-money team can spend. *Portland Press Herald*. Retrieved from www.pressherald.com/sports/dollars-for-draftees-new-rules-limit-what-a-big-money-team-can-spend_2012-06-03.html.

Thurm, W. (2012, November 27). Dodgers send shock waves through local TV landscape. *FanGraphs*. Retrieved from www.fangraphs.com/blogs/dodgers-send-shock-waves-through-local-tv-landscape/.

Townes, C. (2019, October 31). What is really at stake in the WNBA CBA negotiations. *Forbes*. Retrieved from www.forbes.com/sites/ceceliatownes/2019/10/31/what-is-really-at-stake-in-the-wnba-cba-negotiations/#7199dc5450ee.

Tucker, T. (2012, January 26). Terry McGuirk discusses Braves' payroll, ownership, TV deals. *Atlanta Journal Constitution*. Retrieved from www.ajc.com/news/sports/baseball/terry-mcguirk-discusses-braves-payroll-ownership-t/nQQjM/.

Tucker, T. (2019, April 27). Defaults on Falcons' PSLs reach $30 million, records show. *Atlanta Journal Constitution*. Retrieved from www.ajc.com/sports/football/defaults-falcons-psls-reach-million-records-show/YtQHnTqSsn3PPOCPLwQrOJ/#.

USFL v. NFL. 842 F.2d 1335 (2nd Cir. 1988).

Vaccaro, M. (2013, December 15). Finley's free-agency idea was chaotic, but captivating. *New York Post*. Retrieved from https://nypost.com/2013/12/15/finleys-free-agency-idea-was-chaotic-but-captivating/.

Wagman, R. (2008, January 5). Garber's leadership has solidified MLS future. *SoccerTimes*. Retrieved from www.soccertimes.com/wagman/2008/jan05.

Weaver, M. (2019, October 18). What NASCAR's $2 billion ISC merger means in the short term. *AutoWeek*. Retrieved from https://autoweek.com/article/nascar/what-nascars-2-billion-isc-merger-means-short-term.

Weiner, E. (2012, November 9). Was David Stern alone responsible for the NBA's success? *The Sport Digest*. Retrieved from http://thesportdigest.com/2012/11/was-david-stern-alone-responsible-for-the-nbas-success/.

Wesseling, C. (2013, February 28). NFL sets salary cap at 123M, up from 120.6M. *NFL.com*. Retrieved from www.nfl.com/news/story/0ap1000000146046/article/nfl-sets-2013-salary-cap-at-123m-up-from-1206m.

Whiting, R. (1989). *You gotta have wa*. New York: Vintage Books.

Whiting, R. (2004). *The meaning of Ichiro*. New York: Warner Books.

Wile, R. (2017, March 14). The most popular cable channels are the ones you can watch for free. *Money*. Retrieved from https://money.com/cable-prices-most-popular-tv-channels-espn-abc-discovery-hbo/.

Windhorst, B., & Marks, B. (2018, February 5). A big NBA money crunch is coming. Retrieved from www.espn.com/nba/story/_/id/22263630/nba-financial-crunch-coming.

Wojciechowski, G. (2011, April 21). Blame MLB, too, for the Dodgers mess. *ESPN.com*. Retrieved from http://sports.espn.go.com/espn/columns/story?columnist=wojciechowski_gene&page=wojciechowski/110421&sportCat=mlb.

Wojnarowski, A. (2018, June 25). NBA owners' debt limit raised to $325M, increase of $75M. Retrieved from www.espn.com/nba/story/_/id/23906803/nba-raises-owners-debt-limit-325-million.

Woolfolk, J. (2014, February 21). Oakland Athletics: Court agrees to fast-track San Jose's baseball antitrust appeal. *San Jose Mercury News*. Retrieved from www.mercurynews.com/bay-area-news/ci_25195045/court-agrees-fast-track-san-joses-baseball-antitrust.

Year-by-year salary cap. (2010). *NFLCommunications.com*. Retrieved from http://nflcommunications.com/2010/02/24/year-by-year-salary-cap/.

Yellon, A. (2017, December 15). Every MLB owner is getting a $50 million windfall in 2018. Retrieved from www.bleedcubbieblue.com/2017/12/15/16781058/every-mlb-owner-50-million-windfall-2018.

Zimbalist, A. (1992). *Baseball and billions*. New York: Basic Books.

CHAPTER 16

International Sport Finance

Nicholas M. Watanabe

KEY CONCEPTS

academy

administration

Bosman ruling

closed leagues

conglomerate

Co-operative and Community Benefit
    Societies

exchange rates

hybrid system

industrial leagues

membership

nominal exchange rate

open leagues

parachute payments

phoenix club

pre-contracts

private company limited by shares

promotion

protest club

real exchange rate

relegation

solidarity payments

tournament theory

transfer

INTRODUCTION

In the previous chapter, the different structures and ownership styles that exist in North American professional sports were discussed. In recent years, leagues such as the National Basketball Association (NBA) and Major League Baseball (MLB) have placed great importance on growing their brands in other parts of the world, especially as many teams have reached a point of saturation in their local markets. At the same time, international sport leagues have also been growing in recent years, challenging North American teams for popularity across the globe. Thus, the international sport marketplace has now become a hyper-competitive environment where various leagues, teams, federations, and other stakeholders battle one another for the attention and interest of consumers. For example, Major League Baseball scheduled a regular season series in London between the Chicago Cubs and St. Louis Cardinals for the spring of 2020. Although these games were cancelled or postponed because of the COVID-19 outbreak, they were in competition with other matches in London, including European soccer championship group stage matches that were to be played on the same days. Such occurrences are not rare in the international sport marketplace, as the NFL regularly schedules games in London at the same time as top-level professional soccer matches are being played nearby. In this sense, sport leagues from North America are now in constant competition with other teams and leagues around the world, both directly in the same markets, as well as in competing for other resources.

Although top teams and leagues around the world are in competition with one another, there has also been the recognition that they are able to learn best practices from one another. Additionally, as the ownership structure of sport teams has begun to shift away from sole proprietorships to large corporations that often purchase several teams as part of their investment portfolio, such cooperation has now become mandatory for some teams (Andreff & Staudohar, 2000; Fort, 2000). Thus, there is now a need for individuals working in the sport industry to have a solid grasp of the similarities and differences that exist between North American and international sport leagues/teams/organizations. Based on this, the current chapter will introduce you to important concepts in international sport finance, including the differences that exist in league structure, the changing nature of sport team ownership around the world, as well as how new hybrid leagues are breaking traditional molds set by European and North American teams. Finally, the chapter will also highlight some of the financial issues teams face when they deal with sport at the international level, such as the importance of exchange rates, player movement rules, and how the health of industries and the global economy have important ramifications for those within the sport business.

OPEN AND CLOSED LEAGUES

Within the contemporary sport environment, almost all professional sport leagues can either be defined as belonging to an **open** or **closed league** (Buzzacchi, Szymanski, & Valletti, 2010). Specifically, an open sport league is one that allows teams the ability to freely enter the league, while a closed league requires approval from a majority of owners in order to add a new franchise (Noll, 2002; Szymanski & Valletti, 2010). In general, open sport leagues are most often associated with leagues in Europe and South America, especially in sports such as soccer (football), while closed leagues typically correspond to professional leagues in North America (Noll, 2003). Sidebar 16.A examines open and closed leagues in cricket.

SIDEBAR 16.A   Twenty20 Cricket

Cricket has enjoyed great popularity in a number of areas, including India, England, Pakistan, Australia, and the Caribbean. However, one of the major limitations of the traditional form of cricket was the length of the game, with test matches between international teams often lasting for four or five days. With this in mind, limited overs cricket began, which places a limit on the number of overs each team bowls, with different versions typically played between 20 and 50 overs. Needing a short one-day competition to replace the Benson & Hedges Cup in England, the English Cricket Board (ECB) tested out a new format of limited overs cricket called Twenty20 in 2003, where each team bowled to 20 overs. This shorter form of cricket proved to be rather popular, with the match held at Lord's on July 15, 2004 between Surrey and Middlesex having the highest attendance of a counties match in 50 years. Following this initial success, Twenty20 began to be adopted by both professional and international competitions around the world, often drawing great interest in these shorter matches. For example, in Australia the first Twenty20 match in 2005 sold out a ground that had not had a sellout in approximately 30 years (CricInfo, 2005).

In 2007, the International Cricket Council (ICC) hosted the first Twenty20 cricket world championship in South Africa, the popularity of which quickly led to the creation of several professional leagues. The most popular of these new leagues is the Indian Premier League (IPL), which was founded in 2008. Although professional cricket leagues in other countries such as England have used the open league system, the IPL followed the North American franchise model, and started with a closed league composed of eight teams spread across the country. Within a decade of its founding, the IPL quickly grew into one of the most popular and valuable professional sport leagues in the world. In 2018, the league averaged 32,800 spectators per game, a better average than Major League Baseball, Nippon Professional Baseball, and top-flight Spanish professional soccer (La Liga). Utilizing the short format of cricket that typically allows fans to watch a match in under two hours, the league has also been innovative in its use of technology to broadcast games to fans in India and around the world, becoming the first major professional sport league to stream games on YouTube (Hoult, 2010). With growing popularity and a television contract that has approximately quintupled from $102 million a year to $510 million, the IPL has made a strong case for the use of a closed league system and innovation as a suitable way to start professional sport leagues outside of North America (Gollapudi, 2017).

One important distinction that exists between open and closed leagues is the use of **promotion** and **relegation** as part of a multi-tiered league system (Sloane, 2015). For example, in examining the hierarchy of soccer leagues in England, one can see that the top level is the English Premier League (EPL), followed by the English Football League (EFL) Championship, then down to League One, League Two, and eventually the National League System. In such a structure, teams can be promoted to higher leagues by being one of the teams that places in the top of the league at the end of the season (Hughes, 2018). On the other hand, those teams that do not perform well and finish near the bottom of the league are relegated down to lower leagues. As such, open leagues with promotion and relegation reward teams who perform well and punish those who do poorly. Counter to this, closed leagues provide benefits to teams at the bottom of a league through rewarding them with the top draft picks.

Promotion and Relegation

The use of promotion and relegation is an important part of open leagues, as this is the main mechanism that allows for new teams to enter the league system, and then to work their way up the ladder if they are able to perform well (Jasina & Rotthoff, 2012). One notable example of the benefits of the open system is evidenced in the formation of AFC Wimbledon, a club based in the outskirts of London. In 2002, it was decided by the Football Association (the governing body of soccer in England) that Wimbledon FC would be allowed to relocate to Milton Keynes, about 60 miles away (White, 2003). The loss of the club founded in Wimbledon in 1889 was highly controversial, and angered many long-time supporters of the club. In response to this, fans of Wimbledon FC formed together to create AFC Wimbledon in order to have a club in the local community. The team began play in the Combined Counties League Premier Division in 2002–2003, which is the ninth level of the pyramid in English soccer (Williams, 2019). In the following years, AFC Wimbledon continued to perform well and move up the ladder, and eventually earned promotion to League One, the third level of the pyramid, by winning the 2016 playoff final. In a moment of glory, AFC Wimbledon moved ahead of the Milton Keynes (MK) Dons in the English soccer pyramid only 15 years into their existence when the MK Dons were relegated from League One to League Two in 2017 (Williams, 2019).

The above example of AFC Wimbledon highlights the benefits that can come from an open league system that uses promotion and relegation. In closed sport leagues, when teams relocate, fans are typically left with no ability to bring a new team to town, and thus rely on wealthy individuals or corporations to try and gain approval from a league to either move another franchise or start a new team. For example, the city of St. Louis has had the Cardinals leave to move to Arizona in 1987, and then replaced them with the Rams in 1995. However, under the ownership of Stan Kroenke, the Rams relocated back to Los Angeles for the 2016 season, leaving St. Louis and its fans without a local NFL team to cheer for (Brennan, 2016). As such, even though teams will not be guaranteed to play at the top level of competition immediately, the open league system does at least provide an avenue for local communities and fans to be part of a league system without having to rely on approval from the league and the owners of other franchises.

Financial Effects of Promotion

The financial effects of promotion and relegation can mostly be tied to the size of the television/media contracts that leagues have, as well as the potential for increased demand that may come from playing in higher-level competitions (Szymanski & Valletti, 2010). Generally, it is argued that gaining promotion to higher leagues will increase revenues for a team, while being relegated will lead to a decline in the financial performance of a team. However, this picture is complicated by the realities of being able to run a club in a top-flight division (Noll, 2002). Not only is there a certain expectation in regard to the size and quality of the stadium and facilities for teams at the highest level of competition, there is also the need to spend money on quality players to ensure that a promoted club will be able to compete against other first division teams.

So what is the financial impact of gaining promotion into one of the most lucrative leagues in the world? With the EPL having some of the largest media rights deals in the world, the gain for a Championship (second division) club being promoted to the EPL in 2019–2020 is said to be worth at least $100 million dollars. Where does this value come from? To begin with, every club that made it into the Premier League in 2018–2019 was guaranteed "**solidarity payments**" of $54.4 million from international television rights, $43.4 million in equal share payments from domestic television rights in the UK, as well as an additional $6.2 million that comes from other commercial deals (Kelly, 2019). When adding in the minimum performance bonus of approximately $2.4 million for the team finishing in last place, this means that, at a minimum, even if a promoted team were to come in last place they would make at least $106.4 million in revenue from television rights and performance. This revenue would not include other sponsorship deals that would certainly increase in value with a team being promoted to the top division, as well as the additional potential revenue from increased ticket and merchandise demand (Kelly, 2019).

To get a better understanding of the impact that promotion to a top division can have on the finances of a club, Exhibit 16.1 displays the revenue for Newcastle United in 2017 when they were in the Championship, and 2018 when they played in the Premier League. In examining the difference between 2017 and 2018, it is evident that the significant growth in club revenues occurred in broadcasting and commercial (sponsorship and marketing) revenue. At the same time, although the club moved to a higher league, their match day revenue showed almost no change. Although revenues for the club (turnover) more than doubled when entering the Premier League, their expenses only increased by about 11%. Thus for clubs that are promoted, although there is a slight change in expenses, the growth in revenue helps to boost the club from having losses to being profitable.

In further considering the profit and loss account for Newcastle United, two specific details should be noted. First, it is the case that out of the 24 clubs that are in the Championship, 21 of them operate in the red. Although many have argued this is a sign of poor financial management by second division soccer clubs in England, most of the teams that have debt are taking on these burdens purposefully. That is, the debt is typically provided as cash infusions by the wealthy owners of these clubs, who provide the money at little to no interest, and it is used to purchase players to improve a team's talent level. In this sense, much of the debt from second division clubs is owed directly to their owners, who are providing this capital as an investment to improve teams so that they can have a better chance of being promoted to the Premier League (Kelly, 2019). When teams with debt are promoted back into the top flight, owners are then able to have these debts paid back to them, as well as enjoy additional gains in terms of increased profitability and franchise value of their clubs. Because the amount of debt taken on by clubs is often quite substantial, owners will typically not be able to recoup their investment within a single season after promotion. As noted in the Newcastle example, the team was able to reduce their debt by almost 5 percent, while also creating 33.8 million in cash reserves to help with either paying off more debt or strengthening the team through player purchases. The second aspect of the Newcastle United accounting sheet that should be focused on is that the club managed to cut their operating losses

EXHIBIT 16.1 Newcastle United profit and loss statement.

	2017	2018	GROWTH	% GROWTH
Match Day	23.4	23.9	0.5	2.14%
Broadcasting	47.4	126.4	79	166.67%
Commercial	12.1	26.7	14.6	120.66%
Other Income	2.7	1.4	–1.3	–48.15%
Commercial	14.8	28.2	13.4	90.54%
Turnover	85.7	178.5	92.8	108.28%
Wages & Salaries	80.3	93.6	13.3	16.56%
Other Expenses	25.2	24	–1.2	–4.76%
Expenses	105.5	117.6	12.1	11.47%
EBITDA	–19.8	60.9	80.7	
Player Amortization	35.8	41.3	5.5	15.36%
Depreciation	3.5	2	–1.5	–42.86%
Non-cash Flow Expenses	39.2	43.3	4.1	10.46%
Operating Profit/(Loss)	–90.9	17.6	108.5	
Profit on Player Sales	42.3	3.6	–38.7	–91.49%
Profit before Interest & Tax	–48.7	21.2	69.9	
Net Interest Receivable	1.9	1.8	–0.1	–5.26%
Profit/(Loss) before Tax	–46.7	22.9	69.6	
Taxation Credit	5.5	–4.3	–9.8	
Profit/(Loss) after Tax	–41.3	18.6	59.9	
Wages to Turnover	94%	52%	–42%	
Gross Debt	152.3	144.8	–7.5	–4.92%
Cash	0	33.8	33.8	
Net Debt	152.3	110.9	–41.4	–27.18%
Average League Attendance	51,108	51,992	884	1.73%
TV Deal	40.9	123	82.1	200.73%

almost in half through selling players in 2017. Specifically, the team managed to earn 42.3 million by selling players, and thus reduced the potential losses from being close to 80 million down to 41.3 million. This shows that while owners are willing to take on debt to improve the quality of their team when they are in lower divisions, there are still cuts that need to be made in order to ensure financial stability of a team in the long run.

Financial Effects of Relegation and Parachute Payments

At the same time, it needs to be acknowledged that clubs that are relegated from leagues, especially those that are demoted out of the top division, often experience severe financial strain. For example, the German club TSV 1860 Munich was relegated from the top-flight Bundesliga at the end of the 2003–2004 season (Kleinmann, 2017). Following this, the team experienced financial difficulties stemming from a lack of revenues and increased costs of operating the club, including player salaries and debt taken on for the development and construction of a new stadium. In the end, 1860 was required to sell their 50% share of the development of Allianz Arena to rival Bayern Munich for a mere 11 million euros. Although this ensured the club had enough cash flow to be granted a license to continue playing in the second division, it came at the sacrifice of a 50% share of a state-of-the-art facility (Kleinmann, 2017). This was not the end of the financial difficulties, with the club requiring an 18 million euros bailout in 2011 to stay financially solvent. However, eventually investors were no longer willing to put money into the club, and the team was relegated down to the fourth division in 2017 for their inability to pay for a license that would allow them to continue operating as a professional club (Kleinmann, 2017).

Such stories of teams having financial troubles after relegation are rather common in open leagues, and is one of the major drawbacks of using this type of league structure. In many cases, when a team has financial issues that come about from relegation, it can lead to a cascading effect of multiple relegations in a short period of time. For example, German soccer club SC Paderborn 07 gained their first promotion to the top-flight Bundesliga in 2013–2014, and then were subsequently relegated two seasons in a row, and only avoided being demoted to the fourth division in 2017 when TSV 1860 Munich failed to be licensed to play professionally in the following season (Kleinmann, 2017). Although teams in closed leagues can also experience financial issues and can likewise go bankrupt, the lack of a relegation mechanism protects them from being moved to another league with lower revenue potential. As such, where open leagues allow teams to enter leagues and work their way towards being in a top level of competition without paying hefty expansion fees, there are also drawbacks to having promotion and relegation.

To try and reduce the financial impact of relegation, the Premier League introduced a new mechanism called "**parachute payments**" in 2006, where teams that were relegated out of the Premier League would continue to receive some financial assistance to help clubs adjust to the financial realities of playing in the Championship (Kelly, 2019). Specifically, parachute payments are paid to relegated teams over a three-year period, with a relegated team receiving 50% of a normal media share in their first year after being relegated, the amount of the share then going down to 45% in the second year, and 20% in the final year (Kelly, 2019). Additionally, if a club is relegated after only one season in the Premier League, they only receive two years of parachute payments, and all payments cease for any club that manages to gain promotion back to the top flight. Considering that media rights payments to Premier League clubs are worth at least $97.8 million, this would mean a team demoted to the Championship would receive additional payments of $48.9 million in year one, $44 million in year two, and $19.5 million in year three. These payments, which are in addition to revenues paid out from playing in the second division, are designed to allow clubs time to be able to sell players with expensive salaries, and thus prevent teams from going into bankruptcy, or what is called "administration" in the UK.

To gain a better understanding of the impact of relegation and parachute payments on club financials, Exhibit 16.2 presents the profit and loss account for Middlesbrough. In examining the revenues (turnover) from the club, it is clear that there is a major decline in revenues from 2017 to 2018 when the club was relegated. Although the club's broadcasting and total revenue both declined by approximately 50%, the presence of the parachute payment of 41.3 million from the Premier League played an important role in the club's financial health. Without this revenue, Middlesbrough, who went from a profit of 11.5 million in their last year in the Premier League to a 6.6 million loss, would have had much greater losses or would have needed to have sold off the best players on their squad. As such, even though this instance shows that clubs can still go into debt when receiving parachute payments after relegation, the additional revenue does play an important role in helping clubs transition to being in a lower division.

Despite the benefits that come from parachute payments, there has been criticism of this mechanism as being a reward for failure, and that it provides incentives to teams to jump back and forth between divisions. Specifically, recent research has found that the parachute payments create a revenue imbalance in the Championship, and thus reduce the overall competitive balance of the second division of English soccer. Another side effect of the parachute payments is that it creates a group that are often called "**yo-yo clubs**" in England, or "elevator clubs" in Germany. Specifically, these terms refer to teams that are regularly promoted and relegated. Although it is possible to have yo-yo or elevator clubs in any league, country, or sport that utilizes promotion and relegation, parachute payments have the ability to exacerbate this type of behavior. For example, between 2002 and 2010, the English club West Bromwich Albion (West Brom) was promoted to the Premier League four times, and relegated back to the Championship three times (Doyle, 2017). Notably, 2011 was the first time in over a decade when the club was not involved in either a promotion or relegation. The source of the club's volatile movement between divisions can be traced to its fiscal policies and parachute payments. The owner of West Brom, Jerry Pearce, laid out strict financial guidelines for the club in regard to the amount of money that they were allowed to spend on purchasing players. Because this budget was lower than most Premier League clubs' budgets, West Brom was unable to sign enough talented players and thus was not able to compete with most clubs in the league, and thus was often relegated (Doyle, 2017). On the other hand, because of the parachute payments, West Brom was able to spend more money than most of the clubs in the Championship, and thus

EXHIBIT 16.2   Middlesbrough profit and loss statement.

	2017	2018	GROWTH	% GROWTH
Gate Receipts	8.7	7.1	−1.6	−18.39%
Premier League Broadcast	100.6	41.3	−59.3	−58.95%
Championship Broadcast	0	5	5	
Cup Competitions	0.9	0.3	−0.6	−66.67%
Broadcasting	101.5	46.6	−54.9	−54.09%
Sponsorship & Commercial	8.2	5.7	−2.5	−30.49%
Merchandising	3	2.6	−0.4	−13.33%
Commercial	11.1	8.3	−2.8	−25.23%
Turnover	121.4	62	−59.4	−48.93%
Other Income	0.1	0.1	0	0.00%
Wages & Salaries	64.9	48.7	−16.2	−24.96%
Other Expenses	19	6.3	−12.7	−66.84%
Expenses	83.9	55	−28.9	−34.45%
EBITDA	37.6	7.1	−30.5	−81.12%
Exceptional Items	−10.5			
Player Amortization	−24.4	−24.5	−0.1	0.41%
Player Impairment	−4			
Depreciation	−2.9	−2.9	0	0.00%
Non-cash Flow Expenses	−31.3	−27.3	4	−12.78%
Operating Profit/(Loss)	−4.1	−20.2	−16.1	392.68%
Profit on Player Sales	11.3	15.3	4	35.40%
Profit before Interest & Tax	7.2	−4.9	−12.1	−168.06%
Net Interest Receivable	−0.3	−1.5	−1.2	400.00%
Profit/(Loss) before Tax	6.9	−6.4	−13.3	−192.75%
Taxation Credit	4.6	−0.3	−4.9	−106.52%
Profit/(Loss) after Tax	11.5	−6.6	−18.1	−157.39%
Wages to Turnover	79%	53%	25%	

(continued)

EXHIBIT 16.2 Cont.

	2017	2018	GROWTH	% GROWTH
Gross Debt	102.1	100.7	–1.4	–1.37%
Cash	0.2	0.5	0.3	150.00%
Net Debt	101.9	100.1	–1.8	–1.77%
Average League Attendance	30,449	25,544	–4,905	–16.11%

was able to constantly secure a strong enough finish to be promoted back into the Premier League. As such, the mixture of the club's financial management and revenue from parachute payments essentially had the club stuck in terms of not being good enough to be in the Premier League, but too good to be in the second division. Although the club managed to stay in the Premier League for a number of years after 2011, the club was demoted to the Championship for the 2018–2019 season, where it again began receiving parachute payments, and just missed out on promotion back to the Premier League ("West Brom relegated," 2018).

Administration/Bankruptcy

Overall, although there are many criticisms of the use of parachute payments, including that it provides a reward for failure that is counter to the philosophy of the promotion and relegation system used by open leagues, the mechanism does provide important financial stability for teams. Creating financial stability for teams that are demoted is of importance, as the open system relies on the presence of lower leagues in order to have a place for teams that do not perform so well to play. At the club level, when teams are demoted and unable to sell off players, it creates a dire financial situation that often could not be rectified without parachute payments. This is especially the case in open leagues with promotion and relegation, as when teams become financially insolvent, they are placed under **administration**, which in England means that a business has been placed in the control of accountants who will try to stabilize the financial situation (Farquhar, 2008). Essentially, once a club has been placed into administration, it means that the operations of all business matters of the club are controlled by accountants, with only coaching of players and decisions about who will play games left to the previous staff (Conn, 2019).

Indeed, financial issues are seemingly more common in open sport leagues when compared to closed leagues. Part of this is a natural extension of the fact that open leagues will naturally involve many more teams, and thus will lead to the success and failure of organizations. For example, in English football, 42 clubs have gone into administration in the last two decades (2000–2019), with four of these clubs being dissolved, and thus no longer in existence. However, researchers have found that teams in open leagues tend to overinvest in players, and thus the cost associated with being in an open league typically is greater when compared to franchises in closed leagues (Dietl, Franck, & Lang, 2008). This is certainly witnessed not only in the large sums that are spent by clubs in the Premier League, but also by the debt that is taken on by clubs in lower divisions as they try to obtain the talent to become more competitive. Although there is the potential for large financial gains for clubs that are able to successfully build a strong team and gain promotion, it needs to be noted that some of these clubs also risk going into administration.

Despite the large number of clubs in England that have gone into administration, teams playing for other countries are not immune to financial issues. Perhaps the most dire financial situation of any professional sport league currently exists in Italy, where a combination of factors has led to a number of soccer clubs going bankrupt over the last two decades. The first signs of trouble in Italy came in 2002 when Fiorentina, one of the most well-known and historic soccer clubs in the country, was unable to pay wages and was around $50 million in debt. Despite the efforts of the owner to bring in investments, the club was placed into administration controlled by the courts, which prevented the club from receiving a license to play in any league, and thus led to the club becoming defunct (Kirsch, 2019). Although Fiorentina was quickly reestablished and has since gained promotion back into the top-flight Serie A, other clubs in Italy soon began to display similar financial struggles in terms of increasing costs and debts. One of the major problems for Italian clubs has been the fact that many of them still play in old stadiums that lack revenue potential, and television deals for the league have not kept pace with the revenue growth in other top leagues. For example, while Juventus and Inter Milan were both rated in the top 30 in terms of revenue from broadcast rights in Europe (Football Italia, 2018a), the amount they received for media deals was on par with smaller clubs in England such as Stoke City and Middlesbrough (Conn, 2018). This is notable, because Juventus and Inter Milan both received significantly more revenue than other clubs in Italy because of their participation and success in the Champions League, indicating that the broadcast revenue for the average club in Italy is much lower (Baxter, 2018).

Thus, when pairing the relatively low revenues for the league with the growth of wages and the costs of stadium development, Italian clubs have been placed in a difficult financial reality. Based on this, 152 clubs in Italy have gone bankrupt since Fiorentina went out of business, meaning that an average of eight clubs a year enter bankruptcy (Football Italia, 2018b). It is worth noting that, in some cases, clubs such as F.C. Bari 1908 and Reggiana have gone bankrupt multiple times during this time period (Chiarelli, 2018). Notably, in the case of F.C. Bari, the club first went bankrupt in 2014 when debts exceeded 30 million euros. When the club was placed for bankruptcy auction, the first attempt had to be abandoned for lack of serious interest by investors, and the second auction likewise had no bids that were high enough to take over the club's debts. Finally, the club was eventually sold off to a group for 2 million euros in the third auction, where it was taken over by a group led by former referee Gianluca Paparesta, who was most famous for being implicated in the 2006 Italian football scandal that led to the end of his career as a professional referee ("Soccer-troubled Bari," 2014). Bari was involved in further scandal when the next group that took over the club, in 2015, was investigated for possible participation in money laundering (Chiarelli, 2018). Finally, in 2018 Bari was one of three clubs in Serie B that went bankrupt, forcing the league to have to try and start the 2018–2019 season with 19 instead of the usual 22 clubs ("Serie B: Officials," 2018). Because of the financial issues of these three teams, regional courts initially ordered that the league had to be suspended because of the missing teams, and only came to a formal agreement allowing the season to be played three days before the start of the competition ("Serie B suspended," 2018).

The above example highlights the symbiotic relationship that exists between teams in a league, and shows that when clubs go into administration, it not only has the potential for causing financial stress for the club, but also can put other clubs or leagues in danger. The reason for this is that football clubs often are in debt to other clubs because of the sale of players between the teams. Thus, if one club which has purchased a number of players from other clubs goes into administration, it is possible that the clubs that sold the players will not receive part of the payments they expected to receive, and this could put them into financial danger. Precisely because of this, the "Football creditors rule" was established in England in 2003, which required teams that went into administration to place a priority on all debts that were owed to other clubs or players before the club was able to gain approval to play league matches (Farquhar, 2008). This rule, which was passed as part of the Enterprise Act 2002, changed the laws around bankruptcy in England so that rather than the government being able to recover unpaid taxes before other companies, football clubs now were first in line to receive payments when they were creditors to other clubs. Although the British government's tax collection agency Her Majesty's Revenue and Customs (HMRC) challenged this rule in court several times as breaking from precedent where assets from an insolvent company should be paid back first to the government and then to companies in a proportionate manner, the courts have continued to rule in favor of the football creditors rule (Scott, 2010).

In open leagues, the penalty for going into administration in open leagues is often quite severe, with clubs usually penalized by docking a significant number of points (earned from wins and draws). In English football, the penalty for going into administration is 10 points in lower divisions, and 9 points in the Premier League, with such penalties often leading to teams being relegated into lower divisions. The previously mentioned parachute payments serve as an important mechanism that helps clubs to avoid financial issues when they are demoted out of a top-flight league (Liddle, 2019). Because these additional revenue payments have been considered a successful way in which to help demoted clubs, other top football leagues in Europe, including Germany, Spain, Italy, and France, have now adopted the practice. Even with the inclusion of mechanisms such as the football creditors rule and parachute payments, it is evident that there is a growing revenue and resource imbalance in professional sport leagues around the world.

OPEN LEAGUES AND MULTIPLE COMPETITIONS

Another important attribute that is typically found in open leagues, and tends to be absent from closed leagues, is the concept of multiple competitions. Notably, most teams in professional soccer leagues around the world participate in more than one competition during their season. For example, a team in Serie A, the top flight of Italian football, will be guaranteed to compete in both the league (Serie A) and the national cup (Coppa Italia). The number of competitions that teams compete in will depend on the league and country in which they play; for example, a team in the EPL will participate in their league, a league cup (Carabao Cup), as well as the national Football Association (FA) cup. Additionally, the number of competitions can also be dependent on how well a team performs in the league, as placing high enough in a league can gain a team entrance into continental competitions where they compete against top teams in other leagues. Examples of such competitions include the Champions League in soccer or the EuroLeague in basketball.

Having multiple competitions has important implications for the financial health of teams, especially in soccer. Similar to the television media rights deals for leagues, the additional competitions can also present a vital source of revenue for clubs. This is especially the case for Champions League soccer in Europe, where qualification to the competition's group stage provides a guaranteed appearance fee of 15.25 million euros (McCartney, 2019). Additionally, teams are able to earn bonuses for winning (2.7 million euros) or drawing (0.9 million euros) matches. Furthermore, as clubs progress in the tournament, they receive additional payments for each round, with appearances worth 9.5 million in the round of 16, 10.5 million in the quarterfinals, and 12 million in the semifinals. Finally, appearance in the final guarantees 15 million for the runner-up and 19 million for the winners. Overall, playing in the Champions League can thus provide significant financial rewards, especially to the winners, with 2019 champions Liverpool expected to receive a grand total of $84.83 million in prize money (McCartney, 2019). However, there are dangers in regard to having multiple competitions, especially when teams stake their financial future on playing in and advancing in tournaments with large payouts. Similar to the broadcast payments provided to teams in the Premier League, if a club loses out on revenue they expect from qualifying for a specific competition, it can alter the club's future plans, and even send them into financial disarray.

The most famous example of this in recent years is the case of Leeds United, an English football club whose name became synonymous with poor financial management. Leeds United were historically known as a powerful team in the 1960s and 1970s, and won several domestic trophies under the management of Don Revie. In the late 1990s, Leeds United's management began a bold strategy of taking on debt to acquire new players and pay high wages in order to compete with other top clubs in England and continental Europe. The logic behind this plan was that through improving the strength of their squad, Leeds would place high in the Premier League, allowing them to not only receive a large performance bonus, but also qualify for the lucrative UEFA Champions League. In the initial phases, Leeds's strategy was a success: after playing the UEFA Cup in the previous two seasons, the club managed to qualify for the Champions League for the 2000–2001 season. In this competition, Leeds managed to make it to the semifinals; however, due to their finishing fifth in the Premier League, the team did not qualify for the Champions League for the following season.

Lacking the guaranteed Champions League revenue, Leeds United were forced to begin to sell off most of their top players in the summer of 2001, as they no longer had the revenue that they had expected in order to make payments on the massive loans that had been taken out to pay for players. While the club managed to remain successful in the following season, they were soon in danger, narrowly avoiding relegation in 2002–2003. However, due to the large percentage of revenues that needed to be directed towards loan payments and the lack of additional revenue from the Champions League, the club found itself in deep financial trouble in late 2003, and was taken over by a group led by a specialist in corporate recovery, who then began to sell off the club's assets ("Leeds sell ground," 2004). Inevitably, because of the lack of quality players, Leeds were relegated from the Premier League at the end of the 2003–2004 season. In the second division, Leeds continued their downward financial spiral, and when they were unable to obtain additional backing from investors, the club was forced to sell its stadium (Elland Road) and training ground at the end of 2004 ("Leeds sell ground," 2004). Although the club continues to play in the ground, it was forced into a 25-year sale and leaseback deal, as a last resort to stay financially stable while also maintaining a stadium to play in.

In the following year, Leeds were sold for the small sum of 10 million pounds to former Chelsea football club chairman Ken Bates ("Bates completes takeover," 2005), with the goal of turning the club's fortunes around. The club seemed to initially be on the right track, qualifying for the Championship playoff and just narrowly missing out on promotion back to the Premier League. However, despite all of the desperate moves made by the club to reduce their financial issues, the team went into administration in May 2007. Interestingly, Ken Bates put together a consortium that offered to pay back eight pence for every pound of debt (or to pay off 8% of the existing debts of the club), which was accepted by the administrators, allowing Bates to take over the club for a second time ("Leeds United resold," 2007). This move technically freed Leeds from all of its debts, but led to fans protesting Bates's ownership and control of the club. Eventually, Leeds worked their way back from the third division to gain promotion to the Championship League in 2010, and Bates promptly sold the team off to GFH Financial Group, based in Bahrain. Because of their poor financial management and their drop from the Champions League semifinals to the third division in less than a decade, Leeds became synonymous with poor financial management by a football club (Wilson, 2003). In England, the term "doing a Leeds" was coined to describe teams whose poor decision making leads to them experiencing financial difficulties (Robson, 2009).

Multiple Competitions and Prize Structures

The prize structures that are utilized in top competitions in open leagues (such as the aforementioned UEFA Champions League) are a good example of **tournament theory** in action. Specifically, tournament theory is the economic theory that prize money should be structured to elicit more effort from competitors (Lazear & Rosen, 1981). In this case, rather than providing a uniform prize across each stage of a competition, tournament theory suggests that competitions should use increasing prize money. By designing a competition in this way, it provides a financial reward system that should give incentives for teams to qualify for the competition, as well as to put effort into winning matches. The use of this type of prize structure is especially important when teams are involved in multiple competitions throughout a season, and thus may not always have the proper motivation to field their best squad in all matches. Indeed, top clubs in European soccer are often faced with the need to compete in three to four different competitions (league, league cup, domestic cup, and European cup), with sometimes only two to three rest days between matches (Page & Page, 2007; Pawlowski, Breuer, & Hovemann, 2010). Because of the need to rest and rotate their squad, teams may often be strategic in determining when they will field their star players, versus when they will use only a few top players or even field their entire reserve team. Although these decisions are often driven by injuries and the importance of certain matches, the financial incentives still play an important role in motivating teams to try and win matches. That is, teams will tend to put emphasis on fielding their best squad for matches that are important in terms of financial outcomes. Typically, this means teams will put strong emphasis on league matches, especially if they are near the top or bottom of the league, as teams at the top can qualify for European competitions to boost their revenue, and teams near the bottom want to avoid relegation and the drop in revenue that comes with it (Drut & Raballand, 2012). In considering the other competitions, top clubs often have little incentive to play strong squads in domestic cups, as not only are the payouts for these competitions lower, but also these teams are often drawn against inferior competition. Thus, because continental cups like the Champions League and Europa League have a better prize structure and stronger competition, they provide more incentive for teams to field strong squads.

At the same time, based on tournament theory, if the prizes for a competition are not high enough or structured in a way that does not make teams prioritize them, the quality of games could potentially suffer. One good example of this occurred in Asian Champions League soccer, where top teams from across Asia play each other to determine the best team on the continent. Although the tournament has great prestige, the prize money for the competition is relatively low. Recognizing this fact, the Asian Football Confederation (AFC) recently increased the prize money, in 2018, with appearances worth $100,000 in the round of 16, $150,000 for the quarterfinals, $250,000 for the semifinals, runners-up receiving $2 million, and the champions getting a prize of $4 million (Asian Football Confederation, 2017). As such, the maximum amount the winner of the AFC Champions League can receive (including win bonuses) is $4.8 million. Although this money is a significant amount for some clubs in Asia, it should be noted that clubs playing in leagues such as the Chinese Super League (CSL) and J-League (Japan) have access to larger revenue sources. Notably, all clubs in the CSL automatically receive around $10 million just for participating in the competition, with additional prize money allocated to teams based on their performance in the final standings. Likewise, all teams in the J-League receive about $3.2 million for participation in the league, with the winners of the J-League championship provided a prize of approximately $15.5 million, paid out over three years. Precisely because domestic prize money for many countries in Asia often far exceeds the potential gains from the Asian Champions League, teams from these countries have not prioritized this competition, and thus match quality has suffered.

Considering the above example of tournament theory in action, it highlights the need for prize money to be structured to elicit more effort from competitors. Although this is a relatively easy process when teams in closed leagues compete in only a single competition, it becomes much more complex for open leagues that require teams to balance their effort between multiple competitions. This relationship is also made more complex by the fact that when teams are involved in more than one competition, there are often different organizers for the tournaments, and thus priorities may change based on this as well. This conflict of priorities highlights another major difference that exists between open and closed sport leagues. Although closed league teams do have instances where players from their leagues will compete in other competitions, such as National Hockey League players competing in the Winter Olympics or Hockey World Cup, these are mostly limited to representing a country at a sport mega-event, and thus only some of the players from a team will be called away (Torres, 2017). That is, when players from a team in a closed league are competing in more than one competition in a season, one is usually for their professional team and league, while the others will be examples of "international" duty where they play for their respective national teams.

Typically, owners and management of closed league teams are not interested in having their players compete in other competitions, unless there is a significant financial gain that can be provided to the team, and not just the players. The reason for this is that the owners of professional sport teams often view their players in terms of the investment they have made in terms of paying salary, signing bonuses, and other forms of compensation. Thus, when a player leaves the team to compete in an event like the Olympics or World Cup, a closed league team will typically not experience any boost in revenues based either on the performance of the player or the national team. Additionally, because professional teams are often the main source of compensation for top-level athletes, owners in closed leagues also see that there is the potential that players could be injured when competing in multiple competitions. If a player's salary is fully or even partially guaranteed, teams would see that injury as a financial loss, as they would have to continue to pay a salary to the player, while also experiencing potential declines in revenue because of the player's absence, all while not gaining any revenue from other competitions.

It is exactly this type of risk versus reward that makes it difficult for the owners of closed league teams to come to agreement with other organizations (such as the Olympics and international sport federations) in regard to having players involved in multiple competitions. Although players from the National Basketball Association are able to compete for their national teams in the summer when the league is not playing, the NBA has tried to keep players from leaving their teams during the season. In the case of the NHL, the league initially came to an agreement to take a break in the middle of their regular season to allow players to compete in the Winter Olympics, starting from the Nagano games in 1998. However, over the years the relationship between the NHL and the Olympics has become more complicated, partly because of the involvement of the rival Kontinental Hockey League (KHL) from Russia, as well as discussion over whether playing in the Olympics provided any benefits for the NHL and its teams. After the completion of the 2014 Winter Olympics, the International Olympic Committee (IOC) announced that they would no longer cover insurance payments or travel costs for NHL players who were participating in the Olympics, and thus the NHL did not allow players to participate in the 2018 Pyeongchang games (Torres, 2017).

The above issues highlight an important distinction that exists between the closed and open leagues in terms of the relationship that leagues/teams have with the respective governing bodies and organizations in their sport. Notably, in open leagues, teams not only compete in multiple competitions, but do so by cooperating with larger governing bodies at either the domestic or international level. A top team in Europe such as Barcelona will potentially have to work with their league, their national football association, the European association (UEFA), and in some cases even the top international governing body for their sport (FIFA). Indeed, in open leagues there has been a long history of cooperation with organizations outside of the league one is a member of, and thus such cooperation has become a natural part of scheduling the competitive season for teams. This is certainly the case in soccer, where there is not only a history of cooperation, but there are also rules in place that professional clubs must release their players for duty in international matches if the player is healthy.

Turning our focus to closed leagues, particularly those in North America, the owners of these teams have long been in charge of the operations and governance of professional sport leagues. Because of this, owners in closed leagues often are accustomed to being the ones holding the power, and are not as willing to share it or the revenues that are generated from their teams. In essence, this captures one of the unique and main differences between leagues using the North American model of professional sport and open leagues around the world (Fort, 2000). Closed league owners want as much control over their product as possible, and are not as willing to cooperate and share resources (Andreff, 2011). Open leagues, on the other hand, have long worked with other organizations to try and build a sustainable cooperative model that allows teams to compete in more than one competition per season. Thus, it was not surprising for the 2018 Winter Olympic hockey tournament to have the top closed league (NHL) ban its players from participating, while players from a number of open leagues such as the KHL and Swedish Hockey League cooperated with the IOC to allow players to represent their respective countries at the games (Andreff & Staudohar, 2000).

Overall, there are certainly advantages and disadvantages to having teams compete in multiple competitions throughout a season. As has been noted in this chapter, additional competitions can add a lucrative and important fiscal component to the revenues of professional sport teams. Indeed, even closed leagues in North America have started considering whether they should have multiple competitions, as they have witnessed the boost in revenue that comes from game day and broadcast revenue for these additional matches (Andreff, 2011). Most recently, NBA commissioner Adam Silver indicated his interest in potentially adding a new tournament competition as part of the NBA season, which would take inspiration from knockout tournaments such as the UEFA Champions League and the NCAA men's basketball tournament. However, even though the NBA is considering adding a competition, their plans are to do so within the closed league structure, where the league would be in control.

Though the financial benefits of adding a competition would certainly be attractive to the NBA, they do need to consider some of the issues that come with having teams involved in various competitions throughout a season. Not only is there the potential issue of injuries to players that has been a primary reason for closed leagues to prevent players from competing outside of their own league, but if the competition and its prize structures are not structured well, it could lead to a product that is suboptimal. Because the fan interest in matches is often related to the quality of a competition (Borland & Macdonald, 2003), producing lower-quality competitions continues to be a problem for open leagues, and is something that North American teams and leagues need to be aware of as they consider expanding their sport enterprises.

OWNERSHIP AND EXPANSION

In international sport, there are a number of styles of ownership that are used, many of which have previously been covered in this textbook. However, what is worth considering is the changing nature of ownership, especially in open sport leagues around the world. In first considering the history of open sport leagues, professional clubs, especially those in Europe, were typically created by groups within a local community (Andreff & Staudohar, 2000). Because some clubs, such as those in England, were based in the local community, they often had investors but not necessarily clearly defined ownership structures. This changed in the late 1800s when the Football Association (FA) in England required clubs to issue shares to investors. The purpose of this was to provide a clear path of ownership and liability in terms of who was in charge of a club, and also remove the FA from being involved in economic and player trades between clubs. As this type of model was utilized throughout Europe, it was the case that most clubs issued shares, but in most cases they were not publicly traded in their early years.

Another ownership style that exists within open leagues in Europe takes the form of clubs, where individuals who are interested in being invested in a club financially are required to purchase a **membership**. Today, this method of ownership is extremely rare, but it is well known, as two of the world's top clubs—Barcelona and Real Madrid—both utilize this system (Llopis-Goig, 2012). In Spain, these members of clubs are called **socios**, and in addition to having provided financial investment in the club, they are able to vote to decide who will be the president that will run the club. Typically, presidents are elected for a multiple-year term (for example, Real Madrid socios elect a new president every four years), and are tasked with development and execution of the vision and strategy for the club during this period (Garcia, 2011). In the case of Real Madrid, it is said that there are close to 80,000 socios, all of whom provide a yearly payment to the club that provides them not only with tickets to games and voting rights, but also special access to some of the club's facilities. In this manner, the ownership of these clubs is made up of hundreds or even thousands of individuals who are willing to invest time and money into the team, but who are not tasked with the daily operations of the team. However, even though socios provide investment into the club on a yearly basis, they do not technically own any part of the team.

The Soccer Business Boom

In the 20th century, the ownership structure of clubs began to change as the shares that were held among the various investors in a community began to be bought up by wealthy individuals who sought to be the majority shareholder (Andreff & Staudohar, 2000). By doing this, these investors were able to install themselves as the chairmen of these football clubs, effectively giving them full control of the daily operations and major decisions within a club. Similar to owners within closed sport leagues, there is some variance among the chairmen of football clubs in open leagues in regard to the level of control that is exerted over the management of the club. In some cases, the owners of soccer clubs have taken a hands-off approach and simply provided a general vision and yearly budget, while others have gone to the level of picking the manager, players, and even telling the manager what style of play they want from the team. In the 1970s and 1980s, although certain clubs such as Arsenal, Manchester United, and Barcelona were relatively well known around the world, most teams were considered to be small local businesses without much reach beyond their own community (Andreff, 2011).

The 1980s became a transformative period for soccer clubs, and international sport business across the globe. During this decade, English soccer began to fall behind leagues in other countries in terms of competitiveness, and perhaps more importantly, revenue. At the time, English teams were mostly playing in older stadiums that did not have many amenities, which prevented clubs from being able to bring in large numbers of fans and generate match day revenues at the rate teams in Spain and Italy were able to. An additional blow to English soccer came in 1985, when Liverpool fans charged Juventus fans inside Heysel Stadium at the European Cup Final. As Juventus fans fled from Liverpool supporters, many individuals were crushed in the panic, resulting in the death of 39 fans and approximately 600 more injured (Vulliamy, 2015). Following this incident, known as the Heysel Stadium disaster, UEFA banned all teams from England from playing in European matches indefinitely, due to the fear and impression that English fans would continue to perpetrate similar incidents across the continent. In this manner, English soccer clubs not only were falling behind their competitors in terms of revenue and performance, but also general public opinion around the world toward English clubs and their fans was quite negative (Brett, 2019).

Realizing there was something that needed to be done, the top five clubs in English football at the time (Arsenal, Manchester United, Everton, Liverpool, and Tottenham) met with the director of London Weekend Television (LWT) in London to discuss potentially breaking away from the English Football League (EFL). Representatives from LWT noted that the control that the EFL had over television rights often prevented some of the big clubs from being on television, and did not provide the top clubs as much from television rights fees as they should be earning (MacInnes, 2017). Following the meeting, Arsenal's vice-chairman David Dein went to meet with the Football Association (FA) to gauge whether they would sanction the creation of a new breakaway league that included the top teams in English soccer. Because the FA and the EFL did not have a positive working relationship at the time, the FA sanctioned the move, believing it would help to balance power in English soccer (MacInnes, 2017).

After the end of the 1991–1992 EFL first division season, all the clubs in the top flight resigned from the EFL, and then collectively created the FA Premier League on May 27, 1992 (MacInnes, 2017). The Premier League was formed as a **private company limited by shares**, meaning that the company is a private corporation that has shareholders, and that the shares of the company are not allowed to be offered to the general public (Porter, 2019). By using this structure, the Premier League has 20 shareholders, with each club serving as one of the shareholders. In breaking away, the Premier League and its member teams were free to not only negotiate a new television contract, but also to sign new sponsorship and licensing agreements (Conn, 2017). Ironically, the LWT representative who set up the meeting that led to the creation of the Premier League was not able to secure the television broadcast rights for the new league, with BSkyB outbidding all other companies with a five-year £304 million deal (MacInnes, 2017). With this new influx of revenue, and the ability to re-enter European competitions, Premier League clubs quickly began to grow in popularity, and by the late 1990s were again competing with the top teams across Europe in terms of viewership, attendance, and revenue (Conn, 2017).

As the Premier League continued to grow, boosted by the profile of the top four teams (Arsenal, Manchester United, Liverpool, and Chelsea), the league continued to expand its television rights deals and became the most viewed professional league around the world. With this boosted profile, it also meant a renewed interest in English clubs from investors who saw various benefits that could come about through ownership of a Premier League team (Wigmore, 2018). Particularly, the interest in the league has come from wealthy individuals and businesses from around the world. Of the 20 teams that played in the 2019–2020 Premier League season, 13 of them either had all or a majority of shares owned by investors from outside of the UK (Conn, 2017). The growth in foreign ownership boomed with the acquisition of Manchester United by the Glazer family, who began purchasing shares in 2003 (Murphy, 2012). Using a holding company named Red Football, the Glazers continued purchasing shares by buying out the stakes of two major shareholders to obtain 57% of the shares of the company on May 12, 2005. This is especially notable, as not only did it make the Glazers the controlling owner of Manchester United, but it also passed the requisite threshold of 30% that is needed to be considered a serious contender for a takeover bid of an English club. The Glazers quickly moved to purchase more shares the next day, and boosted their stake to 74.81%, which was short of the 75% stake they would need to be able to delist the company from being traded publicly (Murphy, 2012). Three days later, the Glazers managed to purchase enough shares to move to 75.7% ownership of Manchester United, thus changing the club from a public limited company to a private one. In a final push towards gaining full control of the team, the Glazers made an offer to all remaining shareholders of 300 pence per share, with the offer lasting until June 13, 2005. At the deadline, the Glazers had managed to grow their share to 97.3%, but were just shy of the 97.6% that is required by English law to trigger a mandatory buyout of all other shareholders for the team ("Glazer extends Man Utd," 2005). Finally, on June 27, the club announced it had managed to obtain the requisite shares needed, and triggered the compulsory buyout, making the Glazers 100% owners of Manchester United.

After the buyout, the value of Manchester United was estimated to be around $1.5 billion, based on the dollar amount that the Glazers spent to buy all shares of the company ("Glazer extends Man Utd," 2005). This move by the Glazers, who already owned the Tampa Bay Buccaneers of the National Football League in the US, highlighted the future potential and value that Premier League teams could have. Following the Glazers, a number of top Premier League teams were purchased by professional sport team owners from closed leagues in North America (Wigmore, 2018). For example, Stan Kroenke, who owned the St. Louis Rams (now the Los Angeles Rams) and whose family owns the Denver Nuggets and Colorado Rapids, purchased a majority stake in Arsenal, Cleveland Browns owner Randy Lerner purchased a 59.69% stake in Aston Villa, and Shahid Khan, who owns the Jacksonville Jaguars, bought all of the shares of Fulham. As Premier League clubs continued to be bought by wealthy owners of North American sport franchises, others who were interested in being involved in high-profile sport leagues also began to invest in soccer clubs. The most famous of these new owners was Russian billionaire Roman Abramovich, who had managed to amass extensive wealth through oil and political power in Russia, and whose purchase of Chelsea football club forever changed the nature of professional football in Europe (Wigmore, 2018). Whereas owners from North American sport leagues saw Premier League teams as an investment that could help them to grow their own personal wealth, Abramovich saw Chelsea as a tool for his own personal glory. Thus, where even the owners of other rich teams placed restrictions on how much their clubs were willing to spend on players, Abramovich financed the purchase of a number of top players using his own money, rather than the club's. Although Chelsea had been a fairly successful club before Abramovich's arrival, the club had never won a Premier League title. After Abramovich's takeover of the club in 2003, the influx of cash to purchase players boosted the team, who immediately won two league titles within the next three years (Wigmore, 2018).

Abramovich's financing, which many fans dubbed as "buying titles," impacted the entire professional soccer marketplace. Those teams that had the resources quickly began to also pay large sums of money for top players, which quickly inflated the value and salaries of players playing in top leagues within Europe (Wigmore, 2018). For those teams that lacked the resources, the options were to either take out loans and gamble like Leeds did to try and win, be content with being a club that would not be able to compete with richer clubs, seek new investors to boost the club's spending power, or sell the club. In many cases, the shareholders and chairmen of English clubs chose the last option, and began to sell off their clubs to individuals or corporations with significant financial backing. Among this next wave of ownership changes was the sale of Manchester City to Shiekh Mansour, who is the current deputy prime minister of the United Arab Emirates (UAE), and is said to be the richest owner in professional sport, with a personal fortune estimated to be worth more than $22 billion (Armistead, 2008). Specifically, Shiekh Mansour was born into the Al Nahyan family, who are one of the six families that rule over UAE, and thus control much of the country's government and resources, including oil production.

In order to purchase Manchester City, Sheikh Mansour used his private equity company named Abu Dhabi United Group for Development and Investment, more commonly known as the Abu Dhabi Group (Armistead, 2008).

Immediately following the takeover of Manchester City, the Abu Dhabi Group provided a major influx of cash that allowed the team to purchase Brazilian star Robinho from Real Madrid. Over the next several years Manchester City continued to subsidize the purchase of players, allowing the team to drastically improve, and win the Premier League title in 2012, the team's first top-flight title in 44 years. After Manchester City's title win, the Abu Dhabi Group continued to invest in football clubs around the world, purchasing New York City FC of Major League Soccer, Melbourne Heart in the Australian A-League (who were renamed Melbourne City FC), as well as minority shares in Girona FC in Italy, Yokohama FC in Japan, and Sichuan Jiuniu in the Chinese second division (Critchlow, 2015). In this manner, using the massive financial resources of Sheikh Mansour, the Abu Dhabi Group has evolved into a **conglomerate**, marking a relatively new form of ownership in sport. A conglomerate is a large corporation that is composed of many different smaller firms. In this case, the Abu Dhabi Group serves as the sport conglomerate that is in control of the overall direction and synergies between the various teams that it owns or is invested in.

As noted in Chapter 10, when a business feels there is synergistic potential from purchasing another business, it will likely place a higher value on the new acquisition. It is important to note that while the Abu Dhabi Group is not the first owner or corporation in professional sport to own multiple teams, individuals or corporations that own several teams tend to purchase them in different sports. As such, while it allows for horizontal synergy by being able to bundle television deals or share arenas and facilities, it does not provide the same type of synergy that one would get from a conglomerate made up of teams from the same sport in different leagues across the world. That is, while owners with teams in a variety of sports can share certain resources, they are not able to shift players between teams. However, with the new emerging conglomerate in professional soccer, teams are able to use the pieces of their various clubs to create competitive advantage, including using subsidiary clubs to transfer players between teams. Furthermore, while Abramovich's investment in Chelsea was heavily driven by an interest in controlling one of the best professional soccer teams in the world, the Abu Dhabi Group's investment in multiple teams has been much more strategic. Specifically, the team has purchased both a top club (Manchester City), as well as clubs in emerging leagues that are in large markets. In this manner, the choice of locations is purposeful, as the Abu Dhabi Group has invested over a billion dollars in real estate and other industries in Manchester to help build up the area around where their team is based, as well as to expand the holdings of the overall company as well. Thus, the choice of purchasing teams in New York City, Yokohama (which is part of the greater Tokyo metropolitan area), Melbourne, and Chengdu (China) presents the potential for the Abu Dhabi Group to expand its holdings through the use of professional sport teams.

Financial Fair Play

Following the Abu Dhabi Group's purchase of Manchester City, UEFA conducted a review of the finances of 655 professional soccer clubs in Europe, and found that more than half of the clubs had losses in the previous season.

The report went on to note that club owners in soccer had too much hubris in terms of their ability to manage and guide a club successfully, especially from a financial perspective. The report also noted that, in the opinion of experts, about 20% of the clubs in Europe were in financial danger, and if significant changes were not immediately made to the system, it could place the entire soccer industry in danger. One of the biggest focal points was the relationship between team success and team spending, with both academic literature and general observations confirming the fact that teams who spent more money were often rewarded with better on-field success. Because of this, more and more clubs were beginning to borrow money or take on debts to improve their performance in matches, with the hope that this would translate to significant increases in revenues that would cover all debts and pay out greater profits to owners. As previously noted in this chapter, such behavior was evident not only in the top-flight leagues across Europe, but also in lower divisions as smaller teams also chased on-field and financial success.

Beyond teams spending beyond their means, the UEFA report also noted there were a small number of teams whose owners were able to make large financial contributions on a yearly basis to allow their teams to continue to buy top players. In the eyes of UEFA president Michel Platini, who called these rich owners "Sugar Daddies," such practices were problematic not only because they caused greater imbalance between rich and poor clubs, but also because the practice was not sustainable and encouraged smaller clubs without money to spend beyond their means as well. In the report, it was also noted that rivalries between teams with rich owners could also cause massive spending in a market, which led to inflated player salaries that raised costs for other clubs as well. With this in mind, UEFA started to work on developing legislation that would place limits on the financial spending of clubs, through a new set of regulations called the Financial Fair Play (FFP) rules.

Originally, the FFP rules were planned to be released in 2010, but they were delayed first until 2012, and then again until 2015, as discussions continued in regard to how long clubs would need to have to prepare for the new regulations. After several years, UEFA made its first rulings on the FFP rules based on examinations of club accounts from the 2011–2012 and 2012–2013 seasons. The rules state that clubs can spend up to 5 million more euros than the revenue the club brings in from a specific set of revenue sources. Specifically, the sources of revenue are defined as those related to match day revenue, television broadcast rights, advertising and merchandising, the sale of tangible assets, financial investments, performance prize money, and money generated from the sales of players. Similarly, UEFA defined costs for a club in regard to the FFP rules as money spent on transfers, employee wages and benefits, amortization of transfers, costs of debt financing, and dividend payments to shareholders. Through setting these regulations, UEFA essentially created a cap system, where the amount that a team is able to spend on transfer fees is roughly equal to the revenue that the club manages to generate in each year. At the same time, but not including the costs of stadiums, infrastructure, and youth teams, the rules allowed teams to continue building large and expensive stadiums.

For the first monitoring period, UEFA allowed teams special exceptions where they were allowed losses up to 45 million euros as long as the team could display that their owner had enough assets, such as cash in hand, to cover those losses. So what happens to a club that is found to be guilty of violating the FFP rules? Technically, UEFA has created an eight-step punishment system, with penalties becoming more strict based on the level at which a club violates the rules. Overall, the lowest-level punishments include warnings and fines for teams that are in violation of the rules, and gradual step up, including withholding of prize money from competitions, a ban on all transfers, and a deduction of points (similar to clubs that go into administration) that could potentially knock teams out of contention for places in the Champions League. Moving further up the list, more severe penalties include a ban or limit on the number of new players a club can register as members of their club (as well as register for European competitions), with the most strict punishment being a ban from European competitions.

The first round of FFP penalties were announced at the beginning of the 2012–2013 season, with 23 clubs having their prize money withheld unless they were able to come into compliance with FFP rules within a month. In the end, 16 clubs were able to settle their remaining debts before the end of the month, and only seven clubs were punished by not receiving revenues from UEFA. UEFA continued to announce penalties each season, but the rules were criticized for many reasons. First off, many pundits noted that the rules did not necessarily create financial equality across all soccer clubs in Europe, but rather provided a status quo where richer clubs were able to continue spending large sums of money, with smaller clubs having no way to compete against them. One notable example occurred in the 2013 season when Chelsea reported losses close to £50 million for the reporting period, but because the club had record revenue of approximately £255 million, they would technically fall within the FFP rules. At the same time, Manchester City was similarly found to have had significant losses, and even when deducting the costs of facilities, had a loss of around £50 million. In the case of Manchester City, however, part of the club's revenues were found to come from the sale of player image rights that had been sold to a company that paid well over the normal market value for these rights (Buschmann & Winterbach, 2019). Ironically, Chelsea manager José Mourinho, who had been part of the team that had taken on large cash payments from its owner to buy players, questioned Manchester City's practices, stating that they seemed to be "dodgy" financial fair play, where other teams were trying to do the right thing (Burt, 2014).

In 2014, UEFA announced that nine clubs across Europe had been found to have violated the FFP rules and regulations for the accounts from 2011–2012 and 2012–2013. The teams that were found guilty of violations were Manchester United, Paris Saint-Germain (PSG) of France, Russian clubs Zenit St. Petersburg, Anzhi Makhachkala, Rubin Kazan, and Levski Sofia, and three Turkish teams (Galatasaray, Bursaspor, and Trabzonspor). Of these clubs, the two significant penalties were handed down to Manchester City and PSG, both of whom were owned by rich conglomerates backed with oil money. Specifically, Manchester City was found to have combined losses almost reaching £150 million over the last two seasons, including a £97 million loss in the 2012 fiscal year. Because of this, UEFA handed down a three-part penalty in which the club was fined £49 million, had its transfer budget reduced £49 million for the summer of 2014, as well as being limited to naming a squad of only 21 players who were available for Champions League duty. Likewise, PSG was punished in a similar manner when it was found that a sponsorship deal with the Qatar Tourism Authority worth £167 million was not deemed to be the fair market value for such deals. Ultimately, the penalties against Manchester City and PSG were reduced as the clubs negotiated a settlement with UEFA before the 2014–2015 European season started (Buschmann & Winterbach, 2019).

Overall, FFP has received a great deal of criticism from owners, coaches, fans, and the media (see Sidebar 16.B). For some, the rules seem to be simply window dressing to make it look as if UEFA is cracking down on teams backed by highly wealthy owners. Indeed, the reduction in penalties against Manchester City and PSG signaled to many that UEFA was not willing to provide harsh punishments to rich and powerful clubs who were in violation of the rules (Buschmann & Winterbach, 2019). At the same time, the supporters of teams who were found to be in violation of the regulations also slammed the FFP rules. For example, after Manchester City's initial penalties, the supporters group for the club came out and noted that Manchester City was being punished for having a rich owner who cared about the club and the sport, and that what Manchester City was doing was something that other clubs such as Manchester United had been free to do for decades. In this sense, FFP's protection of the status quo and its lack of ability to keep clubs from spending large sums of money led to the rules being openly mocked. FFP again came under attack in 2018 and 2019, when German newspaper *Der Spiegel* published a series of articles using information collected from the Football Leaks website showing that Manchester City had possibly used devious tactics and received help from inside UEFA itself to dodge the rules (Buschmann & Winterbach, 2019).

SIDEBAR 16.B   The Fight Against Financial Fair Play

When Manchester City was first found guilty of violating the FFP rules in 2014, the club began to prepare for an investigation and interviews that were to be conducted by representatives of UEFA. However, in reports published by *Der Spiegel*, it was found that Manchester City's chairman Khaldoon Al Mubarak was privately communicating via email with UEFA general secretary Gianni Infantino, who would become the president of FIFA in 2016. At the time, UEFA had been investigating Manchester City and PSG for several months, and publicly Infantino and UEFA president Platini both stated that those teams who were found to have violated the FFP rules would receive severe punishments. Indeed, UEFA investigators were suspicious of the activities of both clubs, as much of the revenue growth that both clubs had experienced seemed to be coming from sources with close ties to the team owners. For Manchester City, it was found that around 84% of the commercial income from marketing and sponsorship was originating from organizations in Abu Dhabi (Buschmann, Dahlkamp, Latsch, et al., 2018a). Likewise, PSG's £167 million deal was found to be problematic, as the tourism authority that was paying the money was found by UEFA investigators to be closely interlinked with PSG's ownership group. However, despite the evidence that UEFA investigators had assembled, PSG and Manchester City were able to use their connections in UEFA to negotiate the penalty for violation of FFP down to 20 million euros each (Buschmann, Dahlkamp, Latsch, et al., 2018a).

However, these actions were not the only ones taken by Manchester City to avoid the FFP rules and the penalties associated with them. Further investigations reported that when the club was short on revenue, in order to be in compliance with FFP, the club would adjust their revenue figures by backdating revenue to the previous year. That is, in order to make sure that the financial accounts were properly balanced, the team had sponsors based in the UAE such as Etihad Airways and the tourism authority pay additional revenue to Manchester City in what was being called a "win bonus." However, *Der Spiegel* reports argue that what was actually happening was that the Abu Dhabi Group, which was owned by Manchester City's owner, would wire money directly to the sponsors, and that they would in turn pay the money to Manchester City (Buschmann & Winterbach, 2019). In essence, the reports accuse Manchester City of using sponsors as a vehicle through which to pass money directly to the team, while also avoiding any direct links to the Abu Dhabi Group or its owner.

Perhaps the most daring of moves from Manchester City was to push some of the costs that typically encumbered professional soccer clubs to outside companies, while also claiming revenues from these transactions. It is alleged that Manchester City created a marketing agency to which they sold the marketing rights of players. Because clubs typically pay players directly for the marketing rights, the club was able to lower its costs by transferring the rights to a third party, and then was also able to claim additional revenue based on the sale of the rights (Buschmann, Dahlkamp, Latsch, et al., 2018b). As such, by using shell corporations as well as organizations with close connections to the owners, it is suggested that Manchester City was able to skirt around the FFP rules, and continue to find ways to provide cash influxes to continue the purchase of players to strengthen the team. Indeed, it is noted that in the four years after PSG and Manchester City negotiated the reduced penalty for FFP violations with UEFA, the two clubs spent close to $1 billion combined on player purchases. In this manner, it would seem that the FFP rules have really only been used to punish a few smaller clubs, while those with the biggest violations were only given an insignificant punishment.

Supporters' Trust and Fan Ownership

In response to the large sums of money that teams and players have been purchased for in professional soccer, a new ownership trend has re-emerged in recent years. Specifically, a number of supporters of clubs have become disillusioned with the big business of professional soccer, and thus have decided to fight against this system by taking a grassroots approach to building new community-based soccer clubs. Specifically, this ownership style is called the **supporters' trust** model (Niven, 2011). Traditionally, supporters' trusts were non-profit organizations created by fans to provide a way for them to have greater influence in the operations of professional sport teams. Supporters' trusts are most common in the United Kingdom, and even though they are typically associated with soccer clubs, they can also be found for sports in other teams such as rugby and ice hockey.

In general, the supporters' trust model is often defined as fan-owned sports teams, however, it is important to note that there are some distinctions between various types of fan ownership. For example, about 80 individuals who are fans of the club hold shares of the Edmonton Eskimos of the Canadian Football League (CFL). Although these individuals are fans, the ownership shares are private and do not allow for democratic operations of the club among a larger fan base. Likewise, the aforementioned socios in Spain do share a number of similarities with supporters' trusts in that they are sold to a larger number of fans and use a democratic process for the election of the club's leadership (Garcia, 2011). Additionally, neither model pays out dividends, as any profits made by a club in either model are expected to be retained within the team. However, socios require that members pay a membership fee each year in order to continue being invested in a club, while supporters' trusts do not expect fans to make yearly payments to a team, outside of purchases of tickets and other club goods (Llopis-Goig, 2012).

Within the United Kingdom, supporters' trusts were originally encouraged to form as Industrial and Provident Societies (IPSs), a legal term for various types of volunteer and business organizations that was used in the UK. Because of changes in the British legal system, IPSs were renamed in 2014 as **Co-operative and Community Benefit Societies** (CCBSs) (Gibson, 2016). In this manner, supporters' trust clubs are now often registered as a community benefits society, where individuals become part of the organization by buying a share in the club which gives them a vote in the organization's elections and decision-making process. Additionally, because CCBSs are governed under strict non-profit status rules, any profits that are generated by the club are considered to be common property of the club, and thus cannot be paid out in dividends, or loaned to the organization or its members (Gibson, 2016). In other words, similar to socio-run clubs in Spain, a supporters' trust that operates in the UK as a CCBS must reinvest all of its profits back into operations and development of the club and its infrastructure. Although the clubs are unable to pay out profits, they are able to bring in capital to work on improving the club, which often comes in the form of donations to the trust (Llopis-Goig, 2012).

Indeed, the community-based grassroots approach has gained great traction in recent years. After fans of Manchester United became angry with the team being purchased by the Glazer family, a large group of supporters formed together to create F.C. United of Manchester, which is now the biggest supporters' trust in England. In the case of F.C. United of Manchester, the team is often described as a "**protest club**," a term used to describe teams that are formed in protest against the governance style or ownership style of another club (Foster, 2016). The previously discussed AFC Wimbledon is considered to be another protest club, as a supporters' trust was used to build the club after the original Wimbledon FC was moved 60 miles away by its owner. In addition to protest clubs, which can also be found in countries such as Croatia and Austria, there are also teams that are described as "phoenix clubs." A **phoenix**

club is defined as a new team that is created by supporters to replace a club that has failed, such as when a club goes into administration and is dissolved (Stone, 2015). Although phoenix clubs are often fan owned, there are examples of teams being rebooted using previous brand names, including teams in Major League Soccer such as the Seattle Sounders and Vancouver Whitecaps, which were both named after previous professional clubs that had become defunct.

As a final point in regard to fan-owned clubs, it is important to consider that while these models of ownership are able to work in open leagues, they are typically incompatible with closed leagues, especially when they are created at the grassroots level. First off, some leagues such as the NFL require that all teams in the league have a majority owner, and thus using an equal-vote supporters' trust model would not be acceptable based on the league's rules. Furthermore, because entry into top-flight closed leagues often requires a significant expansion fee that is at least a few hundred million dollars, entry to these leagues becomes unrealistic for fan-owned teams. At the same time, there are fan-owned teams in North America, such as the semi-professional soccer club Detroit City F.C. Although the team's model has been rather successful in terms of building a grassroots soccer club in a major city in North America, the closed system used by Major League Soccer means that the club has almost no chance of entry into the league (Liddell, 2019). Furthermore, as rich investors such as NBA owner Dan Gilbert look towards investing in an MLS team in Detroit, it presents the realistic possibility that Detroit City F.C. could lose their status as the top team in Detroit because of their lack of monetary resources (Liddell, 2019). Thus, as previously noted in the example discussing AFC Wimbledon, the use of open teams can provide benefits, in that it allows fans to create teams and try to build them up into professional clubs that are well integrated with the local community.

From Industrial Leagues to Hybrid Leagues

Typically, within a country there is usually only one type of structure used by all professional leagues. For example, even though professional soccer leagues around the world tend to use the open league system, Major League Soccer in the US is a closed league, following the same structure as other major leagues in the country. Likewise, even though hockey in North America uses a closed system, the leagues in Europe tend to employ a tiered system with promotion and relegation. However, there are some countries that utilize a **hybrid system** where there is a mixture of both open and closed leagues within the country. Such a structure is predominantly found in Asia, where professional sport leagues have grown out of older semi-professional **industrial leagues**, which were often funded by large corporations that were interested in competing not just in business, but also in sport (Humphreys & Watanabe, 2015). One good example of an industrial league turned into a professional league is the J-League in Japan. Before the formation of the J-League, the Japan Soccer League (JSL) was formed of teams that were named after the companies that owned them such as Mitsubishi Motors, Yamaha Motor, Nissan Motors, Hitachi, etc.

Beyond the interests of corporations, industrial leagues have been important in the creation of sport leagues and the development of the hybrid system in several ways. First off, founding a professional sport league without any teams can be an expensive affair, and is often met with failures and delays. For example, even though the US has been the top economic power in the world for the last several decades, there have been a number of issues in creating professional soccer leagues in the country. Not only did the North American Soccer League (NASL) eventually perish because of financial issues, but even the MLS was unable to get enough financial backing when it was started, and had to push its kick off date back from 1994 to 1996. As such, considering that developing a professional league is a difficult and costly affair, the use of an industrial league helps to establish a league that is not fully professional and helps to put the infrastructure of the league into place. Additionally, because industrial leagues tend to require that corporations subsidize teams, it avoids the issue of having to find investors to fund all of the teams in the league. This was certainly a problem in the early days of MLS, as the league had trouble getting investors, to the point where almost every team in the league was owned by either Phil Anschutz (Anschutz Entertainment Group) or Lamar Hunt (Hunt Sports Group). This in itself was a problem, as the league suffered in terms of fan perception because of the large amount of control held by these two owners, even though the league's commissioner, Don Garber, argued that this structure helped saved the league from going out of business (Wahl, 2014).

Even though many corporations involved in industrial leagues are powerful international corporations, it is the case that most of these corporations have little to no experience in terms of running a sport business. As such, in what has become a common practice for industrial leagues, the leagues have turned to the countries where the sport is most popular and successful to imitate their business models. Thus, while Asian soccer leagues in Japan, China, and South Korea follow the structure and organization of open leagues from Europe and South America, the baseball teams in these same countries are closed leagues following the MLB business model (Jang & Lee, 2016). At the same time, even though hybrid leagues copy the methods of operation and structure from other leagues, they also sometimes make changes to try and design competitions in a manner they feel is suitable to the environment and market they exist in. One notable example of this can be found in NPB, where the league decided to use a draft to select amateur players similar to MLB. However, because NPB felt that having a reverse-order draft would lead to teams not giving their full effort, they have altered the format of the draft to encourage teams to not tank at the end of the season to improve their chances of getting a top draft pick. Instead, NPB uses what is called a contested draft system, where the first round is composed of each team naming a player they would like to draft. If a team names a player and no one else names them, then that team gets the rights to that player. However, if a player is named by more than one team, then that player is contested, and all the teams that named that individual are entered into a random draw, with the winner obtaining the player. In this manner, teams will continue to pick players and draw lots to see who gets the player, randomly, until everyone gets a player of their choice in the first round. After this, NPB teams then enter into three more rounds that then use the typical reverse-order draft system that is used by MLB.

There are drawbacks that exist from the hybrid model, especially in relation to leagues developed out of previous industrial leagues. Perhaps one of the major issues is that when these leagues transfer from being an industrial league to a professional league, because powerful corporations with significant financial backing own most teams, it can create a system that is restrictive to other smaller teams in the league (Gong, Watanabe, Brown & Nagel, 2019). This effect can be especially pronounced in closed leagues, as corporations will expect that if extra teams or owners are to be added into the league via expansion or new investment, it should come from corporations that are of equal status from an economic and social standpoint. For example, in the Korean Baseball Organization (KBO) league, nine out of the ten teams are owned by and named after major conglomerates, with the final team being an investment group that sells the naming rights of their team (the Heroes) to other corporations. What is especially notable about this example is that the KBO initially began with six teams, and then expanded to ten by adding teams that were backed by other conglomerates (Jang & Lee, 2016).

Another problem arising from being formed by an industrial league is that the on-field parity in the league can be disrupted by the presence of corporations that have certain synergies that allow them to generate more revenue than others, and thus create financial imbalance between teams. This had been a major issue in NPB, where the Tokyo Giants are a subsidiary of the Yomiuri Group which owns two newspapers and a major television station (Yamamura & Shin, 2008). Because of its control of a large media outlet, the Yomiuri Group has created an environment where the Giants receive a large amount of media attention, and are paid significantly more for television broadcast rights than other teams in the league. Thus, the synergy between the Giants and the Yomiuri Group allows the team to have significantly more financial resources than other teams in the league, and provides a significant competitive advantage when trying to attract free agents (La Croix & Kawamura, 1999).

Additionally, when teams are reliant on corporations as financial backers for a sport league, it can cause problems when there are downturns in the economy. That is, if corporations are heavily subsidizing the operations of teams, when the corporation is faced with economic uncertainty, the team will likely be required to make cuts by trading or selling off players to other teams to reduce costs. Another problem with having backing from large corporations is that, while they look to other leagues for best practices, they often do not understand the realities of the sport business. In this sense, some corporations will simply see the sport teams that they own as part of their marketing and outreach, and thus will provide them with financial resources, but may not necessarily run them as businesses. Such practices are evident in a number of sport leagues across Asia, where teams sustain heavy losses, but do not change their operations or management, as the corporation as a whole may consider sustained losses as acceptable (see Sidebar 16.C). As such, because of the corporate ownership, teams can be inefficient and thus this model of sport team ownership may not be one that other leagues should look to emulate.

SIDEBAR 16.C   The Emergence of the Chinese Super League

The Chinese Super League (CSL) is the top flight of professional soccer in China. The CSL is actually a rebranding of the previous professional league in China that was named Jia-A. However, due to a number of scandals, including the bribing of referees and match-fixing, the league decided it was best to change its name and expel those teams, players, coaches, referees, and officials who were found guilty of match-fixing. Although traditional clubs such as Beijing Guoan and Shanghai Shenhua have long been popular within China, the league quickly developed alongside the growth of China's economy in the 21st century. The club that has set the new standard for teams in the CSL is Guangzhou Evergrande, a team that is currently co-owned by the Evergrande real estate corporation and Alibaba, the world's largest e-commerce retailer. Notably, Evergrande real estate group purchased the team in 2010, when it was a small second division club in China League One (Watanabe & Soebbing, 2017). Backed by billionaire Jiayin Xu, who has a net worth of approximately $30 billion, the team used its new financial power to purchase star players from other countries, as well as to hire former World Cup winning coach Marcello Lippi to be the team's manager. Following their promotion to the Chinese Super League in 2011, Evergrande would go on to win every league title for the next seven years, losing only 24 league matches of 210 they would play during this time.

Following Evergrande's model of investment and subsidization of clubs, a number of teams in the CSL were either purchased by large corporations, or sought investments in order to compete. Alongside this investment has been an increase in fan interest in soccer in China, with the league's average attendance having approximately doubled from 10,838 in its first season (2004) to 24,107 in 2018. This growth has also translated into increased revenue potential for clubs, with new media rights deals growing to be some of the most lucrative for professional soccer in all of Asia. Because of the influx of cash from rich owners, as well as the growth in match day and broadcast revenue, the CSL has also become a significant player in the global transfer market (Watanabe, Yan, Soebbing, & Fu, 2019). In the winter 2017 transfer market, CSL clubs made headlines around the world as they purchased a number of top players in their prime from clubs in Europe, and ended up spending more than teams from any other league. Although the Chinese Football Association has stepped in to put in place rules to curb the massive spending by teams, the CSL has used backing from large corporations to grow into a formidable player in the international soccer market (Watanabe, et al., 2019).

TRANSFERS AND PLAYER MOVEMENT

Another way in which North American and international sport leagues differ is in the way players are acquired and moved between teams. In North America, most teams in closed leagues use a reverse-order draft to select players. In the rest of the world, players are typically developed through **academy** systems. Specifically, each club will operate a youth academy, which will be in charge of scouting and identifying talented players at a young age. These players are then brought to the academy to be trained and provided an education as well. If a player manages to advance through the academy system, they will eventually be offered a professional contract with the team, and will thus transfer from being an academy player to being part of the official professional team. If a team feels a player does not fit their needs or is not of the quality they would expect, the player will be released by the academy and will be free to sign with any other team or academy that is willing to take them.

The academy system has its advantages over the draft, in that if a team is good at scouting and developing players, it does not need to worry about other teams taking players they need before them in the draft. On the other hand, the draft system benefits professional teams in North America in that they do not have to operate expensive academy and youth development systems, and are able to shift some of these costs to high schools and colleges. Some teams using the closed league system, such as those in MLB and NPB, have recognized the benefits that can come about from developing academies. Where these teams do not operate youth academies in their respective countries, they have begun development of youth baseball academies in the Caribbean. Recognizing that there is a large interest in baseball, a talented pool of young players, and relatively low costs to their own organization, the Hiroshima Carp was the first Japanese baseball team to establish an academy in the Dominican Republic. From this academy, the Carp were able to identify and train players such as Alfonso Soriano and Timo Perez, who would play for the Carp before going on to careers in MLB ("Carp debutant Batista," 2017).

Beyond obtaining amateur players, there are also significant differences in how players move between teams in closed versus open leagues. Typically, closed leagues move players between teams by conducting trades for other players, draft picks, exchanging cash, or future considerations (such as players to be named later). On the other hand, open leagues tend to use the **transfer** system, where players are simply sold for a mutually agreed upon value (O'Hanlon, 2019). Although there are swap deals in the transfer system where players are exchanged for one another, this is done by agreeing on a set value that the players are both worth, and then transferring the players without exchanging any cash. As has been noted throughout this chapter, the transfer system plays an important role in the sport business. Notably the transfer system can help clubs that do not have a good academy system to obtain players they think will be able to help them perform better on the field. Likewise, smaller clubs that are good at developing players are able to use the transfer rule to develop and sell players to big clubs, thus providing them with an important source of revenue to maintain financial stability.

However, as was noted in the discussion about the Financial Fair Play rules, and Sidebar 16B about Manchester City, the transfer system has also been the source of a number of problems in professional soccer over the last two decades. Because players are not traded, as is done in North America, teams are often free to spend large sums of money to try and improve their squad. The increase in television revenues and wealthy owners has continued to cause the transfer values of players to increase, thus leading to a number of clubs taking on debts to buy players in order to be more competitive. At the same time, players have often been critical of the transfer system, with some equating the practice of simply buying and selling human beings with being a modern-day form of slavery (Taylor, 2008). Indeed, where North American leagues had generally started moving towards free agency in the 1980s, there was no such thing as free movement between clubs until 1995. In what became known as the **Bosman ruling**, Belgian player Jean-Marc Bosman sued his former team with whom his contract had expired, because they had asked teams that wanted to sign him to pay £500,000. After a lengthy trial, Bosman was granted the ability to move to a new team without them having to pay a transfer fee, and thus created what is known as a Bosman (or free) transfer (Taylor, 2008).

Perhaps the most foreign aspect of the transfer system to those familiar with player movement rules in North America is the ability for players to sign **"pre-contracts"** with another team before the end of their contract. In most North American leagues, if a team even gives hints that they are interested in the players of another team, they would be charged with tampering by the league, and would likely face stiff penalties and fines. However, in international soccer, when a player is near the end of their contract and is past the last period in which they can transfer for a fee, they are free to negotiate a pre-contract with another team. For example, when Arsenal star Aaron Ramsey's contract was coming to an end in June of 2019, he was able to negotiate with teams starting in January, and signed a deal with Juventus that would come into effect after his contract with Arsenal came to an end ("Arsenal's Aaron Ramsey," 2019).

One last oddity of the international soccer system is the concept of **third-party ownership**, which has been an extremely controversial issue. Third-party ownership is when the economic rights of a player are not owned by him or a club, but by a third party such as a marketing agency, football agent, or even a single investor (Richards, 2016). The practice of third-party ownership is most evident in South American soccer, where investors often purchase shares in a player, with the money going to help pay for various expenses associated with the training of the player. If the player becomes good enough that they are able to be sold to another club, rather than the club receiving most of the transfer fees, these fees often are paid to the third party. One of the more famous incidents of third-party owners occurred when West Ham United of the Premier League purchased Carlos Tevez and Javier Mascherano in 2006. When it was found that a third party owned the players' economic rights and that this had resulted in issues with their contracts, West Ham was fined by the Premier League. Following this incident, the Premier League moved to ban all third-party contracts in 2008, and FIFA followed suit in 2015, noting that these types of deals pushed the transfer system close to appearing like human trading or slavery (Richards, 2016).

EXCHANGE RATES

Exchange rates can be defined as the value that a nation's currency has, and are displayed as the numerical rate at which a country's currency can be exchanged for another (Tenreyo, 2007). For example, the exchange rate for US dollars (USD) to Canadian dollars (CAD) on June 5, 2019 was 1 to 1.34, indicating that if one was to exchange currency, one would receive 1.34 Canadian dollars for every US dollar. Because exchange rates play an important role in international trade, and are often seen as representing the economic strength of a country or region, they are at the core of international finance. This is certainly the case in the realm of sport, where teams and leagues that conduct business with international partners must be aware of how exchange rates could influence decision making. For example, in international soccer, where players are mostly bought and sold (transferred) between teams, the exchange rate can play a vital role in determining the gains or losses for the parties involved in a transfer involving clubs using two different types of currencies. Although agreements will often be made in a currency such as the euro (Tenreyo, 2007), for a team in China or England, the timing of when this value is paid out could impact how much the club actually pays for a player.

In a similar example, the exchange rate also plays an important role in the National Hockey League (NHL), as all players in the league are paid in US dollars. In this manner, teams that are based in Canada must be cognizant of not only the current exchange rates between US dollars and Canadian dollars, but also of the future prospects for both currencies. On one hand, if the Canadian dollar becomes stronger, it will mean that Canadian teams will have to pay less in their own currency for player salaries. On the other hand, if the US dollar increases in value relative to the Canadian dollar, it would mean greater expenses for Canadian franchises. In further considering the exchange rates between the USD and CAD, the exchange rate between the currencies was once almost on par, with one USD worth 1.06 CAD on July 11, 2014. However, when the price of oil plummeted in 2015, the value of the Canadian dollar began to decline drastically in relation to the US dollar. On October 9, 2015, two days after the beginning of the NHL season, the exchange rate was one USD to 1.29 CAD. This rate continued to grow through the first part of the season, reaching a maximum of one USD to 1.45 CAD on January 15, 2016. Overall, this represented about a 12% change in the value of the Canadian dollar, meaning that the franchises in Canada were required to pay a higher salary cost because of the fluctuation in exchange rates.

To better understand exchange rates, it is important to note that there is a difference between the **nominal exchange rate** and the **real exchange rate** (Grilli & Kaminsky, 1991). For most of us who have exchanged money at the airport or a bank when traveling to another country, we are familiar with the nominal exchange rate, which is simply the market values that are displayed on any given day. Thus in the previous example when it was noted that the value of the USD to CAD reached a ratio of 1 to 1.45 on January 15, 2016, this rate is the nominal exchange rate. On the other hand, the real exchange rate takes into account the different levels of inflation that exist between two countries. In order to calculate the real exchange rate, the following calculation is used:

$$\text{RER} = \frac{e * P^*}{P}$$

where RER is the real exchange rate

e represents the nominal exchange rate

P^* is the domestic price of a good,

P is the foreign price of the same good.

Using the example equation, let's calculate the real exchange rate for hockey sticks between the US and Canada, with the assumption that we live in the US. Looking prices up online, we can see that a specific model of Bauer hockey stick sells for 44.99 USD, with the same stick costing 69.99 CAD. If we use the exchange rate of 1 USD to 1.33 CAD from June 12, 2019, we would set up the calculation given above by writing:

$$RER = \frac{1.33 * \$44.99}{\$69.99} = 0.85898$$

This gives us a real exchange rate of about 0.86. Because the value is less than 1, it indicates that the price of the hockey stick is cheaper in the US than in Canada when taking into account the exchange rate. To better understand the real exchange rate, it should be noted that the rate should be calculated over time so as to consider a trend (Lastrapes, 1992). If the value of the real exchange rate increased from 0.86 to 0.93, it would tell us that the rate is rising, and thus the price of the good at home is rising faster than it is abroad. On the other hand, if the value were to decline from 0.86 to 0.73, it would suggest the opposite, that the prices of goods in Canada are rising faster than they are in the US. For teams that deal with currency exchange rates and the movement of goods and players between two or more countries, having a grasp of the nominal and real exchange rates is important because it can lead to better financial decision making.

Because of fluctuations in currency exchange rates, many NHL players based in Canada keep two bank accounts, one in US dollars which is where they receive their pay, and another in Canadian currency which is used to pay bills and their everyday expenses. Because the currencies fluctuate back and forth, those players who are financially savvy are able to use the changes in exchange rates to their advantage. For example, when the Canadian dollar was strong, many of the players kept their money in US dollars, and only moved money to their Canadian accounts to pay for necessities. However, when the value of the Canadian dollar dropped in comparison to the US dollar, players quickly began to convert their US currency to Canadian dollars in order to maximize the amount of CAD that they could gain. In some cases, players who had held their salary for years in USD were able to move them to CAD accounts, and essentially gain 10% extra purchasing power in Canada by waiting for the exchange rates to change in their favor.

Although NHL teams also participate in similar practices, the reality is that they are required to pay contracts of players (and coaches in some cases) in USD, meaning that when the currency drops, they experience increased costs. One mechanism that NHL teams in Canada are able to use that helps them avoid losses based on sudden drops in currency value is the ability to lock in exchange rates for a season. However, because local revenues such as ticket sales, concessions, etc. are paid to Canadian teams in Canadian dollars, the value that they receive from local revenues also goes down in comparison to their competitors in America. For teams with deeper pockets, such as the Toronto Maple Leafs and Montreal Canadians, while the currency changes do influence the team's bottom line in the short term, they do not necessarily affect these teams' ability to pay lucrative salaries to attract top players. However, for teams in other Canadian markets, the devaluation of the Canadian dollar is a much more serious issue, as it creates a difficult financial situation for teams, especially when they are forced to lock in rates with the uncertainty that further changes in currency value could stress the teams financially.

CONCLUSION

A number of important topics in international sport finance were introduced within this chapter. However, it is important to note that because of the complicated nature of international business and relations, there are also social and political forces that can impact businesses. Although these topics were not fully covered within this chapter, it is important that sport managers be aware of events happening around the globe. Certainly, by observing the operations and practices of other leagues and teams, there are lessons to be learned. For example, leagues in North America have slowly incorporated the practice of including sponsor names and badges on the front of team jerseys, thus increasing the revenue potential of teams. However, it is also important to be aware of global events, as things such as elections in other countries can impact the global economy in a number of ways. Perhaps one of the biggest looming issues is the matter of Brexit, where citizens of the UK voted to leave the European Union (Levitt, 2019). The constant negotiations and political maneuvering between politicians in the UK and Europe have had a number of impacts on the economy, including fluctuations in the currency exchange rate for the British pound. The changing value of the British currency coupled with the fact that it may now be harder for individuals from other countries to be granted a visa to work in the UK has been a primary concern for professional sport teams in the country (Levitt, 2019). In this sense, having a good grasp of finance and politics at the international level can help provide important information for those working in sport, and allow them to strategize and plan to create competitive advantage for their organization.

Concept Check

1. What is an open sport league? How does it differ from a closed league in terms of structure and organization?
2. What advantages does the open league system have over the closed league system?
3. What are the disadvantages in using the open league system compared to closed leagues.
4. What is the promotion and relegation system? Comparing it to the systems used in closed leagues, what type of advantages does it have? What are its disadvantages?
5. What are parachute payments, and why are leagues around Europe adopting this mechanism?
6. What are yo-yo (or elevator) clubs, and what problems does their existence pose for professional sport leagues?
7. What is administration, and why has it become a problem in recent years, especially in professional soccer in Europe?
8. Similarly, why are professional teams in promotion and relegation leagues more likely to go into administration when compared to their North American counterparts?

9. Why do teams in closed leagues tend not to participate in multiple competitions? Please provide details in regard to why there is a lack of participation.

10. What is tournament theory? Why is it important for professional sport leagues to be aware of tournament theory?

11. What are socios (or memberships), and how are they different from other types of sport team ownership?

12. Describe the "supporters' trust" ownership of sport teams, and why this method of ownership has become popular in recent years.

13. What is the difference between a protest club and a phoenix club?

14. What is a conglomerate, and how has it changed the landscape of professional soccer around the world?

15. Why did UEFA create the Financial Fair Play rules?

16. What is the hybrid system of professional sport? Do these leagues strictly copy the leagues they adopt practices from?

17. What are some advantages to a professional sport league of having been formed from an industrial league? What are some disadvantages?

18. What is a transfer? How does it operate differently from the system of player movement in North American professional sport leagues?

19. What is a Bosman transfer? Why is the Bosman transfer important in European soccer?

20. What is third-party ownership, and what problems does it pose for professional soccer?

21. What is the nominal exchange rate? What type of important information does this value provide?

22. What is the real exchange rate? How does it differ from the nominal exchange rate? Why is it important for organizations involved in international business to be able to understand this rate?

Practice Problems

1. On June 1, the euro was trading at 1 to 1.12 US dollars. A professional sport team in the US negotiating a contract with a free agent from Europe offered the player $10,000,000.
   a. Please calculate the player's value on that day using the nominal exchange rate.
   b. The player's agent replied that they wanted the equivalent of 9,000,000 euros three days later. On that day, the exchange rate of the euro moved from 1 to 1.09 US dollars. Based on this, how much more or less will the team have to pay in US dollars compared to the original offer of $10,000,000?
   c. If the exchange rate had remained at 1 to 1.12 (euros to USD), how much more would the team need to have paid the player?
   d. Based on this, how much did the team save in total based on the change in the exchange rate?

2. On May 27, 2016, before the Brexit vote occurred in the UK, the pound was trading at 1 = 1.46 USD. A company in the US selling a device that allows teams to track the movement of players had priced the system at $3,000,000, and was also selling the device at £2.1 million in the UK.

a. Based on this information, calculate the real exchange rate for this device.
b. Based on the real exchange rate that was just calculated, is the product cheaper or more expensive in the US?
c. On October 28, 2016, a few months after the Brexit vote, the value of the pound plummeted, ending trading at 1 pound = 1.22 USD. Assuming no change in the price of the device, calculate the new real exchange rate.
d. Comparing the real exchange rate from June to the one in October, how has the value of the product changed? Is this good or bad for the company?
e. Considering that customers would see the change in the value of the product, the company has decided that they are going to adjust the UK price using the real exchange rate from June to restore the rate to 0.9874. Please calculate the new UK price. Assume that the exchange rate is still 1 pound to 1.22 USD.
f. Reconsidering, the company has now decided that they would like the price in the US to be equivalent to that in the UK, and thus it should have a real exchange rate of 1. Based on this, calculate the new UK price, assuming the US price is $3,000,000 and the exchange rate is 1 pound to 1.22 USD.

References

Andreff, W. (2011). Some comparative economics of the organization of sports: Competition and regulation in North American vs. European professional team sports leagues. *The European Journal of Comparative Economics*, 8(1), 3–27.

Andreff, W., & Staudohar, P.D. (2000). The evolving European model of professional sports finance. *Journal of Sports Economics*, 1(3), 257–276.

Armistead, L. (2008, September 2). Sheikh Mansour bin Zayed Al Nahyan has a deep love of sport and deeper pockets. *The Telegraph*. Retrieved July 12, 2019 from www.telegraph.co.uk/sport/football/teams/manchester-city/2664795/Sheikh-Mansour-bin-Zayed-Al-Nahyan-has-a-deep-love-of-sport-and-deeper-pockets-Football.html.

Arsenal's Aaron Ramsey signs Juventus pre-contract agreement. (2019, January 17). *SkySports*. Retrieved June 13, 2019 from www.skysports.com/football/news/11095/11609843/arsenals-aaron-ramsey-signs-juventus-pre-contract-agreement.

Asian Football Confederation. (2017, December 7). AFC increases prize money for 2018 club competitions. *The-AFC.com*. Retrieved June 3, 2019 from www.the-afc.com/news/afcsection/afc-increases-prize-money-for-2018-club-competitions.

Bates completes takeover of Leeds. (2005, January 21). *BBC Sport*. Retrieved June 10, 2019 from http://news.bbc.co.uk/sport2/hi/football/teams/l/leeds_united/4191871.stm.

Baxter, K. (2018, August 18). With soccer's biggest star and a lucrative TV contract, Serie A is back in top form. *Los Angeles Times*. Retrieved July 12, 2019 from www.latimes.com/sports/soccer/la-sp-serie-a-soccer-20180818-story.html.

Borland, J., & MacDonald, R. (2003). Demand for sport. *Oxford Review of Economic Policy*, 19(4), 478–502.

Brennan, C. (2016, January 6). Brennan: Stan Kroenke betrays St. Louis in bid to move Rams. *USA Today*. Retrieved July 11, 2019 from www.usatoday.com/story/sports/columnist/brennan/2016/01/06/st-louis-rams-los-angeles-nfl-relocation/78355204/.

Brett, D. (2019, July 10). 'I try to trigger all the senses': The artist behind the banners at Anfield. *The Guardian*. Retrieved July 12, 2019 from www.theguardian.com/football/2019/jul/10/artist-banners-anfield-liverpool-fan-kop-art-peter-carney.

Burt, J. (2014, February 1). Chelsea manager Jose Mourinho reveals fears over 'dodgy' Financial Fair Play tactics. *The Telegraph*. Retrieved July 12, 2019 from www.telegraph. co.uk/sport/football/teams/chelsea/10612099/Chelsea-manager-Jose-Mourinho-reveals-fears-over-dodgy-Financial-Fair-Play-tactics.html.

Buschmann, R., Dahlkamp, J., Latsch, G., Meyhoff, A., Naber, N., Schmitt, J., Weinzieri, A., Wille, R., Winterbach, C., & Wulzinger, M. (2018, November 2). How oil money distorts global football. *Der Spiegel*. Retrieved June 12, 2019 from www.spiegel.de/international/world/financial-fair-play-manchester-city-and-psg-pact-with-the-sheikhs-a-1236414.html.

Buschmann, R., Dahlkamp, J., Latsch, G., Meyhoff, A., Naber, N., Schmitt, J., Weinzieri, A., Wille, R., Winterbach, C., & Wulzinger, M. (2018, November 2). Chapter 2: The secret 'Project Longbow'. *Der Spiegel*. Retrieved June 12, 2019 from www.spiegel.de/international/manchester-city-and-the-fight-against-financial-fairplay-a-1236347. html.

Buschmann, R., & Winterbach, C. (2019, March 1). Man City accused of using shadow firms to flout rules. *Der Spiegel*. Retrieved June 12, 2019 from www.spiegel.de/international/world/manchester-city-accused-of-using-shadow-firms-to-flout-rules-a-1255796.html.

Buzzacchi, L., Szymanski, S., & Valletti, T.M. (2010). Equality of opportunity and equality of outcome: Open leagues, closed leagues and competitive balance. In S. Szymanski (Ed.), *The comparative economics of sport* (pp. 174–197). London: Palgrave Macmillan.

Carp debutant Batista blasts his way into history. (2017, June 5). *The Japan Times*. Retrieved July 13, 2019 from www.japantimes.co.jp/sports/2017/06/05/baseball/japanese-baseball/carp-debutant-batista-blasts-way-history/#.XSpn4ihKiUk.

Chiarelli, M. (2018, January 21). Soldi e crac, le manovre di Gianscaspro. *La Repubblica*. Retrieved June 11 from https://ricerca.repubblica.it/repubblica/archivio/repubblica/2018/01/21/soldi-e-crac-le-manovre-di-giancasproBari03.html?refresh_ce.

Conn, D. (2017, July 23). How fans were betrayed as Premier League club owners made fortunes. *The Guardian*. Retrieved July 13, 2019 from www.theguardian.com/football/2017/jul/23/premier-league-at-25-sky-tv-deal-club-owners-fans-betrayed.

Conn, D. (2018, June 6). Premier League finances: The full club-by-club breakdown and verdict. *The Guardian*. Retrieved June 9, 2019 from www.theguardian.com/football/2018/jun/06/premier-league-finances-club-guide-2016–17.

Conn, D. (2019, June 19). 'We never got that money': The inside story of Bury's road to financial ruin. *The Guardian*. Retrieved July 12, 2019 from www.theguardian.com/football/2019/jun/18/bury-inside-story-financial-ruin-winding-up-petition-loans-car-park.

CricInfo. (2005, January 12). Sellout at WACA for Twenty20 match. *ESPNCricInfo.com*. Retrieved June 14, 2019 from www.espncricinfo.com/australia/content/story/145226.html.

Critchlow, A. (2015, December 1). Manchester City deal is good business in China. *Reuters*. Retrieved July 13, 2019 from http://blogs.reuters.com/breakingviews/2015/12/01/manchester-city-deal-is-good-business-for-china/.

Dietl, H.M., Franck, E., & Lang, M. (2008). Overinvestment in team sports leagues: A contest theory model. *Scottish Journal of Political Economy*, 55(3), 353–368.

Doyle, P. (2017, November 19). West Brom owners and fans pile pressure on beleaguered Tony Pulis. *The Guardian*. Retrieved July 12, 2019 from www.theguardian.com/football/2017/nov/19/west-brom-owners-fans-pile-pressure-tony-pulis.

Drut, B., & Raballand, G. (2012). Why does financial regulation matter for European professional football clubs? *International Journal of Sport Management and Marketing*, 11(1–2), 73–88.

Farquhar, G. (2008, March 20). Football administration. *BBC Sport*. Retrieved July 13, 2019 from http://news.bbc.co.uk/sport2/hi/football/7305998.stm.

Football Italia. (2018a, January 17). Serie A second for TV revenue. *Football-Italia.net*. Retrieved June 10, 2019 from www.football-italia.net/115724/serie-second-tv-revenue.

Football Italia. (2018b, July 18). Epidemic of calcio bankruptcies. *Football-Italia.net*. Retrieved November 18, 2020 from www.football-italia.net/124648/epidemic-calcio-bankruptcies.

Fort, R. (2000). European and North American sports differences (?). *Scottish Journal of Political Economy*, 47(4), 431–455.

Foster, R. (2016, October 3). Why are so many football fans protesting against club owners? We asked them. *The Guardian*. Retrieved July 14, 2019 from www.theguardian.com/football/the-agony-and-the-ecstasy/2016/oct/03/football-fans-protest-club-owners-blackburn-coventry-charlton.

García, C. (2011). Real Madrid Football Club: Applying a relationship-management model to a sport organization in Spain. *International Journal of Sport Communication*, 4(3), 284–299.

Gibson, O. (2016, January 19). Government fan plan on club strategy will be written into league rules. *The Guardian*. Retrieved July 13, 2019 from www.theguardian.com/football/2016/jan/19/manchester-united-premier-league-fans-supporters-trust-deal.

Glazer extends Man Utd deadline. (2005, June 14). *BBC*. Retrieved June 12, 2019 from http://news.bbc.co.uk/2/hi/business/4090612.stm.

Gollapudi, N. (2017, September 4). Star wins IPL rights for US $2.55 billion. *ESPNCricInfo.com*. Retrieved June 14, 2019 from www.espncricinfo.com/story/_/id/20570244/star-india-wins-ipl-rights-us-255-billion.

Gong, H., Watanabe, N.M., Brown, M.T., & Nagel, M.S. (2019). The impact of the Chinese Basketball Association's Asian-born player policy on competitive balance. *Journal of Global Sport Management*, 4(2), 128–148.

Grilli, V., & Kaminsky, G. (1991). Nominal exchange rate regimes and the real exchange rate: Evidence from the United States and Great Britain, 1885–1986. *Journal of Monetary Economics*, 27(2), 191–212.

Hoult, N. (2010, January 20). IPL to broadcast live on YouTube. *The Telegraph*. Retrieved June 13, 2019 from www.telegraph.co.uk/sport/cricket/twenty20/ipl/7033597/IPL-to-broadcast-live-on-YouTube.html.

Hughes, M. (2018, November 14). Championship clubs led by Leeds and Derby threaten EFL breakaway in row over TV rights. *The Times*. Retrieved July 12, 2019 from www.thetimes.co.uk/article/championship-clubs-led-by-leeds-and-derby-threaten-efl-breakaway-in-row-over-tv-rights-zxw9tw2lc.

Humphreys, B., & Watanabe, N.M. (2015). The history and formation of East Asian sports leagues. In Y.H. Lee and R. Fort (Eds.), *The sports business in the Pacific Rim* (pp. 3–24). Cham: Springer.

Jang, H., & Lee, Y.H. (2016). A business analysis of Asian baseball leagues. *Asian Economic Policy Review*, 11(1), 95–112.

Jasina, J., & Rotthoff, K. (2012). A model of promotion and relegation in league sports. *Journal of Economics and Finance*, 36(2), 303–318.

Kelly, R. (2019, May 23). What are Premier League parachute payments & how much do teams get? *Goal.com*. Retrieved July 12, 2019 from www.goal.com/en/news/what-premier-league-parachute-payments-how-much-teams-get/ndpbojgz6szj1ojgn3p7jlbuo.

Kirsch, N. (2019, June 6). U.S. cable billionaire Rocco Commisso buys Italy's Fiorentina football club. *Forbes*. Retrieved July 12, 2019 from www.forbes.com/sites/noahkirsch/2019/06/06/us-cable-billionaire-rocco-commisso-buys-italys-fiorentina-football-club/#40a613ab4190.

Klinemann, P. (2017, May 5). Tabula rasa bei 1860: Ayre weg, Cassalette auch. *Kicker.de*. Retrieved July 12, 2019 from www.kicker.de/679217/artikel/tabula-rasa-bei-1860_ayre-weg-cassalette-auch.

La Croix, S.J., & Kawaura, A. (1999). Rule changes and competitive balance in Japanese professional baseball. *Economic Inquiry*, 37(2), 353–368.

Lastrapes, W.D. (1992). Sources of fluctuations in real and nominal exchange rates. *The Review of Economics and Statistics*, 74(3), 530–539.

Lazear, E.P., & Rosen, S. (1981). Rank-order tournaments as optimum labor contracts. *Journal of Political Economy*, 89(5), 841–864.

Leeds sell ground after bid fails. (2004, November 12). *BBC Sport*. Retrieved June 10, 2019 from http://news.bbc.co.uk/sport2/hi/football/teams/l/leeds_united/3995041.stm.

Leeds United resold to Ken Bates. (2007, July 11). *BBC*. Retrieved June 11, 2019 from http://news.bbc.co.uk/2/hi/business/6292746.stm.

Levitt, D. (2019, February 19). How might Brexit affect the Premier League? *The Guardian*. Retrieved July 12, 2019 from www.theguardian.com/football/ng-interactive/2019/feb/14/how-might-brexit-affect-premier-league.

Liddell, G. (2019, March 31). Love of soccer bridges huge cultural divides in diverse Michigan city. *USA Today*. Retrieved July 13, 2019 from www.usatoday.com/story/news/2019/03/31/michigan-soccer-team-yemen-sports-hamtramck/3328049002/.

Liddle, R. (2019, June 23). Newcastle fans deserve stability at their club. Instead it's the same, sad old story. *The Times*. Retrieved July 12, 2019 from www.thetimes.co.uk/article/newcastle-fans-deserve-stability-at-their-club-instead-its-the-same-sad-old-story-px0qlq26h.

Llopis-Goig, R. (2012). From 'socios' to 'hyper-consumers': An empirical examination of the impact of commodification on Spanish football fans. *Soccer & Society*, 13(3), 392–408.

MacInnes, P. (2017, July 23). Deceit, determination and Murdoch's millions: How Premier League was born. *The Guardian*. Retrieved July 13, 2019 from www.theguardian.com/football/2017/jul/23/deceit-determination-murdochs-millions-how-premier-league-was-born.

McCartney, A. (2019, July 11). UEFA announce huge European prize pot in financial boost for Man City and Manchester United. *Manchester Evening News*. Retrieved July 12, 2019 from www.manchestereveningnews.co.uk/sport/football/football-news/uefa-announce-huge-european-prize-16571307.

Murphy, A. (2012). *The official illustrated history of Manchester United: The full story and complete record, 1878–2006* (5th ed.). London: Sterling Publishing Company, Inc.

Niven, A. (2011, August 4). Football supporters' trusts provide a model for a more democratic Britain. *The Guardian*. Retrieved July 13, 2019 from www.theguardian.com/commentisfree/2011/aug/04/football-supporters-trusts.

Noll, R.G. (2002). The economics of promotion and relegation in sports leagues: The case of English football. *Journal of Sports Economics*, 3(2), 169–203.

Noll, R.G. (2003). The organization of sports leagues. *Oxford Review of Economic Policy*, 19(4), 530–551.

O'Hanlon, R. (2019, July 11). What if Mbappe and other stars ran down contracts and opted for free agency? *ESPN.com*. Retrieved July 12, 2019 from www.espn.com/soccer/blog/tactics-and-analysis/67/post/3897822/what-if-mbappe-and-other-stars-ran-down-contracts-and-opted-for-free-agency.

Page, L., & Page, K. (2007). The second leg home advantage: Evidence from European football cup competitions. *Journal of Sports Sciences*, 25(14), 1547–1556.

Pawlowski, T., Breuer, C., & Hovemann, A. (2010). Top clubs' performance and the competitive situation in European domestic football competitions. *Journal of Sports Economics*, 11(2), 186–202.

Porter, C. (2019). Structures of supporter ownership: Strong points and fault lines. In *Supporter ownership in English football* (pp. 207–235). Cham: Palgrave Macmillan.

Richards, A. (2016, September 27). What is third-party ownership and does it affect transfers? All you need to know. *Mirror*. Retrieved June 13, 2019 from www.mirror.co.uk/sport/football/news/what-third-party-ownership-how-8921397.

Robson, L. (2009, March 25). Damned to football. *The Times*.

Scott, M. (2010, November 5). HMRC challenge to creditors rule could cause chaos in football. *The Guardian*. Retrieved July 13, 2019 from www.theguardian.com/football/2010/nov/05/hmrc-football-creditors-rule-challenge.

Serie B: Officials deny Italian second tier has been suspended amid legal row. (2018, September 18). *BBC Sport*. Retrieved June 11, 2019 from www.bbc.com/sport/football/45566113.

Serie B suspended, awaiting appeal of decision to have 22 teams. (2018, September 18). *ESPN.com*. Retrieved June 11, 2019 from www.espn.com/soccer/italian-serie-b/story/3637600/serie-b-suspended-awaiting-appeal-of-decision-to-have-22-teams.

Sloane, P. (2015). The economics of professional football revisited. *Scottish Journal of Political Economy*, 62(1), 1–7.

Soccer-troubled Bari bought by former referee Paparesta in auction. (2014). *Reuters*. Retrieved June 10, 2019 from https://uk.reuters.com/article/soccer-italy-bari/soccer-troubled-bari-bought-by-former-referee-paparesta-in-auction-idUKL3N0O63X820140520.

Stone, S. (2015, July 10). Phoenix from the flames: How do you resurrect a football club? *BBC Sport*. Retrieved July 14, 2019 from www.bbc.com/sport/football/33470801.

Szymanski, S., & Valletti, T.M. (2010). Promotion and relegation in sporting contests. In S. Szymanski (Ed.), *The comparative economics of sport* (pp. 198–228). London: Palgrave Macmillan.

Taylor, D. (2008, July 11). I am a slave, says Ronaldo as he pushes for Madrid move. *The Guardian*. Retrieved June 13, 2019 from www.theguardian.com/football/2008/jul/11/manchesterunited.premierleague1.

Tenreyro, S. (2007). On the trade impact of nominal exchange rate volatility. *Journal of Development Economics*, 82(2), 485–508.

Torres, A. (2017, July 13). Russian players leaving NHL for KHL due to decision not to send players to 2018 Olympics. *The Washington Post*.

Vulliamy, E. (2015, May 27). Heysel stadium disaster: 'I saw the rows of bodies piled high'. *The Guardian*. Retrieved July 12, 2019 from www.theguardian.com/football/2015/may/27/heysel-stadium-disaster-30th-anniversary.

Wahl, G. (2014, December 3). 15 years of The Don: Under Graber, MLS stayed afloat, has taken strides. *SI.com*. Retrieved June 12, 2019 from www.si.com/soccer/planet-futbol/2014/12/03/don-garber-mls-commissioner-major-league-soccer.

Watanabe, N., & Soebbing, B. (2017). Chinese Super League: Attendance, pricing, and team performance. *Sport, Business and Management: An International Journal*, 7(2), 157–174.

Watanabe, N.M., Yan, G., Soebbing, B.P., & Fu, W. (2019). Air pollution and attendance in the Chinese Super League: Environmental economics and the demand for sport. *Journal of Sport Management*, 33, 1–14.

West Brom relegated from Premier League after Southampton beat Swansea. (2018, May 8). *BBC Sport*. Retrieved July 12, 2019 from www.bbc.com/sport/football/44046183.

White, J. (2003, January 10). Pitch battle. *The Guardian*. Retrieved June 1, 2019 from www.theguardian.com/football/2003/jan/11/clubsincrisis.sport.

Wigmore, T. (2018, May 24). Why foreign owners find Premier League football so irresistible. *iNews.co.uk*. Retrieved July 12, 2019 from https://inews.co.uk/sport/football/premier-league-foreign-owners-glazers-manchester-united-abramovich-chelsea-money/.

Williams, A. (2019, May 9). Bangor City fans follow AFC Wimbledon and FC United of Manchester example. *BBC Sport*. Retrieved June 2, 2019 from www.bbc.com/sport/football/48214424.

Wilson, P. (2003, March 23). Catchy Toon could be a classic. *The Guardian*. Retrieved June 11, 2019 from www.theguardian.com/football/2003/mar/23/sport.comment2.

Yamamura, E., & Shin, I. (2008). The influence of a leader and social interaction on attendance: The case of the Japanese professional baseball league, 1952–2003. *The Journal of Socio-Economics*, 37(4), 1412–1426.

APPENDIX
TIME VALUE OF MONEY TABLES

APPENDIX A.1 Future value of $1.00 at the end of n periods.

$FVIF_{i,n} = (1+i)^n$

PERIOD	1%	2%	3%	4%	5%	6%	7%	8%	9%	10%	11%	12%
1	1.0100	1.0200	1.0300	1.0400	1.0500	1.0600	1.0700	1.0800	1.0900	1.1000	1.1100	1.1200
2	1.0201	1.0404	1.0609	1.0816	1.1025	1.1236	1.1449	1.1664	1.1881	1.2100	1.2321	1.2544
3	1.0303	1.0612	1.0927	1.1249	1.1576	1.1910	1.2250	1.2597	1.2950	1.3310	1.3676	1.4049
4	1.0406	1.0824	1.1255	1.1699	1.2155	1.2625	1.3108	1.3605	1.4116	1.4641	1.5181	1.5735
5	1.0510	1.1041	1.1593	1.2167	1.2763	1.3382	1.4026	1.4693	1.5386	1.6105	1.6851	1.7623
6	1.0615	1.1262	1.1941	1.2653	1.3401	1.4185	1.5007	1.5869	1.6771	1.7716	1.8704	1.9738
7	1.0721	1.1487	1.2299	1.3159	1.4071	1.5036	1.6058	1.7138	1.8280	1.9487	2.0762	2.2107
8	1.0829	1.1717	1.2668	1.3686	1.4775	1.5938	1.7182	1.8509	1.9926	2.1436	2.3045	2.4760
9	1.0937	1.1951	1.3048	1.4233	1.5513	1.6895	1.8385	1.9990	2.1719	2.3579	2.5580	2.7731
10	1.1046	1.2190	1.3439	1.4802	1.6289	1.7908	1.9672	2.1589	2.3674	2.5937	2.8394	3.1058
11	1.1157	1.2434	1.3842	1.5395	1.7103	1.8983	2.1049	2.3316	2.5804	2.8531	3.1518	3.4785
12	1.1268	1.2682	1.4258	1.6010	1.7959	2.0122	2.2522	2.5182	2.8127	3.1384	3.4985	3.8960
13	1.1381	1.2936	1.4685	1.6651	1.8856	2.1329	2.4098	2.7196	3.0658	3.4523	3.8833	4.3635
14	1.1495	1.3195	1.5126	1.7317	1.9799	2.2609	2.5785	2.9372	3.3417	3.7975	4.3104	4.8871
15	1.1610	1.3459	1.5580	1.8009	2.0789	2.3966	2.7590	3.1722	3.6425	4.1772	4.7846	5.4736
16	1.1726	1.3728	1.6047	1.8730	2.1829	2.5404	2.9522	3.4259	3.9703	4.5950	5.3109	6.1304
17	1.1843	1.4002	1.6528	1.9479	2.2920	2.6928	3.1588	3.7000	4.3276	5.0545	5.8951	6.8660
18	1.1961	1.4282	1.7024	2.0258	2.4066	2.8543	3.3799	3.9960	4.7171	5.5599	6.5436	7.6900
19	1.2081	1.4568	1.7535	2.1068	2.5270	3.0256	3.6165	4.3157	5.1417	6.1159	7.2633	8.6128
20	1.2202	1.4859	1.8061	2.1911	2.6533	3.2071	3.8697	4.6610	5.6044	6.7275	8.0623	9.6463
25	1.2824	1.6406	2.0938	2.6658	3.3864	4.2919	5.4274	6.8485	8.6231	10.8347	13.5855	17.0001
30	1.3478	1.8114	2.4273	3.2434	4.3219	5.7435	7.6123	10.0627	13.2677	17.4494	22.8923	29.9599
35	1.4166	1.9999	2.8139	3.9461	5.5160	7.6861	10.6766	14.7853	20.4140	28.1024	38.5749	52.7996
40	1.4889	2.2080	3.2620	4.8010	7.0400	10.2857	14.9745	21.7245	31.4094	45.2593	65.0009	93.0510
50	1.6446	2.6916	4.3839	7.1067	11.4674	18.4202	29.4570	46.9016	74.3575	117.3909	184.5648	289.0022

13%	14%	15%	16%	17%	18%	19%	20%	25%	30%
1.1300	1.1400	1.1500	1.1600	1.1700	1.1800	1.1900	1.2000	1.2500	1.3000
1.2769	1.2996	1.3225	1.3456	1.3689	1.3924	1.4161	1.4400	1.5625	1.6900
1.4429	1.4815	1.5209	1.5609	1.6016	1.6430	1.6852	1.7280	1.9531	2.1970
1.6305	1.6890	1.7490	1.8106	1.8739	1.9388	2.0053	2.0736	2.4414	2.8561
1.8424	1.9254	2.0114	2.1003	2.1924	2.2878	2.3864	2.4883	3.0518	3.7129
2.0820	2.1950	2.3131	2.4364	2.5652	2.6996	2.8398	2.9860	3.8147	4.8268
2.3526	2.5023	2.6600	2.8262	3.0012	3.1855	3.3793	3.5832	4.7684	6.2749
2.6584	2.8526	3.0590	3.2784	3.5115	3.7589	4.0214	4.2998	5.9605	8.1573
3.0040	3.2519	3.5179	3.8030	4.1084	4.4355	4.7854	5.1598	7.4506	10.6045
3.3946	3.7072	4.0456	4.4114	4.8068	5.2338	5.6947	6.1917	9.3132	13.7858
3.8359	4.2262	4.6524	5.1173	5.6240	6.1759	6.7767	7.4301	11.6415	17.9216
4.3345	4.8179	5.3503	5.9360	6.5801	7.2876	8.0642	8.9161	14.5519	23.2981
4.8980	5.4924	6.1528	6.8858	7.6987	8.5994	9.5964	10.6993	18.1899	30.2875
5.5348	6.2613	7.0757	7.9875	9.0075	10.1472	11.4198	12.8392	22.7374	39.3738
6.2543	7.1379	8.1371	9.2655	10.5387	11.9737	13.5895	15.4070	28.4217	51.1859
7.0673	8.1372	9.3576	10.7480	12.3303	14.1290	16.1715	18.4884	35.5271	66.5417
7.9861	9.2765	10.7613	12.4677	14.4265	16.6722	19.2441	22.1861	44.4089	86.5042
9.0243	10.5752	12.3755	14.4625	16.8790	19.6733	22.9005	26.6233	55.5112	112.4554
10.1974	12.0557	14.2318	16.7765	19.7484	23.2144	27.2516	31.9480	69.3889	146.1920
11.5231	13.7435	16.3665	19.4608	23.1056	27.3930	32.4294	38.3376	86.7362	190.0496
21.2305	26.4619	32.9190	40.8742	50.6578	62.6686	77.3881	95.3962	264.6978	705.6410
39.1159	50.9502	66.2118	85.8499	111.0647	143.3706	184.6753	237.3763	807.7936	2,619.9956
72.0685	98.1002	133.1755	180.3141	243.5035	327.9973	440.7006	590.6682	2,465.1903	9,727.8604
132.7816	188.8835	267.8635	378.7212	533.8687	750.3783	1,051.6675	1,469.7716	7,523.1638	36,118.8648
450.7359	700.2330	1,083.6574	1,670.7038	2,566.2153	3,927.3569	5,988.9139	9,100.4382	70,064.9232	497,929.2230

$$\text{FVIFA}_{i,n} = \frac{\left((1+i)^n - 1\right)}{i}$$

PERIOD	1%	2%	3%	4%	5%	6%	7%	8%	9%	10%	11%	12%
1	1.0000	1.0000	1.0000	1.0000	1.0000	1.0000	1.0000	1.0000	1.0000	1.0000	1.0000	1.0000
2	2.0100	2.0200	2.0300	2.0400	2.0500	2.0600	2.0700	2.0800	2.0900	2.1000	2.1100	2.1200
3	3.0301	3.0604	3.0909	3.1216	3.1525	3.1836	3.2149	3.2464	3.2781	3.3100	3.3421	3.3744
4	4.0604	4.1216	4.1836	4.2465	4.3101	4.3746	4.4399	4.5061	4.5731	4.6410	4.7097	4.7793
5	5.1010	5.2040	5.3091	5.4163	5.5256	5.6371	5.7507	5.8666	5.9847	6.1051	6.2278	6.3528
6	6.1520	6.3081	6.4684	6.6330	6.8019	6.9753	7.1533	7.3359	7.5233	7.7156	7.9129	8.1152
7	7.2135	7.4343	7.6625	7.8983	8.1420	8.3938	8.6540	8.9228	9.2004	9.4872	9.7833	10.0890
8	8.2857	8.5830	8.8923	9.2142	9.5491	9.8975	10.2598	10.6366	11.0285	11.4359	11.8594	12.2997
9	9.3685	9.7546	10.1591	10.5828	11.0266	11.4913	11.9780	12.4876	13.0210	13.5795	14.1640	14.7757
10	10.4622	10.9497	11.4639	12.0061	12.5779	13.1808	13.8164	14.4866	15.1929	15.9374	16.7220	17.5487
11	11.5668	12.1687	12.8078	13.4864	14.2068	14.9716	15.7836	16.6455	17.5603	18.5312	19.5614	20.6546
12	12.6825	13.4121	14.1920	15.0258	15.9171	16.8699	17.8885	18.9771	20.1407	21.3843	22.7132	24.1331
13	13.8093	14.6803	15.6178	16.6268	17.7130	18.8821	20.1406	21.4953	22.9534	24.5227	26.2116	28.0291
14	14.9474	15.9739	17.0863	18.2919	19.5986	21.0151	22.5505	24.2149	26.0192	27.9750	30.0949	32.3926
15	16.0969	17.2934	18.5989	20.0236	21.5786	23.2760	25.1290	27.1521	29.3609	31.7725	34.4054	37.2797
16	17.2579	18.6393	20.1569	21.8245	23.6575	25.6725	27.8881	30.3243	33.0034	35.9497	39.1899	42.7533
17	18.4304	20.0121	21.7616	23.6975	25.8404	28.2129	30.8402	33.7502	36.9737	40.5447	44.5008	48.8837
18	19.6147	21.4123	23.4144	25.6454	28.1324	30.9057	33.9990	37.4502	41.3013	45.5992	50.3959	55.7497
19	20.8109	22.8406	25.1169	27.6712	30.5390	33.7600	37.3790	41.4463	46.0185	51.1591	56.9395	63.4397
20	22.0190	24.2974	26.8704	29.7781	33.0660	36.7856	40.9955	45.7620	51.1601	57.2750	64.2028	72.0524
25	28.2432	32.0303	36.4593	41.6459	47.7271	54.8645	63.2490	73.1059	84.7009	98.3471	114.4133	133.3339
30	34.7849	40.5681	47.5754	56.0849	66.4388	79.0582	94.4608	113.2832	136.3075	164.4940	199.0209	241.3327
35	41.6603	49.9945	60.4621	73.6522	90.3203	111.4348	138.2369	172.3168	215.7108	271.0244	341.5896	431.6635
40	48.8864	60.4020	75.4013	95.0255	120.7998	154.7620	199.6351	259.0565	337.8824	442.5926	581.8261	767.0914
50	64.4632	84.5794	112.7969	152.6671	209.3480	290.3359	406.5289	573.7702	815.0836	1,163.9085	1,668.7712	2,400.0182

13%	14%	15%	16%	17%	18%	19%	20%	25%	30%
1.0000	1.0000	1.0000	1.0000	1.0000	1.0000	1.0000	1.0000	1.0000	1.0000
2.1300	2.1400	2.1500	2.1600	2.1700	2.1800	2.1900	2.2000	2.2500	2.3000
3.4069	3.4396	3.4725	3.5056	3.5389	3.5724	3.6061	3.6400	3.8125	3.9900
4.8498	4.9211	4.9934	5.0665	5.1405	5.2154	5.2913	5.3680	5.7656	6.1870
6.4803	6.6101	6.7424	6.8771	7.0144	7.1542	7.2966	7.4416	8.2070	9.0431
8.3227	8.5355	8.7537	8.9775	9.2068	9.4420	9.6830	9.9299	11.2588	12.7560
10.4047	10.7305	11.0668	11.4139	11.7720	12.1415	12.5227	12.9159	15.0735	17.5828
12.7573	13.2328	13.7268	14.2401	14.7733	15.3270	15.9020	16.4991	19.8419	23.8577
15.4157	16.0853	16.7858	17.5185	18.2847	19.0859	19.9234	20.7989	25.8023	32.0150
18.4197	19.3373	20.3037	21.3215	22.3931	23.5213	24.7089	25.9587	33.2529	42.6195
21.8143	23.0445	24.3493	25.7329	27.1999	28.7551	30.4035	32.1504	42.5661	56.4053
25.6502	27.2707	29.0017	30.8502	32.8239	34.9311	37.1802	39.5805	54.2077	74.3270
29.9847	32.0887	34.3519	36.7862	39.4040	42.2187	45.2445	48.4966	68.7596	97.6250
34.8827	37.5811	40.5047	43.6720	47.1027	50.8180	54.8409	59.1959	86.9495	127.9125
40.4175	43.8424	47.5804	51.6595	56.1101	60.9653	66.2607	72.0351	109.6868	167.2863
46.6717	50.9804	55.7175	60.9250	66.6488	72.9390	79.8502	87.4421	138.1085	218.4722
53.7391	59.1176	65.0751	71.6730	78.9792	87.0680	96.0218	105.9306	173.6357	285.0139
61.7251	68.3941	75.8364	84.1407	93.4056	103.7403	115.2659	128.1167	218.0446	371.5180
70.7494	78.9692	88.2118	98.6032	110.2846	123.4135	138.1664	154.7400	273.5558	483.9734
80.9468	91.0249	102.4436	115.3797	130.0329	146.6280	165.4180	186.6880	342.9447	630.1655
155.6196	181.8708	212.7930	249.2140	292.1049	342.6035	402.0425	471.9811	1,054.7912	2,348.8033
293.1992	356.7868	434.7451	530.3117	647.4391	790.9480	966.7122	1,181.8816	3,227.1743	8,729.9855
546.6808	693.5727	881.1702	1,120.7130	1,426.4910	1,816.6516	2,314.2137	2,948.3411	9,856.7613	32,422.8681
1,013.7042	1,342.0251	1,779.0903	2,360.7572	3,134.5218	4,163.2130	5,529.8290	7,343.8578	30,088.6554	120,392.8827
3,459.5071	4,994.5213	7,217.7163	10,435.6488	15,089.5017	21,813.0937	31,515.3363	45,497.1908	280,255.6929	1,659,760.7433

APPENDIX A.3 Present value of $1.00 due at the end of *n* periods.

$$PVIF_{i,n} = \frac{1}{(1+i)^n}$$

PERIOD	1%	2%	3%	4%	5%	6%	7%	8%	9%	10%	11%
1	0.9901	0.9804	0.9709	0.9615	0.9524	0.9434	0.9346	0.9259	0.9174	0.9091	0.9009
2	0.9803	0.9612	0.9426	0.9246	0.9070	0.8900	0.8734	0.8573	0.8417	0.8264	0.8116
3	0.9706	0.9423	0.9151	0.8890	0.8638	0.8396	0.8163	0.7938	0.7722	0.7513	0.7312
4	0.9610	0.9238	0.8885	0.8548	0.8227	0.7921	0.7629	0.7350	0.7084	0.6830	0.6587
5	0.9515	0.9057	0.8626	0.8219	0.7835	0.7473	0.7130	0.6806	0.6499	0.6209	0.5935
6	0.9420	0.8880	0.8375	0.7903	0.7462	0.7050	0.6663	0.6302	0.5963	0.5645	0.5346
7	0.9327	0.8706	0.8131	0.7599	0.7107	0.6651	0.6227	0.5835	0.5470	0.5132	0.4817
8	0.9235	0.8535	0.7894	0.7307	0.6768	0.6274	0.5820	0.5403	0.5019	0.4665	0.4339
9	0.9143	0.8368	0.7664	0.7026	0.6446	0.5919	0.5439	0.5002	0.4604	0.4241	0.3909
10	0.9053	0.8203	0.7441	0.6756	0.6139	0.5584	0.5083	0.4632	0.4224	0.3855	0.3522
11	0.8963	0.8043	0.7224	0.6496	0.5847	0.5268	0.4751	0.4289	0.3875	0.3505	0.3173
12	0.8874	0.7885	0.7014	0.6246	0.5568	0.4970	0.4440	0.3971	0.3555	0.3186	0.2858
13	0.8787	0.7730	0.6810	0.6006	0.5303	0.4688	0.4150	0.3677	0.3262	0.2897	0.2575
14	0.8700	0.7579	0.6611	0.5775	0.5051	0.4423	0.3878	0.3405	0.2992	0.2633	0.2320
15	0.8613	0.7430	0.6419	0.5553	0.4810	0.4173	0.3624	0.3152	0.2745	0.2394	0.2090
16	0.8528	0.7284	0.6232	0.5339	0.4581	0.3936	0.3387	0.2919	0.2519	0.2176	0.1883
17	0.8444	0.7142	0.6050	0.5134	0.4363	0.3714	0.3166	0.2703	0.2311	0.1978	0.1696
18	0.8360	0.7002	0.5874	0.4936	0.4155	0.3503	0.2959	0.2502	0.2120	0.1799	0.1528
19	0.8277	0.6864	0.5703	0.4746	0.3957	0.3305	0.2765	0.2317	0.1945	0.1635	0.1377
20	0.8195	0.6730	0.5537	0.4564	0.3769	0.3118	0.2584	0.2145	0.1784	0.1486	0.1240
25	0.7798	0.6095	0.4776	0.3751	0.2953	0.2330	0.1842	0.1460	0.1160	0.0923	0.0736
30	0.7419	0.5521	0.4120	0.3083	0.2314	0.1741	0.1314	0.0994	0.0754	0.0573	0.0437
35	0.7059	0.5000	0.3554	0.2534	0.1813	0.1301	0.0937	0.0676	0.0490	0.0356	0.0259
40	0.6717	0.4529	0.3066	0.2083	0.1420	0.0972	0.0668	0.0460	0.0318	0.0221	0.0154
50	0.6080	0.3715	0.2281	0.1407	0.0872	0.0543	0.0339	0.0213	0.0134	0.0085	0.0054

12%	13%	14%	15%	16%	17%	18%	19%	20%	25%	30%
0.8929	0.8850	0.8772	0.8696	0.8621	0.8547	0.8475	0.8403	0.8333	0.8000	0.7692
0.7972	0.7831	0.7695	0.7561	0.7432	0.7305	0.7182	0.7062	0.6944	0.6400	0.5917
0.7118	0.6931	0.6750	0.6575	0.6407	0.6244	0.6086	0.5934	0.5787	0.5120	0.4552
0.6355	0.6133	0.5921	0.5718	0.5523	0.5337	0.5158	0.4987	0.4823	0.4096	0.3501
0.5674	0.5428	0.5194	0.4972	0.4761	0.4561	0.4371	0.4190	0.4019	0.3277	0.2693
0.5066	0.4803	0.4556	0.4323	0.4104	0.3898	0.3704	0.3521	0.3349	0.2621	0.2072
0.4523	0.4251	0.3996	0.3759	0.3538	0.3332	0.3139	0.2959	0.2791	0.2097	0.1594
0.4039	0.3762	0.3506	0.3269	0.3050	0.2848	0.2660	0.2487	0.2326	0.1678	0.1226
0.3606	0.3329	0.3075	0.2843	0.2630	0.2434	0.2255	0.2090	0.1938	0.1342	0.0943
0.3220	0.2946	0.2697	0.2472	0.2267	0.2080	0.1911	0.1756	0.1615	0.1074	0.0725
0.2875	0.2607	0.2366	0.2149	0.1954	0.1778	0.1619	0.1476	0.1346	0.0859	0.0558
0.2567	0.2307	0.2076	0.1869	0.1685	0.1520	0.1372	0.1240	0.1122	0.0687	0.0429
0.2292	0.2042	0.1821	0.1625	0.1452	0.1299	0.1163	0.1042	0.0935	0.0550	0.0330
0.2046	0.1807	0.1597	0.1413	0.1252	0.1110	0.0985	0.0876	0.0779	0.0440	0.0254
0.1827	0.1599	0.1401	0.1229	0.1079	0.0949	0.0835	0.0736	0.0649	0.0352	0.0195
0.1631	0.1415	0.1229	0.1069	0.0930	0.0811	0.0708	0.0618	0.0541	0.0281	0.0150
0.1456	0.1252	0.1078	0.0929	0.0802	0.0693	0.0600	0.0520	0.0451	0.0225	0.0116
0.1300	0.1108	0.0946	0.0808	0.0691	0.0592	0.0508	0.0437	0.0376	0.0180	0.0089
0.1161	0.0981	0.0829	0.0703	0.0596	0.0506	0.0431	0.0367	0.0313	0.0144	0.0068
0.1037	0.0868	0.0728	0.0611	0.0514	0.0433	0.0365	0.0308	0.0261	0.0115	0.0053
0.0588	0.0471	0.0378	0.0304	0.0245	0.0197	0.0160	0.0129	0.0105	0.0038	0.0014
0.0334	0.0256	0.0196	0.0151	0.0116	0.0090	0.0070	0.0054	0.0042	0.0012	0.0004
0.0189	0.0139	0.0102	0.0075	0.0055	0.0041	0.0030	0.0023	0.0017	0.0004	0.0001
0.0107	0.0075	0.0053	0.0037	0.0026	0.0019	0.0013	0.0010	0.0007	0.0001	—
0.0035	0.0022	0.0014	0.0009	0.0006	0.0004	0.0003	0.0002	0.0001	—	—

$$PVIFA_{i,n} = \frac{\dfrac{1}{i-1}}{i(1+i)^n}$$

PERIOD	1%	2%	3%	4%	5%	6%	7%	8%	9%	10%	11%
1	0.9901	0.9804	0.9709	0.9615	0.9524	0.9434	0.9346	0.9259	0.9174	0.9091	0.9009
2	1.9704	1.9416	1.9135	1.8861	1.8594	1.8334	1.8080	1.7833	1.7591	1.7355	1.7125
3	2.9410	2.8839	2.8286	2.7751	2.7232	2.6730	2.6243	2.5771	2.5313	2.4869	2.4437
4	3.9020	3.8077	3.7171	3.6299	3.5460	3.4651	3.3872	3.3121	3.2397	3.1699	3.1024
5	4.8534	4.7135	4.5797	4.4518	4.3295	4.2124	4.1002	3.9927	3.8897	3.7908	3.6959
6	5.7955	5.6014	5.4172	5.2421	5.0757	4.9173	4.7665	4.6229	4.4859	4.3553	4.2305
7	6.7282	6.4720	6.2303	6.0021	5.7864	5.5824	5.3893	5.2064	5.0330	4.8684	4.7122
8	7.6517	7.3255	7.0197	6.7327	6.4632	6.2098	5.9713	5.7466	5.5348	5.3349	5.1461
9	8.5660	8.1622	7.7861	7.4353	7.1078	6.8017	6.5152	6.2469	5.9952	5.7590	5.5370
10	9.4713	8.9826	8.5302	8.1109	7.7217	7.3601	7.0236	6.7101	6.4177	6.1446	5.8892
11	10.3676	9.7868	9.2526	8.7605	8.3064	7.8869	7.4987	7.1390	6.8052	6.4951	6.2065
12	11.2551	10.5753	9.9540	9.3851	8.8633	8.3838	7.9427	7.5361	7.1607	6.8137	6.4924
13	12.1337	11.3484	10.6350	9.9856	9.3936	8.8527	8.3577	7.9038	7.4869	7.1034	6.7499
14	13.0037	12.1062	11.2961	10.5631	9.8986	9.2950	8.7455	8.2442	7.7862	7.3667	6.9819
15	13.8651	12.8493	11.9379	11.1184	10.3797	9.7122	9.1079	8.5595	8.0607	7.6061	7.1909
16	14.7179	13.5777	12.5611	11.6523	10.8378	10.1059	9.4466	8.8514	8.3126	7.8237	7.3792
17	15.5623	14.2919	13.1661	12.1657	11.2741	10.4773	9.7632	9.1216	8.5436	8.0216	7.5488
18	16.3983	14.9920	13.7535	12.6593	11.6896	10.8276	10.0591	9.3719	8.7556	8.2014	7.7016
19	17.2260	15.6785	14.3238	13.1339	12.0853	11.1581	10.3356	9.6036	8.9501	8.3649	7.8393
20	18.0456	16.3514	14.8775	13.5903	12.4622	11.4699	10.5940	9.8181	9.1285	8.5136	7.9633
25	22.0232	19.5235	17.4131	15.6221	14.0939	12.7834	11.6536	10.6748	9.8226	9.0770	8.4217
30	25.8077	22.3965	19.6004	17.2920	15.3725	13.7648	12.4090	11.2578	10.2737	9.4269	8.6938
35	29.4086	24.9986	21.4872	18.6646	16.3742	14.4982	12.9477	11.6546	10.5668	9.6442	8.8552
40	32.8347	27.3555	23.1148	19.7928	17.1591	15.0463	13.3317	11.9246	10.7574	9.7791	8.9511
50	39.1961	31.4236	25.7298	21.4822	18.2559	15.7619	13.8007	12.2335	10.9617	9.9148	9.0417

12%	13%	14%	15%	16%	17%	18%	19%	20%	25%	30%
0.8929	0.8850	0.8772	0.8696	0.8621	0.8547	0.8475	0.8403	0.8333	0.8000	0.7692
1.6901	1.6681	1.6467	1.6257	1.6052	1.5852	1.5656	1.5465	1.5278	1.4400	1.3609
2.4018	2.3612	2.3216	2.2832	2.2459	2.2096	2.1743	2.1399	2.1065	1.9520	1.8161
3.0373	2.9745	2.9137	2.8550	2.7982	2.7432	2.6901	2.6386	2.5887	2.3616	2.1662
3.6048	3.5172	3.4331	3.3522	3.2743	3.1993	3.1272	3.0576	2.9906	2.6893	2.4356
4.1114	3.9975	3.8887	3.7845	3.6847	3.5892	3.4976	3.4098	3.3255	2.9514	2.6427
4.5638	4.4226	4.2883	4.1604	4.0386	3.9224	3.8115	3.7057	3.6046	3.1611	2.8021
4.9676	4.7988	4.6389	4.4873	4.3436	4.2072	4.0776	3.9544	3.8372	3.3289	2.9247
5.3282	5.1317	4.9464	4.7716	4.6065	4.4506	4.3030	4.1633	4.0310	3.4631	3.0190
5.6502	5.4262	5.2161	5.0188	4.8332	4.6586	4.4941	4.3389	4.1925	3.5705	3.0915
5.9377	5.6869	5.4527	5.2337	5.0286	4.8364	4.6560	4.4865	4.3271	3.6564	3.1473
6.1944	5.9176	5.6603	5.4206	5.1971	4.9884	4.7932	4.6105	4.4392	3.7251	3.1903
6.4235	6.1218	5.8424	5.5831	5.3423	5.1183	4.9095	4.7147	4.5327	3.7801	3.2233
6.6282	6.3025	6.0021	5.7245	5.4675	5.2293	5.0081	4.8023	4.6106	3.8241	3.2487
6.8109	6.4624	6.1422	5.8474	5.5755	5.3242	5.0916	4.8759	4.6755	3.8593	3.2682
6.9740	6.6039	6.2651	5.9542	5.6685	5.4053	5.1624	4.9377	4.7296	3.8874	3.2832
7.1196	6.7291	6.3729	6.0472	5.7487	5.4746	5.2223	4.9897	4.7746	3.9099	3.2948
7.2497	6.8399	6.4674	6.1280	5.8178	5.5339	5.2732	5.0333	4.8122	3.9279	3.3037
7.3658	6.9380	6.5504	6.1982	5.8775	5.5845	5.3162	5.0700	4.8435	3.9424	3.3105
7.4694	7.0248	6.6231	6.2593	5.9288	5.6278	5.3527	5.1009	4.8696	3.9539	3.3158
7.8431	7.3300	6.8729	6.4641	6.0971	5.7662	5.4669	5.1951	4.9476	3.9849	3.3286
8.0552	7.4957	7.0027	6.5660	6.1772	5.8294	5.5168	5.2347	4.9789	3.9950	3.3321
8.1755	7.5856	7.0700	6.6166	6.2153	5.8582	5.5386	5.2512	4.9915	3.9984	3.3330
8.2438	7.6344	7.1050	6.6418	6.2335	5.8713	5.5482	5.2582	4.9966	3.9995	3.3332
8.3045	7.6752	7.1327	6.6605	6.2463	5.8801	5.5541	5.2623	4.9995	3.9999	3.3333

INDEX

Note: References to exhibits are in *italics*.

MLB (Major League Baseball): academies in
620; and antitrust law 22, 31; bankruptcies
of teams 77, 115, 530; collusion between
owners 558; commissioner 519–20, 538;
competition for 538; and COVID-19 557;
debt rules 529–31; deferred compensation in
116; drafts in 540; financial information for
346–9; franchise ownership 159; free agency
in 547–9; and gambling 578; global brand
of 589–90; and government involvement
149; impact of Great Recession on 24, 93–4;
insurance in 154–5; Japanese players in 526;
lack of salary cap 556; loan pool 95; luxury
tax 561, 566–7; multi-year contracts in 116–17;
names of franchises 284; new stadiums
274, 308; non-profit status 21; ownership
structure 617; price-to-revenue multiple 344;
price-to-revenue ratio 340; restrictions on
franchises 145–6; revenue sharing in 98–9,
568–70, 573; salary slotting 543–4; secondary
ticket market 576; signing bonuses 172;
synergistic ownerships in 335; television
contracts 29; territorial disputes 536–7; ticket
prices 111; valuation of teams 103, 104, 346,
348–50, 359
MLB.com 259
MLBAM (Major League Baseball Advanced
Media) 104, 569
MLBPA (Major League Baseball Players
Association) 547, 549, 556–8, 561, 573
MLGW (Memphis Light, Gas, and
Water) 303
MLL (Major League Lacrosse) 518
MLS (Major League Soccer) 518–19; Austin
franchise 393; new stadiums 380; ownership
structure 20–1, 522, 527, 540, 616–17; phoenix
teams in 616; salaries of 20; salary cap 343,
556; valuation of 325, 338–44, 341–2
Mnuchin, Steve 95
Mobil 1 355
Modell, Art 150, 286, 517, 528, 571
Mohegan Tribe 35
monetary policy 164–70
money, time value of see time value of money
money markets 5
money supply, monitoring 168–70
Moneyball 43–4, 549
Montana 173
Montgomery County, MD 294
monthly payments 133, 166; calculating in
Excel 134, 135–6
Montreal Alouettes 152
Montreal Expos 145, 179, 264, 530, 536
Montreal Impact 339
Moody's 80, 231
Moore, Maya 535
Moreno, Artie 159
Moricle Society 507
Mourinho, Jose 612

MRP (maturity risk premium) 80–2, 100, 222–3
multiple owners/private investment syndicate
model 16–17
multiple owners/publicly traded corporation
model 19–20
multiplier effect 410–11
multi-year contracts 116–17
municipal bonds 92, 231, 310, 440–2, 445, 450,
451
Murdoch, Rupert 334
Murray, Kyler 546
mutual funds 221
Myers, Wil 558
MZBB (modified zero-based budgeting)
211–13; advantages and disadvantages 215;
starting point 212; steps in 213–14

NAIA (National Association of Intercollegiate
Athletics) 465–6
NAICS (North American Industrial
Classification System) 11, 12–13, 14
naming rights 90, 191, 274–5, 286; in corporate
demand analysis 384–8; Dallas Cowboys
24; during Great Recession 95; future
revenue from 315; for high school sports
438; Indianapolis Colts 225; Minnesota
Twins 4; in NFL 103; for parks and recreation
455–6; and paying off bonds 294; in stadium
funding 309, 310; for television stations 569
NASCAR (National Association for Stock
Car Auto Racing) 519; impact of economic
crises on 28–9; owners of racetracks 48;
ownership structure 21, 524–5; political
support for 31–2; television contracts 29
NASDAQ (National Association of Securities
Dealers Automated Quotations) 45, 48,
161–2, 229, 237, 338, 524
Nashville Predators 97, 146, 180, 524;
funding of home arena 291, 294; government
funding 225
NASL (North American Soccer League) 617
Nassau Coliseum 30
Nationwide Arena 31, 305
natural disasters 165
NBA (National Basketball Association): and
ABA 115–16, 120; and antitrust law 22; and
Atlanta Spirit LLC 17–18; commissioner
527–8; competitors of 539; and COVID-19
557; debt rules 311, 529; draft lottery 541–2;
and gambling 578; global brand of 589; loan
pool 94–5, 532; luxury tax in 560, 561, 562–4;
market demand analysis for 389–90, 391–2;
and multiple competitions 604–6; ownership
model 21, 524, 527; price-to-revenue multiple
344; public and private funding for venues
285; revenue sharing in 99; salary cap 550–2;
salary slotting 543; television contracts 29,
94; valuation of franchises 360; and WNBA
20, 35